A most inspiring book! It encompasses a holistic approach to innovation management and case studies enrich the textbook, covering a wide range of industry sectors and countries. This new edition is a strongly recommended textbook for students and academics. – **Ana Martins, Associate Professor in Leadership, Graduate School of Business & Leadership, University of Kwazulu-Natal, Westville, South Africa**

In the third edition Goffin and Mitchel display an up-to-date knowledge of the innovation management field which helps students and managers to understand and put into practice the difficult, but important task of managing innovative activities. The clear structure of the book and a number international cases assist students to learn and reflect effectively. – **Kristian Philipsen, Associate Professor, Department of Entrepreneurship and Relationship Management, University of Southern Denmark**

This comprehensive textbook is an excellent resource for those exploring innovation for the first time. Equally, it covers a breadth of modern management theory and principals of practice which make it just as relevant for the experienced manager. A key feature of the book is the interesting and informative case studies which connect with the real world practice of innovation and highlight key concepts for the reader. – **Scott Gordon, PhD Director, Entrepreneurship, Commercialisation and Innovation Centre, The University of Adelaide, Australia**

With *Innovation Management*, Keith Goffin and Rick Mitchell present a sensible theoretical and practical guide to one of the burning challenges of this century – how to manage **for** innovation. Using numerous cases and practical examples, connecting strategic to operational matters, they provide an important and invaluable toolbox to students and practitioners. – **Dr. Christoph Johann Stettina – Research & Innovation, Centre for Innovation, Leiden University, The Netherlands**

This book by Goffin and Mitchell gives an insight into innovation management of today. For us in academia who work as innovation support professionals it gives knowledge about different tools and serves as an inspiration in our work. – **Pirkko Tamsen, Director, Uppsala University Innovation, Sweden**

Goffin and Mitchell have provided a comprehensive analysis of innovation management. The reader is presented with a multi-faceted framework approach to the topic. Each facet is dealt with in an easy to understand manner and supported with a collection of industry related case studies. An important contribution to the book is the chapter on innovation performance and capability. The book is an essential read for students of innovation management as well as those charged with the task of driving innovation forward. – **Colman Ledwith, Lecturer, Dundalk Institute of Technology, Ireland**

THIRD EDITION

INNOVATION MANAGEMENT

EFFECTIVE STRATEGY AND IMPLEMENTATION

KEITH GOFFIN AND RICK MITCHELL

With case studies contributed by John Christiansen and Claus Varnes (Copenhagen Business School); Julian Glyn-Owen (Aluris, UK); Ian Kierans (Advanced Organisation, Ireland); Lloyd He (China Institute for Innovation); Mohamed Khater (Cambridge University); Claire McBride (Dublin Institute of Technology); Jawwad Raja and Thomas Frandsen (Copenhagen Business School); Jan Rosier (University College Dublin); Evy Sakellariou (The American College of Greece); Hendro Tjaturpriono (Prasetiya Mulya Business School, Jakarta); Chris van der Hoven (Wits Business School, South Africa); and Tatiana Zalan (American University in Dubai).

First edition 2005
Second edition 2010

Published 2017 by
PALGRAVE

Red Globe Press in the UK is an imprint of Springer Nature Limited, registered in England, company number 785998, of 4 Crinan Street, London, N1 9XW.

Red Globe Press is a global imprint of the above companies and is represented throughout the world.

Red Globe Press® is a registered trademark in the United States, the United Kingdom, Europe and other countries.

ISBN 978–1–137–37343–4 paperback

This book is printed on paper suitable for recycling and made from fully managed and sustained forest sources. Logging, pulping and manufacturing processes are expected to conform to the environmental regulations of the country of origin.

A catalogue record for this book is available from the British Library.

A catalog record for this book is available from the Library of Congress.

BRIEF CONTENTS

CONTENTS

PREFACE

This is the 3rd edition of a book that has been written for both students and managers. It has been designed for those who want a practical but academically rigorous guide to innovation management. The book is based around a framework of innovation management – the *Innovation Pentathlon Framework* – which was developed from our research and has been used extensively in our work with companies. Aligned to the framework, we have selected the key concepts and theories from the field of innovation management together with the tools and techniques that managers can use to improve performance. As in previous editions these are extensively illustrated by case studies. We have also introduced the use of separate "Theory Boxes" to make it possible to explore key topics in extra depth without interrupting the flow of the text.

Students and managers have always liked the emphasis we have placed on case studies in the two earlier editions. For this edition, we have further increased the number of cases – many of which have been written based on our personal contacts – and have invited colleagues to contribute their favourites. All the cases have been carefully selected to illustrate the points made in the main text.

There are 77 half-page 'mini cases' and one 'main case study' per chapter, a total of 86 in all. In selecting these cases, we have sought to achieve a wide international spread as well as parity between the manufacturing and service sectors because, too often, the service sector is not given sufficient attention in writings on innovation management. In this edition we have also added some cases to illustrate innovation in the public and not-for-profit sectors. Additional teaching material such as study questions, teaching notes and slides are provided on the associated website.

Innovation management is a relatively new and fast-developing area and so we have been careful to review the recent literature and to include much new material in this book. But it should be remembered that even for the topic of innovation, there is much from the past that remains valid and useful. So we have not hesitated to include material from older publications and case studies where it is appropriate. The 'new' is not always the 'best', even in innovation.

Similarly, there are no 'quick fixes' in the complex field of innovation management. Therefore, the challenge for managers is not just to adopt the ideas in this book but to adapt and blend them to fit the context their organizations face. We wish them every success in meeting that challenge. Similarly, we hope that this book will help students quickly learn the aspects of innovation management that will make them more effective and successful in their careers.

LIST OF CASE STUDIES

Innovation management is a very practical subject. And so many managers and students reading previous editions have commented that it is the case studies that both bring innovation to life and make the concepts more understandable.

Each chapter includes at least five 'mini cases' and one 'main case study', each of which is closely linked to the chapter's text; the cases are designed to reinforce the main discussions. The main case studies cover the main themes raised in the chapter and they have a set of 'Reflective Questions'. In addition, at least one case in each chapter includes a link to a video interview with the main protagonist. These specially arranged interviews allow readers to 'meet' the managers described in the cases discussing innovation management.

The table below summarizes the cases per chapter, indicating the main sectors covered, the country or region the organization is most active in, the company and topic, and indicates those cases with video interviews.

(Continued)

(Continued)

LIST OF THEORY BOXES

In this edition we have occasionally used "Theory Boxes" to expand or elaborate on particular tools or theories without interrupting the flow of the main text. These are listed below.

ONLINE RESOURCES

Visit **www.palgravehighered.com/gm** to access a wealth of materials to support your course and use of the textbook.

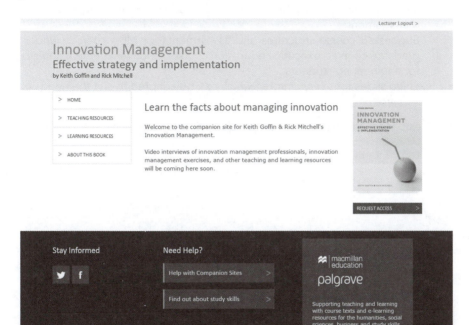

For students:

- Video interviews to accompany select case studies, in which managers expand upon the issues discussed in the case
- Guideline answers to the 'Questions for Students' that appear at the end of each chapter
- Chapter summaries to aid with revision
- Links to multimedia material to support your studies
- Bonus Appendix: Innovation Auditing
- Bonus Case Study: Integra: Digital Content Services.

For lecturers:

- A comprehensive **instructor's manual** that provides the tools needed to adapt *Innovation Management* to your own course. It offers:
    - Teaching notes on every chapter, including learning objectives, suggested discussion topics and practical exercises, teaching notes to accompany the case studies, and recommended multimedia material
    - Tips on teaching, where both the authors and faculty members from leading institutions share their experience and advice on teaching innovation management
    - Suggested course structures and assessments for MBA courses, undergraduate courses, executive education courses, and management courses for engineering students.
- Teaching slides for every chapter, which can be adapted to suit the needs of your course

- A testbank featuring multiple choice questions to accompany every chapter.

ABOUT THE AUTHORS

KEITH GOFFIN, BSc, MSc, PhD

Keith is Professor of Innovation and New Product Development at Cranfield School of Management in the UK.

He graduated from Durham University in 1977 with a first class honours degree in Physics and subsequently obtained an MSc in Medical Physics from Aberdeen University. For fourteen years he worked for the Medical Products Group of Hewlett-Packard (HP), starting as a support engineer working on new product development. In subsequent management roles, he gained extensive experience in international marketing and, for example, took HP's defibrillator products from a 5 per cent market share to market leadership position within a year. Parallel to his management responsibilities, Keith studied part time for a PhD at Cranfield. The results of his research on customer support have been applied at Ford, NCR and HP. In 1991 he became Product Marketing Manager at HP and focused on developing the intensive care market in Asia Pacific, before leaving HP in 1994 to join Cranfield.

At Cranfield, Keith lectures on the MBA and Executive Programmes and has developed many new courses on innovation management. Keith regularly lectures at other schools, including Bocconi University, Mannheim Business School, the Technical University of Hamburg-Harburg, Stockholm School of Economics and KoreaTech, South Korea. From 2002 to 2004 he worked as Academic Dean at Stuttgart Institute of Management and Technology.

His research interests are identifying customers' hidden needs, innovation leadership, tacit knowledge in R&D, project-to-project learning and portfolio management. He has published three books, 14 major reports and over 40 academic papers in a number of journals, including the *International Journal of Operations & Production Management*, the *Journal of Product Innovation Management*, the *Journal of Operations Management* and *Research-Technology Management*. In addition to his work at universities, he regularly acts as an innovation management consultant to companies including Agilent Technologies, Altro, Bosch, Mölnlycke Health Care, Philips, Reckitt-Benckiser, Roche, Sanofi, Sony, Ludvig Svensson and Welding Alloys.

RICK MITCHELL, MA, PhD, CEng

Rick is Visiting Professor of Innovation Management at Cranfield School of Management and Visiting Fellow in the Engineering Department at Cambridge University.

He has a degree in Natural Sciences from Cambridge University and he joined Philips Research Laboratories in 1965 when he worked on thermal imaging, acoustic wave devices, and radio system design, publishing 20 papers and receiving 26 patents. Parallel to his work at Philips, Rick studied for a PhD in Electrical Engineering, which he received from Queen Mary College in London in 1971.

After three years as a Corporate Planner for Philips Electronics, Rick moved to its Pye Telecommunications subsidiary as Radio Systems Division Manager for four years, before becoming International Development Manager for all Philips' mobile radio business in 1986.

Joining Domino Printing Sciences, a world leader in industrial printing equipment, in 1988, Rick managed the R&D and Quality functions and developed the company's expertise in new areas such as laser-based equipment. He joined the main board of the company in 1994 as Group Technical Director, with responsibilities across four R&D sites and 12 subsidiaries, retiring in 2003. In 1990 he co-authored the book *How to Profit from Innovation*. In February 2001 Rick joined Cranfield School of Management and the Institute for Manufacturing at Cambridge University. He takes an active role in research and in designing and presenting courses on technology and innovation management.

ACKNOWLEDGEMENTS

To write a book aimed at students and practising managers requires a high level of contact with both these groups, in order to understand their needs. In our teaching and research, we are fortunate to come into constant and extensive contact with excellent students. We also work constantly with senior managers, who are not only very good at what they do but are also reflective on the issues they face. We benefit enormously from interacting with both these groups, and from their ideas, probing questions and the experiences they share with us. This 3rd edition includes many ideas based on feedback from our students and work with executives.

The Pentathlon Framework, which provides the backbone for this book, was originally developed from research generously supported by the Anglo-German Foundation. Thanks also to the many managers who were interviewed as part of this research and contributed many of the ideas about how a framework for innovation management could be used. In the past 15 years, the framework has been applied extensively and we have received very useful feedback from many other managers.

The work of our current and former doctoral students helped in identifying the literature on specific aspects of innovation management and by providing the new ideas, which emerged from their own research. Thanks to Nitish Khetavath, Dr Ian Kierans, Dr Ursula Koners, Dr Bertram Lohmüller, Professor Jan Rosier and Hendro Tjaturpriono.

A large number of managers in industry have given up precious time to help us with the case studies, or have provided material and ideas through being regular guest speakers at our lectures. Thanks to the following:

Mohammad Alkhas – Aramex
Jörg Asbrand – time:matters
Mirjam Berle – time:matters
Aleksei Beznosov
Dr Alex Bogdanov
Seth Bishop – KD UK
Richard Blackburn
Ciaran Black – Coillte
Nigel Bond – Domino Printing Sciences
Simon Bradley
Simon Bransfield-Garth – Azuri
Erik Chang – Ericsson
Danu Chotikapanich – Cobra International
Vorapant Chotikapanich – Cobra International
David Cope
Lars Cosh-Ishii – Mobikyo

Martin Cserba – 21TORR Agency
Dr Olaf Dietrich – Miele
Anastassios Dimopoulos – Intracom Telecom
Andrew Dobson – Tetley Tea
Peg Dyer – Allstate Insurance
David Epps – Amey
Klaus Fischer – Fischer GmbH
Massimo Fumarola – Fiat Iveco
David Gluckman – Lumkani
Jeff Gould – RNLI
Sreejith Govindan, Integra
Dr Edmond Harty – Dairymaster
Erik Hoppenbrouwer – Organon/Fagron
Nick Huang – Haier
David Humphries – PDD
Mariam Ismail – INFIT
Tsubasa Itani – Former database marketer at All Nippon Airways
Synthiea Kaldi
Dr Amin Khan – MASkargo
Hans Jørgen Klein – Grundfos
Corina Kuiper – Antwerp Management School
Dr Matthias Langhorst – Zeiss
Michael Levie – CitizenM Hotels
Steen Lindby – Rockwool
T. Linganathan – Texas Instruments Malaysia
Amulya Malladi – Radiometer
Isabelle Mari – JCDecaux
Steve Marriott
Werner Mayer – Bosch
Lee Metters – Domino Printing Sciences
Liam Mifsud – Equant
Franz-Joseph Miller – time:matters
Dr Edwin Moses – Evotec
Sachin Mulay – Wipro Technologies
John O'Neill
JS Oh – Bixolon
Wim Ouboter – Micro Mobility
Martin Oxley – BuzzBack
Roger Parker – Allstate
Dr Michael Peterson – Deutsche Bahn
Dr Mario Polywka – Evotec
Christian Rasmussen – Grundfos
Spyros Sakellariou – Intracom Telecom
Pierre Olivier Schnerb – Cobra International
Dr Magnus Schoeman – Atos
Daniel Scuka – Wireless Watch Japan

Karim El Showeikh – Magdi El Showeikh
Dipali Sikand – Les Concierges
Klaus Stemig
Yoshimoto Tanaka – All Nippon Airways
Alexandros Tarnaris – Intracom Telecom
Fiona Taylor
David Teng – Haier
Carsten Tessum – Radiometer
Kym Thompson – Cobra International
Kilala Tilaar – Martina Berto
Martha Tilaar – Martina Berto
Chris Towns – Clarks
A. Vasudevan – Wipro Technologies
Katja van der Wal – Philips
Dr Xinming Wan – Haier
Zhengtao Wang – Haier
Tove Weigel – Mölnlycke Health Care
Catherine Whelan
Howard Whitesmith
Bernard Widjaja – Martina Berto
David Williams – Richardson Sheffield

A number of colleagues shared ideas and teaching material with us, which was greatly appreciated. Many thanks to:

Professor Pär Åhlström – Stockholm School of Economics
Dr Nicky Athanassopoulou – Cambridge University
Dr Mattia Bianchi – Stockholm School of Economics
Lloyd He – China Institute for Innovation
Professor Mark Jenkins – Cranfield School of Management
Dr Tim Minshall – Cambridge University
Dr Letizia Mortara – Cambridge University
Dr Eoin O'Sullivan – Cambridge University
Dr Rob Phaal – Cambridge University
Dr Tazeeb Rajwani – Cranfield School of Management
Dr Anders Richtnér – Stockholm School of Economics
Dr G. Chris Rodrigo – George Mason University
Dr Clive Savory – Cranfield School of Management
Dr Richard Schoenberg – Cranfield School of Management
Dr Matthias Seiler – HT Group
Professor Marek Szwejczewski – Cranfield School of Management

We are very pleased that a number of colleagues have contributed mini cases to this edition. Thanks to Professor John Christiansen and Dr Claus Varnes (Copenhagen Business School); Julian Glyn-Owen (Aluris, UK); Dr Ian Kierans (Advanced Organisation, Ireland); Lloyd He (China Institute for Innovation);

Dr Mohamed Khater (Cambridge University); Dr Claire McBride (Dublin Institute of Technology); Dr Jawwad Raja and Dr Thomas Frandsen (Copenhagen Business School); Professor Jan Rosier (University College Dublin); Dr Evy Sakellariou (The American College of Greece); Hendro Tjaturpriono (Prasetiya Mulya Business School, Jakarta); Professor Chris van der Hoven (Wits Business School, South Africa); and Dr Tatiana Zalan (American University in Dubai).

In preparing the 3rd edition, we decided that it would be worthwhile to meet on a regular basis. Exactly halfway between Rick's home and Cranfield is The Gandhi restaurant in Sandy, Bedfordshire – thanks to them for providing our monthly backroom table for meetings and excellent meals.

Lauren Zimmerman, our Development Editor at Palgrave, read and commented on our work and provided many useful ideas on how to develop the style and layout of the book. Our anonymous academic reviewers also took the time and effort to make many useful and concrete suggestions. Copies of major drafts were organized by Maggie Neale, which really helped. Later in the process, Tiiu Sarkijarvi, Ursula Gavin, Isabel Berwick, and Aine Flaherty took the lead in the production process and helped maintain momentum.

And last but not least, many thanks to our two families for their patience when the answer to the question 'Is it finished yet?' was not (yet) affirmative.

Keith Goffin and Rick Mitchell
Cranfield, UK, August 2016

PUBLISHER'S ACKNOWLEDGEMENTS

The publisher and the authors would like to thank the organizations and people listed below for permission to reproduce material from their publications:

Amey, for permission to reproduce Figure 9.3 'Amey's Version of a Stage-Gate® Process for Services.' Copyright © Amey.

AXA Ireland, for permission to reproduce Figure 3.2 'AXA's Innovation Quadrant.' Copyright © AXA.

Dr. Martin Barnes, for permission to reproduce and adapt Figure 7.6 'The Project Management Triangle.' Adapted from the original version set out by Dr. Martin Barnes. Copyright © Dr. Martin Barnes.

Bureau of Labor Statistics (BLS), for permission to reproduce the data in Table 3.3 'Employment in the Service Sector in the US, 2012.' From Employment by major industry sector, www.bls.gov/emp/ep_table_201.htm This is in the public domain.

Central Intelligence Agency (CIA), for permission to reproduce the data in Table 3.1 'Selected International Economic Comparisons, 2014.' From *The World Factbook* 2014–15. Washington, DC: Central Intelligence Agency, 2015. The *Factbook* is in the public domain. https://www.cia.gov/library/publications/resources/the-world-factbook/index.html

NTT DOCOMO, for permission to reproduce Figure 1.9 'DOCOMO's Partnership Concept – The 'Ecosystem'.' Copyright © NTT DOCOMO.

Domino Printing Sciences plc, for permission to reproduce Figure 4.17 'Relationship between Maximum Line Speed and Character Height for Continuous Inkjet Printing,' Figure 4.18 "Crossing the Chasm': Domino Lasers Unit Sales' and Table 6.5 'Domino Lasers' Risk Assessment Tool.' All copyright © Domino Printing Sciences plc.

Grundfos, for permission to reproduce Table 6.6 'Grundfos' Score Tool to Separate Strategic and Tactical Projects.' Copyright © Grundfos.

Houlihan Lokey, for permission to reproduce and adapt Figure 7.10 'Types of Partnership.' From Margulis, M.S. and Pekár, P. Jr. *The next wave of alliance formations: Forging successful partnerships with emerging and middle-market*

companies. (Los Angeles, Houlihan Lokey Howard & Zukin 2003). Reprinted with permission from Houlihan Lokey. Copyright © 2003 Houlihan Lokey.

Kano Quality Research Office (KQRO) and Dr Noriaki Kano (with additional thanks to Secretary Ms Yoko Oyama), for permission to reproduce and adapt Figure 4.10 'Kano's Model of Product (or Service) Features' and Figure 4.11 'Matrix for Allocating Product Features to their Kano Categories.' From Kano, N., Nobuhiko, S., Takahashi, F. and Tsuji S. 'Attractive Quality and Must-be Quality' (1984), Hinshitsu – Journal of the Japanese Society for Quality Control, Vol. 14, No. 2, p. 39–48. Copyright © 1984 Dr Noriaki Kano.

Martina Berto (MB), for permission to reproduce Figure 6.11 'MB's Bubble Diagram Showing the Seven Brand Groups.' Copyright © Martina Berto.

Michael E. Docherty, CEO, Venture2 Inc., for permission to reproduce and adapt Figure 2.4 'The Open Innovation Funnel.' Copyright © Venture2 Inc.

European Union, for permission to reproduce data from the EU Industrial R&D Investment Scoreboard, in Table 2.1 'R&D Investment in Different Industries, 2013' and Table 3.4 'Service Organizations Ranked Top for R&D Investment, 2013.' Copyright © European Union, 1995–2016.

HarperCollins Publishers and Geoffrey A. Moore, for permission to reproduce and adapt Figure 2.3 'Adopter Categories for Innovations.' From "The Revised Technology Adoption Life Cycle" (p. 21) from Crossing The Chasm, Third Edition by Geoffrey A. Moore. Copyright © 1991, 1999, 2002, 2014 by Geoffrey A. Moore.

Harvard Business Review, for permission to reproduce and adapt:
– Figure 1.3 'The Innovation Ambition Matrix.' From The Innovation Ambition Matrix, in 'Managing Your Innovation Portfolio' by Bansi Nagji and Geoff Tuff, May 2012. Copyright © 2012 by the Harvard Business School Publishing Corporation; all rights reserved.
– Figure 5.7 'Selecting a Lead User Group.' From Networking to Lead Users, in "Creating Breakthroughs at 3M" by Eric von Hippel, Stefan Thomke and Mary Sonnack, September–October 1999. Copyright © 1999 by the Harvard Business School Publishing Corporation; all rights reserved.

Harvard Business School Press, for permission to reproduce and adapt:
– Figure 4.15 'Value Gap Analysis for Circuses and Cirque du Soleil.' From Blue Ocean Strategy: How to Create Uncontested Market Space and Make the Competition Irrelevant by W. Chan Kim and Renée Mauborgne. Boston, MA 2005, pp 43. Copyright © 2005 by the Harvard Business School Publishing Corporation; all rights reserved.
– Figure 4.16 'The Development of Sustaining and Disruptive Technologies.' From The Innovator's Dilemma: When New Technologies Cause Great Firms to Fail by Clayton M Christensen. Boston, MA 1997, pp 11. Copyright © 1997 by the Harvard Business School Publishing Corporation; all rights reserved.

IEEE, for permission to reproduce and adapt Figure 7.2 'The Spiral Model for Agile Development.' From Boehm, B. W., 'A Spiral Model of Software Development and Enhancement', Computer, 21(5) (1988), 61–72. Copyright © 1988 IEEE.

International Trade Centre, for permission to reproduce the questions in Table 9.5 'Innovation Audit Questions Recommended for the Service Sector.' From Riddle, D., 'Managing Change in Your Organization'. International Trade Forum, 2 (2000), 26–8. Copyright © 2000 International Trade Centre: All rights reserved worldwide.

John Wiley & Sons, Incorporated, for permission to reproduce and adapt:
– Table 1.2 'Success of Different Degrees of Innovation.' From Markham, S. K. and Lee, H. 'Product Development and Management Association's 2012 Comparative Performance Assessment Study', Journal of Product Innovation Management, 30(3) (2013), 408–29. Copyright © 2013 John Wiley & Sons, Incorporated.
– Figure 4.3 'Scenarios for Entry-level Vehicle Design, Detroit 1980.' From Schwartz and Ogilvy in Ch. 4 of: L. Fahey and R. Randall (eds) Learning from the Future: Competitive foresight scenarios (Chichester: John Wiley, 1998). Copyright © 1998 John Wiley & Sons, Incorporated.
– Figure 4.9 'Business Model Canvas.' From Osterwalder, A. and Pigneur, Y., Business Model Generation: A Handbook for Visionaries, Game Changers, and Challengers (Hoboken, NJ: John Wiley, 2010). Copyright © 2010 John Wiley & Sons, Incorporated.

Kimberly-Clark, for permission to reproduce Figure 9.4 'Job Description for Manager Innovation Capabilities at Kimberly-Clark. Copyright © Kimberly-Clark.

Dr Bob Lillis, Dr Chris van der Hoven, and The Case Centre, for permission to adapt Main Case Study (Chapter 3) 'CitizenM Hotels – Attention to Every Detail.' From CitizenM Hotels: Service Operations & Business Model Innovation, The Case Centre. Copyright © 2012 Cranfield University.

Manifesto for Agile Software Development, for permission to reproduce Theory Box 7.1 'The Agile Manifesto.' Copyright © 2001 Manifesto for Agile Software Development.

McGraw-Hill Education, for permission to reproduce and minimally adapt Figure 5.5 'Johari Window.' From Luft, J., Group Processes: An Introduction to Group Dynamics (USA: McGraw-Hill Education, 1984). Copyright © 1984 McGraw-Hill Education.

Merriam-Webster's Collegiate® Dictionary, 11th Edition, for permission to reproduce the definition on page 2. Copyright © 2016 by Merriam-Webster, Inc. (www.Merriam-Webster.com).

Pearson Education Limited, for permission to reproduce Figure 8.2 'The Cultural Web.' From Figure 9.1 on page 138 of *Exploring Techniques of Analysis and Evaluation in Strategic Management - 1st Edition* by Veronique Ambrosini, Gerry Johnson and Kevan Scholes, Pearson Education Limited. Copyright © 1998 Prentice Hall Europe.

Peters Fraser & Dunlop (www.petersfraserdunlop.com) on behalf of the estate of Arthur Koestler, for permission to reproduce and minimally adapt Figure 5.3 'Creativity as the Intersection of Two Different Frames of Reference.' From Figure 2 in Act of Creation by Arthur Koestler. Copyright © 1964 estate of Arthur Koestler.

Dr Rob Phaal, for permission to reproduce:
– Figure 4.4 'Strategic Landscape Structure for a Study of Urban Mobility.'
– Figure 4.5 'Compiling a Strategic Landscape.' From Phaal, R., Farrukh, C. and Probert, D., *Roadmapping for strategy and innovation – aligning technology and markets in a dynamic world*, (Institute for Manufacturing: University of Cambridge, 2010.)
– Figure 4.6 'Generic Roadmap Structure.'
– Figure 4.7 'Cascaded Matrices Linking Market and Business Drivers to Technology Requirements, via Product Features.'
All copyright © Robert Phaal.

Portland International Center for Management of Engineering and Technology (PICMET), for permission to reproduce and adapt Table 6.3 'Some Generic Examples of Factors for Application-focused Projects,' Table 6.4a 'Examples of Scaling Statements for Opportunity,' Table 6.4b 'Examples of Scaling Statements for Feasibility,' and Figure 6.9 'Types of Project on an Opportunity/Feasibility Matrix.' From Mitchell, R., Phaal, R. and Athanassopoulou, N. "Scoring Methods for prioritising and selecting Innovation projects." Proceedings of the Portland Conference on Management of Engineering and Technology (PICMET) Kanazawa, Japan 2014. Copyright © 2014 Mitchell, Phaal and Athanassopoulou.

Sage, for permission to reproduce and adapt Figure 5.6 'Example of a Repertory Grid Interview' and Mini Case 5.6 'Equant – Repertory Grids in Practice.' From Goffin, K., 'Repertory Grid Technique', in D. Partington (ed.) Essential Skills for Management Research (London: Sage, 2002). Copyright © 2002 Sage.

Professor Jagdish Sheth, for permission to reproduce and adapt Figure 2.1 'Drivers of the Need for Innovation.' From Sheth, J.N. and Ram, R., *Bringing Innovation to Market: How to Break Corporate and Customer Barriers*, (New York: Wiley, 1987). Copyright © 1987 Jagdish Sheth[22].

Stage-Gate Inc., for permission to reproduce and adapt the Stage-Gate® Process in Figure 7.9 'A Five-stage Stage-Gate® Process.' Stage-Gate® is a registered trademark of Stage-Gate Inc. Copyright © Stage-Gate Inc.

Quality Press, for permission to reproduce and adapt Figure 7.3 'The House of Quality.' From ReVelle, Jack B., *Quality Essentials: A Reference Guide from A to Z*, (ASQ, 2004), pp. 9-11, House of Quality image. Copyright © 2004 ASQ, www. asq.org. No further distribution allowed without permission.

Industrial Research Institute, www.iriweb.org (http://www.tandfonline.com), for permission to reproduce and adapt:

– Figure 5.9 'Scouting Organization and a Typical Cross-functional Scouting Team,' Figure 5.10 'Schedule for Scouting Activity: the 3-3-3 Approach' and Main Case Study (Chapter 5) 'Mölnlycke Health Care – Innovation Scouting.' From Weigel, T. and Goffin, K., 'Creating Innovation Capabilities: Mölnlycke Health Care's Journey', *Research-Technology Management*, 58(4) (2015), 28–35. Copyright © 2015 Industrial Research Institute.

– Figure 6.7 'Comparison between Two Projects Using their Confidence Value Distributions,' Figure 6.8a 'Decision Tree for RFID Project for Embraer,' Figure 6.8b 'Monte Carlo Simulation for Decision Tree by Embraer,' Figure 6.8c 'Comparison of Three Strategies for RFID Implementation' and Mini Case 6.2 'Embraer Aerospace – Using Decision Trees.' From Mitchell, R., Hunt, F. and Probert, D., 'Valuing and Comparing Small Portfolios', *Research-Technology Management*, 53(2) (2010), 43–54. Copyright © 2010 Industrial Research Institute.

World Trade Organization, for permission to reproduce Table 3.2 'GATT Classification of Services.' www.wto.org Copyright © World Trade Organization.

We would also like to thank everyone who has given up their time to be interviewed for the case studies. We really appreciate your generosity and support. Please see the individual case studies for the names of the interviewees.

UNDERSTANDING INNOVATION AND INNOVATION MANAGEMENT

innovation – n., the introduction of something new
From Merriam-Webster's Collegiate® Dictionary, 11th Edition copyright © 2016
by Merriam-Webster, Inc. (www.Merriam-Webster.com).

INTRODUCTION

As consumers we are constantly bombarded with advertisements for new products. So think innovation, think new products? No: although new products are essential, other types of innovation, such as new services and new business models are just as important. And because customers are more demanding and competition stronger, companies need to be good at managing all types of innovation.

Nearly 20 years ago management guru Peter Drucker said that how to manage innovation was an unanswered question.[1] Even today, when most companies think innovation is the best way to achieve growth, how it can best be managed is still not fully understood. So insights into how to manage innovation (and courses on it) are in demand. Consequently, the volume of publications on innovation has rocketed over the past decade. But therein lies the problem: innovation management is developing so fast that it is becoming increasingly difficult to gain an overview of its most critical aspects.

With new tools and techniques being promoted as 'the solution' to innovation issues, it is no wonder that companies adopt the latest innovation management idea. But there are 'no quick fixes, panaceas or one-size-fits-all solutions'[2] and so managers must identify which innovation management tools are relevant for their organization. It is not simply a case of *adopting* best practice; managers always need to *adapt* innovation management techniques to their company's specific business environment.

This book was written to meet the needs of managers and students interested in innovation and innovation management. It presents an integrated view of the skills, tools and techniques needed to successfully develop new products, services, processes and business models. Innovation is an exciting topic because successful innovation cuts across functional boundaries – from research and development (R&D) to marketing; it relies on different disciplines – from creativity to organizational behaviour; and it challenges managers' and employees' thinking – going much further than just 'thinking outside the box', as we will see in Chapter 5.

This book is relevant to organizations in the manufacturing and service sectors but it also discusses topics that have been recognized as salient in the public sector.[3] The choice of tools and techniques we present is based on an extensive review of the literature, our personal experiences in industry, and 20 years' teaching, research and consultancy. Many examples and case studies from different organizations around the world are discussed in this book; since innovation is a practical subject, we think that practical examples are an essential and interesting way to understand it.

Too many companies focus on just one aspect of innovation management – typically, ideas generation – although other aspects are equally important. Leading organizations take a broader view and consider a range of issues, including selection, implementation and business culture. Based on our research, we have identified five key elements of innovation management, which we refer to as the

Innovation Pentathlon Framework. We draw the analogy that managing innovation is like competing in the Olympic pentathlon; excellent performance in one sport will not guarantee a gold medal. Therefore companies need to achieve high performance in each of the five areas identified by the framework. The Pentathlon Framework has been used extensively in our teaching and our work with many leading organizations. It is a tool to help organizations develop their *innovation capability* – the ability to achieve growth through innovation.

Both the nature of innovation and the ways in which it can be managed are often unclear. So in this chapter we define exactly *what innovation is* and in the rest of the book we pragmatically explain *how to manage innovation*. This chapter covers:

- Understanding innovation.
- Understanding innovation management.
- The Innovation Pentathlon Framework.
- The structure of this book.
- A main case study on NTT DOCOMO, a Japanese company in the service sector, which shows how a broad approach to innovation can lead to sustained growth.

UNDERSTANDING INNOVATION

Innovation is a ubiquitous term – Google currently identifies no less than 498 million 'hits' for 'innovation' – but it is often misunderstood. A common misconception is that innovation in business is just about new products. Recognizing such misconceptions is not just of academic interest; because if employees and managers misunderstand innovation, then they will fail to contribute to it. Therefore this section will define innovation and explain what we will call the *dimensions*, *degrees* and *drivers* of innovation.

Definitions of Innovation

The dictionary definition of *innovation* – introducing something new – is clear, but a broader one is needed to help managers or employees understand business innovation. A definition is needed that gives insights into the following issues: What are the most important types of innovation? How can innovation lead to sustainable competitive advantage? What is the most effective way to boost the innovation performance of an organization?

Managers and employees may have a range of opinions on the nature of innovation in their business environment. An R&D manager of an industrial safety equipment company told us: 'If I ask five different people at our company what innovation is, I will get at least five different answers.' Diverse views on innovation arising from different functional perspectives can hinder the implementation of innovation strategy. For example, employees in operations might think that innovation is the sole responsibility of R&D. Such an attitude would mean that operations would not actively contribute to innovation (see Mini Case 1.1 to understand the contribution manufacturing operations made to Tetley's competiveness).

> **MINI CASE 1.1:** *Tetley's Teabags – Rounding on the Competition*[4]
>
> Tetley is a leader in the world teabag market and originator of the round teabag. On the face of it, the round teabag was only an incremental change from the traditional square version. However, through the process innovation required to support the production of the new product, Tetley gained sustainable competitive advantage. When the company developed the round teabag, it knew that with suitable marketing, this new product could capture significant market share. Advertising copy promoted the idea that round teabags allow the tea to go round in circles and therefore make a better brew. But Tetley knew that competitors would quickly try to copy this product innovation. So the company decided not to discuss round teabags with its supplier of manufacturing equipment. Instead, it hired Cambridge Consultants Ltd to develop a completely new manufacturing line for round teabags. When the new product was introduced, competitors were unable to obtain similar manufacturing equipment and Tetley maintained its lead.
>
> Tetley became part of Tata Tea in 2000, forming the world's second largest tea company. Tata Tea, now called Tata Global Beverages, is itself a subsidiary of the Tata Group, a successful, growing conglomerate with a reputation in India for doing business responsibly. As well as tea, Tata also has interests in a broader group of beverage companies, which includes Eight O'Clock Coffee in the US and Mount Everest Mineral Water in India (its Himalayan brand of mineral water).
>
> Andrew Dobson, director of global innovation at Tetley, says: 'Innovation is critical. It's really important to continually bring new and fresh things to market which surprise and delight, whether that's simply a new blend or flavour, an entirely new product or a new route to market.' Tetley also recognizes that it is vital to stand out from the crowd and consistently communicate what makes the Tetley brand unique and better than its competitors: 'A good product is one thing but in our competitive environment, it is equally important to be innovative at getting our message over to consumers', says Dobson.
>
> The objective of the Tetley innovation programme is to be one step ahead of competitors and develop brands and products that offer consumers both functional and emotional benefits. Dobson says:
>
> > We've built a reputation as pioneers in the tea industry – we were the first to launch the teabag; the first to 'change the shape of the market' by introducing round teabags in 1989 and then the 'no-drip' drawstring bags in 1997; and the first big 'black tea' brand to really branch out into new and exciting varieties such as green tea and rooibos. We're always looking for new ways to revolutionize the tea industry.
>
> And the latest innovation from Tetley is functional green 'super teas', which the European Food Standards Agency has verified as reducing tiredness and fatigue.

Over time, the understanding of innovation has evolved. The importance of understanding innovation was recognized in the 1930s by Austrian economist Joseph Schumpeter. His work on innovation strongly influenced the field of economics, as will be discussed in Chapter 2. Schumpeter considered different aspects of innovation and, although it was developed 80 years ago, his definition has five components that are still relevant today:[5]

1. 'The introduction of a good (product), which is new to consumers, or one of increased quality than was available in the past.

2. Methods of production, which are new to a particular branch of industry. These are not necessarily based on new scientific discoveries and may have, for example, already been used in other industrial sectors.
3. The opening of new markets.
4. The use of new sources of supply.
5. New forms of competition, which lead to the restructuring of an industry.'

Schumpeter's view of innovation was broader than new products; for example, it indicated the importance of manufacturing methods. An example of a company whose manufacturing prowess is as important as its new products is the Swedish furniture giant Ikea (it can produce durable products at low cost). This company has also innovated in opening new markets, such as China.

Michael Porter defined innovation as including 'both improvements in technology and better methods or ways of doing things. It can be manifested in product changes, process changes, new approaches to marketing, new forms of distribution, and new concepts of scope … [innovation] results as much from organizational learning as from formal R&D.'[6] This definition covers similar points to Schumpeter's but indicates that innovation can originate from marketing, distribution and an organization's learning. That is, innovation does not only emerge from R&D.

Both Porter and Schumpeter use the word 'new' in their definitions, but it should be noted that many commercial innovations are not totally new. Everett Rogers, an expert on how innovations spread through markets, showed that innovation 'is an idea, practice, or object that is perceived as new by the individual or other unit of adoption'.[7] So the *perception* of newness is as important as originality. This definition helps companies to remember that ideas for innovation are not necessarily brand new. Ikea's 'invention' of selling furniture in flat packs is credited with playing a big part in its success. But the idea goes back much further; to at least the Thonet chairs that were popular in Viennese coffee houses from 1859. As the chairs became fashionable throughout Europe, they were dispatched in kit form. This example should remind managers that previous solutions can be valid and starting from 'a blank sheet' is not necessarily the most efficient way (in Chapter 5 we will discuss how existing knowledge can be an important component of ideation).

The definition of innovation from the Organisation for Economic Co-operation and Development (OECD)[8] is: 'the implementation of a new or significantly improved product (good or service), or process, a new marketing method, or a new organizational method in business practices, workplace organization or external relations'. Similar to Porter's, the OECD definition indicates different sorts of innovation and identifies the role of business processes and external partners.

In the service sector, the term 'innovation' can refer either to the service product or how it is delivered[9] (this will be discussed in detail in Chapter 3). Only leading service companies have departments focused on driving innovation; for example, Bank of America has its Innovation Development Team and Singapore Airlines has its Product Innovation Department. A useful definition is: 'innovation in the service sector comprises new services and new ways of producing or delivering services as well as significant changes in services or their production or delivery'.[10]

Comparing the various definitions of innovation, it can be seen that there are several common elements: *what* is changed (such as product or manufacturing process changes); *how much* is changed (whether the innovation is brand new, or just perceived as new, or is significantly different); and the *source* of the change (often science and technology).

Dimensions of Innovation in the Manufacturing Sector

The definitions discussed above describe *what* is changed but it is also useful to refer to what we call the *dimensions of innovation* (Figure 1.1). These dimensions are the areas in which an organization can potentially innovate and sometimes the term *types of innovation* is used. *Product innovation* is the first and most obvious dimension and many companies tend to focus on products and their features (see Mini Case 1.2 on Gillette). However, companies should avoid being one dimensional, that is, only focused on products, in their approach to innovation.

The second dimension is *process innovation*, which normally refers to improvements in a manufacturing process. (Other business processes can be improved but they will be referred to later.) Process innovation is particularly important as it can make a product hard to copy. The Mars Group, owner of the Pedigree brand of pet foods, has improved its manufacturing processes to the level that it is the world leader at producing complex shapes. These shapes cost more to manufacture but give the product a marketing advantage. For example,

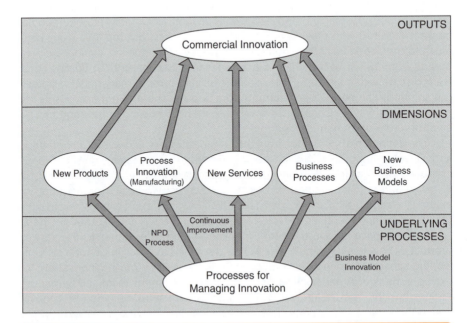

FIGURE 1.1: Example Dimensions of Innovation for a Manufacturing Company

the shape of dog biscuits has been carefully designed to clean dogs' teeth. So the process innovation supports the marketing of the product. In service companies, the equivalent of manufacturing is the service production and delivery process. For example, fast-food companies have sophisticated equipment to ensure that their food is of consistent quality, wherever it is sold.

Service innovation is the third dimension. Companies producing complex and technical products can create services to help differentiate their products. For example, the manufacturer Rolls-Royce is known for its aero-engines and its excellent after-sales service. One of its services is that its engines have sensors that predict the need to replace parts. Any replacement parts needed are delivered in advance to an appropriate airport, where they can be exchanged.

Companies can also use *business process innovation*, the fourth dimension. This optimizes internal processes, for example supply chain management, and the external processes that make it easier for customers to do business with the company, for example order fulfilment. Many supermarket chains now offer internet shopping and, for example, Tesco in the UK has been very successful at designing this process and growing sales. Part of its approach includes four giant 'dark stores' in London – stores that are closed to the public, where Tesco's employees select items from the shelves to match customers' internet orders for home delivery.

Finally, *business model innovation* (BMI), the fifth dimension, can be a key source of commercial innovation. BMI has become a much talked about aspect of innovation in recent years and so we will discuss it many times in this book but particularly in Chapter 2. A business model is the way in which a company *creates* and *captures value*. Probably the best-known examples of BMI are low-cost airlines, such as EasyJet, Southwest and Ryanair, which have revolutionized short-haul passenger travel with minimum ('no frills') service included, and everything else at extra cost. An example of a company that is experimenting with business model innovation is BMW. The car manufacturer has just launched a car-sharing scheme in London.[11] With research showing that car ownership is a lower priority with young people, car manufacturers are experimenting with such pay-as-you-go schemes.

Studies show that when new products or services are being developed, the business model that supports them is seldom considered.[12] In contrast, AkzoNobel, a leading manufacturer of marine coatings, not only developed a new high-tech product for coating the bottom of oil tankers but also changed its business model: selling the product in advance by predicting when a ship would need a new coating. AkzoNobel made a new product much more successful by linking it with a new business model.[13] This shows the importance of an organization understanding the full opportunities for innovation and not assuming that it is only related to the product itself.

Across industries, a number of generic business models have been identified. One of them is the so-called 'razor and blades' model. Companies such as Gillette sell their razors at a low price but make money on the continuous demand for the blades. This model has been transferred to other sectors by companies such as HP, which price their printers low and then make significant revenues and profits on selling ink and toner.

> **MINI CASE 1.2:** *Gillette – Blade Runner*

Some managers perceive innovation to be inextricably linked to a first-to-market strategy. Breakthrough products such as the iPad have captured the imagination of many people, who now perceive innovation as consisting of first-to-market, new products. Unfortunately, this view can lead managers to forget the biggest downside of being first to market – competitors can quickly copy your innovation if you have not thought of ways to protect it. Worst of all, competitors may learn from the limitations of the first-to-market product and make their 'copy' better than the original.

The Gillette 'Mach 3' razor was a first-to-market product. At very high cost, Gillette developed this advanced razor, with its characteristic three blades set at different, very precise angles. A UK supermarket chain quickly introduced a good copy of the product at a fraction of the development costs. This made Gillette more dependent on expensive television advertising to try and protect sales of its product.

When products are easy to copy, competitors can 'leapfrog' the original features. Thus, Wilkinson Sword introduced a four-blade razor. Then Gillette introduced its 'Fusion' product with five blades. This was quickly copied in a much cheaper form by the US Rite Aid pharmacy chain. But all good things come to an end (there can only be so many blades on a razor). So now the focus of competition seems to be switching from the number of blades to features such as automatic skin hydration.

Most products are relatively easy to copy and patents seldom give sufficient protection. For example, Canon worked round several hundred patents owned by Xerox in the development of its first, and very successful photocopier. So, companies that are *one dimensional*, focusing only on product innovation, miss opportunities for sustainable competitive advantage. Combining the different dimensions, a *multidimensional* approach, can be powerful. For example, complementing new products with special manufacturing processes can make products harder to copy[14] (contrast Mini Case 1.1 on Tetley's with Mini Case 1.2 on Gillette). Overall, companies need to find creative ways to ensure that their innovations are not easy to copy[15].

As we have stressed, combining the different dimensions leads to competitive advantage. For example, 10 years ago Volkswagen planned a new version of the Golf GTX, the target segment being young people (25- to 30-year-olds). Although the design of the product was updated and some new performance features added, these were essentially incremental. However, with the new version of the product, VW redesigned the manufacturing process. A major part of this was bolt-on, as opposed to welded, side panels, to make repairs more cost-effective. This process innovation was focused on the most common accidents of the target segment, which are city front offside collisions. In advance of the product launch, VW contacted insurance companies and the significantly lower repair costs enabled it to negotiate a lower cost of insurance for young drivers of the Golf GTX. By allowing VW to work with partners in a unique way, the manufacturing innovation supported a breakthrough in the business model. By considering not just the product innovation dimension, VW surprised the competition and gained significant market share. The innovation was hard to copy because other manufacturers such as Ford could not make similar design changes, due to the exorbitant costs of reconfiguring their existing production lines. Making changes to other dimensions can make a relatively bland, incremental product successful, as the VW example shows.

The dimensions suggested in Figure 1.1 might not be sufficient for every market. An example is the gourmet food market, where packaging is so important that managers in this market consider it to be a dimension of innovation. Similarly, packaging is crucial for Unilever's personal hygiene products and the company has just spent 40,000 hours developing a smaller deodorant aerosol.[16] Apple is famous for its design-led innovation (with attractive and easy-to-use products) and some would argue that the company has used design as an extra dimension of its innovation. Thus every organization needs to identify whether additional dimensions are relevant in its markets.

Management needs to drive the underlying processes that stimulate innovation within a company (see lower portion of Figure 1.1). Some of these will be formally defined and documented, such as the new product development (NPD) process. Others will be less tangible, such as idea generation, or the management of company culture. The OECD says that innovation management 'consists of all those scientific, technical, commercial and financial steps necessary for the successful development and marketing of new or improved manufactured products, the commercial use of new or improved processes or equipment or the introduction of a new approach to a social service. R&D is only one of these steps.'[17]

In a modern manufacturing company, line operators are not simply responsible for manufacturing products. They are also given full responsibility for constantly improving the manufacturing processes (through continuous improvement and other means). Some companies even talk about their operators being 'process owners'. Senior managers need to see themselves as the process owners for innovation management and not simply as managing new products and services. With this different perspective, managers should view the innovation processes within their organizations as the way they can create a capability for growth.

Dimensions of Innovation in the Service Sector

Typically, the dimensions of innovation are different in the service sector and they vary from one market to another. For example, the interaction with the customer is an important dimension, and can be via the internet, by telephone or face to face. Thus there are many opportunities for innovating how a service is delivered (see Mini Case 1.3 on Les Concierges). We will discuss the dimensions for a specific sector.

We worked with an insurance company that decided to examine its overall innovation performance. A group of senior and product managers took part in a workshop to identify all the dimensions of innovation relevant to their markets. To stimulate the team to come up with ideas, the discussion was based on the parallels to innovation in manufacturing companies (Figure 1.1).

The workshop results are summarized in Figure 1.2. New products – which for this company meant new insurance policies – are important. However, a range of other dimensions was identified. This included the customer interface and the way service products are 'delivered'. The management team immediately

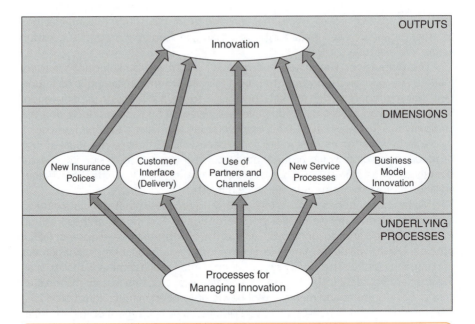

FIGURE 1.2: Example Dimensions of Innovation for an Insurance Company[18]

developed a number of ideas to improve service delivery and linked this to customer profiling (analysis of customer data to identify market segments). Other dimensions where the managers perceived that the company could innovate were working with partners (as most of the insurance policies were underwritten by suppliers) and the use of different sales channels (including banks, brokers and the internet). Completely new service processes and business models were the other dimensions identified.

As a result of the workshop, the insurance company recognized that it had more innovation possibilities – dimensions – than previously thought. Now, as each new product is developed, the company looks at each of the dimensions shown in Figure 1.2, with the goal of creating more unique insurance products, which are 'hard to copy'.

> **MINI CASE 1.3:** *Les Concierges – High-tech, High-touch*[19] *with video interview*

Have you ever said to yourself, 'I just wish I had someone else to take care of this for me'? Les Concierges is that someone else. People with demanding jobs have limited spare time, and so sometimes struggle to meet their many personal and family commitments. Finding the right way to help them has enabled Dipali Sikand, the founder of Les Concierges, to build an international business.

Continued...

The company was started in 1998 in Bangalore, India (the centre of the country's IT industry) and it has grown significantly. Currently, it serves 1,600 corporate clients across nearly 2,000 international sites, with 1,600 concierges. The idea behind Les Concierges may be simple – helping professionals with their daily tasks – but recognizing the need and developing a 'high-tech, high-touch' solution are real innovations. Where did the original idea come from? Sikand says: 'For me it was "necessity is the motherhood of invention". As a young working mother, I faced the challenge of achieving a work–life balance and realized that corporates want to help their employees.' So, although the company assists busy professionals, Les Concierges, as a business, targets corporations rather than individuals.

Corporations benefit because their employees can focus more on their work. Les Concierges often posts one or two of its staff to companies ('onsite concierges'), often in the IT industry. The host company provides a desk and an intranet connection for Les Concierges and then the 'help desk' can go live, offering four categories of service: shopping, everyday tasks, entertainment and travel. The host company pays a retainer each year based on its number of employees but it sees the return through increased employee productivity. A transaction fee is paid by employees, who save precious time in their busy schedules. An onsite concierge 'can be employee's personal assistant, travel guide, entertainment adviser, home maintenance guru, errand runner, and party planner … all rolled into one', says Sikand.

The interaction with customers is crucial and Sikand refers to this as 'high touch', even though the company deals with over 2.1 million requests for help per year. She has hired many women, as she feels that they are more sympathetic to customers' needs. With such empathy, Les Concierges can often delight its end-customers by coming up with original ideas for birthday presents and so on. Les Concierges staff take absolute pride in solving difficult challenges. According to Sikand: 'Our commitment is to do anything, anytime, and anywhere. The only limit to our services is your imagination and we take on any request, provided it is legal and ethical.'

The importance of the behind-the-scenes 'high-tech' organization is also recognized. Sikand's team have concentrated on making the service delivery high tech and slick – proprietary software tracks each customer transaction and coordinates the many tasks that are passed to outside suppliers every day. Although it is a 'people business', this has not stopped Les Concierges making significant and regular investments in technology.

As Sikand says: 'Innovation for us means thinking of novel ways to not only solve the customer's problem but also to delight them in the process. We always want to do it the way you would have liked to have been treated yourself.' The close relationship that Les Concierges maintains with its end-customers also means that it can keep ahead of market trends. 'Increasingly, our customers' needs are moving from requests for "errands" to more "aspirational" requirements. The company has introduced a range

of proactive products, for example, we have arranged financial services advice for professionals at a major corporate.' And it has extended the concierge concept to address new markets, such as 'residential concierges', who work with property managers to help them acquire and retain tenants. Les Concierges places strong emphasis on innovation, and it has created the role of 'VP product development' (which is still unusual in a service company). As Sikand says: 'We keep inventing new services, and new standards of delivery. It's our expertise and passion for pre-empting customer needs that leaves the competition behind.'

Now visit www.palgravehighered.com/gm to watch Dipali Sikand discussing the unique role of VP Product Development at Les Concierges.

Degrees of Innovation

Innovations can be dramatic. Breakthroughs such as the iPad and the iPhone are the examples that people most often mention when they talk about innovation. However, it is important to recognize that there are different *degrees of innovation* that apply to each of the dimensions of innovation. For example, an incremental new product might be combined with a new service that makes it very competitive.

There is no generally accepted terminology for the degrees of innovation. In one of the earliest classifications, consultants Booz-Allen and Hamilton proposed six degrees of product innovation: from the improvement of an existing product to 'new-to-the-world' products that create entirely new markets.[20] However, the six are somewhat unwieldy and most innovation discussions now use a smaller number. Table 1.1 introduces the terminology we use throughout this book, which has three degrees and so is easy to apply.

Incremental innovations are improvements to existing products, services and processes (such as manufacturing). They target companies' *core* customers and markets, and can enable growth through gaining market share. It is easy to identify opportunities using traditional market research, where customers are simply asked what their preferences are. Examples of incremental innovations include washing machines that require less water and power, and bank accounts allowing mobile access.

Next, there are *breakthrough innovations*,[21] which are products and services that are based on substantial changes through, for example, new technology or by addressing previously unmet customer needs. They are new to the customer and create new categories. It should be noted that companies attempting to develop breakthrough products and services face a far greater challenge than with incremental ones. For instance, 'traditional market research and development approaches [have] proved to be particularly ill-suited to breakthrough products'.[22] Similarly, it takes time for customers to understand the benefits of breakthrough products and so it takes time to build sales. Importantly, breakthroughs help companies move from their core to *adjacent markets*, expanding and achieving growth. Examples of breakthrough innovations include two-drawer dishwashers (that allow single people to wash smaller amounts of crockery, or more if they have visitors), and the way Les Concierges helps busy professional people arrange their personal lives.

Most dramatically, there are *radical* innovations (sometimes called *transformational* innovations), which are game changing. These are rarer as they create new businesses and major new categories, or completely redefine the competitive environment. Ideas such as iTunes and the Tata Nano car capture the headlines.[23] The former innovation has reached its full potential but the low-cost car developed in India has not yet succeeded. Another example of a radical innovation is Uber, the internet-based taxi service. This new business model has hit the headlines in nearly every country, as local taxi drivers have protested against it.

Some observers will view certain innovations as radical, whereas others will perceive them as incremental. This discourse is often heard in academia, but the

TABLE 1.1: Degrees of Product Innovation

	Degree of innovation	Explanation		Investment (percentage)
1.	Incremental innovation	• Improvements to existing products, services and processes, such as line extensions • New products or services that address the same existing markets • Easy to develop based on customer needs • Growth only possible through taking market share	The Golden Ratio	70
2.	Breakthrough innovation	• New products or services with unique features that provide real benefit to customers • Difficult to develop, as they require deep customer insights • Generate growth through opening new, adjacent markets • May take time to generate sales		20
3.	Radical innovation	• Develops products, services for markets that do not yet exist • New business models that transform markets • Rare and difficult to develop		10

search for an unambiguous definition is probably not a productive one, since the degree of innovation is context dependent. In practice, discussing the degrees of innovation makes organizations aware of where there is extra potential for innovation.

Although managers often aspire to radical innovation and successes capture the imagination of the public, a lower degree of innovation is more common. Research investigating over 100 companies in 1997 showed that 84 per cent of product innovations were 'line extensions' (that is, incremental innovation) and that, on average, 62 per cent of revenues came from such products.[24] As might be expected, however, 38 per cent of revenues (and 61 per cent of profits) came from breakthrough product innovations. A 2014 survey of 1,500 top managers showed that only 13 per cent of companies achieve breakthrough innovation.[25]

Innovation Ambition and the 'Golden Ratio'

The *innovation ambition matrix*[26] (Figure 1.3) is a useful tool to stimulate managers to decide on the intended role of innovation in their organization (their 'innovation ambition'). Along the x-axis of Figure 1.3, increasing degrees of innovation and more dimensions are added. Thus the axis moves from modifications of existing products and services (on the left) to development of combinations of new products, services and business models (on the right). Combinations are important because, for example, 'breakthrough products and services increasingly need to be part of a broader business model'.[27] As we stressed earlier, a greater market impact can often be achieved by combining different dimensions, for example a new product with a new service, and this is shown by the markets addressed on the y-axis (moving from existing markets and customers, via adjacent ones, to new markets and customers).

The first key message of Figure 1.3 is that organizations need to decide on their innovation strategy – what they want to achieve from innovation – and from this divide their innovation budgets across the categories *incremental* (optimizing existing products and services for existing customers), *breakthrough* (creating new benefits for existing customers) and *radical innovations* (innovations for completely new markets). Thus a company with an ambition to grow through developing new markets might divide its innovation budget across these *strategic buckets* in the 'ratio' 70:20:10 (as shown in Table 1.1), whereas a more conservative organization might decide that the 'ratio' 90:5:5 is appropriate. Some managers stress the importance of the balance selected by referring to it as the *golden ratio*. This term refers to the fixed proportions underlying many beautiful works of art.[28] In this, it is somewhat misleading because there is *not* a single golden ratio that innovative companies should adopt. However, the concept is useful because it forces organizations to consider what their current ratio is, and what they aspire to. How an organization's innovation ambition needs to match the choice of innovation projects is discussed in Chapter 6.

Figure 1.3 conveys a number of other messages. With core markets, much of the innovation will focus on incremental improvements. So, in the bottom left-hand corner, the well-established techniques of quality management, such as the work of the quality management guru Deming, can be used.[29] Continuous improvement to manufacturing processes or service delivery can be used to achieve higher quality output at lower cost. Many companies have and continue to reap rewards from continuous improvement – *kaizen* in Japanese. Continuous improvement is important but it cannot lead to growth in new markets. For that, breakthroughs and radical innovation are essential.

'Innovation is hard. Breakthrough innovation is even harder'[30] because completely new products and services require deep customer insights. Only with such insights can unique features with real benefits be developed. Often, business process innovation is needed to support breakthrough products, as new markets demand different approaches from core markets. The biggest strategic contrast between incremental, breakthrough and radical innovations is that the latter two allow companies to expand into new markets and so provide the potential for more growth.

The top right-hand corner of Figure 1.3 is the realm of radical innovations. These require not only new products or services that bring new customer benefits but also new business models. For example, crowded cities make car ownership less attractive and so product innovations like the Tata Nano will need to be matched with new business models. Developing new markets is challenging

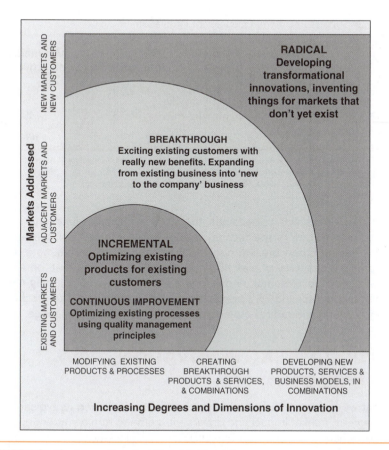

FIGURE 1.3: The Innovation Ambition Matrix

Source: reprinted by permission of Harvard Business Review. Adapted from The Innovation Ambition Matrix, from 'Managing Your Innovation Portfolio' by Bansi Nagji and Geoff Tuff, May 2012. Copyright © 2012 by the Harvard Business School Publishing Corporation; all rights reserved.

and can take as much effort as developing the innovation itself, and can require an existing organization to adopt a new organizational structure. We refer to this as *collateral changes*, where the innovation is so different that an existing company cannot manage it without significant changes to its processes and structure. Radical innovation is rare and difficult to achieve but can, as the name implies, transform a whole company. Think of Virgin's move from selling records to transatlantic travel.

In Figure 1.3, the area between the two extremes (bottom left-hand and top right-hand corners) is the main focus of innovation management. Here, research and practice now provide many useful tools and insights and a coherent approach to managing innovation is emerging. Some argue that incremental improvements are not innovation; we believe that there is no value in agonizing over where the boundary between incremental improvement and innovation lies. However, the further one moves up the diagonal on Figure 1.3, the more difficult

TABLE 1.2: Success of Different Degrees of Innovation

	On time (%)	On budget (%)	Met technical objectives (%)	Met market objectives (%)
Incremental	57.9	62.3	72.9	68.0
Breakthrough	43.6	49.1	66.3	58.7
Radical	29.2	31.7	53.1	46.3

Source: adapted from Markham, S. K. and Lee, H. 'Product Development and Management Association's 2012 Comparative Performance Assessment Study', Journal of Product Innovation Management, 30(3) (2013), 408–29. Copyright © 2013 John Wiley & Sons, Incorporated. Reprinted with permission[31].

the management challenge becomes, the more crucial cross-functional thinking becomes, and the more the techniques presented in this book are required. Table 1.2 illustrates how breakthrough and radical innovations are more difficult. Based on a major survey of over 450 manufacturers, it shows that, on average, 57.9 per cent of incremental innovations are 'on time', whereas only 43.6 per cent of breakthrough and 29.2 per cent of radical projects meet their schedules. So, breakthrough and radical projects are more challenging to manage.

UNDERSTANDING INNOVATION MANAGEMENT

Now that we have established what innovation is – including its typical dimensions, degrees, market impact and drivers – it is time to turn our attention to how it can be managed. This is a complex topic and it will fill the rest of this book but this section gives an overview, covering:

- The typical phases of an innovation
- The business functions involved
- Top management's view of the challenges with managing innovation
- Trends in innovation management research
- The need for a framework for innovation management.

Phases of an Innovation

Every innovation must be managed through a number of *phases* before it is commercially viable. All innovations begin with the generation of ideas and the road to implementation and commercial success can be a long and difficult one. Some ideas will, and should, fall by the wayside. An extreme example is the pharmaceutical industry. Ideas for new drugs are based on novel chemical structures called 'new chemical entities' (NCEs). These take years to develop, test and launch onto the market. The majority of NCEs are rejected along the way for one reason or another, for example side effects, and typically only one NCE in a thousand will be commercially successful. A recent study of other manufacturing sectors showed that successful companies take one in four ideas to market, whereas less successful companies only manage to take one in eight ideas to market.[32]

Figure 1.4 shows the typical phases of an innovation. A funnel of ideas is created and these will cover all dimensions of innovation; that is, there will be ideas for new products, services, processes and business models. Since it is considered to be hard (fuzzy) to manage, this phase is often called the *fuzzy front end* or *ideation*. Some ideas are filtered out immediately, whereas others progress further and are developed into *concepts*. Such a concept might be prepared by a small team from different functional areas of the business working together part time over a few weeks. More complex concepts will take longer to develop. At the concept stage, the size of the potential market and the best way the innovation can be designed will have been considered (although these questions will not have been fully answered). Similarly, each concept will have been analysed as to the investment required and the initial estimate of potential returns.

Normally, senior management decides which concepts will be selected to become *projects* and enter the implementation phase. Certain concepts may be rejected as currently uninteresting, to emerge later as 'recycled ideas'. The way concepts are selected is an important part of managing innovation.

The analogy to a funnel used in Figure 1.4 has been used for many years. Kim Clark and Steven Wheelwright from Harvard Business School have also used

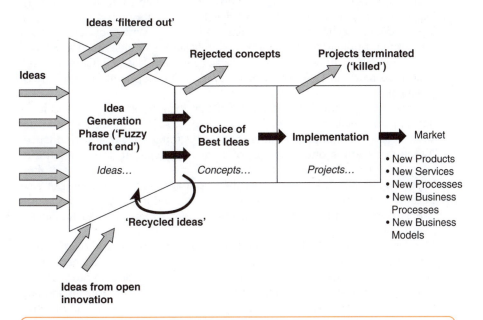

FIGURE 1.4: The Typical Phases of an Innovation: 'The Development Funnel'[33]

it as a basis for discussions with managers on the typical phases of innovation.[34] They had managers draw their own versions of the funnel and found that managers perceived that the different phases often overlap, problems are common and so iterations are necessary. The funnel structure is, of course, a simplification. For example, ideas may well be modified and refined several times as they are turned into usable concepts, so the boundary between the *idea generation phase* and the *choice of best ideas* may not be clear-cut. And a project may be modified or cancelled during *implementation* if new information comes to light, although most companies make a firm 'go' decision before implementation starts.

Innovation and Business Functions

Any organization that wants to be innovative must ensure that all business functions actively contribute. Innovation should not only originate in the R&D department, or the strategic planning group. Managing innovation cuts across functional boundaries. The following functional areas should be involved in product innovation:

- *Research and development:* for many managers, R&D is *the* source of innovation and it is true that this function should drive many of the ideas for new products and services in a company. However, companies that rely solely on R&D can fall into the trap of producing sophisticated products that the market does not require. This has been recognized by a leading economist who said: 'the proper management of innovation is much more than establishing and maintaining a research and development laboratory that produces a great deal of technical output'.[35] Service companies may not have an R&D department but leading ones have the equivalent, with titles such as Service Innovation Group (time:matters, a logistics company based in Germany; see main case study in Chapter 8) or Innovation Development Team (Bank of America).
- *Industrial design:* this is the department that focuses on the form and function of products and services. Design – think of Apple – leads to more successful products, competitive advantage and stronger financial performance. Although design is often thought of as relating solely to the aesthetics of a product, it can contribute at a more fundamental level. Consumers often buy products not only because of their appearance and function but also because of their emotional and symbolic value. Getting designers and engineers to work together effectively can be exigent, as they have such different perspectives.[36]
- *Marketing:* this function has a key role to play in innovation. It should identify customers' needs, through creative forms of market research. It needs to be involved throughout the whole process of innovation, including product definition, pricing decisions, positioning and product launch. Good marketing should make the difference between a promising and a successful product, particularly in the case of breakthrough and radical innovations, where new markets need developing.

- *Sales:* this function is often excluded from the innovation process, as many companies are worried that sales executives will stop selling existing products when they know what is in the pipeline. More astute organizations involve selected salespeople because of their market knowledge and their ability to help develop new markets. The latter point is important because breakthrough and radical innovations address new markets that require market development. This is where selected top salespeople can help. For example, Agilent Technologies, manufacturer of chemical test equipment, actively involves sales in advising how to develop the markets for its chemical test equipment.

- *Operations:* this function, often called *production* or simply *manufacturing* in the manufacturing sector, should also contribute to innovation. Unfortunately, many operations managers do not perceive that they have a key role in driving innovation. This limits the ability of a company to obtain longer term competitive advantage, as process innovations are harder to copy than product innovations. Service sector companies often underestimate the potential of operations to contribute to innovation, although the service experience is crucial to customer satisfaction.

- *Finance and accounting:* this function is able to make a contribution to innovation. It can provide essential support in calculating return on investment (ROI) for innovation projects,[37] so aiding the selection process. That said, during the early stages of breakthrough and radical projects, it is impossible to calculate ROI and so good finance directors know the importance of using other ways of assessing projects (see Chapter 6 for full discussion on this). At Verigy, manufacturer of computer chip testing equipment, financial controlling plays a key role in determining which projects offer the best combination of low risk, high return and a good match to the available resources. The finance function can also help develop effective pricing packages. An example of this is the 'power by the hour' leasing offered by Rolls-Royce.

- *Human resource management:* hiring, developing and motivating good people are essential aspects of innovation management. The creative atmosphere of small teams can easily be lost as organizations grow and so the HR function can and should proactively support the maintenance of a culture of innovation in the organization.

- *Senior management:* needs to build the capability to innovate within an organization. This requires key processes – such as new product development and business model innovation – that need the support of different functional areas. Researchers have identified the friction and lack of understanding that commonly arise between different functions, particularly marketing and R&D.[38] Breaking down functional barriers ('silos') is part of management's role. Akio Morita, the late chairman of Sony, recognized this, saying: 'this is the job of top management – to arrange good communications [between functions]'.[39]

- *Outside resources:* these have been recognized as essential for open innovation.[40] For example, suppliers in the automotive industry conduct significant parts of the product development for car manufacturers. Similarly, universities and research institutes can enable small organizations to economically partake in the development of new technologies, and develop new core competences.

Now that we have discussed the phases through which an innovation must be managed and the functional areas that need to be involved, we will explain the difficulties that managers perceive with managing innovation.

Top Managers' Views

The world's best-known management consultancies, including Arthur D. Little, BCG, IBM, McKinsey and PwC, all publish biannual reports on top managers' views on innovation. These are based on large surveys; for example, IBM conducted 1,700 one-to-one interviews with CEOs in 2012. Therefore, the reports give useful insights into the challenges of managing innovation.[41]

Several of the latest reports show that innovation is viewed as the most viable path to corporate growth, rather than alliances, mergers and acquisitions. For example, top companies that are effective at breakthrough innovation can generate between 15–25 per cent of their revenues from products that are less than one year old. But to achieve growth, managers must ensure that their organizations have the right processes to support innovation. As PwC consultants have said: 'It is a common misconception that innovation is a serendipitous and unstructured activity that cannot be planned for, forced, or disciplined.'[42] In the various reports, several innovation processes are highlighted that need to be developed – from idea generation through to commercialization.

Most organizations are only good at incremental innovation (see the bottom left-hand corner of Figure 1.3). This focus on incremental innovation means that many companies' 'innovation operating models are inadequate for the desired growth'.[43] However, some organizations are good at both incremental and breakthrough innovations and a good example is Singapore Airlines (see Mini Case 1.4).

To create the ideas that will lead to growth, IBM's report recognized that companies need to be 'far more adept at converting [customer] data into insights and insights into action'.[44] Ideas can come from internal brainstorming sessions, collecting ideas through the internet (crowdsourcing), and customer data. Collecting ideas from other organizations – open innovation – has become the most popular way of managing innovation in recent years.

Some ideas will be rejected (see Figure 1.4) and selecting the most promising ideas is challenging. Incremental ideas are, by their nature, more familiar to managers, less risky and thus more attractive. Radical ideas need more patience and cannot be evaluated in the same way as product improvements. The first part of innovation strategy is to decide how much innovation is needed by an organization (its ambition) and this sets the appropriate ratio of radical/breakthrough to incremental efforts.[45] Finally, the business areas in which to compete must be selected. Selecting an appropriate strategy and allocating the right performance measures are things that many organizations struggle with.

> **MINI CASE 1.4:** *Singapore Airlines – Overhead and Ahead*[46]

Singapore Airlines (SIA) is regularly recognized as an excellent airline. In fact, 20 times in the last 21 years *Condé Nast Traveler*, the travel industry's leading magazine, has voted it the best. The quality of SIA's service is legendary. Its business strategy is based on a solid service product and constant improvement in its delivery. A first-to-market innovation strategy has been an important part of SIA's approach for years.

SIA's air travel, its product, is based on wide choice of routes, enhanced through alliances with other airlines. The way the service is delivered is designed to give exceptional customer satisfaction. It blends people-based and technology-based innovation. Cabin crew are renowned for being empathetic and helpful and this has been strongly promoted through the Singapore Girl advertising. Cabin crew receive longer and more detailed training than that given by other airlines. For example, all cabin trainees spend time in homes for the elderly, in order to empathize with the problems faced by older travellers (a growing segment worldwide).

On-board technology is also a focus. It is constantly updated and the aircraft fleet is one of the most modern in the industry. Having more modern aircraft has helped SIA differentiate its service product; passenger areas have larger than average seating, and a French fashion house designed the décor and the service ware (including the tableware). In-flight services are constantly being enhanced and the list of firsts here is long: in-flight telephones; in-flight fax machines; Dolby surround sound and personal video screens in coach class; electronic tickets (but SIA is flexible in also allowing flight confirmations by telephone, fax or email).

Service companies like SIA need to make their innovations hard to copy. Competitors have quickly copied SIA's technology-based innovations, whereas the quality of the service provided by its staff has been harder to match. SIA recognizes that customer satisfaction is crucial and so it invests 40 per cent of its innovation budget in staff training. Being perceived as a service leader is important but behind the scenes 30 per cent of the innovation budget is spent on process improvement and it has some of the lowest costs in the industry. The final 30 per cent of the innovation budget is invested in the Product Innovation Department, developing new products and services.

The surveys of top managers show that they perceive commercialization to be difficult. The process of launching a new product or service on the market becomes more risky the more radical the idea is. Successful commercialization can depend on the right partners, as the aim may be to provide solutions rather than stand-alone products and services. Many companies do not allow innovations the time they need to be successful.

Innovation depends on the contributions of many functions and people and so the culture of innovation is important: 'Establishing and fostering an innovation culture is a subtle mix of encouraging the right behaviours and giving people the means to take ownership of their innovation efforts.'[47] Overall, the reports show that top managers perceive innovation as challenging. This is because it includes a range of tasks, such as ideation and market development.

Trends in Innovation Management Research

This section gives an overview of what that research has found; how it can be applied will be covered in later chapters. Innovation is an area in which both economists and management researchers have been active.

Innovation has been studied at the *macro*, *micro* and *project levels*. Macro-level research investigates the sources and impact of innovation within economies and industries. The micro level studies how companies manage innovation and the advantages that it brings them in terms of revenues and profits. The project level looks at the management of innovation projects, such as new product development or new service development. In this book, we are primarily concerned with the micro (company) and project levels.

Figure 1.5 shows the eight topics that have dominated innovation management research at the micro and project levels over the past 20 years (the x-axis). These topics were identified by checking the keywords used in abstracts in six top journals that publish on innovation (including *Harvard Business Review*, *MIT Sloan Management Review*, and the leading academic journal, the *Journal of Product Innovation Management*).[48] By focusing only on the top journals, it enabled comparative data on the number of research articles published year by year (y-axis) to be generated and it excluded the effect of the increased number of journals publishing on innovation. Some topics have been researched steadily over the years but with few papers published each year. Other topics have emerged strongly in recent years.

The first topic we will consider is Stage-Gate® new product development.[49] This is the process that defines different stages of NPD, such as 'business case' and 'test' and defines the responsibilities of different departments at these stages; for example, marketing would need to estimate the market size for the

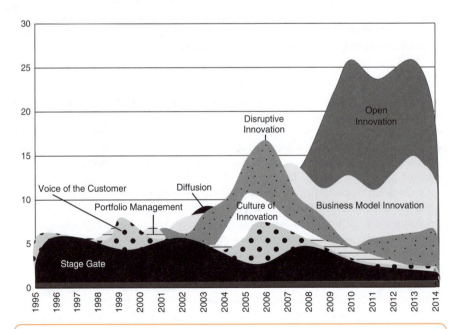

FIGURE 1.5: Trends in Innovation Management Research, 1995–2015

business case, whereas finance would have to estimate the costs of the technologies proposed by R&D. Stage-Gate® has been actively researched from the 1990s, with typically up to five papers in the key journals a year, as can be seen from Figure 1.5. There is a need for a clear process, which defines the responsibilities of different functions, such as R&D and marketing, at different phases of NPD. Robert Cooper and Elko Kleinschmidt of McMasters University in Canada have published definitively on this. In Stage-Gate® NPD, management meets at the end of each stage of product development and has to approve the progression to the next stage. Most companies have developed formal processes based on Cooper and Kleinschmidt's recommendations.[50]

Voice of the customer (VOC) research is a broad term that covers the many different ways that customer insights can be generated. It showed peaks in 1999 and 2006. One of the early key papers on this was by Abbie Griffin and John Hauser.[51] Over the years many different methods have been developed for identifying customer needs and we will discuss them in Chapter 5. One of the discussions in the innovation literature is that 'traditional market research is not a good predictor of success'.[52] Various methods for identifying customers' needs have been promoted, with authors claiming their idea is the 'best' method. In reality, each technique has both advantages and limitations. For example, *quality function deployment* is a Japanese method that stressed the value of VOC but this method is not a panacea.[53]

Portfolio management is the term used by researchers to describe the processes – formal and informal – that organizations use to select ideas. It is an important topic but it has never generated a large number of papers, and so it is hardly visible in Figure 1.5. This is surprising as the importance was recognized by *The Economist* magazine, which said: 'one of the biggest thoughts emerging from innovation research in recent years: neither idea generation nor execution is as important or as tricky as the filtering process that links the two'.[54] A recent paper that did research the topic said 'the innovation portfolio was only vaguely guided by corporate strategy'.[55]

Diffusion of innovations (the factors that influence market uptake – covered in detail in Chapter 2) was made popular by Everett Rogers of the University of New Mexico. His ideas have interested researchers since his classic book, *Diffusion of Innovations*, was published in 1995[56] and this interest peaked in 2003 but is now waning. The best-known aspect of the work of Rogers is that the *early adopters* of innovations such as new products have particular characteristics. They are normally very open to new ideas and readers might consider if they know someone who always has the latest technology, such as the newest mobile phone.

Although a significant part of managing innovation is about defining and managing processes, it should never be forgotten that processes make things possible but people make them happen. This requires setting the right atmosphere in which innovation can flourish: 'To lead innovation ... you must carve out the mental space within which the innovation process can be carried out [and] setting the expectations that innovation will push boundaries.'[57] Although managers recognize the need for a *culture of innovation*, this is not an area where there has been much research since the peak in 2006, although a number of papers have identified the most important factors related to culture.

Disruptive technology is one of the three topics that have prompted the most research and it peaked in 2006 with 16 papers. The topic explains how every technology reaches its natural limits and it is inevitable that another technology will, at some stage, overtake it. Think, for example, how vinyl was replaced by CDs, which have now lost their popularity because of digital MP3 files. Disruptive technologies change markets and can destroy companies that fail to move from one technology to the next at the right moment. Disruptive technology became popular through the work of Clayton Christensen of Harvard, following his 1995 co-authored *Harvard Business Review* article[58] and his book *The Innovator's Dilemma*. Although it is not as popular as in 2006, disruptive technology is still the subject of about five papers a year in the top journals. We cover it in Chapter 4.

Figure 1.5 shows that *business model innovation* (BMI – covered in detail in Chapter 2) is also being heavily researched today, as scholars catch up on the huge wave of practitioner interest in the topic. The popularity of BMI with practitioners is demonstrated by over 1 million sales of the book *Business Model Generation*, co-written by Alexander Osterwalder and Yves Pigneur; Osterwalder developed the ubiquitous *Business Model Canvas*,[59] which focuses on the nine main elements of a business model. BMI tells us how a company can create value for their customers and capture value in ways that lock out competitors. It should be noted that the ideas about business models, such as finding ways to link closely with key stakeholders, apply not only in business but also in the not-for-profit sector (see Mini Case 1.5 on Lumkani).

MINI CASE 1.5: *Lumkani, South Africa – Fire Alarms for Free![60]*

Lumkani is a social enterprise that has developed an early-warning fire detection device, designed to address the challenges of shack fires in informal settlements in South Africa and across the globe. When David Gluckman, an economics graduate from the University of Cape Town, heard about a low-cost fire detector that had been developed by a fellow graduate (as part of an electrical engineering honours thesis), he was excited. At the time, Gluckman had just left his corporate job to explore a career in social entrepreneurship. He immediately recognized the potential for social impact of such a device, and in March 2014 joined the newly formed Lumkani to help manage R&D and other business-related activities.

The developers of the Lumkani early-warning device had been spurred on by the enormity of fire risk in South Africa's informal settlements: between 2000 and 2010, 250,000 people were displaced because of fires. And as the rate of urbanization increases, so too does the scale of the challenge. Building a low-cost, user-friendly, 'off-the-shelf' device involved regular consultation and engagement with target communities. Thus, the product was designed around real-life situations, not based on assumptions about the end-user. Since smoke-producing cooking is common in informal settlements, Lumkani's detector senses an increase in temperature rather than smoke, which reduces the chance of false alarms and accurately detects hazardous fires. An alarm alerts residents to imminent danger before the fire becomes unmanageable. The devices are wirelessly connected to other devices in neighbouring dwellings in the immediate vicinity, which helps to create a community-wide response to fire hazards.

Continued...

Demand for the device has grown, particularly among communities that have seen the Lumkani 'in action', that is, mitigating loss of life and damage to property in real fires. Since November 2014, the company had distributed detectors to 6,000 households. Funding for the Lumkani project has come from crowdfunding and an award from the Chivas Regal 'The Venture' campaign, a competition that seeks to identify and support promising start-ups worldwide. As a finalist in the 2015 competition, Lumkani was awarded US$75,000. The company's crowdfunding campaign (a requirement for the Venture competition) has raised a further US$22,000.

One of the biggest challenges facing Lumkani is the need to keep the cost of the device as low as possible. Although designed to ensure safety and mitigate against loss of life and property, for many customers the device is not considered a high priority in the face of other pressures, such as school fees and rising food prices. In addition, the battery for the device needs to be changed once a year, presenting a challenge for the company to ensure awareness about this among its end-users.

The next hurdle for Lumkani is to ensure sustainability and the scalability of its business model. As the organization is currently dependent on donations, it is testing devices with new functionality associated services, which could enable a more sustainable funding model. One of the keys to future sustainability would be to attain 'buy-in' from other stakeholders who could benefit from the system, such as local authorities. In the meantime, the company is continuing to develop and enhance its client relationship management systems and GPS software. Boosting its sales and marketing resources, Lumkani aims to consistently increase its reach among customers in South Africa and abroad. And as Gluckman says: 'Social impact business is not so different to everyday entrepreneurship: you really need to know your customer, build something he/she wants and build the sustainable and scalable model around that.'

Case contributed by Chris van der Hoven.

It can be seen that, over the past 20 years, by far the most researched topic is *open innovation* (companies looking beyond their own organization for ideas – explained in detail in Chapter 2). Since the term was introduced by Henry Chesbrough of the University of California, Berkeley in a 2003 *California Management Review* article,[61] up to 25 academic papers have been published per year on this area. Open innovation is as fashionable with practitioners as academics. It is an important way for companies to gather innovative ideas but it is not without drawbacks, such as issues with intellectual property rights. As an approach, open innovation is extremely important but the hype around it has led to the myth that it can address all the innovation issues of an organization. This is not the case and as Julian Birkinshaw of London Business School said: 'open innovation is not the future, but it is certainly part of the future'.[62]

Figure 1.5 shows where researchers have focused their attention and it prompts the question: Which areas of innovation management have practitioners focused on? The review of the management consultants' reports gave us some answers. The internet provides another perspective, albeit far less controlled. Table 1.3 shows the number of 'hits' that the key terms from the research literature generate on the internet. Here, it is interesting to see that 'culture of innovation' appears to be the most discussed term, followed by open innovation and VOC third. Interestingly, business model innovation (BMI) is only in sixth place on internet hits, although there are many academic papers on it – 141 since 2000.

TABLE 1.3: Internet Hits for Innovation Management Terms[63]

Term	Hits (million)	Internet 'hit' ranking	Total academic papers (1995–2014)
Culture of innovation	15.200	1	50
Open innovation	3.220	2	174
Voice of the customer	2.040	3	64
Disruptive technology	0.530	4	103
Diffusion of innovations	0.450	5	98
Business model innovation	0.448	6	141
Stage-Gate	0.330	7	46
Portfolio management	0.019	8	53

There is a danger that 'management fads' can overtake innovation management, as has been a problem in other areas of management.[64] So managers and researchers need to exercise a healthy scepticism, be more critical of the tools and techniques, and 'beware [of] the next big thing' in innovation management.[65] The discipline of innovation management is still relatively new; for example, it is not as advanced as the area of quality management, which has a well-accepted set of tools and techniques and clear ways in which these can be applied in organizations. The first key interpretation of Figure 1.5 is that it shows that different innovation management topics emerge and become popular. Some achieve such status that they are wrongly attributed as being 'solutions' to all innovation management problems. A key message for managers is that not everything good in innovation management is new – the latest is not (necessarily) the greatest. Relating this to Figure 1.5, the latest wave of innovation management thinking does not devalue those that have gone before. Good innovation management requires a combination of approaches, rather than just the latest idea. Open innovation cannot solve all the issues a company faces, and so it is with BMI, or disruptive technology. This is not to detract from any of these concepts – they are important and we will assign them significant coverage in this book – but their limitations must be understood, and be weighed against their advantages.

As the discipline of innovation management advances further, the way concepts and tools are viewed is changing. *The Economist* recently stated that innovation management is no longer an art and is 'becoming a practical science'.[66] Certainly, in the past 10 years, there is wider recognition that managers need to be cautious of concepts and tools that are being oversold. We will exercise caution in how we discuss tools and techniques; the advantages, limitations and contextual factors will be considered.

THEORY BOX 1.1: *Contingency Theory – One Size does not Fit All*

It might seem obvious that the circumstances facing a company (its internal issues and external business environment) have a fundamental influence on the type of management needed. However, back in the 1950s, management researchers were looking for leadership styles that could be universally employed and the tradition of *scientific management* was influential. It was largely sociologist Burns and psychologist Walker working at the University of Edinburgh, UK who recognized that universal approaches to management problems were unlikely – that there was not a single (best) way of solving such problems. Burns published his book *The Management of Innovation* in 1961. *Contingency theory* (also referred to as a *situational* approach) has three key tenets:

1. Organizations require management to address internal needs and adapt to the business environment (context).
2. There is no single one best way of managing and organizing. This is because the most appropriate approaches depend not only on the task but also on the business environment.
3. Different forms of organization are needed to match different types of environments.

Where contingency theory helps with innovation management is that it reminds us to recognize contextual factors and be sceptical about universal solutions – one of the key messages in this chapter. Contingency theory should also prompt a closer consideration of the contextual factors in deciding when and how to address a management problem.

Examples of Innovation Research Using the Theory

Two examples of where innovation management researchers have used the theory concern new product development (NPD) projects (see also Chapter 7). It has been found that the context of the project has a bigger impact on whether it will be successful or not, than just the process used.[67] Recent research has stressed that the type of NPD process needs to be carefully chosen to match the context of the project.[68]

The Need for a Framework

Another interpretation of Figure 1.5 is that different topics in the research literature are treated as largely separate from another. This is largely because researchers have limited time and focus on one or two topics that interest them. This means that how the topics relate to one another is ambiguous. An example of this is how open innovation impacts the culture of innovation in an organization. Philips, the Dutch electronics company, found to its expense that focusing strongly on searching for outside ideas had a detrimental impact on R&D motivation. So the links between the topics are as important as the topics themselves. This is the reason an overall framework for managing innovation is necessary.

Innovation management often requires managers to match 'technical' expertise, in areas such as technology, project management and finance, with 'soft' skills in managing people and creativity. The skills needed for technology management relate closely to engineering and the physical sciences, whereas the soft skills are closer to the social sciences, and finance is covered in business education. Few managers have been educated in all these areas. The eclectic mix of skills required is what makes innovation management fascinating.

Our own research back in 1998 used a survey and 16 in-depth case studies in Germany and the UK to study how senior managers approach innovation. It emerged that managers identify many facets to managing innovation: they cite strategy (for example whether it is better to be first to market, or to follow); people management (for example motivating teams); and good project management (for example in striving to meet challenging time-to-market goals).[69] Integrating these facets of innovation management is difficult and the director of one manufacturing company said he really needed a 'systematic way to encourage and manage innovation'. From this and similar views of others interviewed, the Innovation Pentathlon Framework emerged.

THE INNOVATION PENTATHLON FRAMEWORK

Figure 1.4 (the development funnel) illustrates the process of idea generation, selection and implementation. But it does not show the link to a firm's strategic intent (the importance of which emerged from our discussion of drivers of innovation), or the link to company culture.

Starting with the development funnel, two extra elements – *innovation strategy* and *people and organization* – needed to be added. As its name suggests, the *Innovation Pentathlon Framework* identifies five *areas* or *elements* of innovation management, as shown in Figure 1.6. In each of the five areas, there are a number of key topics to be managed:

- *Ideas generation:* The raw material for innovation is ideas. Managers need to create an environment that supports creativity at the individual and team level, and makes use of creativity techniques. Creativity can be managed – it is a myth that it is based on solely eureka moments of inspiration[70] – and it should harness the knowledge within and outside the organization. Good ideas blend technical, customer and market requirements but traditional market research is not effective for generating breakthrough ideas, so new approaches are needed.[71] Ideas come from recognizing problems that, when solved, help customers greatly. As innovation includes new products, services and new or improved processes, and business models, the scope for idea generation needs to be kept wide and external sources need to be involved.

- *Selection:* an effective process is required to ensure that the best ideas are chosen, first for development into business concepts and then into new products, services, process innovations and business models. The finite resources available for innovation projects need to be carefully divided across the most promising projects. This requires suitable tools to decide on the merit (risk and return) of individual projects. It is also important not to fall into the trap of looking for the big winners.[72] For such radical projects, it is difficult to use financial measures as there are many unknowns.[73] The challenge with breakthrough and radical projects is similar to that faced by investors such as venture capitalists.[74] In portfolio management, executives need to collate the information across the range of projects, to check that the portfolio of

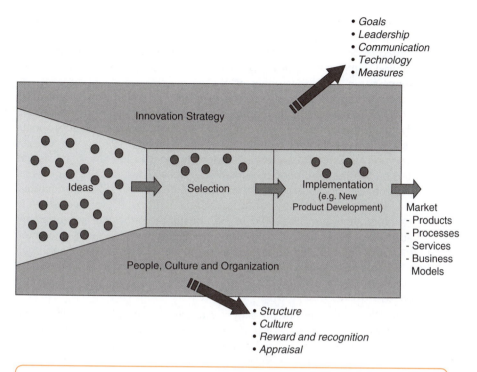

- *Goals*
- *Leadership*
- *Communication*
- *Technology*
- *Measures*

Innovation Strategy

Ideas

Selection

Implementation
(e.g. New
Product Development)

Market
- Products
- Processes
- Services
- Business
  Models

People, Culture and Organization

- *Structure*
- *Culture*
- *Reward and recognition*
- *Appraisal*

FIGURE 1.6: The Innovation Pentathlon Framework
Source: originally developed from research supported by the Anglo-German Foundation.

innovation projects is balanced and matches company strategy. Collecting information on portfolio decisions helps strengthen future decision-making by learning from experience.

- *Implementation:* this phase should focus on quickly and efficiently developing new products, services, or processes, or business models, or any combination of these. Faster development times can be achieved through effective cross-functional teams, prototyping and testing. Commercialization is the last step in implementation and the market launch is crucial. Increasingly, new products need to be complemented with new business models. The more radical the innovation, the more work needs to go into achieving commercialization and, as the surveys of top managers showed, this is difficult. The implementation process is an area where companies can learn from each project, so that the future performance can be greater. And 'breakthrough innovators differentiate clearly among projects with a low and high degree of innovativeness and use different processes for radical and incremental R&D projects'.[75]

- *Innovation strategy:* developing and implementing an innovation strategy requires top management to identify the big opportunities and threats. Assessing market trends and determining how these drive innovation in the company's chosen sector(s) is the first step. The role of technology, the opportunities it can open, and how to acquire expertise in the relevant technologies need to be considered. Management needs to communicate the role of innovation within a company – product, service, process and business process innovation – and this means establishing a common language.[76] It also means matching the resources to the strategy. For example, first-to-market approaches require particular capabilities in R&D and market development. Lastly, gauging innovation performance, through the use of appropriate measures, is essential.

- *People, culture and organization:* underlying innovation are many issues related to the management of human resources. These include hiring and training policies, job design, and creating effective organizational structures, which will increase innovation outputs. Creating a *culture of innovation* in which employees are motivated to be constantly innovative is fundamental and senior executives should take an active role in coaching innovation teams. Such interactions 'motivate talent and reinforce the innovation culture'.[77] Effective reward and recognition programmes need to be maintained.

The Pentathlon Analogy

Overall, the Pentathlon Framework allows us to divide a complex topic into more understandable and manageable parts. It allows the problems with innovation management in an organization to be separated out and diagnosed. But each of the five elements is, in itself, a complex area. Each element overlaps to a certain extent with the others and impacts them. For example, a 'blame culture' will negatively impact the generation of ideas.

Innovation management has been previously compared to a marathon.[78] It certainly needs enduring practice and, in this sense, the analogy is valid. However, the implication that innovation management is – like a marathon – top performance in a single discipline is misleading. Managing innovation requires good performance in a number of areas. A better analogy is the pentathlon, where good performance in five disciplines – the five elements of the framework – is essential.

Top performance in one area alone will not lead to long-term competitiveness. For example, in the late 1990s, one leading German manufacturer was very good at implementation, as it had a highly efficient new product development process and was faster to market than its competitors. However, it was not good at generating unique customer-oriented ideas and so, overall, it was first to market with 'average' ideas and was not successful. Now, it has an enviable reputation for generating ideas based on deep customer insights and getting these to market fast.

We emphasize that the Pentathlon Framework focuses on the innovation processes within one organization. Strong links are required to the outside world (just as the Olympic pentathlon did not exist in isolation: there were spectators, stadia and training camps). The context in which innovation occurs – the business situation – has a strong influence on innovation management. This is shown in Figure 1.7, where the market and other forces directly impact how

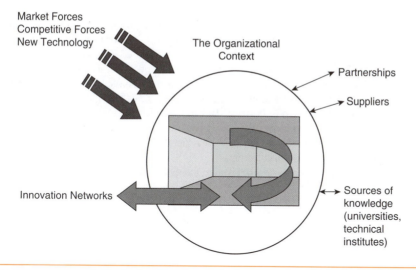

FIGURE 1.7: The Innovation Pentathlon Framework in Context

an organization should manage its innovation. Figure 1.7 also indicates that an organization must look outside its boundaries to increase innovation levels and the concept of open innovation links with suppliers and technical institutes (the main case study at the end of this chapter on NTT DOCOMO looks at partnerships and alliances). Chapter 2 looks at innovation in context in detail.

Applying the Pentathlon Framework

The Pentathlon Framework helps identify the strengths and weaknesses of an organization's innovation management. To demonstrate this, two short examples will be given, one from the service sector and one from manufacturing. Each of these has been disguised, to ensure confidentiality.

EXAMPLE 1: *International Bank – Innovation Processes*

A business division of a major international bank spent time considering the lessons it could learn from innovation management in the manufacturing sector. Two conclusions were quickly reached: the bank's innovation strategy needed to be rethought and new service product development needed a better process.

Having observed that most manufacturing companies have Stage-Gate® Processes, the bank identified that its NPD was weak and slow. The approach was bureaucratic, with many approvals required; for example, more than 10 managers needed to agree to new advertising copy.

Continued...

Consequently, a new process was designed for developing new service products, including streamlined approvals and clear responsibilities. This included formally assigning NPD to cross-functional teams led by marketing.

Idea generation was also identified as a weak element in the bank's innovation management. Regular cross-functional workshops were introduced to generate initial ideas. The bank's management was impressed by the way leading manufacturers used prototype products to get qualified feedback from customers. Consequently, the bank focused on turning ideas as quickly as possible into 'service prototypes' (with, for example, material on explaining the new service to customers and proposed advertising). An important part of the service prototypes the bank developed were the 'role play' discussions of how the new products would be explained to customers.

The improvements at the bank were also closely linked to the overall innovation strategy, which was then clearly communicated to all staff.

EXAMPLE 2: *VehicleCo – Cross-functional Creativity*

Setting the right atmosphere for creativity is essential and the physical environment, the people and the business culture can all play a role. At a UK specialist vehicle manufacturer, which we will call VehicleCo, such is the legacy of the charismatic founder who still takes an active role in generating technical ideas and ensuring that they are commercially feasible. By asking critical questions about new products – acting in some ways as a devil's advocate – he has created a culture that blends three distinct elements. A focus on developing first-to-market technical solutions is blended with a strong commercial awareness in R&D, and an emphasis on constant 'prototyping'. Prototypes are used as the basis for internal discussions on new concepts and for making discussions with customer groups more concrete.

The factory has an ideal physical environment for creativity; it is open plan with marketing and R&D sitting together, separated from production by a glass wall. Similarly, only a glass wall separates the workshop used for producing prototypes and so its work is visible for all to see.

At VehicleCo, cross-functional teams are used to develop all ideas. For example, although most companies use continuous improvement teams, these are normally only staffed by manufacturing employees. Marketing and other functions are represented in continuous improvement projects, to bring a commercial focus and 'outside ideas' to brainstorming sessions. Similarly, production people are present in NPD discussions. Brainstorming has become synonymous within the company with mixing different functional perspectives. With such a strong cross-functional orientation, it is not surprising that the functional R&D organization has gone – replaced by business teams where R&D and marketing are combined in small groups with clear target markets. Over the past decade, the organization has been changed several times and is expected to change again. Employees see this as inevitable and not negative; it means the organization is flexible enough to react to market changes.

It would be wrong to leave the impression that VehicleCo has no issues with innovation management. It had to modify its NPD process to solve problems with the quality of new products and transfer to production. Similarly, it has yet to introduce a review process to determine what can be improved from one project to the next.

Limitations of the Pentathlon Framework

The Pentathlon Framework categorizes the main elements of innovation management but it has some limitations. First, it is not a predictive model of innovation performance, although it provides a means for assessing all aspects of innovation management within an organization and it can be used as a diagnostic tool (Chapter 9 gives a set of questions to 'audit' performance against the framework). Second, the interaction between the elements of the framework, for example how changes in a company culture will influence the generation of ideas, is hard to predict and often context specific. So the five elements should not be treated as independent factors and we will constantly refer to the linkages. Within these limitations, the framework enables clearer discussions on the nature of innovation (just as the development funnel enabled managers to better understand how ideas are developed into products). It also can be used as a communication tool, to explain to employees why, where and how improvements in innovation management are to be made.

THE STRUCTURE OF THIS BOOK

The structure of this book is based around the Innovation Pentathlon Framework with chapters as follows:

- *Chapter 2: Innovation in Context* explains the economic and social contexts of innovation.
- *Chapter 3: Service Innovation* discusses the innovation management issues in the service sector, the manufacturing sector, the public sector, and not-for-profit organizations. It also introduces much of the terminology of innovation management.
- *Chapter 4: Developing an Innovation Strategy* provides an overview of what an innovation strategy is and the most important management tools for selecting the right strategy for an organization.
- *Chapter 5: Generating Innovative Ideas* discusses how to generate ideas for new products, new service products and new processes. It covers approaches to improve individual and organizational creativity.
- *Chapter 6: Selecting the Innovation Portfolio* discusses how to select the best ideas for commercialization and achieve a balanced portfolio.
- *Chapter 7: Implementing Innovations* explains how innovation projects can be quickly and efficiently implemented and commercialized.
- *Chapter 8: People, Culture and Organization* covers the last element of the Pentathlon Framework. It explains the importance of recruiting and managing people, teams, creating a culture of innovation, and choosing the right structure.
- *Chapter 9: Innovation – Performance and Capability* discusses how to set the right working environment for innovation, including the role of human resource management.

Figure 1.8 illustrates the structure of this book, showing that five chapters – 4, 5, 6, 7 and 8 – are directly related to specific elements of the pentathlon. The outer circle indicates that Chapters 1, 2, 3 and 9 discuss topics that are related to the whole topic of innovation management.

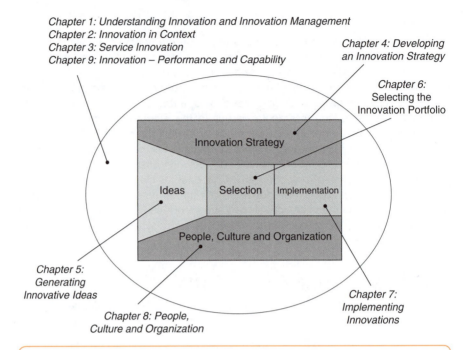

Chapter 1: Understanding Innovation and Innovation Management
Chapter 2: Innovation in Context
Chapter 3: Service Innovation
Chapter 9: Innovation – Performance and Capability

Chapter 4: Developing
an Innovation Strategy

Chapter 6:
Selecting the
Innovation Portfolio

Innovation Strategy

Ideas   Selection   Implementation

People, Culture and Organization

Chapter 5:
Generating
Innovative Ideas

Chapter 7:
Implementing
Innovations

Chapter 8: People,
Culture and Organization

FIGURE 1.8: Chapter Structure and the Pentathlon Framework

Format of the Chapters

Each chapter follows a similar style:

- The issues and the most relevant concepts, management tools and techniques to address them are explained. The tools and techniques have been selected based on an extensive review of the literature, and our own experience of managing innovation in commercial organizations.
- Important terms related to innovation management are first shown in italics and then their meaning is explained.
- Occasionally, we use a 'theory box' to discuss relevant management theories, tools and techniques.
- The theory and tools are backed by examples, including five or more international 'mini cases' (mini case studies) per chapter. These have been selected to illustrate key aspects of how companies manage innovation in services, manufacturing, the public sector and the not-for-profit sector. They have also been carefully chosen to give broad geographical coverage.
- At the end of each chapter, a longer case study is given with a set of questions for readers to consider. These main case studies have been carefully selected to illustrate the challenges facing companies, how solutions have been developed, and the main learning points from each chapter. Half the chapters have main cases based on manufacturing companies and the other half focus on the service sector.

- A summary recaps the main points.
- Short recommendations for managers are given.
- Discussion questions are provided to help students reflect on what has been discussed in the chapter.
- A few annotated recommendations for readings, either books or papers, are given, for readers who want to go deeper into the topics covered in the chapter.
- References for each chapter are listed at the end of the book. We have deliberately provided a comprehensive list of sources, so that readers can find the evidence on which our arguments are based and source material if they are conducting academic assignments. Over 150 references have been added in updating this edition.
- The website **www.palgravehighered.com/gm** provides additional notes and material for each chapter.

For this introductory chapter, our main case study looks at the innovation management challenges facing NTT DOCOMO, the Japanese mobile telephony service provider.

Summary

Many reports and articles continue to be published on innovation management. However, improving performance of a company is still a real challenge for managers because the latest techniques for managing innovation will not, on their own, be enough. Managers need to address a broad range of factors in managing innovation, from stimulating the ideas through to implementing the best ones. This chapter showed that there are five main dimensions of innovation – product, service, process, business process, and business model innovation. Companies need to identify which dimensions are important for them. Similarly, innovation has different degrees. It consists of incremental improvements to existing products and services, which many companies focus on. However, breakthrough and radical innovation give the greater opportunity for growth, as they address unique needs and open adjacent and new markets.

Extensive research has shown that innovation management is complex and multifaceted. Its scope is wide, ranging from business strategy, managing technology and new product development, to organization and people management. Based on this, the Pentathlon Framework is a tool for managing innovation. This book aims to identify the ways in which an organization can improve both its *innovation performance* (its output of new products, services and so on) and its *innovation capability* (an organization's ability to manage innovation effectively).

Management Recommendations

- Determine the intended role of innovation in your organization – your innovation ambition – and clearly communicate this to employees.
- Consider how innovation can be enhanced from contributions throughout the organization.

- Use the Pentathlon Framework to pinpoint the areas of innovation management that your organization needs to improve.
- From the analysis using the Pentathlon Framework, identify how your organization can build a capability for breakthrough and radical innovation.

Questions for Students

1. What are the advantages of combining process innovation, for example manufacturing, with product innovation?
2. Why do many organizations get caught in the incremental innovation trap?
3. Open innovation has become a popular innovation management topic in recent years. Which elements of the Pentathlon Framework does it impact?
4. Why is fast and efficient new product development not enough for a company to become the market leader?
5. Are you personally an early adopter when it comes to new products? Why, or why not?

Recommended Reading

1. 'Something New Under the Sun: A Special Report on Innovation', *The Economist*, 13 October 2007. Excellent overview of key issues in managing innovation and technology. Written in the characteristic style of *The Economist* – clear and to the point.
2. Anthony, S.D., Duncan, D.S. and Siren, P.M.A., 'Build an Innovation Engine in 90 Days', *Harvard Business Review*, 93(12) (2014), 61–8. Good coverage of the challenges of managing innovation in a corporation, although what they claim can be achieved in 90 days is optimistic.
3. Birkinshaw, J., Bouquet, C. and Barsoux, J.-L., 'The 5 Myths of Innovation', *MIT Sloan Management Review*, 52(2) (2011), 43–50. Critical review of innovation management tools and techniques.

▶ MAIN CASE STUDY

NTT DOCOMO, JAPAN – WATCHING THE MOBILE MARKET[79]

NTT DOCOMO is the top Japanese mobile telephone service provider. The company was formed in 1992 when the Japanese government dissolved Nippon Telephone and Telegraph's (NTT) monopoly. The name comes from an abbreviation of **Do Co**mmunications over the **Mo**bile Network, and a play on *dokomo*, the Japanese word for 'anywhere'. Increasingly, users want a huge variety of what the industry refers to as 'content' (information and services) available anywhere and everywhere.

DOCOMO struggled initially but it has developed a successful business model that has been copied by famous names such as Apple. Lars Cosh-Ishii, Director of Mobikyo and publisher of Wireless Watch Japan, has been focused on this segment since 2001. As an industry expert he has gained deep insights into local market strategies and says:

> Considering the explosive growth of global telecommunications activity over the last decade, Japan is widely recognized within the industry for pioneering the most advanced and successful test market for building next-generation mobile products and services. Japan introduced the original mobile internet platform, developed the first camera-phones and built the world's first commercial 3G network, long ago. Most people likely do not realize how widely Japanese technology enables their daily lives; each time the majority of some 4 billion mobile phones worldwide connect to the network, they use 'essential patents' developed by DOCOMO and its partners. We should also note that a significant portion of critical internal components, display screens and cameras for example, are produced by Japanese companies for all major international handset brands.

One of the unusual characteristics of the Japanese mobile telephone market is that there is no direct channel by which mobile telephone ('handset') manufacturers can market their products. Every handset in Japan is provided as part of a service contract. This has led DOCOMO to take a broader view of innovation than many of the other network providers around the world and, in particular, to push for the design of handsets – *keitai* in Japanese – for specific market segments.

Integrating Handsets, Coverage and Mobile Services

To understand its target segments, DOCOMO undertakes regular market research. Market research reports have looked at urban usage of mobile phones,[80] how adolescents use wireless services and the functions they most want in their handsets.[81] Cosh-Ishii observes: 'DOCOMO has very strong in-house technical R&D capacity: their spec. was adopted by ITU for LTE(4G), and the company conducts extensive "lifestyle" research focused on end-user daily needs in order to develop new content and service offerings.' What is unusual is that DOCOMO openly publishes the results of its market research because it is keen to share its insights with its partners, and to make sure it can offer the optimum combination of handsets, coverage and mobile services to the consumer.

Handsets – Silver Segment

With ageing populations worldwide, many companies are trying to target what is often called the 'silver [haired] market' or 'silver segment' but DOCOMO has been particularly successful. Millions of new senior subscribers have adopted the Raku-Raku ('easy-easy') range of mobile telephones. In advertising the Raku-Raku, DOCOMO highlights the technical features but cleverly links these to emotional benefits, says Cosh-Ishii: 'For example, their adverts show grandparents operating the handsets easily and keeping in touch with their families. The three big button design, for making quick calls to select pre-programmed contact numbers, also adds peace of mind for everyone concerned.'

Today, there are six models of Raku-Raku aimed at the 22 per cent of Japanese owners of mobile phones who are over 50 years of age. The silver segment handsets were developed for DOCOMO by Fujitsu with:

- Larger keyboards and text on the display.
- Simple user interfaces.
- 'Enhanced audibility' for the hard of hearing – advanced signal processing reduces background noise and can even slow down the speed at which someone's speech is heard on a handset.
- A pedometer function on some versions. This measures how far the person carrying the phone walks, which 'is particularly relevant to users wishing to regularly update their doctors with this data'.

Handsets – Outdoor Segment

Japan has extensive mountains and hill-walking and mountaineering are national passions. This segment has been addressed with handsets like the 'Geofree II'. Users' ideas provided the inspiration for the handset, supplemented by research looking at developments in the digital watch industry, where rugged designs combined with 'outdoor' features had been very successful. Combining a range of features in a handset offers outdoor sportspeople added safety – easy access to weather and local information and emergency services. DOCOMO was able to get these insights by researching outside its own industry.

The outdoor handsets:

- Are lightweight, float, are water resistant and shock-proof.
- Have an extremely robust large (1.8 inch) liquid crystal display.

- Provide easy access to emergency services.
- Support 'i-Area', a function that gives local information, such as the weather, based on the actual base-station in which the handset is located.

Handsets – Kids & Juniors Segment

Mobile phones must address the next generation's needs and DOCOMO offers 12 different versions. These cover a wide range of requirements based on an international comparison of children's use of mobile phones.[82] Cosh-Ishii observes: 'They really focus on target client needs, from the hardware design and easy interface to pre-loaded fun and useful learning content for youngsters, while making sure that parents, who are key purchase decision-makers, understand and endorse the clear value proposition.'

The Kids & Juniors handsets have:

- Specially conceived colours and designs, from renowned Japanese designer Kashiwa Sato.
- A wristwatch remote that can help locate a lost phone by making it beep within a range of 10 meters.
- Content specifically developed for kids. This includes cartoons, games and learning (and over 400,000 users subscribe to this at $3 a month).[83]
- An emergency ripcord. If the child pulls it: a 100-dB alarm starts 'screaming'; the camera automatically takes a photograph of the scene; the phone dials a voice call to the parents (or another preset number); it also emails recent photos to a preset address; and starts an 'emergency GPS tracking'. (And if someone thinks that pulling the phone battery will stop the alarm, they are wrong, because the handset designers have thought of that.)

Coverage

Of course, handsets are useless without the right coverage and internet services. Increasingly, coverage is being perceived by customers not just in terms of signal availability but in terms of uninterrupted, perfect reception of television on the move. Cosh-Ishii notes: 'And of course, more efficient data transmission provides the services Japanese mobile consumers want, and more revenues for DOCOMO.'

Over 1,100 engineers are employed in DOCOMO's R&D and spending on development has increased fourfold since 2000. This investment pays for a wide range of projects on achieving ultra-fast mobile communications, higher capacity and a fifth-generation mobile communication system (5G), which aims at over 10 Gbps data rates. Network availability at peak times is a key concern in Japan, as the country suffers from regular tremors. Following the recent tsunami, there was extreme usage of mobile telephones, as people checked whether relatives were OK. Therefore, network capacity needs to match these 'spikes' in usage.

DOCOMO R&D has adopted a central coordinating role, stimulating innovation between the equipment manufacturers, content providers (websites) and platform vendors (network providers), as shown in Figure 1.9. Wireless Watch Japan stresses that DOCOMO has a clear strategy: 'They view their market as an ecosystem, in which all of the partners should have a fair share of the margin. So DOCOMO share both development risk and gain.' DOCOMO encourages independent programmers to create a wealth of internet-based content.

Integrated Services

Mobile telephone service providers worldwide have often talked about finding the 'killer app' – the service that mobile telephone users will use constantly, and that will generate significant revenue growth for providers. DOCOMO is different in that it is not searching for one solution. Instead, it is looking to coordinate the best combination of handsets, an extremely reliable network, and innovative services – the content that customers will find essential to everyday life.

'Non-voice services' (data rather than voice transmission) have become the cornerstone of DOCOMO's strategy. Initially, these services were simple ones, such as downloadable, changeable ringtones, and DOCOMO introduced its most prominent non-voice service in February 1999. Today, the 'i-mode' (internet mode) makes mobile internet access so easy that DOCOMO has over 60 million users. It was also the first to create a new business model in which access is priced on the amount of information downloaded rather than the access time.

Seven categories of services are highlighted by the DOCOMO website:

- Connecting with people: email and voice calls.
- Entertainment: from games to TV, to reading and learning.

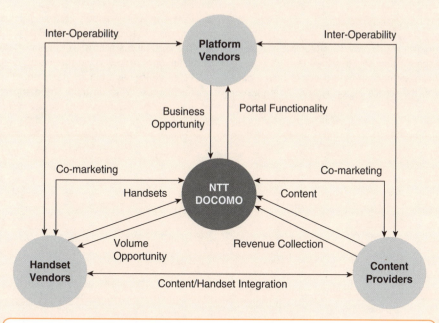

FIGURE 1.9: DOCOMO's Partnership Concept – The 'Ecosystem'
Source: copyright © NTT DOCOMO. Reprinted with permission[84].

- Peace of mind at all times: disaster warning, child protection, easy ways to deal with phone theft and so on.
- Phone personalization: from its appearance to customized information.
- Reference services: including international and local news.
- Convenience: including mobile shopping (with recommended bargains), banking, health and insurance.
- International calls and roaming.

Each of these categories links to a number of websites providing content. DOCOMO has carefully selected content partners for the quality of their services, a willingness to optimize their websites for mobile access, a willingness to accept site development risk, and an interest in forming a partnership (in which DOCOMO brings more traffic to the content provider in return for a commission on the information charges levied).

DOCOMO is now selling over 100,000 products via mobile shopping. However, Kazuhiro Yoshizawa, CEO, aims to add new types of integrated services, saying: 'I look to strengthen the company's relationships of mutual trust with partner corporations. Identifying various issues still yet to be addressed and mustering the business assets of our partners and DOCOMO will enable us to co-create new solutions and offer new value to customers and society as a whole.'[85]

Cosh-Ishii of Wireless Watch comments:

DOCOMO has built an ever faster and more dependable network. They pioneered the build-to-order handset strategy which enabled mass roll-out of valued services (embedded NFC payments and television broadcasting for example) and designed the original managed content platform for third-party vendors. In the spirit of Kaizen (continuous improvement) we are looking forward to the future advancement of this ecosystem in the decades ahead.

Reflective Questions

1. Why did network provider DOCOMO decide to have specific handsets developed?
2. How can partnerships and alliances help a company in the service sector achieve its innovation strategy?
3. How can a service provider make it harder for competitors to copy innovations?
4. The unusual characteristic of the Japanese mobile telephone market is that there is no direct channel by which handset manufacturers can sell their telephones. What do think is the impact of this on DOCOMO's international competiveness?

INNOVATION IN CONTEXT

INTRODUCTION

In Chapter 1 we analysed innovation management and introduced the Pentathlon Framework as a way of clarifying and addressing its main components. Our aim in this chapter is to set the practice of innovation in the broader context and introduce some themes that pervade the book. We start by briefly discussing the economic background and the role of innovation in economic theory and development. This leads to a discussion of the key factors that drive the need for innovation. We then introduce a number of themes that cut across the elements of the Pentathlon and which will reappear in various ways in the chapters that follow. Two of these, the way markets develop and mature, and the way innovations diffuse through populations, used to be considered mainly of academic interest because their timescales were beyond the typical business planning horizon. But the accelerating pulse of business life means that they are now becoming directly relevant to innovation practice. The two other topics, open innovation (OI) and business model innovation (BMI) are, to a considerable extent, also driven by the increased speed and connectivity of business. And, as we showed in Chapter 1, they have recently been the focus of a great deal of academic study. We introduce them here and discuss how to apply them to specific issues in later chapters.

This chapter covers:

- The treatment of innovation in economic theory.
- The factors that drive innovation in business.
- How the evolution of industries and markets interact with innovation.
- Diffusion of innovations.
- Open innovation.
- Business model innovation.
- A main case study on Aravind Eye Hospitals.

ECONOMICS AND INNOVATION

Innovation has not always been a popular idea. The philosopher Edmund Burke said that: 'Innovation is generally the result of a selfish temper and confined views',[1] and George Washington's dying words are said to have been: 'Beware of innovation in politics.' But economists have been more approving. A major influence has been what became known as the Austrian School of economic thought. The earliest work was in 1839 by A.F. Riedel, who recognized that new products have a significant impact on the economy. Surprisingly, he did not identify the importance of process innovation even though the Industrial Revolution had included process innovations that made a big impact, such as the power loom and the spinning jenny. The most significant work on innovation from the Austrian School came a century later with Joseph A. Schumpeter, who later moved from Vienna to become a professor at Harvard University. His work, which was already mentioned in Chapter 1, laid the foundations for our understanding of the nature and impact of innovation, and his book *The Theory of Economic Development*[2] is one of the classic economics texts. It discusses the importance not only of product innovation but also of process innovation, such as new manufacturing techniques that can drastically alter the costs and structure of an industry. Our main case study for this chapter, Aravind Eye Hospitals, gives a dramatic example of this.

In the following sections, we consider in more detail how innovation is linked to economic growth, business cycles, investment and company size.

Innovation and Economic Growth

The measure of macroeconomic progress that is most relevant to human welfare is the economic output per person. There is general agreement among economists that the main drivers of this are: *physical capital accumulation* (machinery, buildings, fertile land and so on); *human capital* (improvements in skill and education); and *technical progress*, a term that embraces not only technological innovation but also improvements in business methods. Technical progress cannot be measured directly, so it is usually estimated simply as the remainder, or *residual*, between the observed growth in economic output and that part of it that can be explained within classical economics by increases or improvements in labour and capital. In the 1950s, a number of studies found that only about half the observed growth in the US economy could be accounted for by the growth of capital and labour. In a 1957 paper that helped to win him the Nobel Prize, Robert Solow[3] estimated that technical progress generated as much as 88 per cent of the growth in output per man-hour between 1909 and 1949. Other studies have shown different results but the 'residual' is always significant. It is perhaps unfortunate for economics that a large part of the explanation of economic growth should be outside economic theory and many attempts have been made to address the issue by means of proxies such as patents and spending on R&D. More recently, it has been recognized that in most parts of the economy, capital accumulation is itself largely the result of technical progress because in manufacturing, new ideas lead to the design of new machines that supplant older generations, while in the IT and communications industries, demand for capital is driven by innovations in software. Of course, political structures and institutions can be important facilitators but it is clear that, in general, innovation is the dominant factor in economic progress.[4, 5, 6]

There has been much concern in the Western press about the dangers of developed countries losing their position of leadership in fundamental science and technology to the rising economies of Asia. The importance of science to technical innovation is obvious but that is not the same as saying that leadership in *research* is necessarily vital for leadership in innovation. In an influential book,[7] Amar Bhidé of Columbia University argued that although technical progress depends on science, basic discoveries quickly become available to all, either through publication or licensing, and most of the benefits go to the users of those discoveries and their customers. For example, the transistor was invented at Bell Laboratories (based on original work in Germany) but Sony was the first company to exploit it, and most of the benefits of the transistor have not gone to Bell, nor yet to the US. Does it matter that the computer was invented in America (or perhaps England), the internet in Geneva, or Skype in Estonia? Ultimately, the countries that best apply a new technology benefit the most. In this, one sees parallels with open innovation at the company level where companies collaborate on innovations or buy them from each other. The important thing is not where the invention comes from but the ability to understand and adopt it. Of course, this ability is no small matter: it requires a deep level of knowledge and expertise to master an emerging technology, apply it successfully in practice and then maintain its competitiveness over time. A high level of technical education is still necessary for a company or country to profit from technological progress.

Innovation and Business Cycles

Writing in 1939, Schumpeter believed that in addition to improving economic performance, innovation also drives long-term cyclical patterns of growth and decline, not only within individual markets but in whole economies.[8] According to Schumpeter, the introduction of an innovation is followed by two main phases. First comes the *diffusion phase*, in which the innovation leads to new products with higher utility and often reduced production costs. This radically changes customers' expectations and often disrupts the pricing structure and employment in the existing market (he called this *creative destruction*).[9] Successful innovation in one field may also enable faster innovation in other fields, as the ideas are copied. Entrepreneurs are able to generate higher profit levels through the enhanced value that innovations offer and this stimulates economic growth. As others follow, adoption becomes easier as barriers are broken and experience is accumulated. In this, Schumpeter anticipated modern ideas of diffusion and the adoption lifecycle, which we discuss below.

In the second phase, once innovations have diffused throughout an economic system, they lose their power as a source of growth, and an equilibrium state is reached in which the value of products and their pricing is largely stable. This market stagnation (Schumpeter also called it *depression*) continues until new technologies emerge. Here, Schumpeter anticipated the modern theory of 'S'-curves (see Chapter 4).

More controversially, Schumpeter believed that clusters of technologies also drive repetitive cycles in the whole economy. In this, he was building on the earlier work of Kondratiev,[10] who claimed to have identified larger scale patterns (*long waves*) of technology-driven development lasting about 50 years (see Theory Box 2.1).

A number of points are noteworthy for managers:

- Being first to market with an innovation may bring increased profits.[11] The improved product utility or significantly reduced process costs disrupt the pricing structure of markets and allow the innovating companies to earn higher profits.
- The increased profits achieved by entrepreneurial organizations will quickly attract interest and innovations will be copied. So they must make it as difficult as possible for a competitor to copy an innovation for example by

patenting it, by embedding it in a new business model, as discussed later in this chapter, or through a new manufacturing or service delivery process (see Mini Case 1.1 on Tetley's Teabags).

- As innovations diffuse to more companies, competition increases and prices are forced down. In this phase, the overall business competence of companies (their *complementary assets* – see Chapter 4) rather than their innovative ability often determines who will benefit most from the innovation in the longer run.

- When the equilibrium/depression stage is reached, companies must be on the lookout for alternative technologies or new business models to start a new cycle.

THEORY BOX 2.1: *Kondratiev Long Waves*

The Russian economist Kondratiev observed that one may identify a number of so-called 'long waves' of innovation driving economic development in cycles. In his 1925 book, he identified two such cycles, lasting from about 1790 to 1850 and from 1850 to 1896, the first driven by steam and mechanization (the Industrial Revolution) and the second by railways and steel. He believed a third was underway at the time. Later commentators have broadly – but by no means unanimously – agreed that the third cycle should be identified with electrification and the chemical industry, and the fourth with cars and petrochemicals. The timing of the fifth, computing and IT, is less certain: is it at its peak or its end? And there is no agreement whether the next such cycle should be expected to be based on nanotechnology, biotech, healthcare, robotics or renewable energy.

Some commentators have found evidence of a cyclical variation in global GDP of about the right frequency,[12] although the effect is not dramatic. There is no compelling theory that suggests that these waves are inevitable or predictable, and since there have, at best, been only four complete cycles of Kondratiev waves, they 'constitute an interesting interpretation, but one that cannot be taken as a well-established fact; there haven't been enough of them to serve as convincing evidence'.[13] Certainly, although a group of technologies may have driven regular cyclical behaviour in a small group of Western economies a century or so ago, there is no compelling reason to assume that the same thing will happen in the more technically diverse and international economies of the 21st century. We must just wait and see.

Innovation and Company Size

Are small companies more innovative than large ones, or is it the other way round? The evidence is not clear. An investigation of nearly 600 companies in the US showed that the size and age of companies are determinants of the number of new products produced per dollar of sales.[14] Other studies found, perhaps not surprisingly, that R&D expenditures increased almost in proportion to firm size,[15] and that larger companies were awarded more patents than small ones.[16] However, research by the London Business School concluded the opposite: that small firms are the most important innovators.[17] Yet other studies have found no difference between the innovation performance of large and small companies, apparently because although larger companies can have higher R&D expenditures, small companies may have more innovative employees; for example, young graduate scientists bringing with them the latest scientific knowledge and ideas.[18] It must be remembered, however, that although small companies may have inventiveness and flair, they may lack some of the core business disciplines required for commercial success. For example, Mini Case 2.1 shows how the launch of a new drug by Biogentex failed because of a lack of key customer knowledge. Of course, the survey findings depend on the business sectors studied and the measures of innovation used. But overall, for established companies, the relationship between company size and innovation is simply inconclusive.[19] Yet large companies do have many advantages: resources, funding, knowledge of markets and technologies, management experience and so on. So why are they not overwhelmingly the main source of innovation? The fundamental reason is probably that as a company grows and becomes increasingly competent, so its culture and processes become more and more specialized to the type of business it does. This is exactly what allows large companies to survive so well but it inevitably makes a serious change of direction more difficult. It is rightly said that great companies often fail by learning the lessons of success too well.

One type of small company is, almost by definition, innovative: that is, the *start-up*. Such companies have to have something new to offer in order to compete and this is probably the reason why most people instinctively think of small companies as innovative. There are many examples where start-ups, rather than the market leaders, have been responsible for breakthroughs. For example, the bagless vacuum cleaner was developed by James Dyson, an entrepreneur-innovator, rather than a market leader such as Hoover. One study showed that small companies backed by venture capital are disproportionately successful,[20] probably because they have to go through a very demanding approval process to obtain venture capital. This has helped companies to recognize the value of tough approval processes for innovation, and Texas Instruments, Philips and others have mimicked the approaches used by venture capitalists in their internal new venture approval processes.

MINI CASE 2.1: *Biogentex – Moving Molecules to Market*[21]

Biogentex is a European biopharmaceutical company established on the back of academic research that identified several interesting new molecules with high potential as neurological drugs for treating seizures. The founder of the company, a professor in molecular pharmacology, approached the university's technology transfer office and it was agreed that the university's patents on these molecules could be transferred to the newly established company.

Continued...

The company then approached various venture capitalists and some agreed to support the company with its first injection of venture capital, which allowed it to take the new drugs into a first phase of clinical development. Of all the drugs that entered the development pipeline, only two reached the end of the first phase successfully, and even then there were several major hurdles in sight. At that time, the CEO of the company (a medical doctor with considerable biotech experience) and the CSO (a pharmacology professor) explored new market opportunities and found – to their surprise – that the drugs in development could also be used for the treatment of severe lower back pain.

Next, the CEO approached the board of directors and argued that it would be good for the company to widen the market opportunities by exploring two alternatives in parallel: the seizures and the pain markets. The CEO thought that investigating the two alternatives would keep their options open. However, not everybody on the board agreed with the CEO's arguments and a difficult discussion ensued. Eventually, the board decided that the painkiller opportunity, with its bigger potential market, was the only one that Biogentex should target. So the company completely reoriented towards pain treatment and built expertise in this area. It then took the company six years to gain regulatory approval. Biogentex R&D and management were exhilarated when the drug was approved.

The product was named Pretira and it was launched in 2014. Sales gradually increased as doctors became convinced about the efficacy and safety of the product for treating back pain. However, after the first year, Pretira fell short of its sales and financial targets. It became clear that there were serious problems but the board of directors, the investors, the company's management and its R&D function were all baffled. How could such an effective product not be selling? The company's marketeers looked into the matter further and found, to their surprise, that orthopaedic surgeons could make more money by conducting surgical interventions than by prescribing Pretira to their patients. And Pretira has not been as widely adopted in the market as the company hoped – successful diffusion has not been achieved.

Case contributed by Jan Rosier.

Investment in Innovation

The most obvious measure of the level of effort going into innovation is companies' spending on R&D. Table 2.1 shows the spending, in absolute terms and as a percentage of sales, of the five companies that invest most in R&D in each of six important market sectors, worldwide. The figures are for 2013. As would be expected, different sectors show different levels of R&D expenditure, reflecting the state of their markets and technologies, and the opportunities and threats they face. There is also considerable diversity within the sectors because these are broadly defined and may include companies with quite different ambitions and business models. Moreover, innovation is not restricted to the product and service dimensions, so not all of it involves R&D; and even when it does, expenditure on joint ventures, collaborations and acquisitions may not be included.

Certainly, every company should carefully compare its own investment on innovation with what its direct competitors are reporting. If they are significantly different, alarm bells should ring; but the real meaning must be sought at a level of detail deeper than the gross figures for expenditure.

TABLE 2.1: R&D Investment in Different Industries, 2013

Top five companies in sector by R&D investment	R&D spend (€ billions)	R&D intensity (% of sales)
Aerospace and defence		
1. Airbus	3.6	6.0
2. Boeing	2.0	3.2
3. Finmeccanica	1.7	10.7
4. Bombardier	1.4	10.9
5. Safran	1.2	8.0
Automobiles & parts		
1. Volkswagen	11.7	6.0
2. Toyota	6.3	3.5
3. Daimler	5.4	4.6
4. General Motors	5.2	4.6
5. BMW	4.8	6.3
Banks		
1. Banco Santander	1.2	3.0
2. Royal Bank of Scotland	1.1	4.6
3. Barclays	0.74	2.2
4. Deutsche Bank	0.66	2.1
5. HSBC	0.53	1.1
Chemicals		
1. BASF	1.8	2.5
2. DuPont	1.6	6.0
3. Dow Chemical	1.3	3.1
4. Monsanto	1.1	10.3
5. Syngenta	1.0	9.4
Software and computing		
1. Microsoft	8.2	13.1
2. Google	5.7	13.2
3. IBM	4.1	5.7

TABLE 2.1: Continued

Top five companies in sector by R&D investment	R&D spend (€ billions)	R&D intensity (% of sales)
4. Oracle	3.7	13.5
5. SAP	2.3	13.6
Pharma and biotech		
1. Novartis	7.2	17.1
2. Roche	7.1	18.6
3. Johnson & Johnson	5.2	11.5
4. Merck	5.2	16.2
5. Sanofi-Aventis	4.8	14.4

Source: data © European Union, 1995–2016[22].

DRIVERS OF INNOVATION

The need – or opportunity – for innovation is driven by five factors. Four of these come from the world outside: technological advances; changing customers; competition; and the changing business environment. The fifth, strategic intent, relates to the company's own aspirations. These factors are illustrated in Figure 2.1, which is based on the work of Sheth and Ram,[23] with the strategic intent factor added.

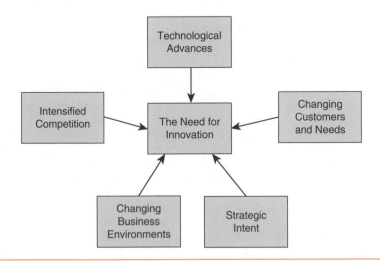

FIGURE 2.1: Drivers of the Need for Innovation
Source: adapted from Sheth, J.N. and Ram, R., Bringing Innovation to Market: How to Break Corporate and Customer Barriers, (New York: Wiley, 1987). Copyright © 1987 Jagdish Sheth. Reprinted with permission.

Technological Advances

There are endless examples of new technologies having a major influence on businesses, from the internal combustion engine to float glass to the internet. More recently, 'big data' (using sophisticated computer analysis to identify trends in customer habits) has become the buzzword in the information technology (IT) industry. Nanotechnology is increasingly being used in products, such as easy-to-clean surfaces, and is making an impact in paints and clothing. The impact of autonomous vehicles is yet to be felt.

New technologies can create new industries and new applications of established technologies are constantly emerging, most obviously in computing. Multinational companies that used to conduct all their own basic research often cannot keep abreast of all the developments, using their internal resources alone. This is one reason that *open innovation*, the sourcing of ideas and technology across organizational boundaries, has become so popular.

Technology is equally important for service companies and R&D is increasingly having a major impact on how service companies do business. For example, a Japanese bank has just introduced robot front-office 'tellers', which can advise customers in 19 languages. FedEx, the leading courier services company, has always recognized the importance of investing in technology and led much of the development of hand-held barcode readers, which enabled it to provide the first parcel-tracking capability. Bank of America (Mini Case 7.7) and other leading service organizations have created innovation departments to monitor new technology and test it with actual customers. Such *rapid prototyping* is just as important for services as it is for product development (see Mini Case 2.2 on Metro AG).

▶ MINI CASE 2.2: *Metro AG – Super Supermarkets*[24]

Technology in the service sector can give customers a better service experience. In the retail trade, RFID (radio frequency identification) 'smart tag' technology is having a big impact. Chip manufacturer Intel and supply chain software giant SAP have joined forces with the German company Metro AG, the world's fifth largest retailer, to create a fully working prototype of the supermarket of the future, in the small town of Rheinberg, Germany.

Products in the supermarket are all labelled with RFID in order to automate stock keeping and make shopping easier for customers. Each shopping trolley has a touch screen computer with a scanner and, as the customer selects each item, it is scanned in. The computer displays a range of useful information. This includes detailed product information on the item scanned, the total amount spent, special offers, the customer's 'standard' shopping list, and a map with the customer's position in the store. The biggest advantages are that the map helps shoppers find their grocery items faster and the items in the trolley do not need to be unloaded at the cashier's desk, saving the customer time. The trolley's computer automatically indicates the total amount to be paid and, having paid the cashier, the customer can simply push their trolley out to their car. Queuing is virtually eliminated and smartphone technology has been linked into the system to enable contactless payments.

Continued...

Metro has called the project the Future Store initiative, and through the extensive use of technology is looking for not only increases in supply chain efficiency but also a better customer experience. It has been recognized that the latter needs constant testing with real users. Smart tags are still relatively expensive and so are not viable for every item in every supermarket but as the cost of tags continues to fall, they will become ubiquitous in retail.

Manufacturing companies often use prototypes to gain detailed customer feedback on new products. Extending the idea to the trial of a new service concept is a bold approach that few service companies have yet contemplated. Metro's prototyping has helped it identify the 'real advantages for both the retail industry and consumers'. The initiative now involves 75 partner companies and helps them improve 'their processes and reduce their costs ... [and] tailor their range of products and services to the consumer needs'.

Is Future Store an expensive, one-off experiment? It does not appear so, as a second store was recently equipped with the same technology. This has proved that the IT investment is viable, as customer numbers and satisfaction levels at the refurbished store have increased significantly.

Changing Customers and Needs

The second driver of innovation is the changing characteristics and requirements of customers. For instance, the ageing populations in the West and China are increasing the needs for products for the older generation, such as 'toys that entertain the elderly' – software-based pastimes that can help with the loneliness generated by most of their younger relatives working and living in the cities.[25] In contrast, other Asian markets are largely made up of young consumers with different aspirations. As earnings in newly industrialized countries soar, the demand for particular products and services will develop. Normally, companies design products for the developing world and simplify them for other countries. The Whirlpool Corporation developed the Ideale, one of the world's cheapest automatic washing machines, retailing at $150, specifically for countries such as Brazil and China.[26] Products developed at a price point suitable for newly industrialized countries are also starting to be popular in other countries – referred to as *reverse innovation*.[27]

Changing customers also means that traditional market segments can disappear or fragment and companies will need to adjust their product ranges accordingly. For example, car manufacturers now target over 15 key segments in the US, as opposed to only five in the late 1960s. And within each segment, endless variations and colours are offered, a far cry from Henry Ford's 'any colour provided it's black'. At the same time, there is the pressure for more environmentally acceptable products and services. As basic needs are met, there is an additional challenge to innovation – determining the more subtle factors that nevertheless affect customers' choices, the so-called *hidden needs* (see Chapter 5).

Competition

The third driver shown in Figure 2.1 is growing competition. For example, logistics costs have plummeted thanks, among other things, to the container revolution in shipping. Consequently, 'home markets' are being threatened by foreign competition, and margins are under pressure. Companies may also face competition from sources normally outside their industries. An example of this is the bicycle industry in Japan where Nippon Bicycle has taken a significant share of the market by offering made-to-order, highly customized mountain bikes with a fast delivery time. Nippon is owned by the consumer electronics company Panasonic, which has made use of its expertise in logistics to become successful in a new market.

Products and services that were competitive when they were introduced quickly become commodities. Philips, the Dutch consumer products giant, has learned from experience that its margins erode within months of every new product introduction, because of competitors' actions. So this commercial uncertainty needs to be carefully considered during new product development.[28]

Today's products and services seldom increase in value with time (with some notable exceptions such as malt whisky and good wines); so constant updates and improvements are required.

Changing Business Environments

Business environments are always subject to change – sometimes gradual and sometimes radical. Trade groupings such as ASEAN and North American Free Trade Association have a great effect on how business is done, as countries joining the European Union have found. Major political change, such as that in China in the 1980s under Deng Xiaoping or in Myanmar at the moment, can transform business opportunities. Governments regularly intervene in the economy with changing regulations and taxation policies. An example of changing regulations that could drastically change one market is the US Food and Drug Administration's planned faster approval of generic drugs.

The ups and downs of the business cycle are also influential. Downturns drive many companies to cut their investments in innovation but the winners that emerge have continued to invest.[29] An example is Corning, the subject of our main case study in Chapter 9.

Strategic Intent

The ambitions of the leaders of a company play a decisive role in determining the amount as well as the type of innovation a company will attempt. We call this *strategic intent*. The most common strategic reason for innovation is to achieve growth, but the *amount* of growth required depends on the level of ambition of the leadership. Some will be aggressive, some more cautious, but the stance is a matter of ambition not calculation. And there may be other strategic imperatives too, such as improved security through diversification or the wish to reduce environmental impact. Public sector and not-for profit organizations – and many commercial ones – may be motivated simply by the wish to do a better job for their customers or make a positive impact on the world. This was what drove Aravind, the subject of the main case study at the end of this chapter, to dramatic innovation. These are all drivers from within the organization, not mere responses to the outside world. Indeed, without strategic intent, there would be no companies at all.

Although most of the drivers of innovation come from outside the organization, they are not necessarily unpredictable. Two particular influences that affect the landscape of innovation and can be broadly anticipated are the changes that occur as technologies progress and the changes in markets as different types of customer adopt an innovation. We now consider these two topics in more detail.

INDUSTRY EVOLUTION

The role of innovation changes as new industries grow and mature. At the start of any new industry, there is usually a period of ferment and experimentation during which the companies try out many different product designs as they try to find the best way to satisfy the need that brought the industry into existence. Eventually, as Abernathy and Utterback point out,[30] a *dominant design* arises that becomes an actual or de facto standard and is eventually adopted by all serious players. In the automotive industry, for example, the early years of the 20th century saw a struggle between steam, electric and internal combustion power units until the dominant design – petrol engine, four wheels, monocoque construction, three pedals plus a gear lever – emerged in the 1920s. It is little changed to this day. Commercial aircraft are now almost all monoplanes with wing-mounted engines after years of exploration of other designs. Once a dominant design emerges, competition on the core performance inevitably slackens (although it may continue for some time) and the competitive focus moves elsewhere: typically to cost, quality, brand value, styling and additional features. For example, competition in the automotive industry has moved on through power-assisted steering and automatic gears to styling, parking sensors, self-parking and collision avoidance systems. This change of focus is illustrated in Figure 2.2: once the dominant design emerges, competition on the core features slackens and attention moves to other factors, and eventually to the performance of the whole

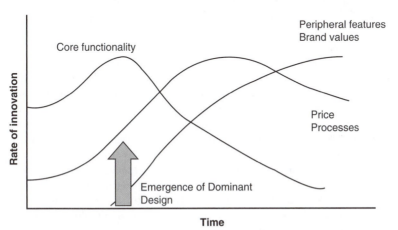

FIGURE 2.2: The Effect of Dominant Design on Product and Process Innovation
Source: Based loosely on Abernathy and Utterback, 1978[31].

company (brand values). Until, of course, a radical new technology appears and starts the process again (see Mini Case 4.5).

Once a dominant design has emerged, it leads to efficiencies of scale and experience among suppliers. As the automotive and PC industries demonstrate, design standardization allows manufacturers to use many common components such as lights, tyres and shock absorbers with all the advantages of volume supply and specialized expertise that go with it. New suppliers can now enter the component market because the interfaces are defined and stable. The whole supply chain rides up a learning curve, incrementally improving efficiencies and trimming costs. All this helps to maintain the advantages of the dominant design, although the specialization that drives the improvement may make it more difficult for companies to adapt if and when an alternative dominant design appears.

A dominant design may emerge simply because it is the best available way to perform the function. Axes, needles, woodscrews and forklift trucks are all examples of designs that are dominant simply because nobody can (as yet) improve on them. Another way for a dominant design to arise is by way of a formal standardization agreement at the national or international level. For example, we all drive on the same side of the road (at least within each country); all postal systems use stamps; rails are now the same distance apart on virtually all European public railways. Such agreements are particularly useful when interfacing between the products of different parties is important. For example, the way mobile telephone systems work has been laid down by international agreement, rather than emerging in the marketplace, because all handsets must work with the same network. Once a standard is set, innovation at the system level necessarily stops and competitive attention moves elsewhere.

A dominant design may also be held in place by *threshold* or *network effects*. A threshold effect operates when a dominant design is held in place by the high cost of making a change. An excellent example is the 'Qwerty' keyboard (see Mini Case 2.3). This design is inherently inefficient but it is so well established that attempts to replace it with a better one have always failed,[32, 33] because anyone who wants to change over has to unlearn a painfully acquired skill and learn a new one. The cost of making the change simply outweighs the benefits. The UK would long ago have changed to driving on the right like the rest of the world if it were not for the cost – not to mention the dangers – of the transition.

Another, more powerful way in which a dominant design becomes locked in place is through so-called *network effects* or *network externalities*. These occur when the value of a design becomes greater the more people adopt it. Telephones, email and Facebook are modern examples of this. The more popular they are, the more valuable they become. The network effect may be direct, when the value is directly related to the number of customers; or it may be indirect, when the value is generated by related products and services. Thus, the VHS video standard and the CD format became unassailable in their time not because of the hardware but because of the huge amount of software products that are available to use on it (see Mini Case 4.8). The same effects dominated in the emergence of DVD and the MP3 standard for music recording. Microsoft's

Windows operating system is an example where the threshold effect of familiarity is supported by the many independent application programs that have been written to run with it.

Where they occur, network and threshold effects both serve to make an established dominant design very difficult to shift. Together they can make an almost insuperable barrier, as people who tried to persuade the world to adopt the artificial new language, Esperanto, found out. The new language is difficult to learn; and it is of no use until many other people have learned it, too.

Clearly, the emergence of a dominant design has major implications for companies. The ideal situation, of course, is to have leadership in the design. Companies in that position will want to hasten its adoption and stimulate network effects if possible to hold it in place. Others may face the costs of changing to it and possibly writing off a lot of investment. And all players will need to think carefully about where their competitive edge will come from in future and in particular which aspects of the design to keep in house and which to subcontract.[34]

MARKET EVOLUTION

When an innovative new product or service is launched, it is seldom adopted at once by all possible customers. Some will pounce on it at once, attracted by the novelty, while others will be more cautious and will consider it only when it is well proven. This applies to companies as well as consumers and is known as the *adoption lifecycle*, illustrated in Figure 2.3. The five adopter categories are as follows:

1. The first adopters are termed *innovators*. They are interested in novelty for its own sake and will have the knowledge and interest to experiment, and to overcome teething problems.
2. Next are the *early adopters*. Typically, they are more interested in the new opportunities the innovation presents. As individuals, they will be financially and socially secure and so able to accept mistakes and failures. As companies, they will be technically competent and will aim to use the innovation for competitive advantage – to get a step ahead of their rivals.
3. The third group, the *early majority*, is particularly important because they are numerous and represent the start of the mainstream market. They are typically more pragmatic and will adopt only when they have clear proof that the idea works and has real value. Unlike the early adopters, who will rely on their own judgement, the early majority will often move only when they can see that others like them are using the innovation successfully.
4. The fourth group, the *late majority*, are typically more cautious and less confident in dealing with novelty so they need plenty of support and often the security of buying from a large company or well-known brand.
5. Finally, the *laggards* will adopt only when they absolutely have to, and then reluctantly. In consumer goods, this is often the stance of the elderly. Among businesses, it may be those in a high-risk business such as oil and gas or nuclear energy, with a well-founded aversion to any kind of risk.

The adoption lifecycle curve has been found usually to be roughly bell-shaped in practice and this has led to the easy assumption that it is 'really' a normal distribution with the boundaries between the adopter categories falling at the standard deviation points, so that the innovators 'should' be 2.5 per cent of the total, the early adopters 13.5 per cent, the early and late majority each 34 per cent, with the laggards making up the rest. There is absolutely no justification for this; in practice, the proportions are bound to vary substantially from case to case.

The adoption lifecycle has had a major influence on marketing theory and practice, and companies will adapt their marketing and sales strategies according to their estimate of which state of the cycle has been reached. A more recent addition to the theory has been Geoffrey Moore's recognition that the transition from one adopter category to another can be problematic, particularly for companies in technology-based markets.[35] He particularly emphasized the difficulty of the transition (now often known as 'crossing the chasm') between the early adopters and the early majority when selling to other companies. The problem is that early adopter companies are interested in innovations that will give them serious competitive advantage. The early majority, on the other hand, will be seeking to make an improvement in their business, not a revolution; and being practical they will demand hard proof that an innovation can deliver it. The problem is that the experience of the early adopters often will not provide the sort of proof that the early majority look for; and anyway they may want to keep it to themselves. The result is that the sales of radically new products often start well but then stall or even collapse at the end of the innovator/early adopter phase. The main case study in Chapter 4, on Domino, provides an example of this. Companies may have to make special efforts to cross the chasm into the mainstream markets.[36]

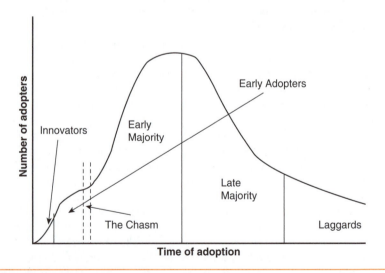

FIGURE 2.3: Adopter Categories for Innovations
Source: "The Revised Technology Adoption Life Cycle" (p. 21) from Crossing The Chasm, Third Edition by Geoffrey A. Moore. Copyright © 1991, 1999, 2002, 2014 by Geoffrey A. Moore. Reprinted by permission of HarperCollins Publishers and Geoffrey A. Moore.

DIFFUSION OF INNOVATIONS

Diffusion is the term used for the way in which innovations spread through populations and market segments. Our concern in this book is mostly with how new products, processes and services spread through markets but many of the most influential studies have been done at the social level: the spread of farming practices in South America, or contraceptive methods in India, for example. The original and most influential study concerned the spread of hybrid seed corn in Iowa in the 1930s.[37] A leading researcher in diffusion studies has been Everett Rogers at the University of New Mexico, whose book *Diffusion of Innovations* is a classic text.[38] It is highly relevant for managers, as it gives indications on how product and process innovations can be planned so that they are adopted more quickly.

The way an innovation spreads through a population depends on several things: the characteristics of the innovation itself; the personal characteristics of the adopters, or customers; the communication channels through which they learn about and evaluate the innovation; and *change agents* – people such as teachers, consultants, public health workers and salespeople, who help adopters to get to grips with the innovation.

The Influence of Features

The characteristics of innovations themselves have a powerful effect on how quickly and readily they are adopted. Rogers[39] identifies six such characteristics, emphasizing that it is the adopter's perception of these that is important:

1. Relative advantage: The extent to which the innovation is perceived as being better than what preceded it. This is where attention normally goes when designing a new product.

2. Observability: The degree to which the results of an innovation are observable to others. Preventive innovations, that is, ones that prevent the occurrence of something undesirable, are notoriously problematic because the adopter can never know whether the risk was there to start with. One of the reasons given for the success of the rat poison Warfarin is that the rats typically come out in the open to die, so the effects of the poison are made clear.

3. Trialability: New products are more readily adopted if there is an easy way for customers to try them out before purchasing. Free downloads provide this service for pop music. Most software is now available in free trial versions. Products where a trial is not possible (or is difficult or prolonged) face more resistance.

4. Compatibility: Innovations that require a significant change of behaviour or attitude tend to be resisted, however great their other benefits may be. Medical innovations (contraceptive methods for example) are an obvious case where cultural norms have a big influence. The demand for telephony grew slowly, partly because it required new social habits, whereas mobile telephony took on quickly because it built on existing practices.

5. Complexity: Innovations that are perceived as complicated or difficult to use are adopted slowly. Major simplifications to an existing idea often spur adoption.

6. Risk: The more risk the customer takes in acquiring the product, the less likely they are to buy. Trialability helps to overcome this. Like many retailers, Amazon benefits from making it as easy as possible for customers to return a product if they have second thoughts.

These factors should be taken into account in designing any new product or service and in planning the launch and promotion. Table 2.2 suggests questions to consider in respect of each one. They are also helpful in considering how to

TABLE 2.2: Factors that Influence the Diffusion of Innovations

No.	Factor	Relationship	Questions to ask
1.	Relative advantage	The greater the perceived advantage, the faster the diffusion	• What new benefits does the innovation offer? • Does the innovation cover all the benefits of the existing product, process or service? • How much better is the innovation, in terms of finances, time saved and other measures?
2.	Observability	The easier it is to observe the advantages, the faster the diffusion	• How can the benefits of the innovation be made as tangible and demonstrable as possible?
3.	Trialability	The easier it is for users to test the innovation, the faster the diffusion	• Is the customer easily able to trial the innovation to perceive the benefits first hand? • Can a trial on a small scale be used?
4.	Compatability	The closer the match to the existing product, process or service, the faster the diffusion	• In what ways can the innovation be made similar to the customer's current way of working?
5.	Complexity	The simpler the innovation appears, the faster the diffusion	• How can an innovation be designed to be simple? • How can extra features and customization be developed in the product, process or service without adding unnecessary complexity?
6.	Perceived risk	The lower the risk, the faster the diffusion	• What are the customer's perceived risks of adoption? • How can they be minimized?

Source: based on ideas in Rogers, 2003

overcome resistance to any kind of innovation, including organizational change; indeed, they are related to the factors in the change equation, which we introduce for this purpose in Chapter 9.

Although these attributes are conceptually distinct, they may overlap somewhat in practice, as Rogers concedes. But they have been tested empirically and these studies certainly emphasize the importance of factors other than the apparent advantage in determining how readily an innovation will spread. The Dvorak keyboard (Mini Case 2.3) is a good example of an innovation that has great functional advantages but has never caught on because although it is potentially faster, it is perceived as too complex and difficult to learn. Conversely, Mini Case 7.2 describes how a new business model made the features ideal for the diffusion of solar panels in Africa.

CHAPTER 2

> **MINI CASE 2.3:** *Keyboards – Dvorak versus Qwerty* [40]

The most common type of computer keyboard is the Qwerty design. However, it is not the most efficient design. A faster alternative, the Dvorak keyboard, was developed years ago but it is still virtually unknown, demonstrating the uncertainty involved in the diffusion of innovations.

Consider the difference in how the two keyboards were designed. The Qwerty version was actually designed to slow the rate at which you can type. This was because it was developed for mechanical typewriters, where there was a problem of the levers catching together and jamming. People who have used typewriters will remember the annoying problem of two levers jamming, and the need to flip the levers back, which nearly always resulted in you getting ink on your fingers. To minimize the chances of two levers jamming, designers looked at the most common sequences of letters in words and deliberately moved letters that commonly come in sequence (for example 'e' and 'r') close together on the keyboard where they will not be pushed simultaneously. The sequence of keys on the keyboard led to its name, Qwerty.

Professor Dvorak, an American engineer, analysed the process of typing with the aim of making it faster. To do this, he considered how the letters could be distributed on the keyboard to take advantage of the fact that most people are right-handed. Therefore, approximately 55 per cent of the work is allocated to the normally stronger right hand, by locating more of the common letters on the right-hand side of the keyboard. The central row of keys was reserved for the most common letters, with the less common letters allocated to keys further away from the strongest fingers. Despite the clever ideas behind the Dvorak keyboard, it has not been widely adopted, although a number of computer manufacturers offer it as an option for touch screens and it is known to reduce the level of repetitive strain injury.

Diffusion theory can be used to understand the failure of the Dvorak innovation. Although once trained, a touch typist may be faster on the Dvorak keyboard, the *relative advantage* of the device is not high. The *observability* and *trialability* of the innovation are low as potential users cannot perceive the advantage that the keyboard can bring to them until they have taken the time to learn to use it. And the *risk* is high that after all that effort it may not live up to expectations. Superficially, the *complexity* of the keyboard is the same as a Qwerty one, but to a user the *compatibility* with their current modus operandi is low.

OPEN INNOVATION

The term *open innovation* (OI) was popularized by Henry Chesbrough in his 2003 book of the same name.[41] It simply means that organizations can, and should, look outside their own doors for innovative ideas and ways of exploiting their own.

Chesbrough pointed out that the scientifically based industries that emerged in the aftermath of the war were generally self-sufficient in terms of technology for the very good reason that they had acquired a near-monopoly of knowledge in their field. Nobody knew more about computing than IBM or more about communications than the Bell Telephone Company. The huge, successful research labs of IBM, Philips and other companies produced a stream of new technologies and products based on ideas produced in their own organizations, which the companies developed and sold entirely by themselves. Anything they could not use immediately could be kept 'on the shelf' for later use. But a number of increasingly strong *erosion factors* have undermined the viability of this 'closed innovation' paradigm:

1. Universities are much more willing to work with others to commercialize their ideas.
2. People generally change jobs more often than they used to and they carry their knowledge away with them.
3. Financing for start-ups is much more readily available thanks to the rise of the venture capital industry.
4. The international spread of industrialization has produced a huge proliferation of small firms, developing new ideas and technologies all over the world.
5. The internet has made it much easier for companies and individuals to access knowledge and contact potential collaborators.

As a senior research manager from Merck said: 'Every senior scientist here running a project should think of herself or himself as being in charge of all the research in that field. Not just the 30 people in our lab, but the 3,000, say, in the world in that field.'[42] William Joy of Sun Microsystems said simply: 'Not all the smart people work for Sun.'[43] With open innovation, the innovation funnel is porous, as shown in Figure 2.4, with ideas and technologies potentially entering and leaving at any point.

Managers who are asked about OI often say: 'we've been doing that for years'. And indeed, companies have habitually licensed whole products from others to complete their offerings in the market, as Microsoft did for the original Xbox (Mini Case 2.4), and many have funded and profited from university research. However, since the 1990s, collaborative modes of innovation have rapidly become much more widespread and deliberate and many companies are adopting OI as a deliberate policy. So, although there may be an element of 'old wine in new bottles', the move to open innovation probably deserves to be regarded as a genuine paradigm shift because until recently it was an unspoken assumption that innovation was mostly something to be kept 'in-house', whereas now the expectation is that, of course, it is likely to involve other parties.

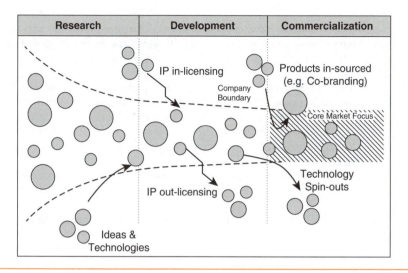

| Research | Development | Commercialization |

IP in-licensing

Products in-sourced
(e.g. Co-branding)

Company
Boundary

Core Market Focus

IP out-licensing

Technology
Spin-outs

Ideas &
Technologies

FIGURE 2.4: The Open Innovation Funnel
Source: adapted from Docherty, M. E., Venture2 Inc. Reprinted with permission[44].

> **MINI CASE 2.4:** *Microsoft – Open Innovation for the Xbox [45]*

Microsoft started work on the Xbox games console in early 1999. It was a response to the perceived threat that the TV would acquire processing and communications capabilities and eventually displace the PC and with it Microsoft's flagship 'Windows' operating system. Gates later said that in the strategic picture Microsoft needed twin pillars, with 'a PC in the den and an Xbox in the living room'. The project was a combination of top-down direction from Bill Gates and his team, and a bottom-up initiative from games enthusiasts in the company.

But Microsoft had little competence in the design of many of the key elements of a games console, such as the audio and graphics chips that deliver the realistic pictures and sound on which the games depended. Nor did it have much experience in designing and manufacturing electronics hardware. And its games division could expect to supply only a fraction (albeit a profitable one) of the games for the console. So, for a successful entry into this established, competitive market, Microsoft would have to assemble a coalition of suppliers, whose work would make or break the project. In such a fast-changing market, the chosen partners would have to be able to drive performance up and price down very aggressively. Sony had already shown the way: it forced the cost of its PlayStation down from $450 to $80 over five years by combining components and simplifying the design as the technology progressed. And when PlayStation 2 was launched, its graphics were 600 times better than those of its predecessor. Microsoft's job would not be easy.

Microsoft had one technical card to play: a suite of software called DirectX that made it easy to write games and other software for PCs. PCs come in a wide range of configurations with different processor speeds, memory sizes and peripherals. DirectX took care of the interfaces between the software and

Continued...

whatever hardware there was, and 'allowed game developers to make use of all the add-on gear that computers had gained without worrying about the particular mix'.[46] Games developers would not have to learn a new set of programming techniques for each new generation of machine – as was the case, for example, with PlayStation.

Microsoft's team approached all the major suppliers of PCs one by one, proposing they join the project as partners and handle the hardware. None found the business attractive because traditionally games consoles are sold at a loss and all the money is made on the games. So, Microsoft now had to take full responsibility for the hardware; but chose to subcontract the complete manufacturing task to an established contract manufacturer, Flextronics of Singapore, which proposed building two new factories to make the Xbox, one in Mexico and one in Hungary.

The support of games designers inside and outside Microsoft was crucial for the success of the project. Even the choice of Nvidia as the maker of the vital graphics chip was heavily influenced by their preferences.

The launch date for the Xbox was originally set for late 2000 but it became clear that the performance that could be achieved at that time would not provide the impact that Microsoft, as a newcomer to the market, required. It was decided to delay the project by a year to allow the use of Nvidia's next generation graphics chips and larger storage capacity.

Microsoft provided only the business and design concept, the finance, the styling, and the core operating software (not Windows, as it turned out). All the key components and the manufacturing were subcontracted. Microsoft would sell the hardware at a significant loss and generate income from its own games and from a $7 licence fee it collected on games from third parties. The business plan forecasted a loss of $900 million, even if all went well, a price the company was prepared to pay to open up a new business area.

The Xbox was launched in November 2001, 18 months after Sony's PlayStation 2 and 6 months after Nintendo launched its GameCube. The Xbox was an immediate success and by mid-2004, 14 million units had been sold. This established Microsoft as a serious player in the console market, and it remains so to this day. It launched the Xbox 360 in 2003 and continues to fight it out with Sony and Nintendo for the top three places in the market. In 2014, Microsoft was selling 11 million units per year compared with 18 million for Sony and 16 million for Nintendo.

As we showed in Chapter 1, there has been a huge amount of academic research on OI in the past 10 years.[47] This has served to give structure to the subject and clarify what can be done, although without, as yet, giving much guidance to practitioners on how to do it well.[48] This is not a criticism: when a new paradigm opens up, it is important to define its scope and possibilities. But more work is still required. One of the difficulties is that most of the applications of OI are relatively recent so although there are plenty of examples of what is being tried, it is too early to say for certain what works and, perhaps more important, what does not work.[49]

The Scope of Open Innovation

Chesbrough's first publication concentrated on two modes of OI: *outside-in*, in which companies seek out innovative ideas from others to employ within their own business model, and *inside-out*, in which they deliberately 'spin out' ideas or technologies for others to use. Gassman and Enkel[50] also pointed out the importance of the *coupled* mode of OI in which companies work together, pooling resources and ideas to produce something of value to both businesses. Outside-in OI overlaps to some extent with user-centred innovation, studied by von Hippel and others, in which companies work closely with individuals or companies who use their products in particularly demanding situations. We discuss this further in Chapter 5. Most of the academic literature concentrates on the outside-in form of OI,[51] despite the fact that for every outside-in innovator, there must also be an inside-out partner.

Inside-out or outside-in OI may operate without any change of business model. In this case, a contract is made between the parties for the transfer of expertise or intellectual property (IP) from one to the other, which allows them to enhance their product without necessarily altering the way they do business. However, if the resulting innovation is radical enough, it may require significant changes to the business model.[52] This is particularly likely in the case of coupled innovation, where the result may be significantly novel for both parties.

Another dimension of the subject is the parties involved and their motivation. The original formulation assumed that OI would be based on normal commercial relations between two businesses, while von Hippel's user-defined innovation assumed one company working with one user without financial inducements. But we now see many variants on these. For example, several companies may work together to develop a commercial ecosystem of benefit to all, as in the collaboration, and mutual dependence, between computer games designers and console manufacturers. The extreme case is perhaps the development of open-source software such as Linux, which involves many individuals and many companies working together non-commercially to develop something that is of benefit to all but owned by none.[53] Table 2.3 summarizes these variations.

We remarked earlier that the academic study of OI has not so far resulted in much guidance on best practice. This is true except for two important lessons. The first is that OI is a significant reorientation of the business, which must be taken seriously and supported at a high level in the organization. The second is simply that OI is possible and can be highly successful. It was reported in 2011[55] that Procter & Gamble had compared the net present value (NPV) of its open innovation projects with its closed innovation projects and discovered that open innovation projects outperformed internal projects, achieving a 70 per cent higher NPV.

Implementing Open Innovation

Some companies have adopted OI as a strategic step, to be driven from the top. A prime example is Procter & Gamble, whose initiative was driven personally by A.G. Lafley, the chief executive, who announced the company's intention to source half of the company's new ideas externally. The Connect and Develop programme, started in 2001, reportedly achieved that aim within four years. P&G could trace a history of technical collaborations going back more than a century but this step still required a major concentration of management effort. Not all companies are, or need to be, so bold. A more usual approach is to start with modest pilot projects where the opportunity arises, and build up the capability more slowly.

TABLE 2.3: Modes of Open Innovation for a Company

With ⟍ OI Mode	One other company	Several parties/ business models unchanged	Multiple parties/new business models	Individuals
Outside-in OI	Firm buys IP from another organization for exclusive use, e.g. patent licensing	Firm buys IP from several others for its product, e.g. Microsoft Xbox	Firm uses others' IP to develop a new business, e.g. Apple's iPod and iTunes store	Firm invites ideas from individuals, e.g. crowd sourcing; authors working with publishers
Inside-out OI	Firm sells IP it doesn't need, or transfers to spin off, e.g. exclusive patent licencing; corporate incubators – Philips, BT, etc.	Firm transfers IP to several others to use in their products, e.g. non-exclusive licensing of CD patents to equipment makers	Firm makes its IP available to others to develop a new business, e.g. IBM and Linux	No known examples
Coupled OI	Companies collaborate, each giving IP to the other for their own products or services, e.g. Sony and Philips developing the CD	Several companies collaborate to develop new opportunities for their products, e.g. games consoles and games; Uber	Collaboration leads to an innovation not owned by either party but of value to both, e.g. open source software	Firm collaborates with skilled individuals to improve product, e.g. Lego Mindstorms

Source: Loosely based on Vanhaverbeke and Chesbrough, 2014[54]

Outside-in

The possibilities for outside-in collaboration range from simple subcontract, through joint development projects to joint ventures, and acquisitions.[56] The extremes, subcontract and acquisition, are well-established approaches; open innovation is newer and concerns primarily the intermediate situation where there is collaboration but no clear ownership. Here, investment is less than that required in mergers and acquisition but the benefits may be greater and more enduring than those from subcontracting. However, such collaborations face special issues. The first is how to manage the partnership, and especially the thorny issue of ownership of the intellectual property. We cover this further in Chapter 5.

The second issue is that of *absorptive capacity*: the ability of the receiving party to absorb and apply the knowledge it receives. This is important and yet often overlooked. Technology is not generally a commodity that can be bought and then forgotten about. For a start there may be operational problems. Who will sort them out? More importantly, the initial version may in time be developed to provide updates, improvements and perhaps whole new opportunities.

Where are these future opportunities? Not in the documentation, but in the half-formed thoughts and ideas in people's heads. So, if the company wants to be able to use and develop the technology into the future – as well as cope with any operational issues along the way – it will have to develop or recruit people with the right expertise. The only alternative is if the partnership with the supplier is so secure that there is no doubt it will continue as long as needed. That normally means at least a formal joint venture, or else merger or acquisition. Mini Case 2.5 shows how an Egyptian company addressed this issue. See also Theory Box 4.1 for a further discussion.

> **MINI CASE 2.5:** *INFIT – German and Danish Technology Made in Egypt with video interview*

INFIT was set up in the 1990s in Egypt as a joint venture with German company Woeste as a manufacturer of galvanized pipe fittings. Over the years, the Egyptian-German joint venture has grown to become the sole manufacturer of galvanized pipe fittings and small job castings in Egypt.

Mariam Ismail, managing partner of INFIT, says: 'From its earliest days the founder of our company Mr Helmy Ismail believed that we needed to compete on the quality of our products.' The company's strategy has been to win orders on local and European markets by demonstrating its ability to combine German technology and quality assurance with the cost advantage of manufacturing in Egypt. The concept of 'German technology made in Egypt' has played a vital role in building the company's solid reputation with its customers.

Underpinning this has been a long process of technology transfer, absorption and internalization. INFIT's focus has been not only on transferring manufacturing technologies but also on working hard to adopt know-how from its German counterpart in all its operational activities. There has been persistent desire to build a strong 'German' organizational culture. The company has sought the help of German engineers to work alongside its Egyptian engineers and operators to ensure a process of exposure to know-how and has built a structured programme of engagement to allow for a systematic transfer of operational and technical knowledge between both parties. This methodical technology transfer process has become an integral part of INFIT and has been applied a number of times when the company was involved in product or process innovation.

INFIT's ability to transfer technology to develop its processes proved to be an important capability when the company was in need of a new DISAMATIC production line due to the deteriorating machine conditions and decreased throughput of the existing line. Ismail explained: 'The DISAMATIC production line is an essential part of our business; it is used for fast manufacturing of sand moulds for sand casting. This process is vital for the mass manufacturing of metal casting; with a low performing DISAMATIC our competitive ability is greatly compromised.' Having identified the need, the management team set out to identify the most suitable provider of this technology:

> When it comes to technology transfer and adoption, we have learnt not just to look for radical new technologies from abroad. We sometimes seek incremental upgraded versions of our existing technology. We prefer strategic collaborations that enhance our manufacturing capability at a rate that we can effectively manage, rather than a disruptive technology that can at times negatively impact other operational capabilities across our company.

Continued...

INFIT opted to cooperate with a Danish company that not only delivered the needed machinery but also had the expertise and reputation for transferring production know-how to its customers. Following its investment in the upgraded version of the DISAMATIC production line, INFIT worked with the Danish counterpart to ensure that engineers and operators had gained sufficient knowledge in the operations, troubleshooting, and preventive maintenance of the line. The company's capability in handling technol-

ogy transfer ensured that the new Danish machinery and know-how were quickly integrated into the company. The company's German and Egyptian engineers joined forces to exercise this capability in organizing on-site training with the Danish team. It wrote a company-specific instruction manual for standard operations and quality assurance of the line, and set clear performance indicators to measure line performance. A large part of INFIT's competitive ability now comes from its capability to understand technology and know-how from its foreign counterparts and explicitly integrate it into its operational processes; this ability has become an integral part of the company culture.

Now visit www.palgravehighered.com/gm to watch Mariam Ismail discussing the steps INFIT took to absorb management and cultural competences, as well as technology, from partner companies.

Case contributed by Mohamed Khater.

Organizations that are looking for ideas or partnerships must go through four stages:[57]

1. *Orientation:* clarifying needs and translating them into a form suitable for the search.
2. *Exploration:* searching for solution providers.
3. *Selection:* deciding on which potential solution providers to engage with.
4. *Engagement:* coming to an agreement.

An increasing range of organizations exist to help enterprises locate possible partners and set up collaborations.[58] Several of them, such as InnoCentive, Nine-Sigma and IXC, offer expertise over all four stages, while others specialize in particular parts. At the time of writing, the EU's Enterprise Europe Network offers free services in finding possible partners and has over 600 centres throughout the EU. Many governments offer similar services.

Inside-out

Many larger companies, such as Philips,[59] British Telecom,[60] Xerox and Lucent,[61] have established corporate venture groups to sell or license technologies they cannot use, or to spin out companies to exploit them.[62] Sometimes, these companies are reabsorbed into the parent when they have pioneered a new application that turns out to be more relevant to their business than had been thought. Mini Case 2.6 describes how Philips founded and developed its technology incubator.

Such 'heavyweight' methods are appropriate for large companies with several opportunities to exploit. Much less has been written about how to do inside-out OI on a smaller scale. Some companies may develop technologies with the explicit aim of selling them on for exploitation by others, in which case they are likely to have a network of targets in mind. For many, however, the opportunity for inside-out OI may come only occasionally. Their best chance lies with using intermediaries.

MINI CASE 2.6: *Philips Electronics – Incubating the Future*[63]

When he became CTO of the Dutch company, Philips, in 2001, Ad Huijser was clear that the long-term future of the company would depend on new markets and technologies that were outside the company's current scope. There had been a number of promising ideas of that sort from the research labs but they often found no ready route to commercialization, for two reasons. First, they did not fall within the remit of any of the existing product divisions. Second, product divisions tended to operate on a large scale and did not have the entrepreneurial approach to manage small, uncertain projects. As Huijser said: 'Start-up companies are all about "future": they simply have no "history". In a large company, you also have to defend your history. Your existing markets have to be served as well.' After studying 10 failed initiatives from the past, Huijser and his colleagues decided that the kind of new technologies they were looking at would have to be managed according to a venture capitalist model. The ventures, rather than the corporation's management, would have to determine the direction of activity.

So, in 2002, Huijser set up an incubator to take ideas from the research labs and develop them as potential start-ups:

> I started the technology incubator in Philips to change the conditions of a large company to those of a small company. All that I say to these people is: 'Listen, you have a chance to make it a success, but I will stop it if you do not deliver the next steps at that and that moment.' Then it becomes a survival game in the same way as it is for start-up companies.

It was expected that projects would usually spin out of Philips but in 2005 the board asked Huijser to look out for opportunities for projects to 'spin up', that is, back into the company.

The incubator was managed by Jelto Smits, as CEO, with a CFO. He adopted the role of venture capitalist, using much the same criteria for selecting projects, except that the rapid growth and cash flow that venture capitalists normally require was de-emphasized. Philips was in this for the long run. It turned out that a much higher proportion of projects that applied for entry to the incubator were accepted than would be typical in the venture capital market. The reason was that in the market many proposals are rejected because of the quality of the teams rather than the proposal itself. Here, all the team members had already worked successfully in the company for some years and had a good understanding of the business; and the incubator management could help recruit new members where necessary.

Eleven projects entered the incubator in the first two years. Five years later only one had closed, five remained and the other five had either spun out, with Philips retaining a minority shareholding, or spun up back into the company.

Continued...

The incubator concept was working and the venturing idea was better understood in the product divisions. The next step was to manage the spin-out and spin-up candidates separately. The existing incubator was transferred to the lighting and cleantech divisions and two new incubators were set up in 2006 under the management of healthcare and lifestyle. Philips formed a joint venture with Prime Ventures, an experienced venture capital company, to manage future potential spin outs as well as the minority stakes in the existing ones. As Corina Kuiper, the director responsible at this point, says: 'In Philips we used to say "if it doesn't work, kill it". Now we have a plan B. But we cannot spin out efficiently by ourselves. It's partners, partners, partners.'

BUSINESS MODEL INNOVATION

Business model innovation (BMI) has come to prominence in the academic literature in recent years, as we showed in Chapter 1, but it is not a new idea. For example, the first self-service store was opened in 1916, transforming retailing from a low-volume/high-margin/labour-intensive business model to the opposite;[64] and Thomas Cook ran the first European package holiday in 1855, even introducing the 'circular note', a forerunner of the traveller's cheque, in 1871. But the idea of the business model as a focus of innovation in its own right is only recently gaining momentum.[65] Mini Case 2.7 shows how Coillte, the Irish forestry company, introduced a process for BMI, while Mini Case 7.2 shows how a business model innovation released the potential of solar power in rural Africa.

> **MINI CASE 2.7:** *Coillte – Making BMI Happen*[66]

Coillte is a commercial company established in 1988 and owned by the Irish state. Named after the Gaelic word for forest, Coillte owns 7 per cent of the land in Ireland. It has a group structure with three divisions focused on forestry, wood products and land added value – renewable energy, recreation and land development.

In May 2012, Coillte's CEO launched a group strategy, which emphasized growth – through current or new markets with innovative business models (BMs) – and cost reduction. The group had accumulated a collection of ideas for growth, mostly in the previous 12 months, but some had languished for years. Many ideas were radical enough to need to be unconstrained by current strategies and divisional boundaries. Consequently, management recognized the need to select some promising growth opportunities and apply a BMI perspective to them.

Stemming from the group strategy, Coillte developed a process for generating new BMs based on identifying unmet customer needs; innovatively configuring its resources; working differently with its network partners; and technological inventions. Several projects to generate new BMs for existing businesses and create new businesses were initiated. This process even enabled the company to venture from its core business area (business-to-business, B2B) – wood and wood products – into the business-to-consumer (B2C) market with recreational services for children.

Continued...

It is notoriously difficult to conduct market research on services, and particularly experiential ones such as recreation. Therefore, to gain deep insights on value, Coillte used different methods to gain customer insights and continuously prototyped and tested its BM thinking.

Coillte has come to recognize that the 'capability' to create new BMs is crucial as it can be applied time and time again. The company's experience offers three main lessons for other established organizations seeking to create breakthrough business models:

1. *Developing innovative business models requires more than a workshop with the management team.* Initial ideas from senior managers were found to be too similar to existing businesses and diverse teams were needed to take the task further. Selecting the right team, with the right perspective and knowledge for the BM task, and making the appropriate resources and expertise available are challenging but crucial.

2. *Customer insights require the right tools at the right time.* To develop an alternative value proposition, deep customer insights are needed. Initially, Coillte conducted interviews but later went much deeper. Others have suggested observing customers but Coillte found that more systematic, probing techniques were necessary. For example, these allowed Coillte to identify parents' expectations of what they wanted their children to learn from recreational activities in the forest.

3. *Experimentation and learning are essential.* The Business Model Canvas (see Chapter 4) is only a representation of a business model and a real prototype is needed to check customers' and partners' perceptions of value. Generating a robust business model requires a hypothesis-testing mentality. For example, Coillte offered full 'prototype' recreational activities to test the reactions of children and parents before the final products were launched. Executives responsible for selecting business models need to avoid a common tendency to reject proposals that deviate from what they know.

Having gained deep customer insights and having decided how to create a high-value set of recreational service products, Coillte had to develop the wider business model. This required continually refining and testing the value proposition and, critically, the value delivery system to deliver that value proposition. In the case of Compass Club – a service that provides schoolchildren with fun learning experiences in the outdoors – recruiting, training and managing school teachers to act as qualified Compass Club leaders was critical. This involved partnering with a number of specialist external providers. This service is now launched throughout Ireland and is targeting 40,000 children within its first few years of operation. So far, the response has been very strong, with unsolicited requests for additional services to different schoolchildren segments, with different sets of needs.

Coillte has come a long way in the past four years. It has built a number of new business models for its wood products; it has launched a set of recreational service products; and, crucially, it has built an innovation capability. And the strength of this capability is demonstrated by the fact that the recreational products are B2C, a big step for a traditional B2B company. Ciaran Black, group director of innovation, noted that: 'What was once considered radical (i.e. a children's recreation business) is now widely accepted and the new service concepts currently being created are considered as natural extensions to an existing recreation service platform.'

Case contributed by Ian Kierans.

Broadly, a business model is the system of interdependent activities that determines the way a company does business with its customers, partners and stakeholders. It is a concept that has received little formal attention from economists or, until recently, business academics. According to Teece:[67] 'The concept of a business model lacks theoretical grounding in economics ... there is not a single scientific paper in the mainstream economics journals that analyses or discusses business models.'

A recent definition by Johnson, Christensen and Kagermann,[68] which we will use as a starting point for this discussion, views a company's business model as comprising four interlocking elements:

- A customer value proposition (the job to be done for the customer)
- A profit, or value capture, formula that allows the company to retain some of that value

and in support of these:

- The key resources required and the business processes employed.

The concept of the business model has been explored in a practical way by Osterwalder and Pigneur, whose hugely popular book is one of the key references in Chapter 4.

HP's approach to the home printer business – selling printers at or below cost and making money on the consumables – is an example of business model innovation, as is the combination of the Apple iPod with the iTunes music subscription service. The Beatles changed their business model from the traditional one of live performances supplemented by record sales to concentrate wholly on recording – relying on brand image and their ability to make more innovative music in the studio. Supermarkets offer a much reduced level of personal service than traditional retailers but lower costs and a much wider range of merchandise.

A business model is not the same as a strategy. A strategy is a direction of travel, a set of aims and intentions for a company, while the business model is the way the chosen strategy is embodied in the business. In a sense, it sits between tactics and strategy. A new strategic direction will often require a new business model but the strategy comes first. For example, when Richard Branson decided to take his Virgin Group from a media business to a transatlantic airline, it required a new business model but the strategic decision came first and was then *embodied* in the business model.

Why has the world been so slow to recognize the potential of BMI? Probably because the business model of a company is so fundamental that it is mostly unnoticed and unchallenged, its origins lost in the mists of institutional memory. Most people just take it for granted and will intuitively alter proposed innovations to make sure they fit into it. Indeed, 'few companies understand their existing business model well enough – the premise behind its development, its natural interdependencies, and its strengths and limitations. So they don't know when they can leverage their core business and when success requires a new business model.'[69] A particularly challenging situation is when the business has drifted into a new shape that requires the existing model to be changed in situ. This is the situation faced by Mahdi El Showeikh in Egypt, described in Mini Case 2.8. Such a change will affect most parts of the business and so may meet a lot of inertia on the way. The upside of this, however, is that an effective new business model may be difficult for competitors to emulate. Competitors may invent a product that is technically superior to the iPad but the combination of the iPod and iTunes will be difficult to displace.

> **MINI CASE 2.8:** *Magdi El Showeikh – Soft Garments to Software*

Magdi El Showeikh & Co is a textile manufacturer located in Egypt. The company was established as a family business in 1986, and has grown to become one of the lead manufacturers of garments in the east of Egypt. The company prides itself on being able to manufacturer high-quality garments made from the finest Egyptian cotton at a reasonable price.

Yet the company's greatest pride is its ability to develop new products and production processes to enable it to grow and enter new markets. Over the years, the company has developed a reputation for being able to customize products to meet customers' quality and cost requirements. Karim El Showeikh, the company's youngest director, says: 'This unique reputation has been the result of a continuous capability building exercise aimed at company staff, equipment, and production processes to ensure that no customer order would be refused because the company couldn't meet the technical or cost requirements of that customer.'

A key capability of the company has been the ability to write in-house software for its knitting machines. Over a period of 10 years, the company built a repository of software for delivering customized specifications and production settings for meeting challenging demands. According to El Showeikh:

> We don't just run our knitting and dying machines on off-the-shelf programs like the rest of our competitors; we create our own programs that pay attention to every small detail in the processes. This enables us to make extremely customised pieces of cloth that meet the exact requirements of our customers.

This capability saved the business in 2011 when, due to political changes in Egypt, the company was faced with a shrinking local market for its products as consumer spending tumbled, while access to international markets became impossible. Competitors were slashing prices in a fight over whatever limited orders there were. Magdi El Showeikh had to innovate once again to survive. This time, however, there were no new orders to innovate around nor was there a way to make its production process any more efficient or cost-effective. The company had to innovate around its business model.

El Showeikh had been the main catalyst in building the company's software repository, and for many years he had attempted to convince management that the company should be leveraging its software capability as a product but his request had been refused as it was seen as a divergence from the company's main business. He explained:

> However, with business at a standstill and the company needing to generate more cash flow, I was finally given the green light to test my new business model. We immediately began to reach out to competitors who had won orders and convince them that we could get their production lines to work better and cheaper. It wasn't hard to do because we had a great reputation for getting the job done and competitors were eager to learn how we do it so well.

In the six months after gaining management support, El Showeikh organized a new business unit aimed at evaluating the specialized software and deciding which programs could be sold to competitors without compromising the company's competitive advantage. He also organized a sales unit that would access the new market, and an engineering team that would deliver the software solution. Karim's business model innovation had given birth to a new line of business for the company, with the whole suite of services now tailored around assisting other textile manufacturers to meet the complex requirements of their customer orders.

Case contributed by Mohamed Khater.

The Customer Value Proposition

A compelling customer value proposition is the core of any successful business. Clearly, the topic is as broad as business itself, so we will simply emphasize here three avenues for value proposition innovation that have risen to prominence since the first edition of this book in 2005; all are treated more fully in later chapters.

The first is the concept of *hidden needs*. It used to be assumed that to find out what people need, all you have to do is to ask them. In fact, people will usually mention only features that they have already seen elsewhere or at least can easily imagine. Nobody ever asked for a telephone or a television until they had actually been demonstrated, but the needs that they meet are real enough. Understanding the needs that people have but do not readily articulate takes considerable subtlety, but can provide a rich source of ideas for new value propositions, as we show in Chapter 5.

The second possibility is *disruptive innovation* (see Chapter 4). Most companies will naturally seek to make their products or services more competitive by improving their core performance, or perhaps by adding additional features. However, all features reach a point of diminishing returns when further improvements are of little benefit to the customer. A new value proposition may then be possible, providing less of the expected performance but other benefits (such as lower price or operational simplicity) that attract a different range of customers. Familiar examples are supermarkets and low-cost airlines, which give much reduced customer service (previously regarded as a key aspect of competition) but instead offer lower prices and a wider range of products/destinations.

A third, related possibility is to provide an entirely new value proposition. This approach is called *blue ocean strategy* and is described in more detail in Chapter 4. One example is the out-of-town cinema complex providing multiple screens, easy parking and other facilities, replacing the traditional city-centre sites. Another is Zara's innovative approach to fashion retailing, offering a rapid, flexible response to changing fashions by bringing clothes manufacturing back from East Asia to Europe so as to shorten the supply chain (Mini Case 4.3).

Value Capture

Although there is probably an infinite number of possible customer value propositions, there is a limited number of ways for a company to capture part of that value. Stefan Michel of IMD lists a total of 15,[70] some of which we list below with our own comments. Others summaries are also available.[71] The message for managers is that it is worth reviewing the range of available possibilities and choosing deliberately rather than simply defaulting to a familiar model.

1. The pricing process
   Many products and services are purchased with a single payment by the customer but this does not have to be on the basis of a fixed price list. For example, many products are bought by auction over the internet or elsewhere and the price of many airline tickets varies with demand. A more recent variation is that used by Priceline, which reverses the traditional roles of supplier and customer. Here, potential customers name the price at which they are willing to purchase goods, or services, such as room rental. Potential

suppliers can then accept or reject the proposal, while the use of the internet keeps the pricing confidential on both sides.

2. The payer
The use of a product or service sometimes delivers benefits to several parties and it may be possible to change which one pays. Many European cities now have free-issue newspapers (such as London's Metro), whose large circulation allows them to be funded entirely by advertisers. Vestergaard, the makers of LifeStraw, a filter for cleaning and sterilizing drinking water, recognized that its product would prevent rural communities from having to boil water for drinking. It has now provided filter systems to provide drinking water for 4 million people in rural communities in Kenya, funded from the carbon credits that the company can claim when the product is used.[72]

3. The basis of payment
When Xerox introduced its first commercial copying machines, it faced the problem that its machines were expensive and customers were not sure how much they would use them. The solution – innovative at the time – was to provide the copier at a nominal rent and charge users by the number of copies they actually made. A variant on this is to keep the product cost low and charge significantly for the consumables used, as with the ink for inkjet printers and the blades for razors. Netafim, an Israeli maker of sophisticated drip-feed irrigation systems, overcame the reluctance of small farmers to invest in its complex product by providing the installation free and taking payment by a proportion of the increased yield.[73]

4. The price carrier
Many products provide a range of benefits that can be charged for separately or together and finding new ways to bundle (or unbundle) them can be a useful competitive advantage. Package holidays come in a wide range of varieties depending on what aspects of the total experience are included and this allows the companies to craft many variations targeted at different customer groups. In other circumstances, unbundling (specialization) may be a relevant approach, particularly if competitors may find their own offering difficult to alter. Hence the proliferation of vehicle servicing companies specializing, for example, in tyres or exhausts, which they can provide more quickly and efficiently than generalized garages. Aravind Eye Hospitals, the main case study for this chapter, applies the same principle to its branch of medicine.

Linking the Components

An essential attribute of a good business model is that its components should be reinforcing so that the whole is significantly more than the sum of the parts. A good example is the low-cost airline business of which Ryanair is an exemplar. The key customer value proposition is the low cost, which generates a high volume of business. The low cost is sustained by interlocking aspects of the business model. Restricting the business to short-haul flights allows a lower standard of comfort and service, which reduces variable costs and allows fast turnaround times, which in turn improves the utilization of the aircraft. It also

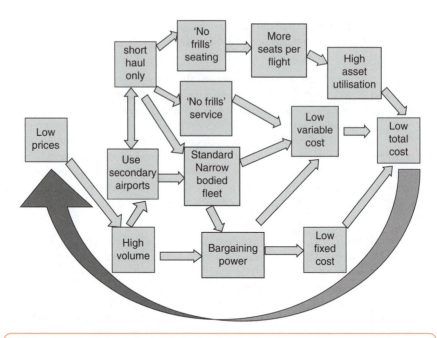

FIGURE 2.5: Aspects of Ryanair's Business Model
Source: based loosely on Casadesus-Masanell and Ricart, 2011[74]

allows a standardized fleet of relatively small aircraft, which gives operational flexibility and, together with the high volume of traffic, allows the use of provincial airports with significantly lower operating costs. The standardization also gives bargaining power with suppliers and more efficient support services. This is illustrated in Figure 2.5.

This tightly interlocking business model has proved difficult for incumbent airlines to copy, although several tried and subsequently withdrew. It simply required too large a change from their existing way of operating.

Summary

In this chapter we have explored a number of factors that set the context of innovation in business and which will recur as themes in later chapters.

Innovation is the primary source of growth in a stable economy. Large or small companies may be innovative. Several factors drive their need for innovation, including changes in markets, technology and customers. But the strategic aims of company leaders play a significant role.

The focus of innovation changes as the underlying technologies mature. The emergence of a dominant design marks a point when competition shifts away from the core attributes towards other factors such as quality and services.

As markets develop, different types of customers with different motivations emerge and innovation efforts must adapt accordingly. The way innovations diffuse through a population or market depends strongly on the characteristics of the innovation itself and on the adopters (customers).

Companies increasingly collaborate with others during the innovation process, a practice known as open innovation. Changes to the business model are often valuable to support other innovations and may be a profitable source of innovation in themselves.

Management Recommendations

- Measure the actual growth and profitability benefits arising from your innovation investments. Don't rely on input measures alone to assess your innovativeness.
- Think about the possibilities for open innovation. Look around for opportunities to benefit from partnerships with other companies and organizations.
- Apply the insights provided by diffusion theory to individual innovation projects.
- Be ready to modify the focus of innovation as your market develops.
- Understand your own business model and consider carefully how new products and services may be supported and enhanced by alternative business models.

Questions for Students

1. Use the ideas of diffusion theory to design the launch campaign for a new type of electronic reader similar in concept to a Kindle but based on thin flexible plastic displays.
2. Compare and contrast the problems facing small and large companies in working in partnership on an innovation project.
3. Plot a diagram like Figure 2.4 to show the links between the components of the business model for a supermarket on the outskirts of a town.
4. You are about to launch an innovative and surprising new type of motor transport, which you anticipate will eventually become widely adopted. How will you seek to update the product and the way it is marketed as it moves through the adoption lifecycle?
5. If the ideas of Amar Bhidé were applied fully at the national level, what changes would it imply for policy on education and research funding?

Recommended Reading

1. Rogers, E.M., *Diffusion of Innovations* (New York: Free Press, 5th edn, 2003). One of the classic texts on innovation, with a wealth of fascinating examples of innovations in the manufacturing and service sectors.
2. Abernathy, W.J. and Utterback, J., 'Patterns of Industrial Innovation', *Technology Review*, 80(7) (1978), 40–7. The original work on dominant design.
3. Chesbrough, H., Vanhaverbeke, W. and West, J. (eds) *New Frontiers in Open Innovation* (Oxford University Press, 2014). Good, up-to-date review of this developing field.

4. Special issues on business model innovation in *Harvard Business Review* (Jan-Feb 2011), *Long Range Planning* (2010, 2013) and *R&D Management* (June 2014).

◗ MAIN CASE STUDY

ARAVIND EYE HOSPITALS – PROCESS INNOVATION IN HEALTHCARE[75]

Aravind Eye Care was founded in 1976 by Dr Govindappa Venkataswamy with the mission to eliminate needless blindness in India. 'Dr V' was inspired by two things. First, the knowledge that 5–10 million people in India, and 50 million worldwide, suffer bilateral blindness, much of which can be prevented or treated. Second, surprisingly, was the McDonald's hamburger chain. In this, Dr V saw an example of how good disciplined processes could turn a variable, skill-based service into a product that could be delivered with high quality and low cost in any culture: 'The McDonald's concept is simple. They feel they can train people, all over the world irrespective of different religions, cultures … to produce a product in the same way and deliver it in the same manner in hundreds of places.' His colleague, Professor Fred Mason says: 'His vision of what was possible was way beyond what was reasonable!' Yet today the Aravind Eye Care system is the largest eye care facility in the world, with 10 hospitals treating 3.5 million outpatients and doing 400,000 sight-restoring operations a year. The company runs at a profit, generating all the surplus funds it needs to finance expansion; yet each paying patient subsidises two more who cannot afford to pay. The clinical results are at least as good as those achieved in the Western hospitals.[76]

To make all this possible, Dr V had to take a radically different approach to the eye care process. The success of Aravind is based on three principles: excellent administration; a conviction that carefully designed processes can often substitute for human skill; and, above all, a culture that emphasizes service, humility, kindness and equality. The underlying business model is one of the oldest, inspired by McDonald's: increase volume, build efficiencies and reduce costs. All employees know that every rupee saved helps in treating more patients.

Recognizing that the doctors', and especially the surgeons', time is the key constraint in a specialist hospital, Aravind sets out to maximize the efficiency with which it is used. As many as possible of the subsidiary tasks, such as refraction testing and counselling, are done by paramedical staff (there are six nurses to every doctor), leaving the doctors free for medical advising and operations. Recruiting and training the right calibre of paramedical staff is vital for Aravind. In the words of Dr Natchair, who is in charge of training paramedical staff:

> We recruit girls from a rural background … with the right attitude. Knowledge and skills are important, but not so much as the right attitude. After recruitment we give them two years' training. The training is excellent and is recognised in the US, and the government of India is considering adopting our syllabus.

Blind people are often unable to make the trip to hospital unaided, so much of the initial diagnosis, scanning and counselling is done in camps in the countryside; Aravind currently run 1,500 a year. It also pioneered the use of broadband radio and webcams in remote rural areas allowing doctors to assess and diagnose eye conditions remotely. Part of the service is to bus patients into hospital on the day of their appointment. On arrival, it takes two minutes to book a patient in, thanks to an efficient IT system. They then see a doctor for a definitive diagnosis and a paramedical counsellor to help them decide what action is best for them. Those who need surgery usually have their operation on the same day, unless they prefer not to. Those who need spectacles can have them made and fitted on site within four hours.

The operating theatres have four tables on which two surgeons work, aided by a team of nurses. While the surgeon is operating on one patient, the next is being made ready by the theatre staff on an adjacent operating table. As soon one operation is complete, the surgeon can move straight to the other table where he will find the patient fully prepared and sedated, the surgical instruments laid out and the magnifying microscope focused on the patient's eye. The next patient, who has been waiting on a chair, then takes up the vacant table and is sedated ready for their operation. In ordinary hospitals, multiple use of an operating theatre would be considered hazardous because of cross-contamination but it is possible in the special circumstances of Aravind, thanks to excellent procedures and because the patients are otherwise entirely healthy. Surgeons at Aravind conduct an average of over 2,000 operations a year (10 times the national average), yet they operate only in the mornings, leaving the afternoons for outpatients and research. The high throughput of patients also means that doctors get more clinical experience in a month at Aravind than they would in a year elsewhere. As one said: 'In Delhi, where I studied, we did not have so many cases of varied nature. There we did one or two cases of surgery a month; here we do some 30 cases a day!'

Follow-up counselling is provided by specially trained paramedical staff, keeping doctors free for medical work.

Although doctors and nurses are paid at competitive rates, the efficiency and high throughput of patients keeps costs low. The large number of patients also gives doctors far more experience of diverse eye conditions than they would normally obtain. As Dr V says: 'Doctors are not paid more because they do more operations but ours is a teaching institution and the more patients we have the better the training can be.' Aravind has now established two training centres and is currently working with 150 other hospitals interested in introducing its methods.

Up to 75 per cent of blindness in the developing world comes from cataracts, which can be cured by replacing the affected lens with an artificial one. This procedure accounts for much of Aravind's surgical work. The cost of these lenses used to be $250, barely affordable in India, so in 1991, Aravind set up a separate activity called Aurolab to make the lenses at lower cost. This, too, was highly successful and today Aurolab manufactures intraocular lenses for $5–10 each, for local use and export internationally.

Prahalad, in his book *The Fortune at the Bottom of the Pyramid*,[77] points out that in providing products and services for the very poor, companies have to reverse the usual operational logic. The usual approach is: 'Work out the cost, add the necessary margin and that determines the minimum price that must be charged. Now go and find somebody who will pay it.' In these markets, the opposite applies: 'Work out the maximum that customers can afford to pay, subtract the necessary margin and that determines the maximum cost. Now go and find a way to do it.' Aravind Eye Care is a dramatic and inspiring example of where this logic can lead.

Reflective questions

1. What advantages do developing countries have in innovation, particularly in processes and services?
2. What kinds of innovation most require inspiring (rather than effective) leadership?
3. Why has an equivalent of Aravind not yet arisen in the West?
4. If you were to attempt to found an equivalent of Aravind in your own country, how would it be different?
5. What risks might lie ahead for Aravind as India's economy develops?

SERVICE INNOVATION

INTRODUCTION

This chapter looks at managing innovation in four different service sectors: commercial services; manufacturers' services; public sector services; and the not-for-profit sector services. Service innovation is important for four reasons. First, the service sector accounts for over half of gross national product in many countries. Second, manufacturers need services as these play a key role in achieving customer satisfaction.[1] Third, the public sector is faced by decreased funding in many countries and so innovation is perceived as the way to develop new and cost-effective services.[2] Fourth, the distinct characteristics of services – such as their intangible nature – means that their innovations need to be managed differently than product innovation.

Managing services can be challenging because they are intangible and so it is harder for people to articulate their needs about them. For example, many people struggle to name service examples of breakthrough and radical innovations. In addition: 'Despite the dominance of services in modern economics, and their rapid growth worldwide, it is surprising how little research and how few methods and techniques exist to address the unique challenges of service innovation.'[3] Another problem is that researchers have biased their work by applying ideas from new product development (NPD) to the new service development (NSD) domain.[4] Nevertheless, this chapter aims to give a comprehensive picture of how to manage innovation in services, something many organizations struggle with.

This chapter covers:

- The role of services in the economy.
- The generic characteristics of services.
- Specific characterisitics in commercial, manufacturers', public sector and not-for-profit sector services.
- The relationship of services to the Pentathlon Framework.
- A main case study on the management of innovation at a service company, CitizenM Hotels from Holland.

SERVICES AND THE ECONOMY

The service sector is dominant in many countries, as can be seen by looking at its contribution to GDP and its role in providing employment. The importance of services has also been stressed by several recent major reports.[5]

Services and GDP

Table 3.1 shows GDP, population and the breakdown of the economy in 21 selected countries in Africa, the Americas, Asia Pacific and Europe. The far-right column shows the contribution of services and it can be seen that seven of the countries listed generate over 70 per cent of their GDP from services (indicated by bold type). This includes Brazil (71 per cent), the US (77.8 per cent), Japan (72.0 per cent), France (78.9 per cent) and the UK (now a staggering 79.5 per cent). In contrast, the service sector is currently not as significant in countries such as Nigeria (54.8 per cent) and Indonesia (43.3 per cent).

CHAPTER 3

Studies show that as an economy becomes more mature, the proportions of GDP generated by *agriculture*, *industry* and *services* change significantly.[6] (The term *industry* refers to manufacturing, mining, construction, electricity, water and gas.) Developing countries are more dependent on agriculture and it typically generates more than 15 per cent of GDP; for example, 17 per cent in India and 30.3 per cent in Kenya. As the demand for food is met, the call for goods increases. Countries develop by *industrializing* and Egypt (39.9 per cent manufacturing), Mexico (33.8 per cent), China (42.7 per cent) and Indonesia (42.9 per cent) are all examples of this. In parallel to industrialization, agriculture becomes

TABLE 3.1: Selected International Economic Comparisons, 2014

	Country	Total GDP (trillions)	Population (millions)	Agriculture (% GDP)	Industry (% GDP)	Service sector (% GDP)
Africa	Egypt	$0.946	88.4	14.5	39.9	45.6
	Kenya	$0.133	45.9	30.3	19.4	50.4
	Morocco	$0.259	33.2	13.0	29.3	57.7
	Nigeria	$1.053	181.5	20.2	24.9	54.8
	South Africa	$0.707	53.7	2.5	29.5	68.0
Americas	Argentina	$0.951	43.4	10.2	29.5	60.3
	Brazil	$3.276	204.3	5.6	23.4	**71.0**
	Canada	$1.596	35.1	1.6	28.6	69.7
	Mexico	$2.149	121.8	3.5	33.8	62.7
	USA	$17.350	321.4	1.6	20.6	**77.8**
Asia Pacific	Australia	$1.100	22.8	3.8	28.2	68.0
	China	$18.090	1367.4	8.2	42.7	48.1
	India	$7.411	1251.8	17.0	30.0	53.0
	Indonesia	$2.686	256.0	13.7	42.9	43.3
	Japan	$4.767	126.9	1.2	26.8	**72.0**
Europe	France	$2.591	66.5	1.7	19.4	**78.9**
	Germany	$3.748	80.9	0.7	30.4	68.9
	Italy	$2.135	61.9	2.2	23.4	**74.4**
	Netherlands	$0.808	16.9	2.8	22.3	**74.8**
	Russia	$3.577	142.4	4.2	35.8	60.0
	UK	$2.569	64.1	0.6	19.9	**79.5**

Source: The World Factbook 2014–15. Washington, DC: Central Intelligence Agency, 2015[7].

less labour intensive, productivity rises and consequently agricultural products become less expensive. This leads agriculture to account for a lower proportion of GDP. Later, *postindustrialization* sees a shift towards the service sector, as the demand for tangible products saturates and people start to focus on healthcare, education and entertainment.

Mature economies have service sectors that employ the majority of the workforce. Even in the internet age, many services require human interaction. The shift to the service sector is also being accelerated by fewer jobs being available in agriculture and manufacturing, due to automation. Today, most developed countries have more farm tractors than farm workers. Automation is also impacting services. For example, Japanese banks have recently introduced robots to serve customers. Robots mimic the way human tellers interact with customers, even taking account of customers' facial expressions in the way they give advice. But robots also speak multiple languages and do not have 'off-days'.

Categories of Services

The term *services* covers 'a heterogeneous range of intangible products and activities that are difficult to encapsulate within a simple definition'.[8] Consequently, 'measurement of trade in services is inherently more difficult than measurement of trade in goods, inasmuch as services are more difficult to define'.[9] The General Agreement on Tariffs and Trade (GATT) defined 12 major *categories* or *types* of services, as shown in Table 3.2. However, this categorization has not been universally applied and the United Nations (UN) recognizes that this leads

TABLE 3.2: GATT Classification of Services

	Categories
1.	Business services
2.	Communication services
3.	Construction and related engineering services
4.	Distribution services
5.	Educational services
6.	Environmental services
7.	Financial services
8.	Health-related and social services
9.	Tourism and travel-related services
10.	Recreational, cultural and sporting services
11.	Transport services
12	Other services

Source: World Trade Organization, www.wto.org. Reprinted with permission[10] .

to confusion when different reports are compared. The list in Table 3.2 is what we will refer to as *commercial services* but we will also cover *manufacturers' services*, *public sector services* and *not-for-profit services* in this chapter. It should be noted that what are commercial services in one country may be public services in another; for example, in some countries healthcare is largely a public service.

Employment in Services

Table 3.3 is derived from the US Bureau of Labor Statistics. It shows the main categories of services and the levels of employment in different sectors in the US, which has a highly developed service sector. (Note that Table 3.3 uses a

TABLE 3.3: Employment in the Service Sector in the US, 2012

Sector	Categories	Jobs (thousands)	Total (%)
Agriculture, forestry, fishing and hunting	Total	2,113	1.6
Goods-producing, excluding agriculture	Mining	800.5	0.6
	Construction	5,641	3.9
	Manufacturing	11,919	8.2
	Total	18,360	12.6
Services	Utilities	554	0.4
	Wholesale trade	5,673	3.9
	Retail trade	14,875	10.2
	Transportation and warehousing	4,415	3.0
	Information (inc. communications)	2,678	1.8
	Financial services	7,786	5.4
	Professional and business services	17,930	12.3
	Educational services	3,347	2.3
	Healthcare and social assistance	16,972	11.7
	Leisure and hospitality	13,746	9.5
	Other services	6,175	4.2
	Federal government	2,814	1.9
	State and local government	19,103	13.1
	Total	116,068	79.9

Source: data from the Bureau of Labor Statistics (BLS)[11]

variation on the GATT classification – an example of the confusion the UN refers to.) It can be seen that agriculture employs only 1.6 per cent of the US work-force, matching the percentage of GDP in Table 3.1, although note the figures are from different years. 'Goods-producing' industry provides 12.6 per cent of the employment.

In the US, 79.9 per cent of employment is in the service sector, closely matching the 77.8 per cent of GDP (Table 3.1). In the US, the main services include retail (10.2 per cent of employment), financial services (5.4 per cent), professional and business services (12.3 per cent), health and social care (11.7 per cent of employment) and leisure and hospitality (9.5 per cent). Interestingly, federal and local government employs 15 per cent of the workforce (this statistic indicating the opportunity for innovation in public sector services). Other developed countries have a similar mix of categories of services in their employment figures.

R&D in Services

Research and development (R&D) investment is mainly associated with the manufacturing sector and in Chapter 2 we discussed the level of R&D investment as a percentage of revenues (termed *R&D intensity*) for manufacturing companies. The R&D intensity figures for different companies in the same industry are similar: for example, 8–10 per cent is typical in electronics, 4–5 per cent in pharmaceuticals and 6 per cent in automotive. Such patterns are less easy to identify for service companies, as they are more diverse.

Table 3.4 shows the 20 service companies that invest the most in R&D, with Google heading the table. It should be noted that the revenues invested in R&D in the service sector are not always easy to identify, as formal R&D departments with separate budgets seldom exist in this sector. The data in Table 3.4 are from the EU Industrial R&D Investment Scoreboard, and from the second column it can be seen that Google ranked ninth in the world for R&D (behind eight manufacturing companies). Only these 20 service companies made it into the top 250 companies worldwide by R&D investment (with Korea Electric Power ranked 20th in service R&D intensity but 237th out of all companies).

Google is the biggest investor in service R&D but some of that investment is in developing products such as Google Glass (digital glasses, which have now been withdrawn) and its autonomous car. Telecommunications invest 2–3 per cent of their revenues in R&D; for example, NTT in Japan, AT&T in the US and BT in the UK, and banks also conduct service R&D, such as Santander, Royal Bank of Scotland and HSBC. Noteworthy is the level at which some famous names are investing in R&D: Facebook at 18 per cent (eight largest service R&D investor; ranking 101th), Baidu at nearly 13 per cent and Google at 13 per cent. Amazon invested 6.4 per cent of revenues in R&D in 2007 but the figure has dropped to 0.8 per cent. Twitter's spending on R&D is unbelievably high (92.9 per cent) and this has attracted negative comments from investors, who view trying to keep up with Facebook's R&D investment as 'unrealistic'.[13] With increasing competition in the service sector, it is likely that forward-looking companies will use R&D as a means of developing differentiated services.

TABLE 3.4: Service Organizations Ranked Top for R&D Investment, 2013

	R&D investment ranking	Company	Region	Service	R&D € millions	R&D intensity (%)	Sales (millions)	Employees
1.	9	Google	US	Software & computer services	5735.6	13.2	43379.7	47756
2.	24	Oracle	US	Software & computer services	3735.0	13.5	27753.6	122000
3.	46	SAP	Germany	Software & computer services	2282.0	13.6	16815.0	66572
4.	62	NTT	Japan	Fixed line telecommunications	1716.7	2.3	75232.3	239756
5.	81	Banco Santander	Spain	Banks	1229.0	3.0	41035.0	182958
6.	91	Royal Bank of Scotland	UK	Banks	1083.1	4.6	23524.0	118600
7.	92	AT&T	US	Fixed line telecommunications	1079.0	1.2	93359.4	243000
8.	101	Facebook	US	Software & computer services	1026.0	18.0	5708.1	6337
9.	137	BT	UK	Fixed line telecommunications	823.9	3.8	21836.7	87800
10.	154	Barclays	UK	Banks	736.8	2.2	33553.4	139600
11.	162	Deutsche Bank	Germany	Banks	663.0	2.1	31451.0	98254
12.	166	Central Japan Railway	Japan	Travel & leisure	644.1	5.7	11379.7	28619
13.	184	HSBC	UK	Banks	530.1	1.1	47770.3	263000

TABLE 3.4: Continued

R&D investment ranking	Company	Region	Service	R&D € millions	R&D intensity (%)	Sales (millions)	Employees
14. 198	Australia & New Zealand Banking	Australia	Banks	501.4	4.2	11857.3	47512
15. 203	Baidu	Cayman Islands	Software & computer services	488.3	12.9	3795.7	31676
16. 213	Twitter	US	Software & computer services	448.1	92.9	482.1	2712
17. 214	National Australia Bank	Australia	Banks	447.4	3.9	11578.3	
18. 230	Amazon.com	US	General retailers	421.3	0.8	53985.9	117300
19. 236	Unicredit	Italy	Banks	407.9	1.7	23822.4	147864
20. 237	Korea Electric Power	South Korea	Electricity	406.5	1.1	37126.6	

Source: data © European Union, 1995–2016[12].

CHAPTER 3

GENERIC CHARACTERISTICS OF SERVICES

Considering the very different categories listed in Tables 3.2 and 3.3, it might be thought that there is little that can be said about services that applies across the board. Nevertheless, there are generic characteristics that allow services to be better understood. In discussing these characteristics, we will establish a terminology that will be used throughout this book because the concepts of service innovation must be clearly articulated.[14] We also include 11 mini cases to illustrate many different aspects of managing innovation in services.

The Service Product

Most service companies refer to their *products*, which are produced and delivered to the customer. These are best referred to as *service products*. The customer's perception of the quality and utility of a service product is dependent on the *service augmentation* – the production and delivery mechanisms for the service product. Improving the service augmentation is often referred to as *process innovation*. Research shows that competitive advantage is often gained from service augmentation and not the service product itself.[15] The total package, consisting of the service product and the service augmentation, is called the *augmented service offering* (see Figure 3.1), and this is what customers consider

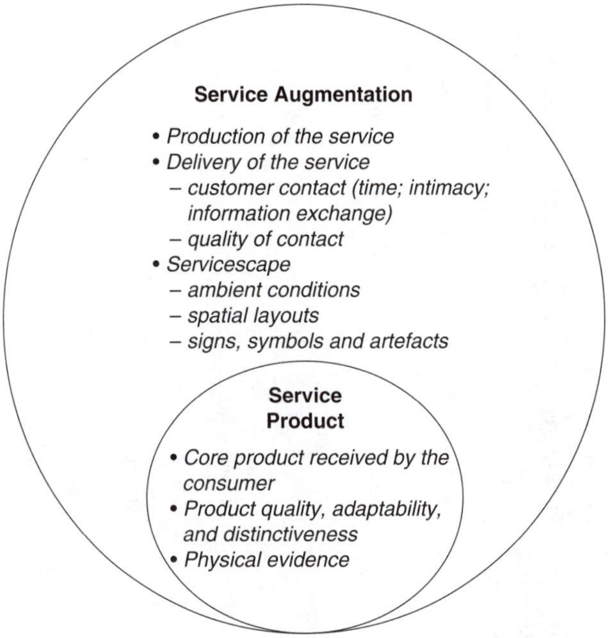

Service Augmentation

- *Production of the service*
- *Delivery of the service*
  - *customer contact (time; intimacy; information exchange)*
  - *quality of contact*
- *Servicescape*
  - *ambient conditions*
  - *spatial layouts*
  - *signs, symbols and artefacts*

Service Product

- *Core product received by the consumer*
- *Product quality, adaptability, and distinctiveness*
- *Physical evidence*

FIGURE 3.1: The Augmented Service Offering (Service Product and Service Augmentation)
Source: based loosely on Storey and Easingwood, 1998

when making judgements about overall service quality. For example, think of a memorable meal with your partner – it will be one where the quality of the service was as good as the food.

In the service sector, innovation consists of *new service products* and *new service augmentations* and these innovations often need to be integrated with *business model innovation*.[16] Innovation in services also includes significant changes in their *production* and *delivery*.[17] Service companies therefore need a *new service development* process (NSD – covered in detail in Chapter 7) and the Halifax building society has a clearly structured one (see Mini Case 3.1 on Halifax).

► MINI CASE 3.1: *Halifax – Building a New Service Development Process*

The Halifax building society in the UK focuses on the fast development of new service products. These include new lending packages for house purchasers, which, for example, allow borrowers to customize repayment levels to their needs over a number of years. After the financial crisis of 2008–9, such packages, which reduce risks for borrowers and the lender, are essential. Halifax has reduced the time to develop and introduce new mortgage packages from six months to a matter of a few weeks. There are four main steps to its development process and in each of these the responsibilities of each department are clearly defined:

1. *Concept development:* This takes account of previous products, competitive products and perceived customer requirements. The concept will be refined, taking particular account of the views of marketing and operations. An initial check is made on whether the concept can be delivered with existing systems or whether it will require changes at the operational level.
2. *Trial:* Customers (in focus groups) are asked their opinions of the new service. This market research largely replaces the market piloting of new mortgage packages, which was common in the industry a few years ago.
3. *Delivery system definition:* The delivery of a new service requires that a suitable system is set up. The *system* means all resources involved in the delivery, which typically will include computer resources (for tracking payment level and so on) and human resources (for marketing and administering the service).
4. *Introduction:* Once the delivery system has been defined, the introduction of the new service largely involves the implementation of training programmes to explain it to staff, preparation of necessary software to run systems and so on.

Sometimes, different service products are necessary to address different market segments and recognizing segments is important in service innovation. An interesting example of segmentation is a restaurant in the departure area of Schiphol Airport in Amsterdam. Here, staff greet customers and then ask them how much time they have before their flight. Dependent on the answer, the service person directs the customer to a specific part of the menu, which is broken into sections based on how much time before the flight, with meals that can be served within these times. Once the order is placed, the customer is given an electronic timer that rings when the meal is ready. Through clever segmentation, the restaurant guarantees that the customer is served and that the customer can enjoy their meal without being rushed.

The Servicescape

Another key concept is the *servicescape* – the environment in which the consumer receives the service.[18] This is important because, as psychologists have identified, social interactions are influenced by the environment in which they occur.[19] The physical environment gives the consumer clues as to the quality of the service and influences customer satisfaction. Again, think of a memorable meal with your partner; it will be one where the ambiance was as good as the food. A functional and pleasant environment can also increase the motivation of service employees and boost their performance, which can mediate increases in consumer satisfaction.

The servicescape has three dimensions:

1. *Ambient conditions*, such as odours, air quality and temperature.
2. *Spatial layout* of the facilities and their suitability for delivering the service.
3. *Signs, symbols and artefacts*, such as the quality of the signage provided to travellers at an airport and the uniforms and appearance of staff.

These three dimensions generate physiological responses in the consumer (in response to the sounds and odours related to a service environment); cognitive responses (consumers' perceptions of a service); and emotional responses (leading to satisfaction or dissatisfaction).

Supermarket design takes account of the ambient conditions. Background music and the smell of freshly baked bread can influence our willingness to purchase. Appropriate spatial layout can make finding goods easier. The French chain Carrefour has researched the order in which customers prefer to buy food and has arranged its stores accordingly. Signs and symbols direct customers through supermarkets and the appearance of staff at the meat counter strongly influences our perception of how fresh the produce is.

The servicescape is an aspect of service management that is often overlooked but should be considered during new service development (see Mini Case 3.2 on Boeing and Airbus). Companies that conduct the majority of their business via the internet need to treat web design as seriously as a company creating a physical servicescape. For example, Grays of Westminster, the renowned specialist London camera dealer, has all customers visiting the website click on a doorbell, giving them somewhat the feeling of entering the physical shop (www.graysofwestminster.co.uk/index.php).

> **MINI CASE 3.2:** *Boeing and Airbus – Creating the Feeling of Space*[20]
>
> Sometimes manufactured products have an impact on the servicescape of service providers. An example is passenger aircraft design. Airlines need well-designed passenger cabins and Boeing and Airbus are being challenged to provide more innovative cabin design within the limitations of the space available. The ambient conditions, such as air quality and temperature, need careful control but the main focus is now on the spatial layout, more comfortable seating and cabins that give the impression of being spacious. Innovations such as luggage bins that lift out of the way provide extra space.
>
> *Continued...*

Perception plays a key role and so the subtle use of décor, mirrors, dividing walls and lighting can give the impression of more space, by reducing shadows and other effects that make passengers feel more cramped. The size of windows also has been found by psychologists to have a strong influence on passenger wellbeing. Airbus and Boeing are strongly competing with each other on cabin design.[21] The latest move in this competitive battle is Boeing's increased usage of composite materials. Composites are materials made by combining different components to create a material with significantly improved properties, such as strength and weight. Light, strong composites have enabled fuselages to be developed that withstand higher cabin pressure. Long-haul passengers will now be able to look forward to a higher cabin pressure (the equivalent of 1,800 metres altitude instead of 2,400), higher humidity and larger windows – all of which will help make long-haul flights less tiring.

The Service Organization

The service sector normally refers to the end-person receiving the service as the *consumer* (the equivalent of the end-user for manufactured goods). Not all the employees in a service company have contact with consumers. Therefore, the terms *front-office staff* (contact with consumers) and *back-office staff* (supporting functions that do not have customer or consumer contact) are commonly used. Note that in the hospitality sector, the terms *front of house* and *back of house* are used.

The front office (also called *service operations*) is normally responsible for most aspects of the production and delivery of service products and managing the servicescape. The attitude and behaviour of these front-office employees are crucial as they directly influence consumers' perceptions of the service. Front-office employees also have the expertise to conduct process innovation – improvements to the way services are delivered. AXA Ireland has been very effective at motivating its front-office staff to improve processes (see Mini Case 3.8). However, service product innovation is normally the responsibility of the back office and some service companies have specific innovation departments, such as Bank of America's Innovation and Development Team.[22]

The Nature of Services

Most innovation management research has focused on the manufacturing sector and studies of service innovation are still rare.[23] So the most effective ways to manage service innovation are still emerging. However, researchers have identified five generic characteristics of services: *intangibility*, *customer contact*, *inhomogeneity*, *perishability* and their *multifaceted* nature. It is useful to recognize the implications these characteristics have for the management of innovation.

Intangibility

Service products are intangible, meaning they cannot be perceived by touch (in contrast to manufactured goods). For example, the ability to collect cash is intangible, although some aspects of the service delivery such as the ATM are tangible. Intangibility means that customers can find it difficult to judge the quality of a service in advance and they will take cues about the quality from the more tangible aspects. Factors such as the servicescape can have a big influence (see Mini Case 3.3 on healthcare).

CHAPTER 3

> **MINI CASE 3.3:** *Innovating in Healthcare – Not Such a Pain*[24]
>
> Healthcare services include some intangible aspects, such as the atmosphere of hospitals. Diagnosis and treatment have traditionally been the focus of hospital managers and the delivery has been overlooked. Consequently, waiting times are long in many healthcare systems, staff members are overworked, many healthcare workers have too little time to spend with informing and assuring patients, and the décor in many hospitals is drab. However, now the impact of the servicescape has been recognized. Research in the US shows hospital departments that had been redecorated in pastel shades and where attractive artwork is on display leads to increased patient wellbeing and, for example, patients require less medication – the amount of painkillers requested is up to 45 per cent lower and significant savings result.

Service intangibility has three main implications for innovation. First, it is difficult to gain deep customer insights because 'customers often cannot specify exactly what they want'.[25] Second, when companies design their service products, they must fully consider the delivery system and servicescape. Third, the intangible nature of services can trap companies into not knowing they need a well-defined NSD process. An effective NSD process is needed, which defines the responsibilities of all departments including the front and back offices (see the discussion on NSD in Chapter 7). All three points also show the need for careful piloting of new services.

Customer Contact

Another characteristic that all services share is they rely on contacts with the customer. Such contacts have a strong influence on customers' perceptions and the terms *moments of truth* or *touch points* are used to emphasize the importance of interaction. Aspects of a negative experience are termed *pain points* (see also Mini Case 9.4 on Deutsche Bahn). An example of a touch point in the luxury cruise business (literally and figuratively) is when the captain of the ship shakes hands with all first-class passengers as they disembark to make them feel special.

Research shows that customer contact can be managed by considering the *contact time* needed, the *intimacy* required, and the *information* to be exchanged,[26] as shown in Figure 3.1 above. Then, the most appropriate levels of contact can be decided – *self-service*, *remote service* or *interpersonal service*. In self-service, customers cooperate by delivering most of the service themselves and contact with the service provider's staff is minimal. Remote services are designed for low contact, such as helplines for answering customers' questions on computer problems. Internet retailers may only have remote contact but they still need to manage it. For example, Amazon tries to develop some intimacy by monitoring purchases and making suggestions on books and music that the consumer will probably enjoy. Managing remote contact professionally can be dependent on good staff training. Some service products require a high degree of contact between the customer and the employees responsible for the delivery. For example, a business consultancy project will normally require extensive interpersonal contact.

Customer contact has three main implications for innovation. First, designing service products with the appropriate degree of customer contact is essential. Innovating the way the customer contact is provided can significantly improve the perceived quality of the service product (see Mini Case 3.4 on DialAFlight). Second, new service products may change the nature of customer contact and staff retraining may be necessary. Third, service prototypes must be tested with real customers, as 'laboratory testing' is not valid.

> ### MINI CASE 3.4: *DialAFlight – Managing Customer Contact*[27]

DialAFlight is an internationally successful internet travel retailer. The company has succeeded in a crowded, competitive and low-margin market through a strategy focused on the interaction with the consumer. Other travel retailers just focus on their websites, offering fast search engines to identify locations, flights and other information. However, DialAFlight says: 'As our name suggests we do not believe in operating an online transactional service but instead DialAFlight offers customers the opportunity to book over the phone which is a more efficient, friendly and customer focused experience.'

Consumers use the website to check initial ideas but then they are directed to 'Speak to an expert. Live in 5 secs', who will answer their travel questions. The travel experts clearly identify themselves by name and, in discussions with the customer, are skilled, personable and enthusiastic in giving advice on travel destinations, flights and budget packages. DialAFlight deliberately hires people who love travel and speak multiple languages. In the event of further questions, it is the original employee who phones back and, similarly, repeat customers are encouraged to return to 'their representative'. Although based on a simple idea, it shows the value of professionally managed customer contact.

Inhomogeneity

The output from service providers varies because it depends on the employees delivering it and the individual consumer receiving it. So service products are *heterogeneous* (but we will use the US term *inhomogeneous*). An example of inhomogeneity in the healthcare business is that two doctors might give exactly the same treatment but one is more empathetic to the patient.

Inhomogeneity can influence service quality positively or negatively and so it must be managed carefully. For example, leading organizations give their front-office staff some discretion to be flexible in matching the service to the individual consumer (see Mini Case 3.5 on the Czech Probation Service). Others aim for *service consistency* – identical service independent of the employee. One way of achieving this is *service scripting*, where service employees are given scripts of what they should say to the customer. This approach can have mixed results if the employees are not motivated (as anyone knows who has been told to 'have a nice day' by a disgruntled fast-food employee). Some organizations prefer not to script their front-office employees' work and let them empathize in their own personal way (see main case study on CitizenM at the end of this chapter).

Inhomogeneity has two implications for innovation. First, service design must take account of different people in the service delivery chain and different consumers. In some businesses, service consistency is the goal but other companies may use the interaction between their employees and customers to deliberately provide inhomogeneous service offerings for certain customer segments. This is often called *personal service* and, for example, taxi companies often offer a premium service for businesspeople being driven to airports. Second, different segments may require not only different service products but also appropriate service augmentations. For example, in education, a university lecturer will teach the same subject in a very different way depending on whether the class is undergraduate or graduate.

> ### MINI CASE 3.5: *Czech Probation Service – Cracking a Difficult Case*[28]
>
> Probation is a well-known alternative to a prison sentence in many countries but can it be effective? In the Czech Republic, probation was failing as shown by the excessively high reoffending rates, particularly for the Roma community. Due to the perception that probation was unsuccessful for Roma offenders, Czech judges often opted for custodial sentences. However, the Roma mentoring programme has changed that. This programme recognized that certain aspects of the service delivery needed to be customized for individuals from the Roma community.
>
> The Czech justice system began investigating why there were so many breaches of probation by Roma people. They discovered that some of the reasons were very basic. It could be, for example, that the family did not have the money to travel and meet the probation officer. To support the work of Czech probation officers, senior members of the Roma community have been appointed as mentors for offenders and have received 100 hours of training. Their work has reduced the difficulties caused by language and cultural differences but, far more, it has allowed the mentor to tailor the meetings with the offender. Also, the peer pressure of someone from their own community checking that the conditions of probation are being met has had a significant impact on the effectiveness of probation. And offenders now receive personal advice. Reoffending rates are now at 60 per cent (much lower than in other countries), showing the importance of services focused on ethnic minorities, addressing the individual's situation, creating contact with respected peers, and generating sound advice for an individual.

Perishability

The production, delivery and consumption of a service are normally simultaneous. Services are perishable – they cannot be stored and so the *location* and *timing* of the delivery are crucial. For example, fast food cannot be kept very long (typically under display lights) before it loses its freshness. Even utilities such as energy companies cannot store energy easily on the grid. Geographical availability must match the distribution of consumers and an example of this is the franchised chains of fast-food restaurants around the globe. A mantra for many managers in the service sector is 'location, location, location' (attributed to the founder of Selfridges, the UK retail chain).

Of course, the internet has altered our understanding of location, as many successful companies have achieved a considerable 'presence' via the web. Traditional companies are mainly based in physical outlets ('bricks and mortar'), whereas 'clicks and mortar' is used to refer to companies where their internet presence is backed up by physical assets such as storage and distribution. Amazon is clicks and mortar, while Facebook is not. Retailing products where physical inspections and trying-on are essential, such as shoes, used not to be effective via the internet.[29] However, fast delivery and the opportunity to easily exchange goods has changed that (see also the main case study in Chapter 8 on time:matters). In the coming decades, internet solutions will no doubt further 'erode' the importance of location.

Perishability has two main implications for innovation. First, the delivery mechanism – location – must ensure easy access for the consumer. Second, front-office staff must be involved in new service development, to advise on the capacity levels needed to meet demand (when and wherever it is), and on how quality can be maintained independent of demand (see Mini Case 3.6 Career Launcher).

> **MINI CASE 3.6:** *Career Launcher – Online Maths*[30]

Career Launcher – CL Educate Ltd – is one of Asia's biggest private educational providers, with 225 learning centres across the world and over 3,000 employees, the majority of whom are teachers or academics by background. The company offers school tuition, vocational training and learning publications.

Chairman and founder Satya Narayanan says that the success of his service is based on experimenting with new ideas. He says it is important to 'do a pilot, do a prototype … let the customers come and tell you [that you] need to do more … that you need to expand'. And expand he has – all the way to the US.

In the US, there is a severe shortage of qualified mathematics teachers and a high demand for tutors. So Career Launcher offers an online tutoring service for school students. In live, one-to-one sessions students can ask about what they did not fully understood at school. In an age when call centres based in faraway countries have acquired a negative image, Career Launcher has been careful to manage its delivery, especially customer contact and availability. Discussions on maths problems are made easier by specially designed software that controls webcams and a tablet PC. These enable more effective discussions, as formulae and diagrams can be easily shared. The India-based tutors are carefully selected, all have degrees in maths or physics, and are well briefed on the curricula in US schools to ensure that they show the right level of knowledge and empathy. The service they provide cannot be stored and due to the time difference with the US, Career Launcher maths tutors cover a night shift.

Service Quality is Multifaceted

Quality for manufactured products is a simpler concept than for services, largely because the customer is able to base their opinions on a tangible product. For services, intangible aspects and customer contact make 'quality' a complex construct (see Mini Case 3.7 on MASkargo). For example, a customer's overall impression of a retail store will be affected by the location, the servicescape, the range of goods and services available and their display, and even the parking.

The multifaceted nature of quality has two main implications for innovation (see Table 3.5). First, customer expectations and perceptions need to be managed and internal perceptions need to directly match those of the consumer, otherwise front-office staff will not meet customer expectations. For example, DHL offers what it terms 'express delivery' but this service is not always fast enough when an important piece of equipment requires replacement parts. This has allowed the company time:matters (see main case study at the end of Chapter 8) to build a whole business addressing this segment. The credo in many service organizations is underpromise and overdeliver. Second, managing service innovation quality requires good cross-functional interaction between the front and back office.

MINI CASE 3.7: *MASkargo – Air Freight Service Quality*[31]

Air freight is a significant business. Currently, one-third of the dollar value of all goods shipped globally is air freight. The competitive Asian market is about half the world market and growing. Typical shipments from Asia include high-value electronics and perishables such as seafood for top restaurants. The region is also particularly dependent on air freight because of the distance to market.

What are the most important factors when shipping air freight? And how can these be addressed in new service offerings? Management at the Malaysian Airlines company MASkargo had their own opinions on the key factors but rather than rely on just internal views, they decided to conduct interviews with 19 senior air freight purchasing managers. An innovative market research technique – repertory grid technique (see Chapter 5) – was used, which revealed 44 facets of air freight services. Many of these were previously unknown and related to service augmentation. This information allowed MASkargo to enhance its service quality through a number of segmented products. Examples include ground handling services which ensure that there are no delays, special temperature-sensitive shipping, shipping for dangerous goods, and dealing with shipments to remote areas.

Table 3.5 summarizes the five generic characteristics of services that have been discussed and their implications for innovation management. It can be used as a checklist, when reviewing service innovations, for example at the key stages of new service development.

TABLE 3.5: Characteristics of Services and their Implications for Innovation Management

Characteristics	Main implications for innovation management
Intangibility	**1.** The intangible nature of services can make it more difficult to conduct effective market research than for physical products, as customers may find it harder to articulate their ideas for improved services.[32] **2.** The design of the production and delivery mechanisms (*augmentation* including the *servicescape*) must be carefully planned at the same time as the service product. The tangible components of services (*physical evidence*) need to be carefully managed to give customers a positive perception of the service product. **3.** Intangible products can easily lead to informal processes. Managers in the service sector need good processes for the development of new services.

TABLE 3.5: Continued

Characteristics	Main implications for innovation management
Customer contact	1. It is essential to design *new service products* with the right degree of customer contact. What is the appropriate level of contact and does this match the expectations? Consider *contact time*, *intimacy* and the *information exchanged*. 2. Innovations in the way the customer contact is managed can improve the perceived quality of the service product but staff retraining may be necessary. 3. Contact can only be tested with customers and 'laboratory testing' is not valid.
Inhomogeneity (heterogeneity)	1. NSD must take account of the dependency of the service offering on the consumer and (often) the main persons in the delivery chain. Either consistency or customization can be a valid aim. 2. Different customer segments can require changes to the service product and service augmentation. It is important to identify the main market segments.
Perishability	1. The production and delivery mechanisms must ensure easy access for consumers. 2. Front-office staff need to plan capacity issues during NSD and ensure that quality can be maintained as demand increases.
Service quality is multifaceted	1. Expectations and perceptions need to be managed. Internal perceptions need to be matched to those of the customer and/or consumer. 2. Managing service quality requires good cross-functional interaction between the front and back office.

CHAPTER **3**

CHARACTERISTICS BY SECTOR

Now that the generic characteristics and terminology of services have been discussed, we will explain some of the characteristics of commercial services, manufacturers' services, public sector services, and the *third sector* – not-for-profit services. These differences are only now emerging as not only has there been a paucity of research on services but also sectors such as not-for-profit have not been considered by innovation researchers.

Managing Commercial Service Innovation

The need for innovation in the service sector is widely recognized as are the challenges.[33] Postindustrialization is driving demand as are demographics; for example, ageing populations need more healthcare. Although demand is high, many new service products are market failures and so good service design is essential. In commercial services, innovation managers need to focus on new service development (NSD), improving delivery mechanisms and developing a real capability for service innovation.

Typically, NSD is not as well structured as manufacturing NPD. Research shows that effective NSD needs a formal process to guide the necessary cross-functional teamwork,[34] including coordination of the front and back offices.[35] Often there are four stages in the development of a new service product: generation of a concept; business analysis and planning; development; and market launch.[36] Some researchers have recommended that NSD processes be based on those used in NPD.[37] However, we think there is a need for a different approach because service companies need to have an NSD process that is appropriate for the category of service. A recent influential review of the research literature came to a similar conclusion.[38] The reason that the category of service is important can be understood by considering the following examples. Career Launcher's coaching service requires IT requirements to be considered (see Mini Case 3.6), whereas DialAFlight's NSD needs more emphasis on designing personal interactions (see Mini Case 3.4). So, the NSD process at these two companies will need a different emphasis.

Our recommended approach to NSD has various elements. First, as service consumers often cannot articulate their needs, NSD needs to give emphasis to the intangible aspects of service products. Many of the methods for identifying customers' needs, which will be explained in Chapter 5, are relevant. Second, the NSD process requires extensive experimentation, to verify that customer expectations (of the service product and the augmentation) are met and also to verify the level of demand.[39] Internet technology can enable such tests and at the same time stimulate faster market demand.[40] Finally, in managing NSD, tools such as the *service concept* and *service blueprint* are useful and so we will explain them in Chapter 7.

Research has shown that innovations that 'radically redefine the delivery of a service are relatively rare'. NSD teams may take this as a challenge. One area where innovations can be made is in the way clients interact with service providers.[41] For example, some US hospitals have found patients are more satisfied if they can have longer appointments with cardiologists, where a group of patients discuss their symptoms together. Ideas for how to improve delivery can come from customers[42] and high-quality market research. In addition to researching customers' views, front-office employees can generate creative ideas.[43]

Companies need the ability to regularly and strategically innovate.[44] Research on innovation in financial services in Germany indicates that only 16 per cent of companies consider how they can innovate through changing their organizational structures to, for example, enhance delivery. This is a missed opportunity, as combining innovation in the core product with innovation in the delivery can lead to sustainable competitive advantage.[45] Another important aspect to consider in NSD is that competitors can quickly copy new service products.[46] Patent protection is difficult but if the way a service is delivered is unique, this can make an innovation harder to copy.

As shown by Table 3.3 above, retail services employ over 10 per cent of people in the US. Innovation management is increasingly important in retail, with leading companies using the internet and physical stores in combination, to offer the best customer experience. Many of the latest retail innovations are technological, such as virtual reality being used to help customers try on and choose clothing and equipment.

MINI CASE 3.8: *AXA Ireland – Unwavering Focus on Innovation*[47]

The French firm AXA is the largest insurance company in the world, with approximately 166,000 employees, 103 million clients and €98,534 million in revenues. Its Irish subsidiary has high market shares in the motor and household insurance markets. Generally, the insurance sector is not known for innovation but it is one of AXA's core values. In Ireland, the focus started in 2000, when AXA became one of the first companies in the world to recruit an 'innovation manager'. The role was broadly defined as 'to raise the innovation capability of the organization through staff involvement and shared knowledge'. The task was challenging as there had been no previous incumbent but the innovation manager had the full support of the CEO, whose aim was to grow AXA Ireland through innovation.

The innovation focus led to the transformation of the AXA product range. This included service products for specific segments, such as packages for young drivers (including insurance that gives discounts if they do not drive late on Friday and Saturday nights), female drivers and students, and specific packages for executive cars to classic cars. In addition to new service products, AXA has focused on innovating delivery through its TaskMasters programme. This recognized that front-office employees responsible for a task are the process experts, rather than management.

TaskMasters empowered employees to focus on service delivery mechanisms that can be implemented quickly and at low cost. To foster enthusiasm and encourage participation, improvements were rewarded and recognised which led to innovation becoming an essential part of employees' everyday activities. TaskMasters has, for example, resulted in improvements which mean that clients' insurance claims can be dealt with following one single phone call, as opposed to the many calls required in the past. TaskMasters has also led to organizational changes being made to improve service delivery, such as more cross-functional teamwork to support faster resolution of customer claims.

AXA recognized that a clear understanding of the meaning of innovation is essential within a service organization. To address this need, the innovation manager developed the Innovation Quadrant (Figure 3.2), as a categorization of the types of ideas that lead to successful innovations. The figures in Figure 3.2 indicate the percentage of ideas successfully implemented over the first few years. It can clearly be seen that 'create' – new service products – represented only 10 per cent of the implemented ideas. In

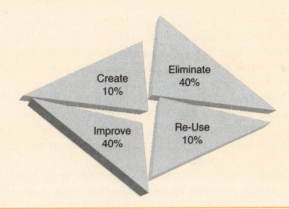

FIGURE 3.2: AXA's Innovation Quadrant
Source: copyright © AXA. Reproduced with permission.

Continued...

contrast, the elimination of non-value-adding steps has had a major impact on many areas of the AXA business, representing 40 per cent of the implemented ideas. Similarly, many improvements to existing service products have been made. AXA's experience illustrates the value of innovation in the service product, the delivery process and the organization. Some years later, AXA swapped the goals for 'eliminate' and 'reuse' because it had eradicated most of the unnecessary 'stuff', demonstrating how innovation strategy must develop over time.

Managing Manufacturers' Service Innovation

Manufacturers should not focus solely on products; they should also consider developing services to help customers gain maximum value from the use of products. Focusing on services is often referred to as *servitization*.[48] For example, car manufacturers offer maintenance, repair, and leasing and other financial services. Services that help the customer derive maximum value from their purchase are normally referred to as *after-sales service*. Good after-sales service is essential to achieve customer satisfaction; for example, 50 per cent of car owners who switch brands do so because of frustration with after-sales service.[49] Service products also make a significant contribution to revenue, with profit margins normally higher than those for products.

Manufacturers normally have highly developed NPD processes but only a few give enough attention to developing suitable service products to match their products (see Mini Case 3.9 on Jura). To design such services, manufacturers need to understand their customers' service needs and to design services to address these, in parallel with NPD.[50] Manufacturers of complex equipment need to have a deep understanding of their customers' businesses. For example, leading manufacturers of factory equipment will often be called on to help their customers not only maintain production lines but also advise on how to increase output.[51]

Manufacturers may also need to manage servicescapes. For example, a large number of European customers purchasing Mercedes personally collect their new cars from the factory at Sindelfingen in Germany. The Sindelfingen customer centre has been carefully designed not only to make the collection process easy but also to be impressive. The building supports the overall impression of Mercedes quality and customers are encouraged to take a factory tour. So the customer centre and the factory both form the servicescape and influence customers' perceptions. Similarly, Jura, the Swiss coffee machine manufacturer, has an impressive 'repair factory' where customers can bring their machines for maintenance and repair.

Caterpillar Inc. has a worldwide reputation for its range of innovative, robust earth-moving equipment. However, Caterpillar also has a long tradition of focusing on serviceability. It even talks of 'negative downtime' for some products – its largest earth-moving equipment includes an extensive remote monitoring capability, which monitors performance and arranges for preventive maintenance before a problem even occurs.[52]

> **MINI CASE 3.9:** *Jura – Cappuccino 'Made in Switzerland'*[53]

Do you like a good cappuccino? The Swiss company Jura designs premium coffee machines for private and professional use. For example, the top-selling Impressa Z5 was the first machine to make a cup of really frothy cappuccino at the press of a button. Jura was founded in 1930 and its first product was an electrical iron. In 1937, it designed its first coffee machine and it has grown into an international business. It now has 685 employees worldwide and revenues of €357 million/$393 million.

The Impressa Z5 was developed to make the very best-tasting coffee. Jura's R&D has expertise in coffee grinding, brewing and producing excellent frothy milk. All this requires expert knowledge in a number of disciplines, from mechanical engineering, to the physics of foams, to control software. In addition, Jura uses distinctive design and its industrial designers were inspired by the shape of a coffee bean in drawing the unique lines of the Z5. Jura also designed the product to make after-sales service easier and has designed a complementary service product. The Z5 is designed for easy maintenance. For example, in contrast to many other products on the market, the grinding mechanism is self-cleaning. The Z5 also has an array of sensors that prompt owners to refill the coffee beans, or change the water filter, descale, or initiate the cleaning cycle.

But Jura has not just created an amazing product, it delivers an excellent after-sales service. Should owners have a problem, a dedicated Z5 hotline number gives access to immediate advice. Experienced and professional service personnel carefully explain how to get the Z5 working again, with sharing tips such as using a toothpick to readjust a faulty detector. If the machine has a fault that cannot be solved over the telephone, the hotline operator will organize extra fast collection, fast repair and fast return (ensuring that coffee enthusiasts do not have to do without 'their Z5' and their daily cappuccino for long). Swiss owners have another possibility. They can drive to Jura's state-of-the-art 'service factory' (a servicescape in itself), where they can personally watch while the problems with their machine are diagnosed and the repair costs estimated.

Fast maintenance and repair are foremost in Jura's after-sales service strategy but the company is also careful to maintain customer contact. Many manufacturers send advertising and other material to owners registered through warranty schemes. Often such marketing is intrusive but Jura focuses on just one communication a year – Z5 owners receive a Christmas card with new coffee recipes. To support premium products, manufacturers need to be just as good at designing services as the products themselves. Few do it as well as Jura.

Managing Public Sector Innovation

The need for innovation in the public sector has only emerged in the past few years. Pressure on funding and the increasing demand for public services mean that many governments are trying to deliver 'more for less'.[54] As described earlier, the number of people employed in government and public services can be high (15 per cent in the US) and so innovation in the way these people work potentially can have a big impact. Thus governments need to design new ways to deliver public services. Managing public sector innovation requires a clear understanding of the context and its potential for innovation, generating suitable ideas, and designing a process for implementation.

An important factor is recognizing the nature of innovation in the public sector: it consists of ways to create value for society through new services, new processes for service delivery, and new contractual models (see Mini Case 3.10 on the Met Office). New contractual models are partnerships with the private sector to generate economic value from a public sector asset. (They are an example of open innovation in this sector.) Commercial partnerships can enable government departments to earn money, which is, of course, an advantage for taxpayers. However, as was noted in Chapter 1, organizational culture must be considered and in the UK it has been found that civil service employees are not trained in commercial negotiation and so are not well prepared for such partnerships.[55] Therefore, successful innovation can require new staff skills in the public sector.

The delivery of services can also be innovated through co-development (citizens are involved in designing new services), co-management (services are delivered collaboratively), and co-governance (citizens or other agencies are involved in planning and delivery). Examples of these are the Danish government involving citizens in service design, the way the UK government has citizens calculate their own tax (using online tools), and the Welsh government's involvement of citizens in the planning of better internet services for Wales.

A recent book by Christian Bason[56] focuses entirely on innovation in the public sector and identifies the need for the sector to take many ideas on how to manage innovation from the commercial sector. For example, open innovation, which was described in Chapter 2, can be useful for public sector innovations.[57] Other important sources of ideas can be frontline staff and best practice from other similar organizations.[58] Bason stresses the need for public sector agencies to cooperate across departmental boundaries more effectively with the public – its 'customer'. It should be noted that cross-departmental (or cross-agency) working is the public sector equivalent of cross-functional working in manufacturing NPD. For example, the Warwick Justice Centre is a single building that houses the police, the courts and social services, which has enabled closer and more effective cooperation between the main agencies involved with delivering justice.

> **MINI CASE 3.10:** *The Met Office – Not Catching a Cold*[59]

In 1854, the British government formed a new department to investigate whether it was possible to forecast the weather for shipping purposes. Later, this department became the Met Office (the UK Meteorological Office), which is best known for its BBC weather forecasts. In 2001, the Met Office developed a model to forecast the demand for healthcare based on weather conditions. This looked at how cold weather makes respiratory conditions worse. A free-of-charge service for hospitals was launched that helped them predict the demand for emergency services for respiratory problems. However, when government funding ran out and hospitals were asked to pay for the service, the vast majority ceased using it.

The Met Office started discussions with Medixine, a small Finnish tele-health company. Working together, they created an automated telephone system that alerts at-risk patients of upcoming adverse weather conditions, checks if they have adequate medication, and advises them to wrap up warm and stay indoors. This service has proved a big success, with around 40,000 patients using it. Medixine markets the service and earns revenue for every patient it signs up, which is shared with the Met Office. In addition, the NHS benefits from a significant reduction in costly hospital admissions. The service demonstrates that public sector and commercial partners can benefit from commercialization.

Managing Not-for-profit Innovation

The rising cost of delivering services is one of the main drivers of innovation in the not-for-profit sector; for example, providing shelter for the homeless in cities is expensive. However, the 'understanding of the innovation process or innovative capabilities in this particular context remains unclear'[60] and so terms such as service products and service augmentation need clarifying. For example, Amnesty International considers its 'service products' to be the offers it makes to prospective members and it realizes the importance of constantly showing new 'value' in this area. Others perceive fundraising and the delivery of their services as an area to focus on (see Mini Case 3.11 on the RNLI). More case studies from the third sector are needed to give more understanding – current research is 'sparse' but shows that a stronger orientation towards understanding the consumer and building networks to other organizations that can assist in service delivery are important.[61] It appears that the issues in the not-for-profit sector are similar to those for public services. In addition, many third sector organizations need to work closely with social services in the delivery of their services. Indeed, the few examples of not-for-profit innovations tend to come from healthcare. For example, multidisciplinary teams in the US have helped cut overall health costs. These teams, led by specially trained nurse practitioners, include geriatric social workers, community health, behavioural health, physical and palliative therapy specialists and, working together, they have been shown to reduce the need for hospital treatment for the elderly and disabled.[62] Forward-looking not-for-profit organizations recognize that they need to innovate in how they generate their funds and how they deliver their services. For example, Emmaus is a charity for homeless people in the UK, which talks about being a 'social enterprise' that generates a significant 'return on investment' through recycling and other revenue-generating work.[63] Similarly, leading charities are looking at how their services can be improved through the emergence of new technology; for example, how robots will revolutionize help for the elderly.[64]

The term *social innovation* is used to describe novel initiatives that cross from the not-for-profit into either the public or commercial sectors. Social innovation can earn more for a charity than can be collected through donations. For example, a farm in Australia employing disabled, homeless and other socially excluded people helped them at the same time as making profits to reinvest.[65] Interestingly, the potential role of profit has not always been clear in the third sector. For example, one idea is for philanthropic work to support micro businesses that aim to address some of the issues that not-for-profit organizations want to address. An example is that Pierre Omidyar, philanthropist and founder of eBay, has invested in the company Ethos Water. This was created to make profits from selling bottled mineral water and invest some of this in making clean water available in Africa and India. Another example is more veiled. Bosch, the German technological leader is a famous company but less well known is that the organization is owned by a foundation aimed at philanthropic and social endeavours, funded by its profits.[66] Motivating not-for-profit organizations such as charities to aim for profits can be difficult, but examples such as Aravind (see main case study in Chapter 2) illustrate how earning profits can help charitable organizations achieve more of their goals. Such a step will require a significant cultural change for some charities, where making profits has not traditionally been perceived as appropriate.[67]

MINI CASE 3.11: *RNLI – Blue Ocean Innovation*[68] *with video interview*

The Royal National Lifeboat Institution (RNLI) is 'the charity that saves lives at sea'. It provides an 'on call, 24-hour lifeboat search and rescue service and a seasonal lifeguard service'. It was founded in 1824 before even the invention of life jackets (lifeboat crew were first issued with life jackets made of cork in 1854) and today it maintains a fleet of 340 lifeboats. These boats, with their characteristic orange and blue colours, operate from 237 stations around the UK and Ireland. In addition, seasonal lifeguards are on duty at many beaches and the RNLI helps over 25,000 people a year who get into difficulties in the sea. RNLI has a long history of helping distressed people and it has conducted many famous rescues, for which its crews (the majority of whom are volunteers) have received prestigious medals. With such a proud heritage, it might be asked: Does innovation have any place in such an organization? Jeff Gould, head of innovation at RNLI, firmly thinks that innovation is essential and says: 'No organization has the luxury of standing still and my role is to ensure that innovation is a central part of the charity's strategy as we look to challenge both the ways of thinking and working for a sustainable future at the RNLI.'

But what does innovation mean in the context of a charity such as the RNLI? The organization has recognized that it needs to bring innovation to the ways in which it generates its funding, the services it offers and the way it delivers them. To enable this, Gould has created a crash course 'Innovate in 90 minutes' for staff and volunteers at the charity. Furthermore, in the RNLI Innovation Lab at its headquarters in Poole, ideas for funding models and rescue equipment can be quickly prototyped. For example, a seaside environment was created in Minecraft (the popular net-based game for children) to help children understand beach safety. This was quickly tested in the lab and found to be very effective, with 8,000 sign-ups in the first week of release. Similarly, the latest technologies – from virtual reality software to rescue drones – are being investigated in the lab and with partners in universities and industry. Many volunteers are also involved in this work because, as Gould says: 'Many of our supporters have experience, skills and ideas that we value just as much as the donations they make.'

Contrary to what the RNLI name maybe suggests, the charity is increasingly international in its outlook. It has identified that drowning claims an estimated 372,000 lives worldwide each year and many of these are children. And, as the majority of these losses happen in low- and middle-income countries, the RNLI is using its experience and working with partners to build capacity in the communities most at risk of drowning, most recently in Bangladesh, Ghana and the Philippines.

Asked what his advice would be for other managers attempting innovation in the not-for-profit sector, Gould has a clear view:

> Most in the not-for-profit sector recognize the need to innovate but it can often be seen as a magic bullet, easily discarded if it misses the target. The key is to align innovation to the business strategy and demonstrate its worth through tackling challenges and presenting future possibilities.

Now visit www.palgravehighered.com/gm to watch Jeff Gould discussing the RNLI Innovation Lab as well as future innovations in the not-for-profit sector.

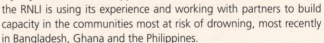

SERVICES AND THE PENTATHLON FRAMEWORK

This chapter has shown how the management of innovation for service products differs from that for manufactured products. The main points about service organizations that should be kept in mind when reading the chapters that follow on the elements of the Innovation Pentathlon Framework are summarized in Figure 3.3. This shows that an innovation strategy can be more difficult to articulate in a service organization because of the intangible nature of service innovation and normally the lack of a single department such as R&D, which is seen as having the main responsibility for innovation. Similarly, technology increasingly impacts the service sector, so monitoring technological advances and identifying potential impacts need to be done. Other differences that are highlighted in Figure 3.3 are the difficulty of discussing intangible service products and the range of sources for ideas (including the front and back offices), the difficulty of choosing the best projects, as service projects are intangible and therefore hard to imagine, the need for a formal NSD process, which ensures that different service departments are coordinated, and the challenge of creating a service culture of innovation.

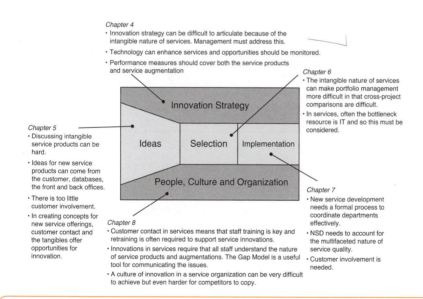

Chapter 4
- Innovation strategy can be difficult to articulate because of the intangible nature of services. Management must address this.
- Technology can enhance services and opportunities should be monitored.
- Performance measures should cover both the service products and service augmentation

Chapter 6
- The intangible nature of services can make portfolio management more difficult in that cross-project comparisons are difficult.
- In services, often the bottleneck resource is IT and so this must be considered.

Chapter 5
- Discussing intangible service products can be hard.
- Ideas for new service products can come from the customer, databases, the front and back offices.
- There is too little customer involvement.
- In creating concepts for new service offerings, customer contact and the tangibles offer opportunities for innovation.

Innovation Strategy

Ideas   Selection   Implementation

People, Culture and Organization

Chapter 7
- New service development needs a formal process to coordinate departments effectively.
- NSD needs to account for the multifaceted nature of service quality.
- Customer involvement is needed.

Chapter 8
- Customer contact in services means that staff training is key and retraining is often required to support service innovations.
- Innovations in services require that all staff understand the nature of service products and augmentations. The Gap Model is a useful tool for communicating the issues.
- A culture of innovation in a service organization can be very difficult to achieve but even harder for competitors to copy.

FIGURE 3.3: Summary of Service Issues to Consider in the Next Five Chapters

Summary

Managing service innovation involves particular challenges. Some of these are generic and some are specific to the service sector under consideration. Ideas on how to manage services are relevant to manufacturers and organizations that only provide services. This chapter has shown the key role of services in many economies, the increasing importance of services for manufacturers, and the need for innovation in the public and not-for-profit sectors. As part of this, products are inextricably linked to their production and delivery – service augmentation. Service augmentation, including the environment in which the service is delivered, has a strong influence on customer satisfaction. The intangibility, customer contact, inhomogeneity, perishability and multifaceted quality of services all have implications for the management of innovation.

Managing innovation and new service development is challenging because of the diverse nature of service sectors and the many categories of services. A suitable management process is required and this must consider not only the product itself but also the augmented service offering. The process also needs to ensure good teamwork, spanning the front and back offices.

Management Recommendations

- Irrespective of whether your organization is in the manufacturing, service, public, or not-for-profit sector, identify the role of services in your business. Consider which customer segments require particular services.
- Identify where innovations in both the service product and the augmentations can lead to competitive advantage. Make these improvements as tangible as possible to customers.
- Recognize the need for an efficient new service development process.

Questions for Students

1. Think about the best restaurant you have eaten in. What are the things about the service product and augmentation that you liked? Did you dislike anything?
2. Did you receive 'good service' when you last had your bicycle/car repaired? What is 'good service' in that context?
3. Analyse the servicescape of your university. Could it be enhanced and what could be the impacts?
4. What was the service delivery process when you received your last passport or driving licence?

Recommended Reading

1. Johnston, R., Clark, G., and Shulver, M., *Service Operations Management: Improving Service Delivery* (London: Pearsons, 4th edn, 2012). Leading textbook on the management of services, including Useful discussions on new service development.

2. Bason, C., *Leading Public Sector Innovation: Co-creating for a Better Society* (Bristol: Policy Press, 2010). Key review of innovation in the public sector.

3. Biemans, W.G., Griffin, A. and Moenaert, R.K., 'New Service Development: How the Field Developed, its Current Status and Recommendations for Moving the Field Forward', *Journal of Product Innovation Management* (2016), doi:10.1111/jpim.12283. Useful summary of the service innovation research literature.

▶ MAIN CASE STUDY

CITIZENM HOTELS – ATTENTION TO EVERY DETAIL

How do you come up with the idea for an innovative hotel chain? Take one experienced hotelier, add an entrepreneur with experience in the fashion industry, a brand boffin, and finally a specialist in market trends and customer offerings. At a dinner together in 2004, four close friends, all successful businesspeople, recognized a gap in the market. Although there were many hotels catering for business travellers, there was no good offering for frequent travellers on a limited budget. As Micheal Levie, CEO and founder, says, the niche is: 'the frequent traveller that is in the mid-segment. So not the ones that have "plenty of wallet"... but really the ones that are either on the corporate rate, or on a "restricted wallet".' The four friends were convinced that the current offerings at this price point did not match the standards travellers were used to in their own homes – in terms of the quality of a night's sleep, the food, the environment and furnishings, and the speed of wireless connection.

The four were so enthusiastic that they decided to design a new hotel, with a unique service product and a novel delivery mechanism. And they decided to start from scratch, rather than looking to purchase an existing hotel. In the summer of 2008, their detailed planning came to fruition when their company CitizenM ('M' for mobile citizen) opened its first 230-room hotel at Schiphol Airport in Amsterdam. In 2009, they opened a 215-bedroom hotel in the city of Amsterdam and today the chain has seven hotels, including London, Paris and New York.

The Service Product

By excluding other segments, CitizenM could develop a clear niche value proposition. At its simplest, the CitizenM offers a good night's sleep at an affordable price. But it is the way the company has designed everything about the product and its delivery that is innovative. CitizenM recognizes that most frequent travellers would rather be at home so it does everything to make staying at its hotels pleasant, relaxed and value for money.

CitizenM aims to provide what customers want, including some elements of luxury at an affordable price. For example, it has king-sized beds and thick, soft towels because it knows these are valued by customers (other mid-budget hotels economize on the quality of beds and use the cheapest towels), whereas other things that mid-budget frequent travellers do not value are eliminated (such as an expensive full-service restaurant). Levie says: 'And we don't have anything else, so they do not pay for anything else. So the end-product you buy is a night's sleep.'

Everything about the customer experience is convenient, quick and efficient. And all the touch points that are important have been tweaked to match frequent travellers' needs. For example, a lot of guests arrive 'from twelve, fourteen hour flights. And all of a sudden their biological clock says it's six o'clock in the afternoon, I need breakfast. So guess what? We're offering 24-hour breakfast', says Levie. A measure of how well the service product is perceived by the customers is the popularity of CitizenM on TripAdvisor, where it is consistently ranked very high and has been voted the trendiest hotel worldwide.

The Service Delivery

The way the CitizenM product is delivered has been planned to a level of detail seldom seen in hotel services. This led to the design of the hotel building, the rooms, the technology used, and the design of every action in the day-to-day running of the hotel. However, in all this, the customer experience is never forgotten. CitizenM hotels are designed based on high-tech room modules produced in a factory. Designing the room modules with full electrical and plumbing connections was challenging but it gives flexibility. Rooms are relatively small but the modules can be then connected together on-site to give the number of rooms required. Constructing a hotel only takes around 15 days, so the construction costs are only 60 per cent of those of a typical 4-star hotel.

The level of detail taken into account in the design of the rooms and furnishing is evident. For example, the king-sized beds fit wall to wall and so changing the sheets would normally be awkward and time-consuming. Not so, because the beds can be raised at an angle on specially designed springs to make changing sheets faster and easier. Levie states: 'I think that we're more efficient and that only comes about when you look at the detail. Every little facet has been specially designed.'

The rooms have some of the latest technology, provided by Dutch electronics giant Philips. This includes the television and special lighting to make the room more relaxing. Working closely with Philips allows the technology to be regularly updated. Other technology enables guests to check in and check out themselves at self-service terminals (but a member of staff will quickly ask if you want help).

Operation of the hotels is lean. Each has a hotel manager, an assistant hotel manager and between one and five 'ambassadors' on duty in any 8-hour shift (depending on the time of day), one of whom also acts as the senior manager. There are three shifts in 24 hours. As well as fulfilling front-of-house duties such as acting as host, receptionist, breakfast server, bar tender and so on, ambassadors also undertake back-office functions, such as preparing booking reports. All the cleaning and housekeeping operations are contracted out to EW Cleaning Operations, Amsterdam.

Compared to a similar sized hotel, CitizenM hotels operate with less than half the staff. More than 50 per cent of bookings are web reservations and CitizenM at Schiphol has a room occupancy rate above 90 per cent per annum. The combination of low construction costs and low running costs means that the hotels can offer reasonable room rates in premium locations and can generate positive financial returns within one year.

Ambassadors, Brand and Customer Experience

Most mid-budget hotels focus on reducing costs and inadvertently remove offerings that customers value. For example, some hotel chains expect their guests to walk to the nearest restaurant. At CitizenM, there is 24-hour service at the bar, which has a full selection of quality chilled meals that are prepared in a microwave. Staff at the bar offer advice and act in their ambassador role, chatting with guests and generally making them feel welcome and relaxed. And they are very good at identifying whether they are dealing with the tired traveller who just wants to eat and then sleep, or the traveller who wants to have a pleasant chat. The interactions with the traveller are a central part of the brand the company has created.

According to Levie:

Most hotels take a logo and they put it on their stationery … We have a brand. And we feel that a brand is something that is your character; it's a life; that is who you are. So our brand lives everywhere in our name, in our attitude, in the way of communication and the way we are. So also on the website where you will most probably meet us first, so it is that character and that way that we come across. Our ambassadors are the most important people, because they deliver the service. We hire and recruit people who have a genuine kindness and friendliness and a big smile.

Recruitment and Training

Recruitment and training typically takes four weeks. Selection days include role-playing exercises to check candidates have the right behavioural skills to deliver excellent customer service. Once chosen, four days of one-on-one sessions with a CitizenM trainer are held, including shadowing a 'buddy' in a live situation. An ambassador is allowed to go 'solo' when the hotel manager is satisfied they can offer the required guest service. Staff turnover is average within the industry, due to the nature of ambassadors – typically young, enthusiastic and internationally mobile people. Levie says:

Our service delivery is not scripted, we hire people with a smile, we train them to be themselves and to have their own culture and beauty come out, and to treat you as a human being. So instead of,

'Did you have a nice trip sir?', you get a friendly 'Hi', but the 'Hi' comes from the heart.

Marius, an assistant hotel manager in Amsterdam, values the flexibility of his role: 'I feel freedom here because I can do what I want. If I want to be on the front desk, I will go on the front desk. If I want to be in the bar, I am in the bar.'

The Future

'We believe CitizenM is very scalable … the core is there', says Levie, who with his partners has plans for further expansion. The company is also very confident about its niche – what it offers and what it does not offer. As the website says:

Here's what to expect from your stay at our Bankside hotel in London: XL king-sized, super comfy bed; wall-to-wall window; rain shower for washing away that jet lag; free movies; free Wi-Fi for Facebooking all your snaps; international plug system. Absolutely no trouser presses, bellboys, or stupid pillow chocolates.

Mid-budget frequent travellers and the world's largest cities are likely to see many more CitizenM hotels in the years to come.

Videos of the CitizenM hotel at Schiphol and interviews with staff can be found at: www.the casecentre.org/CitizenMcase.

Reflective Questions

1. Identify all the ways in which the CitizenM delivery mechanism was designed to reduce start-up and running costs.
2. Which aspects of the CitizenM hotel concept would be easy to copy and which would be more difficult?

Source: based on www.citizenm.com/, several stays at the CitizenM Schiphol, Amsterdam, and CitizenM Hotels: Service Operations & Business Model Innovation, The Case Centre. Adapted with permission from co-authors Bob Lillis and Chris van der Hoven, and The Case Centre. Copyright © 2012 Cranfield University[69].

For another case study on innovation at Integra in India, visit www.palgravehighered.com/gm

DEVELOPING AN INNOVATION STRATEGY

INTRODUCTION

Innovation strategy is part of overall business strategy. It determines when and where innovation is required to meet the aims of the organization and lays out in broad terms how it is to be achieved. It is a key element of the Pentathlon Framework, shaping and influencing all the other elements, as shown by Figure 4.1.

Innovation strategy guides idea generation through setting goals for internal work, approval of research programmes and sponsorship of partnerships with others to explore new opportunities. It guides project selection and prioritization through the criteria used in selecting projects, and perhaps directly by earmarking funds for strategically important work. Innovation strategy also guides training and recruitment and provides the framework for major investments in implementation.

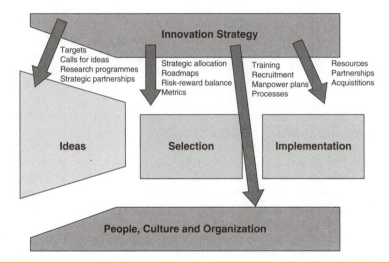

FIGURE 4.1: The Influence of Innovation Strategy on Other Elements of the Pentathlon

The need for innovation comes ultimately from a mismatch between the aims of an organization and what it can actually expect to achieve by continuing with its present policies. The logic of strategic analysis is illustrated in Figure 4.2. It involves making a prediction of the future, bearing in mind the effects of the key drivers of innovation mentioned in Chapter 2 – technology, customers, competitors and the wider business environment – and asking whether the result is acceptable (see Mini Case 4.1 on Aramex). If it is not, then the extent and manner of the mismatch points to what kind of innovation is required.[1] For many organizations, the main strategic impetus comes from the needs of customers and the demands of investors for growth and profitability, but the ambitions of the leaders of the company often play a vital role, as the fortunes of Microsoft

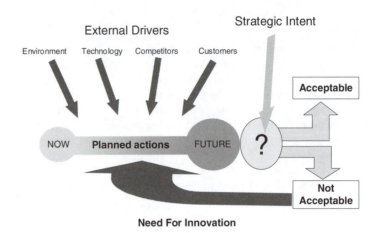

Need For Innovation

FIGURE 4.2: The Need for Innovation Arising from the Gap between Acceptable and Unacceptable Projections for the Future

under Bill Gates, the Virgin group under Richard Branson and Apple under Steve Jobs attest. This vital component is shown as *strategic intent* in Figure 4.2.

Innovation strategy must take a long-term view. Many of the most serious threats and opportunities arise slowly and it is important to look far enough ahead to see them coming. Moreover, significant innovation is likely to need a lot of preparation work involving studies, trials and experiments before the best approach is found. So work must begin well before the need becomes pressing. For this reason, we give considerable attention in this chapter to how long-term trends, particularly in technology, customer behaviour and competition, can demand and shape innovative responses. Mini Cases 4.2 and 4.3 relate how two companies, JCDecaux in advertising and Zara in clothes retailing, reacted to long-term trends of commoditization and increasing competition in their industries. At the time of writing, we can see the Dutch company Philips moving out of consumer electronics, in which it has been a dominant force for very many years. The company judges that the market will be less attractive in future, as it becomes more turbulent and fast-moving, so it is concentrating on other markets such as healthcare, where its strengths are more appropriate. Microsoft is searching for new areas of business knowing that it cannot rely on its hugely successful Windows-related products for ever.

By definition, innovation strategy involves confronting uncertainty, not only about how our world will develop but also, inevitably, about how the innovative responses we propose will actually work out in practice. Most people find this intrinsically uncomfortable to deal with (see Theory Box 6.3). Much of this chapter concerns tools to help managers to assess the future, to clarify their options and choose a robust path through the uncertainty.

The increasing speed of development of businesses and markets means that this planning process should be ready to anticipate the evolution of buyer types, the emergence of dominant designs and other trends that might previously have been reckoned outside the normal planning horizon (see Chapter 2).

Innovation Strategy is an aspect of the wider field of business strategy, whose main strands we summarize briefly in Theory Box 4.1.

This chapter covers:

- Tools for strategic analysis.
- Linking strategy to customers' needs.
- Facing the limits of technology or capability.
- Value innovation and blue ocean strategies.
- Disruptive innovation.
- Strategic issues of open innovation.
- Protecting the value of innovation.
- A main case study of Domino Printing Sciences.

MINI CASE 4.1: *Aramex – Delivery Unlimited*[2]

Aramex is a leading provider of comprehensive logistics and transportation solutions based in Dubai, UAE. In 2015 its revenues rose by 5 per cent to AED 3,837 million (just over $1 billion). Fadi Ghandour, a Lebanese/Jordanian entrepreneur, and William Kingson, his American business partner, established Aramex in 1982 as an express courier wholesaler to North American courier companies, including FedEx and Airborne Express. They have led Aramex to become DHL's first real competitor in the Middle East and a major worldwide operator. In the words of Thomas Friedman, the author of the bestseller on globalization, *The World is Flat*, Aramex 'is the example that is worth a thousand theories'. In 1997, Aramex became the first Arab-based company to be listed on the NASDAQ stock exchange and from 2005 it has been listed on the Dubai Financial Market.

For a variety of historical and cultural reasons, innovation is not what the Middle East region is famous for. But innovation has been at the centre of Aramex's success. The company's first business idea was not at all original: according to Ghandour: 'You copy, paste, and then you innovate.' Aramex essentially replicated what other competitors such as DHL, FedEx and Airborne Express were doing at the time, although offering a price advantage. It was the only way the small Jordanian start-up without brand recognition could compete. Ghandour realized, however, that competing on price could not last long, as the incumbents would match the start-up's cost structure and squeeze it out of the industry. So, the only way forward was to innovate.

One of the successful innovations is the Shop and Ship service, a product of the Lebanese Civil War, when security concerns closed many travel routes in the region. It was a simple formula: customers could do their shopping online in the US or the UK and get their packages delivered to a local address assigned by Aramex. Based on this, Aramex consolidated shipments and brought them over to the region. With the spread of e-commerce, and relying almost solely on word of mouth, the service has been growing at a double-digit rate year on year. Another recent innovation is InPost-Aramex Lockers, which enable consumers across the Middle East and Africa to access private automated parcel lockers for all e-commerce activities, a revolutionary concept for the region.

Aramex's business model is asset light, with IT being the largest investment; in the words of Mohammad Alkhas, CEO for the Gulf Cooperation Council (GCC) group of countries at Aramex: 'it's like Uber for shipments'. Much of Aramex's success can be attributed to the company's culture, with its focus on the customer, flat hierarchy, agility, teamwork and learning. It is imbued with the values of Ghandour, the entrepreneurial co-founder. While these practices and organizational structures are common in modern

Continued...

organizations, in the early days they were a novelty and did not go down well with many senior managers who eventually left the organization. Says Ghandour:

> I didn't go to a business school, so I didn't have any preconceived ideas about how the organization should be run … It is a requirement for every single person that comes to the organization … before he does anything else, he learns this is who we are, these are our values, this is our culture, and this is how we conduct ourselves in the organization.

Alkhas believes that companies need to listen to customers who can be a big source of innovation: 'Great ideas are not coming from the head office, they are coming from Aramex's employees on the front line, they are in touch with customers, they are the ones who know best what keeps disrupting the business.' Creative thinking is a core value at Aramex. In 2014 the Aramex Innovation Centre 'Redlab' was launched, which, through an interactive online platform, allows employees to submit, discuss and vote on ideas.

Today, Aramex employs more than 17,000 people in over 500 locations in more than 70 countries across the GCC, the Levant, Africa, Asia and Asia-Pacific, Europe and North America. And it is not only parcels that it delivers; the company has delivered double-digit growth in profits for the past decade.

Case contributed by Tatiana Zalan.

TOOLS FOR STRATEGIC ANALYSIS

Many tools are available for strategy formulation. The appropriate choice depends, above all, on the degree of uncertainty to be faced. Courtney et al.[3] suggest four levels of uncertainty:

1. Clear enough future: Here, there is no great uncertainty as to how the external world is moving. The uncertainty to be confronted is primarily about the development and impact of any proposed innovation.
2. Alternate futures: Here, there are a small number of discrete possibilities. Examples might be the possible collapse of a major competitor, the pending possibility of restrictive legislation, or political change, such as Scotland leaving the UK.
3. Range of futures: Here, there is a wide spread of possible outcomes within a definable range, as, for example, at the launch of a radical new product, such as 3D television, or introducing an existing product line into an unexplored market.
4. True ambiguity: There is really no basis for predicting the future. Examples would be launching a radical new technology (such as television) or entering the Russian market after the fall of communism.

In this section we describe four tools that are helpful in building an innovation strategy in the first three situations. We do not know any useful tools for analysing true ambiguity, and in any case this is likely to require protective action rather than innovation. The four tools are:

1. *Scenario planning*: a way to explore alternate futures; or a range of futures if the main uncertainty is confined to a small number of variables.

2. The *strategic landscape map*: a convenient way to map out the future of a company within one of the possible futures and identify opportunities and threats where innovation may be required.
3. *Roadmapping*: allows more detailed exploration of particular innovation opportunities and is also useful for innovating within a 'clear enough' future.
4. The *Business Model Canvas*: a helpful tool for reviewing the completeness and coherence of the business model for an innovation.

All these tools should be used in a workshop environment involving all the key players and then communicated more widely as appropriate. This is a management activity, not a job to be delegated to a group of specialists.

THEORY BOX 4.1: *Strategic Management Theory*[4]

There are not many theories directly connected to innovation management – disruptive technology and diffusion are the most notable ones. In contrast, strategic management is an area where theory is more developed and widely discussed: 'Strategic management is the process and approach of specifying an organization's objectives, developing policies and plans to achieve and attain these objectives, and allocating resources so as to implement the policies and plans.'[5] The essence of strategy formulation is coping with the competition but it goes further by gaining more power through relationships with suppliers and customers. Researchers in the field of strategy have identified six main theories:[6]

1. *Profit-maximizing and competition-based theory* views the purpose of a company to maximize profits by achieving a long-term competitive advantage. An organization's market position vis-à-vis the competition is seen as the most critical factor influencing competitive advantage and performance. Michael Porter's *five forces model* is a key model of competition, which has been hugely influential.
2. *Survival-based theory* stresses that an organization constantly needs to adapt its resources and capabilities in order to survive in changing environments.
3. *Human resource-based theory* differs from the survival literature in that it places more emphasis on human resources, as a crucial part of developing strategy.
4. *Agency theory* regards the relationships between shareholders, owners and managers as important to the success of an organization.
5. *Contingency theory* (explained in detail in Theory Box 1.1) stresses that there is not one best way for an organization to be managed – the unique circumstances a company faces require unique responses.
6. *Resource-based view* (RBV) is very popular in the literature. In contrast to the competition-based view, it believes that competitive advantage is based on the internal resources an organization possesses. Resources that are more **v**aluable, **r**are, **i**nimitable and **n**on-substitutable (referred to as *VRIN characteristics*) enable companies to achieve sustainable competitive advantage.[7] The RBV has been criticized for not providing a deeper understanding of what 'resources' are and for regarding them as static. To deal with changing business environments, *dynamic capabilities* are needed. These are 'an organization's ability to build, integrate, and reconfigure capabilities to address rapidly changing environments'.[8]

How can these theories assist managers? They should be regarded as different perspectives on the same problem: How can an organization in a changing environment react and gain competitive advantage? The first five theories point to the range of factors to consider in developing and implementing an innovation strategy (as part of business strategy).

Continued...

The RBV and the concept of dynamic capabilities bring to the fore the need to think broadly about what an innovation strategy needs to achieve. Innovation strategy should cover not only *innovation performance* (the desired output of new products, services and business models) but also *innovation capability* (the sum of the underlying processes that enable innovation). Innovation capability should be viewed as a dynamic capability; that is, something that needs constant management attention and improvement. Business environments change and, today, companies need the capability to design and implement new business models. Chapter 9 focuses on how companies can build their innovation capability.

Scenario Planning

Scenario planning is designed to help organizations grapple with a future that could develop in a small number of alternative ways. The guiding principle is that although the future is unpredictable, cause and effect will still apply and this limits the range of possibilities. For example, a future in which global warming is a reality is pretty sure to have rising sea levels; a reduction in private motoring in the US would depress the motel business; and driverless cars will certainly reduce demand for taxi drivers. So assumptions about a few key variables lead not to unlimited possibilities but to a restricted number of likely future states, or *scenarios*. Each of these is, in Michael Porter's words: 'An internally consistent view of what the future might turn out to be – not a forecast, but one possible future outcome.' Developing scenarios opens the mind to alternative possibilities but in a disciplined way, seeking to:

- Understand the range of futures that might plausibly occur.
- Find indicators that can be used to give early warning of which scenario is evolving.
- Prepare the way, if only mentally, for possible disruptive changes.
- Avoid strategies that could be disastrous in some possible scenarios.
- If possible, find some strategies that are valid for all likely scenarios.

If only a small number of plausible scenarios are found, it may be appropriate to do more detailed plans for each one.

Scenario planning first arose after the Second World War. Its use was pioneered by oil giant Shell, which used it to examine what would happen if there were to be a political change in the Middle East leading to a sudden rise in the price of oil. This work did not allow the company to predict the Yom Kippur War of 1973 but did leave it prepared for the price shock and able to react faster and more effectively than its competitors.[9]

Scenarios have mostly been used to examine the impact of major geopolitical and social changes but they can be used on a smaller scale to analyse the consequences of, say, the collapse of a competitor, a major regulatory change, or a significant shift of customer behaviour. Each scenario is a description of how the world would be if the uncertainties under consideration turned out in a particular way.[10, 11] The scenarios are made as complete as possible and are presented in a colourful and compelling way so as to stimulate interest. The quality depends very much on the skill and knowledge of those participating in its definition. The key steps are:

1. Identify the issues of concern and the timescale of interest.
2. Analyse the internal and external forces at work and identify assumptions that apply to all.
3. Identify trends in key factors and extrapolate to the chosen time.
4. Identify a small number (usually two or three) of high-impact factors whose outcomes are uncertain.
5. Consider all possible combinations of the key factors. Reject any combinations that are incompatible or contradict other assumptions.
6. Analyse the remaining scenarios in depth and propose preparatory actions.

Figure 4.3 is a highly abbreviated summary of scenario work done in the 1980s looking at design criteria for future automobiles in the US. Fuel price and consumer values were thought to be the major uncertainties influencing the kinds of vehicles customers would want in the next two decades, and the combinations of these led to the four scenarios illustrated. This work was influential[12] in combating the assumption in Detroit that the big auto companies should continue with their policy of producing cars with only stylistic differences, for similar markets (a scenario called 'Long Live Detroit'). At the time of writing, it appears that the market may be heading towards the opposite scenario ('Green Highways').

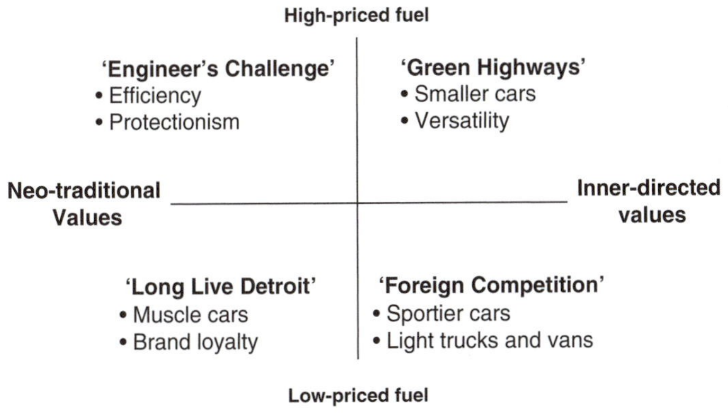

High-priced fuel

'Engineer's Challenge'	**'Green Highways'**
• Efficiency	• Smaller cars
• Protectionism	• Versatility

Neo-traditional Values ——————————————— **Inner-directed values**

'Long Live Detroit'	**'Foreign Competition'**
• Muscle cars	• Sportier cars
• Brand loyalty	• Light trucks and vans

Low-priced fuel

FIGURE 4.3: Scenarios for Entry-level Vehicle Design, Detroit 1980
Source: adapted from Schwartz and Ogilvy in Chapter 4 of: L. Fahey and R. Randall (eds) Learning from the Future: Competitive foresight scenarios (Chichester: John Wiley, 1998). Copyright © 1998 John Wiley & Sons, Incorporated. Reproduced with permission[13].

The Strategic Landscape Map

The *strategic landscape map*,[14] a derivative of the roadmap, is a simple and useful tool for taking a broad view of the future. Companies often use it as the first step in thinking about strategy. The map is simply a diagram divided horizontally into several layers, which together represent all the significant aspects of the business that will remain important over the period being examined. These may be product lines, technologies, customer segments, competitors, core competences and so on. The horizontal axis is time. An example of the structure used for exploring urban mobility issues is shown in Figure 4.4.

The team considers each layer in turn and populates it with the developments, possibilities and challenges they expect at various times. They then look for links and influences within and between the layers and so identify opportunities or issues where innovation may be appropriate. These issues are then taken away by smaller groups for closer analysis, for example using *topic roadmaps*. Some serious preparation is needed to make the process work well. In particular, the layers of the map must be carefully chosen, to ensure that they represent all the continuingly important strands of the business. It is also helpful if a number of key players prepare a brief and structured presentation on the key issues facing the organization in the various layers in the short, medium and long term.

Like many strategy tools, the strategic landscape is best applied in a workshop situation, with responsible senior managers present, allowing participants

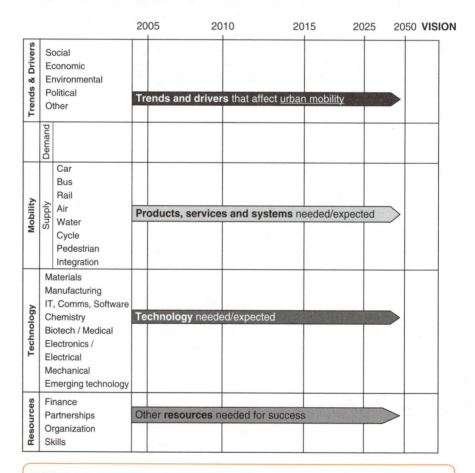

FIGURE 4.4: Strategic Landscape Structure for a Study of Urban Mobility
Source: copyright © Robert Phaal. Reproduced with permission.

FIGURE 4.5: Compiling a Strategic Landscape
Source: Phaal, R., Farrukh, C. and Probert, D., Roadmapping for strategy and innovation – aligning technology and markets in a dynamic world, (Institute for Manufacturing: University of Cambridge, 2010). Copyright © Robert Phaal. Reproduced with permission.

to explore options and share perceptions and hopefully to build a consensus about key issues (Figure 4.5).

Roadmapping

The components of strategy must be linked together in a coherent way that commands the understanding and engagement of all those involved and clearly identifies the actions that will make it happen. An effective way of achieving these aims is to construct a *topic roadmap* that displays and links the aims of the organization, the means it will use to deliver them, and the new resources needed to make it all possible, in a single document. Roadmaps have been most frequently used for product (or service) strategy but the basic approach is effective for any type of new activity. The emphasis will be on developing a coherent and structured approach to the issue, linking between the layers to show how the main strategic goals are supported by the activities necessary to make them happen. A roadmap is always a working document and at any time it may include question marks and alternatives as strategy develops. The elements are usually shown not as single points but as bars indicating how long they may take. A roadmap is in many ways like a Gantt chart but at a rather high level of abstraction, the emphasis being on the logical structure and interdependencies rather than on completeness of detail.

The upper layer of the roadmap typically shows specific business aims such as a planned entry into a new market sector. Below this might be the physical or service products the company would need to achieve these aims; and below that the capabilities, resources or technologies it would have to develop to deliver them. For a product roadmap, appropriate layers will usually be those shown on the left of the diagram. Roadmaps for other purposes will use different layers within the more generic descriptions on the right: *know-how* (capabilities), *know-what* (deliverables), *know-why* (aims) and *know-when* (timing). The horizontal scale is always 'time' – too often absent in strategy presentations. A simple, generic example is shown in Figure 4.6.

The first consistent use of roadmapping in business was by Motorola and Corning in the 1980s.[15] The technique was adopted by a number of electronics companies in the 1990s, notably Philips,[16] BP,[17] Lucent and HP, and this led to its use by communities of companies collaborating to plan the evolution of technologies for complete industry sectors. The roadmap for the semiconductor industry is perhaps the best known of these.[18] It has certainly been influential in guiding the progress of this industry. Subsequently, roadmapping has been applied to even broader topics at the national level, such as the UK Foresight activities for transport and other sectors[19] and even, less formally, in international politics.

The basic structure of the map can be varied in many ways to reflect the task in hand but it will usually retain the layered structure with links showing interdependencies, and time as the main dimension.

Building a Roadmap

In our experience, representatives of all relevant technical and commercial departments must be involved because the purpose is to stimulate understanding and debate about how the parts of the strategy work together; and ultimately to generate commitment to the plan. And it must have the active participation of

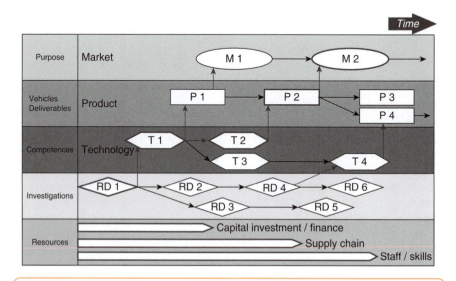

FIGURE 4.6: Generic Roadmap Structure
Source: copyright © Robert Phaal. Reproduced with permission.

the management team responsible for the aspect of the business under review. After all, the subject is nothing less than the future of their business.

The act of building the map is itself a learning process so it usually takes several iterations and much review before the plan settles down into a stable and accepted form. It is wise to do a rough draft quickly and refine and improve it as understanding grows rather than to try and perfect each part separately before putting it all together. Much of the understanding comes from seeing the whole picture. Moreover, building the map takes a lot of effort and it is motivational to have an output early on so that participants can see the sense of what they are doing. Roadmaps gain much of their value from the process of review and critique.

Although it is easy to imagine how useful a roadmap could be, getting started on it may not be so simple. Researchers at Cambridge University[20] have devised a quick way to generate a coherent 'first-cut' roadmap, particularly for planning product or service strategy (see Theory Box 4.2).

THEORY BOX 4.2: *The 'Fast Start' Process for Roadmapping*

The process of constructing a product roadmap consists of four stages, the first three of which are concerned with identifying the key market drivers, product features and technologies. A pair of *cross-impact matrices* is used as an analytical tool (Figure 4.7) in a similar way to that used in quality function deployment for products, as described in Theory Box 7.2.

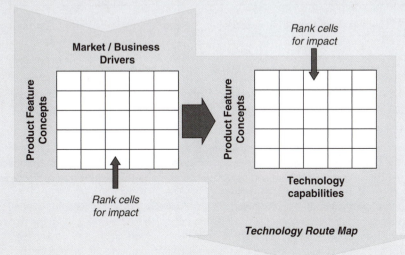

FIGURE 4.7: Cascaded Matrices Linking Market and Business Drivers to Technology Requirements, via Product Features
Source: copyright © Robert Phaal. Reproduced with permission.

In the first stage, a prioritized set of market and business drivers is chosen and each is given a weighting out of 10 according to the team's view of their importance. These may be factors such as price, reliability, environmental impact, suitability for the distribution network and so on.

Continued...

In the second stage, participants consider the features or benefits of the product that drive competitive advantage. The first cross-impact matrix is used to check how well they support the key market and business drivers. Each feature is given a score according to the strength of its influence on each driver and these scores are multiplied by the weighting factor of the driver to give an overall score. This score shows how well that feature contributes to satisfying the set of drivers. This is a useful check that the right features have been chosen and that all the drivers are addressed, but it is highly approximate so the precise rankings should not be taken too seriously. Any surprises should, however, be carefully reviewed. This process is illustrated in Figure 4.8.

Driver Weight	4	10	2	6	6	10	8	4	
	Market Driver 1	Market Driver 2	Market Driver 3	Market Driver 4	Market Driver 5	Business Driver 1	Business Driver 2	Business Driver 3	Score
Feature 1	✓✓✓	✓		✓✓		✓✓✓	✓		72
Feature 2	✓	✓✓✓						✓✓	42
Feature 3			✓		✓✓✓	✓	✓		38
Feature 4	✓	✓		✓	✓	✓		✓✓	44
Feature 5	✓	✓✓✓		✓✓		✓✓✓	✓✓✓	✓	104
Feature 6	✓✓			✓✓✓		✓	✓✓	✓	56

FIGURE 4.8: Cross-impact Matrix Relating Market Drivers to Product Features in the First Stage of the Quick-start Process for Product Roadmapping

In the third stage, a similar analysis is done linking the product features (which now have weights derived from the first process) to the competences or technologies that the company has available. This shows what the critical competences are and how they contribute to the performance of the products and so to the needs of the company and the market.

In the fourth stage, the information derived in the first three is used to generate a first roadmap: the market drivers being on the first level and the contributing technologies in the third, while the discussion of the important features gives the team a start on defining the products. The key market events and their timing, the number of product lines and the frequency of new products also have to be considered and included.

For a product roadmap, a good starting point is for the participants to estimate what level of performance is achievable for each of the key product features at various times in the future. The team must also be aware of any possible limits to progress and must make some assumptions about what level of resources they can employ. In practice, the performances proposed are unlikely to be entirely acceptable, so the debate begins, trade-offs are made, and the team eventually agrees on a set of performances features that are adequate and achievable. During the debate, managers should apply the Kano analysis, which we describe below, to assess how far it is useful to advance each feature. It may be that some will have reached a point when further improvement is not profitable.

Keeping a Roadmap Alive

Roadmaps are sometimes used as a way of analysing individual issues, but more often they are intended to have a continuing life as part of the organization's strategy debate. If this is so, then one cannot overemphasize the need to review and update regularly. There are four principal reasons for this:

1. The world changes, often rapidly. A roadmap is not a page from an atlas but a sketch-map of a changing battlefield, so the assumptions behind it are constantly being made obsolete by the march of events and the roadmap must adapt.
2. Our own understanding of the world changes as we learn, think and debate with colleagues. The roadmap must adapt to these new insights.
3. The process of thinking about strategy is more important than the strategy document. General Dwight Eisenhower wisely said: 'I have always found that plans are useless, but *planning* is indispensable' (italics added). Reviewing the roadmap deepens understanding and reinforces commitment to what has been agreed and so prepares us to meet the next challenge.
4. Old colleagues move on and are replaced with new. The act of reviewing the strategic roadmap with newcomers is an excellent way to acquaint them with the strategic thinking.[21] A research-based company we recently worked with displayed a large copy of its roadmap in the corridor to its canteen. Although some believe a roadmap should be confidential, the CEO of this company says the value of everyone understanding the strategy and knowing how they can contribute to it far outweighs any downside.

The Business Model Canvas

As we constantly emphasize, breakthrough and radical innovations are likely to call for changes, and perhaps further innovations, in many aspects of the business. A helpful tool for visualizing this context is the Business Model Canvas, proposed by Osterwalder and Pigneur and illustrated in Figure 4.9. Their book gives a number of examples of its use.[22] The canvas depicts all the main elements of the business model, allowing managers to assess the complete proposal in the round. It's helpful in checking for incompatibilities and possible missed opportunities. Managers should ask:

- Can the value of the core innovation be enhanced by changes to other parts of the business model?
- Can the innovation be made more defendable?
- Are the parts of the business model mutually reinforcing?

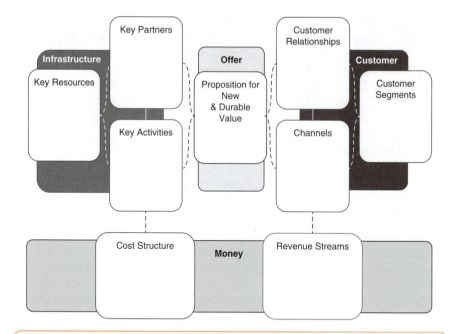

FIGURE 4.9: Business Model Canvas

Source: adapted from Osterwalder, A. and Pigneur, Y., Business Model Generation: A Handbook for Visionaries, Game Changers, and Challengers (Hoboken, NJ: John Wiley, 2010). Copyright © 2010 John Wiley & Sons, Incorporated. Reprinted with permission.

INNOVATION STRATEGY AND CUSTOMER SATISFACTION

All organizations aim to satisfy their stakeholders, and particularly the most important of these: the customer. Thus, strategy must include an analysis of the important benefits that an organization offers to its stakeholders and how their value is to be maintained and enhanced into the future. The influential work of Noriaki Kano, a Japanese quality guru, provides a framework for thinking about customer satisfaction and helps to address two major strategic issues we discuss in full later on, namely *capability ceilings* and *feature fatigue*.

Kano's Feature Analysis

Kano originally presented this analysis as a quality management tool and it is certainly most powerful as a way to link product (and service) features to the satisfaction of end-customers.[23] However, it can also throw light on how well the company serves other stakeholders such as staff, suppliers and distributors. Kano classified the features of a product or service into three categories according to the effect they have on customer satisfaction.

1. Basic features: These are attributes without which a product or service would be unacceptable. Cars must start readily, window-glass must not distort the

view, and restaurants must be hygienic. All these features are expected and failure to provide them would cause great dissatisfaction. However, providing extra performance beyond the basic requirement gives no extra satisfaction to the customer and may be expensive and even counterproductive. A car must start reliably but a failure once in 15 years gives no competitive advantage over once in 10 years; and the diners' experience in a restaurant would not be enhanced by the extra cleanliness provided by rubber gloves and face masks for the waiters.

2. Performance features: These are features that provide a real benefit to the customer, and the more they get, the better. Typical examples would be: low price, ease of use, fuel economy, battery life in a mobile phone, and size of dividends for shareholders. Performance features are particularly important because they are the long-term focus of competition in any market. Companies gain competitive advantage and profitability, perhaps over many years, by moving up the curve faster than their competitors. Every step is the basis for the next advance.

3. Delighters, or excitement features: A customer is unlikely to demand these features because they are not part of the way the service is normally viewed, but when offered them, they may be surprised and pleased. Such features often respond to *hidden needs* (see Chapter 5). They give an extra, unexpected value and may be attractive out of all proportion to the objective benefits they give. When it was first introduced, the remote control on a TV was a classic example of a delighter. We doubt that many people had gone into their TV shop to complain about the chore of getting out of the seat to change channels, but once it was available, it quickly became indispensable. The 'tilt' feature on Apple's iPhone (changing the display automatically from portrait to landscape as the phone is turned) is another example. An unexpected new initiative such as an acquisition or expansion into a new market may have the same effect on investors in a company. Some delighter features are easily copied and so give only short-term advantage to the innovator, but some introduce a whole new dimension of customer satisfaction and competitive advantage.

Figure 4.10 illustrates Kano's classification of features in schematic form. The horizontal axis is the level to which the feature is taken and the vertical is the customer satisfaction conveyed by it. The three categories of feature follow different curves reflecting their different effects on customer perception. A successful product needs to have an appropriate combination of basic, performance and delighter attributes. Customer or stakeholder *satisfaction* comes from the basic and performance features, while their *loyalty* depends on delivering consistently superior performance, possibly accompanied by some excitement features.

The features of a company's product may be allocated to the Kano categories by a simple questionnaire in which customers are asked how they would feel about a significant increase or decrease in its level of implementation (or possibly its presence or absence). The answers are interpreted using the matrix shown in Figure 4.11. Thus, a feature is clearly a delighter if a respondent is unconcerned if it were reduced (or absent), but pleased if it is improved/present. If they are uninterested in an improvement, but would be unhappy with a reduction, then it is a basic feature. Features that fall into the central box (shaded grey) cause

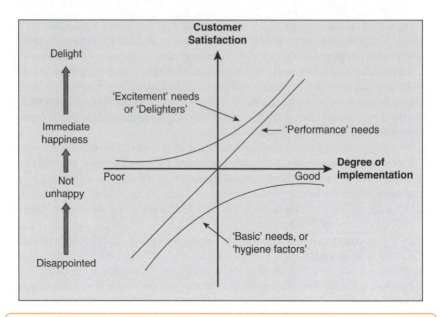

FIGURE 4.10: Kano's Model of Product (or Service) Features
Source: adapted from Kano, N., Nobuhiko, S., Takahashi, F. and Tsuji S. 'Attractive Quality and Must-be Quality' (1984), Hinshitsu – Journal of the Japanese Society for Quality Control, Vol. 14, No. 2, p. 39–48. Copyright © 1984 Dr Noriaki Kano. Reproduced with permission[24].

		"How do you feel about having less of this feature?"		
		Good	Don't care	Bad
"How do you feel about having more of this feature?"	Good		Delighter	Performance feature
	Don't care	Delighter when absent	Indifferent (Possibly an overprovided feature)	Basic
	Bad	Reduction is performance feature		

FIGURE 4.11: Matrix for Allocating Product Features to their Kano Categories
Source: adapted from Kano, N., Nobuhiko, S., Takahashi, F. and Tsuji S. 'Attractive Quality and Must-be Quality' (1984), Hinshitsu – Journal of the Japanese Society for Quality Control, Vol. 14, No. 2, p. 39–48. Copyright © 1984 Dr Noriaki Kano. Reproduced with permission[25].

no particular response either way so might perhaps be reduced or eliminated. A deeper understanding may be reached by repertory grid or conjoint analysis, as described in Chapter 5.

A key strategic question for any organization is how it can enhance the value it delivers to stakeholders as time goes on, so strategic analysis should include a review of how key features may move on the Kano diagram during the planning period. This raises two vital questions. The first is whether the organization can continue to enhance the performance features of its products and services at the rate the stakeholders require, or, at least, as fast as competitors do. The second, and more subtle, issue is whether stakeholders, particularly customers, will continue to demand the same balance of features in future. We consider these two challenges in the following two sections.

Capability Ceilings and Technology S-curves

The first strategic challenge that can be illustrated by Kano's analysis is the *capability ceiling*. This arises when an organization can no longer move its products and services up the performance curve on the Kano diagram as it would wish. If key capabilities are approaching the limits of what they can do, the organization may be vulnerable, especially to competitors with a better approach.

Every technology has a natural upper bound on performance, beyond which it simply cannot be pushed, and the same applies to working methods or other capabilities. We will use the terms 'technology' and 'competence' more or less interchangeably in what follows.

Viewed over a sufficient length of time, the progress of any technology is likely to follow a recognizable path,[26] as illustrated in Figure 4.12. On the vertical axis we plot the performance of a key characteristic. It might be a physical attribute of a product, such as speed, price or comfort; the scope of a service, for example the number of customers a salesperson can serve in a day; or any other parameter that is of value to the customer. On the horizontal axis is the cumulative investment made in developing that aspect of the technology. The curve tends to be S-shaped (see Theory Box 4.3). In the early stages, when the technology is in its infancy, the performance is modest and the rate of progress is relatively slow; but each advance provides the basis for further improvement and so progress accelerates and the slope of improvement becomes steeper. This improving trend may go on for a long time, but eventually it comes to an end when some natural limit is approached. As a technology approaches this ceiling, progress becomes slower, investment becomes less and less productive, and the organization becomes vulnerable to attack. The various stages of development have been labelled: *emerging* when it is in the experimental phase; *pacing* when it is developing rapidly; *key* when its progress drives competition in the field; and finally *base* when it is essential but no longer a source of competitive advantage.[27]

History is full of examples where this drama has been played out. For example, commercial sailing ships showed steady improvement from Roman times through the Middle Ages and into the 19th century, but the flowering of the great clipper ships like the *Cutty Sark* in the second half of the century signalled the top of their S-curve. Further attempts at improving their speed were unsuccessful,

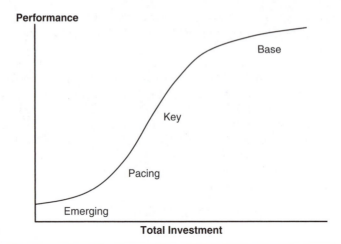

FIGURE 4.12: The Technology (or Competence) S-curve
Source: based on Foster, 1996[28]

and indeed counterproductive: the only possibility was to add more sail, which led to a number of well-publicized disasters when the overdeveloped monsters capsized in a side wind. Sail could improve no more, and gave place to steam.

A similar thing has happened in many modern instances: propeller aircraft reached an absolute speed limit and jets took over for faster travel; waxed cylinders gave way to vinyl discs which in turn gave way to CDs as each reached its limit of audio fidelity; trains replaced canals and so on. 'Just in time' manufacturing has replaced batch-based methods and even in sport the 'straddle' method of high jumping gave way to the downward-facing Western Roll and its cousin the Fosbury Flop.

An organization that relies on a capability that is approaching the top of its S-curve is vulnerable. It is therefore imperative to understand key capabilities well enough to be clear where their limits lie and what the alternatives might be. A maturing technology is always potentially at risk of replacement but the threat is *real* only if the limit to the capability is truly unavoidable *and* there is a genuine market demand for further improvement. It is *real* and *urgent* if an alternative technology is at hand that does not have disadvantages that outweigh its benefits.

The question of possible disadvantages of a competing technology may be illustrated by two contrasting examples. The first concerns the chemical phthalic anhydride, which is an important feedstock for the manufacture of a number of other chemicals used in plastics and paint manufacture.[29] The original process for making it, using naphthalene, was challenged by a new one, using orthoxylene. This new process offered only a 10 per cent improvement in performance but the naphthalene process could not match it. Over $100 million was spent on efforts to raise the yield but to no avail because the technology had simply reached its limit. Although the new process offered only a relatively small improvement, it had no disadvantages and quickly took over the market.

A contrasting example is the introduction of fluorescent lights. The ordinary incandescent lamp reached the limit of its efficiency as a source of light around

1940. Fluorescent lamps were significantly more efficient when they were introduced and quickly became almost 10 times better. However, they were *not* a direct replacement for the incandescent: they had a higher initial cost, a different quality of the light and, perhaps most important, they would not, for a long time, fit into the existing light sockets. As a result, the two types coexisted for many years until pressure for energy conservation gave fluorescent lights a decisive advantage (just in time to be themselves overtaken by LEDs).

Of course, technologies are not vulnerable to replacement *only* if they are reaching the top of their S-curve. Sometimes, a better alternative appears while there is still plenty of scope for improvement in the incumbent technology. The arrival of a new technology may itself trigger a burst of improvement in the old one that delays the switchover (the 'sailing ship effect') and the two may then jostle for leadership for some time until one becomes dominant.[30] Sometimes, hybrids emerge: many early steamships had auxiliary sails. We see this scenario being played out at the moment in the automotive industry where the arrival of the electric car and fuel-efficient diesels has stimulated a great improvement in efficiency of the petrol engine, and also generated electric–petrol and electric–diesel hybrids.

The idea of a capability ceiling has traditionally been applied to technology-based products but we stress that services are equally dependent on capabilities that reach a limit of capability and can be superseded. Mini Case 4.2 describes how the advertising company JCDecaux foresaw and overcame the limits of the traditional billboard offering. Service companies need to be aware of how the fundamental limits on their competences may make them vulnerable to new competition.

The S-curve is a powerful metaphor and illustrates an important principle that innovation managers must be alert to. But the shape of the curve cannot generally be used for quantitative prediction and the upper limit may be difficult to predict, although it was possible for Domino Printing Sciences, the subject of this chapter's main case study.

THEORY BOX 4.3: *Generalizing the 'S'-curve*

Gordon Moore, one of the founders of Intel, pointed out in 1965 that the number of transistors on an integrated circuit chip typically doubles every two years or so (Figure 4.13). Although it may now at last be coming to an end, 'Moore's law' held true for more than four decades, and has formed the basis for much of the strategic planning in the semiconductor business. The progress it describes has, of course, been of immense importance in all fields of electronics and computing.

This so-called *geometric* rate of change, in which each increment is a percentage rather than an absolute amount, leads to an accelerating, *exponential* improvement. This is difficult to show effectively on a linear scale so it is usual to use a logarithmic scale, as in Figure 4.14. In fact, many other technologies such as the density of magnetic data storage and the cost of decoding a genome have been found to show a steady percentage change year on year, although presumably investment must be the driving factor, rather than time. Of course, the slope of the curve is different for each case. A related phenomenon is the 'factory learning curve', in which the cost of producing an item tends to reduce steadily with every doubling of production experience. It seems, therefore, that the early upward swing of the S-curve is perhaps exponential, so that plotted on a logarithmic scale, the curve would look like Figure 4.14. (The dotted square shows where the centre of the classic curve lies.)

Continued...

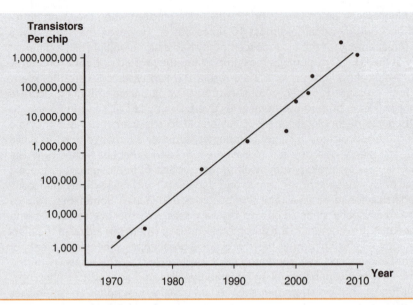

FIGURE 4.13: Moore's Law: Growth in the Number of Transistors per Integrated Circuit Chip, 1970–2010
Source: data from manufacturers Intel, AMD, Zilog and IBM

The S-curve is not a precise, nor a universal, predictor.[31] Nevertheless, the simple truth is valid and important: whatever route it takes, *any* technology or capability eventually reaches a limit, which will be a point of threat to a company that is dependent on it. Managers must be ready to take action well in advance of the critical point.

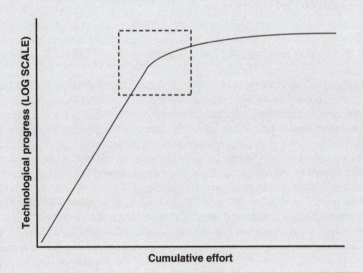

FIGURE 4.14: The S-curve on a Logarithmic Scale

Responses to a Maturing Capability

As a core capability or technology moves up the S-curve, attention will be on pushing forward the performance and exploring the new applications that the extra capabilities open up. At this stage, the company typically seeks to gain a strong market share and the marketing message concentrates on the functional advantages of the product. Then, as the technology reaches its later stages, attention inevitably moves away from the core performance (which has gone about as far as it can) to emphasize related aspects such as price, quality, reliability and service. At this stage, a company has a number of options (which may be pursued simultaneously):

1. Seek new technologies or capabilities that can continue the development of the core competence in some other way, thus starting a new S-curve.
2. Add new delighter features to retain competitive advantage.
3. Hone the effectiveness of all parts of the business and position itself as a competent and reliable supplier in the long term, not only of the product itself but also perhaps of a range of supporting products and services.
4. Look for alternative ways of delivering value to its customers by *value innovation*, the subject of the next section.

CHAPTER 4

MINI CASE 4.2: *JCDecaux – Billboards and Bus Shelters*[32]

JCDecaux's story began in Beauvais, France in 1953. Jean-Claude Decaux, who was born into a modest family of shoe shop owners in 1937, took the initiative to display advertising posters for the family shop in the city. This initiative, which was rare in the 1950s, enabled him to gain recognition and become a poster sticker for other Beauvais retailers seeking to promote their businesses.

Decaux set up his own billboard company at the tender age of 18. The young entrepreneur employed six colleagues to display large-format roadside billboards, as strong competition prevented him from gaining access to towns. However, the 1964 French Finance Act, which planned to impose higher taxes on roadside advertising displays, made him rethink his strategy. He devised an innovative concept: providing and maintaining bus shelters that provided sites for advertising. The mayor of Lyon was the first to adopt this new public service, in 1964. The advertising bus shelter and the JCDecaux business model were born.

Since then, the group has continued to innovate, designing new types of street furniture with advertising space. The range now includes information panels, public toilets, public litter bins and large-format scrolling panels. The philosophy of its founder has remained intact: to provide local authorities with street furniture financed through advertising. The business is increasingly digital. JCDecaux now operates more than 49,300 digital screens across 30 countries. These can be found at London's Waterloo station, airports such as Singapore, Los Angeles and Dubai, and shopping malls such as the Villagio Mall in Doha. Street furniture is also being digitalized, as illustrated by the advertising bus shelters in Paris and London, smart advertising clocks in São Paulo and large-format screens in Chicago. Some of the sites now provide other services and sources of revenue with the installation of free Wi-Fi in Dusseldorf, Germany, and 4G relay masts in the bus shelters of Amsterdam. JCDecaux is now the largest outdoor advertising company in the world, with over 12,000 employees and a presence in more than 75 countries, reaching over 390 million people every day.

VALUE INNOVATION AND BLUE OCEAN STRATEGY

Most innovation happens within an existing industry or market space. It consists of doing broadly the same things, or at least addressing the same aims, but better – perhaps startlingly better. However, competing in the same game is not always the best policy. Sometimes, the best innovation strategy is to outflank the competition by offering a significantly different mix of benefits and perhaps defining a new market space. This rather broad principle is called *value innovation* or *blue ocean strategy*,[33] and is especially attractive when players are competing head to head with similar offerings – as happens when feature fatigue has set in and no new delighters are available, or when the defining competence has met a capability ceiling that cannot be breached. Mini Cases 4.2 on JCDecaux, 4.3 on Zara and 4.4 on Hotel Formule 1 are examples of value innovation.

> ## MINI CASE 4.3: *Zara – A Revolution in Fashion*[34]

The Spanish retailer Zara, the chief brand of the Inditex group, has made a great success by overturning the long-established practices of the mass fashion business. Low margins at home and low-cost labour overseas have driven European clothes retailers increasingly to obtain supplies from the East Asia, shipping them, in the main, by sea. But this makes the supply chain long and slow. Zara, a fashion retailer, has reversed the trend by switching back to local manufacture. With the aid of sophisticated logistics, it can bring the latest fashion trends to the high street in a fraction of the time of its competitors. This opens a new market space that is difficult for competitors to invade.

The majority of Zara's products are now made in its own factories in Spain and Morocco, from where it ships them by truck or air to over 2,000 stores worldwide. Maria J. Garcia, a spokeswoman for Zara, says: 'The vertical integration of our production system allows us to place a garment in any store around the world in two to three weeks, provided the fabric is in stock.' The norm in the sector is five to 10 *months*. No sooner has a new look made the headlines than it is on the hangers in Zara – weeks or months ahead of anyone else, and at a premium price. Moreover, the company's speed of response means it can closely follow the ups and downs of demand. Twice-weekly deliveries mean that Zara shops are seldom short of popular lines and yet need to hold very little stock. So, when demand turns down, they simply switch immediately to the next thing. The company typically introduces 10,000 new lines a year.

By contrast, the much longer lead times elsewhere in the sector mean that competitors have to place orders months in advance. Forecasting that far ahead is almost bound to be wrong in such a fast-changing market and the result is a huge cost in obsolete stock that must be discounted or scrapped; a cost that Zara avoids.

Zara's business model ensures loyalty and premium prices by always offering its customers the most up-to-date designs. It has been noted that a Spanish woman will visit a typical clothing store three times a year, but 17 for Zara. The cost of making the clothes in its highly automated European factories is certainly higher than it would be to buy them from off-shore suppliers but the higher margins and savings in inventory costs and discounts more than compensate for this and give the company a unique positioning in its market.

The brand is very profitable – its return on sales has been as high as 15 per cent, five times the typical level in the sector. It is also growing strongly: from its foundation in 1975, it had a turnover of over

Continued...

$14.8 billion in 2015. It was described by Daniel Pielle of Louis Vuitton as 'possibly the most innovative and devastating retailer in the world'. Zara is now the largest fashion retailer in the world and its owner Inditex is one of the largest clothing retailers in the world. In 2015, Forbes listed the Zara brand as one of the most valuable in the world, at $9.4 billion.

The scope for a blue ocean strategy may be highlighted by value gap analysis.[35] This compares the perceived value or attractiveness of the key product features offered by all competitors in the market to see where there are gaps that might be exploited. (It may also serve to highlight how similar their offerings are!) Needless to say, a value gap analysis should be based firmly on the perceptions of customers. Formal techniques such as repertory grid analysis (Chapter 5) may be helpful. Figure 4.15 summarizes the offerings of traditional circus companies, contrasted with that of Cirque du Soleil, a Canadian company that, in 1984, introduced a contemporary form of circus without animals but with an overall artistic theme and storyline. There are currently 20 shows running in major indoor venues worldwide, grossing around $1 billion. Before then, the circus business was generally in decline.

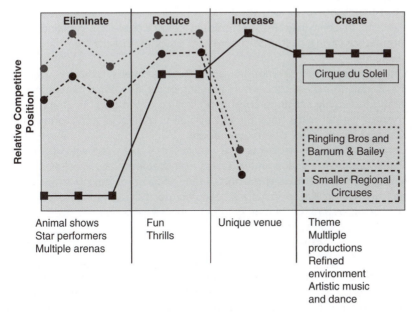

FIGURE 4.15: Value Gap Analysis for Circuses and Cirque du Soleil
Source: reprinted by permission of Harvard Business School Press. Adapted from Blue Ocean Strategy: How to Create Uncontested Market Space and Make the Competition Irrelevant by W. Chan Kim and Renée Mauborgne. Boston, MA 2005, pp 43. Copyright © 2005 by the Harvard Business School Publishing Corporation; all rights reserved[36].

The search for a blue ocean strategy starts with an understanding of which of the existing features might be *enhanced*, *reduced*, *increased* or *created* (ERIC makes a convenient mnemonic). Often, a Kano analysis based on interviews and questionnaires will show the opportunities, but in a well-established market more subtle tools such as conjoint analysis (Chapter 5) may be needed to cut through the preconceptions of customers and managers. The other side of the task is to create new customer value by creating new features. Kim and Mauborgne give a number of possible strategies for finding these opportunities, which we summarize briefly below.

- Look for ideas from other segments of the market and combine the most attractive features of both, eliminating the rest. Curves is a US company that operates fitness facilities targeted at busy women who would normally be users of home exercise videos. Its low-cost, women-only fitness clubs have relatively basic facilities but offer a large choice of locations so they are convenient to get to and provide the supportive atmosphere of a health club at low cost.
- Look across to other industries that provide the same type of function in a different way. Low-cost airlines aim to provide the speed of air transport with the cost, simplicity and multiple destinations of a bus.
- Target a different part of the buyer chain. Thanks to the internet, many services that used to be provided through an intermediary can now be sold direct to the end-user. For example, in Europe there is a growing trend of farmers supplying customized boxes of produce directly from farms to the consumer.
- Offer a different mix of emotional and functional needs. QB House (Mini Case 8.4) is making a great success of providing quick, functional haircutting, eliminating the costly and time-consuming service of the traditional approach. In contrast, health clubs have thrived by building a social atmosphere around the strict functionality of the gymnasium.
- Consider the other products and services that are used with the product. Dyson has built a successful business from bagless vacuum cleaners, eliminating a tiresome related product. Many shops are moving towards home delivery. Caterpillar, originally a manufacturer of earth-moving equipment, now provides a range of management services for users.

Feature Fatigue and Disruptive Innovation

The second strategic issue illustrated by the Kano diagram is that the position of features tends to change in a predictable way with time. Delighters eventually lose their impact and become performance features and these themselves eventually become basic. This trend leads to important strategic challenges.

Consider the typical lifecycle of a new performance feature such as a TV remote control or a camera in a mobile phone. When it is first offered, it causes admiring comment and generates well-deserved sales advantage for the originator. But in the course of time it is copied by competitors and loses its special impact. Its existence is then no longer a surprise and the scramble starts to make improved and refined versions. It may now become a performance feature, the focus of competitive improvement. Often the improvement continues until the performance of the best products completely meets the needs of even the most demanding of users. The performance of products in the market will now be spread out along the performance line and customers can choose which level they are willing to pay for. Eventually, the market becomes so used to the feature that it is no longer a competitive element and drops below the axis as a basic need. Table 4.1 gives some other everyday examples of these movements.

When a core performance feature starts to run out of steam as a competitive advantage, it heralds a structural change in the competitive landscape. Basically, the product or service is heading towards becoming a *commodity* and the company must seek new features either in the product itself or in other parts of the business model to maintain advantage. Companies often find it difficult to adapt to this change because the old focus of competition may be effectively built into the fabric of the organization. It may be its core competence, and may very well be where management has habitually looked to protect and enhance margins. As a result, companies often fail to notice that the game is changing and may continue to develop the familiar features of its products well beyond the point of interest to its customers. Customers themselves may not be helpful, either. When asked about the relative importance of various features, they will continue to rate basic features highly. Are comfortable seats important in a car? Of course customers will say they are. But that is not the same as saying that further padding will make a customer choose one car rather than another.

A further complication to the picture is that customer preferences may change as the market moves through different adopter categories (see Chapter 2). The later, more conservative adopters may be less interested in high levels of performance features, hastening the onset of feature fatigue.

Continuing to develop basic features as if they were still performance features can be disastrous on three counts. First, the extra but useless performance can add unnecessary cost or complexity to the product (users of the Windows operating system may feel familiar with this); second, the chance to pursue features that will be of real interest to the customer is foregone; and, third, the company may become vulnerable to an alternative, so-called *disruptive* approach.

TABLE 4.1: Examples of the Evolution of Product Features on the Kano Diagram

Delighters that became basic features	Performance features that became basic
• Starter motors and heaters in cars	• Accuracy of clocks and watches
• TV remote controls	• Size of portable phones
• Seat-back TV on long-haul flights	• Resolution of printers
• 'Cash back' at supermarket tills	• Fidelity of audio systems
• Predictive text	• Resolution of cameras in phones
• Cameras in phones	• Speed of cars
• Internet banking	• Reliability of home appliances

DISRUPTIVE TECHNOLOGIES AND BUSINESS MODELS

The concept of *disruptive innovation*, or *disruptive technology* as it was originally called, was first identified by Clayton Christensen at Harvard.[37] It is, in fact, a special example of value innovation. His papers generated a wave of research that peaked in 2005, as we showed in Chapter 1. Christensen pointed out that companies often fall prey to a new technology or a new business model whose performance is actually inferior to that of the incumbent companies but which has other advantages. This can happen if a performance attribute that has previously been the focus of competition is starting to exceed the needs of a significant part of the market. In other words, the feature is dropping from the performance category towards basic. Then a new approach can alter the basis of competition in a dramatic way. An example is budget hotels such as Hotel Formule 1 (see Mini Case 4.4), which provide simple and comfortable sleeping at much lower cost by doing away with the restaurants, public spaces and other facilities that are usual in hotels. Another example is CitizenM (the main case study in Chapter 3).

Disruptive technologies, which change the basis of competition, are distinguished from *sustaining technologies*, which maintain the current focus. Sustaining technologies may undergo major transitions as one technology runs out of steam and is replaced by another, but essentially they represent 'business as usual', so they tend to be well managed by competent companies. Disruptive technologies, on the other hand, change the competitive focus of the business and are much more difficult for established companies to adapt to. Mini Case 4.5 discusses the role of electric power as a disruptive technology in the automotive business.

Christensen's initial research was conducted on computer disc drives, a fast-moving market sector in which product lifecycles are shorter than most. But further investigations have shown that the principles apply in other sectors from retail to earth-moving equipment. His ideas were based on the following observations:

- Companies succeed by serving their customers in markets they understand well. They seek to improve the performance of their products to stay ahead of competition and protect their margins.
- The pace of technology development often exceeds the demands from the bulk of the market. This may be because the technology is developing particularly fast, driven by the requirements of the most demanding users, or because the need for improvement is reducing.
- Disruptive technologies initially offer products that have poorer performance on the accepted features but other advantages such as price or size. They are first used either among the least demanding users in the lower tier of the market or in new markets currently too small, or offering too low margins, to attract established companies.
- In the course of time, a disruptive technology may improve enough to offer performance that is acceptable to most of the customers in the established market – even if never fully matching that of the existing approach. It can then

compete fully with the established technology while its other features can catastrophically change the basis of competition.

Figure 4.16 illustrates the concept. The sustaining technology, introduced at time t_1 improves rapidly over time, enabling the product performance in respect of feature 'A' to increase from level L_3 to L_1. However, the needs of both 'high-end' and 'low-end' users (indicated by the shaded area in Figure 4.16) increase more slowly. Nevertheless, companies that develop products with improved performance will often be successful and their market shares will increase.

The disruptive technology is very different. On its introduction at time t_2, its performance is not adequate for this market so its first use may be in other applications, where its other attributes are an advantage. However, when it improves to level L_2, it starts to appeal to low-end customers. At this point, the new technology will start to disrupt the established market and customers may switch in significant numbers. Typically, established companies will then tend to relinquish the lower end of the market and migrate upwards where margins are better, not recognizing the existential threat until too late. Think of Kodak and film.

Since Christensen's original work, the concept of disruption has been expanded to include not only technology but new processes and, especially, business models. For example, supermarkets were disruptive to the retail sector. They were typically sited away from town centres so were less convenient to get to, and offered less customer service than smaller shops or department stores. But their low prices and a wide choice of goods were an attractive option. They have since moved upmarket by improving customer service, in store and online, and offering more specialized merchandise. Meanwhile, many use their huge purchasing power to take their low prices to open smaller, more convenient

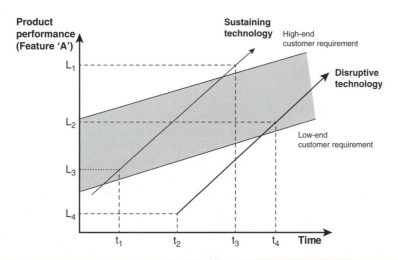

FIGURE 4.16: The Development of Sustaining and Disruptive Technologies
Source: reprinted by permission of Harvard Business School Press. Adapted from The Innovator's Dilemma: When New Technologies Cause Great Firms to Fail by Clayton M Christensen. Boston, MA 1997, pp 11. Copyright © 1997 by the Harvard Business School Publishing Corporation; all rights reserved[38].

outlets. Similarly, airlines such as Southwest and EasyJet have opened new markets for low-cost air travel by offering only short-haul, 'no frills' services (see Chapter 2).

Christensen's work on disruptive innovation is undoubtedly one of the most valuable new insights in management theory in recent years. But it is not without its critics and has been somewhat overhyped.[39] Disruption is a potential threat but only in specific circumstances, as we have outlined above. And even when the threat is real, there are several possible responses.

> **MINI CASE 4.4:** *Hotel Formule 1 – A Different Strategy for Customer Satisfaction*[40]

In the early 1980s, the board of Accor, a French hotel chain, challenged its managers to come up with a new concept for low-cost hotels. They were asked to reconsider what customers really valued from a night's stay and to see whether it was possible to find a better overall value proposition than the one generally on offer. The analysis showed that a number of features that were traditionally provided by even the lowest cost hotels were of comparatively little value to customers making an overnight stop. These included lounges, eating facilities, availability of a receptionist and spacious rooms. Such features were important for people staying in two- or three-star accommodation, for whom a hotel stay was, in part, a cultural experience. However, most users of low-cost hotels simply wanted a good night's sleep. The other features were being oversupplied.

By moving to small rooms with only basic facilities, cutting out lounges and restaurants, and having receptionists available only at peak times, the company was able to reduce construction and operating costs for the new hotel chain significantly. But rather than merely reducing the price, it also used the money to raise the standards of the features most important for overnight customers – comfort, cleanliness and quietness in the rooms – well above that usually available in the sector. The result was a new value proposition, giving a much higher level of customer satisfaction. The Hotel Formule 1 chain, launched in 1985, quickly became the market leader in the sector. Within 10 years its market share exceeded that of its five nearest rivals combined. A new market sector had been created, which flourishes to this day.

Responses to a Disruptive Threat

The future of a company that faces a threat from a disruptive technology or business model sounds bleak. It seems as if they must either pour investment into something that cannot be used in the current business or stand back while it develops elsewhere into an overwhelming threat. This is too alarmist. Of course, a disruptive business *may* be able to fully replace the old but more usually the incumbent will have some desirable features that the disrupting one does not, so the two may coexist,[41] sharing the market according to the different sets of capability. Wessel and Christensen[42] propose that the future track of a disruption may be predicted by examining what they term the *extendible core* of the disruptor: that is, the part of their business model that could be applied if they chose to move upmarket. In the case of the PC, a disruptive innovation in the computer industry, the operation of Moore's law (see Theory Box 4.3) would clearly provide a rapid improvement in its extendible core – the microprocessor – allowing the

PC eventually to invade the space of the larger and more complex mini and mainframe computers. However, it is equally clear that budget hotels cannot move upmarket without destroying their own business model. Companies facing a disruptive threat have three responses:

1. Find an immediate application: If the disruptive technology is not suitable for the existing market, the company may be able to find a way to operate in a new market where it is. Typically, this is done by setting up a new division kept separate from the main company so that it can develop its own business model. HP took just this approach with its inkjet printers. When first introduced, inkjet printing could not rival the quality of laser printing, but it had other attributes such as low cost, low noise and low power consumption. Rather than trying to get existing customers to buy the inferior technology, HP set up a separate division tasked with exploiting inkjet printing in whatever applications it could find, operating whatever business model allowed it to make money. The strategy paid off handsomely when the quality of inkjet printing eventually rose to be good enough to displace laser from much of the desktop market. But if the improvement had not happened, HP would still have had a profitable, if modest, business. IBM did a similar thing with the PC, setting up a new activity in Florida, well away from the company's base in New England.

CHAPTER **4**

> ## MINI CASE 4.5: *Automotive – Electric Power*

The petrol-based internal combustion engine has been the overwhelmingly preferred power supply for personal transport since it won a brief struggle for dominance with electric, diesel and steam power in the first decade of the 20th century. A dominant design emerged in the 1920s: a 4-6 cylinder petrol engine, hydraulic brakes, 3-5 gears and a steel body shell. The diesel engine retained a niche position in buses and trucks, and electric power hung on in a handful of specialist applications. Now, a century later, the industry is going through another period of creative turmoil as it tries to deal with the pressure for a less polluting means of transport.

There are many contenders for the new dominant design. They range from traditional designs powered by plant-derived ethanol at one extreme, to high-efficiency diesel engines, petrol–electric hybrids, plug-in hybrids, hydrogen power, and fuel cells with fully battery-powered cars at the other. The battle is peculiarly intense because as one moves along the list, less and less of the established architecture remains. A hybrid vehicle is architecturally similar to a normal vehicle, with a central power unit supported by gears, clutch and transmission. But a fully electric car may consist only of a battery, four electric motors and a computer (together with steering and brakes and a cabin for the occupants). The power train – engine, clutch, gearbox, transmission – has gone, and with it 75 per cent of the manufacturing cost, as well as the value of much of the design, manufacturing and support infrastructure on which the established companies have so long relied for their competitive position. This is a full-scale architectural revolution. It is not surprising that although Daimler AG, Toyota and Ford are now active in diesels and hybrids, the new wave of fully electric cars was pioneered by Tesla and other start-ups.

Electric vehicles are an example of a disruptive technology. For years, the technology existed in a few niche applications but did not have the performance to compete in the mainstream. Now, market

Continued...

requirements have changed to make low pollution and running costs very attractive, at least to some sectors. As their performance and range improve, electric vehicles will surely take a significant market share, even though they may never match petrol vehicles on the traditional criteria. But it is a competence-destroying innovation: the incumbent companies must embrace electric traction but the more successful it is, the more it erodes their added value and destroys their core competences.

2. Focus on the existing business: If the disruptive technology does not precisely replace the incumbent one, an aggressive response may be successful, emphasizing and enhancing the features of the existing business that are not shared by the new one. Examples of this are all around us: many big department stores are thriving by emphasizing their differences from supermarkets; cinemas remain in business after the arrival of television with ever more impressive visual and sound experiences, served with ice cream and giant popcorn; and our clothes are *not* all made of artificial fibres. Disruptive technologies do not always win all the business.

3. Attack back – disrupt the disruption: A final strategy is for incumbents not only to emphasize and enhance their intrinsic advantages against the new entrant, but to add further ones, changing the basis of competition yet again. The Swiss watch industry is the classic example. Its success had been based on a long tradition of craftsmanship in making clockwork timepieces that were more accurate and reliable than any others. This advantage was wiped out by the arrival of extremely accurate electronic watches based on quartz crystals that were also very much cheaper. Faced with this dramatic change, the Swiss did not attempt to follow the new competition. Instead, some companies re-emphasized their upmarket Brand position while others redisrupted the market by turning to a new way to compete – on style. Swatch became a byword for novel visual design, a fashion accessory rather than a timepiece. To retain its valuable brand name, Swatch re-engineered the design of the watch, reducing the number of assembled components by 40 per cent so that it could still be made cost-effectively in Switzerland.

STRATEGY AND OPEN INNOVATION

Innovation strategy must include decisions about the role of open innovation, a topic introduced in Chapter 2 and further elaborated in Chapters 5 and 7. We deal here only with the strategic issues involved.

There can be great advantages in incorporating the cutting-edge capabilities of other organizations into one's service or product offering; indeed, there may be little choice. But the loss of control that this may imply can be a problem in the longer run.[43] Henry Chesbrough, writing with David Teece of the University of California at Berkeley, makes a distinction between *autonomous innovations* that affect only part of the product and *systemic innovations* that affect several parts of the design simultaneously.[44] Autonomous innovations can usually be safely and efficiently outsourced – the lamps on a car or transport to and from a hotel are examples. Systemic innovations, on the other hand, tend to relate to the architecture of the product or service and the owner in effect has control of the offering itself. Aircraft designers do not outsource design of the wings, and supermarkets do not subcontract control of their supply chain. And IBM made a big mistake when it left ownership of the operating system of its PC with its supplier, a small start-up called Microsoft.

Protecting Strategic Value

In launching an innovation, particularly a new product or service, companies need to consider right from the start how best to defend their position against competition. Intellectual property – patents and trademarks – is the way that most readily comes to mind and we discuss this in some depth in Chapter 5. In fact, solid intellectual property that really blocks out competition is comparatively rare, although where it exists, it is obviously very valuable. Many companies do build up and maintain a strong patent position as a matter of strategy. But in planning a new initiative, one is more likely to make use of a pre-existing patent portfolio than to set out to create one from scratch. Managers cannot simply instruct engineers to 'go and get some patents'. Moreover, it is the patentee's responsibility to detect and prosecute infringements, which is likely to be difficult and expensive, and can put small companies at a disadvantage against large ones. It is therefore worth considering what other ways are open to companies to protect their innovations from rivals.

The simplest way to prevent competitors copying an innovation is to keep the knowledge secret. This can be an effective strategy for process innovations, or others, that are not visible to people buying the product. And some companies, such as Coca-Cola, can use it to protect the formulation of their product. Agreements with participants in the supply chain can also give at least a temporary monopoly position. For example, QB House (Mini Case 8.4) obtained deals to give it exclusive rights to place its innovative hairdressing outlets in key Japanese railway stations and airport concourses, blocking out the competition, at least for a while. Many specialist shops do the same in railway stations and other semi-public places. Signing up exclusive deals with key distributors can also work, for a time.

Some companies rely explicitly on their deep knowledge of a market to keep ahead by continuous innovation, as Mini Cases 4.6 on Micro Scooters and 4.7 on Cobra, illustrate.

> **MINI CASE 4.6:** *Micro Scooters – When Patents Don't Help*[45]

Its popularity may have waned but the urban scooter was a smash hit that continues to be in demand. What used to be considered as simply a child's toy has become a high-tech product, aimed at a range of age groups. The story behind this phenomenally successful product is an interesting one, which shows the need for innovative marketing, fast product development and the limitations of international patent protection. Surprisingly, the product idea itself almost failed to get to market.

Continued...

Wim Ouboter is the Swiss inventor of the original Micro city scooter. He studied international marketing in the US and had worked in banking in Switzerland and textile manufacturing in the US. However, it was his love of sports – windsurfing and cycling – that helped him to identify a niche in the transport market. Over 20 years ago, Ouboter recognized that, when he wanted to go out for a drink or a meal in the evening, it was often too far to walk but not far enough to warrant getting his bicycle out of the cellar, or to drive. Later, he was to coin the phrase *microdistances* for these sorts of journeys. As he often travelled microdistances, he set about designing a solution to the problem. He considered a skateboard but decided on a scooter, as it would be easier to ride. So he hand-made himself a simple scooter that turned out to be two to three times faster than walking, and which could be folded together, so that it would be easy to take into a bar. This prototype worked well and turned heads in Zürich. Ouboter said: 'When I was on it, people always used to stop and stare at me. So much so that I started to think that it wasn't very "cool" to be seen riding a scooter! So I stopped riding it during daylight hours.' Soon, the prototype fell into disuse and the whole idea might have died, had not Ouboter still believed that there was a need for such a product.

Then, in the summer of 1996, the prototype was spotted by neighbours' children, who asked if they could try it out. They were hooked immediately. From then on, throughout the summer, up to 20 kids per day took turns to use the scooter: 'They just kept coming to borrow it and my wife kept saying there really is something in this idea.' The success with the local neighbourhood finally convinced him and his wife to take the idea further. At the time, the launch of the Smart car, with its advertising slogans of 'Reduce to the Max' and 'The Future of Mobility', inspired Ouboter to make a video of his prototype and approach the car manufacturer. The Smart organization was impressed and considered integrating a scooter within the boot of the car as an ideal combination – a city car with the city scooter for the last lap of the journey. However, it eventually backed out so Ouboter turned to Southeast Asian manufacturers looking for a source of funding. He found a partner company with enough faith in the project to fund the tooling and other set-up costs and who helped find a Japanese retail partner willing to try the product, with an opening order of 20,000 scooters. These sold immediately and the market grew quickly to sales of 75,000 units per week – almost an instant success.

City Bug UK Ltd handled the UK marketing. Seth Bishop, one of the partners, says they quickly realized that: 'the product was great but it would attract competitors quickly. And without many international patents it would need a strong brand to maintain a market leadership position.' This was difficult because City Bug did not have the 'marketing spend' of a big company. Therefore, it adopted what some marketing professionals now refer to as *stealth marketing* – finding novel ways to reach their target segments, without resorting to conventional advertising. The marketing plan concentrated on establishing the profile of Micro as a premium product: 'We wanted it to achieve cult status quickly, to make it stand apart from the copies.' Therefore, the marketing team concentrated on getting fashion journalists interested so that they would write articles in magazines such as *The Face* and selecting distribution channels such as design shops as opposed to retail chains. From the start, the Micro product was promoted as a top design.

The high labour content made it uneconomical to produce the Micro product in Switzerland so it is manufactured in China even though Ouboter knew that, by the time production of the Micro had ramped up, the word would have spread and a host of Asian copies would be inevitable. Patent cover would not be helpful in this case because it typically takes up to two years to be granted a patent, during which time a host of copies would be on the market, many from countries where patent rights are difficult, or even impossible to enforce. Ouboter states:

> The difference between innovation in my market and, for example, the pharmaceutical sector is timescales. Product lifecycles are typically six months for me and so the market moves much

Continued...

faster than the bureaucracy of patents. And so I need to compete through constant product innovation, not through lawsuits.

With sales in over 80 countries, Micro has finally achieved the 'cool' image and broad market appeal that Ouboter intended. Yet crucially, the company continues to innovate both in the design of new and existing products and branding. They now sell a wide range of goods, including, from 2017, a small, Italian-made electric car.

MINI CASE 4.7: *Cobra, Thailand – Technological Expertise as a Market Strategy*[46]

Based in Chonburi in Thailand, Cobra International was founded in 1985. It is a leading manufacturer of robust products aimed at a wide range of water sports, from surfing to windsurfing, and from jet-skis to kayaks. The company has always had a policy of building manufacturing capabilities based on new technologies and its strength in composite materials has allowed it to move into the automotive and motorcycle components markets.

Overall, Cobra's strategy is based on its manufacturing expertise, its closeness to customers, its adoption of new technologies, and its ability to venture into new markets, including service products. Cobra is focused on quality consistency, and is the only manufacturer in the industry with ISO 9001:2000 certification. This is one of the reasons that it has become a world leader, with over 50 per cent market share, as an original equipment manufacturer supplying the top brands. Windsurf boards must withstand tremendous loads, as top windsurfers can launch their boards up to seven metres off rolling surf. Making boards that can withstand such a buffeting requires not only good manufacturing but also an intimate knowledge of fibre-reinforced composites. Cobra is constantly developing the 'combination of methodologies and materials', says Pierre Olivier Schnerb, vice president of technology. 'For example, Cobra Tuflite® technology applies techniques learnt from windsurfing to surfing.'

Another element of the company's strategy is to hire employees with an intimate knowledge of the sports for which Cobra manufactures the equipment. Kym Thompson, an Australian, has been a champion surfer, winning multiple state titles dating back to the late 1960s. He has been a member of the Australian surfing team and has worked as a professional surfboard designer since 1969. A highly skilled artisan, he has extensive experience in manufacturing and because of the quality of his boards is a living legend within the international surfing industry. At Cobra, Thompson is constantly improving quality while seeking to expand the methods and technologies used in surfboard manufacturing. Many other employees are active sportspeople and bring product and design ideas into the company. Being users themselves has helped Cobra to develop top designs and build close relationships with nearly all the top brands.

Vorapant Chotikapanich, founder and current president, thinks innovation and technology are absolutely essential for the company's competitiveness:

We are currently organized according to technology rather than industry. So, for example, the thermo compression molding division manufactures everything from windsurf boards, surfboards, wakeboards to kiteboards. It is important to apply our technical expertise across all our products, based on our own competences and those of our network of customers, suppliers and designers. It is these sorts of approaches that also us to enter new markets.

Continued...

Danu Chotikapanich, Vorapant's son and the CEO of Cobra since 2005, has developed the company's expertise to the level that it now sells engineering services. He explains: 'Our team continuously experiments with new techniques and technologies and so the Cobra engineering team has the capability to perform a full range of services for customers, including custom-designing new products or re-engineering production processes.'

Whether the technology is called 'RTM', 'low-temperature prepreg', or 'bio-source materials', Cobra International is the expert. This means it is already using these technologies in its products and also using its expertise to sell engineering services and break into new markets.

Disruptive technologies and value innovations are initially shielded from competitive response simply because they alter the whole business model so that competitors take time to recognize the threat and may find it difficult to adapt their ways of working. British Airways and KLM both started low-cost companies to compete with Ryanair and EasyJet but ended up selling out to them when the internal contradictions in running such contrary business models proved too great to handle.

Such strategies give, at best, temporary protection. In the long run, and earlier if the innovation can be copied or the patents 'worked round', a company's ability to profit from an innovation generally depends on its strength in the many other business capabilities that are necessary for success. Teece calls these factors *complementary assets*.[47] They may be generic assets, such as marketing, distribution, manufacturing expertise or brand image, which could be applied to a range of projects, or specifically adapted to the product in hand, for example a dedicated servicing activity or a capital-intensive factory. If the innovator lacks the required complementary assets for the long run, then it is vital to use the period of protection to build them up. For example, companies may push for a dominant market share that can be defended by the cost benefits of large-scale manufacturing or procurement.

Network effects (see Chapter 2) can be a powerful factor in holding a dominant design in place, and companies can seek the same effect for their own products by encouraging others to develop complementary products to use with it. The better such supporting offerings are, the more secure the main product becomes. This is a strategy used by games console manufacturers who seek to sign up the most creative game inventors to support their product. Philips and Sony used it with the CD standard and Microsoft with Windows. Support of film companies was a major factor in the battles for dominance in the video player market (Mini Case 4.8), and more recently for high-definition DVDs.

Products with network effects show a characteristic adoption curve: slow at first but reaching a rapid 'take-off' point when enough people have adopted it so that network effects kick in. If two or more standards are competing, the network effect may be enhanced by the competition so that a 'tipping point' is reached,[48] when one first emerges as the acknowledged leader and then grows rapidly at the expense of the others.

> **MINI CASE 4.8:** *Home Video – From Betamax to Blu-Ray*

The tussle for supremacy in the home video recording market illustrated the power of network effects in a mass-market product.[49] The video tape recorder was pioneered for professional purposes by RCA and Ampex in the US, with the latter eventually emerging as the dominant player. Many companies, including Philips, Sony, JVC and Matsushita took an interest in the technology from the 1950s but competition quickened in 1971 when Sony brought out the U-Matic, a cassette model that was suitable for semi-professional users, such as schools, although not yet for home use. Sony, Matsushita and JVC agreed to cross-license their patents in 1970 and the race was on to open up the domestic market.

Sony launched the Betamax, the first home video recorder, in 1975. JVC followed with the VHS a year later. Although they used incompatible cassettes and recording formats, neither had a fundamental advantage in cost or technology. Sony had the advantage of being first to market but its one-hour recording length was felt by many to be too short. VHS offered two hours from the start and a number of major companies, including Matsushita, decided to wait for it. In fact, Sony launched a two-hour machine only five months after the launch of VHS and thereafter the two formats matched each other with innovations, neither drawing ahead for more than a few months at a time.

The market for VCRs grew dramatically, from around 20,000 units a year in 1975 to nearly 20 million in 1983 and 40 million in 1987. Sony's sales also grew but its initial 100 per cent market share dropped to 61 per cent when VHS arrived in 1976 and was down to 50 per cent in 1978, 30 per cent in 1981/2 and below 10 per cent by 1985.[50]

Sony did not lose its initial advantage because of significant price or product disadvantages; its problem was that JVC, a much smaller and perhaps less arrogant company, gave much greater emphasis to signing up partners and distributors. It consequently gained a small but significant market lead early on, which was amplified into greater dominance by network effects. These became particularly strong in the early 1980s when the market for prerecorded videotapes took off. Its higher market share made the VHS system the more attractive format for suppliers of the software. In turn, the better range of prerecorded films made VHS machines more popular and so an upward spiral developed that turned JVC's 60/40 lead in terms of installed base (total machines sold) into a monopoly within a few years.

Another player in this market was Philips. It introduced its own video recorder, the 1700, in 1975/6 but did not market it aggressively. The technically superior 2000 system followed in the late 1970s but it was too late to stem the rise of VHS and was eventually withdrawn. But Philips learned the lesson of the importance of network effects and when, in 1979, it launched the CD it was in partnership with Sony. The companies immediately licensed the format widely and on favourable terms, creating a standard that was never threatened.

The VHS/Betamax battle was nearly repeated in January 1995 when Philips/Sony and Toshiba (in partnership with Warner Brothers) both announced competing video disc recorders. This time the power of the software providers and potential licensees operated directly: they combined to push for a single standard and, within the year, both parties had agreed to adopt a common format, the DVD.

THE SUCCESS TRAP

A company that makes an innovative strategic change will itself be changed by the experience. As the new capability moves up its S-curve, the competitive focus of the company typically moves away from dramatic service or product innovation towards improvements in business processes.[51] Financial, quality and manufacturing disciplines tighten, and organization, capital investment and margins dominate management discussions. The disciplines of running a mature organization are challenging and they become deeply embedded in the culture and thought patterns of the company. The trouble is that these habits can be quite wrong for handling something really novel. The most successful companies often find change most difficult because they have the most to change.

Indeed, in established companies, the structure of the firm itself reflects its way of doing business and this in itself may pose a huge barrier to radical change. Whole divisions of the organization may be formed to specialize in one module of the product. For example, Airbus makes the fuselage of its aircraft in France and the wings in Great Britain, a division of labour that admittedly has political as much as technical origins. Recently, a radical new aircraft design was proposed: a flying wing with the passengers and cargo inside. Needless to say, the proposal came from Boeing, not Airbus. It is almost impossible to imagine Airbus proposing, let alone developing, a concept that would destroy the very structure of the company. Any well-established company faced with a major change to the architecture of its product or service may face similar issues.[52]

A study[53] of 27 firms that faced a radical innovation and adopted it, found that only seven were successful. Their own established approaches, divided loyalties and the priority given to existing businesses all stood in the way of the success they sought. Experience of spin-outs at Xerox[54] found that radical new activities kept within existing divisions seldom prospered because professional managers tried to force the new businesses to work within the patterns of the old. HP had the same experiences with small disc drives.[55]

In summary: 'An unhappy by-product of success in one generation of technology is a narrowing of focus and a vulnerability to competitors championing the next technological generation … firms seem to fail by learning the lessons of survival in the short term too well.'[56]

Summary

This chapter has covered the first element of the Pentathlon Framework – innovation strategy. We have discussed the various factors, some subtle and some not so subtle, that demand innovative change. These have the common feature that they stem from the blocking of pre-existing routes to competitive advantage either through loss of scope for improvement or through satisfaction of market demand. Different analytical tools are appropriate depending on the type of uncertainty being faced, for example Scenario Planning, Roadmapping, Strategic Landscape mapping and the Business Model Canvas.

Innovation strategy must look well into the future because the need for innovative change often comes from slowly developing trends, which may be difficult to recognize and respond to. Among these are the competence ceiling and feature fatigue, which opens the threat from disruptive technologies. We introduced Kano's classification as a useful structure for understanding these and discussed responses to them. Business model innovations such as value innovation and blue ocean strategies must also be considered as possible strategies.

Finding barriers such as IPR to defend innovations from competition is important, but strong complementary assets are required in the long run.

Management Recommendations

- Plan well ahead, using tools such as roadmapping and scenarios that encourage participation from all concerned.
- Be ready to innovate in all parts of the business model.
- Understand the limits of your existing technologies or competences and be clear whether these limits may put the organization at a competitive disadvantage.
- Be alert to the possibility that the market's demand for further improvements to existing products and services may be not as strong as it was. Avoid going further than required and find new sources of competitive advantage as the old run out.
- Consider early on how to defend your innovation from competition.
- Recognize how the management style and focus for success in established businesses is inimical to new ones. Set up separate activities for new businesses as far as possible.

Questions for Students

1. Do a Kano analysis of a product of your choice, including at least three examples of each feature category, and then consider how they may move on the diagram in the next five or seven years. What has happened to the features of a mobile phone in the last seven years?
2. Consider which of the following have been sustaining innovations and which disruptive: jet engines; drive-in restaurants; plastic bottles; engineering plastics; containerization in shipping; domestic solar electricity.
3. The British government has decided that the streets of London are too crowded and the River Thames must be used to relieve the congestion. Your company has been asked to bid for the contract to provide high-density passenger traffic by boat. Plot a roadmap for the development of the business in three phases over the next 10 years.
4. Sketch a Business Model Canvas for one of the phases.
5. Online shopping for groceries and other foods is developing fast. Use the concept of the extendible core to consider how far it may go to displace conventional food shops and what these can do in response.
6. It is always assumed that companies should aim to continue for ever transforming themselves as necessary. Why should they?

Recommended Reading

1. Christensen, C.M. and Raynor, M.E., *The Innovator's Solution* (Boston, MA: Harvard Business School Press, 2003). Authoritative review of the theory of disruption. For a shorter account see: Bower, J.L. and Christensen, C.M., 'Disruptive Technologies: Catching the Wave', *Harvard Business Review*, 73(1) (1995), 43–53.

2. Osterwalder, A. and Pigneur, Y., *Business Model Generation: A Handbook for Visionaries, Game Changers, and Challengers* (Hoboken, NJ: John Wiley, 2010). Popular and accessible book on using the Business Model Canvas and related tools. In a good example of open innovation, the authors credit 470 contributors.

3. Phaal, R., Farrukh, C. and Probert, D., *Roadmapping for Strategy and Innovation* (Cambridge University Press, 2010). Complete and authoritative review of roadmapping techniques, including the strategy map.

4. Teece, D.J., 'Profiting from Technological Innovation: Implications for Integration, Collaboration, Licencing and Public Policy', *Research Policy*, 15(6) (1986), 285–305. Seminal paper on the role of IPR and complementary assets in determining the distribution of advantage from innovations.

5. Utterback, J.M., *Mastering the Dynamics of Innovation* (Boston, MA: Harvard Business School Press, 1996). Covers the evolution of markets and technologies, and the concept of dominant design. Good case studies.

6. Kim, W. Chan and Mauborgne, R., *Blue Ocean Strategy. Expanded Edition* (Boston, MA: Harvard Business School Press, 2015). Update on the authors' hugely popular 2005 book.

▶ MAIN CASE STUDY

DOMINO PRINTING SCIENCES: FACING THE LIMITS OF TECHNOLOGY [57] WITH VIDEO INTERVIEW

Domino was founded in 1978 as a spin-out from the technology consultancy Cambridge Consultants. Graeme Minto had led a project developing continuous inkjet (CIJ), a high-speed, non-contact printing technology for a client. CIJ works by making a continuous jet of ink break up into droplets that can be deflected to form characters. It is fully flexible, character by character and can print on surfaces moving at very high speed – up to five metres a second. The client eventually lost interest but Minto believed the technology had promise so he licensed the know-how and set up on his own, working out of the garage of his home.

Fortune favours the brave and by the early 1980s the company was prospering, helped by EU legislation requiring the date marking of perishable goods, an application for which CIJ was ideally suited. In 1985, Minto floated Domino successfully on the UK stock market and set about handing over the reins to a new management team with experience in running large companies. He himself became chairman and after four years moved on to other things,

leaving a thriving company with a technology much in demand, albeit in specialist applications.

Approaching the Limits of Technology

It was in the early 1990s that Domino management started to be concerned about the restrictions that the technology itself would place on the growth of the company. As Howard Whitesmith, Domino's MD at the time, commented:

> CIJ is ideal for printing simple information onto products bouncing along a high-speed production line, like putting codes onto Coca-Cola tins, for example. But it has serious limits: it's low resolution – well below what is acceptable on a printed page – and you can't make images more than about half an inch high. In fact, as the characters get larger, the printing speed goes down sharply [see Figure 4.17]. By the end of the 1980s we'd made a lot of progress with better resolution and bigger images but it was becoming more

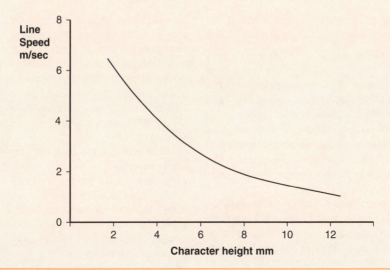

FIGURE 4.17: Relationship between Maximum Line Speed and Character Height for Continuous Inkjet Printing
Source: copyright © Domino. Reprinted with permission.

and more difficult. The technical guys were quite clear that we were starting to push up against the laws of physics.

Many of our customers already wanted to print larger characters, as well as images such as barcodes and logos but with the flexibility of non-contact printing. But we couldn't do it. And there were other things about CIJ that were less than ideal, such as the fact that we used solvent-based fluids, which can be an environmental problem. It's not as fundamental as the print size issue but here, too, we couldn't meet what our customers wanted.

Domino faced both a threat and an opportunity. Without a new technology, its rapid growth could soon come to an end, but there was obviously a demand for better performance if only it could be done. The big danger was that if a competitor moved in with something better, Domino would not only miss out on a new business opportunity but could lose many of its existing customers.

Meanwhile, competition became more intense. As David Cope, Domino's operations director, says:

In the 1980s we could still make regular improvements in product performance but in the 1990s

more competitors were coming in but there was less and less chance to keep a competitive edge in terms of the actual printing. The focus shifted to the reliability of the product, and the back-up we give in service, distribution, and sales competence. And price, of course.

Service was particularly important because if the printer breaks down, it stops a whole production line. Domino invested a great deal of effort in ensuring that its subsidiaries and distributors could guarantee quick and effective service anywhere in the world.

The Search for New Technologies

During the 1990s, Domino staff looked for ways to print larger, higher definition images onto moving products. Steve Marriott, Domino's R&D manager at the time, said:

It wasn't a big, concerted project. We just all knew that about the limitations of CIJ so we kept our eyes open for anything that might be better. We followed up magnetography, ion deposition and various kinds of contact printing. We even played with spraying a light-sensitive layer onto the surface and projecting an image onto it. But we didn't find anything that would replace CIJ.

The nearest thing was 'binary' inkjet, a technology related to CIJ but using over 100 jets for each inch of printing width instead of the single nozzle used in CIJ. It was extremely fast and could be expanded to large printing widths. There were immediate applications in the commercial printing industry for addressing and personalizing magazines and envelopes, markets in which Domino already had some presence. But the equipment would be much too expensive and complex for simpler applications.

Another possibility was 'drop on demand' (DOD), the technology used in desktop printers. It is a high-resolution technology and the printheads could be stacked together to print large images. But it was slow, very sensitive to the distance from the printhead to the surface, and could print only onto paper or cardboard. Not a suitable technology for coding Coke tins. There was huge potential if it could be made fast and robust enough for general purposes but nobody knew if this was possible.

A final possibility was laser marking. This works by rapidly scanning a small spot of laser energy over the product. It makes a mark by removing a layer (for example of printed ink) and exposing the surface beneath; or by changing the colour of the surface itself. This technology would be fast, reliable and environmentally friendly but it wouldn't be suitable for all surfaces. One drawback was that laser marking requires no ink, so Domino would forgo an important source of revenue. Another was that nobody in the company knew much about lasers, either from a technical or marketing perspective.

The Domino board realized that there was no simple solution to their problem. Whitesmith says: 'I don't think we ever asked ourselves how many different technologies we might have to take on, we just took each one on its merits and made separate business cases.' Binary inkjet was easiest to decide because it was within the technical capabilities of the Domino R&D team, and there was a clear market in commercial printing. Developing binary technology proved more of a challenge than expected but Domino launched a product in 1997 that became successful and substantially replaced CIJ in the commercial printing sector.

Laser marking was clearly a case for acquisition. In 1994 Domino bought Directed Energy, a small laser company in California that had a unique small high-power laser tube already in use in marking equipment. Domino's international distribution and knowledge of the marking market coupled with Directed Energy's technical expertise allowed Domino to take the leading position in the expanding laser marking market.

DOD proved more complex. Domino's technical team surveyed all the available examples in the early 1990s and found none that met their requirements. They adopted a 'watching brief', waiting for something suitable to be developed elsewhere. Eventually, Xaar in the UK, Spectra in the US and others brought suitable printheads to the market and Domino began to build them into products. They chose to act as integrators, selecting whatever type best suited each application.

The Difficulties of Becoming a Multi-technology Company

Within a few years, Domino changed from being a single-technology company to one with a variety of technologies and products (see Figure 4.16). Whitesmith stated:

> To start with, we were very aware that the new technologies, especially laser, meant a big change and a big challenge to the company, especially to our distributors. So we set up separate divisions to drive the new products along, complete with their own specialist sales forces. That didn't last long: it was too expensive and our customers sometimes got confused when they got calls from several Domino salespeople apparently in competition with each other! We ended up with a hybrid arrangement where every salesman handled the complete product range but they had local specialists in each technology to call on for support.

Lasers developed well and made up 20 per cent of Domino's business by 2015. It started as a niche business selling very profitably to a number of big 'early adopter' companies such as Anheuser-Busch. Then in 2001 the laser market apparently 'crossed

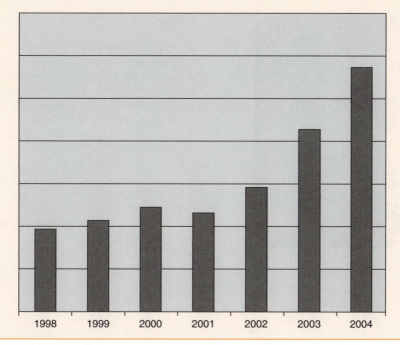

FIGURE 4.18: 'Crossing the Chasm': Domino Lasers Unit Sales

Note: vertical scale not shown.

Source: copyright © Domino. Reprinted with permission.

the chasm' (see Figure 4.18). Simon Bradley, the laser business manager, says: 'Quite suddenly sales took off and we noticed that instead of all coming from our big customers in the US they were suddenly coming from many new customers all over the world.' As the business expanded, Domino started to buy in different types of laser tube for specific applications. Eventually, as the market matured, it became possible to buy all the tubes it needed at competitive prices. The California laser factory was closed and the division was absorbed into the mainline business. The specialist technology of Directed Energy had launched Domino into laser marking but from now on, the company's complementary assets in manufacture, marketing, distribution and service would drive the business forward.

Domino went on to acquire several other companies, each with its specialist competence and technologies, including Print and Apply labels, Thermal Transfer printing and some variants on CIJ. Cope says this all made for a more complex operation 'but that just reflects the real complexity of the markets and products'.

Meanwhile, as anticipated, DOD was steadily developing and starting to be used for printing onto tiles, cartons, and even in small printing houses. It was only a question of time until it would invade the much larger market for general printing. Domino could not compete in these markets through the printhead technology so it invested in acquisitions to build strength in equipment design and application. By 2012, the digital printing market was the company's strongest growth area and had huge potential for the future. In 2015, the board accepted a takeover bid for just over $1 billion from Brother Industries of Japan. Both parties agreed that the next phase of expansion would need the financial muscle of a much larger company.

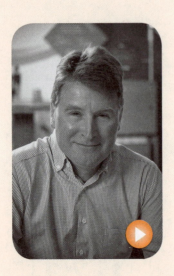

Reflective Questions

1. How can companies recognize that their technology is facing a technical limit?
2. Do such technological limits necessarily matter?
3. What issues face a company adopting a new technology that fully replaces its current one?
4. What problems might a single-technology company expect to face when it adopts new, overlapping products?

Now visit www.palgravehighered.com/gm to watch Nigel Bond discussing the changes in Domino Printing Sciences throughout the years; for example, integrating new technology companies into the group.

GENERATING INNOVATIVE IDEAS

INTRODUCTION

To become more innovative, most companies concentrate intuitively on *idea generation – ideation –* through suggestion schemes and brainstorming. However, there is more to this element of the Pentathlon Framework than simply increasing the number of ideas generated within an organization. Innovation requires not only creativity but also the application of knowledge and effective ways of recognizing customers' requirements. It also may require sourcing external ideas – open innovation – by, for example, canvassing on the internet or licensing ideas from other organizations. And once novel ideas are generated, it is important to consider how to protect them. This early stage of innovation is often referred to as the *fuzzy front end*. It is difficult to manage partly because many commonly held views on creativity and ideas are wrong. For example, although often heard, imploring employees to 'think outside the box' is definitely not a good way to stimulate creativity. So, in this chapter, we will explain how the insights from innovation management research can help us manage the fuzzy front end.

The perspective of customers and users is crucial and termed the *voice of the customer* (VOC). As we discussed in Chapter 1, VOC has been a research topic over the past three decades and it has been recognized that customers often struggle to articulate their needs. Therefore, it is necessary to move from traditional market research, which relies on direct questioning, to enhanced techniques, such as observation and indirect questioning. These can identify breakthrough ideas that either revitalize existing markets or create new ones. And when innovative ideas have been generated, companies must think about how they can protect them.

In concentrating on the fuzzy front end, this chapter covers:

- The key management issues at the front end.
- The way creativity can be stimulated in an organization.
- The types of knowledge that are generated in organizations and how they can be harnessed to increase innovation performance.
- Techniques to identify customers' needs, particularly their hidden needs, and gain ideas through open innovation.
- Protecting the value generated by innovation.
- How the Swedish healthcare company Mölnlycke manages its fuzzy front end.

MANAGING THE FUZZY FRONT END

In the Pentathlon Framework, the front end is the funnel of ideas that are developed into concepts for products, services and business models. These concepts then go through to project selection and some to implementation. An idea is typically 'a mental picture of a possible and feasible solution to a problem'.[1] Note the word 'problem'. The thing that distinguishes an idea from a mere random thought is that an idea has some value, whereas a thought is, well, just a thought. The reason an idea has value is that it can solve a problem. So being open to discuss problems – and their obverse, opportunities – is important.

Without the generation of ideas, there can be no innovation, but without recognizing problems and opportunities, there will be no ideas. As its striking name implies, the fuzzy front end (FFE) is difficult as it challenges executives to manage uncertainty. The FFE is about exploration, and the managers and teams who excel in this phase of innovation tend to be those with the mentality of explorers – they thrive in visiting the unknown, where familiarity, experience, certainty, maps and detailed planning are left behind.

The Scope of Ideation

The FFE should generate ideas for incremental, breakthrough and radical innovations. But growth comes largely from breakthrough and radical innovations. As discussed in Chapter 1, the innovation ambition of a company is the amount of breakthrough and radical innovation it requires to reach its growth targets. So breakthrough and radical ideas are especially needed. A recent survey showed that top companies, on average, generate a successful product from five FFE ideas, whereas less successful companies start with 12 ideas.[2] Thus it appears that successful companies produce higher quality ideas that warrant development.

Much of the research on ideation has concentrated solely on product innovation.[3] However, the FFE also needs to generate ideas for new services, for services that can support products, for processes by which innovations are produced, and for new business models. Generating and protecting such ideas – effective ideation – requires creativity, knowledge, deep customer insights, and involving the user (see Figure 5.1).

Ideation is also impacted by adjacent elements of the Pentathlon Framework (see Figure 5.1). The influence of innovation strategy on the FFE is that it sets the targets (for which ideas need to be generated), and sets the innovation ambition (determining the right balance of breakthrough and radical ideas). If

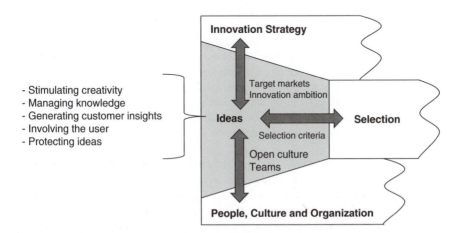

FIGURE 5.1: Interactions of the Adjacent Elements of the Pentathlon with Ideation

targets are not clear, then employees may submit ideas that are original but not useful, as they fall outside the aims an organization wants to address. For example, when Whirlpool, the US domestic appliance manufacturer, challenged employees to submit innovative ideas, one submission was for fitness training equipment.[4] This was rejected as the board perceived it to be too far from its core markets and competences. In defining the scope of ideas to be considered, management teams need to achieve the right balance between being open enough but not wasting time on ideas that will never be adopted by the business. Start-ups face a different challenge: they do not have existing markets and competences to consider but need to commercialize their ideas fast enough to stay in business.

In some organizations prioritization is disconnected from the FFE, in that the people creating the ideas do not know the criteria by which they will be judged. But it has a positive impact on the quality of ideas when the selection criteria by which concepts will be selected are known. For this reason, Richardson Sheffield, a leading manufacturer of kitchen utensils, makes sure that its selection criteria are clear to teams working at the FFE (see Mini Case 6.6). Corporations need to be careful that their selection mechanisms, particularly those based on financial projections (also Chapter 6), do not kill all the breakthrough and radical ideas.[5]

Teams and Organization

Choosing the right teams to work on the FFE and having an appropriate organizational culture will support effective ideation. The emphasis in the ideation phase is on learning and experimentation, so it requires a unique approach and, usually, a dedicated team with the skills to carry out the particular studies that are required. If the innovation opens radically new ground for the organization, it may be wise to recruit new people, or make use of universities and outside consultants.

During implementation, companies use cross-functional teams but during the FFE, the involvement is often restricted to R&D and marketing. But diverse teams are more likely to develop novel perspectives. Swedish healthcare manufacturer Mölnlycke has found it advantageous to involve a full cross-functional team, as the different functional areas had very different perspectives, which led to greater insights.[6] For the same reason, IDEO, a successful design consultancy, has linguists and biologists in its innovation teams. One function that can bring novel ideas at the FFE is industrial design, as designers empathize with customers and know how to design technically and emotionally attractive products and services.[7]

In large, established organizations, radical ideas may meet resistance. Thus to ensure openness to ideas, organizational design plays a role at the FFE.[8] For example, ideation 'will fail unless senior managers create the right organizational structures, provide the proper resources, allow sufficient time for experimentation and learning, and personally engage'.[9] Pharmaceutical company Eli Lilly has found it necessary to develop a separate, parallel organization for developing breakthrough and radical ideas.[10] The company's 'early stage organization' develops concepts for new drugs and concentrates on demonstrating that the concept is viable – so-called 'proof of concept' – before passing the concept to R&D for further work.

Some innovations may even need to be kept secret in large corporations (kept 'below the corporate radar') for a time. This is called *stealth innovation* and it allows ideas to be developed to the stage when they have a better chance of gaining approval.[11] In Germany, companies such as Agilent Technologies (a top manufacturer of chemical text equipment), often allow engineers to work part time on *Schubladen* ('bottom drawer') projects;[12] ideas they want to personally investigate without making them official 'projects'.

Planning

At the FFE, the focus of work is not to deliver the innovation, but to learn what is possible and the best way to go about it. In the broadest sense, it is about reducing uncertainty to the point when either work on the concept is terminated or it can proceed with confidence that the significant risks and uncertainties are clear. Although the effort and expenditure at the FFE may be relatively small, most of the outcomes of any full project or product are essentially determined by decisions made early on. So this is the time when management involvement pays dividends. Sadly, top management attention is too often concentrated in the later stages when the activity and expenditure are highest, rather than when the opportunities are to be found.

The planning of work for the ideation phase is likely to be tentative, hardening up as time goes on. Nevertheless, ideation teams need, right from the start, a clear project charter: a one-page brief that sets out the purpose and key objectives of the project. At the FFE, a project charter is essential but by the time the implementation phase is reached, it must have developed into a clear specification for what is to be delivered.

Early Stage Decisions

The FFE is a dynamic phase in which many ideas are generated, quickly evaluated, developed further into concepts, or rejected. Creativity theory identifies a *divergent stage*, in which many ideas are generated, and a *convergent stage*, at which the many ideas are winnowed down to the most promising ones (see Theory Box 5.1). In the very early stages, the selection will be based on intuition,[13] but the sooner more formal methods are introduced the better, as we discuss in Chapter 6.

FFE decision-making consists of identifying customer problems, defining the nature of these problems, generating ideas of how to solve them, and developing full product (or service, or business model) concepts.[14] An effective product concept will have 'a description of a new product idea, plus its primary features and customer benefits'.[15] Selecting the ideas to progress further into full concepts needs to balance the risk of accepting ideas that look attractive but then fail for technical or market reasons (*false positives*), against the risk of rejecting ideas that looked unattractive but could have been successful (so-called *false negatives*). Even an idea that has previously failed in the market may be worth

CHAPTER 5

reconsidering, as markets often take longer to develop than expected and an old idea may now be attractive.[16]

An example of a false positive is the Sinclair C5 – an early electric vehicle developed by UK inventor Clive Sinclair, which did not sell. A famous example of a false negative is phase contrast microscopy, which Frits Zernike demonstrated to Zeiss, a leader in optics and optoelectronics. One of the company's scientists rejected the idea, saying: 'If this had any practical value, we would ourselves have invented it long ago.' (This is an example of the *not invented here* (NIH) syndrome, where researchers reject existing ideas and prefer to develop their own solutions; see also Mini Case 8.2). However, phase contrast microscopy became the first technology to enable high resolution observation of unstained biological specimens. It won Zernike the Nobel Prize and has since become a standard technique in electron microscopy.[17]

The review processes at the FFE must be flexible and open-minded. This is because at this early stage, it may be absolutely right to change direction as new learning comes to light. Thus reviews should not just check that things are on track but also that the right work is being conducted. And the project team must be held accountable not for reaching the planned result but for doing efficient studies and well-conceived experiments. Such reviews are very different from those for projects at the implementation stage.

THEORY BOX 5.1: *Creativity Theories*[18]

Four diverse topics, which have been researched by psychologists, can give important ideas for managers on creativity:

- Divergent and convergent thinking
- The relationship between intelligence and creativity
- Stages of problem-solving
- Association theory.

The American psychologist J.P. Guilford developed the theory of *divergent and convergent thinking*. The former is the type of thinking stimulated by open-ended questions that can have multiple answers. For example, someone can give many answers to the question 'What moves on wheels?' Convergent thinking, in contrast, is the type of thinking that is required by conventional questions with one answer, such as 'What is the currency of Sweden?' During the FFE of innovation, there is normally a divergent thinking phase where many ideas about customers' needs are being generated, followed by a convergent phase where these are scrutinized.

The relationship between intelligence and creativity has been researched extensively and has been an area of controversy. Some researchers originally argued that there was no difference between these individual attributes. Extensive empirical research has led to *threshold theory*, which views creativity and intelligence as not entirely independent: people with an IQ below a certain threshold will not be creative. Surprisingly, research also indicates that people with exceptional IQ levels may also struggle to be creative. This is because deep expertise can lead to *Einstellung,* a mental block based on assumptions, where an expert sometimes is blind to certain solutions. This can be solved by bringing diverse ideas and opinions to bear. Another important observation from psychology is that certain people are much better

Continued...

at identifying and defining problems than others. Often, clearly defining the problems is a major step towards resolution.

Theory can help with problem-solving. Solving problems is a key application of creativity, and in the 1920s, Graham Wallas was the first to recognize the stages of problem-solving. He delineated:

- *preparation*, in which the problem is identified and defined
- *incubation*, where a problem is internalized and put aside ('sleep on it')
- *illumination*, when a solution emerges (the *eureka* moment)
- *verification*, where the solution is tested and improved.

The incubation stage is somewhat of an enigma – when thoughts emerge, they seem sudden because, often, the mental processing that has occurred has been unconscious. The concept of *insights*, substantial steps in thinking, and how they emerge is useful. An insight can emerge as information is structured and ordered, as visual information is used, when a mental block is overcome, when information is randomly combined, and when an analogy is found. All of these can be seen from the perspective of *restructuring*, where the representation of a problem is changed, sometimes multiple times, until a different understanding emerges. The solution to the 'nine dot' insight problem (discussed below) is an example of how thought needs to be restructured to achieve a solution.

Association theory stresses that the way ideas are generated forms a chain, as one idea leads to another. It indicates that more original ideas often emerge later. The conception that better ideas arise later in the process of creativity means that teams should be allowed enough time to solve problems. Some researchers argue that association is less important than metaphorical thinking and the use of analogies, which allow us to restructure our thinking. Diverse views and teams can help enable the restructuring of thoughts, through different associations.

Overall, creativity theory guides managers to know when to stop divergent thinking; to focus on creativity when hiring new team members or selecting teams; to ensure that problems are clearly defined; and to allow enough time for a chain of ideas to lead to a full solution.

CHAPTER **5**

Generally, the front end is perceived as fuzzy because it requires managers to address themes that are inherently complex and ambiguous. These include managing knowledge, creativity and ideas; gaining deep customer insights; and finding ways to protect intellectual property.

STIMULATING CREATIVITY

There are a number of myths about creativity. Two of the most widespread are: creativity will be stifled by attempting to manage it; and employees should simply be encouraged to think 'outside the box'. This expression, which has gone global and is used in Hindi and Chinese, comes from the popular 'nine dot' puzzle (see Figure 5.2), which has been used in countless seminars and as a test for creative thinking.[19] It requires nine dots to be joined with four straight lines. Many people struggle and miss one dot (see lower left diagram) because they assume that the straight lines must remain within the boundaries of the 'box'. One solution (see bottom right diagram) 'breaks' this assumption, solves the problem, and led to the ubiquitous 'think outside the box'. Here, as so often, it is the hidden assumption that blocks creativity.

Stimulating creativity requires managers to go beyond the myths and have a good understanding of creativity. Then they can begin their management of the FFE. We will cover the following areas:

- The different types of business creativity
- The factors that influence individual creativity
- How group creativity can be managed
- Key creativity techniques.

Types of Business Creativity

It is important to differentiate between business creativity and mere invention. Business creativity goes beyond invention and original thinking to commercialization.[20] A reminder of this important difference is that James Murray Spangler invented the first portable electric vacuum cleaner and was granted a patent in 1908. But it took the business mind of William Henry Hoover to make it a commercial success.

There are three types of business creativity: *exploratory*, *normative* and *serendipitous creativity*. Exploratory creativity is closest to most people's understanding of creativity – the identification of new opportunities – and is particularly necessary during the FFE. It is 'unconventional thinking, which modifies or rejects

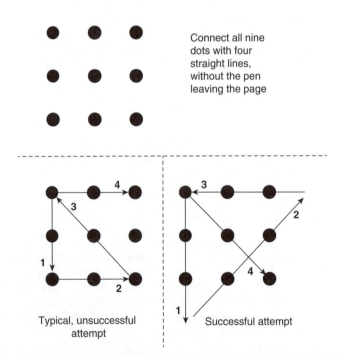

Connect all nine dots with four straight lines, without the pen leaving the page

Typical, unsuccessful attempt

Successful attempt

FIGURE 5.2: The Nine Dot Puzzle

previous ideas, clarifies vague or ill-defined problems in developing new views, or solutions'.[21] Exploratory creativity requires divergent thinking (see Theory Box 5.1).

The most important characteristic of normative creativity is that the problem to be solved is clearly defined. Problems are often articulated in a vague or indirect way and only certain individuals possess the skills to identify and exactly specify problems. Therefore, an important task for managers is to clarify the essence of the problems that their employees should focus on but without narrowing the focus too much, so as to leave scope for real originality. Normative creativity is needed to solve the many problems that arise in developing technological solutions to customers' needs during new product development (NPD).[22] James Lovelock, famous inventor and creator of the Gaia theory of the earth, said he is always surprised about how often he invented something in response to someone asking: 'Can you think of a way to do …?'[23] It is also often required for process innovation, for example when a manufacturing facility is not delivering high quality. The opportunities for normative creativity are enormous in the service sector and solving customer problems is a catalyst of service innovation.

Serendipitous creativity acknowledges the role of accident and good fortune in, for example, discovering a new application for an existing idea. The most famous example is 3M Post-it notes, where a glue that was being developed for permanent fixing failed but for which a very successful alternative use was found. Serendipitous creativity, by definition, cannot be managed easily, although looking for ideas from different sectors or bringing in experts from other fields can help because 'the best innovators aren't lone geniuses. They're people who can take an idea that is obvious in one context and apply it in not-so-obvious ways to a different context.'[24] Managers can help by emphasizing the important issues that need an answer so that staff will be ready to grasp the serendipitous idea when it occurs.

Knowing the three types of business creativity gives managers a greater ability to increase innovation. For example, asking employees for ideas for new products and services gives them an exploratory task, whereas specifying a customer problem that the product or service needs to solve gives employees a normative task (which is easier to respond to). Depending on the task involved, the most appropriate combination of individual and group creativity techniques can be selected.

Individual Creativity

The creativity of key individuals plays an indispensable role in many organizations. But individual creativity is a contentious subject in the academic literature. Some researchers take an elitist perspective and argue that most of the creativity in an organization originates from a few individuals. Others contend that creativity is a social process, and everyone has the potential to be creative under the right circumstances. We will discuss the factors that influence individual creativity and then how individuals' potential for creativity can best be unleashed in teams. The importance of linking individual and team creativity is exemplified by the following quote from the Economist Intelligence Unit: 'Innovations may begin in the mind of a single individual, but if they are to generate valuable products or services they need to be developed by a community of thinkers.'[25]

From his extensive research, Mihaly Csikszentmihalyi, a psychologist at the University of Chicago, stresses the importance of *knowledge* to make creativity possible. Both individuals and teams need to be able to access relevant information and experts (*knowledge domains*) to be creative.[26] For example, in the complex field of pharmaceutical research, where hundreds of chemicals may be considered in the search for an effective medication, the volume of ideas being considered makes it necessary to have good data management – even highly talented individuals with good memories simply cannot remember all the data that might be relevant. For this reason, Evotec AG, a German-owned provider of chemical services to the pharmaceutical sector, has created a database of the thousands of chemical experiments it has conducted. Similarly, with the growth of material being published, it is becoming increasingly difficult for scientists to have a grasp of more than their own specialized field. So, knowledge management is increasingly important to support creativity, which is why we will discuss it later in this chapter.

The myth has developed that individual creativity results from a flash of inspiration and the metaphor of the light bulb – invented by the American Thomas Edison – has become inseparable from creativity. One element of the metaphor is the instantaneous way a bulb lights and, for many, this stands for how creativity happens: without precedent, or planning. The view that creative ideas emerge spontaneously originates from the romantic era, where poems and other great works of art were credited by their authors to moments of inspiration. For example, Samuel Taylor Coleridge claimed that he wrote his famous poem Kubla Khan in one attempt, rather than through hard work over a period of time. Closer scrutiny of the many similar stories about spontaneous creativity shows them to be untrue (and earlier drafts of his poem were found in Coleridge's papers after his death).

Psychologists have been interested in the relationship between creativity and intelligence (see Theory Box 5.1), and creativity and personal traits. Much of the research looking for the typical traits of creative individuals is inconclusive. Csikszentmihalyi's work does show, however, that extremely creative individuals have 'complex personalities', by which he means that such people display contradictory traits. For example, they may switch quickly from being humble to being proud, introvert to extrovert, and traditional to being rebellious. This may make the job of managers harder but if this is the price to pay for more highly creative individuals, it is almost certainly worthwhile. Csikszentmihalyi's and others' work shows that managers should nurture the creativity of their key individuals by:

1. Giving them full access to the knowledge domains related (directly and indirectly) to their work. This means ensuring that company research scientists attend the leading conferences in their field and even allowing them to spend time at universities each year. In service, it would mean having key individuals visit leading service companies in other sectors, to gain a different perspective.

2. Motivating them to develop a passion for the subject on which they are concentrating.
3. Providing the time for them to immerse, even indulge themselves, in the issues. Initially, the process of creativity is divergent, when ideas, information and alternatives are being collected. Then the process becomes convergent, as some possibilities are rejected. Providing sufficient time is often difficult because of the focus on business results, but managers need to avoid extreme time pressure, as this is detrimental to creativity.[27]
4. Avoiding personal uncertainty. For example, the prolonged threat of a downsizing has a massive negative impact on personal creativity.[28]

Team Creativity and Culture

The level of creativity in an organization is not only dependent on individual creativity. Companies need to create an atmosphere and culture in which innovation project teams excel. As this is intimately connected with the management of people (the fifth element of the Pentathlon Framework), we will save our main discussion of this topic for Chapter 8. The vast majority of innovation projects involve teams. The lone inventor, striving to develop a successful product, is a rare phenomenon; although James Dyson, the inventor of the bagless vacuum cleaner, worked in isolation on countless prototypes, before finding the right design.

Research shows that nurturing team creativity is largely a question of avoiding barriers to creativity. Teresa Amabile, a professor at Harvard Business School, has conducted a number of studies and identified the key issues as:

1. Matching the right group of individuals with the right challenge. Too often, the match of people to projects is poor, or the team is not sufficiently diverse.
2. Giving teams the autonomy and the means to meet the challenge they are given but not the freedom to choose the challenge themselves.
3. Vague or ill-defined problems are where discussions should start; such problems often mark the starting point of successful innovations.
4. Project strategy needs to be developed in discussions with employees, as this helps them feel confident about the direction and ensures their 'buy-in'.
5. Making suitable resources available (including time, space and money). A certain amount of time pressure can be positive but team creativity plummets when unrealistic schedules set by management lead to mistrust and employee burnout.
6. Building teams with diverse backgrounds and skills, shared excitement in achieving the goal, and a climate where the contribution of all employees is recognized.
7. Ensuring timely and appropriate supervisory encouragement. For example, if management takes too long to respond to team proposals, this has a negative impact on team motivation.
8. Guaranteeing support from the rest of the organization, particularly for innovation teams working under time pressure. Similarly, protecting teams from organizational politics is important.

CHAPTER 5

Very strong company cultures – *cults* – can decrease creativity.[29] Pressure for uniformity or elitism blocks creativity, especially openness to others' ideas. At the team level, management must avoid *groupthink*, when a team develops an unrealistic view of the issues and disdains opposing views. Authoritarian leadership can make groupthink more extreme.[30]

Diversity helps creativity, as theory tells us and practice shows (see Mini Case 5.1 on Allianz). Process innovation in manufacturing companies has largely been the responsibility of quality teams. Groups of manufacturing employees meet regularly to identify opportunities for improving the efficiency of processes. However, if a group consists only of manufacturing employees, the ideas generated may be too narrow. For this reason, JCB, which designs and manufactures earth-moving equipment, always invites other functional areas to its manufacturing quality meetings. For instance, sales representatives are responsible for stimulating discussion on which of the process improvements are likely to have the most impact for customers.

> **MINI CASE 5.1:** *Allianz Versicherungs AG – Mixed-up Ideas*[31]

Increasingly, companies need to bring in a fresh, outside perspective into the way they define their innovation strategy. Too often, organizations have a too narrow perspective on their markets and this prevents them generating breakthrough ideas. Creativity is often the result of a market being viewed from different standpoints and this approach has been very successful at Allianz Versicherungs.

Allianz is the largest insurance provider in Germany. Dr Karl-Walter Gutberlet, an Allianz board member with responsibility for private customers, also serves on the board of Mondial Assistance Deutschland GmbH. This company is a business-to-business service provider, which runs calls centres for insurance companies, to manage claims made to them. Gutberlet's idea was to add this service philosophy to the insurance viewpoint. The result is an innovative new product that has taken the German market by storm and won an innovation prize from *Capital* magazine.

The new product was officially called 'Allianz Haus- und Wohnungsschutzbrief' (house and home emergency cover) but is better understood as the equivalent of a car breakdown service – a 'household emergency service'. Normal house insurance may cover the costs of solving a problem (for example, a blocked water pipe) but the consumer is still left with the job of finding someone to do the repair. Taking the analogy of the breakdown services available for cars, the new product covers the costs and also provides a hotline at Mondial, which organizes a quick repair by a qualified tradesperson and the payment; and this is for around €5 per month.

Klaus Stemig, a member of the board of Mondial Germany, was appointed to be the project manager for the 24-hour household emergency service. A cross-functional team was assembled for the project comprising personnel from Allianz, Mondial and Agemis, a facility management company that provides part of the service provider network for the product. The kick-off was in July 2003 and the product was introduced (with the full supporting networks of service providers) in April 2004. Despite a time to market of only eight months, extensive market research was used to test and improve the initial ideas generated in brainstorming sessions involving the two companies. Over 400 inputs from interviews and focus groups defined the key product features. The completed product includes cover for heating failures, plumbing problems, removal of wasps' nests, emergency babysitting, emergency pet care and storage of copies of crucial documents such as passports.

Continued...

The cross-functional team had to solve many unexpected problems during the development, but having all functions represented and both companies' networks meant that these could be quickly addressed. Stemig says:

> For example, information technology is typically the bottleneck in the development of insurance and service products but our representatives from IT were on board from the beginning … We are proud that we not only developed a new concept but that we developed it on time, matching a very challenging schedule. For example, it wasn't easy to create a new network of tradesmen set up to respond 24 hours a day across all of Germany but we did it.

The product sold more than double the first year's goal of 25,000 policies and has established a reputation for Allianz as an innovative player in a conservative market. Spotting strategic opportunities is often about bringing in a different perspective and it is management's role to ensure that an organization's paradigms are challenged. Allianz is continuing to try and do this and is rolling out further new products, such as 'Accident 60 Active' for senior citizens who need not only health insurance but also help in finding and organizing the health services they require.

Creativity Techniques for Innovation

Many creativity techniques can be used during innovation projects. The choice of which technique is most appropriate depends on the type of creativity needed, for example normative or exploratory, and the number of individuals involved. J. Daniel Couger, from the University of Colorado, describes 22 creativity techniques, with recommendations on which work best with individuals or teams, and which can be used for exploratory or normative creativity.[32]

The constant use of only one creativity technique can lead employees to lose interest and so it is disappointing to learn that a survey of executives found that *brainstorming* was by far the most popular technique for generating ideas.[33] Companies that are aware of different techniques have two advantages: they can choose the most suitable techniques to match the issue at hand, and provide variety for their employees. We will discuss five creativity techniques that can be helpful for innovation, both during the FFE and later. Effective creativity consists of not only encouraging employees to think differently but also bringing different fields of knowledge into consideration (see Theory Box 5.2).

CHAPTER **5**

THEORY BOX 5.2: *Koestler's Frames of Reference*[34]

Arthur Koestler wrote a classic book on creativity in the 1960s and his central premise provides a useful tool for innovators.[35] When we think, we do so using frames of reference – using particular ways of thinking (rules, habits, associative contexts and so on) that have been useful in the past. These are the mental equivalent of the physical reflexes and movements, which our bodies apply, unconsciously, to particular situations. For example, an engineering frame of reference includes a strong focus on measurements to describe the workings of a system. Frames of reference are efficient ways of thinking but they can be difficult to shake off. According to Koestler, the creative act is bringing a new, previously

Continued...

unassociated, frame (F_2 – Figure 5.3) to bear on a topic with an existing frame of reference (F_1). Frames of reference are similar to the philosopher Thomas Kuhn's concept of paradigms: patterns and rules that define boundaries, and shared sets of assumptions. Koestler's theory reminds managers of the importance of bringing diverse views and knowledge from different domains together.

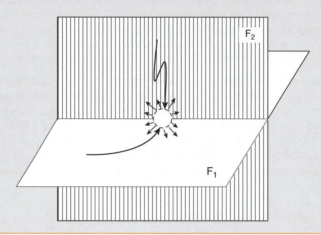

FIGURE 5.3: Creativity as the Intersection of Two Different Frames of Reference
Source: Figure 2 from Act of Creation by Arthur Koestler reprinted by permission of Peters Fraser & Dunlop (www.petersfraserdunlop.com) on behalf of the estate of Arthur Koestler. Copyright © 1964 estate of Arthur Koestler.

Brainstorming and Brainwriting

The original and most widely known creativity technique is *brainstorming*, which was developed in the 1950s for use with groups. A group of people are asked to describe any ideas that come to mind as solutions to a problem (normative creativity), or as opportunities for new products, services of businesses (exploratory creativity). The ideas are written on a flip chart where everyone can read them and one idea leads to another (association – see Theory Box 5.1). An experienced moderator typically records the ideas and reflects these back to the group to stimulate further discussion (leading to association and restructuring). The evaluation of each idea is suspended during the idea collection phase, so that potentially good ideas are not prematurely rejected (preventing 'that will never work' judgements). For example, IDEO, a Californian design consultancy, encourages employees to ring a small bell if they hear someone unduly criticizing an idea.

Brainstorming is based on the assumption that people are naturally creative and that by deferring judgement on the quality of ideas until a sufficient quantity has been collected, some really good ones may emerge (c.f. association theory's recognition that better ideas often emerge later). The limitations of brainstorming are that certain people may dominate the discussion and the first idea that emerges strongly influences all subsequent discussions (see Theory Box 6.3). The more effective variation is *brainwriting*. In this, individuals are given a couple of minutes to think of their ideas and write them down. Each idea is then shared with the group; this ensures that a large number of ideas are generated and moderates the dominant idea and person in the group.

Left–Right Brain Technique

The *left–right brain* technique ensures a 'whole-brain' approach to identifying an opportunity or solving a problem. Typical left-brain functions include speaking, writing, calculating, logic and deliberating and so on. In contrast, our right brains control our abilities for intuition, spatial perception, art and visualization. A creativity task can be formulated to drive thoughts from both our left and right brains and two columns on a flip chart are used to summarize the contrasting ideas.

For example, the improvement of a service product can be analysed from a left-brain (analytical) perspective, asking questions such as: What is the core product? How quickly is it delivered? What are the key performance indicators? In contrast, the right-brain (emotional) approach would lead us to ask questions such as: How do they feel about the service? Can we paint a picture that captures the customer's perspective of our service? The contrast between the insights gained from left- and right-brain focused questions help to generate new ideas.

Five Ws, One H Technique

The *five Ws, one H* technique is a versatile technique that can be used at all stages of innovation. It helps enhance our understanding of a problem or an opportunity by asking five 'W' questions ('who', 'what', 'where', 'when' and 'why'?) and one 'H' ('how'?). Specific W and H questions are developed for the topic and the answers to the Ws tell us more about the issues. The answer to the H question provides ways to implement the ideas generated by the Ws. The technique is very useful for investigating reports of product problems.

A medical electronics company received a number of complaints that a widely sold blood pressure measuring device was not working properly. Investigation using the five Ws, one H technique helped understand the problem better. The 'where' and 'why' questions prompted an analysis of what was different about the hospitals that were filing complaints, compared to the majority of hospitals that had no problems. It emerged that the device worked well, except if the patient was shivering. The hospitals that made complaints were found not to heat their recovery rooms (where patients are placed following operations), as a warm ambient temperature slightly slows the recovery from an anaesthetic. Most hospitals heat their recovery rooms to near normal room temperature. The H question was: How can the device be made to work when the patient is shivering? The answers to this led to improvements in the device and accurate blood pressure measurements in all conditions.

Attribute Association

Attribute association can be used to improve a product, a process, service, or a business model.[36] The starting point is to create a list of its attributes. This can be based on a company's internal views, or on market research exposing the customer's perception. For a vacuum cleaner, the list of attributes would include the ability to clean carpets, flooring, stairs, corners and so on, plus other factors such as manoeuvrability, design and so on. Each of the product, service or process attributes is then reviewed using one of the approaches in Table 5.1: Can an attribute be *modified*, *subtracted*, *multiplied*, *divided*, or *unified*?

TABLE 5.1: Modifying Attributes

	Approach	Explanation	Service and manufacturing examples
1.	Modifying the nature of attributes	Also called *product morphology analysis*, this approach takes the main product attributes and sees how these can be modified	• Home insurance normally covers the costs of repairs. Allianz has gone further and offers a home 'breakdown' service, with fast call-out of qualified tradespeople guaranteed for any household problem (see Mini Case 5.1) • Early domestic coffee machines had a simple glass pot to hold the freshly brewed coffee. However, companies such as Braun have changed this attribute to a vacuum flask, which keeps the coffee warm until needed
2.	Subtraction or simplification of attributes	Removing certain attributes may simplify a product and make it more attractive to certain segments. This is an attempt to prevent what some writers have called *feature creep*, the tendency for development teams to always add more features to products	• Some mobile phone companies have successfully marketed a 'receive calls only' contract, which is popular with parents who want to be able to contact their children but do not want them making too many calls • Not every subtraction attempt will be successful or positively perceived by customers, e.g. the colourless 'Crystal Pepsi' failed when it was introduced to the market in 1993
3.	Multiplication of attributes	An existing product attribute is copied and offered, sometimes with a modification of the function of the repeated attribute, multiple times in the product. The multiplication leads to a specific benefit	• A classic example is the 'Mach 3' razor from Gillette. The three blades all cut but the first two, which are set at different angles, drag across the skin to raise the beard for cutting by the second or third blade. Now the Gillette 'Fusion' has five blades (see Mini Case 1.2) • A service example is Europcar's multiple rental agreement. Busy executives can purchase rental agreements of, for example, five days a month but these can be multiple rentals, such as one day at five different airports

TABLE 5.1: Continued

	Approach	Explanation	Service and manufacturing examples
4.	Division of attributes	This essentially looks at the product architecture and how physical or functional components are grouped together	• In the automotive sector, 'mechatronics' (the combination of software-driven electronics and mechanical components) is making a big impact. Companies such as Daimler AG are moving previously mechanically controlled functions into software, to optimize vehicle performance • DialAFlight, an internet retailer of travel and tourism services, has carefully divided its service augmentation between its website and its call centre to give a personalized service (see Mini Case 3.4)
5.	Unification of attributes	Assigning new functions to existing attributes. This can also lead to simplification	• Toro, a US lawn mower manufacturer, has designed a rotary blade that has an aerofoil shape that cuts grass into much smaller pieces and circulates it longer. So grass cuttings can be left on the lawn and the need for a grass box has been removed. Effectively, a mixture of task unification and simplification

Source: based on Goldenburg et al., 2003[37] and Altshuller, 1996[38]

The process of reviewing and modifying attributes requires practice and there are no hard and fast rules for which of the approaches given in Table 5.1 is the most appropriate for a particular application. Complex products may benefit most from subtraction or task unification. Or an experiential service might benefit from multiplication of its most valued attribute. Of course, the review of product attributes does not simply have to be conducted internally; observing users can give other insights.

MANAGING KNOWLEDGE

Creativity is grounded in knowledge. Over the past 20 years, much has been written on *knowledge management* – how an organization can stimulate and effectively utilize knowledge. One caveat is that creativity researchers have found that deep expertise and knowledge can lead individuals to mental blocks (*Einstellung*) and being trapped by their own experience,[39] and so it is important to bring new knowledge into discussion (see Theory Boxes 5.1 and 5.2). From the vast field of knowledge management, we have selected three topics

CHAPTER 5

we think are important for those responsible for managing innovation. These are the nature of knowledge, how knowledge can be captured, and how it can be transferred.

Nature of Knowledge

Knowledge has two main forms: *explicit* and *tacit*.[40] Explicit knowledge (also known as *articulated* or *declarative knowledge*) is formal and systematic, easily communicated and shared. It can be *codified* – summarized in a written or symbolic format that can be easily shared. Examples of explicit knowledge are instructions manuals, textbooks, standard operating practices (SOPs – detailed descriptions of manufacturing and other management processes), and sheet music. In contrast, tacit knowledge is hard to express, formalize, or write down. It is highly personal, often based on individuals' mental models (which they may not even be aware of themselves), and is usually taken for granted.

An illustration of tacit knowledge is the master craftsman who can create a perfect artefact but cannot readily explain all the steps taken, or the particular ways the materials are chosen, formed, worked, reworked and finished. Master craftsmen have a high level of knowledge, most of which is not written down. Another example of tacit knowledge is the experienced cook who has a favourite dish they can cook without weighing the ingredients, or timing the stages of cooking. In order for the dish to be cooked by someone else, the recipe needs to be prepared, and the timings, weights and other details codified. Tacit knowledge is practical, context specific and not easily shared as it is 'in the heads' of certain individuals. It can be invaluable to a company, as tacit knowledge is difficult to copy but, since it resides with individuals, it is lost if they leave. Customers' tacit knowledge of how they use products can lead to breakthrough products (see Mini Case 5.2 on Miele).

The two types of knowledge reside in various locations within an organization. Databases, computer systems, publications and the internet (including wikis – shared sources of knowledge built collaboratively, such as Wikipedia) are repositories of explicit knowledge. Sometimes, however, what tends to be stored is information as opposed to knowledge. Information alone, without interpretation or experience, is of limited use. Also, the sheer volume of unstructured explicit knowledge can sometimes limit its usefulness (this is particularly the case with much of the internet). Tacit knowledge resides with individuals in organizations, their expertise and heuristics ('rules of thumb'). Stimulating interactions between such individuals, including discussions on their 'routines for doing things', is a way for managers to share tacit knowledge.

To manage tacit knowledge to support innovation, three recommendations can be given:

1. When certain individuals have tacit knowledge that is vital, companies need to ensure that it is shared with colleagues through regular interactions.
2. Key solutions, approaches and so on need to be documented in a way that the organization does not lose vital information if individuals leave.
3. Customers' tacit knowledge needs to be recognized and captured.

> ### MINI CASE 5.2: *Miele – Watch, Listen and Roll*[41]

Miele, the German household appliance manufacturer, is aware that customers cannot articulate exactly what they need. Instead, gaining insights is a subtle process of interpreting the meaning of what is said (and seen). To generate deep customer insights the company regularly uses ethnographic market research. Dr Olaf Dietrich, director of product management laundry care, says:

> We are in constant contact with our users and have a 'watch and listen' philosophy at Miele. By this we mean that we realize that it is essential for our marketing and R&D people to see issues first-hand. You can only really understand customer needs if you were present to see the issues.

In a Miele investigation of the implications of the growing number of people with allergies, a mother was observed carefully 'hoovering' her child's mattress three times. When asked why, she said: 'Because then I know it's clean.' (Note, she did not say: 'I need a vacuum cleaner with a technology that monitors when things are clean.') To solve the need, Miele developed a vacuum cleaner with a hygiene sensor at the nozzle. This has a 'traffic light' indicator, which turns from red, through amber, to green as cleaning progresses. This sensor is a breakthrough feature for the increasing number of people who have allergies; it allows them to know when a room is dust-free, or that an allergic child's mattress is free of house mites. Note, the feature was not developed in response to an explicit customer request. Rather, it was the recognition that the parents of children with allergies spent more time cleaning because they feel guilty if they do not clean enough. And so they adopt a ritual of vacuuming several times just to be certain their child's room is dust-free. The market research behind this product was conducted in close cooperation with an association for people with allergies. Through this, Miele also identified the opportunity for a range of products specifically designed for people with allergies and this link also means that Miele has established a lead over its competitors that makes its innovations harder to copy.

The vacuum cleaner work was several years ago but Miele has not stopped innovating. Dietrich explained:

> We recently observed users regularly 'overdosing' the amount of detergent used in washing machines. They almost never measure the powder correctly. This is because users are not really aware how the load in the drum and the degree of soiling affects the amount of detergent needed. Most people also don't know that too much detergent damages clothes in the long run.

The solution from Miele is called 'TwinDos'. An automatic (liquid) dosage function is integrated into washing machines with two cartridges (a two-component detergent system for whites and coloureds). The user tells the machine the degree of soiling, whereas the load is measured automatically by sensors. The machine determines the exact amount of detergent, which is then pumped in. In this way, the user does not need to dose manually anymore (even for stains).

CHAPTER **5**

Capturing Tacit Knowledge

A leading researcher on tacit knowledge has been Ikujiro Nonaka, a professor at Hitotsubashi University in Tokyo.[42] He recognized the importance of making tacit knowledge accessible, particularly in R&D settings, and identified transfer mechanisms.[43] Tacit-to-tacit knowledge transfer is called *socialization* and an apprentice learns from a master through observation, discussion, and trial and error under supervision. Once the apprentice has learned, their knowledge is also largely tacit. Managers can promote socialization by creating a work environment in which less experienced employees observe and learn from senior colleagues. For example, some R&D departments have new project managers 'shadow' senior colleagues.

Externalization is the name given to the process of converting tacit to explicit knowledge and this may require the development of new symbols and methods of codification. An example of tacit knowledge being converted into explicit knowledge is found in the history of music. Troubadours, travelling medieval musicians, learnt music and lyrics through apprenticeships, travelling with older musicians. Pope Gregory sponsored the development of a musical notation. This enabled the spread of songs and music including the chants named after him. Further developments such as the metronome allowed accurate capture of how fast the composer intended a piece of music to be played.

Individuals with tacit knowledge may be reluctant to support the process of externalization because of the time required for this task. Evotec AG, the provider of chemical services to the pharmaceutical sector mentioned earlier, found that a database of experiments was not enough. It arranged weekly informal tutorials in which scientists explained how they had solved specific problems. This allowed experience to be externalized and passed on to newer colleagues. (This was also much easier than persuading experienced scientists to try to document their knowledge.) Metaphors, analogies and models are often effective means by which insider knowledge can be made understandable for outsiders. Our own research shows that engineers' knowledge can be stimulated by having them base their discussions of problems around metaphors and stories.[44]

Another key concept of knowledge management is *communities of practice* (CoPs). These are groups of people who share a common context to their work, use common practices, share identities and can provide the social context for knowledge transfer across organizational boundaries. For example, engineers form a community with a common background, similar experiences and ideas that can make the communication between engineers in different organizations more effective than between engineers and marketing people within one organization. CoPs are important as they can be viewed as the means by which companies can profit from their employees' exchange of knowledge with broader communities. For example, the ideas for a 'graphical user interface' passed through the community of engineers from Rank Xerox to Microsoft, where they were finally implemented in Windows. Hallmark Cards, US greeting card manufacturer, has created what it calls 'customer communities of practice'.[45] Ideally, about 100–150 interested customers are linked via a website and encouraged to exchange ideas, comments, experiences and diaries. Hallmark's approach is a useful example of how internet technology is being used to stimulate customer ideas.

L'Oreal, the French cosmetics giant, has recognized that tacit knowledge typically stays 'within national boundaries, where workers share a language and cultural and institutional norms and can draw on strong interpersonal networks'.[46] To ensure that tacit knowledge can be passed internationally, the company actively develops and promotes managers from multicultural backgrounds; as it has found that such people can be very effective at spotting the opportunities for innovations in local markets, which people rooted in one culture tend to miss.

Capturing tacit knowledge from key employees is important, as is tapping customers' tacit knowledge on products and services. This latter point will be discussed later in this chapter, when we describe how to develop deep customer insights. Once knowledge has been captured, it needs to be transferred appropriately, to support innovation.

Promoting Knowledge Transfer

Tacit knowledge from internal and external sources, for example customers or universities specializing in a particular technology, can be helpful in innovation. The knowledge that certain individuals or groups possess can be important in solving technical or commercial problems. Customers have tacit product knowledge that needs to be tapped using sophisticated market research techniques. Although tacit knowledge is easy to understand, it is more difficult for managers to take advantage of – or *broker* – tacit knowledge.

An anecdotal study of IDEO, the product design consultancy based in California, showed that it brokered knowledge in four ways.[47] First, by bringing together people with knowledge of different markets, countries, products and technologies, the chance of unique ideas emerging is higher. Second, collections of tangibles, prototypes, toys and multitudes of other items are displayed prominently in the company's offices, to remind people of ideas and stimulate further ones. Third, IDEO focuses on creating new uses for old ideas. For example, in Nike's Air technology (running shoes with shock absorbing soles), IDEO took ideas previously used in medical inflatable splints. Fourth, constant testing using prototypes will show what works and can be commercialized.

As more becomes known about tacit knowledge and its generation and transfer, it is likely that managers will be provided with more concrete tools and approaches. One of the current approaches is known as the *learning organization* (see Theory Box 5.3).

CHAPTER **5**

THEORY BOX 5.3: *The Learning Organization*

The best-known theoretical contribution to the knowledge management debate is organizational learning. This is 'the capability, which enables an organization to acquire and process new information on a continuous basis to elevate knowledge and improve decision making'.[48] Peter Senge, an expert on organizational learning, identifies five key elements of learning organizations:[49]

1. Promote and value the *personal mastery* (expertise) of individual employees. Recognition of individuals helps generate a high level of commitment to the organization and its learning.
2. Encourage *mental models*, which illustrate the way in which an organization and its processes work. Drawing and discussing key processes helps discover new ways of thinking;
3. Promote *team learning*, so that teams continuously adapt successful practices from other teams, both internal and external to the organization.
4. Have a *shared vision*, which is the collective form of personal mastery. This is the level of ambition an organization has to have *the* key expertise in an area. This stimulates the organization's learning, which is only possible if it deeply matters to employees.
5. Utilize *systems thinking*, the ability to understand the cause-and-effect relationships inherent in organizational processes. It is the cornerstone of organizational learning and interlinks Senge's other four elements.

Utilizing Existing Knowledge

Although innovation is normally associated with the 'new', ideation can also build on existing knowledge. As discussed in Chapter 1, some ideas such as Ikea's 'flat pack' are not new but that does not make them any less important. Existing knowledge is particularly important in normative creativity – solving problems. Both databases of patents (documented inventions) and Mother Nature can provide useful pointers for innovators.

Learning from Patents – TRIZ

TRIZ is a form of problem-solving based on patents developed by Genrich Altshuller, the Russian engineer and inventor.[50] Altshuller worked in the Moscow patents office and became interested in the way many patents he read seemed to fit a pattern and solve problems in similar ways. The acronym TRIZ is based on the four Russian words for the 'theory of inventive problem solving'. Since his work in the 1940s, over 2.8 million international patents have been grouped into categories.

Patents document how particular problems are solved and they can be grouped by the generic problem they are solving. For example, an automotive patent might be specifically concerned with engine temperature control but at a generic level it is concerned with methods for cooling. Altshuller grouped patents by generic problems and found that, based on the underlying science, there are a limited number of ways to solve a particular problem. TRIZ databases have been created by consultants and these allow engineers working on a specific problem to look up the generic ways in which such a problem has been solved and to find the use of patents connected to these solutions. In this way, rather than relying on brainstorming (which is dependent on the knowledge around the table), problem-solving based on a TRIZ database ensures that no possible solution is overlooked and provides example ways that problems have been solved (in example patents). TRIZ databases provide access to the explicit knowledge of previous generations of scientists and engineers.

The second use of TRIZ is that it can help identify design trends and opportunities for improvement. For example, physical design tends to start with straight lines, regular folds. Over time, more complex designs using curves emerge. Comparing current products against these trends can generate ideas. Mars Inc. uses TRIZ regularly and a good example is the packaging of the ubiquitous Mars bar. The wrapper used to have straight lines and was sealed like a parcel. Consequently, it was awkward to open. Nowadays, the ends of the wrapper have a serrated edge, which means that they can be torn open easily. Another example is the soles of running shoes, which have increasingly intricate designs to absorb shock

The third way that TRIZ helps is by providing insights into how *design trade-offs* can be managed. Say, for example, a particular component needed to be strengthened to withstand wear but could not be heavier. TRIZ matrices allow designers to look at the ways in which this particular trade-off and many others have been solved previously. Once again, the theory of creative problem-solving provides access to a body of knowledge summarizing millions of inventions.

Somewhere, sometime, somebody has already faced a similar problem and so learning from this is quicker and more effective that starting from scratch.

The Cold War led to TRIZ being largely unknown in the West until relatively recently. Now, it is being widely applied as a way of finding quicker solutions to product design problems. Slowly, TRIZ is also being adapted to the service domain,[51] although currently there is no database of service ideas. Overall, TRIZ is most useful for the type of problem-solving found in NPD but the idea of trends can also generate useful ideas during FFE.

Learning from Nature – Biomimicry

Darwin's theory of evolution stresses that the life forms that have the ability to adapt are the ones that survive. Thus every species on our planet has a rich history of 'research and development', or, in other words, nature can be considered as an endless testing laboratory. *Biomimicry* uses examples from nature to inspire innovation – introducing a new frame of reference, to use Koestler's terminology. There are increasing numbers of examples where product designers have used ideas from nature. One is the 'winglets' at the end of commercial airliners' wings, which mimic birds' wings. Another is a motorcycle crash helmet that prevents injuries at lower impacts through the use of a flexible membrane covering the helmet. This mimics the way the skin on the skull helps deflect minor impacts.

The website www.asknature.org provides an excellent, evolving database of examples from nature. Similar to TRIZ, biomimicry is most useful in NPD but nature can also inspire the divergent thinking needed during FFE. For example, a healthcare manufacturing company has looked at how ideas from nature can be applied to reduce hospital infections.

Ideas from Emerging Markets and Competitors

Moving specifically to creativity in new product and new service projects, it can be noted that many innovations have come from the developed world. However, there is increasing recognition that the challenges faced in the developing world can inspire novel solutions, which can later be applied globally. *Reverse innovations* are products or services that are developed to solve the needs of the developing world but later find global markets.[52] The manufacturer Harman, which produces car 'infotainment' systems (combined radio, navigation and heating controls), launched a project based in China and India to develop a product for Asian requirements and at a third of the cost of similar, Western-developed innovations (see Mini Case 5.3). The company deliberately chose project managers with international experience and who were more culturally aware and moved Western engineers to work in India.[53] Later, many of the cost-saving ideas were successfully transferred back to the West.

Large organizations can harness ideas from remote markets but ideas are often blocked, because headquarters do not recognize the potential. So regional managers need to be particularly adept at explaining the ideas and gaining the necessary backing by acting as *bridgers*. They need to share their understanding of local markets and show how an innovation can be of benefit in more developed markets.[54] The Japanese quality movement uses the word *gemba* to

CHAPTER **5**

mean 'where things actually occur … raw, untainted information'.[55] Originally, this expression was used to stress that manufacturing managers must spend sufficient time on the production floor, if they are to learn how to improve production efficiency. Gemba is analogous to the way ethnographers refer to going out 'into the field' and going to the gemba is also used to describe ethnographic market research.

Note that reverse innovations should not be confused with *reverse engineering*, where a company buys a competitor's product, and takes it apart to identify a competitor's ideas. Reverse engineering has been used by many Japanese companies to gain ideas from their competitors.

MINI CASE 5.3: *The Jaipur Foot – Indian Low Tech*[56]

What is the appropriate level of technology? This question should be asked constantly by product design teams, as the customers and end-users of products and services will seldom be persuaded to adopt a higher level of technology than is appropriate. A clear example of this is the 'Jaipur Foot', which has become a household name in the war zones of the world.

Biomedical engineers have long studied the workings of the body and designed artificial limbs, some of which incorporate microprocessor control and feedback systems. Unfortunately, the demand for prostheses is heavy; a direct result of the millions of antipersonnel mines that have been laid during wars over the past 50 years. Mines are cheap and easy to produce, simple to lay and extremely difficult, dangerous and time-consuming to clear. The civilian populations in war zones pay a heavy price and many people in countries such as Afghanistan have lost and continue to lose limbs as they return to their villages and agricultural fields following conflicts. However, these civilians do not have the money or access to the high-tech devices found in the biomedical engineering laboratories of the West. Enter the Jaipur Foot.

It was not only the cost of conventional artificial limbs that acted against them being adopted, it was also that their design did not fit with the lifestyle of people in Asia, where many people squat, eat and sleep on the floor. The Jaipur Foot is the solution and it is made of simple materials – rubber, wood and aluminum – which are not only readily available but can also be worked by local craftsmen. Typically, it takes 45 minutes to build, lasts five years and costs about $30.

GENERATING CUSTOMER INSIGHTS

Product innovations often fail. One study found that 34 per cent of new product developments do not fully reach their business objectives,[57] while another study found the figure to be 90 per cent.[58] The latest major study showed that in better companies nearly 20 per cent of their new products do not succeed (and less effective organizations have nearly 50 per cent failure rates).[59] A key reason that new products fail is that they are too similar to other offerings on the market; they are not *differentiated*.[60] Service products also need original features (either in the service product or augmentation) to avoid the chance of market failure. Market research is common for consumer products and increasingly business-to-business (B2B) manufacturers are interacting more intensively with their customers.[61] Additionally, organizations that want to develop a new business model – to create and capture value – perceive customer insights as essential in deciding what value should to be created. So the voice of the customer (VOC) is a fundamental part of the FFE (see Mini Case 5.4 on Bixolon).

VOC is fundamentally important in managing innovation. Therefore, we will give an explanation of a wide number of methods for identifying customer needs. We have personal experience of applying many of these methods in B2B and B2C companies. Ideally, a combination of methods should be used.

MINI CASE 5.4: *Bixolon – Printing's on the Move*[62] *with video interview*

Bixolon is a South Korean company that was founded as a spin-off from Samsung in 2002, originally called Korea Printing System. Since then it has grown and won numerous awards, such as the Korean Ministry of Trade, Industry and Energy 'Tower of Exports' awards for $20 million in 2004 and $50 million in 2013. It produces specialist printing devices for retail POS (point of sales) and has developed a reputation for innovation in mobile printing devices.

J.S. Oh, Bixolon's president, says: 'Decision makers for POS systems are normally very conservative. Such systems enable sales transactions and any problems immediately lead to lost revenue. So all the components of the system must be top quality and market-proven. Buyers absolutely insist on that.' Buyers are also very cost-sensitive, which makes it hard to differentiate with technology. However, Bixolon has successfully differentiated itself by constantly spotting key market trends.

One of Bixolon's strategic moves was to recognize the mobile market and one of the products that has enabled its enviable growth was its mobile printer, SPP-R200. This communicates with data processing devices and it had unique features at the time of its market introduction. 'The product concept emerged when we had a customer conference in 2006. Customers told us that demand for printing outside buildings was increasing and current mobile printers made by major American companies like Zebra and Intermec were too bulky.' The key issue was to come up with a compact but rugged design, and a specially selected cross-functional Bixolon team spent a whole year achieving this. The product was a big success and it established the company's reputation as a leading mobile printer manufacturer.

Bixolon was also the first manufacturer to add Bluetooth certification, to enable easy integration of its devices into a wide variety of POS systems.

Innovation is relentless in the POS market, and so the requirement to understand customers' needs is never-ending. J.S. Oh says:

> Except the tier 1 market, with retailers like Walmart, Carrefour and Tesco, the POS market in any country includes a number of small and medium-sized POS system companies. They all have their own requirements for POS hardware. So it is hard to get consistent ideas from customers on future innovation. Our customers' needs are always on the move – so that's why we never stop listening.

Now visit www.palgravehighered.com/gm to watch J.S. Oh discussing market trends and the role of customer insight in creating a new product in more detail.

Identifying Customer Needs – Traditional Approaches

Traditional market research uses *surveys*, *focus groups* and *interviews* to obtain customers' inputs. In surveys, current knowledge of products, markets and customers is used to frame the questions asked and a suitable sample is determined. In selecting the sample, companies strive to identify a representative group of customers whose answers will be indicative of the whole market. It should be noted that in some markets buyers and users may be different persons. For example, in a transport company the buyer is usually not the driver. In addition, the purchase decision might not be made by a single person but by what the marketing discipline refers to as the *decision-making unit* (DMU), which can consist of several people. In B2B markets particularly, the DMU can be complex as the individuals involved can have different expectations and requirements. For example, in the medical electronics market, the DMU for equipment consists of doctors and nurses who will use the products, bioengineers who will maintain them, and hospital purchasing managers who will consider the investment. Each has a different focus but all need to be convinced that it is the right equipment.

Survey methodology is well known and will not be discussed here. Suffice to say that the design of a good questionnaire is not easy and, to be effective, questionnaires need to be *piloted*. For an overview of the crucial aspects of designing and using questionnaires, refer to the classic texts on the subject by Oppenheim[63] and Dillman.[64]

Focus groups are small groups of customers or users who have sufficient experiences in common to discuss a specific topic, related to products or services.[65] Normally, they are invited to meet at a neutral location, the discussion topic is introduced and visual examples of the subject matter are often on display. The discussion is stimulated with a broad question posed by the moderator, who also ensures that all participants contribute equally, and that all topics are discussed, with observers being hidden behind a two-way mirror. Video recordings may also be used. Once the data have been collected, the analysis of surveys or focus groups leads to a list of product attributes required by customers. Traditional methods are fine for confirming incremental needs but they need to be combined with techniques to identify hidden needs.

Traditional techniques such as surveys and focus groups are valuable. But customers may not be able articulate their needs, as their ability to comment on the products and services is limited by their prior experience. This means that traditional methods of market research tend to lead to incremental improvements[66] rather than breakthrough ideas.[67] The requirements that customers find it difficult to articulate are termed *hidden needs* (or *emerging needs* or *latent needs*). Leading companies are particularly good at generating deep customer insights.[68] The best companies are also using more market research tools, such as ethnography, online communities and so on.[69] New approaches to understanding customers have also been found to be needed in the service sector.[70]

Hidden Needs Analysis

Companies with the ambition to develop breakthrough and radical new products, services and business models need to identify customers' hidden needs. Figure 5.4 gives an overview of how different market research techniques and methods to involve the user can be used in combination (see also the main case study on Mölnlycke Health Care at the end of this chapter). When an organization has the ambition to develop breakthrough and radical innovation, this means that, in addition to the traditional survey and focus group research, techniques such as *repertory grid analysis* and *empathic design* (described below) need to be used to supplement traditional ones. As Figure 5.4 shows, market research data collection and analysis lead to insights and ideas (for new products, services, or business models).

Ideas should be tested early on and in a practical way with users through *lead user workshops, experimentation* and *rapid prototyping, crowdsourcing* and *competitions.* Such approaches allow intense interactions with customers and allow ideas to be enhanced. This, in turn, leads to better product definition and then these product attributes can be prioritized using *conjoint analysis.* As shown in Figure 5.4, *hidden needs analysis* should lead to more radical products but it is challenging and the best companies 'are far more adept at converting data into insights and insights unto action'.[71] There are an increasing number of published examples where companies have based successful product innovations on addressing hidden needs that they have identified (but this is an area where there is an urgent need for researchers to investigate how often such approaches lead to breakthrough products).

Surprisingly, the adoption of enhanced market research techniques has been slow. A survey of 70 Finnish companies producing B2B products showed the usage to be very low: 58 per cent of respondents do not use any techniques and 27 per cent use only one technique.[72] It was found that companies were not using innovative approaches to market research because they did not have the expertise and perceived the data difficult to collect and analyse. Specialized consulting companies, such as BuzzBack (see Mini Case 5.5), IDEO, PDD and WhatIf!, are the vanguard. We will look at the enhanced techniques in detail, starting with repertory grid technique, so as to understand their potential for discovering hidden needs.

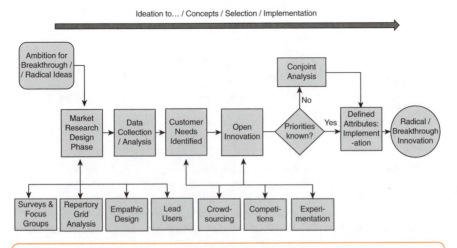

FIGURE 5.4: Hidden Needs Analysis in Product Development

> **MINI CASE 5.5:** *BuzzBack – Qual with the Quant*[73] *with video interview*

BuzzBack Market Research was founded in the US in 2000, with offices in London and a team of 40 experts. The company helps both corporations and emerging brands to develop new product concepts, position their brands and select their communications strategy. It has a broad range of clients from fast-moving consumer goods, healthcare, financial services, restaurant chains and advertising.

Some managers think that market research faces a dichotomy: deep insight methods such as ethnography can only be used with small numbers of consumers, while corporates want the reassurance that insights are based on large samples. BuzzBack is squaring this circle with clever online approaches that aim to combine the best of qualitative and quantitative research.

Martin Oxley is MD BuzzBack Europe, a veteran of top market research companies, and a fellow of the Market Research Society. He and his colleagues have built a set of tools that enable consumers to share their (innermost) thoughts about products – be they rational, irrational, or emotional. BuzzBack is careful that its approaches are based on good (social) science. For example, the company uses the 'Johari window' (see Figure 5.5), a theory on group dynamics developed in 1955 by psychologists **Jo**seph Luft and **Har**ry Ingham. Oxley says:

> Applied to market research, the Johari window illustrates that consumers can be helped to go beyond the usual rational responses since they do not have full knowledge or willingness to express their emotional views and opinions. Therefore, subtle projective and enabling techniques are needed to tease out such views and feelings. With this in mind, we provide a portfolio of online methods, which can be scaled from small to large samples. We know people are more honest with a computer.

	Known to others?	
	Yes	No
Known to Self? Yes	**Known Self** Things we know about ourselves and others know about us	**Hidden Self** Things we know about ourselves but are hidden to others
Known to Self? No	**Blind Self** Things others know about us that we do not know	**Unknow Self** Things neither we nor others know about us

FIGURE 5.5: Johari Window
Source: adapted from Luft, J., Group Processes: An Introduction to Group Dynamics (USA: McGraw-Hill Education, 1984). Copyright © 1984 McGraw-Hill Education. Reprinted with permission.

The tools that BuzzBack uses to surface consumer feelings and perceptions are based on a mix of proprietary ideas, and ideas from social science. All of them make it possible for people to easily share their views and feelings online. For example, 'Concept Focus' is a tool by which consumers can highlight the text they find most important in a new product concept description. Similarly, the tool 'eCollage™' allows people to select from a collection of images to convey their 'collage' of feelings. Another example

Continued...

is BuzzBack's 'Blobs' tool, which was based on the ideas of the therapist Pip Wilson, who developed ways to help abused children articulate their thoughts. In market research, it allows people to characterize their mood and feelings by selecting amorphous cartoon figures and adding text.

The tools are constantly in use for client companies. Recently, they have been applied to investigate perceptions in different countries around 'indulgence' – the sort of foods that consumers perceive as a treat. This made it possible for a dairy manufacturer to better under-stand the opportunities for its products, including the most likely times of day they would be eaten and by whom. Oxley concludes:

> We find that management teams are more willing to give their support to projects where the market research has been conducted with significant numbers of customers. So online methods are crucial but we strive to make sure that the quantity does not compromise the quality of insights.

Now visit www.palgravehighered.com/gm to watch Martin Oxley discussing deep customer insight and using new tools for market research in more detail.

Repertory Grid Technique

Repertory grid technique (RGT) is a powerful market research tool for identifying customer needs. The technique was developed for use in psychology. It enables interviewees to articulate their perceptions of products and services and taps their tacit knowledge. The technique is a structured form of interviewing that leads to a matrix of quantitative data – the *repertory grid*. Surprisingly, even though the potential of the technique has long been recognized, it is rarely used. This is partly because of the skills an interviewer needs to conduct interviews.

To understand how the technique works, we will explain how an IT service provider used it to improve its service offering. These service providers install and maintain computer networks for companies, including tasks such as upgrading PCs and training employees in the operation of software. Interviewees would be managers at client companies who have experience of the services they had outsourced, for example purchasing managers. The interviewee would be asked to name six outsourced services with which they are familiar – these we will call service products A, B, C, D, E and F. The services are what are termed the *elements* of the test and each is written on a separate (postcard-sized) card, as shown in Figure 5.6(A). A wide range of services can be selected and Table 5.2 shows that the interviewee has chosen an assortment, including facility management and financial auditing. The IT service provider's own service is also on the list (Service B), as is one direct competitor (Service E).

Note that the cards have been prenumbered in a random sequence (5, 1, 4, 3, 2 and 6), to enable the selection of a random sets of cards. From Figure 5.6, it can be seen that the name of the first service (A) has been written on the card numbered 5, whereas Service B is written on the card numbered 1. After the cards have been annotated with services, the interviewee is presented with a set of three

TABLE 5.2: The Augmented Service Offerings Chosen by the Interviewee

Service products
Service A – Facility management (security and cleaning)
Service B – IT services (IT service provider)
Service C – Data warehousing
Service D – Financial auditing
Service E – Competitor's IT services
Service F – Employee training seminars

cards (termed a *triad*). Figure 5.6(B) shows the triad consists of Cards 1, 2 and 3, corresponding to Services B, E and D respectively. The interviewee is asked: 'How are two of these services similar and different from the third?' A typical response (a *construct* in RGT terminology) – a service attribute – could be that two of the

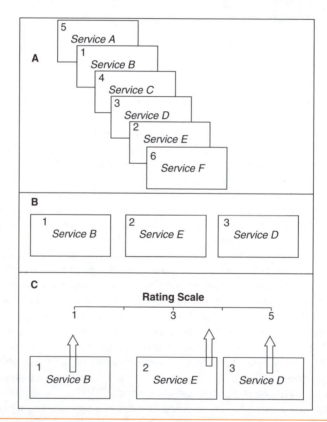

FIGURE 5.6: Example of a Repertory Grid Interview

Note: A – the elements of the test, services, written on cards; B – the first triad presented to the interviewee; C – the rating of the services in the first triad.

Source: Goffin, K., 'Repertory Grid Technique', in D. Partington (ed.) Essential Skills for Management Research (London: Sage, 2002). Copyright © 2002 Sage. Reprinted with permission.

service providers are 'easy to work with, good communications', whereas working with the third 'is difficult'. The way in which the interviewee differentiates between the elements in the triad reveals how they perceive the different services. Each of the three services is then rated against this first attribute. As shown in Figure 5.5(C), this is normally on a 5-point scale, on which Service B has been highly rated on 'easy to work with' (1), whereas Service D was given a minimum rating (5).

Further triads are used to identify further attributes. The interviewee is not allowed to repeat attributes and so each new triad elicits at least one new attribute. As each attribute is determined, the interviewee is asked to explain what they mean by, for example, 'fast response' and they will give details such as timings and the actions they expect. RGT interviews are normally recorded, as this captures the customer's exact words. Following each construct, the interviewee is required to rate all the services against it using the same 1–5 rating scale. These ratings form the repertory grid, as shown in Table 5.3.

In Table 5.3, the six elements of the test – Services B to F – are shown across the top of the grid. Down the side are the attributes identified during the interview. The stars around the ratings indicate which cards were in the triad that elicited particular attributes. For example, the first attribute was elicited using a triad consisting of Cards 1, 2 and 3 (indicated by the ratings with stars: *1*, *4*, *5*). It can be seen that the Service B is rated as 1 ('easy to work with, good communications') but Service D is difficult to work with and received a rating of 5. Looking at the ratings, it can be seen that on the attribute 'fast response', Service C is rated mid-scale (3) but rated as poor (5) on the attribute 'absolutely reliable service (guarantee)'. The ratings tell us not only about how an interviewee perceives services; they also give us information on the importance of particular attributes. For example, the ratings on the attribute 'clearly defined service product' are

TABLE 5.3: A Repertory Grid on Outsourced Services

Attributes	Card 1 Service B	Card 2 Service E	Card 3 Service D	Card 4 Service C	Card 5 Service A	Card 6 Service F	Poles
Easy to work with, good communications	*1*	*4*	*5*	5	1	1	Difficult
Fast response to problems	1	4	5	*3*	*4*	*4*	Slow
Professional employees	*2*	5	*3*	4	*1*	1	Little knowledge
Clearly defined service product	3	*2*	1	*3*	1	*1*	Poorly defined
Service is good value for money	*3*	*3*	5	1	*5*	5	Expensive
Absolutely reliable service (guarantee)	5	4	*4*	*5*	5	*5*	Less reliable

not as widely spread (they only range from 1 to 3) as those for 'good value for money' (where the ratings range from 1 to 5). This shows that this latter attribute differentiates more strongly between the elements. Hidden needs tend to be indicated by low ratings for all elements.

> **MINI CASE 5.6:** *Equant – Repertory Grids in Practice*

One company that has used the repertory grid technique extensively is Equant, the world's largest data network provider – offering network design, integration, maintenance and support services in over 180 countries. The company always placed a high emphasis on being 'customer focused' and regularly reviewed the results of customer satisfaction surveys, comparing its performance to competitors. Although such surveys provided useful 'benchmarks', Equant recognized that it did not measure performance against the criteria that were most important to customers.

In the late 1990s, the company offered excellent network performance and global service availability. Consequently, it received better ratings than its competitors in surveys and this could have led to complacency. However, a project was launched to investigate whether there were aspects of service quality that were important to customers but were not covered by the surveys. Liam Mifsud, business support manager at Equant, designed and conducted repertory grid interviews, in which the elements of the grid were a range of the customers' current service providers. Interviewees (IT directors and managers) were asked to name six suppliers that their companies did business with, and these elements were presented in triads. Since the suppliers named covered a wide range of companies, from IT, to reception services, to office cleaning, respondents generated interesting constructs. These included a far wider range of service quality criteria than those covered by the customer satisfaction surveys.

The results showed that customers' perceptions of service quality were not solely based on technical measures, such as coverage or network performance. Equant was able to identify 10 new criteria on which its performance was being judged. For example, customers emphasized intangible elements of service quality, such as the responsiveness and flexibility of account management teams, and the quality and competence of the support staff they came into contact with. Mifsud says: 'This provided us with a valuable means of understanding the changing needs of customers.'

Source: Goffin, K., 'Repertory Grid Technique', in D. Partington (ed.) Essential Skills for Management Research (London: Sage, 2002). Copyright © 2002 Sage. Reprinted with permission.

The grid also can be used to derive a *cognitive map* of an interviewee's perceptions of products and services. Deriving and interpreting this map is beyond the scope of this discussion but it can give further insights for product and service designers. Further details can be found in the book *Identifying Hidden Needs: Creating Breakthrough Products.*[74]

Repertory grid technique can also be used to generate ideas for manufactured products. HP's Medical Products Group first used repertory grid interviewing over 20 years ago and it helped the company identify the emerging importance of product attributes, such as 'easy to set up' and 'easy to clean', in the medical equipment market.[75] A focus was placed on these factors in all subsequent developments. Mini Case 5.6 on Equant gives an example from the service sector.

Ethnographic Market Research

Dorothy Leonard-Barton, professor at Harvard Business School, has promoted *empathic design* and defines it as 'the creation of product or service concepts based on a deep (empathic) understanding of unarticulated user needs'.[76] The term *ethnographic market research* is more widely used, indicating that the data collection and analysis methods are largely drawn from ethnography. The foundation of the technique is *systematic observation* but it also includes *discrete observation, contextual interviews*, and what we will term *empathy building*. Empathic design can help organizations design products and services for people in developing countries, as these can be very different to the products and services of the West (see Mini Case 5.7 on SEWA). For example, GE, the US conglomerate, has recognized that innovation teams need to be located in developing countries, to ensure that there is a deep enough understanding of local needs. This has led to the development of medical equipment that can function in rural areas where there is only intermittent electricity. Beth Comstock, chief marketing officer at GE, says: 'We've established customer innovation centers close to where new solutions are needed, and we help our employees there abandon their assumptions about what customers need. Instead, they observe how people actually live and work.'[77]

> ### MINI CASE 5.7: *SEWA Bank – Cash, Loans and More*[78]

It is a shocking statistic but more people in India have to live on less than $1 a day than the entire population of the US. The cash-poor segment of the market is ignored by institutions in many countries but the emergence of India as a powerhouse for low-cost innovation is changing views. The *base of the pyramid* (BOP) market is now attracting significant interest. But to design products that fit BOP needs requires companies to develop a deep understanding and empathy with people in developing markets. Innovations in products and services are starting to be offered that until recently would have been thought unimaginable. In products, the Tata Nano car remains poised to be a low-price breakthrough but has not quite made it. In the meantime, in the world of personal finance, dramatic changes have taken place.

Microfinance – small loans for very poor people – has been very successful through the Grameen Bank in Bangladesh and the SEWA Bank in India. The SEWA Bank was opened by the Self-Employed Women's Association (SEWA) in 1974, to help self-employed people gain access to working capital and loans to grow their businesses, without having to resort to extortionate moneylenders. The bank specializes in loans for women, as women have been found to utilize loans more effectively than men, and save some of their earnings. Ela R. Bhatt, the bank's founder, says that: 'The Bank should go to poor women and not expect these women who are busy and insecure to come to the Bank … Poor women are vitally concerned with the livelihood of their households … they are the most eligible borrowers, although they are been excluded from mainstream banking.' Enabling poor people to save and borrow has allowed many self-employed women to become financially more robust and the bank now also offers a range of services. Although customers are very poor, the bank recovers 98 per cent of loans and in 2013 generated revenues of €27 million and net profit of €276,000.

Microfinance is poised to develop further. As low-cost ATM technology becomes widely available, through internet kiosks known in India as *sanchalaks*, insurance and other financial services previously unavailable to the poor will also enter the market. And as the *sanchalaks* and other IT solutions proliferate (for example, Vortex Engineering, an Indian technology company, has designed an ATM that does not need air conditioning and comes at a quarter of the normal cost of a terminal), access to healthcare and other services for the poor will improve.

CHAPTER 5

Systematic Observation

Systematic observation assesses the use of products and services directly, rather than relying on customers' reported perceptions.[79] Systematic observation is time-consuming, the analysis is complex and difficult to learn, and significant preparation is needed, but it can bring key insights.[80] It is for this reason that market research companies are increasingly hiring ethnographers, whose training enables them to observe and interpret effectively, that is, accurately, unambiguously and in an unbiased way.

The key to effective observation is the preparation of a good *coding scheme*. This is a list of the factors the researcher expects to observe, such as problems and frustration using a product. Such a scheme is based on the research question: What is the observer looking to understand? Usually, in product innovation studies, observation aims to understand how customers use products in their day-to-day environment and to identify the unarticulated problems they face with these products. For example, a manufacturer might watch people operating washing machines in their own homes and this would yield a large amount of data on where (in the house), how (the process), and when (time of the day) washing machines are used. Such observations showed that families with young children in London often use their washing machines daily – for them, the time-honoured British 'weekly wash', or 'Monday washing day' is not viable. Much of the advantage of ethnographic market research is that it looks for deep understanding of customer segments because, in many ways, a customer segment has its own 'culture'. Ethnographers look to understand tribal culture, whereas ethnographic market researchers look to understand the culture of segments. For example, Sainsbury's, the UK supermarket giant, used ethnography to understand the needs of families with children suffering from food allergies. Observing that such customers often have separate shelves for specific foods led the company to create complete 'allergy-free' shelves in its supermarkets, so that families could find all the special foods they needed faster.

In the service sector, observations can be used to determine the typical stages of consumption of a service. The coding scheme gives the observer points to watch for and should highlight *touch points* (key interactions) and *pain points* (stages that do not match expectations). This is particularly important, as the clues to unarticulated needs may be nonverbal. Coillte, an Irish company investigating recreational needs of families and the opportunities to offer outdoor recreation, recognized the importance of adults receiving specific feedback on their child's 'performance' at a particular activity (Mini Case 2.7).

Table 5.4 gives a generic coding scheme for observation and has eight categories of data; from the observed triggers for product usage up to the unarticulated needs. It gives the main types of events to look for and the additional columns can be annotated with the timings of when these are observed and additional notes. Under 'product usage', it can be seen that it helps to identify the so-called *job to be done*, because 'by thoroughly mapping the job a customer is trying to get done, a company can discover opportunities for breakthrough products and services'.[81] It can be seen that the eight categories of data

TABLE 5.4: Generic Coding Scheme for Observational Studies

	Data categories	Events to look for	Observed?	Timings	Notes
1.	Triggers for acquiring the product or service	• Why, when and how?			
2.	Triggers for product usage	• Who, what, where, when, why, how?			
3.	The environment	• Physical layout/objects • Actors • Activities/events • Time sequence			
4.	Interactions with user's environment	• Physical interactions • Social interactions			
5.	Product usage	• 'Job to be done' • Wasted time • Doing things right • Doing things wrong • Misuse • Confusion • Dangerous situations, e.g. physical damage or data loss			
6.	Intangible aspects and unarticulated needs	• Emotions • Frustration and wasted time • Fears and anxiety • Linguistic signals • Extralinguistic signals • Nonverbal signals, e.g. body language • Spatial signals			
7.	Contradictions	• Actions differing from explanations • Answers with 'gloss' or sweeping statements			
8.	User customization	• User modifications of the product • User modifications of the (normal) process			

Source: based on Leonard-Barton and others

CHAPTER **5**

force the observer to look not only at how the product fits into the user's overall environment but also to look for signals that indicate unarticulated needs. For example, identifying the triggers for use can give insights. For a vacuum cleaner, the trigger for use could be the weekly clean of rooms, or something spilled. The latter trigger for use brings different requirements, such as speed, which may influence product design; for example, Black & Decker created the well-known hand-held 'Dustbuster' vacuum cleaner to address the need for quick cleaning.

As shown in Table 5.4, frustration with services or products can indicate that a current design does not meet the user's needs, or it may indicate a poor user interface. A good observer will look for signs of frustration, such as subtle *extralinguistic signals*, for example the speed and emphasis in speech, *nonverbal signs* such as body language, and *spatial signals*, for example the proximity of a user to others or objects. Another clue to unarticulated needs can be that users have modified the equipment to better meet their needs. Users may also modify their working pattern to get around the limitations of current products or services. Due to the multidimensional nature of good observation, the best solution is to make video recordings. These can be viewed offline by a number of people all looking for different clues. The disadvantage of video recording is that filming may influence the user's actions and so this needs to be allowed for in the analysis.

MINI CASE 5.8: *Clarks – These Boots are (Really) Made for Walking*[82]

Clarks Shoes has been renowned for the quality and comfort of its products for over 175 years. The company was aware that the market for leisure footwear was significant and growing fast, and decided to enter, what was for it, a new market – walking boots. As this was a market about which it had no detailed knowledge of customer needs, it worked closely with PDD, a London-based market research consultancy. Chris Towns, innovations manager, said: 'I needed to understand the buying habits, end use and expectations of our new consumer. Understanding the motivations of walkers can only be guessed at from within the confines of your own office.'

PDD specializes in ethnographic studies and it conducted contextual interviews with walkers in UK national parks, home interviews with people who were members of walking and rambling clubs, and observed customers buying walking boots. The insights obtained from this market research allowed Clarks to clearly identify its target segments and, for these, to understand customer priorities. For example, 'comfort', 'fit' and 'safety' were quickly identified from interviews as important product attributes. However, the contextual interviews in the national parks allowed the design team to understand the real meaning of each of these terms and develop product characteristics to meet them. Much of the development involved experimentation with prototypes and this was conducted directly with walkers. Similarly, systematic observation of customers in shops found that they always felt the tongue of walking boots before they tried them on. Therefore, it appeared that the tongue was a feature of a boot that customers closely associated with comfort. This insight led Clarks to produce a particularly well-padded tongue in its final product. The Clarks range of 'Active' walking boots has been well received by hobby and professional walkers and ramblers and is selling well.

The massive amount of data collected in systematic observation must be analysed and summarized in a form that is useful to management. New technology is helping here and PDD, a market research consultancy in London, produces databases for its clients of key video clips, categorized by customer segment. This database can be made available on a company's intranet to any department involved in product development. This helps to spread the understanding of the customer's world throughout the innovation project team (see Mini Case 5.7 on Clarks Shoes).

Another approach to analysing observations is to identify typical scenarios of how products are used, with associated problems and issues. Descriptive statistics on the number of times particular events occur, for example, can also be a useful way of summarizing data. Simple drawings and storyboards can also be used to summarize triggers for use and problems encountered. Storyboards are useful communication tools with users and internally, to help the whole of the NPD team understand users' needs.

Discrete Observation

Discrete or covert observation, in which users are observed without their knowledge or permission, is only viable for consumer products and services that are used in public. For example, in Japan, Nokia has had employees observe how users operate its products in public. Similarly, car manufacturers have built miniature cameras into cars at shows to observe how potential customers react to their new products. Using discrete observation raises ethical issues. As discrete observation often deliberately eavesdrops on users' conversations, it has been colloquially dubbed capturing 'the murmur of the customer'.[83] It should be kept in mind that people quickly become aware that they are being observed and often react negatively. Obtaining permission in advance is safer.

Contextual Interviews

Contextual interviews are conducted in the user's environment but observation and a number of semi-structured questions are used with systematic observation, to understand the situation in which products are used. Questions collect background information, and then stimulate users to describe their actions. Typical questions are: 'Can you please describe what you are doing?' and 'When is that necessary?' Essentially, this produces verbal data on product usage that might not be generated in pure observation. Having people describe their actions can also unearth their tacit knowledge. Once again, video recording is commonly used. Contextual interviews are particularly useful for gaining insights into how the customer feels during the service delivery process and gaining ideas for improvement.

WhatIf!, a London consultancy, has made contextual interviewing easy for the manufacturers of consumer products, by negotiating access to all the residents in one (long) street in Birmingham. All the houses in 'The Street' can be visited with minimal notice and product managers have been able to observe their products in use and ask questions. Intel has a number of projects that make use of contextual interviewing and employs a team of ethnographers, sociologists and behavioural scientists based in Oregon,[84] responsible for identifying the social backgrounds to product usage.

An important part of analysing market research data is to look for *contradictions*, which is a concept from ethnography. These are the times where a customer has said one thing about how they use a product and yet they do something different. For example, in focus groups, customers often say they measure the amount of washing powder they use but, when observed at home, they just pour in the amount they guess is appropriate. Often, people put *gloss* on their answers, to put themselves in a better light. Another type of contradiction is the sweeping statements some customers make. For example, when discussing a Britvic water filter, one woman said it was very easy to change the filter element. When asked to demonstrate it, she took over nine minutes for this task (finally saying that her husband always changed the filter element). The Irish company Coillte mentioned earlier in this chapter found that Irish parents expressed a preference for half-day recreational events for the whole family. When prototype products were marketed, it was found that only one-day events were fully booked and no full families came (it was mainly one parent and the children). This example illustrates that customers often tell us what they want us to hear (that is, that they are a family that does everything together) rather than what they actually want (a full day where one partner, usually the 'mum', gets the day off). The concept of contradictions is powerful for uncovering hidden needs but is still not a widely known concept.

Empathy Building

Most authors concentrate on the data collection and analysis aspects of empathic design. However, the other side is the need to ensure that product designers develop not only an understanding of customers and users but also fully empathize with them. As yet, there is no formal methodology for this but a number of examples from industry demonstrate the approach. When the Ford Motor Company developed its Focus model, one target segment was elderly people. In order to get the engineers to understand the difficulties older people have in getting into and out of cars, designers wore padded suits that reduced their ease of movement and simulated the restricted movement of later life. Similarly, a mobile phone design team also working on a product for elderly people had its engineers wear thick gloves and glasses smeared with Vaseline for a week, to help them understand how difficult it can be for older people to operate today's products. No doubt in coming years the way in which companies attempt to generate true empathy will develop further. It is a case of finding ways in which the designers can 'step into the customer's shoes'. Massachusetts Institute of Technology (MIT) has a whole lab dedicated to helping 'improve the quality of life of older people and those who care for them'. This group has even developed a suit that mimics the problems older people have, with vision and movement.[85]

Lead Users

Another approach to uncovering hidden needs was developed by Eric von Hippel at MIT. *Lead users* are groups of customers or users who face more challenging requirements than most of the current marketplace (see Mini Case 5.9 on Lego). Their needs can be ahead of the market, by months or years, but they become mainstream over time. An example of lead users is the way the company North Face cooperates with some of the world's top mountain athletes, to design rucksacks and protective clothing, As the market vanguard, lead users face urgent, challenging needs and can benefit significantly from solutions to these. One word of caution is necessary: the theory on disruptive innovation discussed in Chapter 4 shows the drawbacks of solely concentrating on lead customers' needs. Organizations need to be cautious because extreme needs might not be relevant to mainstream customers. However, if applied correctly, the lead user technique looks at the needs of demanding users, collects ideas from users of similar products and services in other markets, and checks the mainstream market for the relevance of the ideas generated.[86]

In contrast to traditional market research, where the sample is chosen to be representative, lead users face particular issues and are not representative of normal users. The selection of a lead user group normally follows four steps. First, a screening process is used with existing users to identify which of them have more demanding needs. Figure 5.7 illustrates the process in which the starting point is screening normal users. From these, the *extreme users* are at the top of what can be perceived as a pyramid of users. They are extreme in terms of the demands they place on products or services and also, normally, in their expertise in dealing with the particular challenges they face. For example, extreme users may have the ability to modify standard products or processes in order to cope with the particular challenges of their working environment.[87] Once the extreme users have been identified, the second and third steps are to identify two analogous fields where similar challenges are faced to the ones in the current market. Fourth, the extreme users and the two groups of analogous users are brought together for a workshop.

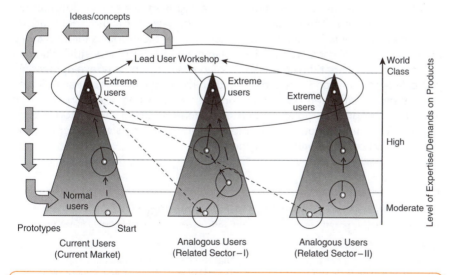

FIGURE 5.7: Selecting a Lead User Group

Source: reprinted by permission of Harvard Business Review. *Adapted from Networking to Lead Users. From "Creating Breakthroughs at 3M" by Eric von Hippel, Stefan Thomke and Mary Sonnack, September-October 1999. Copyright © 1999 by the Harvard Business School Publishing Corporation; all rights reserved[88].*

To understand the process, consider the example of 3M, where lead users helped develop improved medical drapes. Drapes are adhesive films applied to the skin to minimize infections during surgery. The key attributes of the product were discussed with normal users – these were adhesion to skin and infection prevention. The discussions also identified that an increased risk of infection was a worrying trend in many hospitals. Next, extreme users were identified; surgeons who had to deal with higher risk of infection than in normal hospitals. Here, both military field surgeons and surgeons working in developing countries with lower hygiene levels were consulted. Discussions with these extreme users identified two related sectors. The problem of infection is also an issue for veterinary surgeons, who have to operate on animals in non-hygienic environments and have problem fixing drapes on fur and hair. Finally, an unusual second set of *analogous users* was identified; Hollywood make-up artists, who have to attach masks to skin.

Extreme users from the current market and those from related sectors form the full lead user group. For each of the lead users identified, techniques such as observation and contextual interviewing should be used to understand their working environment and issues. One of the advantages of working with analogous users from related sectors is that they usually do not mind sharing their experience, as competitive issues are not involved, and so it is normal to organize a workshop with the lead user group. This is used not only to tap their individual expertise but also to learn from the discussions that result from bringing together users from what can be very different sectors and backgrounds (referring back to Figure 5.3, this can be seen as the bringing together of different frames of reference). The discussions are moderated and produce ideas for products that address the challenging needs facing lead users. The development of these ideas into prototypes can also be conducted in close cooperation – called *co-development* – with the lead users, before the products themselves are tested with normal users. Hilti, a European manufacturer of industrial mounting equipment, found that the combination of a workshop and co-development was particularly effective and less expensive than its normal market research. Recent surveys show that in the US, Japan and the UK, between 3 and 6 per cent of users have modified products,[89] and companies studying these modifications can gain ideas for product improvements. Many consumers will generate product ideas and concepts without payment.[90]

> **MINI CASE 5.9:** *Lego – Mindstorming Toys, for Girls and Boys*[91]

Since its introduction in 1998, the Lego Mindstorms robot kit has been a huge success, selling upwards of 40,000 units a year. The kit includes a large robot brick that can be used in combination with a range of motors, lights, bricks and sensors to build highly intelligent devices – for example a robot that can solve Rubik's Cube in seconds. Writing the control programs for such devices is a complex task, which is conducted on a laptop. The market for Mindstorms has developed into two distinct segments; parents

Continued...

buying the $200 kit for teenagers hooked on engineering, and adult enthusiasts ('geeks') who love programming in their spare time. Geeks love to exhibit their creations at the annual Lego 'Brickfest' conference.

When Lego updates and enhances Mindstorms, it turns its attention to the geeks and gets some of them involved in new product development. After signing a non-disclosure agreement, lead users exchange their ideas in a secure chat room, hosted by Seren Lund, director of Mindstorms. Lead users are encouraged to be in regular contact with Lego, giving a wealth of ideas about how to make significant improvements to Mindstorms. Involving enthusiasts at an early stage has helped Lego develop very successful products, including the EV3 introduced in 2013. Interestingly, although the dedicated enthusiasts have been crucial to the development of Mindstorms and have strongly influenced the design, they are not paid by Lego. Prototype kits, peer recognition and the opportunity to influence the product are motivation enough.

Lego has also conducted ethnographic market research on the way girls play. It has recognized the importance of how girls communicate with their friends and with toys during play. Such insights have led to the successful 'Friends' series, aimed at girls and introduced in 2012. The core idea of the product is mini-sized models of five girls that come in kits matching the fictional 'Heartlake City' suburban environment in which they live – for example apartments, houses and cafes. The five friends are more realistic that Lego's normal 'people' and the whole series comes in predominately purple and pink tones.

Although extremely popular, Lego's 'Friends' has been criticized for stereotyping the way girls play and indirectly contributing to the problem that not enough girls opt for STEM (science, technology, engineering and mathematics) subjects at school and university. In contrast, Mindstorms has been tremendously successful with males. It will be interesting to see if Lego will use its marketing prowess to encourage more girls to use the Mindstorms product, but, as has been pointed out: 'That doesn't mean paint the EV3 pink.'

Open Innovation

Chapter 1 showed that open innovation is currently one of the most researched areas of innovation management and the concept was further explored in Chapter 2. Open innovation is certainly an important set of techniques to be considered. It is the so-called *outside-in* aspects of open innovation, in which companies seek out innovative ideas from others to employ within their own business, that are important at the FFE.

Collecting External Ideas – Crowdsourcing

Some consumers and users submit unsolicited ideas.[92] For some companies, this can give a flood of ideas, many of which are poor, because external people do not have the knowledge of what the company needs. So to manage crowdsourcing effectively, there are four stages: drawing good ideas (through a website, rewards, explanation); shaping the right ideas (by sharing some information from R&D); selecting ideas (initial filter and full evaluation); and managing the use of the ideas (through clarity of ownership and including legal representatives on teams). There are a number of consultancies that can help organize competitions, and crowdsourcing in general.

The main application of crowdsourcing is normative creativity – finding solutions to particular problems – and 'a crowd can be managed in a manner that increases the likelihood of developing better solutions'.[93] The advantage of gaining many ideas quickly through social media include its low cost and access to deep and diverse groups.[94] Swarovski, an Austrian company that produces cut-glass crystal, jewellery and other luxury goods, has co-designed watches with 1,650 of its customers. Similarly, running shoes, wallpaper designs, model railways, baby carriages, towels and snowboarders' backpacks have been designed in this way.[95]

With the popularity of open innovation has come a wave of attempts from companies to tap the thinking power of crowds through competitions (also known as *tournaments*). For example, Cisco, a major technology company that designs networking equipment and software, was interested in gaining ideas for growing the business. An initiative called the 'Cisco I-Prize' asked people to submit business ideas for the company and offering a top prize of $250,000. Over 2,500 people submitted ideas but many were unsuitable and so five filters were introduced: Does the idea address a real pain point? Is there a big enough market? Is the timing right? Does it fit the company? Is the idea of long-term interest?[96] Thus companies using crowdsourcing need to define the challenge on the internet in a clear way and participants need specific instructions (not just 'post your ideas' or think outside the box). Organizations need to adapt tournaments to the type of ideas needed. For example, evolutionary ideas need different approaches to revolutionary ones; the abilities of contributors need consideration; and the real value of answers is not known until they are shared.[97] Another issue is that communication on complex problems can be difficult and companies need to be aware that the best solutions may be buried in the thread of discussions.[98]

In addition to methods to stimulate new ideas, tracking social media can give organizations immediate feedback on existing products. *Big data* – typically large datasets on customers' purchasing decisions – is leading to analytical approaches for finding trends. Similar analytics also help spot relevant trends in social media communications and can extract the relevant information for product developers (see Mini Case 5.10 on All Nippon Airways).

▶ **MINI CASE 5.10:** *All Nippon Airways – Big Data, Small Numbers*[99]

The main business of All Nippon Airways (ANA) is scheduled passenger flights (domestic and international) but it also has businesses for non-scheduled flights, freight, buying, selling and leasing aircraft, and ground support services. It has approximately 12,000 employees, a fleet of 234 airliners and it serves about 3.8 million passengers a month. Many of these passengers are members of its frequent flyer scheme, the 'ANA Mileage Club'. Unusually, this club allows families to combine and redeem their miles, having recognized the demotivation of multiple family members just failing to collect enough miles before they go out of date.

One of the current buzzwords of marketing is 'big data'. Companies are investing in complex algorithms to analyse their customers' buying habits. Big data can be used to identify which products to

Continued...

recommend to customers, and to generate ideas for new products. However, ANA has recognized that to really understand big data, small numbers are also important.

ANA has a significant database on its frequent flyers and, similar to many airlines, it has used 'data mining' – analysing buying patterns – to generate customer insights. For example, cluster analysis showed that ANA customers could be grouped into 10 main segments. What is different at ANA is that it has gone further than the number-crunching. ANA selects small numbers of people, randomly selected from each of the clusters, to attend focus groups. This enables ANA to investigate motivation and behaviour more deeply. Tsubasa Itani is a mathematician and data-based marketing expert who helped in the cluster analysis and arranging the focus groups. He says:

> Before you meet the people you have your own assumptions about their motivations as a customer; you have your hypotheses based on the data. But it is when you meet the people that the clusters come to life – you understand their behaviour and how you can design new offers to meet their needs.

An example insight was about the 'sponsor'. Whether a customer is travelling to visit relatives, travelling for pure leisure or for business, the sponsor paying for the flight has a big impact on buying behaviour.

Yoshimoto Tanaka is director of the data-based marketing team, which uses data mining and focus groups to keep ANA's service offering at the leading edge. For example, the insights gained from cluster analysis have enabled ANA to determine causes of a 'slump'. This is when 'precious groups' of customers who have used the airline regularly in the past suddenly stop booking with ANA. Now ANA targets them with limited special offers. Another example is by identifying the different characteristics of each flight route (using big data and focus groups in local cities), ANA has optimized its fleet resource. Mr Tanaka says: 'When ANA makes its strategic decisions it always places the customer at the centre, and we support that process with scientific research. Marketing decisions must be based on data and reliable insights, not just on instincts.'

Virtual Communities

The worldwide web has enabled groups of people with common interests to exchange their ideas easily and such virtual communities are being tapped by companies looking for ideas to help in developing products. *Online communities* have been defined as a group of customers who have a high level of interest and knowledge about a particular group of products.[100] Beiersdorf, the German company that owns the Nivea skin care brand, uses its website to collect ideas directly from consumers, and the idea of using virtual communities to improve NPD is gaining popularity.[101]

At its simplest, the use of online communities involves online surveys that customers can voluntarily complete and which can give insights into their needs (obviously such questionnaires have limitations such as their validity). However, a range of interactions are now being used, from interactive question-and-answer games (which are designed to gain understanding of how products are perceived and used), to *user design software*, where customers can participate in the design process. *Open source software* is a prime example of where users and customers are intimately involved in product development but other examples are emerging. Facebook was able to have its website translated into different languages by allowing users to do the work and video games companies have also had their customers help in major development projects.[102] One of the main advantages to web approaches is that they can tap the collective intelligence of users;[103] so it is an emerging type of market research that is likely to be an important complement to the other methods we have described.

Experimentation and Co-development

Users are often unable to describe the sort of product solutions they require, as they do not have sufficient technical knowledge. A creative exchange of ideas between the user (their needs) and the designer (potential solutions) is needed.[104] This needs to be an iterative process, as potential solutions need to be tested and modified to be effective. Therefore, it is useful to produce *physical* and *virtual prototypes* that can be tried out and discussed by users and customers. This process is also sometimes called *co-development*, as noted earlier, and takes advantage of the much improved technologies for the production of prototypes. Whether it is 3D printing of physical models, computer simulations of car crash scenarios, or virtual reality mock-ups of products, which allow users to interact with them, there are many possibilities. Co-development is also being adopted by the service sector, as customer inputs are critical to good service product design. Allowing customers and users to try and test products at an early stage means that it is still possible to make changes to the final product or service design (for ideas on how this can be implemented, see the section on Agile Project Management in Chapter 7).

Most people think of product (physical) prototypes but the retail sector is increasingly using prototyping and experimentation.[105] For example, J.C. Penney, the US retailer, regularly conducts experiments and assesses its sales initiatives, as they are one of the key elements of its service. (See also Mini Case 7.1 on how the insurer Allstate researched the best way to sell an innovative new product.) In designing these tests, control groups and other ideas about research design are crucial. Amazon will also often test two different offers in parallel. So experimentation can also be an important way of selecting the right innovation, and, as such, should be seen as a valid adjunct to prioritization methods (see Chapter 6).

Identifying Priorities – Conjoint Analysis

Essentially, all the techniques discussed up until now identify product or service attributes. Once these are clear, the priorities from the perspective of the customer can be determined using *conjoint analysis*, as indicated in Table 5.5. Conjoint analysis (or *stated preference technique* or *trade-off analysis*) is one of the more widely applied scientific approaches to market research. Provided the product attributes have been appropriately elicited from customers, conjoint analysis is a useful method for understanding the *utility* of each of them. Conjoint analysis can be used in the service sector to understand the trade-offs that a customer is willing to make between elements of the service product and service augmentation.

There are three main stages in conjoint analysis:

1. Identifying the characteristics of each of the product attributes and hypothetical product descriptions.
2. Interviewing a suitable sample of customers.
3. Calculating the customer's perceived value of each attribute (the utility).

To understand this, we will consider the example of the development of a laptop computer. 'In this market there are now different segments: for example, the business 'on the road' laptops (small and lightweight) and sophisticated machines for gaming enthusiasts (which have excellent graphics capability but are much heavier). Various methods will have been used to identify product attributes and it should be stressed that for breakthrough innovation, attributes not currently on the market will have to be identified.

Let us assume that seven attributes were identified in market research with gamers: 1) Display size; 2) RAM; 3) Hard disk capacity; 4) Processing speed; 5) Physical size and weight; 6) Graphics card and; 7) Price. An important question during product development is: on which of these attributes does the customer place most value? Only with this information can development priorities be effectively set. For example, how much emphasis do users place on weight reduction or in developing or sourcing a better battery from a leading supplier?

The first stage involves the identification of levels for each of the attributes and the typical range of values of existing products. For example, the weight of a laptop is typically around 3 kg. Once the attribute measures and their ranges have been determined, the next stage is to prepare descriptions of a hypothetical set of products. Table 5.5 shows the specifications of Products A, B, and… N (typically about six would be defined). Naturally, attributes change over time and

TABLE 5.5: Attribute Levels[106]

	Product attribute	Product A	Product B	Product N
1.	Display size	13 inch	14 inch	15.6 inch
2.	RAM	8 GB	16 GB	32–64 GB
3.	Hard disk capacity	512 GB	256 GB	1128 GB
4.	Processing speed	2.5 GHz	2.6 GHz	2.7 GHz
5.	Physical size and weight	2.04 kg (4.5 lbs)	1.93 kg (4.25 lbs)	2.90 kg (6.4 lbs)
6.	Graphics card	Nvidia GeForce GTX 965M	Nvidia GeForce 970M	Nvidia GeForce GTX 1070
7.	Battery rundown	3 hrs 55 min	5 hrs 42 min	3 hrs 18 min
8.	Price	€1,299	€1,999	€2,099

in a fast-moving market such as gaming laptops, the price and performance will need to be checked regularly. There are many possible combinations of attributes and so many hypothetical products can be developed, although only three (Product A, Product B... Product N) are shown in the table. The number of hypothetical products that need to be considered depends on the number of attributes and their possible levels. For example, six attributes, each with at least three levels (as shown in Table 5.4), result in $3^8 = 6,561$ theoretical combinations but far fewer will be used in data collection).

The next stage is to interview customers and to present them with alternative products. The sample of customers to be interviewed needs to be representative of the target market. In the so-called *pairwise* version of conjoint analysis, the customer would be presented with simplified descriptions of Products A and B and would be asked: 'Which do you prefer?' Each product has advantages and disadvantages; although Product A has a bigger hard drive, it is more expensive than B and has a smaller display. Therefore, the customer makes trade-offs between the values of the attributes in choosing their preference. Next the customer is presented with another two products and asked the same question. The process of presenting the products and collecting answers is made easier by conjoint analysis software packages (such as the widely used ACA developed by Sawtooth Software), where this is automated and many researchers now administer conjoint analysis via the internet.

The interviews collect a significant amount of data on how customers view attributes and make trade-offs. Conjoint analysis software takes this data and uses mathematics to determine the value or utility a customer places on each attribute. Figure 5.8 shows the typical output of conjoint analysis, for the attributes weight and battery rundown (capacity). Graphs of the utility versus the attribute levels are shown and the slope of this graph indicates the importance

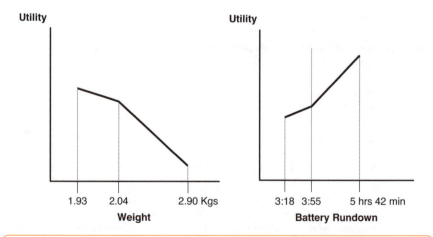

FIGURE 5.8: Conjoint Analysis Utility Graphs for a Laptop Computer

of the attribute. For example, the utility drops slowly from low to medium weight but then drops sharply, as users do not like a machine of nearly 3 kgs. Battery capacity appears to be very important as the utility increases significantly for a machine with over 5 hours battery rundown.

Utility graphs can be derived for all attributes and give an understanding of how customers make their trade-off decisions, which in turn allows product development decisions to be made more effectively. In addition, analysis of the results pertaining to price can allow pricing decisions for new products to be made. For readers who want to know more about conjoint analysis, we recommend the textbooks of Caroll et al.[107] and Gustafsson et al.[108]

Referring back to Figure 5.4, conjoint analysis is shown as one of the last steps in gaining insights and designing a full product, service or business model concept. It should be stressed that although conjoint analysis is an effective method, it is completely dependent on the identification of product attributes that are pertinent to customers (including hidden needs).

Choosing Insight Methods

To help choose the most appropriate approaches for a specific piece of market research, Table 5.6 gives the advantages and limitations of the eight techniques discussed in this chapter. To achieve effective results and uncover hidden needs, a combination of techniques is almost always needed.

For example, one of Robert Bosch's business units, which designs and manufactures production line equipment, used observation of operators working in their customers' factories and repertory grid interviews, thus gaining insights into product requirements. A survey was then used to collect data from a representative sample of users and the results are now being incorporated into a new product design. Real customer insights are often the result of using a blend of techniques.

PROTECTING THE VALUE OF IDEAS

In Chapter 4 we discussed some of the ways to protect strategic value, such as network and threshold effects, or linking a new product or service to a particular process innovation (to make it harder to copy). *Intellectual property* (IP) – patents and trademarks – is the way that most readily comes to mind to protect ideas, although solid IP that really blocks out competition is comparatively rare.

Most countries in the world have laws that protect IP – ideas, designs, works of art, literature or music – for a period so that their originators can benefit from their investment. The field of *intellectual property rights* (IPR) is complex, constantly changing and varies to some extent from country to country. It is a matter of civil, not criminal, law and companies have to police their own IP and take action at their own expense to protect it. In this section, we will concentrate on the aspects of importance to managers, but we stress the importance of taking legal advice before making serious commitments or investments in IPR. The four main kinds of IP are patents, trademarks, copyright and design right, and these are discussed below.

TABLE 5.6: Different Approaches to Identifying Customer Problems and Requirements

	Approach	Overview	Applications/advantages	Limitations
1.	Survey research	• Widely used method of collecting customer inputs • Use of direct questions to determine customers' views on what they think are their requirements	• Open-ended questions allow respondents some freedom to give creative ideas • Can be applied as a postal survey, telephone or direct interviews	• Questionnaires are often thought to be easy to design. In fact, the opposite is true and many surveys are poorly designed and so produce equivocal results • Response rates often low, which raises the question of whether the results are representative of the market • Respondents may find it difficult to articulate their answers to open questions
2.	Focus groups	• Small groups of selected users or non-users, paid to discuss product needs • Discussions are stimulated by an initial question and by having example products in the room • A moderator guides discussions • Market researchers often observe the discussions through a two-way mirror	• Help to define customer problems and give background information, rather than identifying solutions • As users are taken outside their normal environment, this guarantees that they are not distracted and spend time discussing products	• The somewhat artificial nature of the situation can limit the effectiveness • Particular individuals can dominate the discussions. Thus good moderation is required • Some companies try to save costs by using inexperienced moderators; this wastes the potential of focus groups discussion
3.	Repertory grid technique	• Users or customers undergo a structured interview • Interviewees are stimulated to identify product attributes by being asked to compare triads of different products and/or services	• Repertory grid technique is powerful at enabling users and customers to articulate their issues • The technique taps tacit knowledge of hidden needs	• The technique is not well known • Interviewers need to have experience with 5/6 different products and services to make the technique work • Interviewer needs specific training in the technique, although it is easy to apply • Time-consuming interviews

TABLE 5.6: Continued

	Approach	Overview	Applications/advantages	Limitations
4.	Empathic design	• A range of approaches of which the main ones are systematic observation, contextual interviews and putting product designers 'in the shoes of users'	• Becoming more popular • Gives an in-depth understanding of customers' and users' product use models • Contextual interviews are in vivo and the environment gives valuable information	• Systematic observation is not easy and using specialists may be the best approach; otherwise base studies on a suitable coding scheme developed from Table 5.4 • Vast amounts of qualitative data may be generated, which requires effective analysis strategies
5.	Lead users	• Identification of users who have extreme needs in your current market • Further identification of analogous users in related sectors • It is usual to run a workshop with extreme and analogous users, to develop product concepts	• Workshop brings together very different users and stimulates creative discussions • Can be combined with experimentation, to test the concepts identified in the workshop	• Difficulties in identifying lead users • Workshops are time-consuming and lead users may need to be motivated to give their time • Workshop is outside the normal working environment (although it can be combined with a visit to a lead user environment)
6.	Experimentation	• Customers are presented with early prototypes of products (or services) and base their suggestions on these • Can be an extension of the lead user approach	• Observing in a realistic scenario how customers react to tangible product ideas • Seeing and using a tangible product often enables customers and users to articulate their views better	• May require expensive virtual prototyping equipment • Superficially, services cannot easily be prototyped. However, leaders such as HSBC Bank prototype their services and collect reactions

CHAPTER

5

(Continued)

TABLE 5.6: Continued

	Approach	Overview	Applications/advantages	Limitations
7.	Open innovation	• Companies place their focus on accessing ideas from outside the organization. These can be collecting ideas from customers, from other companies, and from 'crowds', accessed via the internet • Should stimulate the use of a range of approaches from tracking social media, to launching tournaments	• Can help a company becoming too internally oriented and relying on technology-push as a strategy • Theory tells us that different, that is, external, views will stimulate creativity • Well-managed crowdsourcing gives a company access to expertise that it would not normally be able to tap into	• Open innovation has been 'oversold' and it is not a solution to all a company's innovation issues • Internal cultural issues need to be considered – NIH syndrome (see Chapter 8) can lead some employees not to want to adopt ideas generated externally
8.	Conjoint analysis	• Customers are presented with descriptions of products or service products and must choose their preferences • Identifies the trade-offs customers make in deciding between different products	• Identification of the product attributes that customers perceive as their key priorities • Development of pricing models	• If the wrong attributes are fed into the analysis, the prioritization will not be useful (it will encourage a continuing focus on incremental products) • The somewhat artificial nature of the decisions can limit the accuracy of the findings • Relatively complex method that usually needs expert support

Patents

A *patent* is a 'legal right granted to exclusive commercial use of an invention, normally for a limited period of time'.[109] Its power comes from the fact that it protects the very idea itself, not just the way it happens to be used. Patents are very important. It is argued that one of the reasons why the Industrial Revolution began in Britain was it was the only large country with a patent system that gave less wealthy inventors such as James Watt the chance to spend time and effort working on their inventions, secure in the knowledge that they could profit from them later.[110] Abraham Lincoln (the only US president to have been granted a patent) said: 'The patent system added the fuel of [self] interest to the fire of genius.'

The patentee has to pay a fee and make a full disclosure of the idea, including a clear description of at least one way that it can be embodied in practice so that others will be able to use it when the patent expires. Protection typically lasts for about 20 years, depending on the country, but often with renewal fees to be paid at intervals, which get steeper as time goes on. An important point to note is that a patent cannot be granted if an idea has previously been discussed in the public domain.

Patents are granted separately in each country where protection is required (although a single patent covers the EU), so such protection can be expensive. The initial cost for writing a patent and following it through is typically several thousand pounds per country (and may take several years) followed by renewal fees of a further five or ten thousand over the first 10 or 12 years. The decision to patent is not one to be taken lightly.

What Can be Patented?

To be patentable, an idea must pass four tests. It must be *novel*; it must involve an *inventive step*; it must have a *practical application*; and it must not be in an *excluded category* (which includes, among other things, scientific theories, mathematical methods and, in many jurisdictions, methods of doing business). As discussed above, the most demanding test from the management point of view is that the invention must not have been publicly revealed before the filing date of the patent. A patent application for a means of raising sunken ships by filling them full of small airbags was refused because the idea had been shown (using table tennis balls) in a Disney cartoon in the 1940s. The patent office will search existing patents but this does not guarantee that the idea has not been published in some other way. Management must ensure that everyone involved in innovation understands the need to keep any invention absolutely secret until a patent is filed. If it is necessary to talk about it to third parties, make sure that a formal confidentiality agreement is in place.

Infringement of Patents

If another company manufactures or offers for sale a product incorporating a patented idea, they are said to infringe the patent. The owner, or licensee, of the patent can force them to stop and may be able to extract substantial damages, particularly if the infringer was aware of the problem. This is the primary power that a patent gives. However, a company granted a patent may find that enforcing its right in a foreign country is a difficult and costly affair.

Infringement is a quite separate matter from patentability. For example, suppose long ago Company X invented the first chair with a back and was granted a patent on it. If Company Y already had a patent on a stool (an essential constituent of a chair), then Company X would infringe this if it actually sells any of its chairs. It would need to seek a licence from Company Y before it could market its product. But its own patent could still be valid, and Company Y (or any other) would have to seek a licence from Company X to sell a stool with a back.

A company that wants to use a patented idea has a number of options. One is to seek a licence to use it. Another is to challenge the validity of the patent, particularly if it can find a prior disclosure of the idea. The third, which is often possible, is to work round the patent by finding a way to perform the same function but outside the legal scope of the patent. The full disclosure required in the patent document often helps competitors 'design around' the patent and copies proliferate.[111] A survey of 600 European companies showed that 60 per cent had suffered from copies of their products but only 20 per cent went to trial.[112]

The Business Use of Patents

Patents have four main uses in a company. The first, as noted above, is to enforce a monopoly by taking legal action to prevent others using the idea. This can create a competition-free and possibly very lucrative market. The second is to license the patent to others in return for a fee, or royalties, or both. The third is as a bargaining counter in relations between companies: large companies often agree to swap rights to each other's patent portfolio, each one using its own IPR to gain access to that of the other. Finally, small companies use their patents as objective proof of their technical depth and inventiveness so as to enhance their value on sale or flotation.

Patents are a vital protection but, sadly, they may be less useful for small companies than for large. A survey of European small and medium-sized enterprises (SMEs) found that patents are used less than they might be, although many respondent companies had suffered financially when copies of their products and services were made, often by larger companies.[113] The perceived limitations were that patent protection took a lot of effort to acquire and, in practice, gave only limited protection because legal action was expensive and seldom successful. Because of this, SMEs and larger companies often adopt other strategies to protect their position, including relying on their inventiveness to keep ahead of the competition or making innovation hard to imitate.

Trademarks

A *trademark* is defined as 'any sign capable of being represented graphically, which is capable of distinguishing goods or services of one undertaking from those of other undertakings'.[114] It can be a name, a symbol, a special font or script, a colour, or, more often, a combination of them. There are many familiar examples: the names Coca-Cola and Google, the Mercedes logo and so on. A registered trademark can be obtained through a patent office and separate protection is needed in each country but the fees are quite modest. Protection is granted separately for different, broad categories of product so the same name may be used in different context. There is generally no problem in using 'Windows' in house-building, for example. Failure to trademark in different countries can cause problems. For example, La Chemise Lacoste, the international clothing company, has a right-facing crocodile trademark. Crocodile International, a Singapore-based clothing manufacturer, registered its own left-facing crocodile motif across Asia. When Lacoste sought to dominate the high-end Asian market, the two companies became locked in a number of legal actions.[115]

A trademark may not be purely descriptive (like 'bread' or 'washing powder'), or too similar to another one already in use for the same category of product. So it is important to check the availability of the proposed name of a new product or service if you may want to trademark it later.

There are two reasons for seeking protection for a trademark in a particular country. One is to be able to prevent other companies using it and so 'passing off' their products as yours. The other is to establish your own right to use it there; because, unlike other types of IP, trademarks are, by and large, granted to the first applicant in each country (the US and Canada are notable exceptions). Thus, if you do not register early, you may lose the chance to do so later. Similar to trademarks, there is an issue with registering your website before 'website squatters' take the domain that matches your company name and then try to sell it to you.

Copyright

Copyright protects writing, music, computer programs, electronic circuit layouts, web pages, photographs, works of art and so on from unauthorized copying for commercial use. It protects the wording or appearance of the work but not its meaning (if any). Limited copying for personal use or study (that is, non-commercial usage) is allowed: typically one chapter of a book, one article from a journal, a short excerpt from a piece of music; this is known as *fair use*. In the UK, copyright for musical and artistic works lasts for 70 years following the death of the creator.

Copyright is created automatically when the work is complete and requires no registration or payment. Generally, the copyright for anything done by an employee in the course of their job would belong to the company, but there may be ambiguity about work done by contractors or freelance workers, or university lecturers.

One defence against an allegation of copyright infringement is that the work was separately created and appears the same merely because there was little choice in how the function could be performed. This may be plausible in software and so some programmers deliberately include sections of code that have no function as a way of proving if their program has been copied.

It should be noted that in the internet age copies of text and pictures are much easier to make. The ready access means that some companies do not show respect for copyrighted material. For example, a Swedish manufacturer of agricultural equipment found that not only had its products been copied but one of its Asian competitors had also copied its 'terms and conditions' one by one. The other impact of the internet is that such copying and plagiarism are easier to detect and a German manufacturers' association has introduced annual 'awards' for the worst cases of product plagiarism – to try and shame the culprits.

Design Right

Design means the appearance of all or part of a product, especially its shape, colour, texture or ornamentation (or a combination of them). Design protection can prevent another company copying the product directly, or marketing an apparently identical one, even if they can show that they designed it themselves. It is a useful way to protect an original piece of design, and the brand recognition that may go with it, such as the Coca-Cola bottle shape. In services, aspects of the *servicescape* can be used to strengthen the brand, such as McDonald's double arches.

In many countries, an *unregistered design right* exists that gives some protection against copying. More powerful is the *registered design right*, which gives a monopoly right to the design for up to 25 years, and can apply internationally. The design has to be registered through a patent office and it is granted only to designs that are novel and would be viewed as 'fresh' by an 'informed user'. Expert advice is essential. There is a one-year period of grace after public disclosure so it is possible to test market a design before registering it.

It is extremely important to clarify the ownership of IPR in any collaboration with third parties.[116] Managers should always insist on a legal agreement on who owns the IPR in innovation projects; it can be embarrassing to find that a subcontractor owns the copyright to the manual produced for you, the artwork for your sales campaign, or the computer program that runs your new product (says one author speaking from bitter experience). Design consultancies will often expect to retain some rights, for example to use patented ideas in applications that are not relevant to the company's business. It is also important to establish clearly who will be responsible not only for paying the costs of filing and maintaining it, but also for choosing countries to file in, for detecting and taking action on infringements, and for defending the patent if it is attacked.

Summary

This chapter covered the second element of the Pentathlon Framework – generating innovative ideas at the fuzzy front end (FFE). It explained the challenges of the FFE, such as the need for the right teams to work on this difficult phase of innovation; and the difficulties of planning work on breakthrough and radical innovation, which, by definition, is work that has not been conducted before. It also explained that decisions on which ideas are most promising is an art more than a science at this early stage.

Next, the role of creativity is generating ideas was covered, with explanations of some of the most relevant theories. The importance of giving clear direction rather than the typical 'think outside the box' approach was stressed. The most effective ways for individuals and teams to be creative, including a number of techniques in addition to brainstorming, were explained.

Managing innovation is fundamentally about generating new knowledge and so explicit and tacit knowledge and their impact were discussed. Managers need to look for effective ways to stimulate the exchange of knowledge in their organizations. Sometimes, existing knowledge can give teams new ideas of how they can solve their challenges. For example, patents summarize how specific problems have been solved previously and TRIZ databases can be a rich source of ideas. Similarly, biomimicry uses nature as a source of ideas.

One of the most effective ways to generate ideas for innovation, be it product, service or business model innovation, is through the generation of deep customer insights. Here, traditional market research has serious limitations and, therefore, companies need to understand and adopt appropriate enhanced approaches. More sophisticated methods for market research such as ethnography and crowdsourcing are particularly useful for capturing the elusive voice of the customer.

This chapter also discussed various approaches to protecting innovative ideas and the value they create. Patents, trademarks, copyright and design rights were all described but other forms of protection, such as the use of process innovation – which is hard for competitors to copy – were suggested. Finally, the main case study for this chapter, on Mölnlycke Health Care, looks at the link between the strategy and idea generation.

Management Recommendations

- Foster an understanding of the different types of creativity in your organization and use this to stimulate a constant flow of ideas.
- Encourage staff to recognize the importance of actively collecting ideas from outside sources.
- Take active steps to establish and maintain a 'culture of innovation' that supports idea generation.
- Promote the exchange of knowledge within and between innovation project teams. Recognize and protect knowledge that is vital to the organization.
- Employ an appropriate combination of market research techniques to identify your customers' hidden needs.
- Identify suitable ways to protect innovative ideas from competitors.

Questions for Students

1. What is the most innovative product you have experienced and how do you think the idea for this emerged?
2. What insights does creativity theory give us into the limitations of managers asking their employees to 'think outside the box'?
3. Why does traditional market research often lead to incremental innovation?
4. Should a small company engaged in international business focus all its efforts to protect IP on patents?
5. How do animals navigate and what is its relevance to innovation? (Use www.asknature.org.)

Recommended Reading

1. Squires, S. and Byrne, B. (eds) *Creating Breakthrough Ideas: The Collaboration of Anthropologists and Designers in the Product Development Industry* (Westport, CT: Bergin and Garvey, 2002). Interesting perspectives on how product design studies can be improved through ethnographic methods.
2. Runco, M.A., *Creativity, Theories and Themes: Research, Development, and Practice* (Amsterdam: Elsevier, 2007). Everything you will ever need to know about creativity.
3. Floren, H. and Frishammer, J., 'From Preliminary Ideas to Corroborated Product Definitions: Managing the Front End of New Product Development', *California Management Review*, 54(4) (2012), 20–43. Academic review of the front end.

▶ MAIN CASE STUDY

MÖLNLYCKE HEALTH CARE – INNOVATION SCOUTING

Mölnlycke is a leading provider of single-use surgical and wound care products. The company name comes from the small town of Mölnlycke, Sweden, not far from Gothenburg, where the company was founded as a textile manufacturer in 1849. It introduced its first wound care product in the 1940s and its first surgical drape in the 1960s. Current products include: Safetac wound dressings and Avance negative pressure wound therapy; single-use surgical products, such as Biogel surgical gloves; and operating room ProcedurePaks. The company has 7,500 employees and generated revenues of $1.29 billion in 2013 from sales to hospitals worldwide. It manufactures in Europe, Malaysia, Thailand and the US.

Mölnlycke Health Care's growth targets have led it to focus on building corporate capabilities for breakthrough innovation. One crucial capability is 'scouting' – generating the customer insights needed to develop new products and services, using specialized techniques and high-performing, cross-functional teams. Building this capability required interventions at the team, organizational, cultural and process levels.

Building an Insights Capability

Many corporations start their innovation journey by launching idea generation schemes, only to find that these do not generate good breakthrough ideas.

Management at Mölnlycke's surgical division also recognized that deep customer insights were particularly important because increased competition meant that new products had to address unmet needs, to provide differentiation. Therefore, the company focused its efforts on what it termed 'scouting', small teams sent out to look for – or scout for – customer insights and new business areas.

The scouting capability was created to address two questions: What do we really know about our customers' needs? Do we have enough evidence to support these views? The direct engagement with customers meant that marketing needed to be involved in the process as well as R&D. Marketing and R&D worked together to identify appropriate market research tools, develop a process, and create a suitable organizational structure. In order to ensure the buy-in of both departments and signal the importance of cross-functional work in generating customer insights, it was decided that the scouting capability should report not only to R&D but also to marketing (see dotted line in Figure 5.9). Scouting was managed by Tove Weigel, in her new role as concept and innovation director.

Weigel quickly recognized that different market research techniques offer different perspectives and, used together, they give a fuller picture of where business opportunities lie. Thus a combination of techniques was used (just as a detective uses

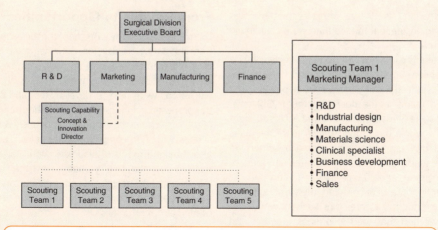

interviews, forensic analysis, database searches and other resources to solve a crime). Three approaches were used that were found to be simple, practical and effective: repertory grid technique, ethnographic market research and lead user workshops.

Generating Insights

To initiate the process, a cross-functional pool of nearly 40 people was trained on the new techniques. This pool was then divided into five teams, each with a deliberate mix of skills – typically a product manager, a clinical specialist, an industrial designer, an R&D engineer, a materials specialist, a finance representative, a manufacturing specialist, business development, and a sales representative. Each team was headed by a marketing manager (to strengthen the links between scouting, R&D and marketing) and had to identify customer needs in a particular area.

A 3-3-3 approach was used, consisting of three days of training on customer insight techniques, three months of data collection, and three days of data analysis (Figure 5.10). Within that structure, each team focused on a current or potential market. Most of the team members worked on the projects part time, typically two days of fieldwork, and

a team meeting every two weeks – this time was reserved to ensure that the scouting work could build momentum.

The teams carried out ethnographic research and RGT interviews at 20 hospitals, filming surgical procedures and conducting interviews, a process that immersed teams in the operating room (OR) environment. One Swiss hospital allowed access to eight ORs for a whole day, during which team members observed hip, open-heart and stomach surgery. In total, the teams collected approximately 20 hours of video recordings and 30 repertory grid interviews.

After the data were collected, the scouting teams came together for a three-day analysis workshop. Teams watched the video recordings together and analysed them in a systematic way based on ethnographic coding techniques. RGT interview responses were categorized into product features, product benefits and the emotions related to the OR environment. Each team focused on its own assigned area but presented its findings to everyone, adding energy to the analysis phase.

Workshop attendees were discouraged from talking about solutions during the first two days. Instead, they focused on identifying the issues customers face. They analysed the emotions of staff working in the OR and considered the culture of that environment. On the third day, teams were tasked with prototyping potential product solutions to address the issues and challenges they had identified in the first two days. The solutions were then discussed with healthcare professionals in an informal lead user workshop, which marked the end of the customer insight process.

The teams found the data collection and analysis experience surprisingly powerful. Taking direct part in ethnography was effective because, as a concept designer said, you 'have to experience it to learn from it – just being given the facts is not the same'. Those who attended the analysis workshop were intrigued by the way customer insights emerged from finding and interpreting clues to customer needs. A designer who attended said: 'different people saw different things ... there were lots of "aha moments" ... You could recognize that you were finding new things.' Similarly, a Mölnlycke clinical specialist (a surgeon with many years of experience) said: 'It surprised me how much information we gained; it led to so many opportunities. We found so many hidden needs.'

From Insights to Opportunities

Following the analysis workshop, the ideas generated from the data were developed further, to ensure that they represented real business opportunities. There were two strands to this work. First, a number of workshops were held to develop, test and optimize the proposed solutions. These workshops engaged a range of techniques, including biomimicry and interactions with non-competitor companies. There was also a second round of lead user workshops, which focused on generating solutions rather than generating insights into needs. Second, a healthcare economist helped the teams determine the size and value of market opportunities.

Teams reported their progress in evaluating ideas to the surgical division executive board each month. This helped the executives to provide the right level of support and guidance, balancing the need for time to allow an idea to develop and the need to maintain sufficient business focus. A member of the executive board commented that: 'Looking back, I recognize that focus is crucial – not starting too many demanding projects at once because "more can be less".' Generally, the aim was to select 'the opportunities that made sense ... killing others while there was time to kill them', said a business development manager.

The scouting process has now been applied to gather insights in approximately 10 different market areas. Mölnlycke has now analysed nearly 200 RGT interviews and 50 hours of video, eliciting hundreds of insights. Three radical and two incremental ideas identified from scouting activities are currently in the development and approval process. Other insights have been highlighted in Mölnlycke's recommendations to customers or addressed through other means. For instance, after OR observations identified a number of medical procedures that created physical stress for medical staff, the company introduced training materials to address these problems. Due to the exhaustive regulatory approval process for medical products, no radical new products originating from the scouting process are yet on the market.

One surprising discovery for Mölnlycke has been that deep customer insights are not only applicable to radical products. The process of interacting with customers through RGT interviews, ethnographic visits and lead user groups has produced crucial ideas for improving existing products, by adding exciting features that the competition does not offer. As a result, there has been a faster than expected payback time from the investment in building the insight capability.

Creating a Wider Culture of Innovation

Beyond the direct benefits of the scouting activity, the pool of employees trained in the process has had a very positive cultural impact on the surgical division as a whole, creating an environment in which seeking new opportunities, focusing on customer needs, and working across functions are the norm. In addition, Mölnlycke's management has sought to engage every employee in contributing to the new focus on innovation and build on the momentum provided by the customer insight process.

One mechanism for this effort was the surgical division's Innovation Days, which were held several times. At these events, employees were presented with a number of unmet customer needs that had emerged from the scouting process and asked to brainstorm and prototype possible solutions. The commitment and energy generated by these events was enormous. Employees still talk of their amazement at, for example, seeing the procurement director, HR director and a receptionist working together to create solutions to a user problem. Senior managers' participation in the event was important for a number of reasons: it signalled the importance of innovation to the organization, helped management understand the link between insights and opportunities, and highlighted the experimental nature of innovation.

Weigel is an industrial designer by background and has always had a focus on customer needs. In reflecting on the initiative, she said: 'The new scouting capability has not only expanded the company's ability to investigate new market areas; it has also had an impact on team performance and corporate culture.'

Reflective Questions

1. Why should different market research techniques be used in parallel?
2. What advantages did Mölnlycke find in having a full cross-functional team involved in the market research?
3. Was it important to have scouting reporting to R&D and marketing?

Source: copyright © 2015. Adapted from Creating Innovation Capabilities: Mölnlycke Health Care's Journey by Tove Weigel and Keith Goffin. Reproduced by permission of the Industrial Research Institute, www.iriweb.org (http://www.tandfonline. com)[117].

SELECTING THE INNOVATION PORTFOLIO

INTRODUCTION

Any organization is likely to have a number of innovation projects running at any one time. Allocating resources between them to achieve optimum value is always difficult, the more so when some have high levels of uncertainty. Managers face three challenges: the first is deciding which individual projects are intrinsically worth doing in themselves; the second is choosing the set of projects, or *portfolio*, that best meets the overall needs of the organization; the third is retaining the understanding and commitment of the people involved (especially those whose projects are rejected), and of those who may be affected. Choosing and managing a portfolio is a dynamic activity because innovation projects change as they proceed and, as a result, some may have to be pushed forward, some delayed and some dropped altogether.

A healthy portfolio in a company looking for growth will include a mix of relatively easy, incremental projects and more challenging breakthrough and radical ones. Many companies get caught in the so-called *incremental trap* – only selecting projects that match their core business and are low risk.

The overriding problem in selecting innovation projects is that much of the information on which the decision should be based will be unknown, or at least uncertain, at the outset, and yet decisions must be made. Some candidates may be rejected at once but for the others acceptance will often be provisional, subject to further investigations and perhaps experiments. Project selection is, therefore, often not a single decision made at the start of the project, but rather a preliminary selection followed by an investigation and a further review and so on until eventually a 'point of no return' is reached. So, although prioritization is shown as a separate section of the funnel in the Pentathlon Framework, it is actually a rolling process extending through the ideas element as well. Often, companies use separate teams, or even departments, for exploring new concepts and for the more focused and disciplined activity of implementation that follows.

The more novel ideas in the innovation funnel may require a great deal of work before it is possible to take the final decision to proceed. Thus, it is inevitable that some effort will be 'wasted'. Many companies find it difficult to accept this; but an organization that is not prepared to invest properly in the early process of investigation and risk reduction will either produce only incremental innovations or will end up cancelling projects later on, when far more money has been invested. Carefully targeted expenditure ensures that the less promising projects are weeded out quickly, leaving a manageable group of strong projects to work on. 'Fail soon to succeed quicker' is a good motto.

In making decisions about project selection, attention properly concentrates on avoiding projects that are likely to fail. The fact that a failed project will be all too visible to one's colleagues and superiors certainly concentrates the mind. But managers must remember that the eventual impact of missing out on a good project may be far greater than that of wrongly choosing a bad one.

As each project progresses and the uncertainties unravel, managers will face not only unanticipated obstacles but also unexpected opportunities. There will be upsides to exploit as well as downsides to manage. This requires a flexible

CHAPTER 6

and open attitude backed up with some strong management disciplines, and a few simple tools.

This chapter covers:

- The principles of portfolio management.
- Financial and non-financial ways to evaluate and select projects.
- Selecting and balancing a portfolio of projects.
- Management processes.
- A main case study on Grundfos.

PRINCIPLES OF PORTFOLIO SELECTION

The overall purpose of portfolio management is to ensure that the collection of innovation projects delivers the best value (however that is defined) over time. The key issues that must be considered are:[1]

- *Project value:* Each individual project should in itself represent good value to the organization.
- *Portfolio balance:* There may also be a need to ensure that the portfolio of projects is balanced in various ways, for example between long-term and short-term projects, between high-risk and low-risk projects, or between parts of the business.
- *Strategic fit:* In addition to value and balance, the portfolio must also respond to the organization's strategic priorities.

It is also important that the process of deciding whether to proceed with a project, and especially when to cancel one, should be as objective and transparent as possible. Mini Case 6.1 describes how the World Bank redesigned its selection process to achieve these aims.

An inadequate portfolio management process leads to slow decisions, a tendency to choose only low-impact projects, and a failure to stop those that have lost their way. The typical results of these are summarized in Table 6.1.

MINI CASE 6.1: *The World Bank – The Vision for Selecting Programmes[2]*

Most people expect innovation to be particularly difficult in large, bureaucratic organizations. The World Bank, with its headquarters in Washington DC, might be seen as such an organization and not a hub of innovation. However, appearances can be deceptive, as the World Bank has, in fact, built a reputation for being creative and innovative. How?

Much of the credit must go to the team at the corporate strategy unit, who have radically changed the way projects are chosen for World Bank funding. The aim of the bank is to alleviate poverty, and traditionally only large, relatively conservative programmes were funded. Large amounts of money were involved so everybody wanted to make the best use of the cash available and avoid funding anything with a high risk. The decision process was normally complicated, conducted at the highest levels in the organization, and slow.

Continued...

The bank has now completely changed the way it selects the best proposals from the myriad it receives. The vision was to base the selection process on the way venture capitalists make funding decisions in stages and spread their risks over a range of projects rather than 'just going for the big one'. Initial funding is now available for the first stages of a programme and subsequent financing is dependent on defined results being achieved in a set time frame. The bank is experimenting more, and running pilot programmes to test radical ideas. The range of projects being considered and the selection process have also become highly transparent: decisions are made by a panel of judges drawn from industry and a variety of not-for-profit organizations, such as Oxfam and World Vision, and centre on a Development Marketplace. This is a day on which proposals are presented and selected in the style of an industrial show, with booths set up for each proposal, presentations and so on. Not only does this make the selection process transparent to all employees and applicants but the resulting exchange of ideas spurs everyone involved towards the production of better proposals, year on year.

TABLE 6.1: Business Impact of Poor Project Selection Processes

Management issue	Resulting problems
Slow decision-making	• Projects that start late will be late to complete • Late to market means lost profit • Rush to make up for lost time causes excess cost and temptation to cut corners • Frustrated staff
Unadventurous, low-impact projects	• Poor profitability • Lost opportunities to gain market share • Poor morale
Too many projects	• Resources stretched so that some or all projects run late • Lack of management attention • Bottlenecks
Poor projects not killed early	• Unnecessary waste of money and time • Lack of resources for good projects

CHAPTER 6

EVALUATING INDIVIDUAL PROJECTS

Figure 6.1 shows the innovation funnel, already introduced in Chapter 1 (see Figure 1.4). Here we have removed the demarcation between the ideas and selection phases to emphasize that although the distinction is important in principle, in practice the process of selection happens continuously as ideas are investigated, reviewed and sometimes rejected. Breakthrough and radical innovations (see Chapter 1) will start to the left while incremental innovations will start

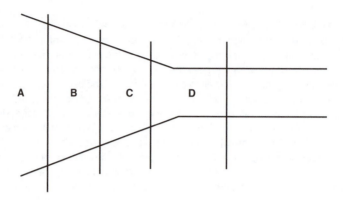

FIGURE 6.1: The Innovation Funnel

further to the right. Projects move to the right as work proceeds and it becomes clearer exactly what they can deliver and what the best application might be. Different selection tools are needed at different stages along the funnel. For the purpose of discussion, we show four separate regions along the funnel but we emphasize that their exact positions will vary very much from case to case.

At the left of the funnel (region A), when the first gleam of an original idea appears, there is nothing better to go on other than the intuition and enthusiasm of the creator. Soon after that, managers will want to inject more objectivity into the selection process. At this stage, any attempt at financial analysis will be little more than guesswork but choices may have to be made anyway. Non-financial decision aids are required and the tool of choice here – in fact, virtually the only option – is *multi-criteria analysis*, in which projects are assessed against a variety of criteria that are pointers towards likely success. In region B, as we show later, the criteria used will usually be very company specific, but later (region C), as the commercial focus sharpens, many companies will use similar criteria. As projects move along the funnel towards full development, multi-factor methods should give increasing emphasis to financial measures until eventually (region D) a formal business plan is required; in the words of Nagji and Tuff:[3] 'Eventually a company must focus on the hard economics … but that can wait until there's something ready to pilot.'

Financial methods are the most familiar and frequently used approaches, so we will start by discussing them and then review the different tools that must be used for projects further back up the funnel.

FINANCIAL ASSESSMENT METHODS

Financial analysis is the most common and, often, the only method used.[4] The analysis can be done with varying degrees of sophistication, and somewhat different methods are appropriate for simple and for complex projects. In discussing valuation methods, it is convenient to distinguish three generic types of project:

1. The simplest is a *single-stage project*, which is expected to run through from start to finish without interruption, as shown in Figure 6.2a. Small or low-risk projects are generally treated in this way.
2. The second is a *multi-stage project*, which is conducted in phases, with a progress review after each one when a decision (shown as a diamond in Figure 6.2) is made whether or not to continue. This is obviously appropriate for breakthrough and radical projects where preliminary investigations are likely to be needed to establish what can (or should) be done. It may be possible to estimate the probability of cancellation at each phase. These figures can be useful in valuing the project, as we will show later.
3. The third type is the *network project* (Figure 6.2c), where decisions after each phase may lead to alternative courses of action, rather than a simple go or stop decision. Diagrams such as 6.2b and 6.2c are, for obvious reasons, called *decision trees*.

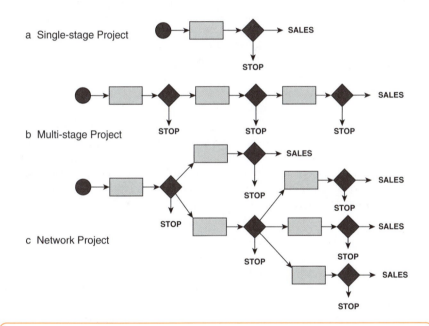

FIGURE 6.2: Single-stage, Multi-stage and Network Projects
Note: Boxes are activities, diamonds are decision points.

Single-stage Projects

Calculating Value

The most straightforward and most commonly used way of determining the value (V) of a project is simply to estimate the income (I) accruing from it and subtract the costs (C) to give a net value.

$$V = I - C \qquad\qquad\qquad \text{Equation 6.1}$$

Many levels of sophistication are possible in estimating the components of this simple equation, but it is worth remembering that extra sophistication does not necessarily make for better decision-making. If the basic data are inaccurate or uncertain, as they are likely to be for innovative projects, elaborate computation will not make it any better. Remember the old adage: garbage in, garbage out.

That said, some enhancements are certainly useful. The first is to take account of the time-related value of money. Income today is worth more than income next year because money in hand today could be invested to earn a year's worth of interest. For the same reason, early expenditure is more costly than later. The first modification of Equation 6.1 is therefore to take account of this effect by using *discounted cash flow* (DCF). In this approach, every element of income or expenditure is discounted by a factor that takes account of when it occurs.[5] An income or cost in one year's time is multiplied by a discount factor $1/(1 + s)$, where s is the yearly cost of money: so if money costs 5 per cent a year, the discount is $1/(1.05)$, or 0.95. Income made in two years' time is multiplied by a discount factor of $1/(1.05)^2$, or 0.91, and so on.

When discount factors are included for both income and costs, the value of the project is called the *net present value* (NPV):

$$NPV = M_1 + M_2/(1 + s) + M_3/(1 + s)^2 + M_4/(1 + s)^3 + \ldots \qquad \text{Equation 6.2}$$

Here, M_1, M_2, M_3 etc. are the cash flows (costs or incomes) into the project in the first, second, third time periods and so on. The discount rate, s, should be the average cost of capital to the organization and should include the cost of equity and debt in the proportions found in the balance sheet.[6] Some financial managers choose a higher discount rate on the income stream as a way of taking account of a high level of risk in the project but this practice is subject to three criticisms:

1. The particular figure used tends to be a 'gut feel' that can seldom be justified.[7, 8]
2. It makes the assumption that uncertainty is always a negative factor, which is wrong. Uncertainty simply means that a project faces a range of possible outcomes and this range may well include results that are better than hoped as well as worse.
3. Risk is not merely an aspect of value. It is an entirely different thing, requiring specific management. Burying risk in a financial discount number hides it from scrutiny and so undermines the management process.

NPV is widely used and is worth the comparatively small amount of effort involved in the calculation, especially if the timescales of the project are long or money costs are high.[9]

Measures of Robustness

The next enhancement is to check how sensitive the valuation is to the key assumptions that have been made. The simplest approach is to rerun the financial calculations several times with different assumptions about the major component parts such as sales levels, timing and so on. This valuable step is surprisingly often omitted, even in these days of easy spreadsheet analysis. Yet the information may be critical in deciding whether to go ahead with a project if it turns out to be particularly sensitive to some factor that cannot be relied on. It is also useful as the project progresses because it highlights which elements the project manager must control to ensure financial success.

Another approach to robustness is to calculate how quickly the project delivers its results. A convenient measure for this is the 'payback time', or *time to break even* (TBE). The financial returns from most projects will follow a curve like that shown in Figure 6.3, starting with a period of loss when expenditure is made but income has not yet begun, moving to the 'break-even point' when the income balances the expenditure, and then on to overall profit. Other things being equal, a project with a short TBE is more secure than one that takes longer, simply because there is less time for unexpected things to happen.

A more subtle approach, commonly used in assessing acquisitions, is to calculate the *internal rate of return* (IRR), which is the value of the discount factor, s, in Equation 6.2 that would reduce the NPV of the project to zero.[10] The high discount rate has the effect of depressing later costs and incomes: in Figure 6.3, this would pull the curve down so that the maximum just reaches the axis, as shown. Clearly, the higher the IRR, the more financially robust the project: an IRR of 25 per cent would mean that money would have to earn 25 per cent a year before keeping it in the bank would be a better option than investing in the project. Companies often reject projects that do not meet a threshold value for TBE or IRR.[11]

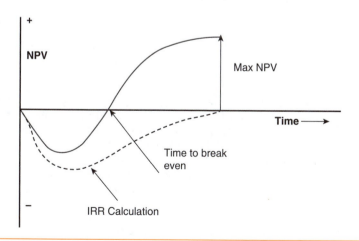

FIGURE 6.3: Development of the NPV of a Typical Project with Time

THEORY BOX 6.1: *Estimating and Using Probabilities*

The objective assessment and management of risk is a relatively recent development in the history of human thought, let alone in business management.[12] The modern concept of probability was not formulated until the mid-17th century by Pascal and Fermat, who built on the earlier work of Galileo, Huyghens and others.[13, 14] The fact that such illustrious names were involved should remind us that this is not an easy topic to think clearly about. Even today, we are easily misled, as the number of people who believe in winning systems and 'runs of luck' at roulette makes clear.

What do we really mean when we say: 'I give this project a 30 per cent chance of success'? Thirty per cent of what? And what use is the number? Let us start with the question of how probabilities are estimated.

In most games of chance, the probability of an event can be worked out just from the logic of the situation: the chance of drawing a king from a well-shuffled pack of cards has to be 4/52 because there are four kings in a total of 52 cards. In the business world, such logical simplicity is rare. Thought alone will not tell us the probability that the dimensions of a part made in a factory will fall in a particular range, or that a certain number of people will go on skiing holidays this year. These must be deduced from measurements of what has happened in the past. *Sampling theory* is the study of how the characteristics of a population can be calculated from measurements of a restricted sample of cases. Three considerations are important:

1. The samples must be representative, that is, from the relevant factory or ski resort.
2. The situation must be stable. If new machinery is introduced into a factory, it is likely to change the process and new samples must be taken.
3. The accuracy of the estimate depends on the number of samples taken. Typically, about 100 are needed to give 10 per cent accuracy, and opinion pollsters have to interview over 1,000 people to get an accuracy of a few per cent.

In estimating probabilities for innovation projects, one relies on comparisons with similar ones from the past. But most people are familiar with very few projects, and fewer still that are genuinely comparable to the one in hand. So, these are not probabilities but expressions of confidence based on a combination of experience and judgement. There is nothing wrong with this: it is all we have. But such confidence assessments are *very* approximate. Not only are they based on restricted information but they are subject to the personal attitudes and biases of those involved (as discussed in Theory Box 6.3 below). They can be improved by pooling the views of several people but they remain expressions of confidence, not calculations of probability in the strict sense.

When asking managers to estimate confidence levels, one useful trick, used by Embraer (Mini Case 6.2) for determining confidence levels in a decision tree, is to give them a small number of tokens with which they 'bet' which branch the project will take. This emphasizes that the estimate is subjective and rough, and avoids pointless discussions about precise numbers. For example, for a two-branch decision, 6 tokens allow people to allocate their tokens equally (3 and 3) to each branch, or 2 or 4 or 1 and 5 either way, making a 5-point scale for each branch, which is probably a realistic level of accuracy. Eight tokens makes a 7-point scale. For a three-branch decision, 9 tokens make a 5-point scale.

Single-stage Projects with Possibility of Failure

Innovative projects often face the possibility of cancellation before they reach the end. How does one include this in the valuation? First, one must put a figure on the likelihood, or probability, of cancellation. This issue is discussed further in Theory Box 6.1, but suppose for now that our confidence in a successful outcome is expressed as a percentage, p. There are two possible outcomes: a loss equal to the costs ($-C$) if the project is stopped; and a profit equal to the difference of income and cost ($I - C$) if not. The classical approach is to add the two possible outcomes multiplied by their probabilities. This gives the mean or, in statistical terms, the expected outcome or *expectation*:

$$\text{Expectation} = p(I - C) + (1 - p)(-C) = I.p - C \qquad \text{Equation 6.3}$$

The result, as one might expect, is simply to reduce the income by the factor p. Notice that the effect on profit can be quite severe: a healthy 50 per cent profit margin is reduced to zero if p is 50 per cent.

But what actually is the expectation? It is the average result that would be obtained from repeating the same project a large number of times. But for an individual project, the result will be *either* a profit of $I - C$ or a loss of $-C$. It will never actually be $I.p - C$; so for a single project the expectation is meaningless. One is reminded of the British trade union leader, who said: 'Don't talk to me about 8 per cent unemployment. If it's you, it's 100 per cent.' He might have added 'or 0'. Certainly, faced with 8 per cent unemployment, few people ask themselves how they can manage on 92 per cent of their salary. The average figure has meaning for governments who are interested in the population as a whole but not for individuals. Similarly, averages are useful for large portfolios of projects but not for small portfolios or individual projects.

Risky or uncertain projects have, by definition, a range of possible outcomes. A single 'average' figure together with a 'probability' tells one nothing other than that the figure is unreliable. It is much better to retain the useful information about what the range of uncertainty is likely to be and use it in making selection judgements.

Multi-stage and Network Projects

In a multi-stage project, managers can take action to deal with problems as they arise and, if necessary, abandon the project if its prospects become unattractive. They can also recognize good fortune and capitalize on it. Management intervention during the course of a project can radically improve its potential value, as we now show.

Consider a project, which we will call Project Alpha, which has four stages, with decision points between. Each stage has a different cost and at the start of the project, managers estimate their confidence of each being a success, in the sense that progress will be good enough for the project to continue. These are shown in Figure 6.4. If the project comes to fruition, the expected income, appropriately discounted, is €75m.

The total discounted cost of the project is €(2 + 6 + 12 = 20)m and the overall confidence in success is 0.5 × 0.7 × 0.75, or about 26 per cent. If the project goes ahead with no intervention, the expected revenue is 26 per cent of €75m, or €19.5m. With costs of €20m, the outcome is projected to be a loss of €0.5m, so the project looks thoroughly unattractive.

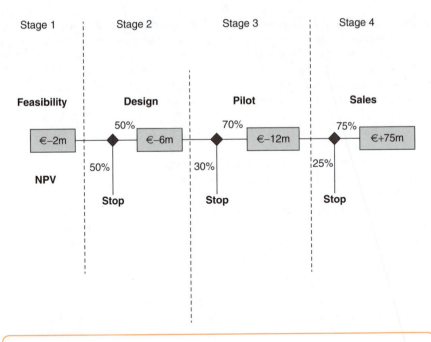

FIGURE 6.4: Decision Tree for Project Alpha
Note: Boxes show activities and their (discounted) cash flow.

The picture changes dramatically if we take into account the option for management to stop the project after each stage if the prospects look poor. The cost of the first stage must be included in full but there is only a 50 per cent chance that the cost of the second stage will actually be incurred. The third stage cost will occur only if the first and second phases are successful, confidence in which is 35 per cent (0.5 x 0.7). The correct calculation for the likely costs is therefore

$$€(2 + 0.5 \times 6 + (0.5 \times 0.7) \times 12)m = €9.2m \qquad \text{Equation 6.4}$$

Thus the project as a whole really has a projected value of

$$€(19.5 - 9.2)m = €10.3m \qquad \text{Equation 6.5}$$

This compares with the previous figure of –0.5m. Clearly, neglecting the possibilities for choice and action during a project can lead to serious undervaluation and the likely rejection of potentially excellent opportunities.

The estimated value for a multi-stage project derived in this way is known as the *expected commercial value* (ECV)[15] and the process of analysis itself is called *decision tree analysis* (DTA). Clearly, it is more realistic than a simple DCF calculation for such projects, although one must always remember that the figures used are estimates, not facts.

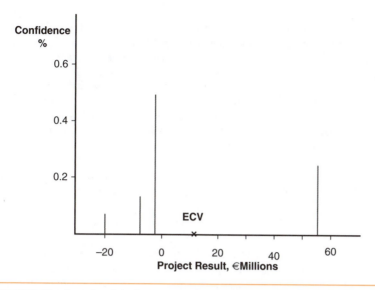

FIGURE 6.5: The Four Possible Outcomes of Project Alpha

The ECV calculation yields a single figure for the value of the project, taking into account the confidence levels ascribed to the outcomes at the various stages. It is convenient to have a single value but it is not a prediction of what one would get in practice. Project Alpha would actually have just one of four outcomes: a profit of €55m if it went to completion; or a loss of €2m, €8m or €20m if it stopped at an intermediate stage. This is illustrated in Figure 6.5. For a single project, the ECV of €10.3m is not itself a possible outcome at all. It will never happen.

The calculation can be made more realistic by replacing the single values for the costs of each phase by a range of possibilities. For example, instead of putting €6m for the cost of phase two of Project Alpha, one would allow, more realistically, a distribution of cost between perhaps €4m and €7m. The analysis then becomes more complex and a Monte Carlo simulation is required (see Theory Box 6.2). Figure 6.6 shows the result of a simulation of a project similar to Project Alpha, where ranges of costs and income have been allowed in place of the single-point estimates to generate a more complete picture.

THEORY BOX 6.2: *Monte Carlo Simulation*

The range of possibilities for a project can be explored more completely using a Monte Carlo simulation, named for the city in Monaco famed for its casinos. This used to be considered a rather esoteric technique but it can now be done easily using a spreadsheet and a simple application package. The idea is to run a large number of calculations using a random number generator to represent the statistics for the confidence levels in the decision tree.

Continued...

For example, the confidence in success of the first phase of Project Alpha is 50 per cent, so the simulation generates a random number between 0 and 100 and if this is less than 50, the phase is deemed to have failed so the simulation records a project loss of €2m and stops. Otherwise, it stores the €2m cost and generates another random number to decide whether the next phase is successful. The confidence level for this is 70 per cent, so if the random number is less than 30, the second phase has failed and a project loss of €8m is recorded. Otherwise, the accumulated cost would increase by €6m and the simulation would move to the next phase, and so on until completion. The simulation is then repeated. Each run will generally have a different outcome, but repeating the process a large number of times and accumulating the results generates a full view of all the possible outcomes and how relatively often they occur.

The Monte Carlo simulation is a helpful and surprisingly easy technique to use. It has the healthy effect of showing the full range of possibilities that management may actually face on the particular project.

Decision trees emphasize that innovation projects usually proceed in stages that generate options that may or may not be taken up. They are very helpful, especially for network projects (Figure 6.2c), in demonstrating where the risks and expenditures occur, and will often point the way to a redesign of the project, for example to remove as much risk as possible early on. However, the complexity of diagrams such as Figures 6.5 and 6.6 may seem daunting when it comes to making comparisons between several projects. But there is a simple way, illustrated schematically in Figure 6.7.[16] First, it is necessary to establish the upper and lower limits of the value for each project; that is, the best and worst outcomes that are reasonably likely to happen. In Figure 6.5, they are –€20m and +€60m but if one makes a full distribution using Monte Carlo techniques, one will generally need

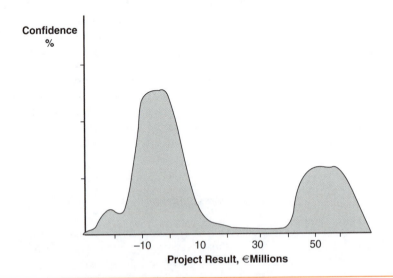

FIGURE 6.6: Result of a Full Monte Carlo Simulation for Project Alpha

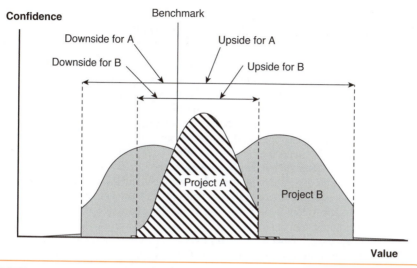

FIGURE 6.7: Comparison between Two Projects Using their Confidence Value Distributions

Source: copyright © 2010. From Valuing and Comparing Small Portfolios by Rick Mitchell, Francis Hunt and David Probert. Reproduced by permission of the Industrial Research Institute, www.iriweb.org (http://www. tandfonline.com).

to make a judgement about how realistic the outer tails are likely to be in practice and truncate the distribution accordingly, as in Figure 6.7. A simple approach is to reject the upper and lower 5 or 10 per cent of the distribution.

The appropriate measure of downside is the lower edge of the truncated distribution because this is the amount the project stands to lose in the worst case; it is the budget managers must commit for the project. The upside measure requires a bit more thought. Managers are usually uncomfortable using the upper edge of the distribution, which is the maximum return the project is ever likely to make. A more conservative measure is to use the area (or integral) under the curve to the right of the threshold, which represents the *probability-weighted upside*. This was the measure chosen by Embraer in Mini Case 6.2.

The ratio of the upside to downside is a measure of how good a prospect each project is, and a rational portfolio can be selected simply by choosing projects in the order of upside/downside until the available budget is used up. Note that in this approach, the concept of risk as a separate variable disappears entirely. Risk is seen merely as a way of thinking about the range of outcomes that each project faces. There is no question of 'balancing' risk and return.

It is worth emphasizing that this approach to prioritization can be used without resorting to Monte Carlo methods by simply taking the upsides and downsides from diagrams such as Figure 6.5, which are derived directly from the decision tree. This is not as accurate as a full simulation would be but it is much quicker and simpler; and may be perfectly adequate if the uncertainties in the costs are not too great.

MINI CASE 6.2: *Embraer Aerospace – Using Decision Trees*

Embraer, the Brazilian aerospace company, wanted to determine the most effective way to introduce radio frequency identification (RFID) technology into part of its operations – a process innovation. The key question was whether it would be better to introduce this innovation via one or two trial implementations to minimize the risk, or to go for a single stage with no preliminaries.

A group of managers first constructed the three decision trees working as a team. They then made their own individual estimates of confidence levels and cost and income data. Recognizing that their estimates could only be approximate, they agreed to set the confidence values on the tree by allocating 12 tokens between the tree branches, representing their relative confidence in each of the outcomes. They estimated costs or incomes (suitably discounted) for each stage as upper and lower limits with either a triangular or flat distribution between them. Finally, the estimates were pooled and discussed as a team to come to agreed values. This process took a few hours. The Monte Carlo analysis was then done offline and the resulting value distributions presented to the team the next day for discussion and review. In this case, it was agreed to truncate the distributions by simply removing the 5 per cent tails at either end. One of the decision trees and the associated Monte Carlo results are shown in Figures 6.8a and 6.8b.

Figure 6.8c compares the main parameters of the confidence distributions for the tree implementations. This shows that although the expectation value is highest for the two-pilot implementation, the one-pilot case gives the best ratio of upside to lowest likely value, which, as argued above, is a more secure basis for choice. This is the implementation the company chose to follow.

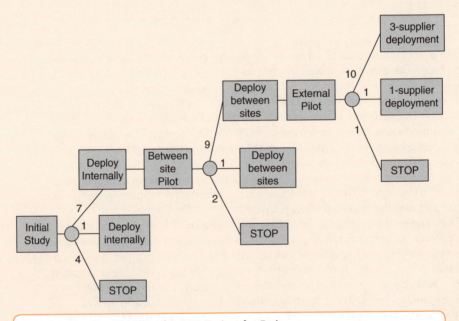

FIGURE 6.8a: Decision Tree for RFID Project for Embraer

Source: copyright © 2010. From Valuing and Comparing Small Portfolios by Rick Mitchell, Francis Hunt and David Probert. Reproduced by permission of the Industrial Research Institute, www.iriweb.org (http://www. tandfonline.com).

Continued...

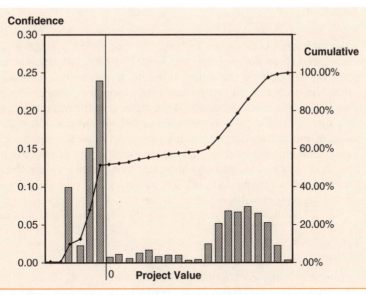

FIGURE 6.8b: Monte Carlo Simulation for Decision Tree by Embraer
Note: The simulation generates confidence levels as a histogram.
Source: copyright © 2010. From Valuing and Comparing Small Portfolios by Rick Mitchell, Francis Hunt and David Probert. Reproduced by permission of the Industrial Research Institute, www.iriweb.org (http://www.tandfonline.com).

	Highest likely value (HLV) $	Expected Upside/ Downside	Mean $	Expected Upside/ Lowest likely value (LLV)
No pilot	475	3.1	135	1.0
1 pilot	765	3.2	160	1.25
2 pilots	697	5.3	190	1.0

Best Expectation   Most secure choice

FIGURE 6.8c: Comparison of Three Strategies for RFID Implementation
Source: copyright © 2010. From Valuing and Comparing Small Portfolios by Rick Mitchell, Francis Hunt and David Probert. Reproduced by permission of the Industrial Research Institute, www.iriweb.org (http://www.tandfonline.com).

Source: copyright © 2010. Adapted from Valuing and Comparing Small Portfolios by Rick Mitchell, Francis Hunt and David Probert. Reproduced by permission of the Industrial Research Institute, www.iriweb.org (http://www.tandfonline.com)[17].

Real Options

Many authors have noted that innovation projects have some similarities with financial instruments called *options*. An option on a stock is a contract that allows, but does not compel, the holder to buy that stock at a fixed price at some agreed point in the future. If the price of the stock rises above the option price, the holder of an option can make money by exercising the option and then selling the stock. However, if the stock goes down, the option holder loses only the cost of purchasing the option itself, which is usually much less than the value of the stock. Many innovation projects have the same logic in that they give management an option, but not the obligation, to take the project forward after each stage. This analogy suggests that the theory developed for valuing financial options might be applied to valuing the flexibility that managers have in managing projects. This is known as the *real options* approach to valuation.[18, 19]

An influential theory of option valuation for financial stocks was worked out in the 1970s by Fischer Black, Myron Scholes and Robert Merton (BSM). The full treatment involves an elegant partial differential equation, the Black–Scholes equation, which allows analysis of a large range of varied cases.[20] The analysis has been extremely influential in the financial community but attempts to apply it to innovation projects have not been particularly convincing because the financial and project domains are seldom closely comparable.[21] The first discrepancy is that in the BSM model, the value of the stock is assumed to follow a 'random walk' path, with its possible range spreading upwards and downwards as time goes on. This implies that the possibility of gain from holding an option increases over time, so that the value of a 'long-dated' option is greater than a 'short-dated' one. By contrast, the value of an innovative idea and the options it provides is more likely to decline with time because of competitive pressures, expiry of patents or market lifecycle. If it were not so, managers would be observed diligently slowing down their innovation projects.

The second discrepancy is that the BSM analysis relies on being able to identify a *hedge position*. In essence, a hedge is a financial asset whose value tends to move in the opposite way, its value going up in conditions that would drive the stock down, and down in conditions that would make it go up.[22] In the world of innovation projects, however, much of the risk will be within the project itself (so-called *specific*, or *private*, risk) and cannot usually be hedged. Real options may be useful in evaluating 'real' projects where the risks are mostly in market conditions but not for the majority of innovation projects where most of the risks are internal. Another cogent objection is that the workings and assumptions of the model are not easily accessible to the user so it is difficult to discuss and justify the results to those affected.

NON-FINANCIAL ASSESSMENT METHODS

In an ideal world, financial calculations would be all you need in selecting projects in a portfolio. Unfortunately, the financial information available in the early stages of a project may well be incomplete or unreliable, or, more likely, both. This is particularly so with breakthrough and radical projects. There are two reasons for this: first, the completion date may be some way in the future and so there may be considerable uncertainty about what can be achieved, and what the customer's reaction will be. Second, developing a reliable financial forecast requires a detailed business plan and companies may feel the effort is not justified when the project is still in the concept stage. This fact is well attested by research. In a wide-ranging study, Robert Cooper and colleagues[23] found that of all the possible ways of selecting early-stage projects, practising managers had the least faith in purely financial projections. So what is to be done?

Many companies rely heavily on the intuition of experienced managers in selecting early-stage projects. Some business leaders seem to have a knack for choosing winners. Or perhaps they are just lucky. However, work in the field of behavioural economics has shown that intuition can be surprisingly fallible.[24] Certainly, the intuition of an expert can be quite astonishingly powerful and subtle: an art historian can know at a glance whether a painting is original; a clinician can make snap diagnoses with great certainty; and we can all tell in a second when a friend is angry. But these skills are developed over a long time and with a great deal of practice and feedback. When we confront unfamiliar situations (and innovations are likely to be so), our intuition is surprisingly easily misled (see Theory Box 6.3). Thus, where hard data are scarce, we need tools and process to help make our decisions as rational as possible. It is also helpful to involve several people, not only because they may bring different knowledge and experience to bear but also to balance out the intuitive biases.

THEORY BOX 6.3: *The Pitfalls of Intuitive Judgement*

Classical economics has assumed that people are generally rational and consistent in the choices they make. Jacob Bernoulli proposed that gamblers, and by extension investors, make decisions rationally; although they attach different 'utility'[25] to gains depending on their total wealth: a gain of $10,000 is more valuable to someone whose worth is $20,000 than to someone whose wealth is $2m. In classical economics, humans are held to be 'selfish, rational and consistent'. However, in the past 20 or 30 years, a body of study, so-called *behavioural economics*, has undermined belief in this 'homo economicus' by showing that we are all subject to consistent biases in our intuitive judgements. We all need to be aware of these and never more so than when we are making business judgements.

The field was given major impetus by the work of Daniel Kahneman and Amos Tversky in the 1970s and 80s, work for which Kahneman received the Nobel Prize in 2002, Tversky having died in 1996. They pointed out that the intuitive mind has a strong tendency to use short cuts, or *heuristics*, in decision-making and that although these are often efficient, they can lead to systematic and serious errors. The most relevant ones are:

1. Framing: The way a proposition is presented can have a significant effect on one's reaction to it. For example, people place more value on (and indeed are more willing to take risks for) avoiding a loss than achieving a gain. The way the proposition is presented influences decisions.[26]
2. The halo effect: One well-rated aspect of a proposition improves the rating given to other aspects, even if they are unrelated. For example, appearance or physique affects how we judge a person's opinions: the views of a handsome or impressive person tend to command respect. More powerfully, the opinions of high-status individuals such as senior managers tend to carry more weight than those of others, even in subjects where they have no special expertise.

Continued...

CHAPTER 6

3. The law of small numbers: Human beings are not natural statisticians. We tend to assume that a small number of samples, for example our own experiences, gives a much more accurate picture of an uncertain reality than it does. Interestingly, this applies just as strongly to professional statisticians when not acting professionally. One of the effects is to make us believe that our own experience, even if very limited, is a good measure of how things are.

4. Anchoring: When presented with a fact, especially a number, we tend to use that as the starting point for subsequent estimates. This is well verified by experiment. An example we often use in teaching is to ask a group: 'Do you think the highest point in Australia is more or less than 4,000 metres?' Having answered that question, the group is asked to estimate what the height actually is. Another group is asked the same question but with a suggestion of 2,000 metres. The responses of each group are typically around 3,500 and 2,500 metres respectively. According to Kahneman,[27] this is typical: the difference between the estimates is regularly about a third to a half of the difference between the anchor values, unless, of course, the participants are already well informed. (We would use a different example if in Australia.) The effect of anchoring is particularly strong if combined with a halo; for example if a senior manager offers a view at the start of a discussion.

5. Groupthink: Janis[28] showed that the desire for harmony or conformity in a group can result in irrational or dysfunctional decisions, often held with high confidence.[29] Arguably, this has led to several high-profile poor decisions such as those that led to the *Challenger* Space Shuttle tragedy of 1986.

6. Availability: When asked to judge how likely or common something is, we are strongly influenced by how readily instances of it can be called to mind. Recent experiences, or things often read about or discussed, tend to bias decision-making.

Although it is risky to rely on intuition alone, there are also risks in going too much the other way. In the early stages of an innovation project, decisions have to be made using very inadequate data. Overly elaborate models, and especially those whose workings are hidden in complex mathematics, obscure the assumptions and can perhaps confer a spurious authority.

The limitations of both intuition and financial projections have led companies to adopt a more broadly based approach in which financial data may be included but as only one of several factors. This is *multi-criteria analysis*, often simply called *scoring*. In this, projects are assessed against a number of factors, or criteria (the terms are used interchangeably), that are pointers to likely success. For a new product, for example, these might include things like: the size of the market; the level of competition; how well differentiated the product was from rivals; the R&D effort required and so on. Potential projects are scored according to how well they meet each factor, and the scores are added to give an overall value. It is not strictly a valuation method but it gives a way of comparing projects against each other, and against a benchmark, while avoiding the dangers of relying too heavily on any one, fallible indicator. An extension of the basic idea, known as *analytical hierarchy*,[30, 31] allows each factor to be itself scored against appropriate sub-factors (see Theory Box 6.4). The *balanced scorecard* approach to measuring total company performance is another related technique.[32]

Clearly, there cannot be one set of factors suitable for all circumstances. Those for selecting early-stage technology projects are bound to be different from those for choosing new sales outlets; and there will be differences between companies. Multi-factor tools *always* have to be customized for the task in hand.

The criteria may simply be used as a checklist to guide the review process and ensure that all relevant factors are being considered. There is considerable value in this, particularly if the list of projects is long and one needs to make a rough selection (*triage*) before a more detailed analysis. However, much clearer insights can be obtained by a more precise tool and it is worth taking the trouble to design one, particularly if it will be used regularly as part of an ongoing process of reviews. For early-stage projects (region B in Figure 6.1), the eventual commercial application may not yet be clear, so projects will tend to be judged against the company's strategic aims, rather than expected market size or other commercial considerations. The factors used will therefore tend to be company specific. However, further along the funnel (moving into region C in Figure 6.1), a point will be reached when the likely commercial application becomes clear. Many projects will, of course, start here. Such projects can generally be assessed against criteria for commercial success that are, to some extent, common to most businesses. We start by considering this situation and return to the early-stage case later.

Designing a scoring tool

The published literature on how to go about designing a scoring tool is surprisingly sparse and there are no published examples that can be regarded unequivocally as representing best practice.

Table 6.2 shows an illustrative example of a scoring tool, compiled from published examples.[33] Scores were allocated against each of six factors, using the statements in the boxes as guidance. (These statements are sometimes called *anchoring statements* but the term *scaling statement* is preferable to avoid confusion with anchoring in the sense introduced in Theory Box 6.3.) Results were then added to give an overall score for the project. Conventional measures such

TABLE 6.2: Example of a project scoring tool

WEIGHT	SCALE / FACTOR	15	10	3	Weighted score
6	Strategic alignment	Fits Strategy	Supports	Neutral	
6	Market size	>$20M per year	$10M per year	> $3M	
3	Competitive advantage	Strong	Moderate	Slight	
2	Fit to supply chain	Fits current channels	Some change	Significant change	
3	Time to break even	<3 years	3-5 years	> 5 years	
6	Net present Value	> $5M	$3M	< $1M	
				TOTAL	

as NPV and Time to Break Even may be included, as here, but they are augmented (perhaps one should say diluted) by broader considerations.

The above example prompts a number of questions, which lead us to the key steps in designing a scoring tool:

1. Structure: Is one set of factors appropriate, and should the factor scores be added, or perhaps multiplied?
2. Factors: How many factors are needed and how should they be chosen?
3. Scaling statements: How many are appropriate, and how should they be designed?
4. Weightings: Should the factors all count the same or is there a case for giving a higher emphasis to some, for example by multiplying their score by a weighting factor? If so, how should the weightings be chosen? Our example also uses a nonlinear scale. What is the justification for this and how nonlinear should it be?
5. Uncertainty: How can uncertainty be included without making the process unduly complicated?

Structure

As already observed, once projects have matured to a stage where a commercial application is foreseen, the overall aim becomes essentially the same for all business projects; namely commercial success. This is made up of two parts: the potential profit, and the investment required to reach it. In financial terms, the ratio of these – return on investment (ROI) – is a fundamental measure of any project and this will often be used explicitly in making the final decision. In the earlier stages, when financial measures are not available, the more general terms *opportunity* and *feasibility* are appropriate.

With this in mind, it is best to create separate scoring tools for opportunity and feasibility. Opportunity is a rough measure of the value that may result from the project. Feasibility is a rough measure of how attainable that might be for the company and hence the effort or investment that may be required to bring it about. The product of the two scores, opportunity x feasibility, is, in fact, a rough indication of the potential ROI of the project:

Opportunity × Feasibility = Opportunity/Difficulty = Value/Investment = ROI

In fact, many familiar appraisal tools, such as McKinsey's market attractiveness/business strength matrix, A.D. Little's risk/reward matrix, and the familiar SWOT analysis (strengths, weaknesses, opportunities, threats), make essentially the same distinction: market attractiveness, reward and opportunity are all broadly synonyms for opportunity, while business strength, risk and strengths refer broadly to feasibility.

How Many Factors?

There are two conflicting considerations in choosing the number of factors. The first is that the managers making the decisions will be subject to all manner of uncertainties in assessing the factors, depending on their different experience, knowledge and assumptions. Their errors in scoring each of the different factors will, to some extent, be uncorrelated, so taking the average of many factors should give a better estimate than using one alone. In this respect, more is better. On the other hand, the more factors that are used, the less attention a scorer will give to any one factor. Between five and eight criteria seems a good compromise in our experience of working with companies on portfolio management.

Choosing the Factors

Since all businesses have certain features in common, it is not surprising to find a considerable similarity in the factors cited in the literature for populating multi-factor tools.[34] In particular, Cooper and co-workers have studied the factors underlying the success of new products.[35] In Table 6.3, we give examples

TABLE 6.3: Some Generic Examples of Factors for Application-focused Projects

Factor	OPPORTUNITY Explanation
Market size	Size of potential market, or number of potential adoptions, reasonably available to us
Our sales potential in a given time	Sales volume of number of adoptions anticipated in a defined time (say, 5 years)
Synergy opportunities	Possible additional benefits to other projects or activities; or the possiblity of new opportunities in combination
Customer benefit	Identifiable benefit to customers (internal or external) or potential adopters
Competitive intesity in market	Number or significance of the competition
Increased margin, or benefit per unit	Improvement in product margin (e.g. by cost reduction or price premium) compared to existing products; or benefit to us per adoptions
Business cost reduction or simplification	Contributes towards cost reduction or simplification of business process
Industry / market readiness	How easy will it be for customers or adopters to take up the product; do they have to change their behaviour or processs?
Market growth	Anticipated growth rate of market
Future potential	Product is a platform for future products or could open new markets beyond the project time frame
Learning potential	Will imporve the knowledge or competence of the business
Brand image	Will imporve the image of the company with investors, customers or other stakeholders
Customer relations	Project is important for retaining key customers

CHAPTER **6**

TABLE 6.3: Continued

Factor	FEASIBILITY	
	Explanation	
Product differentiation	How well the product is differentiated from those of major competitors	
Sustainability of competitive advantage	Our ability to sustain our competitive position (e.g. IPR, brand strength)	
Technical challenge	How confident are we that the proposed product is technically feasible at all?	
Market knowledge	Our understanding of size and requirements of the market	
Technical capability	Do we have the required technical competences to complete the project?	
Fit to sales and/or distribution	Fit to our sales competences and/or distribution chain	
Fit to manufacturing and/or supply chain	Ability to manufacture or supply the product	
Finance	Availability of finance for the project	
Strategic fit	How well does the project fit our compamy strategy?	
Organizational backing	Level of staff or management backing at an appropriate level	

Source: Mitchell, R., Phaal, R. and Athanassopoulou, N. "Scoring Methods for prioritising and selecting Innovation projects." Proceedings of the Portland Conference on Management of Engineering and Technology (PICMET) Kanazawa, Japan 2014. Copyright © 2014 Mitchell, Phaal, and Athanassopoulou. Reprinted with permission.

of appropriate factors from the literature and our own experience.[36] These may be used as a starting point but we emphasize that managers should consider carefully which are relevant to their situation and alter them or add others as appropriate.

Scaling Statements[37]

Each factor should be scored against a scale and the scaling statements are used to give some clarity to what a particular score might mean in practice. Scaling statements are a vital part of any scoring tool. They not only help ensure consistency when several people collaborate in the scoring, but also help to define what the factors actually mean. The following principles are important:

1. Scaling statements should be should made as concrete as possible. This means avoiding vague terms like Strong, Moderate and Weak and instead using statements that could, at least in principle, be observed, checked or demonstrated (as for Market Size in Table 6.2, and most of the examples in Mini Case 6.3). If you find it difficult to express the scaling statements for a

factor in concrete terms, you may need to reconsider whether that factor is appropriate at all. Can it really be useful if you cannot define it?

2. Do not make the outer scaling statements too extreme because this will mean that the scores for most projects will group in the middle of the scale and so will not be well differentiated. Choose statements that might quite probably be met in practice, not ones that represent the outer extremes of what is possible. An unusually good (or poor) project can always be scored outside the range. Why not?

3. It is important that the scaling statements for the various factors should be aligned with each other so that as far as possible a score of, say, 5 on one factor is an equally good pointer to the likely success of the project as a score of 5 on another. This may not be an easy task but it is vital. In fact, any attempt at comparing projects always involves considering them from various aspects and making some judgement as to how one aspect compares with another. Usually, this is done intuitively. By aligning scaling statements, one is attempting to make it as objective as possible. A good approach is to start with one factor, the *base* factor, which clearly has significant impact and for which fairly clear and objective scaling statements can be designed. Then choose the midpoint, or *pivot* statement. This should indicate an unexceptional or 'middle of the road' case, such that if this were the only measure available to judge a project, it would be difficult to decide whether to accept or reject it. Next, choose scaling statements for the two outer levels and ideally for two intermediate points. Once the statements for the base factor have been defined, the others are chosen by reference to it. Imagine two projects, one described only by the base factor and one described only by a second factor. Then, for each scaling statement of the base factor, choose one for the second factor that is equivalent; that is, is at a level that would make it difficult to decide between the two projects. Three scaling statements are a minimum; five can give more precision. Tables 6.4a and 6.4b gives some examples of complete scales for projects aimed at commercial outcomes. See also the main case study on Grundfos at the end of this chapter.

Weightings

Many authors propose that the factors in a scoring tool should be allocated different weightings, to reflect their relative importance. This makes sense if the only consideration is whether the factor is met or not. For example, for a technical innovation, one might ask: 'Do we hold a patent?' But if a factor is measured on a continuous scale, as is usually the case for project selection, any weighting must depend on the scale used. In Table 6.2 it could not be true that Strategic Advantage is <u>always</u> worth 3 times more than Fit to the Supply Chain; it all depends on the measurement scale as defined by the scaling statements. So why not choose the scales to be equivalent, as described above? Logically, separate weightings are then unnecessary.

TABLE 6.4a: Examples of Scaling Statements for Opportunity

Factor	Score					
				Scaling statements		
	0	3	6	9	12	
Our sales potential in a given time	> 1,000 units in 5 years (Gross margin £300k)	3,000 units in 5 years (Gross margin £1m)	10,000 units in 5 years (Gross margin £3m)	20,000 units in 5 years (Gross margin £6m)	50,000 units in 5 years (Gross margin 15m)	
Customer benefit	No obvious benefit to customers	Some benefit to some customers	Clear customer benefits within existing norms; worth visiting existing customers to promote	A significant advance in more than one key feature of interest to customers	Eye-catching new benefits; a talking point at shows; entry to competitor accounts	
Competitive intensity in market	4 or more strong competitors	2 strong competitors	Usual competition; or 1 strong competitor	We will be alone in the market		
Business cost reduction or simplification	<£300k	£1m	£3m	£6m	£15m	
Industry/market readiness	No expressed demand OR requires major change of customer behaviour	Some customers have asked for this but requires some change in customer behaviour	Definitely attractive to most customers; no change to customer behaviour required	There is pent up demand for this		
Market growth	Stagnant market	<5% per year	5–10% per year	20% a year	>50% per year	
Future potential	Update of an existing product	May lead to further variants or applications	Will definitely lead to further produt variants or applications	Could lead to a new product line or several applications	This is the beginning of a major new business OR many further applications are foreseen	
Learning potential	None	Useful learning	Corrects one or more core competences where we are currently weak	Class leading learning in competences vital for 50% of future business		

Mitchell, R., Phaal, R. and Athanassopoulou, N. "Scoring Methods for prioritising and selecting Innovation projects." Proceedings of the Portland Conference on Management of Engineering and Technology (PICMET) Kanazawa, Japan 2014. Copyright © 2014 Mitchell, Phaal and Athanassopoulou. Reprinted with permission.

TABLE 6.4b: Examples of Scaling Statements for Feasibility

Factor	0	3	Scaling statements 6	9	12
Product differentiation	No features that are better than competition	At least one feature is better than offered by the competition	We have some minor features that are better than the competition	At least one important feature is significantly better than the competition	Several important features are much better than the competition
Sustainability of competitive advantage	Key differentiating features will be easy to copy, Or serious concerns about IP against us	We are 6-12 months ahead of the competition. No serious IPR concerns	Competitive advantage can be maintained with continous effort	We are at least 2 years ahead of the competition	Key features are protected by IPR or unique capabilities that are not easy to copy
Market knowledge	Market size not supported by data and requirements not yet checked with customers	Market estimated within a factor of 2 or 3 with some data support	Enough data to size the market to +/–50% and requirements are supported by discussions with sales force	Market size known to +/–20% and customer view established by formal survey	
Strategic fit	Project is clearly outside our strategic intent and fits no product vision	Some doubt about how this fits into existing strategies	Fits strategic intent and a specific product vision	Fits strategic intent at a high level of ambition and meets more than one specific product vision	
Technical capability	We will have to buy in new major capabilities, OR recruit a new technical team, OR rely on a partner	We lack some important capabilities and a plan is needed to acquire them	Exiting staff can acquire capabilities in 3 months or less, or by recruiting one or two new people	Some new skills required but they can be acquired in time	Well within our capability. No new skills or knowledge required
Fit to sales and/or distribution	Entirely new distribution channel required. OR requires new sales skills that at least half the sales force will struggle with	Changes to sales or distribution will need special attention	>75% of sales force could sell it with training or >75% of existing distribution applicable	Some changes to sales or distribution but within our capabilities in the time	Well within competence of existing sales and distribution
Organizational backing	There is opposition from several stakeholders	We have some persuading to do	We do not anticipate trouble gaining support for this	Strong support from all important stakeholders	

Source: adapted from Mitchell, R., Phaal, R. and Athanassopoulou, N. "Scoring Methods for prioritising and selecting Innovation projects." Proceedings of the Portland Conference on Management of Engineering and Technology (PICMET) Kanazawa, Japan 2014. Copyright © 2014 Mitchell, Phaal and Athanassopoulou. Reprinted with permission.

CHAPTER

6

Risk, Uncertainty and Confidence

The level of risk or uncertainty is obviously an important factor in assessing a project. The term *risk* is widely used in portfolio selection, but is often ill-defined. To say that a project is 'high risk' may mean many things. It may mean that the project could lead to catastrophic consequences, in which case they need to be spelled out. But, more usually, a 'high risk' means that it is quite likely to be cancelled before completion or simply that its outcome is difficult to predict at the moment. These are not good decision parameters in themselves. A project with a relatively high risk of being stopped, but for which the decision can be made early and cheaply, may well be preferable to a less risky prospect where the uncertainties will be clarified only after much time and expenditure.

Decision theory makes a clear distinction between risk and uncertainty.[38] The term *risk* is used when probabilities of the various possible outcomes are known, either a priori, as for most card games, or from objective data, as would be the case for health risks for exposure to toxic chemicals. *Uncertainty* is used where no such objective probability data are available. Clearly, innovation projects, being unique, fall into this category so the term 'uncertainty' is to be preferred. The word 'risk' also has a negative connotation that is unhelpful in this context. The fact that a wide range of outcomes is possible means not only the possibility of a relatively poor outcome but also the chance of a very good one, which may be a good reason for doing it.

The possible range of outcomes is very important information and must be included explicitly in any assessment of value. For individual projects or small portfolios, the best approach to uncertainty, as already seen in the treatment of decision trees, is to identify the most reasonable upper and lower extremes – the plausibly best and worst case values, or *confidence limits* – and retain them in the judgement process. Using confidence limits to express the uncertainty is logical and practical.

Participants in the scoring process should therefore select the plausibly best and worst case values, or confidence limits, for each factor rather than a single point value. Where several people collaborate to score projects, they should compare their values and agree on their overall confidence limits. This retains important information that would otherwise be lost. And we have found that, in practice, people often find it easier to agree on confidence limits than on a single value. The upper and lower limits agreed for each factor lead to upper and lower limits on the opportunity and feasibility for each project. We discuss below how these can be incorporated into the decision-making process.

One way in which uncertainty should emphatically *not* be introduced into scoring tools is as a separate factor such as 'commercial risk' or 'technical risk'. Any truly innovative project will inevitably be risky initially, in the sense that the outcome is as yet unclear. That is not a criticism, merely a statement that much is still to be learned. We recall managers in a large, technically based company in the UK saying that they had given up using a scoring tool because it 'always rejected the really novel ideas'. On examining their tool, it became clear why – the first three (out of six) criteria were commercial risk, technical risk and financial risk.

Multi-factor Scoring Tools for Early-stage Projects

For projects with a definable application in view, the factors in scoring tools usually relate to the commercial opportunity and feasibility. As observed above, the measures for these are much the same for most businesses. However, very early-stage projects investigating new technologies or capabilities are likely to be driven, not by commercial opportunity and feasibility, but by the policy aims of the company: for example, operational flexibility, environmental aims, complexity reduction, or generic product improvements such as weight reduction.

If each policy aim has an allocated budget, then all that is needed is to design a separate scoring tool for each one.[39] However, if there is a single budget, there must be a way to compare projects serving one aim with those serving another. The same is true if some projects serve more than one aim. There are two ways to do this. The first is to select the base factor of one of the tools as a reference and then align all the others to that. Alternatively, one can design the tools separately and then allocate weights to them by cross-comparing the base factor scales. For example, if a scaling statement for one aim that rates a score of '5' is felt to be comparable to one that scores '10' for another aim, then the second aim would be given a relative weight of 0.5.

THEORY BOX 6.4: *Analytical Hierarchy Process*

The *analytical hierarchy process* (AHP), developed by Saaty,[40] is a structured, multi-factor decision-making technique that has received considerable attention and several software tools have been developed for it. The key concept is to structure the decision into a nested hierarchy of considerations. For example, suppose a company has established three criteria against which to assess projects: financial benefits, strategy alignment, and new markets. Each of these may be broken down into contributing sub-criteria. For example, financial benefits might be broken down into long term and short term, while contribution to strategy might be broken down into sales efficiency, operational flexibility and cost reduction.

The next step is to allocate relative weights, subjectively, to the main criteria. It is generally recommended to do this by making pairwise comparisons between them. Let us suppose that the weights assigned to our three main criteria are 0.5 for finance, 0.2 for strategy and 0.3 for new markets. We then do the same for each group of sub-criteria. Thus, for finance, short term may be rated 0.7 and long term 0.3.

Projects are then given a score against each of the sub-criteria to which they contribute and weighted accordingly. So, a project that scores 2 for long-term finance and 6 for short term would have a weighted score of $2 \times 0.3 + 6 \times 0.7 = 4.8$. This score is then multiplied by the finance weighting of 0.5 to give a total of 2.4.

The literature on AHP is quite extensive and the method is well adapted to decisions where the contributing criteria can be expressed in binary form: for example 'Do we have distribution in the territory?' or (for pharmaceuticals) 'Is FDA approval required?' and so on. However, for appraising innovation projects, it suffers from the issues discussed above, namely, how can the weightings be assigned without reference to the scales on which the criteria are measured? If the scales are made explicit and aligned, as we propose above, the nested weightings would become unnecessary.

CHAPTER **6**

Ranking and selecting projects using scoring

When a scoring tool is used as described, each project will have two pairs of scores representing the upper and lower confidence limits for opportunity and feasibility. These can be displayed on an *opportunity/feasibility grid*, as shown in Figure 6.9. In principle, each project ought to be represented by a rectangle but this makes the diagram difficult to interpret. The key information is retained by showing the points for: best opportunity, best feasibility; and worst opportunity, worst feasibility, as in Figure 6.9.

The dotted curve shown is one of a family that can be plotted showing where the product of opportunity multiplied by feasibility is a constant (36 in this case). This one passes through the midpoint of Figure 6.9 where O = 6 and F = 6, so if the scaling statements have been well chosen, it separates the diagram into two regions representing, roughly, projects whose ROI is attractive or unattractive. Those falling entirely below and to the left of the line will generally be rejected and those entirely above the line will be candidates for acceptance. The projects that span the line need further consideration. Where the key uncertainties lie may be seen in the details of the scoring.

If you do need to have a single score for each project – for example in order to plot them on a bubble diagram as described later – the upper and lower scores for O x F may be combined to give a single figure by which projects may

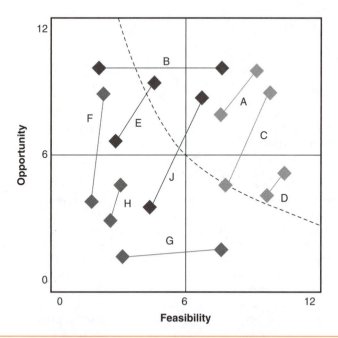

FIGURE 6.9: Types of Project on an Opportunity/Feasibility Matrix
Source: Mitchell, R., Phaal, R. and Athanassopoulou, N. "Scoring Methods for prioritising and selecting Innovation projects." Proceedings of the Portland Conference on Management of Engineering and Technology (PICMET) Kanazawa, Japan 2014. Copyright © 2014 Mitchell, Phaal and Athanassopoulou. Reprinted with permission.

be ranked, depending on how aggressive a portfolio is required. For example, if the primary motivation is to avoid missing any good opportunities, projects may be ranked simply according to their upper scores. This is the so-called *maximax* solution, maximizing the upside potential of the portfolio. Alternatively, ranking by the minimum score minimizes the downside risk of the portfolio. This would be the *minimax* solution. Between these extremes is a range of possible selections obtained by combining the upper and lower scores with different weightings. For example, a single moderately aggressive score for a project might be:

$$(3(\text{Maximum score}) + (\text{minimum score}))/4 \qquad \text{Equation 6.6}$$

while a moderately conservative single score might be:

$$((\text{Maximum score}) + 3 \, (\text{minimum score}))/4 \qquad \text{Equation 6.7}$$

The value of scoring systems often lies as much in the discipline of collecting and discussing information on all aspects of the project as in the final scoring. Helpful as they are, these are rough-and-ready methods designed to aid decision-making in highly uncertain situations. If one project should score a few points more than another, recognize that the precision of the tool is not enough to differentiate them. Find another consideration – the quality of the project manager or the morale of the team, perhaps – to separate them.

Ongoing review

Managers will need to review the portfolio of projects on a regular basis to ensure that it continues to deliver the value expected. As projects mature they will inevitably not turn out exactly as was initially expected, so the portfolio balance will shift if it is not regularly monitored. One key point to be checked is whether the expected ROI of the projects in hand is still attractive. A plot of the annual expenditure of projects against the expected return will show whether the portfolio is drifting towards too many low-return projects.[41]

In the immediate term, progress may be limited by the availability of specialist staff, such as good software specialists or analytical chemists, and in practice, resource issues can lead to complex interactions between projects. Portfolio selection then has to include making the best immediate use of these bottleneck resources. Mathematical optimization techniques are available to calculate how to select the group of projects that will produce the best financial return subject to the constraints on several different resources, although they do not appear to be very popular,[42] probably because the mathematics is obscure. Managers cannot readily review or justify the results, nor adjust or amend them to take account of other factors.

BALANCING THE PORTFOLIO

Choosing the projects that can deliver the best value to the organization is obviously a key aspect of project selection but managers may also wish to ensure that the portfolio of projects produces an appropriate balance of activities across various other aspects of the business. The most obvious is timing. There will be a limit to how much change – innovation – an organization can manage at any one time so a spread of delivery dates is desirable. On the other hand, several new products may be required together for a trade show or an exhibition. Whatever the reason, the timing of the projects in the portfolio must be considered and managed.

There are many other kinds of balance that companies may seek. For example: among markets or divisions of the business; between high risk and low risk; between growth and cost reduction; or between incremental, breakthrough and radical innovations. Martina Berto (Mini Case 6.4) looked for a balance of innovation activities across its main product types.

Bubble Diagrams

Plotting the projects on an appropriate two-dimensional matrix often provides a helpful way to visualize aspects of portfolio balance. We illustrate this with a popular example, the *risk/reward matrix*, illustrated in Figure 6.10.

It may seem odd that any organization would actively seek to have risky projects even in the precise sense discussed above, let alone in the common, pejorative sense. One reason for seeking a risk/reward balance is that organizations may be willing to take on some highly uncertain projects only if they have a sufficient number of low-uncertainty projects going on at the same time to provide security. Many companies also worry that they are 'risk-averse' and do not undertake enough radical projects. 'Risky' is probably taken to mean 'radical', or 'outside our comfort zone'. The notion of risk/reward resonates with managers for obvious reasons. The key is to bring some clarity to it by carefully designing a scoring tool for placing projects on the matrix. Mini Case 6.3 (Domino Lasers) gives an example of this in practice.

The risk/reward matrix, shown in Figure 6.10, shows the balance of the portfolio between four quadrants. These are often named: *bread and butter* (low risk but

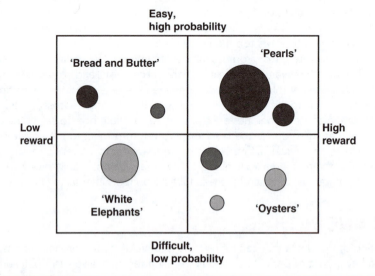

FIGURE 6.10: Risk/reward matrix

low rewards); *pearls* (low risk and high rewards); *oysters* (high risk but potentially high reward); and *white elephants* (high risk, low returns – and proverbially difficult to kill). In bubble diagrams such as this, the area of the circles can be used to represent the investment in the current phase of each project and so the diagram shows the distribution of effort over the whole portfolio. Colour or shading can be used to show how near the projects are to launch, or for any other distinction; for example, to show which market sector or part of the business they relate to.

The fact that projects may be found in any part of the risk/reward diagram emphasizes the point we made in the section on real options: the world of projects is very different from the world of financial stocks. In the financial world, the way the market works ensures that low-risk stocks generate a low reward and high reward goes only with high risk. Innovation projects are generally quite different because the assets they represent are not traded openly. No market mechanism operates against pearls or white elephants.

▶ **MINI CASE 6.3:** *Domino Lasers – Risk/Reward Scoring*[43]

Simon Bradley, the MD of Domino Lasers, a manufacturer of laser systems based in the US and Germany, became concerned that the company was concentrating too much on small, low-impact projects, possibly to the exclusion of larger but riskier ones. The company typically had between 10 and 15 projects in hand, some quite mature but others in the early formative stages.

Bradley wanted to include the management of the newly acquired German subsidiary in the review of the project portfolio to ensure that there would be support from all parts of the company for any changes that had to be made. But it would not be easy, as it was clear that managers in the two parts of the company had different tolerances of risk. The two teams also tended to emphasize different aspects of the market, the Americans being more used to seeking high volume opportunities while the Germans tended to pursue applications with lower volume but higher margins. Doing a portfolio analysis together could help to align the views of the two management teams but there would have to be a clear structure to guide the discussion.

Bradley spent some time in preparing a structured risk/reward analysis. It had to be applicable to early-stage projects, where detailed financial information was not available, as well as to ones that were close to being ready for the market. Carefully defined scales were clearly needed to help align the approaches of the two teams. The tool used for assessing risk is shown in Table 6.5. A trial run for the scoring system quickly revealed a problem. While all the participants were familiar with some of the projects, almost nobody really understood them all. The review could not go ahead without more shared information. Accordingly, three of the participants undertook to collect data on all the projects and circulate it for comment and review so that, at the next meeting, everyone would start from an agreed set of facts.

The teams met by video link to discuss the projects and assign scores for risk and reward to each one. Richard Blackburn, manager of the US factory, explained:

> We started out trying to reach a consensus on each factor but we quickly decided that if there really was a range of opinion about something then we ought not to lose sight of that. So we discussed the facts of each project and then scored them individually. Then we discussed the scores. Sometimes people changed their minds when they understood where the others were coming from, but not always. At the end we recorded the range of each score as well as the mean. People felt much more comfortable not trying to force a consensus.

Continued...

Bradley comments:

> The most useful thing about the scoring system was that it forced us to think about all the aspects of the projects – not just the cost and technical feasibility, which had tended to dominate our thoughts before. For example, we had a couple of research projects where the biggest risks were actually to do with the market acceptance. So we decided to put effort into the market research first and hold off on the technical work for the moment.

TABLE 6.5: Domino Lasers' Risk Assessment Tool

Rating	0	4	7	10	Total
Key Items					
Size of technical step in at least 1 parameter	New concept or order of magnitude change	Step change short of order of magnitude or significant novelty of method	Less than 50% change. No major novelty	Incremental improvement	
Technical uncertainty	Many major technical uncertainties or very high complexity	Several significant technical uncertainties or high complexity	Technical solution defined but uncertainties remain	A defined and straight-forward technical risk	
Demonstrated feasiblity	Have not yet been able to demonstrate feasibility	Limited demonstration achieved. OR outline plan for cost reduction	Almost demonstrated. Full demonstration planned. OR detailed plan for cost redcution	Full technical feasibility clearly demonstrated	
Knowledge of market for this product	Pure guesswork	Rough estimate available but no specific study yet done	Specific study done but more work needed. (e.g. market known within a factor of 2)	Market size well defined. No further work needed (e.g. +/–20%)	
Market readiness	Extensive market development required. No apparent demand	Need or benefit must be highlighted to customers	Clear relationship between product and customer need; or substitutes a competitor product	Meets a clearly expressed customer need; or substitutes one of our products	
Channel capability	No relevant experties or experience in our channels	Some relevant experience or expertise	Considerable relevant resources available	Leverages our existing skills and resources well	
Comments					Total %

Source: copyright © Domino. Reprinted with permission.

An alternative, and perhaps more logically coherent, approach can be the *innovation ambition matrix*, introduced in Chapter 1. Here, projects are shown on two dimensions representing the degree of novelty in the product or service, and the degree of novelty in the application or market. This allows innovations to be classified as incremental, breakthrough or radical. The ratio between this has been termed the 'golden ratio' and Ngji and Tuff, its originators, propose that companies should seek an appropriate balance.[44] They propose 70 per cent incremental, 20 per cent breakthrough, and 10 per cent radical for a diversified industrial company, and 80:18:2 for a consumer goods company, but these are only suggestions. In practice, each company must choose its own ratios.

Bubble diagrams can be used to display a considerable amount of information about the state of the portfolio but not to diagnosis how healthy it is. That is left to the judgement of the management team.

MINI CASE 6.4: *Martina Berto: Aligning R&D and Marketing*

Martina Berto (MB) is an Indonesia-based company that started in 1970 from a small salon in a garage and has grown to be one of the largest vertically integrated beauty products companies in Southeast Asia, with $54 million turnover in 2014. The vision of Martha Tilaar, the founder of the company, was that MB should aspire to develop cosmetics harnessing local natural ingredients and based on the value of local culture. In realizing this vision, MB focuses on R&D activities aimed at discovering new herbal ingredients. The company has six product categories, including hair care, skin care, body care, make up base, decorative and herbal, which are marketed in 10 brands serving three different markets, namely *luxury*, *mass* and *masstige* (mass products that are positioned as luxurious ones). The challenge for MB's management is to manage a large number of products from different categories and various brands over the entire processes of creation, selection and development of the product portfolio.

Kilala Tilaar, the marketing and sales director, describes the industry characteristics: 'It's really technology driven, trend driven and also hyper competitive. As they are trendy products, speed in innovation must be really in place, otherwise you will be forgotten.' Coping with these challenges, the company has been building a strong R&D capability, which actively searches for new formulas. Meanwhile, marketing consistently interacts with the market to identify consumer needs and foresee trends. They work together in generating new product concepts, orchestrated by the Martha Tilaar Innovation Center (MTIC). Bernard Widjaja, the MTIC director, says: 'MTIC is a project leader in the *innovation engine*, which coordinates and synchronizes the R&D explorations and market fulfilment, so that the company's innovation can be effectively commercialized.'

The final decisions on which product concepts will continue into the development pipeline are made in the portfolio review meetings, attended by MB's top management. Tilaar explains: 'Focus, attention, control and investment are the main issues considered by management in evaluating all options and making decisions.' Every year, these processes result in a new product development portfolio, which consists of over 150 new stock keeping units from the various brands. The bubble diagram in Figure 6.11 shows the position of the seven brand groups being developed, viewed from reward and success probability dimensions.

Continued...

CHAPTER 6

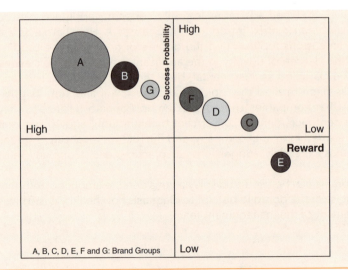

FIGURE 6.11: MB's Bubble Diagram Showing the Seven Brand Groups
Source: copyright © Martina Berto (MB). Reprinted with permission.

Case contributed by Hendro Tjaturpriono.

Strategic Alignment

The portfolio of projects must reflect the strategic aims of the organization. For example, if a company has a long-term aim to move into a new technology or enter a new market, a proportion of its innovation investment must be directed towards that end. This priority may override most others and so must be injected into the portfolio management process by some 'top-down' approach.

There are only two generic ways in which strategic aims can feed into portfolio management. The first is by directly earmarking money for a group of projects, perhaps identified by a roadmapping process (see Chapter 4), that constitute a plan to achieve the required strategy.

The second approach is for management to declare that, as a matter of policy, a certain amount or proportion of funding will be allocated to particular types of project. This approach is known as using *strategic buckets*. It may mean allocating funds to particular market sectors or product types (Figure 6.12) or to certain classes of project. The AXA Ireland insurance company (see Mini Case 3.8) aimed that 10 per cent of its innovation projects should be entirely novel, 10 per cent should be based on the reuse of existing ideas in new applications, 40 per cent should be incremental improvements, and 40 per cent should eliminate unnecessary activities.

Balance or Compromise?

The process of balancing a portfolio seems obvious enough: first agree the strategic buckets; then select an optimum group of projects within each according to their potential value; then modify the selection to provide a balance across

FIGURE 6.12: Strategic Alignment of Project Budgets According to Markets Served

other parts of the business – risk/reward or whatever. But there is a logical problem here. An optimum portfolio for value would be found by listing projects in order of potential value and then selecting from the top until the available budget or resources are used up. If additional criteria are then introduced to 'balance' the portfolio in some way, this is bound to mean choosing a less valuable set of projects. This loss of value is presumably to be made up by some greater utility conferred by the balance. However, to our knowledge, nobody knows how to calculate this, so the whole process is very much a matter of judgement. The neutral term *balance* obscures the fact that the result is always a lower value *compromise*.

Certainly, managers reviewing the portfolio should adjust the project selection by promoting or demoting projects to achieve a better balance, but overall the required results are probably best achieved proactively rather than reactively. That is, by challenging staff to come up with more projects in the underrepresented areas so that the balance is achieved over time rather than at once.

MANAGEMENT PROCESSES

Managers responsible for the portfolio process face three related 'people issues'. The first is the difficulty of getting reliable information on which to base selection decisions. The second is handling the impact of project cancellations. The third is choosing the team, and especially the project manager (see Chapter 8).

Obtaining the Information

The innate difficulty of selecting a portfolio is compounded by the fact that the people who know most about any project are those working on it, and they have a vested interest. Project selection can degenerate into a contest of advocacy skills between passionately committed project leaders. A number of steps can be taken to overcome this.

First, make the collection of the information that is used in the selection process as open and objective as possible, and allocate enough effort to reviewing it. Larger companies can make good use of experts from other departments. A good example is the process used by SmithKline Beecham (now GlaxoSmith-Kline) and described in Mini Case 6.5, in which it took pains to separate the valuation of projects from the final portfolio selection. It may be helpful to allow project teams to present and defend their innovation ideas directly to senior management so that they know they have received a fair hearing and that their work is understood and valued by their seniors. Many companies – Richardson Sheffield (Mini Case 6.6) is one, Philips is another – hold well-publicized exhibitions in which new ideas are promoted and top managers discuss and debate the proposals with the innovation teams before making decisions.

> **MINI CASE 6.5:** *SmithKline Beecham – Selection and Portfolio Management*[45]

When the pharmaceutical company SmithKline Beecham (now GlaxoSmithKline) was formed by the merger of Beecham and SmithKline Beckman in 1989, managers needed to reorient the combined R&D portfolio of more than half a billion dollars in the face of new pressures. Management were unhappy that their selection process appeared to have become politicized, as strong-willed project leaders competed for resources for projects that only they fully understood. The process was seen as neither efficient nor objective. As one manager said: 'Figures can't lie, but liars can figure.' Their aim was to install a process that was much more open and objective and that could gain the support of all concerned.

Their improved approach had three phases. The first was to ask teams to make not one but four proposals: a baseline proposal, to continue the project as planned; a 'buy-up' proposal in which they could ask for larger resources for an enhanced project scope or speed; a 'buy-down' proposal for smaller scope; and a 'minimal' that would close the project but retain as much as possible of what had been learned. This had the effect of moving teams away from 'all or nothing' advocacy towards a more business-centric approach. These new proposals were discussed with senior managers and with the group who would later form the selection panel. In a number of cases, the teams themselves, or the subsequent discussions, produced new approaches that were better than the single track to which the team had become committed. The selection panel now understood all the projects well and were clear that the best routes to success had been chosen.

In the second phase, a common set of information was compiled about each project with the help of consultants and colleagues inside and outside the project. Valuations were produced using decision trees, which resulted in an upper and a lower valuation for each project rather than a single-point valuation. These valuations were reviewed and debated by the selection panel until everyone was content. Only then was the portfolio selected, and this was done by an independent, internal consultancy group who then presented it to the selection panel for review. The selection panel could now concentrate on the portfolio debate, without getting drawn back into valuation issues. The process was reported to be very successful. The careful and open valuation process was accepted as fair. Many projects were changed to the buy-up or buy-down proposal and the new portfolio projected a threefold improvement in return on assets. As a result, management agreed to increase overall R&D expenditure by 50 per cent.

Second, involve a range of different people. For reasons already discussed, it is clearly best not to rely on the view of a single person, but to seek and combine the views of several people, provided they all have the requisite competence. This, in itself, helps to address some of the judgement biases outlined in Theory Box 6.3, such as availability and the tendency to overestimate the relevance of one's own experience.

Third, ask the participants to first form their own opinions privately – and with enough time to think, look up pertinent facts and so on – before discussing with others, to help combat anchoring and halo effects. Participants can put forward their opinions anonymously, as in the Delphi process,[46] or simply announce them simultaneously at a review meeting (*planning poker*).

Fourth, once participants have made their estimates, scores or judgements alone, they should discuss them in a structured meeting whose aim is to understand the facts and reasoning and come to a consensus. It is a mistake merely to take the average of the views because some people with outlying opinions may have sound reasons for them and may persuade the others. However, such meetings can easily be dominated by the participants with the highest status. It is a good principle to start by asking people to give their views in reverse order of seniority.

Handling Cancellation

If the decision is made to cancel a project that has been running for some time, the announcement must be handled with care. A few years of effort that leads nowhere may be insignificant for a company, but is not a trivial matter for the individuals concerned. There must be credit and rewards to people who do good work regardless of whether the project as a whole turns out to be impracticable. Research laboratories do this by allowing their scientists to publish papers so that they can build a reputation for the quality of their work, but other organizations must find their own ways to celebrate good work on failed projects. Innovation is risky but the risk must be borne by the company, not individuals, otherwise the pool of innovators will surely dry up.

CHAPTER 6

▶ **MINI CASE 6.6:** *Richardson's Knives – Portfolio Transparency*[47]

Richardson Sheffield, now part of the House of Fraser, manufactures kitchen knives and scissors. Until recently, the company's success was primarily based on one main product range: the 'Laser' knife. With its fine serrated edge profile, this product had a 25-year 'stay-sharp' guarantee. The Laser with its patents provided the company with a technological advantage that enabled it to grow dramatically from the 1980s. However, in recent years, new entrants to the market, weakening intellectual property rights, and the growing importance of 'fashion' in all kitchen products had started to weaken the company's position.

Continued...

Major problems

One of the key issues facing Richardson was that the company had adopted a strategy of giving every major retailer exactly what they wanted, no matter how difficult the variations were. David Williams, group technical director at the time, explains:

> We had ended up with an increasing number of customer-specific variations – and enormous business complexity, and all within a block of business that actually had not grown at all. We realized we had to stop clinging to old technology and an old definition of what constituted 'customer service'.

The main R&D department had increasingly become overloaded, and one-off special designs were pushing out core product development. The new product introduction process itself suffered from many typical problems; in particular, there was no 'front-end' coordination and control, and no real R&D focus. Williams explains: 'Instead of focusing on major projects, we used to start and develop many projects, and then cherry-pick the best ideas for final design. Many ideas almost got to market before being dropped, because only right at the end did we get any marketing input.' Also, decision-making was very slow and poor. Williams notes: 'All major project decisions were taken by the group's senior executives at regular business review meetings. R&D was only one item on the agenda at these reviews – and usually the last one. Consequently, decisions were often rushed, with executives dismissing ideas and redirecting projects without proper consideration.' Also the reasons why some projects were chosen in preference to others were not transparent to most of the organization, as only those present at the business review meeting were informed.

Another key problem was a poor understanding of the market and consumers. As with many companies that grow through technological dominance, and with products that effectively sell themselves, Richardson Sheffield had lost contact with its customers. As its technological lead diminished, the company found it increasingly difficult to develop new products that met consumers' expectations.

The Innovation Process

The changes to managing innovation at Richardson Sheffield were summarized in the company's three-stage model: this consists of a front-end process, the NPD process, and tooling to production process. The pre-development 'front end' is based around a process framework developed by Williams: 'Essentially, the first key ingredient was to establish that there was only one process … and all projects should follow this route, and be subjected to the same filter screens – no more product extensions, or projects being completed by the back door route.' To enforce this, marketing became the originator of all new product projects, working jointly with R&D to develop product ideas that could be presented to retailers as concepts, rather than simply asking them what they wanted.

A key part of this approach is the offline development of new technology. Williams explains:

> We have found in the past that it is very difficult to get new technologies to work, and impossible to say when the technology will be ready. So we have formalized the approach whereby I keep the technical developments on one side, only pushing them forward when they are ready. Once I have proved the material technology, and if I can sell the benefits to the marketing people – and through concepts to the customer – then the technology is taken up and developed into a full project brief. This way customers are not left waiting for promised new technology, and from the market's point of view the development cycle, from them seeing a technology to the finished product, is very short.

Continued...

For all projects that are to be progressed, the company now appoints a new product manager – from within marketing – who is made responsible for that project, and who works directly with the R&D team once they are given the brief. The coordinated work up-front ensures that only those projects that are likely to have a high market impact come into R&D for development. Williams notes: 'R&D no longer gets bombarded with hundreds of half-baked and badly thought through ideas.' To enforce this, full authority for specific projects has been delegated to the marketing product managers and the development teams. Projects no longer have to be continually assessed by senior executives.

According to Williams:

> Development projects are now very much in the hands of the marketing product managers. Therefore projects are much less likely to be 'political solutions' – a design which tries to harmonize all the division's requirements and customer demands into one product, which often didn't really meet anyone's requirements. The senior executive review now only looks at future product strategy rather than specific projects, and this was again something that we dramatically needed to achieve.

Source: adapted from Goffin, K., Lee-Mortimer, A. and New, C., Managing Product Innovation for Competitive Advantage *(London: Haymarket Publications, 1999). Copyright © 1999 Haymarket Publications.*

Summary

Selecting and managing the portfolio of innovation projects is a difficult but vital part of managing innovation. Failure to make good and timely decisions is bad for efficiency in the short term, and for profit, or even survival, in the long term.

No one set of tools suits all situations; the choice depends on the information available, the type and complexity of the projects involved, and how close they are to commercialization. For early-stage projects, those well to the right in the innovation funnel, information will be sparse and financial approaches are usually unhelpful; multi-criterion scoring is the best approach. The key to a good scoring tool is careful definition and alignment of the scales. Opportunity and feasibility aspects should be assessed separately. Financial methods of varying degrees of sophistication take centre stage when projects become better defined.

Particular care is necessary in treating risk. Risk in the sense of uncertainty should not be regarded as a negative aspect of a project, merely an indication of the need for investigation. It is a mistake to use single estimates of value such as the mean; the range of possible outcomes must always be considered.

The portfolio of projects selected must not only represent the best possible use of resources, but must also be balanced in terms of risk, timing and strategic impact. Various tools such as bubble diagrams are available to help this but the choices are ultimately intuitive and the result is always a compromise.

Selection decisions for innovation projects always involve intuitive judgements. But managers should be aware of the pitfalls of intuition and design the decision-making processes to avoid bias by strong personalities or anchoring effects.

Management Recommendations

- Choose project valuation tools that are appropriate for the types of project: using subjective measures such as scoring when uncertainty is high, but emphasizing financial measures more as commercialization approaches.
- Keep valuation tools simple and transparent so that the decision process remains open to review, and leaves scope for management judgement.
- Treat numerical measures of risk with caution; they are always approximate.
- Avoid making single-point estimates. Try and understand the range of possibilities open to each project.
- Understand the possible errors and biases of individual decision-making. Give close attention to ensuring that the evaluation process is objective and that unsuccessful innovators are rewarded for their efforts.

Questions for Students

1. You have been asked to convene a meeting of student representatives to decide on the style and venue for a major social event. How would you prepare and structure the discussion to minimize the effects of the biases described in Theory Box 6.3?
2. People sometimes express the value of a proposed project as a mean value, together with a standard deviation. What criticisms would you make of this?
3. Find out more about the analytical hierarchy process and construct a hierarchy for deciding where to site a new factory in South America.
4. Board members in companies are often concerned that their staff do not bring forward enough radical or challenging proposals. Why might this be so? Give at least four factors that can make people too conservative in their thinking about future business possibilities.
5. Design a scoring tool that a family with two small children might use for selecting a house and neighbourhood.
6. Find out more about the theory of option valuation and write a brief summary of your conclusions. In what circumstances would the theory be most applicable for evaluating innovation projects?

Recommended Reading

1. Bernstein, P. L., *Against the Gods: The Remarkable Story of Risk* (New York: John Wiley, 1998). Excellent and readable account of the history and ideas of risk and risk management.
2. Boer, F.P., 'Financial Management of R&D', *Research-Technology Management*, 44(4) (2002), 23–34. Good survey of the available methods for valuing innovation projects.
3. Cooper, R.G., Edgett, S.J. and Kleinschmidt, E., *Portfolio Management for New Projects* (Cambridge, MA: Perseus Books, 2nd edn, 2001). Complete and authoritative review of portfolio management practices.
4. Kahneman, D., *Thinking, Fast and Slow* (London: Allen Lane, 2011). Readable survey of the psychology of decision-making including a full treatment of heuristics and biases.

▶ MAIN CASE STUDY

GRUNDFOS – PRIMING THE PUMP [48] *WITH VIDEO INTERVIEW*

Grundfos, based in Bjerringbro, Denmark is the largest manufacturer of pumps in the world, employing 18,000 people and manufacturing over 12 million pumps a year. The company spends over €7 million a year on R&D. In 2011, the company reorganized its new business development organization. There had been trouble with projects running late because of technical issues so a new 'front loading' department was created whose job was to ensure that all the major technical and marketing issues had been sorted out before the project went into the main product development process. The separate technology department would continue to do longer term studies.

With three phases of work and a large number of projects, Grundfos needed to improve its project selection process. It had previously used an externally sourced scoring tool but the team realized that, to have credibility, they would now have to design their own selection tool that people could see really reflected their specific needs. Christian Rasmussen, manager of the technology department, was given the task of creating the tool: 'We decided that front loading was the place to start because their projects had to be evaluated against a broad range of criteria, not only technical. It was too early to use financial analysis.' Grundfos makes a distinction between relatively long-term strategic projects and shorter term tactical ones. Different management and governance processes are used for each type and the first requirement was for a simple but objective method to allocate proposed projects between the two streams. A single factor set was used for this, as shown below:

For the project:

1. How well is it defined?
2. How well would it fit into development (the 'streams') later on?

How well would the potential product:

3. Fit the sales process?
4. Fit the distribution channels?
5. Fit existing supply chain and production?

And

6. How new would any service aspects be to the company?

For each factor, the pivot statement was chosen so that higher scores would suggest a strategic project and lower scores a tactical one. The tool worked well and gave the team the confidence to move on to develop a selection tool for the tactical products, shown in Table 6.6.

Rasmussen says:

It took two days in all to design and present the first tool – later on, with experience, we found we could design a tool for a new requirement in a couple of hours. You need to involve several people in this, especially for the anchoring statements, which are the key to the whole thing. The pivot statement is the most important. We also found that people need to understand the theory behind the method, otherwise they don't feel comfortable; so you have to do some explaining. And it's helpful to score some projects together, at least the first time, to make sure that everyone has the same interpretation.

Grundfos already had a standard form for collecting information on each project, which provided everyone with an objective set of information to start off with. Scoring separately was important as 'it allows people to access information that they didn't know rather than be embarrassed by not knowing and make a silly guess'. The team found that it took a team of four about half an hour to review and score each project for opportunity and feasibility and collate the results; a total effort of two person-hours per project. Says Rasmussen: 'That's not a lot compared with the time we used to take, debating round and round – and considering the importance of the task.'

Grundfos' production department soon adopted the approach for choosing process improvement projects. Hans Jørgen Klein, head of the production technology department, says:

We use scoring tools for three types of projects: internal ideas; external ideas (from universities and other industries); and things which can produce a

TABLE 6.6: Grundfos' Score Tool to Separate Strategic and Tactical Projects

Factor	0	5	10
How would the project fit into the product development organization later down the road	The technology is outside the scope of the streams	The stream could be expected to handle the project after six months	We could imediately say which stream it fits into
How well is the project aim defined	No written statement yet	Core features have been demonstrated, possible applications have been established but no PFMP	Customer view in PRMP is in place
How well would the potential offering fit the sales process	Competences not available in sales or require new customer segment	Some of the existing sales representatives could handle it with training	Previous generation can be found in CAPS
How well would the existing distribution channel fit the offering	Entirely new distribution channel needed	75% of the distribution can be fulfilled with existing channels	Can be supplied through existing distribution without change
How well would the offering fit existing supply chain and production	Major part of the supply chain would have to change and/or new production technology required	Changes in supply chain and production are required but within our capability	Scale up of existing production line and uses existing supply chain
How new would the service be to Grundfos	A new kind of service would be needed to enable the offering	A new but not unfamiliar service setup would be required	If service is needed, the service business exists

Source: copyright © Grundfos. Reprinted with permission.

direct benefit for our customers. Our problem is that we have a lot of project ideas, typically 15 a month, and we have to find an efficient way to make the initial decision whether to investigate an idea further or to park it for the moment.

It took a couple of four-hour discussions with a group of four colleagues, plus quite a bit of work on his own, to design a tool they all felt happy with. It uses separate assessments for opportunity and feasibility. Klein states:

The way our process works is that the project proposer writes a proposal and then reviews it with an independent colleague. Once both of them are happy they also score the project together, giving upper and lower scores on the opportunity and feasibility dimensions. Their proposal and scoring go to the monthly evaluation meeting where they discuss them with the five panel members who decide what to do. The structure of the tool and the anchoring statements makes for much more concrete discussions than we used to have. We get a lot of 'buy-in' from this process.

Klein is still working to improve the process. He finds that project scores tend to be less well differentiated than they would like:

For some reason, people don't feel happy giving very high or very low scores. Maybe it's a mistake to start with the project owners proposing the scores. They won't want to give low scores and probably feel modest about suggesting high ones. Maybe it's a Danish cultural thing. Anyway we can always present the results on a narrower scale to emphasize the differences.

Multi-factor scoring has taken root in Grundfos, but Rasmussen says:

> We never follow the scoring slavishly. The important thing a carefully designed tool does is to clarify and present the information so that you can have a reasonably objective discussion. It may point the way but it can't decide for you. You could say that we use it as a guide but not as a master.

Reflective Questions

1. How could Grundfos evaluate the success of its selection processes?
2. How might it best share the experience and pass it on to others?
3. What review processes might be appropriate?

Now visit www.palgravehighered.com/gm to watch Christian Rasmussen discussing in more detail how he designed the multi-factor scoring process at Grundfos and how people reacted to using it.

IMPLEMENTING INNOVATIONS

INTRODUCTION

Innovation is often thought of in terms of mould-breaking new ideas and inspirational new perspectives. But the great inventor Thomas Edison rightly said: 'Genius is one per cent inspiration and ninety-nine per cent perspiration.' Generating and selecting an idea is only the first step on the journey; the real work starts with the implementation.

Turning an innovative idea into reality is bound to be a unique experience that must be treated as a *project*: a finite activity with its own objectives and resources, and, above all, its own leadership. Therefore, successful implementation of any innovation requires good *project management*, nowadays properly regarded as a professional discipline in its own right. No project of any size has much of a chance without a well-trained project manager empowered to get things done, and having the support of higher management. It also requires a clear set of management processes appropriate to the degree and type of innovation involved. Most of the processes now in use were invented to help with the design of new physical, *hardware* products, but the growth of the software industry in the latter part of the 20th century has led to new approaches to project management, some of which are also relevant for other types of innovation.

Implementation is shown at the end of the innovation funnel in the Pentathlon Framework but this does not mean that the funnel is a linear sequence of collecting ideas, making a decision and then doing the work. Most innovations, and especially breakthrough and radical ones, require some investigative project work during the fuzzy front end. This work is somewhat different to that of the implementation phase proper, since it is aimed at learning and experimentation rather than delivery, as we have discussed in Chapter 5. Nevertheless, the project management disciplines discussed in this chapter remain important. The implementation phase begins when the major uncertainties have been resolved and a firm decision can be made to take the innovation to market. The emphasis then moves to delivering as quickly and effectively as possible, although uncertainties may remain.

Companies often fail to recognize the change of gear that is needed between the investigation and implementation phases, either not giving enough scope for learning and experimentation in the front end or failing to tighten the estimating and planning disciplines as they move to implementation.

All innovations, even incremental ones, are likely to require cross-functional cooperation involving many different parts of the company. Companies usually have a standard process for new product (and service) introduction (NPI) to facilitate this cooperation so that although the products are new, the process makes this kind of innovation to some extent 'business as usual' (see Mini Case 7.4 on Pizza Hut). However, managers must be alert to the possibility that more radical product innovations may require significant innovation in parts of the business not normally included in the standard process. For example, Mini Case 7.1 shows how Allstate Insurance experimented successfully with selling methods for a radical new product and Mini Case 7.2 describes how a business model innovation released the potential of solar power in Africa. Such changes disrupt the work of the departments affected and may generate resistance. This is all the more true

CHAPTER **7**

of the more radical non-product innovations for which there may be no standard process. Recognizing and managing the resistance that innovation generates is an important part of the implementation process.

This chapter covers:

- Different models of project management.
- Project management processes.
- Managing risk.
- Organization issues.
- Recognizing and overcoming resistance.
- A main case study on Wipro Technologies, India.

MINI CASE 7.1: *Allstate Insurance – Innovation in Selling* [1]

It was on a flight from Philadelphia to Chicago in 2002 that Ed Biemer and Roger Parker of Allstate Insurance came up with the idea for a radically new vehicle insurance product. Instead of offering the usual simple balance between cover and price, Universal Auto would offer a combination of variable features at different prices, with variable sales commission and profit. The new features would include forgiveness for accidents at various levels, and cash rewards for making no claims. Customers would have a wide range of options to choose from and agents would have more chance of pleasing a customer and making a sale.

Insurance companies do not often launch radical new products so Allstate had no standard process for new product introduction. Biemer asked Parker to spend time building a coalition of support for this new concept and so over the next six months he and his colleagues spoke to most of the managers in the company, gaining their support and fleshing out the concept with their ideas. Finally, they put the idea to the President, Rick Cohen. He was enthusiastic and allocated $1 million to it.

At this point, Parker moved to a job in marketing and the project was taken forward by a new team. It turned out to be difficult to accommodate this radically different product in the company's IT system but a simplified, preliminary version was launched in 2003 for trial in three US states. It had only limited success. Nevertheless, the CEO, Tom Wilson, offered his support and authorized them to push ahead with a full implementation. It was clear that the product needed improvement, so Peg Dyer, leader in marketing, asked Parker to rejoin the project and do some serious quantitative studies with customers. This was an innovation in itself; previous product variants had been based on actuarial data, not customer input. Parker says:

> The focus groups were a revelation. We literally did hundreds of them and as they went on it dawned on us that the thing that the customers really liked was the sense of reciprocity. It wasn't all 'take' from us; they could get something back, too. We simplified the product to offer only four packages and the testing suggested that 60 per cent of customers would prefer the new product to the old.

The new product, now called Your Choice Auto, was launched in 2005. The take-up was about 15 per cent, which was useful, but not the major success they had expected. All the salespeople and agents had been trained on the product, but maybe the sales process itself needed to change? Parker and his colleagues brainstormed the problem and came up with five possible sales approaches:

1. Explain all the options and leave the customer to decide.
2. Work with customers to understand their needs and help them to decide what was best for them.

Continued...

3. Offer the option priced just below what they were currently paying and explain the others if needed.
4. Start with the lowest priced package and sell up.
5. Start with the highest priced package and work down.

It was not obvious which way would be best, so once again they conducted a careful quantitative experiment. Groups of salespeople and agents were incentivized to work with one of the five options exclusively for a period and then the results were compared. Parker said:

> It was more difficult than we'd expected, because the agents were so used to the traditional sales approach that they kept dropping back to it. We had some cases when the agent would tell us he followed the script but a colleague at the next desk would butt in and say 'no, you don't!' The best trials were at the call centres where we could listen in and help them keep on track.

The outcome was a shock. The fifth approach was easily the most effective, although it had been rated lowest before the trial. With the evidence in place, it was now easy to persuade the salespeople and agents to adopt the new sales method and the result was dramatic: the take-up rate for Your Choice Auto rose to the anticipated 60 per cent, with improved margins and a higher renewal rate. Allstate's product innovation was a great success but much else in the company had to change to make it work.

▶ MINI CASE 7.2: *Azuri Technologies – High Tech in Rural Africa²* *with video interview*

The Cavendish Laboratory at the University of Cambridge pioneered the development of electronics based on semiconducting plastics. This led to the launch of several companies including, in 2010, Eight19, charged with completing the panel development and taking the technology to market. The company's name is derived from the time, 8 minutes and 19 seconds, it takes for the sun's light to reach earth.

At the time of writing, the technology development is still not complete but a new and unanticipated aspect of the business is already booming. Early on, the management team researched various possible Western markets including greetings cards but quickly realized that the most compelling business case was for off-grid electricity supply in the developing world. Rural communities rely on kerosene lamps for lighting, which are dim, costly on fuel and often hazardous, so solar could make economic sense even in the poorest households. The problem was the high capital cost: the target customers typically have little or no savings and no access to credit. The answer caused the launch of a new company, in 2012, only two years after Eight19 started.

The novel solution is a form of 'pay as you go'. The customer pays $10 for the installation of a solar panel together with a battery and low-energy LED lights. To start it working, they buy a scratch card for $2, which reveals a code. When this is sent by phone to the local agent, the customer receives a customized code that unlocks their system for a week. At the end of the week, the customer buys another card, using the money now saved from not buying kerosene, to unlock it for another period. After 18 months, the last code unlocks the system permanently. Simon Bransfield-Garth, the CEO of Azuri, says: 'The business model was the innovation and we realized it would work without our new technology. So the company split in two: a technology development company centred on IPR and a cash-generating distribution company, Azuri Technologies.' The company assembles its own product using the best available panels, batteries and LEDs together with its own control system and distributes it through partners. The information on usage that comes through the payment system and from visits to customers helps optimize distribution. Adequate lighting can transform lives by extending the working day and allowing

Continued...

CHAPTER **7**

children to study and adults to read in the evenings. Each system also has a mobile phone charging point. The scratch card payment method is still in use but many customers now pay by phone.

Bransfield-Garth adds:

> By getting quickly into distribution we've learned a lot about customer needs that we would never have known concentrating on the technology. For example, sometimes in the rainy season there is not enough sun to fully charge the battery, but we've learned that continuity of lighting is more important for our customers than its brightness. So our new systems learn the family's normal pattern of use – some use it only at night, some need a bit in the morning – and adapts the brightness to suit. The human eye is very nonlinear so you get 80 per cent perceived brightness with 50 per cent of the power. Our customers in rural African villages have far more advanced lighting than we get in Europe.

The Azuri business model has the classic features to assist rapid diffusion: it is simple to use and understand; it is easy to trial; and it has immediate benefits that are readily visible to other potential customers. By the end of 2015, over 60,000 systems had been installed in 11 different countries and the business is doubling year on year.

Now visit www.palgravehighered.com/gm to watch Simon Bransfield-Garth discussing in more detail how he developed the innovative business model at Azuri Technologies and how he found his first customers.

PROJECT MANAGEMENT MODELS

Project management is at the core of the implementation phase of innovation. There are several different approaches and it is important to match the method to the type of innovation concerned.

The Staged, or Sequential Model

The earliest paradigm of project management was the so-called *sequential model*. In this, the project is divided into phases, each of which is essentially self-contained and finished with a defined deliverable to be handed over to the next stage. The *waterfall model*, introduced in 1970,[3] was a variant to the sequential model, specifically for software development, recognizing the need for iterations but only between adjacent stages. In NPI, the phases are normally stated as initiation, definition, design, development and implementation (Figure 7.1).

This model is still the basic structure of most types of projects except those based purely on software. One thing has changed, however; at one time, each stage of the NPI process would be the responsibility of a different department. For example, marketing would define what was to be done, engineering would design the product, production engineering worked out how to make it, manufacturing made it, and handed it over to sales to sell. This 'over the wall' approach had the advantage of allowing the specialist departments to develop and deploy deep expertise; and the relatively formal handover between departments

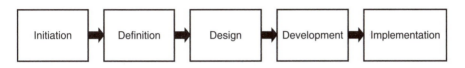

FIGURE 7.1: Staged or Sequential Project Management

provided good overall control. But it could be slow and inflexible. It could also be very inefficient for innovative projects because since each stage was done in isolation, it was difficult to take account of opportunities or requirements arising from later stages; for example, to alter the design to make manufacturing easier, or change the requirement to take advantage of newly emerging technical capabilities or market knowledge.

The Cross-functional Team

The deficiencies of the 'over the wall' model were addressed in the 1970s and 80s by use of *cross-functional teams* headed by an empowered project manager. This was acknowledged in academic publications from 1986 starting with the work of Takeuchi and Nonaka[4] and is a key component of the vast majority of innovation projects. We have more to say about this later in the chapter and also, in more depth, in Chapter 8. The team should include representatives from all the parts of the company that would be affected by the innovation – sales, marketing, R&D, operations and so on – working together, ideally in the same location but at least in close communication. In its extreme form, the team is deliberately separated from the main organization in a separate building or location and given a great deal of autonomy over what they do and how they do it. Radical innovations may need this kind of isolation to allow teams to develop new approaches and perhaps business models free from too much influence from the established business. The challenge, autonomy and feeling of shared responsibility can be very motivational and lead to high levels of energy and commitment. This is how IBM developed the PC and Canon the first copier for personal use. However, most innovations need to be more closely integrated into the home organization. For example Grundfos, a major European pump manufacturer, operated a system of independent project teams with great success for many years but eventually found that the independence led to an unnecessary proliferation of design types, generating costly complexity in the organization. A move to more standard platforms and modules required a change to the project management structure (the main case study at the end of the chapter, on Wipro, also illustrates this issue).

Agile Models

The term *agile project management* came to prominence in 2001 to describe a new approach to software design that had been developing in the 1990s.[5] The concept is now increasingly applied to certain types of hardware project.

The original motivation for agile methods came from the design of software for consumer use. Such applications are difficult to specify fully in advance

CHAPTER 7

because it is impossible to predict exactly how the user will react to them. Designers found that however hard they tried, customer feedback after launch always called for a long series of updates and modifications. As Boehm observed:[6] 'Standards have pushed many projects to write elaborate specifications of poorly understood user interfaces and decision support functions, followed by the design and development of large quantities of unusable code.'

In the agile approach, complete and exhaustive specifications are not attempted at the outset. Instead, attention concentrates on the risky elements or those that require prototyping. The easier parts are done later. A deliberate process of 'trial and error' is used, in which preliminary versions are prototyped and released for testing by potential – or actual – users; modified if necessary and then incorporated into a further, more complete version. The basic model, usually known as the *spiral model*, is shown in Figure 7.2. This is highly appropriate for software development where prototyping is easy and cheap. The application to projects involving physical constructions is more problematic, although not impossible, as we describe below.

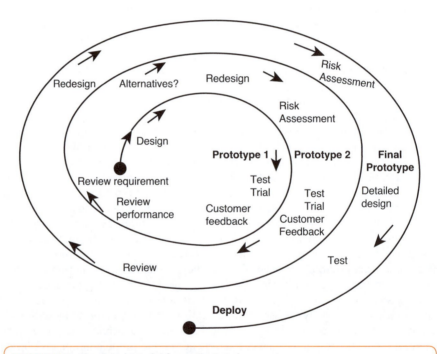

FIGURE 7.2: The Spiral Model for Agile Development
Source: copyright © 1988 IEEE. Reprinted and adapted, with permission, from Boehm, B. W., 'A Spiral Model of Software Development and Enhancement', Computer, 21(5) (1988), 61–72[7]

Scrum Model

The *scrum model*[8] is an extreme example of the agile approach and can be incorporated within phases of the spiral model. It involves a complete rejection of formal specification and work planning. The idea is that a small team, usually fewer than seven people, works collaboratively in a *sprint* to produce a deliverable in a short time, typically a few weeks. The team meets daily to discuss progress and allocate tasks. There is no project manager in the usual sense, although there is a *scrum manager* whose job is to facilitate the work; and there is an overall *owner* who is able to make decisions over what is deliverable. The change in emphasis is away from exhaustive written specifications towards flexibility, close communication and empowering individuals not only to decide how the work is to be done but also what is to be done, and released. This is regarded by some not just as a change of method but as a change of philosophy, as expressed in the Agile Manifesto (Theory Box 7.1).

THEORY BOX 7.1: *The Agile Manifesto*

'We are uncovering better ways of developing software by doing it and helping others do it. Through this work we have come to value:

Individuals and interactions	over	processes and tools
Working software	over	comprehensive documentation
Customer collaboration	over	contract negotiation
Responding to change	over	following a plan

That is, while there is value in the items on the right, we value the items on the left more.'

Source: copyright © 2001 Manifesto for Agile Software Development[9].

Choosing the Appropriate Project Management Model

Agile methods are increasingly the norm in software projects. Many companies are also experimenting with mixing agile and sequential project management models in hardware projects, although there is much yet to be learned about how and where to strike the balance. For complex hardware projects – such as designing an aero engine – it may be quite impractical to build and modify a series of prototypes; and anyway the requirements may be perfectly clear at the outset. A staged process will remain the norm for these. However, agile methods may be appropriate in the investigation phase of innovation projects where the concentration is on gaining knowledge and demonstrating feasibility. The more advanced companies are now using a mixture of sprints and spirals nested within a more formal structure.[10, 11] The boundaries are moving as computer simulation and visualization become commonplace for many mechanical structures – as indeed it has long been for electronics – and virtual reality methods become able to simulate much of the human experience of new products as well. Thus the dividing line between hardware and software design processes will become increasingly blurred; the more so as rapid prototyping methods such as *additive manufacture* become available.

An innovation project can often be thought of as a series of sub-projects nested within an overall framework. The management style for each stage may vary depending on a number of factors, as summarized in Table 7.1.

TABLE 7.1: Factors Determining the Choice of Project Management Model

Factors pointing to use of a staged project management model	Factors pointing to use of an agile project management model
The requirements are clearly defined at the outset and there are no serious technical or other uncertainties	Requirements cannot be fully defined at the outset, either because are many technical or other unknowns, or because demonstrations or prototypes are needed to clarify user needs
Requirements are unlikely to change	Timescales are tight and it is understood that requirements may be renegotiated to meet them
Rapid prototyping and testing are not possible	Rapid prototyping and testing are possible
All key features must be delivered together, either for functional reasons or because the costs associated with the launch are high, e.g. manufacturing start-up	New features can be added and released easily
Teams are spread over several sites and cannot easily meet face to face	Team members can be co-located or can meet easily
The project requires close coordination between different specialisms such as software, mechanical, electrical	Only a single specialism is involved (typically software)

Source: based on pmhut.com

PROJECT MANAGEMENT METHODS[12]

The following is a brief introduction to the essentials of this important subject. Our message to managers is that, whatever project management model you adopt, if you do nothing else to improve your company's implementation of innovations, at least recognize the importance of the right style of project management and make sure that your project managers receive good and appropriate training for their task. And have the active support of senior managers (see Mini Case 7.3).

MINI CASE 7.3: *NZ DoC – Restoring the Dawn Chorus*

Many islands in the South Pacific have been invaded by rats introduced from overseas, and these pests often wipe out indigenous species entirely. As part of its biodiversity programme, the New Zealand Department of Conservation (DoC) looked at the possibility of eliminating rodents entirely from some of the islands. The scientific view was that this was simply not possible, but DoC staff were not convinced: As one staff member said:

> What we were looking at, at the time, was rats invading islands and species going extinct as a consequence … The accepted wisdom was that the best you can do is to go out there and

Continued...

grab what you can and rescue them and take them somewhere else ... You wouldn't have to be involved in too much work before you'd realize there's got to be a better way than that ... Pretty soon you're going to run out of places that you can stick these things.

The mindshift towards trying eradication took place in the early 1980s. The development of new poisons led to experiments on small islands eliminating only a single type of rodent, and moved on later to larger and more complex islands and several species. As more difficult islands were attempted, new techniques were tested and applied. Aerial application of bait was first tried in 1989 and the technique was later developed using helicopters with specially developed underslung baskets. When global positioning systems (GPS) became available, they were adopted to improve accuracy. By 1990, 13 species of rodent had been eradicated from 60 islands. This increased to 20 species by 2001. The biggest operation to date has been the elimination of the estimated 200,000 rats from the 11,000 hectare Campbell Island in 2001 at a cost of $2.6 million.

The vision and passion of DoC staff was one of the most important factors of the success of the pest eradication programme. Although international experts had concluded that eradication was highly unlikely, key DoC staff refused to accept this. Their refusal to give up on the vision led to experimentation and success with small projects which, in turn, bred the confidence to take on more ambitious ones. But the right kind of senior management support was very important. For example, the Campbell Island project was jeopardized when a lorry full of rat poison crashed into the sea. Senior managers stepped in to deal with the consequences and protected the project manager from blame and interference so that he could continue to get on with the job. A common theme in the programme was the need to have a culture of trust, forgiveness and not punishing failures. Management accepted that project teams had to experiment to find the best solutions and that some experiments would fail. Care was necessary to manage expectations. The Campbell Island project manager talked about his strong conviction that the organization trusted him to manage the project and to work through issues without second-guessing or unhelpful interference.

A special team, the Island Eradication Advisory Group (IEAG), consisting of administrative experts and managers from previous eradication projects, played an important role in giving expert advice to project teams and ensuring that lessons were carried forward from one project to the next. The IEAG also helped to protect the team from political interference.

Other countries are now copying the idea. As biologist Sir David Bellamy put it: 'New Zealand is the only country which has turned pest eradication into an export industry.'

When the fuzzy front end is over, there should be a change of gear. The focus shifts from experimenting with new ideas and removing uncertainty, to detailed design and implementation. This will involve people from all over the organization, and may well require significant expenditure on things such as manufacturing, marketing and distribution. From now on, this is a project much like any other.

Well, almost. There should be no show-stopping risks left but this is still an innovation project and parts may be new and not perfectly predictable. Management must be alert to this and have contingency plans in mind when all does not run to plan.

Seven elements are fundamental to successful project management throughout the innovation process and particularly during implementation:

1. Clear aims, including an understanding and management of trade-offs.
2. A breakdown of the work into elements small enough to be planned and managed.

CHAPTER 7

3. A scheduling plan that ensures that tasks are undertaken in the right order and at the right times.
4. A resource plan to ensure that people and facilities will be available to do the tasks as required.
5. Clear understanding and management of risks.
6. An objective staged review process.
7. Active management of stakeholders (the subject of a later section in this chapter).

Companies that rely on a steady flow of new products or services will generally have a formal new product introduction (NPI) process to handle it (see Mini Case 7.4 on Pizza Hut). This will usually be based on a staged review process and will include ways to handle the seven elements just mentioned. A well-managed NPI process is a vital tool but it will usually be designed for more or less incremental innovations and, in particular, in our experience, will tend to assume that a new product will at most require some modifications in production (for products) or back-office processes (for services). Changes elsewhere – in selling, for example (as at Allstate in Mini Case 7.1) – may be overlooked.

Non-product innovations as well as the more radical product cases will not fit into the standard process.

> ### MINI CASE 7.4: *Pizza Hut – New Product Development*
>
> The development of a new pizza might be seen as a trivial selection of a new set of toppings. However, in the fast-food business where product consistency and fast 'roll-out' are essential, it is not that simple. Pizza Hut has a seven-stage NPD process called the Field Ready Product Process (FRPP). This process ensures that a robust product is developed by defining the steps that are necessary to develop the recipe, select suppliers for the ingredients, test the 'manufacturability' of the product in a typical Pizza Hut restaurant, and ensure positive consumer reactions to the new product. Everything is done to ensure that no time is wasted between a product concept being selected and it being available at the majority of the chain's restaurants. Part of the FRPP ensures that employees in the restaurants are adequately trained on the product before it is released. Increasingly, competition in the fast-food industry is based on special meals that are only available for limited periods and matched to major events, such as sport championships, or film releases. In such cases, Pizza Hut has found that a reliable but flexible NPD process is essential, even if the resulting product is 'only' a pizza.

Design Thinking

The overall aims of an innovation will initially be quite loosely expressed and it can be a major task to turn that into 'nuts and bolts' to be implemented. When customers describe what they want from a product, or managers specify the requirements for a new process, it will usually be in terms of the overall performance or experience that they seek, not the way it is achieved. Thus a customer's perspective for a car is likely to be couched in vague terms like 'reliable', 'luxurious' or 'fun to drive', not about what this means in terms of engineering issues such as road-holding, acceleration or acoustics. *Design* is the term for the process that turns customer needs into attractive products or services, taking into account not only their overt features but also the experience users will have in interacting with them, such as the ergonomics and, where appropriate, the aesthetic aspects. For service products, this will certainly include the servicescape. Design is a complete field of study, which we will not attempt to summarize here.

A core aspect of design, which is applicable in all types of innovation, is the need to ensure that users' needs shape and control the choices that are made, and that the elements all contribute effectively to satisfying them. A well-established and effective tool for linking customer needs to the physical features of the product or service is *quality function deployment* (QFD), which we describe in Theory Box 7.2. It is important to remember that the services surrounding the product may also need to be considered as part of the design, as Mini Case 7.5 on Radiometer shows.

THEORY BOX 7.2: *Quality Function Deployment*

The first step in QFD is to understand customers' needs and desires from their point of view. Techniques such as hidden needs analysis, empathic design, repertory grids, contextual interviews and lead user consultation may be used, as described in Chapter 5. The needs elicited by these studies are summarized into simple statements in the language the customer might use. They are likely to be subjective, qualitative and non-technical. These needs, and the responses of the organization to them, are assembled into what is known as the *House of Quality*. In its most complete form, the house can have as many as eight sections, or *rooms*, but we use only five here for the purposes of illustration (Figure 7.3). More complete treatments are to be found in the work of Don Clausing of MIT,[13] and others.[14]

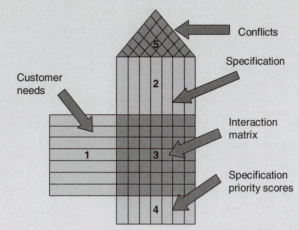

FIGURE 7.3: The House of Quality
Source: ReVelle, Jack B., Quality Essentials: A Reference Guide from A to Z, (ASQ, 2004), pp. 9–11, House of Quality image. Adapted and reprinted with permission from Quality Press © 2004 ASQ, www.asq.org. No further distribution allowed without permission.

Continued...

CHAPTER 7

The first section of the House of Quality contains the customer needs. As an example, we will take the final stages of a postal delivery service, for which customer requirements might be:

- Reliability
- Daily delivery
- Undamaged mail
- Easy to divert mail when I move
- Arrangements for handling parcels when nobody at home
- Low cost.

These requirements are unlikely to be all equally important to the customer, so it may be convenient to allocate a weighting to them to express this. At this point, the Kano analysis of features into basic, performance and excitement categories (see Chapter 4) is useful.[15]

The second section (specification) contains the main performance elements of the product or process in the language of the organization providing it. For a product this would be the technical specification; for the postal service it might include factors that the organization would provide, such as:

- Local distribution points
- Local delivery staff
- Local transport
- Address reading system
- Sorting
- Customer profile information.

The impact of each element of the product performance on customer need is now assessed and noted where the two intersect in the interaction matrix (section 3, Figure 7.3). It is usual to define three levels of impact, which we represent in Figure 7.4, with one, two or three stars. Scores out of 10 are also used; it

		Local distribution depots	Staff quality + incentives	Local transport	Address reading system	Sorting process	Customer profile info.	Low cost
Reliable	7	*	*		*	***		
Daily Delivery	10	**		*	**			
Mail not damaged	9			***	**			
Mail can be diverted	5						***	
Low cost	6							***
Arrangements for absence	4	*	**				***	
		41	100	73	37	63	81	54

FIGURE 7.4: QFD Analysis of Local Postal Delivery Service

Continued...

is usual to give 9 for a high impact, 3 for a medium and 1 for low in order to avoid the situation where a feature providing a very minor impact on several needs is rated more highly than one giving outstanding benefits to only one or two.[16]

These figures are multiplied by the weighting of the customer need (shown alongside each in Figure 7.4) and displayed in the interaction matrix (section 3). The results are added to give overall importance scores for the various features (section 4). The interaction matrix shows at once which features of the specification contribute most to satisfying the various customer needs. The most important must be given priority in the design phase and those with low impact are candidates for elimination. The matrix may also highlight where important customer needs are *not* being served by the product features.

The final part of the House of Quality is the 'roof' (section 5, Figure 7.3), where any conflicts between features are noted (shown by crosses in Figure 7.5). For example, in the postal system case, it may not be possible to install address reading equipment in local depots; and holding customer profile information may conflict with the need for low cost. These conflicts cannot be resolved within existing thinking and so indicate that one benefit must be traded off against another. More importantly, however, this part of the house points to where there are opportunities for innovation that might avoid the trade-off altogether.

Quality function deployment is a valuable tool for ensuring that the detailed features of the product or service really do align with the needs of the customer. Like all such tools, it is an aid to thought not a substitute for it, so much of the value often comes from the discussion it stimulates. The simple and compact form of the presentation is a great advantage.

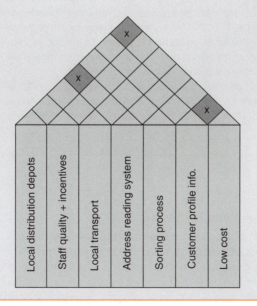

FIGURE 7.5: Conflict between Features in QFD

> **MINI CASE 7.5:** *Radiometer – Blood Testing Every Second of the Day* [17]

The Danish company Radiometer is a world leader in the development and manufacturing of healthcare solutions for blood sampling and testing. The company's products simplify and automate all phases of testing, so hospitals can obtain results with increased speed and efficiency, reducing their workload and the risk of errors. Its products are sold in 130 countries and the company has more than 2,700 employees worldwide.

It is Radiometer's strategy to provide not only excellent products but also excellent service. Amulya Malladi, manager of customer care, sums this up: 'We ensure a smooth installation of our "1st Automatic" system, so that hospital staff can quickly learn how to use it to deliver fast blood test results. The system guarantees the right result, for the right patient, at the right time.' Test results are delivered quickly and barcoding ensures they match the right patient. To ensure this, barcodes are scanned of the patient's ID, the blood sample, and the ID of the healthcare professional taking the sample. This information is then automatically transferred to the blood gas analyser and the database. To collect the patient's blood, healthcare professionals use Radiometer's specially designed '*safe*PICO' syringe. The integrated needle shield allows safe, one-handed needle removal, lowering the risk of needlestick injury, while the innovative '*safe*TIPCAP' facilitates safe removal of air bubbles and seals the sample.

Radiometer has developed the customer care programme based on extensive voice of the customer interviews. Carsten Tessum, global product manager, says this has involved 'asking customers about the blood gas testing process from start to finish and through the lifetime of product. We ask: what are the activities that matter the most to the customer? Where are the potential pain points? What is working and what is not?' Based on this, Radiometer has identified specific areas that are of high importance to the customer and integrated them into its 'LIVE customer care program'. In developing LIVE, Radiometer demonstrates how a full solution could be engineered using a mix of hardware, software, remote monitoring and on-site customer service. This means that the company can proactively help hospitals. Tessum says: 'For example, we can see when equipment is starting to develop problems – for example when it needs to be calibrated more often than usual – and also when consumables are needed. So we can help the customer even before they are thinking about what they need.'

Radiometer knows that developing products and services requires extensive knowledge of how its machines are used by healthcare professionals to analyse blood samples. And across the globe, six blood samples are being analysed by Radiometer machines every second of the day and night.

Case contributed by Thomas Frandsen and Jawwad Raja.

Project Aims and Trade-offs

The content of a project is essentially defined by the task itself, the time allowed, and the cost of doing the work. If something happens to any of these three factors, it can generally be recovered only by changing one of the others. This is illustrated in the *project management triangle* in Figure 7.6. For example, if part of the project runs significantly late, the time can generally be recovered only by assigning more resources to it – which will usually increase the cost – or altering the deliverables. Similarly, a change to the project specification will impact either time or cost. There is no escaping this. The terms of reference for the project should therefore state clearly what the trade-off strategy will be and not leave it to the project team to work out in the heat of the moment when problems arise.

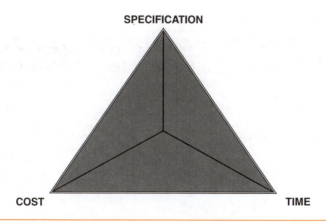

SPECIFICATION

COST

TIME

FIGURE 7.6: The Project Management Triangle
Source: adapted from the Project Management Triangle set out by Dr. Martin Barnes.
Copyright © Dr. Martin Barnes.

The effect of a cost overrun is usually easy to work out but it may be more diffi-cult to work out the impact that a late launch or a reduced specification will have on the commercial benefits. 'Program managers, who know to a penny what an additional engineer will cost and what profits will be lost if the company misses manufacturing cost targets, seldom can quantify the losses associated with a six-month slippage in the development process.'[18] However, the truth is always useful and often surprising.

Studies of new product and service introduction have shown that the time to market often has the greatest impact on profitability.[19, 20, 21] Several factors con-tribute to this; for example, a late launch reduces the total lifetime sales and may reduce the opportunities for premium pricing as a leading product in the market. The reduced sales volume also affects costs, through less efficient use of fixed costs and the loss of 'learning curve' efficiencies that come from accumulated operating experience. Case 1 in Table 7.2 shows how the profitability of a particular industrial project would be affected by various issues arising in the development process.

Such sensitivities are often quoted to emphasize the importance of time in new product development.[22] However, they must be treated with care because they apply to a quite specific case: the product lifetime was five years; the market was growing at 20 per cent a year; and prices were expected to fall by 12 per cent a year. A different set of assumptions leads to quite different conclusions. For example, we calculate that a project to reduce the cost of a product with a five-year life by 30 per cent, in a basically static market with static pricing, shows the sensitivities shown as Case 2 in Table 7.2 (a gross margin of 50 per cent is assumed). In this case, the profitability of the project would be much more sensi-tive to product quality and cost than to the time taken. Timing is probably most sensitive for incremental product improvements where competitive pressures are strong. With breakthrough and radical innovations of all sorts, it may be more important to get all aspects of the project right rather than to rush to market. Clearly, it is important to understand the actual sensitivities for each particular project.

CHAPTER **7**

TABLE 7.2: Project Trade-offs on Two Different Assumptions

Issue	Reduction in project profit (Case 1)	Reduction in project profit (Case 2)
Product introduced 6 months late	31%	10%
Quality problems reduce selling price by 10%	15%	66%
Compatibility problems reduce sales volume by 10%	4%	10%
10% product cost excess	4%	23%
30% development project budget overrun	2%	2%

Work Breakdown Structure

The successful execution of any project requires a reasonably detailed understanding of what has to be done. Without this, it is impossible to estimate the time and resources required or the likely duration of the work. The *work breakdown structure*, as it is known, lists all the tasks, or *work packages*, and the relationship between them. All the tasks should have defined deliverables and people assigned to do them. The level of detail must match the accuracy required of the estimate: if the end-date of the project must be known to within a week, there is no sense in using work packages a month long. The work breakdown is a simple tool and yet is often overlooked, especially in innovative projects where some may say that the uncertainties make such analysis useless. In fact, the converse is true: it is helpful precisely for understanding those uncertainties and addressing them. A review of the work packages is also an effective communication tool at the beginning of a project as it shows everyone the full scope of what is to be done – not just the core design or manufacturing tasks – and highlights how each task depends on others. For example, discussions may clarify what tasks each team member needs to do for the others, the meetings and communication required. Organon, for example, found how important it was to include supply chain issues in the planning (see Mini Case 7.6).

The work breakdown is also vital for monitoring progress. Completed work packages are the only unambiguous measure of what has been achieved.

> **MINI CASE 7.6:** *Organon and Fagron – NPD and the Supply Chain*[23]

Organon is the human healthcare division of AkzoNobel, a Dutch multinational. It creates, produces and markets prescription drugs mainly for reproductive medicine, psychiatry and anaesthesia. Although the majority of its product development is concentrated in the Netherlands, the company has 10 manufacturing sites and over 12,000 employees around the globe, required to provide fast and efficient service to its geographical markets. Organon has learned to plan for demand uncertainty during NPD, to integrate the needs of its manufacturing plants into its product planning process and to design the supply chain alongside the product development.

Continued...

The main risks related to the uncertain demand for pharmaceuticals are overcapacity and lost sales. It is expensive to set up pharmaceutical production facilities and, on the one hand, overcapacity must be avoided. On the other hand, an unavailable product reduces sales and brings a loss in market share that can seldom be recovered. Consequently, Organon product launch plans include different sales scenarios: best, expected and worst cases. Based on these sales scenarios, a number of supply chain design options, including the suppliers to be used worldwide, the manufacturing sites to be used and its inventory strategies, and the delivery logistics selected, are prepared. Each supply chain design option is quantitatively evaluated on five criteria: finance, risk, available resources, flexibility to scale production up and down, and (interestingly) a measure of confidence in the assumptions. Erik Hoppenbrouwer says:

> Early in the NPD process we have added demand and supply scenario planning. We review it regularly and have increased our overall success with product innovations. It is important not only to have an excellent product but also to match it with the best supply chain design. It is not easy as you are often dealing with high uncertainties. Since we have started assessing our confidence in the forecasted figures, we have increased the quality of our decisions. As a result, we can avoid overcapacity while minimizing lost sales.

As supply chain director with Organon for eight years, Hoppenbrouwer was responsible for bringing a greater understanding of how important it is to consider supply chain issues during NPD. Later, he took this expertise to Fagron, where he worked from 2010 to 2015. As the leading company in specialty pharma, Fagron develops innovative concepts and solutions that respond to the specific and individual wishes of compounding pharmacies worldwide. Compounded medications are made based on a practitioner's prescription in which individual ingredients are mixed together in the exact strength and dosage form required by the patient. Hoppenbrouwer says:

> As chief operating officer, my role was to develop and support the introduction of new products. In the first two years we optimized the operations organization, so it would be fast enough and flexible enough to focus on product innovation. Then, between 2013 and 2014, 18 new products were launched successfully.

In 2015, Hoppenbrouwer, who is a Lean Six Sigma Black Belt, co-founded GxPartners (www.gxpartners.eu), a network of Lean and Quality experts. GxPartners supports manufacturing organizations to improve their quality while reducing their costs. Hoppenbrouwer concludes: 'In an environment with stricter regulations and fierce competition, the only way to survive is that companies have their NPD process under control and are agile to adapt, whether in the pharmaceutical industry or in other industries.'

CHAPTER **7**

Estimating

Before any further work can be done, managers have to determine how much effort is required on each task. This is notoriously difficult for innovative projects. There is a school of thought that believes that estimating should be done by a specialist department because those doing the work will give overestimates in order to give themselves an easy life. Our experience, on the contrary, is that enthusiastic specialists more often underestimate out of pride or simple overenthusiasm. What is certainly true is that the key to good estimating lies in taking it seriously: that is, allocating enough time to it and breaking the task down in detail so that nothing is overlooked. Even so, it is difficult[24] and subject to all the pitfalls of intuitive judgement referred to in Theory Box 6.3. One technique that has been found useful is *planning poker* in which a number of people with appropriate experience collaborate in the estimating task. The key aspect is that they first do their estimates individually before sharing them and discussing the reasons for differences. In a recent controlled trial, this was shown to improve estimating accuracy from 45 per cent to 90 per cent.[25]

The Project Schedule

Once the tasks have been identified, it is time to consider the order in which they are to be done. Some tasks may be done at almost any time during the project while others cannot be started until earlier ones are complete, which themselves have to wait for others to be done, and so on. Most projects will contain several such sequences of tasks but there will always be one chain that is longer than the rest. This is called the *critical path* (Figure 7.7). It is important because the sum of the times required to complete all the work packages on the critical path defines the minimum length of the project. Managers will look closely at these tasks to see if any can be rescheduled or speeded up because that is the way to reduce the time the project will take. And they will be ready to assign additional resources to them if required. Once the work is in progress, the tasks on the critical path should be monitored with particular care to ensure that, whatever else happens, they, at least, will be on time.

A wide range of software is available to simplify the task of planning projects. The familiar bar chart, or Gantt chart, is an effective way to summarize the activities in a project for communication inside and outside the project team.

The Resource Plan

The next stage in constructing a project plan is to ensure that the required resources can be made available and that they are used efficiently. In a scrum situation, this is managed on a day-to-day basis with people transferring between tasks as required. However, many projects will require a range of resources and skills, which may not be interchangeable. This first analysis will usually show that the needs vary greatly with time and that peaks occur when some people will be overloaded. This would obviously mean that the tasks would run late. If these are on the critical path, the schedule for the whole project is jeopardized, so extra resources must be found or the plan modified in some other way to reduce the overload.

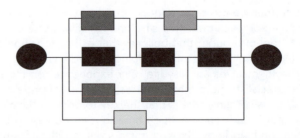

FIGURE 7.7: Schematic Project Schedule Showing the Critical Path (in black)

Managing Project Risks

Types of Risk

Innovation projects often face high levels of uncertainty. We have been critical of the word 'risk' in Chapter 6 but it may be used legitimately here to mean the possibility of occurrences that threaten the ability to meet the project aims, including delivery time and project costs. The whole point of the fuzzy front end is to reduce uncertainty so that when the implementation phase begins, little serious doubt should remain about what can be achieved and what will be its value to the organization. This phase must, above all, identify and resolve any *show-stopper risks*: that is, issues that could affect the viability of the whole project. There should be none of those left when implementation starts.

Of the remaining risks, the most significant are the *pitfall risks*. These are things that might cause the project team to have to stop and redo earlier work that was thought to have been completed. For example, in designing a car, unexpectedly high bodyweight might cause a redesign of the suspension. Clearly, it is important to order the tasks in the work schedule to minimize the possibility of rework. For complex projects, the *design structure matrix* is a helpful tool for doing this (see Theory Box 7.3).

Finally, there are the *minor risks*, which are simply things that are not yet fully clear but will become so in time. Most of these will be dealt with in the course of the project but some may have the potential to have significant impact on the plan. For the more important potential risks, the project team will need to identify a 'Plan B' and (vital but often overlooked) have a way to activate it early enough to minimize the impact. But, of course, in an innovation project nobody can foresee all the risks, so experienced project managers will always plan some 'slack' in the schedule. In simple terms, this means designing the plan to deliver the project early and under budget. It seems obvious but it is too seldom done.

Early attention to risks pays dividends. Toyota reported 30–40 per cent reductions in costs and lead times in R&D projects when it introduced careful risk management processes.[26] Similar results were reported at Xerox.[27]

THEORY BOX 7.3: *The Design Structure Matrix*

The *design structure matrix* is a simple and powerful tool, which may be used for checking the order in which information is required in the course of a complex project, and so helps to minimize the amount of iteration. The matrix shows the design tasks in a project along both axes, in the order in which it is proposed to do them, starting at the top left corner. Then, on the line corresponding to each of these work packages, a cross is put in any column corresponding to a package that will generate information required for successful completion of the task being considered (Figure 7.8).

In Figure 7.8, we can see, for example, that design task E requires information that will be generated by tasks B and C, while task F will require information from tasks A, C, G and H.

This matrix shows quickly where the communication problems will arise in this project. Most of the work packages are correctly ordered because they require only information that comes from tasks that come before them. They have crosses below the diagonal. However, some – B, C, F and G in this example – have crosses above the diagonal, which signals that they rely on information that will be

Continued...

		Information required from:								
		A	B	C	D	E	F	G	H	J
	A	■								
	B	X	■							X
	C	X		■	X					
T a s k	D	X	X		■					
	E		X	X		■				
	F	X			X		■	X	X	
	G	X			X		X	■	X	
	H				X		X	X	■	
	J		X		X		X			■

FIGURE 7.8: Example of a Design Structure Matrix

generated by packages that still have to be done. There is feedback between the tasks, which means that they may have to be revised, possibly more than once, as the facts become available. What is to be done about these? There are five possible approaches:

1. Change the order of tasks: The problem with task C can be overcome by simply doing it after task D, instead of beforehand. Changing the order causes no problems because D does not require information from C. However, there is no such simple solution for the information needs of tasks B and F; for them, other approaches are needed.

2. Concurrent working: Tasks F, G and H all need information from each other and there is no ideal order in which to do them. For example, F requires information from G and H, so if done first, it will have to be revised when they are done. But that revision may, in turn, cause changes to G and H, because they use information from F and so on. The teams involved must work closely together, exchanging information regularly as their parts of the project evolve. Ideally, they would work physically together during that part of the project so that they can deal with the trade-offs and interactions quickly, face to face. If that is not possible, then at least they must set up close and regular communications, forming a 'virtual team', for the duration of that part of the project.

3. Add extra, information-generating tasks: Task B needs information from a much later activity, J, and itself informs many later activities. It may be possible to split task J into two parts: one to be done early on, to release the information required by B, while the rest retains its natural timing. For example, suppose task J is the design of a piece of electronics and B the design of the cooling system for a product that contains it, among other items. Task B requires information about the heat generated by the electronics and this might be worked out separately before the detailed design is done. Adding this extra step removes J from above the diagonal and avoids iteration.

4. Move staff between tasks: An informal alternative to the last may be to second a member of the team working on task J to team B to help them work out what cooling is needed, without making a formal task of it.

5. Use 'working assumptions': As a final resort, the team working on an early task may have to make working assumptions that allow the project to continue. The assumptions may not be optimum but they can be chosen conservatively so that they will not have to be changed later. For a more closely optimized design, the working assumption would have to be refined as the project goes on, requiring some degree of reworking. The project manager must make careful decisions about just how much optimization is worthwhile. Here, too, close communication throughout the team is vital.

Identifying Risks

The first and crucial stage of risk management is to form as complete a picture as possible of the risks facing the project – not just at the start but regularly as it proceeds. This is not at all easy.[28] Nobody likes to be thought of as a pessimist or lacking 'team spirit' and it can be difficult to be negative in the face of optimistic colleagues or a forceful or charismatic boss. There is a well-documented tendency for tight-knit teams, especially of males, to become unreasonably confident in their abilities, a phenomenon known as 'groupthink' (see Theory Box 6.3). No doubt, it all stems from our evolution in hunting groups pursuing large game, where the cohesion would have been an asset, but it has no place in the world of innovative projects. Project managers must find ways to make it easy for people to raise concerns and find a hearing.

One technique for opening up the question of risks at the start of the project is to hold a *premortem* discussion.[29] The team is asked to imagine that they are at some time in the future when the project has finished and it was, in fact, a failure. They then discuss the reasons why this happened as a way to identify the major risks. Another technique is to use an independent person to collect and collate responses from team members anonymously and then present them to the team for open review, carefully facilitating the meeting to keep it objective.[30]

The problem of risk reduction is particularly difficult in service-related projects because important aspects of the customer interaction may only be testable by trialling the complete service. Bank of America addressed this problem by creating a mock banking facility for initial testing and designating some outlets as further test-beds, as described in Mini Case 7.7.

> **MINI CASE 7.7:** *Bank of America – Testing Service Innovation*[31]
>
> When a new chief executive joined Bank of America in 1999, he quickly recognized the need to raise the level of innovation in the bank's services and formed a new Innovation and Development Team (IDT), tasked with spearheading new services and delivery mechanisms. The IDT reviewed ideas for innovations but had the foresight to realize that testing new services and delivery mechanisms is just as important as making physical prototypes is for tangible products. Initial testing was made possible by setting up a mock branch created by the IDT at headquarters. Experimentation to determine the reaction of real customers was the next step, so 20 of the bank's branches in Atlanta were selected as test branches. These were equipped with new systems and the staff received training on the test services that would be offered in parallel to the normal range of services. Through 'live' testing, including the careful monitoring of customers' reactions, the bank has been able to swiftly determine the viability of new services.
>
> Staff members at the test branches were initially highly motivated to support the development of new services. However, problems arose soon afterwards. Staff members are normally paid on a commission basis and so they found that their incomes were dropping significantly because of the time they had to spend being trained on the new services being tested. This was solved by putting the staff on a fixed salary but this caused friction with staff at other branches who felt they were under more pressure on commission. It also meant that the new services under test were not linked to tellers' commission, as were all the existing products at the bank.
>
> *Continued...*

CHAPTER 7

Bank of America's experiences demonstrate two main tenets of new service development. First, it shows the need to iron out design problems in a realistic setting offline, before moving to interact with customers. Second, it shows that the motivation of employees can be a key consideration in the design of new service products.

Phase Gates

It has long been understood that complex projects benefit from having a number of formal review points to ensure that all is going to plan.[32] Much of the most influential work in the field has been done in the context of managing the R&D function. The Stage-Gate® Process of Robert Cooper of McMaster University has been particularly influential.[33] We concentrate here on the formal processes for managing an innovation group; the 'softer' issues including questions of team structure are discussed in Chapter 8.

The basic control and standardization in the management process is imposed through the use of milestones, or *gates*. Each gate is the occasion for a careful and formal review of the project, bringing together the experience and expertise of the organization. Phase review meetings are an important part of the innovation management process for several reasons:

1. They require a formal and objective review of progress, which serves to identify problems and plan the next steps.
2. They allow managers to update their understanding of the wider context of each project. Many innovation projects involve many parts of the business and also outside agents such as suppliers and distributors. The gate reviews are a chance to review these as well as the immediate activities.
3. They give an opportunity to review the environment of the project to check if there have been any changes, such as moves by competitors, which might affect its viability.
4. Their formality prevents projects that are in trouble from dragging on and wasting resources. If all is well, formal approval is given to go on to the next phase; if not, action is taken: the project is stopped, or delayed, or the aims are changed, or a *soft hold* is declared, in which the project continues for a defined time to give a chance to correct the deficiencies.

The Stage-Gate® Process must operate over all the stages of a project, from concept to delivery. How many phases there should be depends on the needs of the organization, the speed and complexity of the projects and, to some extent, the strength of the project management function. Clearly, more gates allow closer scrutiny but at the expense of time spent in preparing for and attending the review meetings. When adopting phase gates for the first time, companies often opt for a large number; we have seen 12- or even 14-phase processes. Experience points to simplicity, however, and a current consensus favours somewhere between four and eight phases. Standard process designs are available in the literature with suggestions for what should be expected by each phase.[34, 35] These are useful but should be used only as a framework. The formal process,

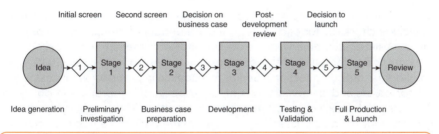

FIGURE 7.9: A Five-stage Stage-Gate® Process
Source: Stage-Gate® Process. Stage-Gate® is a registered trademark of Stage-Gate Inc.[36]

and the checklists that back it up, must suit the organization and, crucially, must evolve to reflect and embody the learning carried over from project to project. Figure 7.9 illustrates a typical Stage-Gate® Process for product development. Most innovative companies will have something of the sort.

The Stage-Gate® Process is well established and almost universally used, but managers must guard against a 'one-size-fits-all' mentality. For very big or innovative projects, a complete and formal process is essential, but small or simple projects need less intervention. Many companies either have two versions or decide at the start of the project which parts of their standard process should be used on this occasion. But managers must beware of changing the process during the project. Many project failures can be tracked back to 'cutting corners' when the project is in trouble. Choose the process at the start and stick with it.

Management Process at the Gates

One key role of the Stage-Gate® Process is to prevent projects rolling steadily forward when they actually contain serious problems not addressed and perhaps not fully acknowledged. This common problem is, of course, a manifestation of tendencies such as 'groupthink' that make risk appraisal so difficult.

A powerful way to avoid overconfidence is the *peer review*. This originated in the practice of *code reading*, in which software engineers read though each other's software to detect flaws of logic. It is more generally known as a *design review*. It brings in a team of colleagues from outside the project to do an in-depth review with the aim of picking up any problems the team may have missed, 'before', as one engineer put it, 'Mother Nature tells us herself'. The members of the reviewing team do not take over, or even share, responsibility for the work. Their job is only to offer advice for the responsible team to use as it sees fit. The role of managers is to check that the reviews happen but otherwise to stand clear. Design reviews should be built into the phase gates so they are expected, as a matter of course, at the critical points, not just demanded ad hoc when management becomes suspicious.

In addition to the results of peer reviews, other documents or evidence of progress may be required at gate meetings. Test results, market survey reports, financial analyses, marketing plans and so on may be expected, and if not available, may stop the progress of the project. Often, it is convenient to include checklists for each gate to remind people of problems to avoid. But these must be brief; otherwise the Stage-Gate® documentation can balloon out of control. The formality of the occasion forces everyone to pause, take stock and address difficult questions. Senior managers can probe for weaknesses and ask for proofs and demonstrations of key aspects of the project. In doing so, they assure themselves that the project is on track; and in giving the formal go-ahead for the next phase, they also assure the project team of their continuing support. The reviews also become a way of passing on lessons from one project to another.

Project Learning

Every innovation management process should include a *post-project review (PPR)*, shown as the final point in Figure 7.9 above, in which project team members discuss how the project was conducted and what could have been improved.[37] Some of this knowledge may then be built into the formal gate process so as to be available for future projects. Although the value of PPRs is well established (see Mini Case 7.8 on Bosch Packaging), research shows that many companies do not use them and therefore miss a learning opportunity.[38] This may simply be because the review process can be quite uncomfortable. There are a number of key points to consider when organizing PPRs:[39]

- *Timing:* It is important that reviews are held relatively soon after the innovation project has been completed, while memories are still fresh.
- *Scope, atmosphere and moderation:* The PPR meeting needs to be effective at uncovering issues and so may need to enter the 'zone of uncomfortable debate'. This normally requires a 'no-blame' atmosphere and a skilled *moderator*. The moderator should normally be from outside the project team and have prior experience of leading probing debate.
- *Learning from success and failures:* PPRs should be conducted for successful and failed projects, as both may have valuable lessons.
- *Learning at different levels:* All aspects of the project should be reviewed. Technical problem-solving is an obvious area but more important lessons may be derived about the process used for running the project. And individuals may have personal lessons to learn.
- *Dissemination of the results:* The time and effort invested in running a review is wasted unless the key findings are efficiently disseminated. The impact is often lost if they are simply documented in (yet another) report. To combat this, many companies now video short 'what I learnt from this project' interviews with project managers and make them available on their intranet. The results of PPRs can be discussed at the start of new projects, and should be a focus for mentoring schemes for project managers.
- *Linking the learning to actions:* Recent research shows the benefit of appointing a *project knowledge broker*, whose role is to concentrate on the transfer of learning between project teams.[40] In particular, this broker is tasked with ensuring that new projects have specific actions linked to the learning from previous projects, in order to avoid repeating mistakes.

Our recent research indicates that some of the most important lessons learnt from innovation projects are closely related to tacit knowledge.[41] For example, handling changes in specifications, managing budgets and solving technical problems are all highly complex. Dealing with them requires a high degree of experience and is based on tacit knowledge. Therefore, senior managers must put suitable mentoring schemes in place that are focused on teaching new project managers these essential skills.

MINI CASE 7.8: *Bosch Packaging Technology – Checklists as Knowledge Catalysts*[42]

The Bosch Group employs over 280,000 people worldwide and is famous for its 'automotive' products, such as engine control systems, and 'at home' products, such as power tools. Less well known but equally successful is Bosch's 'industry and trade' sector, which includes the Bosch Packaging Technology division serving the food, pharmaceutical, cosmetics and chemicals industries. Part of this division, the Bosch factory at Crailsheim (northeast of Stuttgart), designs and manufactures high-tech production line equipment for the pharmaceutical sector. These complex packaging systems are, for example, able to automatically fill hundreds of pre-sterilized syringes per minute. Packaging systems are significant investments for pharmaceutical companies; they typically cost several million euros but provide highly accurate filling capabilities, which ensure that demanding FDA (Food and Drugs Administration) manufacturing regulations are met. Most systems are several metres long, two metres high, and Bosch engineers are proud that the stainless steel equipment not only works efficiently but also looks good.

Filling 500 pre-sterilized syringes per minute requires the syringes to be unpacked automatically, precisely filled with liquid pharmaceutical, sealed and repackaged. The systems that fulfil these functions are based on a complex mix of mechanical engineering, electrical engineering and mechatronics. The R&D laboratory at Crailsheim includes engineers and technicians from these disciplines and Werner Mayer, director engineering/development and documentation, who manages over 70 mechanical designers, perceives the importance of generating and sharing knowledge in R&D.

Long a strong supporter of the need for post-project review, Mayer has clear views about the role of an R&D manager in managing knowledge. He says: 'Don't underestimate what the different members of the team can learn from each other in NPD, particularly at the concept stage. As an R&D manager I need to stimulate the right discussions to enable learning.' There are several aspects of the Bosch Crailsheim NPD process that stand out:

- The culture is one in which engineers are used to openly presenting their ideas to colleagues at 'design reviews' and receiving critical but positive feedback.
- For each NPD stage, Mayer has produced checklists, which are discussed by groups of electrical, electronic and mechanical engineers. Mayer states: 'The questions in the checklists are based on learning from previous projects and act as catalysts, stimulating focused discussions, to uncover issues before they lead to problems.'
- Selected sales personnel are involved in giving inputs, starting at the concept stage; 'good input from sales is essential', says Mayer.
- Everyone involved in the NPD process is required to document the philosophy behind their part of the design, so-called 'functional descriptions'. Such documents are important for pharmaceutical clients, who are eager to ensure that the manufacturing process is 'fail-safe', but Mayer has also found that

Continued...

functional descriptions were an important step in capturing the knowledge of NPD teams. 'It wasn't always easy though', he smiles, 'as good designers want to design rather than write. But now my guys do see the value of this work.'

As well as developing pharmaceutical packaging products, Mayer's team has been given responsibility for optimizing the NPD process within Bosch Packaging Technology: 'It is something that we at Crailsheim are proud of. Not only do we get to design products with innovative features but we also get to contribute to the overall improvement of the NPD process within packaging.'

An innovation management process needs to be regularly reviewed and improved.[43, 44] But it must not become too complex. A surprising number of managers we have spoken to report difficulty with maintaining an effective Stage-Gate® process in the long run. What seems to happen is that the process is put in place, often following a bad experience with projects running out of control, and is initially welcomed. However, over the course of time, more and more checks and balances are added, responding to things learned at the review meetings. At the same time, the process becomes more effective so there are fewer problems with projects, and so people start to question whether all the 'bureaucracy' is actually worthwhile. Eventually, the whole thing falls into disuse. Then another crisis occurs and it is reinstated, usually in a simpler form. The only solution is for managers to resist the temptation to add extra complications except when it is really necessary. The checks at the phase gates are, in the words of the old saying, 'for the guidance of wise men and the blind obedience of fools'. The idea is to remind people of what can go wrong, not to direct their every move. So, for example, there should be checklists of things to consider, rather than a bundle of reports to be written. Each project is unique so the guidance that can be passed from one to another is necessarily limited.

ORGANIZATION ISSUES

Linking with the Rest of the Business

Organizations are not usually designed for innovation, whatever their publicity blurb may say. They are – they have to be – designed, above all, for regular and repeatable performance. Every department will have its goals and incentives, which will be centred on the disciplines of serving customers, improving efficiency and cutting costs. This 'performance engine'[45] poses two challenges to innovation teams. First, they must recognize that however promising their innovation is for the future, the business must go on. So they must work closely with the performance engine, to ensure that the transition will be as smooth as possible, which means involving relevant people in the project early on. Second, the hard-nosed disciplines and incentives of the performance engine need to be relaxed somewhat in innovative projects; very much so in the 'fuzzy front end', but also in the implementation phase because significant uncertainties may remain. Pretending otherwise – the 'just make it happen, OK?' approach – is counterproductive.

Team Organization

As discussed above, innovation projects will usually centre on a cross-functional team of people from various disciplines, possibly from different parts of the company. They may form an entirely autonomous group separate from the rest of the company with a new management structure. At the other extreme, a minor innovation (such as quality improvement) may be handled entirely within one department. The more usual case is intermediate between these, with a project manager running the project with people seconded from various departments. There are several forms of this and we discuss their advantages and disadvantages in Chapter 8.

Managing Simultaneous Projects

Any project organization other than the independent autonomous team is likely to require some members of staff to work on more than one project at a time. This may be inevitable but it raises problems. The most obvious is that individuals often become overloaded if they work for more than one boss, and so their projects will slip.

Another problem is the inefficiency that comes from changing from one job to another. Every change needs a period of readjustment to the new task. This may be no more than recalling the details of the new job, but it may involve meetings, visits, even relocation. All this is, in a sense, time wasted. Wheelwright and Clark report that for engineering work, in the cases they studied, the wastage is such that working on as few as four jobs simultaneously almost halved effectiveness.[46] Interestingly, they found that the optimum was not necessarily to work on only one project because a person working on a single job may have periods of waiting time if the flow of work is not perfectly scheduled, as is quite likely. The figures will obviously vary according to the organization and type of project, but this study does give substance to the intuitive feeling that it is usually better to finish one task at a time rather than to try and keep lots of balls in the air.

A related inefficiency is more subtle and less well recognized. It is the time that is wasted in waiting and queuing due to variations in scheduling. This problem might not arise if all the projects were perfectly scheduled so that each individual or department received a new task at the precise moment when they completed the previous one. But, in reality, this seldom happens because few tasks ever take exactly their allotted time, especially where innovation is involved. In a sequence of tasks, these uncertainties quickly add up so that in the later part of the chain, the actual times have a large random element even though the *average* workload may be as planned. The result is that queues build up and tasks are delayed. This situation is familiar to anyone who has ever queued in a shop or at a motorway toll station.

Maybe the effect is not surprising, but what may come as a shock is just how big it is. A single person dealing with a stream of tasks arriving at random intervals will, on average, have a queue equal to one task (effectively doubling the throughput time) if they are busy, on average, between 50 and 70 per cent of the time, depending on whether the randomness extends to the length of the tasks as well as their scheduling. Delays to projects, however caused, can generate further inefficiencies as managers move people and resources about to try and rescue key projects. We know of departments where as much as 30 per cent of the effort is wasted on this kind of turbulence.

Service companies seldom have an R&D department and so their problem is that employees responsible for innovation often have to do this in parallel to their normal activities, which tend to take precedence, adding a further random element. The result is that neither the normal work, nor the innovation, is done on time. Service managers need to ensure that sufficient capacity is available and reserved for innovation activities.

The inefficiencies that can arise in multi-project departments have been too little studied but it is clear that there are five things managers can do to help:[47]

1. Control the loading of the department to manageable level.
2. Avoid working on too many projects at once, at the department or individual level.
3. Build contingency into the planning process.
4. Arrange flexibility of capacity, for example by arranging for temporary contract staff to be available when necessary to cover transient peaks.
5. Arrange to share work among members of the project team. Transient loads on any one person can be accommodated without extra staff if another team member is also able to do the same work because the chance of both people being overloaded simultaneously is less than for either one alone. This is, of course, one of the innate benefits of the scrum method of working.

Managing Collaborations

As technology and business processes become more sophisticated, companies are driven to concentrate on their core competences and to outsource an increasing range of activities,[48] and it seems likely this trend will continue. Mini Case 2.4 describes how Microsoft used partners and subcontractors for all the major parts of its Xbox product back in 1999. The ability to manage collaborations and alliances is an increasingly important competence for companies to acquire,[49] although there are often good reasons, both of strategy (as we discussed in Chapter 4) and of tactics, for keeping some projects in-house.

The more innovative the project, the more likely it is to require outside resources. The possibilities range from simple subcontracting, through joint development projects and licensing, to joint ventures, equity participation and acquisition,[50] as illustrated in Figure 7.8. The extremes, outsourcing and acquisition, are well established, while the central region is the realm of open innovation, discussed in Chapters 2 and 5. Subcontracting is the most straightforward because it is clear where the ownership lies – at least if the contract has been properly framed. But the contractor must be able to define fully what is required, so this is not an appropriate vehicle for exploratory work. And after the contract ends, the contractor is unlikely to be able to benefit from any later developments in a new technology he has acquired.

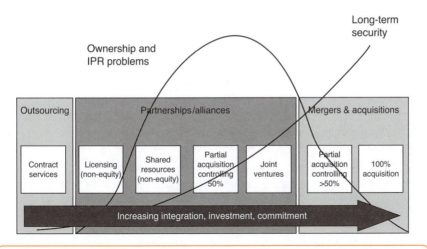

FIGURE 7.10: Types of Partnership

Source: Margulis, M.S. and Pekár, P. Jr. The next wave of alliance formations: Forging successful partnerships with emerging and middle-market companies. (Los Angeles, Houlihan Lokey Howard & Zukin 2003). Copyright © 2003 Houlihan Lokey. Reprinted with permission[52].

Broadly speaking, the security of access to technology in the long term increases the deeper the collaboration is, but inevitably the problems of 'who owns what' (intellectual property, in other words) tend to increase, at least until resolved by acquisition, as shown in Figure 7.10. It is vital to clarify the ownership of IPR in any collaboration with third parties, and also to establish clearly who will be responsible not only for paying the costs of filing and maintaining patents, but also for choosing countries to file in, for detecting and taking action on infringements, and for defending a patent if it is attacked.[51]

Clear contractual relationships are important in managing collaborations but there are limits to what can be written into a contract to ensure success, especially when there is an element of discovery in the work. Alliances typically fail because operating managers do not make them work, not because contracts are poorly written.[53] For this reason, care is needed to ensure that there is a climate of trust and confidence between the partners, that communication is open and frequent, and that the arrangement is clearly understood to be a 'win–win' situation. Of course, this is easier said than done, not least because different companies – particularly different sized companies – may find it difficult to understand each other's very different culture[54] and organization. Consider, for example, these comments from a large and a small company working together:[55]

- *Large company:* 'We ask for simple things like a business case or cash flow projections or reports and they get resentful. They don't see why they should have to justify everything.'
- *Small company:* 'They would ring us up and ask to speak to our Latin America sales director, or ask us to train, like, 20,000 of their consultants. Our whole business was six programmers in one room. They had no clue what that really means.'

A great deal of research is still going on about how best to manage deep collaborations but what is clear is that they must be taken seriously (see Mini Case 7.9 on Philips). This means taking great care to communicate well at all levels (together with clear IPR arrangements to facilitate it) and active sponsorship and guidance from high up in both companies.

> **MINI CASE 7.9:** *Philips – Always Open to Outside Ideas*[56]

Although open innovation has become one of the buzzwords of the moment, Philips, the Dutch-owned lighting and electronics giant, has been a leader in this area for over 20 years. Katja van der Wal is Open Innovation Manager for the consumer lifestyle division, which makes a range of home entertainment, personal hygiene and lighting products. Van der Wal is an expert at the practicalities of making open innovation work.

In working with outside innovators, Philips has developed novel approaches to two of the potential drawbacks of open innovation – namely how to deal with confidentiality and intellectual property issues. In joint innovation work, Philips often needs to search for innovations that could be useful in lifestyle products. These could be promising technologies or even product solutions. However, as a large organization, Philips does not want the message to get out that it is seriously looking at a particular technology or opportunity. Therefore, confidentiality is preserved by using knowledge brokers to scout for interesting products and technologies on behalf of Philips. This is effective and it 'doesn't signal that Philips is working on this or that unmet need', says van der Wal. Working through brokers not only allows Philips to check whether an idea is sufficiently developed but, importantly, also allows it to consider whether the other organization will be easy to work with.

For those organizations that Philips selects on the basis of their innovations and approach, it is important to establish the right relationship from the beginning. Van der Wal says: 'Before you get to legal agreements you must agree some working principles based on establishing trust and transparency between the partners, because without this the contract stage can become a nightmare.'

Once good relationships are established, the benefits of cooperating with outside organizations are multiple and the list of successes that Philips attributes to working with open innovation partners is impressive. For example, the Arcitec shaver's innovative design resulted from working with a mobile phone manufacturer, which, in turn, applied some of the ideas to improve the ergonomics of its handsets. With Nivea, Philips developed a novel electric shaver where skin cream can be applied to the shaving head to give a more comfortable shave. And working with baristas at a connoisseur coffee company gave many ideas for the Senseo range of coffee makers. According to van der Wal: 'It is amazing what is going on outside and we always remind our R&D engineers that there are more people outside Philips who are working on the problems that interest us than there are engineers inside our company.'

DEFINING AND DELIVERING SERVICE PRODUCTS

Everything we have covered in this chapter applies equally to services as to manufacturing. But it is necessary to provide some extra pointers for defining and managing service innovation: 'because services are intangible, variable, and delivered over time and space, people frequently resort to using words alone to specify them, resulting in oversimplification and incompleteness'.[57] In this section, we will present two approaches that can be used to enhance the analysis and hence the management of service innovation projects: these are the *service concept* and *service blueprinting* (see Mini Case 7.10). The former is useful in defining the core product and the latter for optimizing the service delivery. Both are simple approaches that, in combination, allow service products to be better understood and discussed more effectively; and as customers are intimately involved in the service experience, it is fundamentally important to make it easier for them to articulate their ideas on better or improved services.

The Service Concept

The service concept is a useful framework for identifying strategic opportunities for innovation, something too often missed as most service innovations are only incremental.[58] It has four elements: the value, form, nature of the experience, and the outcomes from a service.[59] Table 7.3 shows a number of questions that can be asked in generating ideas for innovative services, looking at each of the elements of the service concept. Often, the best ideas come from looking for unmet needs; optimizing the form and function; improving the customer experience; and making the outcomes more tangible.

Preparing a single sheet description of the service concept will generate ideas for innovation and it can be used in discussions with customers. It also dovetails with the service blueprint, which is a detailed diagram of the form and function of the service.

TABLE 7.3: The Service Concept

Element	Key questions to ask
The value of the service	• What the customer is willing to pay for? • What value does the customer gain? • What hidden and unsatisfied customer needs are there? • Does the customer have to invest too much time or resources to receive the value?
The form and function of the service	• What are the key steps in the delivery of the service? • What does the service blueprint look like? • What opportunities are there to remove stages that are not perceived as value-adding? • What opportunities are there to add stages that add value?
The nature of the service experience	• What are the key steps in which the experience occurs? • What is perceived as negative about the experience with current services? • How are competitors' services perceived?
The service outcomes	• What tangible and intangible outcomes are there? • Are the outcomes clear and tangible? • What additional outcomes would be appreciated? • How can a superior customer benefit be provided?

CHAPTER 7

Service Blueprinting

Service blueprinting was first developed over 20 years ago. A number of organizations in the US have used it very successfully but in many other countries it is not well known. A service blueprint is a flow diagram of the critical interactions between the customer and the service provider[60], starting with the actions the customer takes in deciding to purchase and consume a service. Sometimes, blueprints for complex services will need to be broken into several stages.

Figure 7.11 shows a blueprint for the initial stage in a professional service – business consultancy. The analysis starts with the *customer actions* (second row from the top). It is important to understand these from the customer's perspective, for example by conducting observations and contextual interviewing (see Chapter 5). The first customer action is typically to visit the website and therefore the website is the first physical evidence of the interaction – albeit indirect – with the company (shown in the top row of Figure 7.11). It is important that the site is attractive, easy to use, informative and convincing, for example using case studies and testimonials from previous customers. If the customer is persuaded, then they will probably call the consulting company and their interactions first with the telephone switchboard and then with an expert consultant should all be designed to demonstrate the efficiency, competence and knowledge that the company offers. This should lead to an appointment where the customer visits the consultancy company for the first time.

The first direct contact is when the customer visits the company and encounters the main physical evidence of the company's competence (the servicescape; see Chapter 3). 'First impressions count' and so the consultancy company must ensure that their offices and staff all give the right impression. (Consider, for example, how many companies have security staff running their reception areas and the negative first impression this often makes.) After a welcome, the customer will probably have detailed discussions with a particular consultant, who should be well informed about the client's business and their competitors. The discussions should be an appropriate mix of the consultant asking questions about the client's issues, listening to their explanations and the consultant explaining the different types of services that could be offered. At the end of this discussion, the customer will leave the consultancy company and, if well planned, the consultant will probably accompany them as they leave the building and informally summarize the key points from the meeting and confirm when a written proposal for the consultancy work will be sent to the client.

The customer will then wait for the proposal and it is important that this arrives on time or earlier (not later) than promised. The proposal will be based on back-office work, with input from the support functions. When the actual proposal arrives, it is another type of physical evidence (its style and content) of the quality of work to be expected from the consultancy company.

In the above explanation, the steps will seem relatively obvious, even mundane. However, when service providers use blueprinting, the act of documenting the various steps always, in our experience, leads to ideas for improving the customer experience. The blueprint can easily be combined with video ethnography, to provide visual examples of moments of truth. In addition, the

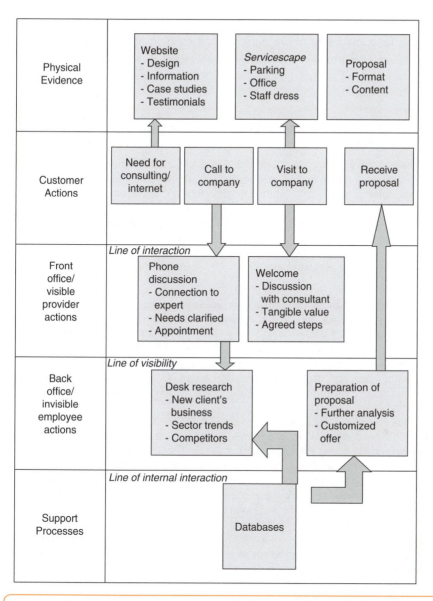

FIGURE 7.11: Example Service Blueprint for Consultancy Services

blueprint can readily be discussed with customers, in collecting their feedback. So, although it is a simple instrument, the power of service blueprinting should not be underestimated.

Using the service concept and service blueprinting always generates ideas for service innovation. In selecting which of these should be implemented, managers should consider whether they are scalable (as business increases), can be made difficult to copy, for example through staff training and a superior customer experience, and how the brand can be established.

MINI CASE 7.10: *Cruise Liners – New Service Development* [61]

Cruising is a big business with an industry turnover of $36 billion in 2013. The number of passengers carried has risen steadily from 7 million in 2000 to 22 million in 2015. A typical guest invests $2,500 for seven nights and the clientele is conservative. Synthiea Kaldi is a former guest relations manager with six years' experience in the industry, working for two of the most successful operators. One of these operators commissioned a new liner and Kaldi's experience on that project shows the critical importance of a cross-functional team being involved from the beginning if the new service concept, always required for a new liner, is to be successful. The problems encountered with the design of the new ship mean that the cruise operator involved is best left anonymous.

According to Kaldi:

> What was good was that the whole service team came together to discuss the new liner as it was being built. Looking back, though, not enough time was spent to iron out problems, and discussing the shipbuilder's blueprints wasn't a very effective way to recognize the issues. We did see some things that had been forgotten such as safety deposit boxes. Fortunately these could still be installed. Other basics were also missing, such as locking cash drawers in the reception desk for the front desk attendants. These were later added but they were never as secure as desired. Customers also noticed the lack of drawer space leading to a regular complaint about the staterooms.
>
> One of the attributes of the new cruise concept was the Food Court. This buffet restaurant was designed to give passengers fast and efficient service in pleasant surroundings. However, it was not as successful as hoped due to a number of factors. The limited number of drink stations slowed the overall service considerably. A serious issue was that the trolleys to bring the food efficiently from the galley, many decks below, did not fit in the lift. Worse still, one of the vents into a main guest corridor captured the sewage-type odour from the water processing plant many decks below. This led to guests perceiving the ship as not being as new or clean as it really was. 'Line of sight' issues in the show lounge were identified too late, although most were remedied before the ship went into service. Again, this was not spotted from the shipbuilder's blueprints and it cost the company hundreds of thousands of dollars as each seat had to be individually elevated and tilted to give a good view of the stage. Once the ship was in service, it was realized that the signage for the toilets, while visible to wheelchair-bound guests, was not visible to those who were standing. It quickly became apparent to the team that line of sight issues are nearly impossible to identify from blueprints and the ship designers should have found a better way to deal with this.

Fortunately, she says, there were also some notable successes built on some good designs for the servicescape (see Chapter 3). The disco was intended to draw the younger, late-night crowd and its decoration, which was pure 1960s, was very effective at achieving this. Kaldi concludes: 'And the ambience chosen for the alternative restaurant, which was only available upon reservation at an additional charge, worked so well that the guests actually felt they weren't paying enough for the experience! It really shows how getting the design right is crucial to the service concept.'

RECOGNIZING AND OVERCOMING RESISTANCE

Whether or not you believe that people are naturally averse to change, it is a fact that significant innovations often cause disruption to the established order of things, which is often uncomfortable or even threatening to those involved. This is why innovation is so often resisted, at least by some. But a bit of thought and planning by the management team can ensure that even a radical innovation meets enthusiastic support by those affected, not obstruction. A particular tool that can be helpful in analysing resistance and planning action to combat it is the so-called *change equation*, which we discuss in detail in Chapter 9. First, however, managers must understand who is interested in the project and how much power they have to affect it. These *stakeholders* may be directly involved in the project or may merely be affected by the ripples it causes in the company or the wider world. The *power/interest matrix*, illustrated in Figure 7.12, separates them into four groups according to the influence they have and the attention they should receive.

These four groups of stakeholders are as follows:

1. The *bystanders* are the least significant stakeholders. They have little interest in the project and little influence over it, so they need no deliberate attention.
2. The *supporters* are more or less keenly interested in the outcome but have little direct power over the project or policy. In a company launching a new product, these might be the shop floor staff, service personnel and perhaps the majority of the sales force. Supporters are not powerful individually but they may carry influence because of their number. They have a right to be kept informed and may turn out to be important in influencing the more powerful stakeholders.

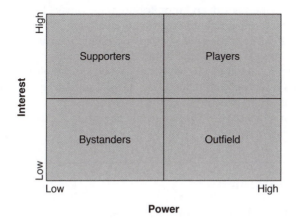

CHAPTER 7

FIGURE 7.12 Stakeholder Mapping: The Power/Interest Matrix
Source: based on Johnson and Scholes, 2009[62]

3. The *players* are clearly the most important group. They have a strong interest in the project and the power to affect it. This group will include the key staff and managers directly involved and often others, such as trade union representatives and key account salespeople, who represent important interests among the supporters. Clearly, they must be kept closely involved and consulted on any major change of direction.

4. The *outfield* are those who have a powerful influence on the organization but are not directly involved with this particular project. Examples may be senior managers, non-executive directors, major investors or key customers. Since they are powerful people, their public endorsement of the project may be helpful, although generally they do not interfere. However, if they feel their interests are threatened, they may suddenly move from a passive position to become key players, and hostile ones at that. The project leader must take care to understand where the project may have knock-on effects that may impinge on the domain or interests of one of these 'big hitters', and then work to avert trouble.

Summary

Managing the implementation of innovations requires all the normal techniques of effective project management augmented with some specialist processes to control the uncertainty that is to be expected in innovation. Managers must choose between several different modes, or models, of project management. Incremental innovations, and the early phases of more ambitious ones, may benefit from agile techniques such as scrum. Otherwise, more formal techniques are usually needed. In addition, a disciplined management process with clear review points, or gates, not only helps the control and monitoring of progress but facilitates learning so that competence in innovation management can mature over time. Managing multiple projects simultaneously demands extra care, especially to avoid overload and shifting priorities.

Increasingly, innovation projects involve collaboration with others and organizations need to develop competence in doing so effectively while not jeopardizing their strategic position.

More radical innovations often demand changes in several parts of the organization, not just the one in which the innovation is centred. For this and other reasons, it is important to understand the resistance that an innovation may generate from the various stakeholders in the enterprise and have a plan to address it.

Management Recommendations

- Ensure that strong project management skills are in place.
- Choose a style of project management and oversight appropriate for the task, recognizing that the needs of the investigation and implementation phases are different.
- Appraise and manage risk.

- Give adequate attention to changes required to support the innovation in all parts of the organization, not just the department on which it is centred.
- Consider the resistance the innovation may generate and manage it.
- Manage the flow of information and avoid unnecessary iterations.
- Install control processes such as the phase gate that allow clear management and facilitate the transfer of learning from one project to another.
- Avoid congestion and overloading when managing a number of projects simultaneously.
- Develop a competence in managing collaborations with others.

Questions for Students

1. What examples can you think of where significant innovations in one aspect of a business called for additional changes in others? Consider innovations in process, product, market position and business model.
2. Do a critical path analysis of a simple process in your business or daily life and use it to suggest an improvement that could speed it up.
3. Consider a change that needs to be made in an organization you know. Identify a key person or group that may be expected to resist the change and plot a strategy for overcoming the resistance.
4. Think of a service you are familiar with. Define the service concept and draw a service blueprint for it. What improvements does this lead you to suggest to the service delivery or the servicescape?
5. Additive manufacture (or 3D printing) is a developing field. What changes could it generate in the way product development is done?

Recommended Reading

1. Wheelwright, S.C. and Clarke, K.B., *Revolutionizing Product Development* (New York: Free Press, 1992). Not new, but an authoritative and readable introduction to the subject.
2. Govindarajan, V. and Trimble, C., *The Other Side of Innovation: Solving the Execution Challenge* (Boston, MA: Harvard Business School Publishing, 2010). Excellent book emphasizing the interaction with the performance engine and the issues of overseeing and motivating the project leaders of innovation activities.
3. Cooper, R.G., 'From Experience: The Invisible Success Factors in Product Innovation', *Journal of Product Innovation Management*, 16(2) (1999), 115–33. Excellent and practical survey of dos and don'ts in managing innovation projects.
4. Keizer, J.A., Halman, J.I.M. and Song, M., 'From Experience: Applying the Risk Diagnosing Methodology', *Journal of Product Innovation Management*, 19(3) (2002), 213–232. Detailed description of a successful process for identifying and managing risks in innovation projects.

▶ MAIN CASE STUDY[63]

WIPRO TECHNOLOGIES, INDIA – OPTIMIZING NPD

Wipro Technologies is a world leader in IT services, with global revenues of $1.2 billion. The company is the world's largest provider of R&D services, with annual revenues of over $270 million and employing nearly 8,000 engineers in this domain. Founded over 20 years ago, it has eight development centres, including a major facility in Bangalore, India. It provides offshore product engineering for a wide range of companies in the electronics and service sectors. The industries where it is active include automotive electronics, medical devices, telecommunications, computing (hardware and software), consumer electronics and industrial automation. The company has an approach it calls 'extended engineering', whereby clients can outsource any part of the value chain, including complete product development, product sustenance and support. The demand for cost-effective product development is high, as companies attempt to design products with faster time to market and lower costs.

The Problem

The downturn in the world economy has limited the amount of money that companies can invest in their portfolio of innovation projects, and heightened the interest in offshore engineering. Advances in IT have made it easier to coordinate outsourced activities and the number of companies taking this approach has increased significantly. Sachin Mulay, strategic marketing manager for the embedded and product engineering group, says there are a number of factors driving companies towards offshore engineering: 'Initially, it was the cost advantage that caught people's attention. That is still important but now there is recognition that offshore engineering can also improve speed to market and the quality of the finished product can also benefit.'

Cost, Quality, Time – Extended Engineering

It has long been recognized that co-location makes NPD teamwork easier. However, as an offshore R&D service provider, Wipro always has to deal effectively with multiple site work and a global delivery model. A. Vasudevan, vice president of VLSI System Design, manages over 600 engineers working on clients' projects. He has clear views on the challenges in NPD and says:

> We must excel at running multiple site projects. To achieve this, we put a lot of emphasis on defining roles and responsibilities at the beginning of projects. We also have a 'handshake' concept, where we put milestones into the schedule where we deliberately check that both parties are 100 per cent satisfied with both progress and communications.

Wipro engineers are not only technical experts but are also highly trained in project management. Vasudevan says: 'As part of our "talent transformation" programme, engineers receive intensive coaching in cross-cultural issues, project management techniques, optimizing communications, and negotiation.'

A recent Wipro project was to develop a human–machine interface for Ixfin Magneti Marelli. This company is the second largest European automotive supplier of what are called 'instrument cluster' products – the instruments and related electronics located around the dashboard, including the entertainment system, air conditioning and so on. Ixfin Magneti Marelli was looking to position itself as the technology leader in its market, offering automotive manufacturers a fully integrated 'infotainment system': an in-car multimedia system with GPS navigation, telephone connections, links to service centres for breakdown and emergency calls, and voice recognition controls for functions such as air conditioning. One challenge was that Ixfin Magneti Marelli had no previous experience of offshore projects. However, extensive communications allowed the transfer of key knowledge to the Wipro team and the timely delivery of a system that was needed for the launch of a new model from Fiat. In fact, in one year of the project, only 2 per cent of the engineering effort was 'on-shore'.

Wipro's expertise was initially seen by clients to be purely technical. That meant that clients' projects were run largely following their own NPD processes. Vasudevan says:

> Increasingly, however, clients are recognizing our process expertise and are interested in us helping them speed up their own processes. We conduct over 500 projects per year and so Wipro has a greater opportunity to learn about the strengths and weaknesses of the product development process than companies working only on their own limited number of projects. After every project we analyse what the technical and managerial lessons are, and in the VLSI/design space we have defined our design methodology called EagelWision. Effective reuse and automation are the basic tenets of this design methodology.

Service Sector

Although Wipro is active in electronics and manufacturing, it also has a rich history of working in the service sector, particularly financial services. These clients are served by a specific organization that has gained significant expertise in the different field of supporting NPD.

Prudential is a leading life and pensions supplier in the UK, with a customer base of around 7 million. The company had numerous call centres spread across diverse locations in the UK, with each call centre dedicated to handling customer enquiries related to a single product line. This meant that customers had separate numbers for each of their products and the call centre consultant sometimes had to transfer them to a different department for each product. As a strategic IT partner, Wipro rationalized Prudential's product categories and business processes, and provided an integrated view of transactions across products. The most important initiative was the integration of multiple front-end customer services applications into a single consolidated system. This will give Prudential's customer service agents a consolidated view of the customer, allowing them to deal with a significantly larger number of transactions. Prudential will be able to deliver on the brand promise of 'one operation', reducing costs and delivering even better customer service.

The Innovation Council and the Future

One of the potential dangers of R&D service consultancy work is that all the innovation at Wipro could be solely in response to clients' specific requirements. Management recognized that innovation should not only be project driven and so three years ago formed the Innovation Council. Mulay says: 'We recognized that we consistently need to push forward our own expertise. Through our own knowledge of a wide range of technologies, we saw that we could identify opportunities.' The Innovation Council evaluates technology development proposals and provides internal funding for the best ones. The resulting projects develop intellectual property that can be licensed to customers and integrated into their products. Vasudevan says:

> Such projects demonstrate our ability to offer leading-edge technology to our customers. They see a roadmap of the components and technologies we are planning and know that it is not just a single product development project where we can serve them but really in the long term.

The Innovation Council is made up of senior managers but the ideas are gathered 'bottom-up'. Vasudevan says:

> It is our engineers and project managers who are immersed in the technical issues who have the creative long-term ideas. Management's job is to choose the best ones, based on our analysis of how the resulting technologies and components will, in turn, both increase the quality and speed of NPD for our customers, and, for example, we have recently developed some key technology for wireless networking.

Although Wipro Technologies was founded as a provider of contract R&D, it has come a long way. It has become a leader by not only developing a technological know-how but also by developing expertise in NPD processes, excelling at communications, becoming adept at spotting technological opportunities, and managing innovation in general. It is a hotbed of NPD learning that is likely to provide a lot of managerial lessons for the future.

Reflective Questions

1. What are the issues when new product development is conducted at multiple sites? How can these issues be addressed?
2. How can the product development process be optimized through learning from each project?
3. What should companies do to stimulate learning that is not just related to specific new product development projects?

This is a reprint of a case study from the 2005 and 2010 editions of this book. For the latest information on Wipro, please see www.wipro.com

PEOPLE, CULTURE AND ORGANIZATION

INTRODUCTION

The fifth element of the Pentathlon Framework concerns people, teams, culture and organization. These people-related issues are crucial because although processes such as new product development make innovation possible, it is the people, teams and organizational culture that make it happen. The *culture of innovation* of organizations is becoming a popular research topic. Senior managers need to accurately 'diagnose' their organizational culture, encourage the right employee behaviour, and give employees the means to drive innovation.[1] Many senior managers have a more positive view of organizational culture and its impact on innovation than employees.[2] So this chapter will investigate ways to manage people, culture and organization in a way that really supports innovation.

Figure 8.1 illustrates how the people and organizational issues underpin the other elements of the Pentathlon Framework. First, the fuzzy front end is dependent on openness, a willingness to take calculated risks, reward and recognition, and a no-blame atmosphere. Second, leadership impacts culture in that a clear innovation strategy and an appropriate corporate structure are essential. Third, people impact project prioritization as financially oriented managers tend to shy away from the risk of radical projects. And project selection is contingent on good team leaders and team members. Finally, research has shown that corporate culture has a direct impact on product innovation.[3] Successful implementation flows from teams, cross-functional relationships, charismatic project leaders, and project-to-project learning.

A survey of over 1,000 US human resource (HR) managers showed that the majority of them recognized the importance of a culture of innovation.[4] The human resource management (HRM) function should play a proactive role in the people-related aspects of innovation management. In practice, few HR

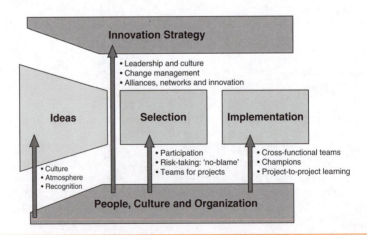

FIGURE 8.1: Links from People, Culture and Organization to other Elements of the Pentathlon Framework

departments actively work creating a culture of innovation and there is significant scope for HR to be more involved in managing innovation.

This chapter covers:

- Organizational culture and innovation.
- People management and innovation.
- Team structure and innovation.
- Leadership and innovation.
- A main case study on the company time:matters.

ORGANIZATIONAL CULTURE AND INNOVATION

Organizational culture has been defined as: 'the set of values, understandings and ways of thinking that is shared by the majority of members of a work organization, and that is taught to new employees as correct'.[5] Extending this, a working definition is: a *culture of innovation* 'cultivates engagement and enthusiasm, challenges people to take risks in a safe environment, fosters learning and encourages independent thinking' in achieving incremental, breakthrough and radical innovation.[6] Some companies, such as 3M, Apple and Google, are known for their innovative culture and the level of freedom they give their employees. So much so, that other organizations often try to copy them (but then find that copying one or two attributes from Google does make them more innovative). It is important to understand how specific attributes impact the culture of innovation (see Mini Case 8.1 on UPS).

> **MINI CASE 8.1:** *United Parcel Service – Bleeding Brown*[7]

UPS is one of only 16 Fortune 100 companies from the year 1900 that have survived to the present day. The company has over 390,000 employees and revenues of over $58 billion. It attributes much of its success to its company culture, which is famous in the US. Some aspects of its culture are tangible. For example, the Policy Book and Code of Business Conduct give specific advice on dealing with customers and solving conflicts. Employees receive feedback from their managers, peers and team members in their annual quality performance reviews. Promotions are largely internal. There is also a focus on communication with, for example, prework communications meetings, where employees informally update each other at the start of a shift.

Less tangible are the drivers of technical innovation at UPS. These can be traced back to the founder Jim Casey, who was the first to modify the Model T Ford for parcel deliveries, the first to utilize conveyer belts for parcel sorting, and made UPS the first logistics company to use air freight (in 1925). UPS is still at the forefront of technology and has recently made significant investments in the development of databases.

A strong culture can, however, have its disadvantages. All the company's processes were focused on providing low-cost shipments rather than premium-priced special and fast deliveries. This led UPS to be

Continued...

CHAPTER **8**

slow to react when FedEx launched its next-day service. Organizational structures need to be reviewed regularly and so does culture. The culture at UPS has now changed and with it strategy: customers are now offered a choice of services (options on delivery and price). And UPS services now include special options to optimize the flow of goods, data and funds, through advanced IT.

Shared ownership was always central to UPS and it generated commitment from employees. The 'Pullman Brown' corporate colour of UPS is such a powerful symbol that employees say they 'bleed brown'. Shared ownership was in their blood and so it was no surprise that, when the company went public, there was criticism and employees' sense of commitment disappeared.

Attributes of a Culture of Innovation

As was discussed in Chapter 1, the culture of innovation is a topic that researchers have looked at for years, and proposed key attributes. We should bear in mind two things in considering this research. First, many papers on innovation culture are based on anecdotal evidence and so their recommendations are not reliable.[8] Second, many studies have been conducted in famous organizations that operate in particular contexts, which means that their attributes may not all be applicable to other organizations. However, as we will show, views on a culture of innovation have remained remarkably consistent over the years.

A major longitudinal study from the 1980s investigated five famous electronics firms: HP, Intel, Motorola, National Semiconductor and Texas Instruments.[9] The results showed that 'a strategy of innovation is contained not in "plans", but in the pattern of commitments, decisions, approaches and persistent behaviours that facilitate doing new things'.[10] The study also identified that a clear innovation strategy, small market-focused business units, and frequent reorganizations (to ensure market alignment and employee flexibility) are important.

In a 1990s study from Harvard,[11] in-depth interviews with managers from Silicon Valley determined the attributes of a culture that promotes innovation. These included people challenging the status quo, reward and recognition, risk-taking, and a positive management attitude towards the inevitable problems that arise. Furthermore, a tolerance of mistakes, teams with the authority to make quick decisions, and sharing information between functions were all identified as essential.

A third major study examined the culture of 11 innovative companies in Asia, Europe and the US.[12] The research elicited that such companies encouraged experimentation, had excellent relationships between marketing and R&D, developed a deep customer understanding, and tapped individuals' and the organization's capacity to innovate. At the companies, which were staunchly proud of their innovativeness, stories acted as a *leitmotif*, such as the story of the inventor of the Post-it ignoring management advice and continuing to develop the product.

These three early studies all mentioned market focus and taking risks. More recent studies we have reviewed showed a strong consistency in what are perceived as the attributes of innovation culture and the seven main ones are listed

TABLE 8.1: Key Attributes of a Culture of Innovation

	Attribute	Ways to build this attribute
1.	Customer-centric	• Be strongly focused on serving customer needs • Train employees in methods to identify customer needs
2.	Openness to new ideas	• Identify company values and preferred behaviours • Ensure high levels of trust • Use appropriate (not excessive) levels of control • Constantly use experimentation
3.	Effective cross-functional teams	• Recruit and work with creative people • Build collaborative and diverse teams, with members from different functions • Protect the time needed for innovation • Build effective communications • Create communities of interest
4.	Well-defined processes	• Have ways to generate ideas • Make idea selection focused on growth (not costs) • Flexible but fast implementation processes
5.	Risk tolerance	• Actively avoid risk aversion • Focus on learning rather than blame
6.	Rewards and recognition	• Provide the opportunity to join challenging projects • Give full and regular recognition • Have appropriate rewards
7.	Appropriate leadership	• Provide a clear vision on the role of innovation • Set appropriate boundaries and select structures • Show executive sponsorship and participation • Give a commitment to innovation in terms of time

Source: based on Barsh, Capozzi, and Davidson, 2008; Jamrog, Vickers and Bear, 2006; PwC, 2013; Wagner, Taylor, Zablit, and Foo, 2014; Rao and Weintraub, 2013[13].

in Table 8.1. Table 8.1 provides a useful comparator for companies that want to build appropriate attributes.

Assessing Culture in the Context of Innovation

There is a widespread opinion that culture is difficult to manage.[14] But it is possible. Many of today's ideas stem from the ground-breaking work of Edgar Schein at the MIT Sloan School of Management.[15] He was the first management researcher to identify the different levels of culture, from the more tangible aspects, for example the formal organization, to less tangible ones such as organizational values. Schein's work led to practical ideas on how managers can recognize, interpret and enhance organizational culture.

CHAPTER 8

Taking Schein's ideas further, the *cultural web*[16] is an effective tool for the diagnosis of cultural issues (Figure 8.2). It is based on ideas from the social sciences, and it identifies six partially overlapping aspects of culture. These are used to identify the *central paradigm* of the organization – the essence of its culture. The key aspects of culture as captured by the web are:

1. Organizational structures: The formal organization is the most obvious manifestation of culture, represented by the *organigram*, or *organization chart*. Formal structures are normally based around what is important to an organization (or what was important in the past). When managers try to change the culture of their organizations, they quickly jump to structure but are unlikely to succeed unless they consider the other elements of the web.

2. Power structures: These are related to the formal organizational structure but are not easily recognizable from organization charts. Certain individuals may have more power than their position in the hierarchy would suggest because of their experience or charisma, or because they are responsible for a particularly important client. Some departments may be more powerful than others, although their managers are at equivalent levels on the organization chart. This may often reflect the central beliefs of the organization; for example, HP was famous in the 1980s for being 'an engineering company' (R&D had more power than marketing). In a service organization, the real power might lie in the back office.

3. Symbols: Just as tribes have symbols that embody their culture, so it is with business organizations. These symbols include advertising and logos, the style of offices, company cars, titles and dress codes. The displays and photographs of a company's products and services in its facilities are always telling. For example, IDEO, the US product development consultancy, is bold enough to display the failed products it developed alongside its successes. As electronics giant HP was being split into two companies at the end of 2015, it is interesting that its advertising used photographs of the garage in which the original company was founded.

4. Stories and language: The language, terminology and acronyms strongly reflect culture. And every organization has stories that capture the essence of key events and share a 'folklore'. Such stories are told to new recruits and visitors and act to reinforce behaviours.[17] FedEx tells a story of an employee who organized a helicopter to get an important package to a customer on time. Although the cost was exorbitantly high, the employee was not disciplined because management was impressed by the dedication to the customer that it demonstrated and recognized the potential of such a story. 3M, the multinational company that makes an eclectic range of products including the ubiquitous Post-it, has several stories about mavericks championing the development of what eventually become successful products, despite initial management opposition.

5. Routines and rituals: *Routines* are the ways employees learn to act towards each other and to process work. Processes enable an organization to run smoothly and, for example, new product development (see Chapter 7) is a crucial innovation process. In addition to formal processes, organizations develop unwritten rules on how different departments interact during the

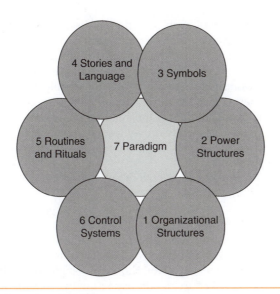

FIGURE 8.2: The Cultural Web[18]

Source: Figure 9.1 on page 138 of Exploring Techniques of Analysis and Evaluation in Strategic Management - 1st Edition by Veronique Ambrosini, Gerry Johnson and Kevan Scholes, Pearson Education Limited. Copyright © 1998 Prentice Hall Europe. Reprinted with permission.

innovation process. These can mean that formal processes are applied very differently from how they are described on paper. Routines can be difficult to change because they are often based on tacit knowledge and may strongly support the overall paradigm of the organization. Organizations also have *rituals*, such as neophyte programmes, sales conferences, regular meetings and traditions, promotion criteria and appraisals, all of which indicate to employees what is valued by the organization.

6. Control systems: These include corporate objectives, measurement systems, and reward and recognition systems. All of them maintain the focus of attention of an organization. The most important control systems for innovation are those used to select ideas and implement them efficiently. Control systems, as shown in Figure 8.2, overlap with routines and rituals, and organizational structures.

7. Paradigm: Reflecting back to the definition of culture given above, the central paradigm is expressed as a statement summarizing the main points about how an organization 'thinks' and 'acts'. The paradigm is the distillation of the points from the six surrounding circles.

Using the Cultural Web

There are three steps to using the web in an innovation context:

1. Determine the current cultural web – how well does the existing culture support innovation?
2. Identify a 'desired' cultural web that supports innovation more effectively.
3. Determine the changes necessary and how they can be achieved.

CHAPTER 8

To determine the cultural web, it is normal for consultants or researchers to talk to a representative sample of employees, taking into account different functions and the hierarchy. Once the elements of the cultural web have been explained, simple open questions can be used to gather each individual's opinions on culture.[19] A workshop with employees can identify the central paradigm. For example, the Hay Group, an international HRM consultancy, conducted a workshop with employees to identify their central paradigm, which led them to recognize from their cultural web that they were narrowly focused on 'job evaluation' services (analysis of remuneration), whereas the market required a broader mix of consultancy services.[20]

To understand how to use the cultural web in an innovation management context, we will give an example.

Determining the Current Web

Figure 8.3 shows the cultural web derived for an international manufacturer of building materials, which we will refer to as 'BuildCo'.[21] Information was gathered in 36 one-to-one interviews and a workshop with employees from five departments. Employees were asked to identify aspects of the cultural web and discussions were used to define the paradigm. Strong alignment was found between different individuals' views on the current culture:

1. Organizational structures: These had recently been changed to link with a Stage-Gate® NPD process and several employees said words to the effect that: 'this has been interpreted by the process managers as [a licence to] "command and control"'. In addition, the strong functional orientation hindered cross-functional teams in NPD.
2. Power structures: These were seen as rigid and centralized and this led to conflicts for the business units. One manager said: 'The parent company's overriding philosophy of being a low-cost commodity company is at odds with a business unit which seeks to add value through the application of technical and market knowledge.' Certain individuals such as process managers and the head of business development had a strong influence. Specifically, the process managers were seen as promoting their processes rather than contributing to projects.
3. Symbols: Although it was relatively new, the gate review board (responsible for assessing the progress of all new product development projects) had already achieved a symbolic status; representing how BuildCo was extending its tight controls into the area of innovation. Moreover, the Stage-Gate® manual had quickly become symbolic of what employees termed 'a reliance on paperwork and red tape'.
4. Stories and language: To improve its NPD, the company had recently implemented the recommendations of a management consultancy (including the Stage-Gate® NPD process). One common story was about the modus operandi of the consultants and their strong influence over top management. Another common story berated the way the board did not delegate responsibility. This was reflected in the power structure, which was concentrated at the centre; employees said the 'parent calls the shots'. Although BuildCo

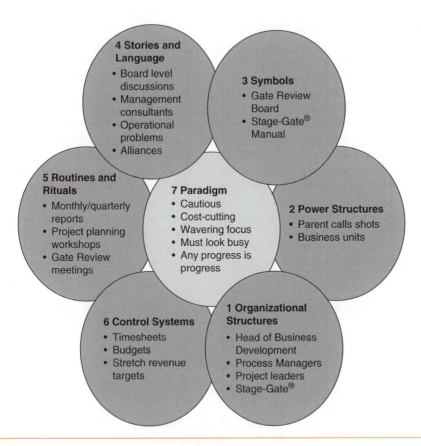

FIGURE 8.3: The Current Cultural Web for BuildCo
Source: based on Confidential MBA Thesis, Cranfield School of Management, 2001

was profitable, operational problems were portrayed as inevitable in typical anecdotes. Finally, the story of an unsuccessful alliance reinforced the view that such ventures are risky and therefore undesirable.

5. Routines and rituals: The most important routines and rituals were identified as the monthly and quarterly reporting, gate review meetings, and project planning meetings.

6. Control systems: Matching the hierarchal organization, the company had many control mechanisms, from timesheets for individual employees, to department budget reports, and challenging revenue targets for the business units. BuildCo was tightly controlled.

7. Paradigm: Having identified the different aspects of their culture, the workshop participants described the central paradigm under five headings, including 'cautious', 'cost-cutting' and 'with a wavering focus'. Such a paradigm was perceived as incongruous for a company aiming to be more innovative.

CHAPTER 8

Identifying a 'Desired' Web

The second stage of using the cultural web is to identify an appropriate culture of innovation for an organization. (In developing this, the attributes shown in Table 8.1 are useful.) To achieve this, BuildCo ran a second workshop. A range of employees were asked to define a desirable and achievable new paradigm. Then, they were required to look at the six aspects of culture that would reflect this central paradigm. Their ideas are shown in Figure 8.4. It can be seen that to achieve the central paradigm of an 'innovative, entrepreneurial, responsive and goal-oriented' company, decentralization was deemed necessary.

There was a strong perception that power at BuildCo needed to be decentralized to stimulate innovation. Participants had widely differing views on the most feasible organizational changes and discussions were lively. Market-focused projects and cross-functional teams were seen as the way to start. Connected to this, new symbols of innovation were needed, such as new recruits bringing a fresh wind, seamless business development (across the functions) and a more dynamic R&D function. Successes were needed to spawn stories

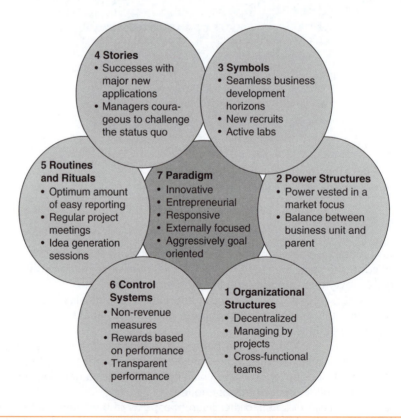

FIGURE 8.4: The Desired Cultural Web for a Manufacturer of Building Materials
Source: based on Confidential MBA Thesis, Cranfield School of Management, 2001

about 'great products', and 'managers having the courage to challenge the status quo'. New routines and processes were also perceived as necessary to stimulate innovation.

Effecting the Change

The final step in using the cultural web is to gather ideas on how culture can be moved to the desired state. The main ones that emerged within BuildCo were:

- The CEO should communicate a clear innovation strategy, and give autonomy to the business units to develop new products and markets.
- Reporting should be streamlined and aligned to the goals of each business unit.
- Cross-functional teams would become an integral part of development projects and project managers would be selected who had the ability to drive these projects.
- The process managers should be moved into project management and make a direct contribution.

The results of the cultural web exercise shocked management but it galvanized them into making a range of changes to move towards the desired culture.

In using the cultural web, we stress that it is management's role to create the atmosphere and opportunities for success, so that stories emerge, rather than trying to 'make them up'. It is unwise to make 'grand declarations about innovation' that are not matched by real results.[22] Managing culture needs to be subtle, as illustrated by Texas Instruments (see Mini Case 8.2).

Senior managers need to be aware that too many change initiatives at the same time can lead to the *acceleration trap* – the organizational equivalent of individual burnout. This leads to a drop in performance.[23] We will discuss how innovation initiatives need to be carefully orchestrated in Chapter 9.

▶ MINI CASE 8.2: *Texas Instruments – Not Reinventing the Circuit*[24]

Some organizations focus on being first to market, where the capability to invent is essential. But there can be a downside to inventiveness when it becomes the strongest component of R&D culture – the danger is that it can lead to the proverbial reinvention of the wheel. In dealing with technical issues, solutions to similar problems are often known and so R&D engineers do not always need to start from scratch. Unfortunately, the *not invented here* (NIH) syndrome, where researchers reject existing ideas and prefer to develop their own solutions, wastes resources. Research-intensive companies, including ABB, Aerospatiale, Audi, BASF, BMW, BT, Nestlé, Nokia, Philips, Renault, Royal Dutch Shell, Siemens and 3M, have recognized NIH as a common problem.

Texas Instruments (TI) is a multinational developer and manufacturer of integrated circuits and test equipment. One of its former employees is famous for having received the Nobel Prize for Physics, for his invention of the integrated circuit. Although it was a truly great invention of which TI is rightly proud, there was an unexpected consequence of the award. Quite simply, TI found that after the Nobel Prize,

Continued...

CHAPTER 8

many of its engineers started designing everything from scratch and avoiding taking any ideas from others. Suddenly, every engineer wanted to invent everything. This was found to be enormously costly and to avoid it, an annual 'not invented here but we did it anyway' (NIHBWDIA) prize for R&D was introduced. This is a prize for the employee who takes an idea from somewhere else and makes a significant contribution to product or process innovation. The NIHBWDIA prize has remoulded the culture of innovation at TI. It has also been applied to process innovation, thus encouraging ideas that have reduced unnecessary plant investments.

Ideas for Creating a Culture of Innovation

Table 8.2 below lists practices that can be used to help create a culture of innovation. In applying these, managers should choose the ideas that appear most appropriate and adapt them to their own organization.[25] Managers should also bear in mind that the more breakthrough and radical innovations they aim to achieve (that is, the golden ratio targeted, as explained in Chapter 1), the greater the changes in organizational culture that will be needed. It should be noted that culture is complex and so multiple approaches are needed, which are carefully selected to be relevant and appropriate for the particular organization where they will be applied. First, we outline some ideas for creating a culture of innovation:

1. Organizational structures: Market-oriented structures and regular reorganizations to ensure market alignment have been found to support innovation (in contrast to reorganizations aimed solely at reducing employee numbers – as we will discuss below). Aligning organizations to markets is effective, provided it is matched with the delegation of authority to these so-called *strategic business units*. In large organizations, the role of the CEO is that of an 'organizational architect' who must align the organization with constantly changing markets, and frequent reorganizations are an important approach.[26] At the project level, autonomous teams can be the best way of dealing with radical innovations, which can struggle within the existing organization and using existing processes. One new approach that has not yet received much coverage in the management literature is the creation of 'innovation managers' (see Chapter 9). Having this role creates a figurehead for innovation improvement programmes. For example, GlaxoSmithKline and Zurich financial services both have innovation managers responsible for improving innovation processes throughout their organizations, while P&G has a manager who is responsible for driving open innovation through external sourcing of ideas.[27]

2. Power structures: Both researchers[28] and practitioners have recognized the value of cross-functional awareness. Shin-Etsu is a Japanese-owned manufacturer of silicon wafers, with customers such as Intel and Samsung. In its Malaysian operation, part of the culture is a strong relationship between R&D and manufacturing. This is fostered through *routines*, which lead to a balance of power. A 'freshman's program' for new R&D engineers requires them to learn how to operate manufacturing equipment and actively participate in *kaizen* (continuous improvement) teams; constructive criticism is actively encouraged and sometimes whole teams will transfer from R&D

into manufacturing in a 'cradle to maturity' (from the idea to its routine production) approach – this helps Shin-Etsu avoid the 'over the wall' mentality that exists in many companies (passing of known problems from R&D to manufacturing).[29]

3. Symbols: There are various best practices. Communication, both internal and external, needs to have an innovation focus; for example, HP has adopted the 'HP Invent' slogan in all its advertising. As an internal communication tool, the AXA 'Innovation Quadrant' (see Mini Case 3.8) has been successful and is a symbol of its understanding of four different types of innovation. Displays of product and process innovations can and should inspire. For example, at Unilever, displays of new products at the entrance to manufacturing facilities make innovation highly visible. IDEO, the Californian innovation consultancy, has dozens of gadgets around the workplace to trigger ideas and experimentation (and it even has 'librarians' responsible for collecting artefacts).[30] Outstanding individual contributions can be recognized through plaques and certificates that are visible in the workplace and act as symbols of innovation.

4. Stories: Managers need to use stories, as they can be a useful way to promote innovation in an organization. Research by Buckler and Zien showed that there are four degrees to which managers use stories to promote innovation. Some make no use of storytelling, focusing only on figures (which often do not promote interest). Others relate anecdotes from the 'good old days', which alienates and places innovation in the past. 'Innovative leaders' reshape old stories to inspire the future.[31] Managers can become 'transformational leaders' if they develop and constantly tell enlightening stories about innovation at staff meetings, interviews and outside speeches.

5. Routines and rituals: These can be used to support innovation. Two categories of best practice are promoting new ideas and tolerating mistakes. Joie de Vivre, a leading innovator in the US hospitality sector, has an interesting routine.[32] The 'Fresh Eyes' programme takes advantage of the different perspectives that new employees bring to the business. In most service companies, new employees are evaluated after 30 days by their managers. The roles are reversed at Joie de Vivre and new employees are encouraged to challenge complacency by asking questions such as: 'Why is it done this way?' and giving their evaluation of what they have seen. Motivating employees by giving them more interesting tasks is central to the philosophy of Hamilton Acorn, an award-winning UK manufacturer of professional quality paint brushes. For example, production engineers are encouraged to design and build complex production equipment and not just focus on running existing production lines.[33] Making funding available for new ideas within organizations is a key step in encouraging people to recognize commercial opportunities. Tolerance of mistakes is part of the culture at Johnson & Johnson and enshrined in the founder's maxim that failure is an important 'product'. Other approaches that promote tolerance and creativity include DuPont's use of the phrase 'it was a good try' to avoid negative criticism, and the symbolic burying in the woods of a prototype scanner that was a market failure (this allowed the engineers to vent their frustration) for HP Medical Products Group. Ericsson, the Swedish communications technology

company, has an interesting approach that is symbolic of its encouragement of new ideas. Employees who make a good suggestion for an innovation are given a credit card with $500 on it and a week's time to experiment and demonstrate the viability of their idea.

6. Control systems: There must be mechanisms that enable employees to suggest ideas and obtain the resources to investigate them further. But processes for portfolio management and NPD are also essential. Metrics can be used to measure and promote innovation throughout an organization. Schefenacker, a supplier of automotive mirror systems, excels at this by 'cascading' management goals all the way down to the individual employee.[34] Later in this chapter we will discuss reward and recognition.

Table 8.2 is directly aligned to the cultural web and it summarizes different ways in which steps can be taken to create a culture of innovation. Most of the examples in the literature on innovation culture come from manufacturing rather than the service sector. Bearing in mind the contrasting nature of service companies, the public sector and not-for-profit organizations (see Chapter 3), creating a culture of innovation always needs to be considered in context.

TABLE 8.2: Practices for Creating a 'Culture of Innovation'

	Aspects of culture/best practices	Explanation and company examples
1.	**Organizational structures**	
	• Market-oriented structures	• Market-oriented organizations engender focus and urgency. Strategic business units serve particular markets and include typical business functions, e.g. R&D, marketing and operations. Miele is organized by customer segments rather than technologies
	• Reduced hierarchy	• Fewer levels of reporting increases flexibility, e.g. Google has tried to maintain a flat organization
	• Frequent reorganizations	• Large organizations can stay more adaptable through reorganizations, e.g. Motorola, HP
	• Teams	• Creating autonomous teams for new ventures, e.g. IBM, DuPont, Xerox
	• 'Innovation managers'	• Formally appointing an innovation manager gives focus to performance improvements, e.g. GlaxoSmithKline, AXA, Bank of America, Whirlpool. To tap outside resources more effectively, P&G created the post of 'director of external innovation'
2.	**Power structures**	
	• Training	• Shin-Etsu promotes excellent R&D and manufacturing relationships through its 'freshman's program', thus achieving a balance of power between these functions. 3M trained its top managers to 'let go' and delegate authority more effectively
	• Cross-functional rotation	• Sony managers place particular emphasis on managing cross-functional boundaries

TABLE 8.2: Continued

	Aspects of culture/best practices	Explanation and company examples
3.	**Symbols** • Communication	• Company logos and slogans are a symbol and some companies update them regularly to ensure the typeface and style is modern. HP recently added a focus on invention with the line 'HP Invent', and AXA has developed the 'Innovation Quadrant', which has become an internal symbol of innovation, e.g. as a screensaver, and a tool for communicating the meaning of innovation
	• Displays of innovation successes and other artefacts	• The workplace and reception area should celebrate innovation by displaying relevant product and process innovations: 'artefacts'. Unilever has interesting displays not only of its products but also process innovations. Artefacts are used to encourage experimentation at IDEO, and AXA has an 'innovation corridor' (outside the staff canteen)
	• Symbolic recognition and awards	• Plaques, certificates and other recognition for innovative employees can become symbols. When HP introduced new reporting metrics for NPD,[35] every division manager trained in the approach received a Perspex desk block with a diagram of the metrics
4.	**Stories**	• 3M 'mavericks' and Sony's Walkman. Managers can compare their style to Buckler and Zien's typology, in order to learn how to use stories more effectively
5.	**Routines and rituals** • Promoting ideas for new products, new services and process improvements	• Joie de Vivre's 'Fresh Eyes'; 'tinker time' at 3M; NIH at Texas Instruments (see Mini Case 8.2). Giving a sufficient challenge to employees is essential (Hamilton Acorn). Internal venture management: making finance available for funding entrepreneurial ideas and opportunities
	• Tolerating mistakes	• 'Failure is our most important product' at Johnson & Johnson; DuPont's 'good try' language; 'Bury the dead' party at HP (now Philips)
6.	**Control systems** • Processes	• Ensure that there are simple mechanisms for staff to propose ideas and obtain resources to investigate them (AXA does this). Most companies have introduced Stage-Gate® or other formal NPD processes. Leading organizations have moved more to having a flexible process for the whole of an innovation. Systems and processes to promote entrepreneurial thinking, e.g. Richardson Sheffield (see Mini Case 6.6)
	• Metrics	• Company goals and metrics are 'cascaded to all levels', e.g. Canon sets notoriously tough NPD goals
	• Rewards and recognition	• Rewards and recognition are closely linked to innovation, including employee performance appraisals, e.g. Fischer has an interesting approach (see Mini Case 8.5)

CHAPTER 8

Context needs to be carefully considered in any attempt to apply best practice from one company to another. Consultants recommended that Evotec, a German-owned chemical research services company, adopt 3M's 'rule' that every researcher is free to spend 10–15 per cent of their time to work on their own projects. The CEO was sceptical that this would bring a return on what he perceived was a large investment of time for a small organization. Therefore, the idea was modified and top performers, elected by their peers, were allowed 10 per cent free time for a period of one year. This focused programme was effective at spurring on researchers to achieve peer recognition. Additionally, in the 10 per cent of their time dedicated to 'personal projects', the top performers turned in some ideas that were profitable for the company.[36] The Danish company Rockwool has also developed some interesting approaches to creating its R&D culture by relaxing its control systems (see Mini Case 8.3).

> ## MINI CASE 8.3: *Rockwool – R&D 'Out of Control'*[37]

Rockwool International Inc. is a leader in high-performance insulation materials for thermal, acoustic and fire-prevention applications. It was founded in Denmark in 1909 as a gravel mining company but in 1939 the focus was changed to insulation. Today, Rockwool is the world's second biggest producer of insulation products, with a turnover in 2014 of €2.18 billion. It produces rockwool (melted rock for insulation) but more recently has added fibres for automobile brakes, artificial soil for greenhouses, and frames for high-insulation windows to its portfolio.

The head office is in Copenhagen, where the R&D unit is also located, with around 100 employees. In 2009, a new vice president for R&D, Steen Lindby, was recruited to rekindle R&D efforts: 'R&D was in dire need of reinventing itself. It was out of sync with the market.' Lindby started the renewal process based on his belief that employees, as social individuals, desire recognition from their peers and their managers. His philosophy had implications for the way a new and larger R&D function was to be created.

A new management style was created, with R&D employees being empowered. Instead of R&D managers being *in control*, the approach was that a manager in the R&D unit had to ensure that their work directly contributed more value to R&D. One layer of management was removed and departments in the R&D unit were also closed. A matrix structure was designed, with new positions added such as 'people managers' and 'program managers', and any reporting that was not perceived to add value was removed. Lindby explains:

> A manager in R&D needs to be 30 per cent out of control. This was one of my biggest challenges, particularly as we allowed every employee in R&D access, without prior approval, to a funding account with 10 per cent of the total R&D budget. This proved to be a significant challenge for my managers.

Five years later, this bold move has helped employees feel empowered and has given them the chance to take responsibility, within their teams. Even without managerial control, the free access funding account amounts stays within the 10 per cent target each year. Reporting is much more open and, at a monthly plenum, project managers verbally present the status of their projects and categorize them in a three-colour – green, amber, red – system. Lindby says: 'Nobody likes to be "red" and peer pressure tends to keeps things on track.'

Continued...

The faith in human nature and the confidence that individuals can be self-organizing has changed the entire setup of the R&D unit. The emphasis on empowerment has significantly increased motivation in R&D and the unit has measured a 10 per cent increase in 'effective project hours', with the same number of people. Clearly, managers were one of the biggest barriers to change. Previously, a good manager was in control, now a good manager is expected to add value.

Moreover, the identity of R&D is now evolving around *supporting* production, sales, marketing and customers. New materials with new properties and products are being developed in a more agile way. Lindby says:

> Importantly, R&D is now able to work dynamically, being playful, co-creating 'specs' with customers, and making sense of the sometimes conflicting demands from stakeholders. For instance, we were under pressure from sales to come up with higher spec properties for one of our main products, but we soon realized that by talking directly to customers what they also wanted was cheaper products. So we had to invent a different solution.

Members of R&D have become involved on their own initiative in talking to customers and this has significantly impacted the culture. Previously, R&D saw themselves as 'providers of specs'; now, they see themselves as listening to and empathizing with customers directly. Lindby says: 'We are now good at figuring out just what is at stake.' However, he expresses some concern as to whether the way R&D is organized – orchestrated – at Rockwood will be transferrable if the company keeps growing in overseas markets, requiring R&D to have a local presence. Lindby asserts:

> It will be challenging but one thing we definitely will maintain is the requirement that new ideas cannot be considered unless colleagues have been convinced. At Rockwool, without peer acceptance, a new idea doesn't have enough value to be presented and progressed.

Case contributed by John Christiansen and Claus Varnes.

Promoting Entrepreneurial Thinking

Many organizations want to instil entrepreneurial thinking among their employees. Successful entrepreneurs generate many business ideas, quickly screen out those that do not look promising, and drive the better ideas forward. They make quick assessments, in stark contrast to the decision-making in large organizations. So, there are a number of points that organizations should strive to emulate.

Research has shown that entrepreneurs focus on three areas in their assessment of potential businesses.[38] First, the scope of the venture is important, as the resources (including finance) required can be vastly different, depending on the market to be served. For example, the founder of FedEx needed a dedicated fleet of aircraft and over $90 million investment before opening for business, whereas today many web-based ideas can be launched on a shoestring. Second, entrepreneurs focus on identifying market needs and quickly developing new products and services to address them[39] (see Mini Case 8.4 on QB House). Third, entrepreneurs raise the barriers to competitors to ensure survival.

Over 70 per cent of successful entrepreneurs 'replicated or modified an idea encountered through previous employment'.[40] It also is interesting to note that employees who are frustrated with the working atmosphere at established companies create most entrepreneurial ventures.[41] This means that companies have to find ways to encourage *intrapreneurship* (entrepreneurship in existing

CHAPTER 8

organizations). It can help if employees' innovation proposals can quickly receive funding – this is normally referred to as *internal venture management*. Once good opportunities are found, separate entrepreneurial organizations need to be created and staffed with people with the right attitude and skills.[42]

> **MINI CASE 8.4:** *QB House Barbers – A Snip at the Price*[43]

QB (Quick Barber) House is the largest chain of barbers in Japan and the brainchild of entrepreneur Kuniyoshi Konishi. He was dissatisfied with the expensive and time-consuming traditional hairdressers. Konishi's hunch was that Japanese businesspeople did not want to take an hour for a haircut and did not value the hot towels and other aspects of the traditional approach. A simple market survey showed that 30 per cent of respondents were interested in a fast, low-price alternative, and this led him to open his first QB barbers in Tokyo in 1996. Now he runs over 400 outlets in Japan, with revenues of over $14 million and plans to expand throughout Asia.

The QB House approach is systematic and high tech. Each and every opportunity is used to reduce costs and achieve the target of a haircut in 10 minutes for 1,000 yen (€7.5 or $8). Locations are chosen directly in business districts. Customers can tell the waiting time from green, yellow and red indicator lights mounted outside every shop – special chairs with sensors determine the waiting time. A contribution to both lowering costs and accelerating the process is that customers buy a ticket from a vending machine, thus eliminating the need for a cash register. Customers sit in a small cabin for their haircut (a 'QB Shell'). This has a seat, a sliding door, mirror and just those utensils needed by the hairdresser for fast and efficient hairdressing. For example, a vacuum 'air-wash' tube mounted from the ceiling is used to clean the customer's neck and clothes of loose hair (and eliminate the time for a hair wash). QB Shells have even been installed on railway platforms in Japan.

After some problems finding local partners in other countries and being copied, QB House has successfully opened 30 outlets in Singapore and Hong Kong. The basis of Konishi's business was recognizing a problem faced by many people: lack of time. What is impressive is the way in which he systematically analysed the process flow in a barbers, developed the optimal solution, and drove it to market despite strong opposition from traditional Japanese barbers.

Counterculture of Innovation

All too easily a company culture can emerge that stifles innovation. Strong hierarchical control, lack of recognition and simply not making it clear to employees that innovation is the responsibility of everyone are common faults. Organizational changes, which focus mainly on reducing employee numbers – *downsizing* – are the most destructive. Research has shown that the uncertainty surrounding *anticipated downsizing* lowers creativity levels more than *actual downsizing*.[44] The depressed atmosphere in the workplace reduces creativity and those employees who are still creative keep their ideas to themselves (for personal advantage). For managers, the messages are clear: if downsizing is necessary, then the process needs to be completed as fast as possible and steps need to be taken to prevent a negative atmosphere arising.

Companies that need cultural change often have the least time to go through the necessary stages: identifying the problems, building commitment to change and so on. And companies with hierarchical structures tend to impose more control. That may lead to short-term success, for example cost reduction, but sti-fle flexibility and the building of a culture of innovation.[45] Even in difficult times, organizations need to experiment with new ideas and create new structures.[46]

PEOPLE MANAGEMENT AND INNOVATION

The next element we will consider is people and their impact on innovation. Managing human resources covers several areas, all of which influence innovation performance.[47] These are:

- Recruitment and job assignment
- Managing performance and careers
- Rewards and recognition.

Recruitment and Job Assignment

Organizations hiring new staff have an ideal opportunity to look for people who will introduce more innovation. In a recent survey, 92 per cent of senior managers considered finding the right staff to be a fundamentally important part of innovation management.[48] It is a challenge to find creative employees with the right mindset, and a recent report referred to the 'war' to find the right talent.[49]

In hiring new employees, selection criteria need to match the innovation strategy. The product technology roadmap presented in Chapter 4 prompts an organization to consider how its innovation strategy necessitates new competences. A strategic approach to HRM will include a regular check on how changes in innovation strategy create the need to build or strengthen competences.

Companies may need 'technical' competences, for example on a particular technology, or market, or people who have a natural ability to drive innovation. The latter is difficult to assess. Candidates' track record, willingness to take risks and their problem-solving skills should be assessed. The use of psychometric tests has increased over the past 10 years and specific tests can identify if an applicant is innovative. One test, for example, measures adaptability, motivation towards change, work style, and challenging the status quo.[50] Such tests can be used as part of the interview process but HRM specialists warn against relying on the results of tests alone.[51]

Research shows that true innovators are rare and so companies need to develop and mentor 'high potentials'. The key skills of the innovator are similar to those of an entrepreneur: they are fast analytical thinkers, driven, and they zero in on key data. Developing such people often means giving them challenging positions to give them 'live' experience.[52] In global companies, innovation also requires the ability to understand other cultures.[53] For example, L'Oréal, the French cosmetics multinational, has recognized that managing innovation across national boundaries requires people who have a deep understanding of more than one culture. Such people are able to spot opportunities, and solve communication problems.[54] Consequently, L'Oréal actively recruits managers who have parents from different countries or have lived abroad for long periods.

Certain types of projects require particular competences in teams. Four factors should be considered in assigning employees to roles: their 'technical' expertise; cross-functional team skills; their ability to champion innovative ideas;

CHAPTER 8

and their motivation. Technical expertise is probably the easiest to assess. The assessment of cross-functional skills and the ability to champion ideas must be an integral part of an appraisal and development system, which we will discuss below. If the appraisal system does not look at these factors, then employees will be assigned to roles without good, objective information on their capabilities being available.

Job assignment should take account of employees' job tenure, as it influences motivation and innovation.[55] An employee's perspective goes through three phases:

1. *Socialization* is the phase where an employee is new to their position, is learning their responsibilities and their supervisor's expectations, and making social contacts. This phase is short and the employee is primarily concerned with gaining acceptance.
2. The next phase is called *innovation* (an unfortunately confusing label in a book about innovation management) and starts when an employee feels secure enough to look for more challenging work, to enhance their contribution to the department. Hard work at this stage can enhance visibility and promotion potential.
3. Employees working in the same role for a substantial amount of time transition to *stabilization*. Here, they focus on preserving autonomy and minimizing their vulnerability. Their openness to innovation can drop significantly.

The rate at which an employee moves between the three phases depends on their personality and contextual issues. From an innovation perspective, it is pertinent that employees who have been in their roles for a long time tend to become less creative in solving problems because they are more rigid in their thinking and committed to established processes ('we have always done it that way'). Job rotation and bringing in new team members can help counter this.

Managing Performance and Careers

Managing performance is complex and the theories that have been developed to explain motivation in the workplace are inconclusive, although they do provide a framework for managers to draw on in work situations.[56] Creative people do not necessarily generate ideas on their own accord; they need encouragement, mentoring and support.[57] A recent internal survey at Google determined that employees perceive coaching as the most valuable role of managers.[58] Management theories can also give useful insights into motivation (see Theory Box 8.1).

THEORY BOX 8.1: *Theories on Employee Motivation*

Work performance is a function of an employee's ability and motivation. Two categories of motivation theory have been developed: *content* theories and *process* theories. Content theories concentrate on the factors that motivate people. Process theories stress the process by which motivation is achieved.

Continued...

Content theories include the well-known work of Maslow and Hertzberg. Maslow's greatest insight was that an individual's needs form a hierarchy and once needs such as pay and job security are satisfied, motivation will depend on factors such as esteem, for example status, and self-actualization, for example advancement. Hertzberg's work essentially extends Maslow's ideas. It divides motivating factors into *hygiene factors*, which lead to dissatisfaction if missing, for example adequate pay and job security, and *motivators*, the presence of which leads to job satisfaction and motivation. The empirical evidence on these theories is inconclusive but both have been widely applied by practitioners.

Process theories look at the dynamic relationships between the variables responsible for motivation. *Equity theory* identifies the importance of employees' feelings; if they feel that they are being unfairly treated compared to their colleagues, their motivation will drop. Objective systems for reward and recognition are therefore essential. The concept of the *psychological contract* – the two-way exchange of perceived promises and obligations between an employee and an organization[59] – is useful because it reminds organizations that the relationship with their employees is governed by mutual perceptions, and not just formal contracts. *Expectancy theory* states that 'employees will direct their work effort towards behaviours that they believe will lead to desired outcomes'.[60] It stresses the importance of clear links between performance and rewards, and managers are responsible for clarifying these links (see Mini Cases 8.5 on Fischer and 8.7 on Zenith Electronics).

There are a number of points that managers can take from the above discussion. It is important to understand and meet individuals' needs. As 'lower level' needs are met, recognition and responsibility become more important. Employees' motivation depends on whether they perceive that the psychological contract between them and the organization is being met. Clarifying goals and potential rewards is necessary.

It is useful to *cascade* the top-level innovation goals down the organization, to each and every employee (Figure 8.5). High-level goals like revenues from new products can be linked to a project team's goals, and, in turn, to the goals of each member of the team. In cascading goals, it is important to check that the goals at each level are specific, measurable, achievable, relevant and timed (as represented by the mnemonic SMART).

At the employee level, goals need to be aligned to those of peers, to promote teamwork. This is particularly important in fast-track breakthrough projects that require particular commitment. Teams cannot have individuals focusing on their personal goals, to the detriment of the team's. In Figure 8.5, therefore, Individual A is tasked with not only writing a particular software module but also with ensuring that this links to Module B and incorporates manufacturing test routines. Clear links to rewards at the team and individual levels are also useful in cascading.

Goals should be clear and measurable. Table 8.3 suggests a number of possible goals that can be used to promote and track innovation at the employee level. These include goals directly related to performance but they should also cover the acquisition of new skills.

Employee Skills Development

To innovate, companies constantly need new skills. The skills and competences that a company needs should be apparent from the product technology roadmap

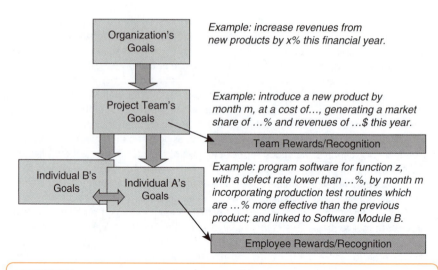

FIGURE 8.5: Cascading Innovation Goals to Employees

(see Chapter 4) and these can be accommodated by hiring or employee development. In the service sector, the ability to design an effective service augmentation is an area where employees may need to be developed through specific training programmes. Public sector organizations are now focusing on innovation and that means public servants need to develop commercial skills, as funding for public sector innovation increasingly involves cooperation with the private sector.[61]

A company's future requirements should be one driver for planning the development of employees' skills. However, of equal importance can be individuals' motivation – for many employees, learning new skills can be hugely motivating.

Appraisals

There are two key aspects to appraisal from an innovation perspective: the topics covered and who conducts the appraisal.[62] Although most organizations perceive the importance of innovation, research has shown that few include it as a criterion in their annual appraisal systems.[63] Choosing innovation as a criterion will certainly put more focus on it within the organization (see Mini Case 8.5 on Fischer). Employees can be appraised by looking at performance versus the agreed goals, such as those in Table 8.3. Note, for example, that these include a focus on business model innovation (BMI), which employees often do not think about, although they may have good ideas about how it can be achieved.

Appraisals can be conducted solely by the employee's direct manager, or alternatively, they can include self-appraisal, assessments by peers, subordinates, or customers. A combination is also possible and the so-called *360-degree assessments* take inputs from supervisor(s), manager(s), peers and subordinates. Assessing an employee's contribution to innovation is not always easy and the advantage of 360-degree assessments is that a broader view is obtained. The

TABLE 8.3: Employee-level Innovation Goals

Area	Metric	Details	Notes on usage
Ideas	Scientific publications	Number published in last x years	Objective measure but only applicable to R&D engineers and scientists. Does not show the real value to the firm
	Patents	Number granted in last x years	Objective measure but only applicable to R&D engineers and scientists. Does not show the real value to the firm
	Ideas generated	Suggestions submitted, etc.	Does not show the real value to the firm. Better to use measures of the ideas implemented and the advantages they brought
	Full product, service, and business model concepts developed	Number of ideas and the experiments made to test them	Encourages employees to think in terms of broader product concepts and business models. Broader concepts such as BMI are often overlooked by employees
Project work	Project goals	Specific time, quality and cost project goals that can be cascaded to the individual	As shown in Figure 8.5, a project's key goals should link to individuals' goals
	Teamwork	Encourages individuals to focus on achieving team or project goals	Is best to link the goal for individuals to be team-oriented by evaluating them directly on team goals
Process innovation	Cost savings	Transactional savings	Largely one-off savings
	Process innovation	Removal of non-value-adding stages from common business processes, e.g. euros saved per year	Objective measure, easy to link to reward and recognition
	Service innovation	Enhancement of the interaction with customers during the service delivery	Can be linked to customer satisfaction metrics. Should cover all aspects of the service augmentation (Chapter 3)
Overall innovativeness	Innovation performance rating	For example, a rating on the scale of 1 ('excellent') to 5 ('poor')	Rating is subjective but discussion is more important than the actual rating. See Mini Case 8.5 on Fischer
Learning	Competences gained	Helps employees focus on supporting the attainment of the organization's innovation goals and personal development, e.g. developing the skills to be a heavyweight project leader	Useful in focusing individuals and teams on capturing the lessons learnt from projects

CHAPTER 8

importance of appraisals in driving innovation is shown by a recent survey of 453 companies from a professional network. This showed that 58 per cent of the more successful organizations had innovation-related objectives in their appraisals.[64]

> **MINI CASE 8.5:** *Fischer GmbH – Fixing Innovation*

Many companies want their employees to become more innovative but do not effectively communicate this message. Fischer, a manufacturer of industrial fixing devices based in southern Germany, was one of the first to take a different approach. The company has a tradition of innovation – it has filed hundreds of patents – and so there has always been a strong focus on R&D generating ideas for new products. However, MD Klaus Fischer has attempted to extend the generation of new ideas across all functions because, he says: 'when we're not innovative across the whole company, then we haven't a chance'. Employees' contributions to innovation are assessed in annual appraisals in different ways. R&D engineers are measured on the number of patents and the speed and effectiveness with which these are converted into products. All employees are assessed on contributions to process innovation – improvements and cost reductions in manufacturing and business processes. And in every appraisal, a rating on a 1–5 scale is used to summarize an employee's overall contribution to innovation. Although the rating is subjective, it stimulates discussion between employees and their managers about innovation. The company has found that the process has been an effective catalyst in increasing overall performance.

Fischer perceives it is central to his role to promote innovation and therefore takes personal responsibility for driving the company's suggestions scheme and maintaining an effective bonus scheme linked to this.

Source: based on Goffin, K., and Pfeiffer, R. "Getting the Big Idea". The Engineer, (4th February 2000), pp. 22–23.

Reward and Recognition

Reward and recognition systems can be used to signal the importance of innovation. Financial reward is not the only motivating factor and individual rewards can compromise collaboration. In many ways, recognition can be a stronger mechanism for promoting innovation than reward.[65] Innovation is intrinsically motivating and so the opportunity to be part of a team working on a radical innovation can be hugely attractive to employees, as was found by Mölnlycke, a Swedish manufacturer of operating room disposables (see main case study in Chapter 5). It found that the people 'scouting' for hidden customer needs found it the most exciting assignment they had ever been given.[66] Equally, it should be noted that some employees struggle with the ambiguity involved with innovation.

There are several decisions to be made concerning reward and recognition: the amount and type of rewards; current performance and sort of behaviour that is desired; the type and recognition to be given; and when to inform employees of new rewards and recognition. Expectancy theory (see Theory Box 8.1) tells us that seemingly unrealistic goals lead to frustration. Goals with no related rewards will not be taken seriously, and good performers will only be motivated by rewards they value.[67]

The level of monetary rewards available is normally driven by profitability. A particular sum may be available for overall pay increases, including cost of living-related increases and a sum available for performance-related increases. In creating a focus on innovation, organizations may decide to reserve an amount for specific innovation projects, or for particularly innovative employees. In shaping a culture of innovation, it is useful to launch and communicate specific schemes for promoting innovation. Here we can learn from expectancy theory and investigate the sort of recognition that good performers themselves value. The full range of reward and recognition mechanisms is listed in Table 8.4. A recent survey[68] showed that stock options and profit sharing were only used by 10 per cent and 18 per cent of companies (respectively), whereas the most widely used approaches were giving the opportunity to work on bigger projects next time (42 per cent of companies) and project completion celebrations (43 per cent). Daring companies are even trying to push entrepreneurial thinking by offering their employees the chance to launch their own ventures within the organization and financially benefit from these (see Mini Case 8.6 on Haier).

A key decision is which reward and recognition schemes are targeted at individuals and which are targeted at teams. Some individuals are unlikely to take on unfamiliar tasks and challenging cross-functional teamwork unless it is rewarded.[69] Saab Group, the Swedish defence contractor, changed its reward structure to put more emphasis on teamwork.[70]

TABLE 8.4: Example Rewards and Recognition for Innovation

Categories	Examples	Comments
Rewards	• Pay increase • Bonus payments • Stock options • 'Project equity' • Time and resources for 'personal projects' • Extra holiday • Company cars • Paid training • Paid education, e.g. MBAs • Promotions • Dual ladder schemes • Ability to lead/profit personally from new ventures	Rewards should always be considered in light of motivation theories and the state of the business environment. They can have certain disadvantages. For example, stock options have little value in low growth periods and can, when allocated to small numbers of employees, lead to equity issues. Equity theory prompts managers to consider how rewards and recognition are allocated. Peer review schemes can be effective at demonstrating objectivity and raising team motivation
Recognition	• Deserved praise from management • Project completion celebrations • Publicity • Plaques and certificates • Peer recognition • Development opportunities • Opportunities to work on the most challenging projects	Content theory shows the importance of not only providing hygiene factors but also motivators, such as esteem and the fulfilment of working on an exciting project

CHAPTER 8

One of the rewards for good performance is promotion, but not every employee has the aptitude to become a good manager. So the *dual ladder* approach recognizes that some employees can have excellent technical skills, for example an engineer may be an expert in certain technologies, but may not have the competence, potential or desire to become a manager. Dual ladder salary schemes at large companies provide motivation for employees to develop their technical competences.

▶ **MINI CASE 8.6:** *Haier – Chinese Whispers: 'They've Reinvented Themselves'[71]*
    with video interview

Haier is the world's number one brand for home appliances, as ranked by the respected Euromonitor International. Haier employs more than 70,000 people worldwide and distributes products in more than 100 countries, with global revenues reaching $32.1 billion in 2014. The company is best known as the world's largest manufacturer of washing machines, air conditioners and refrigerators and is known for its culture of constant manufacturing improvements. It has also been identified as one of China's top 10 global brands by the *Financial Times* (UK).

Internet technology is transforming every industry. Manager David Teng says:

> And as a traditional appliance manufacturer, Haier has struggled with increasing labour cost and market saturation issues in China, which led to decreased margins. Meanwhile, lots of new entrants with a strong internet presence invaded the appliances market. Such companies have an 'internet gene' and so we are facing our greatest challenge.

But Haier is taking steps to change its culture to embrace the internet age. 'We are developing our eco-system – our network with other organizations', says Teng, who now leads what is called the Haier HOPE team (Haier Open Partnership Ecosystem). HOPE aims to 'fill the organization with passion and creativity through turning Haier into an internet-based platform company, made up of several micro-enterprises', says Teng. The intention is to create an organization that is extremely responsive to customer needs, incubates new ideas and innovates quickly. To achieve this, hierarchies have been torn down, so that, according to Teng: 'People with great ideas can find the resources and people to make them happen. Haier will soon consist of hundreds of micro-enterprises owned by Haier employees. They'll be responsible for their own budgets and profit and loss.'

Haier has embraced open innovation for several years and has a platform for exchanging and accelerating innovation through leveraging external resources. Within Haier's Open Innovation Center, Dr Xinming Wan is chief engineer. He has the challenging role of supporting all areas of the Haier business – from washing machines to air conditioning, to refrigeration – in finding the right technologies to solve the technical issues. An example of HOPE's work is that in 2015, Haier launched the world's first pocket washing machine, the CODO. Nick Huang, director of external partnerships, says: 'Its portable design lets users carry it on the go to take care of anything from dirt outdoors to dreaded red wine stains at a party. It is the perfect solution for mid-meal emergencies with its capability to remove embarrassing stains of tea, coffee, ketchup, curry or pickle.' The CODO can be used anywhere and it effectively cleans stains in no time and saves the embarrassment of wearing stained clothes. It is the equivalent size of an electric shaver and weighs just 200g, thus making it convenient to carry in a purse, laptop-bag, briefcase, pocket or your car. This disruptive product is a successful story of a Haier micro-enterprise.

Continued...

The idea was for the CODO was recognized by an R&D engineer in the washing machine business unit. It was quickly adopted and developed by Haier's R&D centre in Japan. When the project team had developed an early prototype with feasible technology, the project leader decided to load this concept on the internet to get consumers' views from an early stage. Consumers provided suggestions on the product, ideas about the product name, packaging and product colour. Zhengtao Wang, owner of the CODO washing machine micro-enterprise, says: 'The website generated thousands of ideas and created many fans for the product. We are happy that the user designed much of the product.'

Haier is reinventing its culture and moving from its manufacturing roots to a stronger focus on innovation. Entrepreneurial self-managing teams, a flat organization structure, open innovation principles, and, above all, involving the user are the tenets of its new culture. And it is not just the CODO product that has emerged from the HOPE initiative. Other new products include the 'Air Cube' and the 'AirBox'. The modular 'Air Cube' is an air conditioner that allows customers to select modules for

the types of air treatment they need – from humidification, to air purification, to aromatherapy. The 'separating dry and wet items' is patented technology to make the produce storage boxes at the bottom of a refrigerator more effective. For example, fresh mushrooms need different storage – humidity and temperature – compared to fresh fruit and the 'Air Box' can provide this. And with so many inventions at Haier, it is no surprise that the company now has an in-house intellectual property team of nearly 40 specialists.

Now visit www.palgravehighered.com/gm to watch Xinming Wan discussing HOPE and managing technology in more detail.

Case contributed by Lloyd He.

Rewards and recognition tend to be set *after the event*, in that they are announced after projects are finished. In some circumstances, it may be beneficial to define and publish the levels of rewards available in advance. Zenith Electronics in the US decided that rewards needed to be known *before the event*, to motivate the team on a particularly challenging project (see Mini Case 8.7 on Zenith).

To fully support innovation, reward and recognition should not only focus on the achievement of business goals but also on encouraging individuals to develop their expertise. For example, few people have the necessary skills to manage a 'skunk works' (see Mini Case 8.9 on Lockheed). Reward and recognition at the chemical company BASF are geared to encourage 'high potential' employees to lead skunk works, and thus increase the innovation potential of the organization.

Reward and recognition systems need to be updated regularly and management time needs to be reserved for this. A common argument from senior managers is that employees are 'expected to be innovative as part of their job' and so no additional reward or recognition is required. In such a case, it is appropriate to ask managers if they are satisfied with current innovation levels. If the answer is 'no', then a change in behaviour can be stimulated by changing reward

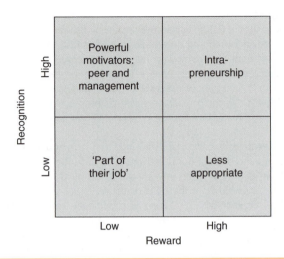

FIGURE 8.6: Innovation Reward/Recognition Matrix

and recognition mechanisms. Figure 8.6, which came out of our consulting work with companies, is a matrix that can be useful in guiding such discussions – an organization can review its current position in the matrix and decide if it is useful to move to another quadrant in the matrix. Recognition, either from peers or management, can be a powerful motivator, whereas reward without recognition is less useful.

MINI CASE 8.7: *Zenith Electronics – Equity Theory in Practice*[72]

US-based Zenith Electronics has used various approaches in providing rewards to employees involved in innovation projects. These were normally 'after the event' awards, given to teams or individuals for top performance. However, a multi-million dollar contract, with high technological risk and a penalty clause for late delivery, led Zenith to take a new approach.

It was decided to create a 'share scheme' for the project with a sum of several hundred thousand dollars reserved for rewarding the large team of over 25 dedicated members and 40 part-time members. At the start, all full-time team members were allocated 200 shares and part-timers received 50. The initial value of the shares was zero but the successful achievement of each milestone and quality target led to set increases in the share value, whereas each day of delay would lead to a defined loss in share value. The rules for calculating the value of shares were all defined up-front and were transparent to the team – so it was clear that, if everything went to plan, a dedicated team member could earn upwards of $15,000 bonus. Discretionary shares were also reserved for allocation to those employees who made extraordinary contributions. Although the scheme required careful up-front definition and explanation, it shows that in forming innovation project teams, the issue of reward and recognition needs to be considered.

Continued...

Zenith developed the high-risk technology on time and was convinced that the adoption of a new reward scheme contributed to meeting the schedule and quality goals. It is now clear to the company that special projects may require special rewards and recognition. In particular, teams facing challenging goals may perceive they deserve more than teams working on incremental innovation.

TEAM STRUCTURE AND INNOVATION

Senior managers need to consider team structure and governance because making teams work is an integral part of innovation. For example, implementation, which was covered in Chapter 7, is dependent on teamwork.

Team Structures

An organization can successfully innovate only if it is efficient at managing teams and developing the necessary leadership skills within the organization. Most of the studies of project teams have focused on their use in NPD but the findings are also relevant to new services, process innovations and BMI. Innovation requires a mix of skills and viewpoints and so the importance of cross-functional teamwork is clear.

There are different types of project team structure, each with advantages and limitations. Therefore, the most appropriate structure for each innovation project must be carefully chosen. The choice should take account of the culture of the organization; it is not realistic to try to move 'overnight' from a strong functional approach to a more autonomous approach. We will discuss five types of teams that are relevant for innovation projects, as shown by the work of researchers such as Michael Martin[73] (Dalhousie University, US) and Steven Wheelwright and Kim Clark at Harvard.[74] These are:

- Functional teams
- Cross-functional teams
- Heavyweight (cross-functional) teams
- Autonomous teams
- Virtual teams.

One word of caution before these team structures are discussed. It is not only the formal structure chosen that influences the success of innovation teams. As the earlier discussion on the cultural web showed, informal power should also be considered. Informal links within and outside the organization need to be supported.[75]

Functional Teams

Although seldom the case, sometimes members from only one function are needed for an innovation project – *functional teams*. Figure 8.7 shows the structure of a typical business unit, with R&D, operations, marketing and finance. A functional team might be formed in any of the functional areas. The best example is the continuous improvement (*kaizen*) team working together to optimize a manufacturing process. In the service sector, groups of operations employees may also work together on improving a process in a function: AXA insurance has

CHAPTER **8**

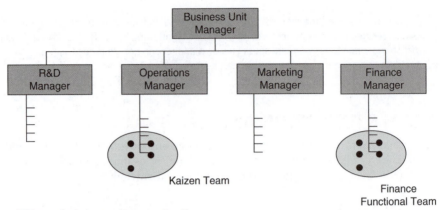

- Team of employees from one function
- Typical example is continuous improvement (*kaizen*) teams in operations
- Team leadership may be provided by a supervisor, or a team member from the same function

FIGURE 8.7: Functional Teams

a 'Taskmasters' programme to encourage teams of employees from operations to identify where they can eliminate non-value-adding steps in key processes.

Functional teams have the advantage that members all have similar goals and so few management actions are required to set the team up. Often the team can nominate its leader and so functional teams do not tie up precious project management talent. The limitations of functional teams are that the perspectives and range of skills included may be too narrow, or a suitable team leader may not be available. In this case, a moderator could be assigned from another function.

Cross-functional Teams

For the vast majority of innovation projects, it is not feasible to rely on inputs from only one functional area. So each functional area needs assigned people. As shown in Figure 8.8, the project manager is normally from one of the functional areas and reports to their normal manager; in this case, the project manager is shown as having been assigned from R&D.

As cross-functional teams include people with different perspectives, it is less likely that key points will be forgotten. For example, team members from operations will start discussions about how a product (or service product) can be produced. The disadvantages of cross-functional teams are that they need management attention to make them work (conflicts of interest often arise between functions), and the project manager does not have direct authority over the team members (normally it is a 'dotted line' reporting relationship). Sometimes, they require management to delegate more responsibility (see Mini Case 8.8 on 3M). And it can be hard to win the full commitment of team members, who still report

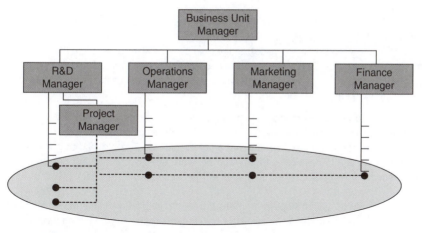

■ Project manager is normally drawn from one of the functions and
  still reports to functional manager

■ Team of employees from across the functions: reporting
  relationship is 'dotted line'

FIGURE 8.8: A Cross-functional Team

to their functional managers. Consequently, the project manager may not have
enough power. Unfortunately, some companies assign their employees to several cross-functional projects in parallel and this exacerbates the problem.

MINI CASE 8.8: *3M – Myth, Mentality or Motivation?*

In the innovation management literature, there is one company that stands out in terms of innovation culture; 3M has been regularly discussed and its practices and products eulogized, including the
ubiquitous 'Post-it'. So much has been said about 3M that almost a myth has emerged surrounding
the way the company manages its people and its innovation. Looking at it objectively, there are three
levels at which 3M has taken steps to stimulate innovation: at the company, team and individual
level.

In the early 1990s, 3M's performance was stagnant. Few enhancements were being made to the
massive portfolio of 60,000 products and to combat this, CEO 'Desi' DeSimone introduced a set of measures of innovation performance at the company level.[76] These goals were that 30 per cent of revenues
must be from products less than four years old and 10 per cent from products less than one year old.
To support this, extra funding, fast-track management decisions on innovative projects, and encouragement to combine ideas across the company's wide range of businesses were introduced. These steps
invigorated innovation in the company and many new products were launched. However, many of these
innovations were only incremental products (such as variations on the Post-it theme) that did not much
impact the market. To drive radical innovation, various steps were taken:

Continued...

CHAPTER **8**

1. The internal view of what constitutes a 'new product' was revised in order to swing the focus away from incremental projects.
2. It was perceived that customers may not recognize their needs or be able to articulate them and the lead user approach (see Chapter 5) was adopted to generate more radical ideas.[77]
3. 3M management stressed that they were expecting innovation in all areas of the business, from the R&D laboratories, to marketing and sales, and after-care.

Although company measures are essential, it is at the team level that projects are conducted and such projects, in aggregate, constitute company performance. Therefore 'action teams' were introduced for NPD.[78] Management recognized the dichotomy that a tight organization could lead to process efficiency but a looser process would devolve authority and be more effective. 3M found not only that the action teams needed training but also top management needed coaching to 'back off' and really empower the team.

At the individual level, 3M has taken steps to promote and reward innovation. In hiring, 3M looks for people who are creative, have broad interests, are self-motivated, energetic, have a strong work ethic, and are resourceful. During the interview process, applicants' problem-solving ability is tested thoroughly in group exercises. A range of approaches promotes innovation through employees. The rule that development people can spend up to 15 per cent of their time on investigating their personal ideas is almost as famous as the Post-it. 'Genesis grants' are available to fund the early investigations of personal ideas. Taking promising ideas further is supported by the Pacing Plus scheme, which motivates by what 3M terms the 'pinball effect' (success gives you the chance to play again); and the Carlton Award is 3M's highest recognition, its Nobel Prize.[79]

Heavyweight Cross-functional Teams

As discussed above, the main limitations of cross-functional teams relate to the conflicts of interest that may arise. If the project manager does not have charisma or persuasion skills, their lack of formal authority can be a problem. As the formal reporting of team members to the project leader is only a 'dotted line', members may give more weight to their functional allegiance. Therefore, a *heavyweight project manager* may be used. Figure 8.7 indicates that this manager has the necessary authority since they are at the same level as the functional managers.

The heavyweight cross-functional team has similar advantages to a normal cross-functional team but the project manager has the authority to drive the project more. One difficulty with heavyweight cross-functional teams is the scarcity of suitable project managers to lead them. Consequently, it is essential that project selection takes account of human resources (see Chapter 6). Also, an influential heavyweight team manager can tend to divert resources from cross-functional teams led by more junior project managers.

Autonomous Teams

Most companies are not good at creating the organizational structure that radical innovation projects and 'highly uncertain work' need to succeed.[80] Studies have shown the importance of the team being placed in a separate location and being led by a high-level manager, freed from bureaucracy.[81] Other research has shown that teams can function better when they are not constantly checked by management.[82]

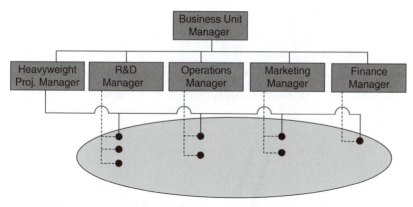

- Team of employees from across the functions report to the heavyweight project manager for the duration of the project
- Project manager reports to top management and is at a similar level to the functional managers

FIGURE 8.9: A Heavyweight Cross-functional Team

In the *autonomous* team, shown in Figure 8.10, an entrepreneurial project manager (*new venture manager*) is selected and assigned a small team, which is deliberately separated from the main organization. Typically, as mentioned in Chapter 7, the team is also allowed to use different processes. Many of the 'rules' of start-ups apply to the design of an autonomous team. It is crucial to have people experienced in certain functions. A small number of participants is ideal and they need to define a simple but effective process for driving an idea to market. A large number of companies, including IBM and DuPont, have used autonomous teams, also called *skunk works* (this term is explained in Mini Case 8.9 on Lockheed).

Autonomous teams have the advantage that they can adopt different ways of working and do not have to fit within the parent's cost structure. There are, however, several limitations. Autonomous teams require an entrepreneurial style of management and finding suitable candidates to lead them may be difficult. (As mentioned earlier, the chemical giant BASF has a management development programme to coach such managers.) The projects allocated to autonomous teams are normally challenging and inherently risky. Consequently, the first project may not be successful but in this case the idea of using such teams should not be rejected.

It has been found that autonomous teams quickly develop their own culture, which may challenge many of the values of the parent organization. There is an inherent danger that autonomous teams working on innovation projects will come into conflict with more operational units of an organization.[83] Other disadvantages can be the disruption to other projects, and the problems with reintegrating members of the autonomous team at the end of the project. Top management needs to be prepared to deal with such issues.

CHAPTER **8**

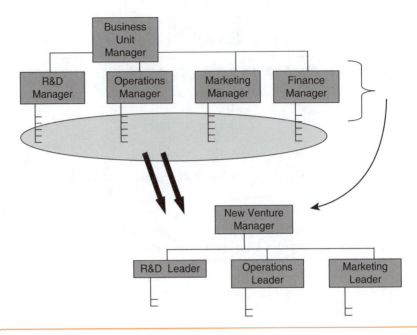

FIGURE 8.10: An Autonomous Team

MINI CASE 8.9: *Lockheed – Stinking of Innovation*[84]

Sometimes, large organizations can stifle innovation through their control systems and routines. Approaches that can help make innovation more efficient, such as NPD processes, can sometimes be constraining. More often, it is the overhead structure of the parent organization that can prevent innovation and so mimicking a start-up is a popular approach, which is normally referred to as starting a *skunk works*.

The original skunk works was created by US aerospace company Lockheed to accelerate the design of a new jet fighter in 1943. Lockheed assigned a team of 23 engineers to the project and freed them from the bureaucracy and the official R&D process. The team was located in a separate building. The name *skunk works* was coined by a team member and came from a cartoon strip featuring an illicit brewery with the same name; it was not named because the 'new organization stinks' (as many people have subsequently assumed). The results for Lockheed were dramatic; the Shooting Star jet fighter was designed in 43 days and was the first American-designed aircraft to exceed 500 miles per hour.

Virtual Teams

For all the types of teams discussed, there may be links to outside suppliers (although these have been omitted from the figures). In many instances, suppliers make major contributions to innovation projects. Sourcing innovation expertise outside (open innovation) is increasingly important and when resources from a number of different organizations are brought together, a *virtual team* is formed.

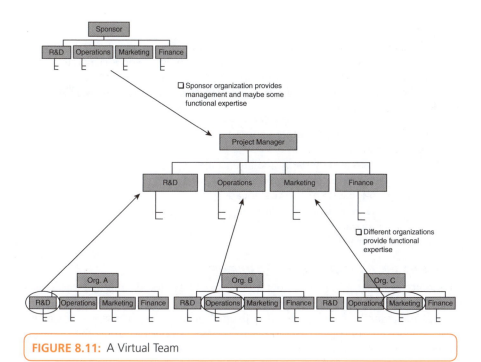

Sponsor

☐ Sponsor organization provides management and maybe some functional expertise

☐ Different organizations provide functional expertise

FIGURE 8.11: A Virtual Team

Figure 8.11 shows a virtual team where the different competences needed are sourced from a variety of organizations but the project management is provided by the organization that launches the project. Increasingly, virtual teams are drawn from a mix of organizations. Creating a virtual team can be appropriate for developing innovations where not all the required expertise exists in-house. Virtual teams are not dependent on an organization's other products, processes and services and they can be entrepreneurial.[85] On the downside, they are not co-located, communication can be difficult, and external resources can be costly (although cheaper in the long term than developing internal expertise).

An example of a virtual team that achieved excellent results is the Wingspan internet bank development team. This pulled together experts from a number of IT companies and launched an online bank within 90 days.[86] The basis of this success included a clear definition of the responsibilities of each of the suppliers, and an 'immersion day' to launch the project, in which all contributors focused on defining the interfaces between their work and that of others. Regular videoconferences kept all the virtual team informed and helped identify problems.

Virtual and globally dispersed teams are common – they are used by about 35 per cent of companies.[87] Their main limitations are that because they are not co-located, communication becomes more difficult and a simple, effective innovation process is needed. Where open innovation is used, outside expertise can be expensive and intellectual property rights (IPR) need careful management.

CHAPTER **8**

Making Project Teams Work

The portfolio of innovation projects needs to be aligned with suitable project teams. Effective empowered teams can reduce the pressure on top management and improve the quality of decisions, as these are made at a more appropriate level in the organization. Ensuring that innovation project teams work effectively involves:

- Choosing the appropriate team structure
- Selecting team members
- Creating a team and managing relationships
- Managing functional and other interfaces
- Managing co-location and virtual location
- Using project leaders and champions
- Launching innovation projects
- Dealing with project failure.

Choosing the Appropriate Team Structure

Different projects require different team structures; for example, radical and breakthrough innovation projects will require a different approach to incremental ones. Cross-functional teams are very useful but they are not suitable for every type of innovation project. Leading companies are adept at using the different types of teams – they are *ambidextrous*, in that they use different types of team to develop incremental and radical innovations.[88]

In Chapter 6, we discussed the significance of having the 'right balance' of innovation projects. By balance, we indicated the mix of innovation projects by their dimensions (product, service, process and BMI), degree (incremental and radical), risks and returns. Achieving the right balance should align innovation strategy with the resources available. One of the scarcest resources is excellent project managers. Project managers take time to learn and so organizations do not have the luxury of being able to assign a top project manager to every project. Team leaders need deep technical knowledge. On breakthrough and radical projects, they also need to be natural risk takers, and be able to create a vision that inspires peers.[89]

The size of the *core team* for an innovation project – responsible for representing the different functional interests and driving the project – should be kept manageable, and research shows that a total of about eight team members is best.[90] A small core team makes the communication channels simpler and speeds decision-making, for those decisions that can be made at the team level; obviously, some decisions require management involvement. Projects in the automotive or aerospace sectors can, for example, have teams consisting of hundreds of engineers. In such cases, special steps are needed to map communication channels and optimize them (see the design structure matrix in Chapter 7).

Table 8.5 summarizes the advantages and limitations of the five types of project teams and can be used as a tool for deciding which type of team is most appropriate for a particular project. An important consideration for teams that cannot be located together is that sharing knowledge becomes much harder.[91]

TABLE 8.5: Choosing the Right Type of Team

	Functional teams	Cross-functional teams	Heavyweight cross-functional teams	Autonomous teams	Virtual teams
Advantages	• Simple to organize. Do not monopolize management time • Ideal for 'tactical' improvements to the day-to-day processes within a function	• Bring together knowledge and responsibilities of all functions • Work well for projects where something similar has already been successfully completed • Require relatively low management commitment	• Due to an experienced manager taking responsibility for the heavyweight team, it has more influence • Can use existing processes and resources • Suitable for breakthrough projects	• Autonomous teams are freed of the bureaucracy and overheads of the parent organization • Separate location reinforces the independence of the team • The team spirit will quickly encourage entrepreneurship • Suitable for breakthrough and radical projects	• Brings together levels of expertise not available in a single organization • Can be much faster moving than projects resourced internally • Such teams are entrepreneurial in nature
Limitations	• Team may miss opportunities, as they have a narrow perspective • Team learning is not applicable to cross-functional projects • Not suitable for breakthrough and radical innovations	• Project manager has little formal power and so may not be able to control cross-functional differences • In competition for resources are likely to lose out to heavyweight teams	• Require an experienced manager to lead the project • May require significant amounts of management time • May not work well for new ventures, as they are too closely tied to the parent organization	• The ideas developed by such teams will test the capacity of the parent organization to accept change • Entrepreneurial management talent is hard to find	• Are not co-located • Need good communication and a simple, effective innovation process • Sourcing outside expertise can be expensive • IPR need to be carefully managed
Recommended application(s)	• Kaizen projects in all functions • Developing a process orientation within the function	• More incremental than radical innovation projects • More complex kaizen projects, where a cross-functional view may add a better understanding	• Radical innovation projects (not recommended for low complexity projects) • Heavyweight teams offer a good training ground for managers with top potential	• New ventures: new products in new markets • Dealing with disruptive technology • Business model innovation	• Development of new technology, where the internal competence does not exist • Essential for effective open innovation

Selecting Team Members

While it is not difficult to ensure that all the relevant functions (or skill sets) are represented in the core team, it is not possible to have the best people from each function. Top people are always in demand so, in practice, the project team will consist of people with different performance levels. In choosing team members, functional expertise and team working ability are important. Higher risk, radical innovations require the highest level of teamwork.

In choosing a team, personality traits should be considered, as these influence team working. It is not simply a case of gathering the cleverest people. Various tests have been developed, such as Myers-Briggs[92] or that developed by R. Meredith Belbin's work at Henley Management College in the UK. These check how the traits of the available individuals compare to those of an ideal team. There is no generally acknowledged 'best' test and so we have selected the Belbin test, as it is easy to apply to innovation teams.[93] Belbin defined a *team role* as a 'tendency to behave, contribute and interrelate with others in a particular way'. He identified nine team roles, summarized in Table 8.6. For example,

TABLE 8.6: Team Roles

Role designations	Characteristics	Typical focus
Coordinator	Positive-minded, self-confident and impartial individual. Often of average intellect	Clarifies objectives, helps allocate responsibilities, articulates team conclusions and seeks consensus
Shaper	Often an overachiever who is impatient, provocative, emotional and outgoing	Articulates the findings in group discussions, presses for agreement and decision-making in their own way
Plant	Intellectual and knowledgeable; individualistic and unorthodox	Makes proposals, generates new ideas
Monitor/ evaluator	Sanguine, cool-headed and clever	Analyses problems and issues, evaluates others' contributions
Implementer	Tough, pragmatic, conscientious	Wants to turn talk into action and effective implementation
Team worker	Team-oriented, gregarious, may be indecisive	Gives personal support to others
Resource investigator	Inquisitive, innovative and communicative	Brings in new ideas, negotiates with outsiders
Completer/ finisher	Attention to detail, conscientious, perfectionist	Emphasizes the importance of meeting schedules and achieving goals
Specialist	Expert in their field. Interested in further building their expertise	Relatively narrow focus on knowledge related to their field

Source: based on many publications about Belbin

the *coordinator* tends to focus on ensuring that the objectives are clear, responsibilities are allocated, and on summarizing team conclusions. The *implementer* pushes for action, whereas the *team worker* is supportive. Typically, individuals have a tendency to a particular team role, with one or two subsidiary traits. Each of the nine roles, with their particular characteristics, brings particular strengths to a team.[94] The best teams have a mix of roles.

A simple questionnaire allows individuals' Belbin roles to be determined and a balanced team to be chosen. Often, ideal team members are not available, and in this case, the Belbin methodology can form the basis of a team 'kick-off' workshop. A moderator explains the Belbin roles, gives the questionnaire to team members and then creates an open atmosphere in which the team members discuss their individual characteristics and how, together, the team can function. For example, if there are no obvious 'completer/finishers' in the team (and in our experience, they are a rare breed), how can this deficit be addressed? It should be stressed that the moderator must set an appropriate atmosphere in the workshop, as otherwise some individuals may object to their results being openly discussed. Applied sensitively, Belbin's typology is a valuable tool for launching and managing teams.

Selection to a particular team is often a strong recognition of an individual's past performance and can be highly motivating. Therefore, motivational aspects must be considered in choosing teams. For example, scientists and engineers often have a strong preference for challenge and want to work on the more demanding projects; a survey of over 1,000 scientists and engineers showed that if they are given an intellectual challenge, they work longer hours and generate more patents.[95] One word of caution though; top scientists sometimes do not look outside their field of knowledge for solutions and this can hinder innovation.[96]

Creating a Team and Managing Relationships

One of the most important aspects of project team management is establishing effective relationships from the beginning. This depends on individual interactions and cross-functional issues. Early research by Bruce Tuckman from the Ohio State University showed that newly created teams typically progress through a number of phases.[97] This is often presented as the *teamwork wheel*, as shown in Figure 8.12.

1. Initially, in the *forming* phase, members tend to be guarded, polite and the team works together cautiously.
2. Next, as the first tasks are tackled, conflicts or personality clashes may occur, or even fundamental disagreements because of different functional backgrounds – this is the *storming* phase. Some of the clashes can be healthy and bring better ideas or identify problems.
3. The team will then move into a *norming* phase, where it addresses the conflicts and develops rules or ways of effectively working together.
4. Lastly, teams should move to and remain in the *performing* phase. Sometimes, new conflicts can move the team back into storming but good team management should move the group quickly back to performing.

CHAPTER **8**

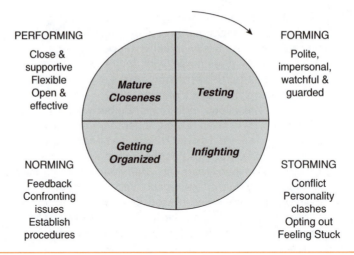

PERFORMING

Close &
supportive
Flexible
Open &
effective

*Mature
Closeness*

Testing

FORMING

Polite,
impersonal,
watchful &
guarded

*Getting
Organized*

Infighting

NORMING

Feedback
Confronting
issues
Establish
procedures

STORMING

Conflict
Personality
clashes
Opting out
Feeling Stuck

FIGURE 8.12: The Teamwork Wheel
Source: based on Tuckman[98]

The teamwork wheel is useful at kick-off meetings and can be used to create team understanding. In the forming phase, teams can develop their own 'ground rules'. Developing such rules early on can minimize the negative aspects of storming and accelerate the transition to performing. Table 8.7 shows a number of suggested rules based on our extensive work with NPD teams. Once teams have been assigned to the innovation task, communication becomes a factor that needs management attention. The fundamental problem is that innovation is about creating new knowledge and so significant amounts of knowledge need to be shared. On the one hand, individuals need to know much about the project they are working on, but on the other hand, if everyone receives all the information about a project, this leads to information overload. Therefore, mapping the flow of information and knowledge within a project can avoid information overload and crucial information not being shared with the right people.

Managing Functional and Other Interfaces

One of the most researched aspects of NPD teamwork is the relationship between R&D and marketing and the 'wall' that often exists between them.[99] It appears to be a perennial issue. In a major study of nearly 300 projects at 50 companies, frequent conflicts were identified.[100] Distrust was found to lead to mutual disrespect and poor consolidation of market and technical ideas. Management needs to lead by example in demonstrating the value of both functions and, particularly, the value of collaboration. Finally, full harmony, where each function is equal partners, can be positive for incremental projects but the 'give and take' attitude may lack the fire that is sometimes necessary to make innovation breakthroughs.

TABLE 8.7: Suggested 'Ground Rules' for Cross-functional Innovation Teams

	Rule	Comments
1.	Respect all team members' opinions and expertise	This should help to avoid cross-functional friction and 'silo mentality'
2.	Customer focus and quality should not be comprised, without a team decision	Stops internal views, or technology-push dominating. The customer's view is accepted as paramount unless there are exceptional mitigating circumstances
3.	Deliver your work on time or warn the team in advance, if you expect problems	Underlines the importance of everyone delivering on time, in order for the whole project not to experience delays. Also encourages individuals to ask the team for support before it is too late
4.	Communicate efficiently and always consider how your work can impact others in the team	Communication is too often poor and the interfaces between different work packages or functions are not sufficiently considered
5.	Question, question, question	Helps teams 'keep an open mind' and be more innovative in their approaches
6.	Assess risk but expect the unexpected	Should allow some problems to be anticipated, the unexpected should be dealt with quickly as some resources are 'reserved' for unseen problems
7.	Make it a winning team	All individuals should focus on making the project team something special and achieving extraordinary results

Although the interface between R&D and marketing is the most commonly discussed, it is not the only one that managers should consider. An other issue is the interface between R&D and the financial controlling function.[101] Complex R&D projects, particularly technology development, require good risk assessment. However, the adequate assessment of risk requires both technical and financial aspects to be considered and this requires excellent working relationships between finance experts and R&D leaders. The interface between these two functions has a significant influence on the effectiveness of portfolio management and is an area where organizations need to concentrate (see Mini Case 8.10 on Intracom Telecom).

Many companies in the manufacturing and service sectors are now focusing on design thinking. However, the interface between R&D and industrial designers also needs careful management.[102] Cross-functional boundaries have been widely recognized as problematic. In addition, the different opinions and 'language' used by management and engineering means that these groups often do not communicate effectively. Organizing effective cross-functional communication is a key management task.[103]

CHAPTER 8

> **MINI CASE 8.10:** *Intracom Telecom – Strategy through Process* [104] *with video interview*

Intracom Telecom, a global telecommunication systems and solutions vendor, was derived from Intracom, a company that began operating in 1977 with 10 employees in Athens, Greece, manufacturing and assembling telecommunication equipment to address domestic needs. Intracom has grown significantly and was transformed into a holding company. The telecommunications business unit was named Intracom Telecom. Intracom Telecom now employs over 1,900 highly skilled professionals, serving more than 100 customers in over 70 countries. The company develops products, solutions and professional services primarily for fixed and mobile telecom operators, public authorities and large public and private enterprises. And its subsidiaries span Europe, Russia and the Commonwealth of Independent States, the Middle East and Africa, Asia-Pacific and North America.

The company recognized that to compete successfully in the global arena, it had to focus its R&D investment on the product categories that address the needs of emerging markets, which have high growth rates. In the late 2000s, management made a strategic change to its product portfolio and organizational structure. Three new business units were created, the Wireless & Network Systems Division, the Telco Software Division and the ICT Services & Solutions Division. On an annual basis, the product portfolio of each of these divisions is evaluated in terms of ROI, the potential for market share cross-selling opportunities and so on. As a result of this, some products have been discontinued or consolidated and a clear portfolio has emerged across the business units. However, to make the strategy viable, process changes were also necessary.

In parallel to the strategic changes, the company has made its processes more agile. For example, the new product/service development process used to take up to three years before market deployment, which was typical in the industry. Now marketing identifies as early as possible the market needs, potential new technologies, and the budgets needed. In response, R&D now develops weekly or biweekly working prototypes. Marketing then shares these new concepts with its customers (in global exhibitions, or by physical visits to the customer's site) to gather input and refine the concepts further. Such fast iteration has allowed Intracom Telecom to achieve much faster release dates.

Spyros Sakellariou, section manager, explains his experience with the agile approach:

> In 2011, the company decided to invest in big data applications targeting the telecom operators in South and Eastern Europe. Initially, the marketing team intended to build a comprehensive big data platform for the telecom sector. However, when we started sharing this idea with our customers, we realized that although impressed with the technology, they did not understand how such a platform could be used. Triggered by this new understanding, we built not only the platform but designed turnkey applications with tailor-made benefits for the telecom operators – such as a 'customer-churn prevention service' and 'customer experience management'.

The agile process allowed Intracom Telecom to avoid unnecessary investment, to help customers understand their own needs based on prototypes, and deliver products ahead of time while engaging the customer. However, applying agile processes entails challenges. The volume of day-to-day tasks, unexpected problems, and the different agendas of marketing and R&D often led the two departments to neglect sharing and exchanging ideas and knowledge. Management realized that the enabler for the agile approach to work was more openness and prioritizing the communication between the two functions, as well as marketing and R&D showing the discipline to deliver their innovation work on time despite the inevitable operational, short-term requests.

Continued...

As the agile process was counterintuitive for some of the existing teams, new ones were created by merging engineers and managers who had experience in agile processes with new hiring or transfers. Anastassios Dimopoulos, general manager and VP of the board of directors, says: 'We now have very short development cycles for our products, very quick deliverables which help us budget our R&D and deliver only what is needed to our customers using our resources efficiently.' The next step for the company is to use its 'devops methodology' to shorten the delivery times of new products and services even further, while guaranteeing the reliability of the technology when deployed in customers' live networks.

Now visit www.palgravehighered.com/gm to watch Spyros Sakellariou discussing the importance of communications and new product development process in more detail.

Case contributed by Evy Sakellariou.

Managing Co-location and Virtual Locations

Co-location is an important mechanism for innovation projects. If all team members can be brought together, then communications and team spirit improve dramatically. Open-plan offices with furniture on wheels make it easier to bring teams together. Email is no substitute for bringing people within speaking distance. Where co-location is not possible, extra effort must be made to integrate the efforts of the various members of the team. Modern high-definition videoconferencing is making the management of virtual teams easier and is starting to be almost as good as face-to-face contact. Skype is much poorer quality but free.

Different physical locations and locations in different time zones make communication more difficult but they can bring some advantages. For example, 21TORR, a German marketing and internet consultancy company, has used separate locations to its advantage. Customers in California have found it useful to choose 21TORR as a service provider, which, because of the time difference, can implement website modifications 'overnight'.

Using Project Leaders and Champions

The importance of innovation project managers cannot be overstated. For incremental projects, the leader must act as a communicator, climate-setter and planner. However, for radical innovation, the team leader must do more, acting as a real *champion*, pushing the cause when the project encounters resistance.[105] Champions also need to be good at managing cross-functional boundaries (see Mini Case 8.11 on Fiat Iveco). Research shows that during radical innovations, champions must have the ability to find unconventional solutions because more radical projects require more novel approaches.[106] A recent study of 212 companies showed that champions need to display different attributes at different

CHAPTER **8**

stages of radical innovations. At the start, they need to create or discover market opportunities, they then need to lead experimentation, before moving to develop the business until it can stand alone.[107] In leading companies, senior managers are also careful to give close, direct support to their innovation champions.[108]

As good project leaders are rare, organizations need to take active steps to ensure that they assign their best managers to the more complex projects. The development of champions takes time and direct coaching of junior colleagues by experienced managers helps. Not everyone has the necessary passion and energy and special rewards and recognition may be necessary to avoid such key employees being lost. It should be noted that many companies 'fundamentally mismanage their innovation talent ... [and] don't provide meaningful growth opportunities for their innovation professionals'.[109]

> ## MINI CASE 8.11: *Fiat Iveco – Innovation Interfaces*[110]

Iveco is the arm of Fiat responsible for manufacturing and marketing commercial and industrial vehicles, buses and diesel engines. Massimo Fumarola has worked as platform development manager in the heavy vehicles division and as business development manager in the engine business unit. In both roles he has been closely involved with considering how Iveco can increase overall innovation performance. Fumarola says:

> In my opinion there are three challenges in managing innovation. The most important one has to do with the organization and there is a dilemma. On the one hand, we want employees to work in structured, methodical ways to produce products in a timely, in fact a very disciplined way. On the other hand, we want people to challenge the established ways of thinking and working. This is a big problem and the only way to solve it is sometimes to take suitable people and break them out from the parent organization and give them freedom not just to act but also to think innovation.

> Getting enough people with the right experience is something we need to work on. We have great functional specialists but not enough people who have worked in several functions and have a deep understanding of the interfaces [between functions]. Unfortunately, in this industry and other ones I talk to, not enough people want to become what I'll call 'cross-functional boundary managers'. It takes time to find, encourage and develop such people.

> Third, it's about getting everyone involved. It's not just the voice of the customer. You also need to involve the truck operators, the suppliers, the regulatory agencies, and all the other stakeholders right from the beginning. Interfaces, not functions, generate most of the problems and we're getting more interfaces to consider. I think that the best managers of tomorrow will be the ones who can maximize innovation performance by minimizing the interface issues.

Launching Innovation Projects

Several times we have mentioned the value of kick-off meetings for innovation teams. Although these have not been researched, a number of highly successful projects have used them and our personal experience is that they are extremely valuable. Bringing the whole team together (even if it will subsequently work virtually) is useful. In addition to team-building, the meeting can establish ground rules, define the work breakdown structure, consider the interfaces between the work packages (see Chapter 7), and consider the implications of the characteristics of the individuals in the team.

Dealing with Project Failure

Although success is the aim of every team, this can be elusive. Studies have shown that many products fail, even those from famous companies; for example, Google Glass digital glasses have been withdrawn and it looks like the Apple Watch may suffer a similar fate in 2016.[111]

Empirical evidence shows that few organizations are good at terminating projects because they do not have clear termination criteria.[112] This can result in resources being wasted and significant demotivation.[113] Team members from unsuccessful projects are likely to feel demotivated and careers can be damaged through association with failure, unless there is a culture that accepts that not all projects will be successful. There must be sanctions for incompetence, but good individual performance should be recognized, even in unsuccessful projects.

Terminations should be carried out as early as possible and the team members need to be reassigned quickly, to reactivate employee motivation. There is much that can be learnt from projects that are not successful and researchers have found evidence that companies that were good at this were able to 'build on this failure' to be successful on subsequent projects.[114]

LEADERSHIP AND INNOVATION

Research points to the importance of the role of the CEO in many aspects of management and it is no different for innovation. The role of the CEO and top management team is to decide on the innovation strategy, clearly communicate it, and create the environment in which innovation can flourish. In providing innovation leadership, CEOs need to recognize that trying to adopt best practice will not help. This is because breakthrough and radical innovations require different ideas, identifying new opportunities, and building novel organizations, rather than applying standardized processes.[115] In the context of innovation, leadership includes: communicating clearly how important innovation is to the organization; demonstrating this importance by investing top management time in supporting projects; selecting the right people and structures; establishing key aspects of the culture, such as the freedom to experiment; and constantly driving projects.

The CEO's Style

The personal traits and management style of the CEO have an influence on innovation. Recent research has shown that CEOs need to be good at questioning, observing, associating facts, experimenting and networking.[116] They also need to be good at dealing with ambiguity because managing innovation involves dichotomies. These include focusing on individual and team performance, supporting employees but knowing when it is appropriate to confront them, being patient but conveying urgency, and leading from the top while stimulating bottom-up ideas.[117]

CHAPTER **8**

Some senior managers are very analytical. For example, numerous CEOs have a financial background. Such managers need to be aware that 'left-brain' analytical thinking can stifle innovation in the early stages, killing the good ideas and encouraging the bad ones.[118]

Vision, Direction and Stamina

The CEO and the top management team need to signal the importance of innovation and repeatedly explain the meaning for their organization. If this is not done, many organizations concentrate only on product innovation and opportunities for service and business model innovation will be missed.[119] CEOs should not try to define their own innovation vision and force others to follow it; rather, they should create a community that generates novel ideas. This involves giving teams tasks that are intellectually and emotionally demanding – diverse teams will need to have heated debate to create the right 'clash of ideas'.[120] Efforts to stimulate innovation are often difficult and results may not be fast in coming, so senior managers need stamina if they are to be successful at leading innovation.[121]

In setting direction, the top management team's most important decision is the balance of radical, breakthrough and incremental innovations in the portfolio, the so-called 'golden ratio' (covered in Chapters 1 and 6).[122] Other areas where leadership is needed are in showing the importance of customer insight, and in honing the processes to ensure that the organization innovates. This means carving out the mental space for employees to innovate and setting the challenge that innovation must push boundaries. In the early stages, CEOs must encourage searching far and wide for insights, identifying important unsolved problems with emotional or social needs, developing solutions via fast prototypes, and experimenting with business models.[123]

Organizational Structure

Earlier in this chapter we discussed the cultural web, which showed that the formal organization has an impact on innovation culture. So the CEO also needs to design the organization in a way that will encourage innovation. This involves considering factors such as hierarchy, the amount of radical innovation planned, and market focus.

The hierarchy of a large organization can negatively impact innovation and it has been suggested that 'control by letting go' is more appropriate than strong controls.[124] Gary Hamel, the famous management thinker, said managers must ensure that a 'pathological hierarchy' does not strangle innovation.[125] Less hierarchy means that companies can create value quicker, by making decisions faster than their competitors.[126]

One of the main points to consider when designing a corporate structure is the amount of innovation required. If breakthrough and radical innovations are needed (which are essential for growth), then managers need to consider whether the corporate structure is conducive to the development of radical ideas. Typically, incremental innovation can be managed within a more hierarchical structure, but when breakthroughs should be developed, highly autonomous teams are needed.[127]

Radical structures may be needed for radical innovation.[128] The team responsible for more radical innovation needs to be freed from some of the restrictions of corporate processes – particularly the financial stranglehold of budget and hurdle rates – but such skunk works will inevitably have culture clashes with the parent.[129] As consultants at PwC put it: 'The operating models and metrics for "business as usual" conflict with those needed to drive innovation, but it was also seen that such units must not become isolated from the core business.'[130] Strong culture can become a barrier to innovation[131] and insightful managers know when it is time to 'let go' and pass responsibility to others (see main case study on time:matters).

Summary

This chapter covered the fifth and final element of the Pentathlon Framework – people, culture, organizational, and leadership issues. It stressed the strategic importance of human resources. Overall, the chapter explained how to create a 'culture of innovation' and discussed the people management practices such as reward and recognition that underlie this. Most innovation work is conducted by teams and five types of teams can be used for innovation projects. Selecting the most appropriate team was shown to be best based on considering the characteristics of the project – for example if it is radical or incremental – planned. The central role of top managers in creating a culture of innovation was shown to be based on their demonstration and stamina for innovation and dependent on their leadership style. Illustrating the above points, this chapter's main case study is about time:matters, a company that has revolutionized 'same-day' shipments. It focused on creating the right culture to generate a constant stream of service innovation.

This and the previous four chapters have proposed a wide range of tools and techniques for innovation management, relating to each of the elements of the Pentathlon Framework. The management challenge is to boost innovation performance by coordinating the improvements across the elements of the Pentathlon Framework and this is the subject of Chapter 9.

Management Recommendations

- Use the cultural web as a diagnosis tool and apply ideas from best practice to create a real 'culture of innovation'.
- Choose the most appropriate team structure for each and every project.
- Manage innovation project teams not only to obtain the maximum returns from projects but also to develop sufficient talent for driving challenging radical projects.
- Link innovation strategy to the development of employees and support this with appropriate reward systems.

Questions for Students

1. Many managers focus on designing a new organizational structure when they want to change culture. Is this sufficient?
2. What are the attributes of someone who will be good at incremental innovation compared to the attributes of someone who could lead radical projects?
3. What are the challenges of developing a new product for Southeast Asia using a team based in Europe?
4. A manager asks you to identify five best practices of managing innovation culture that they can quickly apply. What would your answer be?

Recommended Reading

1. Rao, J and Weintraub, J., 'How Innovative is Your Company's Culture', *MIT Sloan Management Review*, 54(3) (2013), 29–37. Good ideas on how to 'measure' company culture and actions to take to make it more innovative.
2. Tushman, M.L. and Anderson, P. (eds) *Managing Strategic Innovation and Change: A Collection of Readings* (Oxford: Oxford University Press, 1997). Classic collection of readings on culture, leadership and innovation.
3. Flurr, N. and Dyer, J.H., 'Leading Your Team into the Unknown', *Harvard Business Review*, 93(12) (2014), 80–8. Useful review of the strategic aspects of innovation teams.

▶ MAIN CASE STUDY

TIME:MATTERS – AND CULTURE TOO![132]

Spare parts logistics and same-day delivery are big business and the *time-critical* segment is growing fast globally. *Downtime* – when equipment fails – can be disruptive, costly and even life-threatening. Therefore, for a range of shipments from stem cells, to medical devices to turbines, rapid and reliable delivery of spare parts around the globe is essential. The time:matters company is a spin-off from Lufthansa Cargo, formed in 2002 to serve the time-critical segment, through coordinated air, road and rail transportation. In 2014, over 500,000 consignments were made, corresponding to over 10,000 tons of shipments, gross revenues were over €88 million, and the growth rate was 13 per cent. From its beginning to the present day, management at time:matters has always recognized that company culture drives service innovation.

Time Critical A to B

Consider the following scenario. It is 15:48 on a Friday afternoon and the production line of your top customer in Barcelona is down because your equipment has failed. The production manager has just telephoned to say that they must work '24/7 on a crucial order' and the line must be running again by 'tomorrow – latest'. Fortunately, the 80 kg spare part is in stock at your logistics centre in Amsterdam but how can you get it from A to B – Amsterdam to Barcelona –today? Call Germany: +49 (0) 69 9999 2079 and the logistics specialists from time:matters will find a solution.

The client list for time:matters is impressive. It includes IT companies such as IBM and Fujitsu Technology Solutions; medical equipment suppliers such as

Siemens Healthcare; InteraDent Zahntechnik (dental prostheses); virtually all the large logistics players such as DHL, UPS and Kuehne + Nagel; and global players like John Deere, Bosch and Otto (Germany's biggest mail order company). Each of these companies will have one-off problems that need to be solved urgently and ongoing requirements that, once recognized, lead to new business opportunities. For example, InteraDent will have a number of urgent shipments requiring unique solutions throughout the year but, as it produces over 60,000 prostheses per year in the Philippines, it also needs regular European shipments. These must be fast and 100 per cent reliable, so that dentists can provide fast treatment to their patients.

To address the time-critical segment, CEO Franz-Joseph Miller says that spinning off from Lufthansa Cargo was essential because:

> from 1995 to 2001 and as part of Lufthansa, the business grew to €8 million but there was little strategic focus on the specific needs of our target segment. We focus on speed, customized solutions, and 'same-day' delivery in Europe. Same-day in our business means transport times across Europe from initial call to delivery of only 2–8 hours. So our service operations have been designed to enable high-speed transportation through our partner networks; courier delivery when the shipment is so valuable that the customer does not want to let it 'out of their hands'; and customized solutions. A fundamental element is our ability to give seamless tracking, door to door.

Service Innovation

Companies such as FedEx, DHL and TNT provide fast shipments through their own infrastructure of aircraft, delivery agents and tracking systems, using proprietary software and scanning devices to track shipments. In contrast, time:matters has developed 'open architecture' software to allow it to quickly integrate its partners' systems, including those of Lufthansa, Brussels Airlines, Deutsche Bahn (German railways), and small local couriers. Jörg Asbrand is chief operating officer at time:matters and says: 'We are a company with no buildings and essentially no assets. Our ability to innovate and to partner with other organizations is our main asset.' For example,

time:matters has negotiated with partner airlines to enable it to load shipments onto their aircraft up to 10 minutes before departure. It also has an exclusive contract on Deutsche Bahn inter-city express trains for its personnel to take personal care of shipments.

Miller also stresses the importance of constant innovation, saying: 'I believe the CEO must show their passion for innovation and I regularly sit with the project teams. That sends a strong signal and our service innovation group works constantly on updating our service offerings.' The group gathers and selects ideas using a 'survival of the fittest' philosophy, where the originator of the idea needs to show their commitment and compete for resources to develop their ideas into products. There have been a number of major innovations in the past few years, two of which will be discussed.

First, time:matters is focusing on the 'digitization of its platform' – the creation of digital booking processes and standard operating practices – for some of its services. The innovation group has worked with employees who are experts at solving logistical problems, to identify how solutions can be made repeatable, scalable and automated. Expert know-how has always been valued at time:matters but it is now taking standard problem-solving tasks away from its experts, to free their time for more challenging work. To gain support for this change, the experts were integrated into the project team and their fears of becoming less important to the company were openly discussed. Now, many of the solutions that needed to be identified by experts via the +49 (0) 69 9999 2079 number can be found more easily by using the new online booking system.

Second, a major opportunity in an adjacent segment was identified by time:matters employees but it was quickly recognized that it was such a different target segment that it needed to be spun off. In 2014, the company Liefery (the 'delivery factory') was founded. It is a new service, delivering products locally to customers in as little as 30 minutes of them placing an order, or on-demand delivery exactly at the time the consumer wants. This has been launched in 54 German towns and cities with plans to expand further throughout Europe. Customers use an app to specify where their items should be delivered to and the costs for the service start at €6.99. Delivery is quick and punctual because of direct links to online retailers (such as Zalando, REWE or Amazon) and shops in the city where the customer places their order. Miller says: 'The new delivery service makes it easier to shop. It's a quick and straightforward way to get what you need, and Liefery also gives local businesses a way to strengthen their position in the market as online shopping continues to boom.'

Culture Matters

With only 160 employees, Asbrand says time:matters is proud of: 'being small, non-corporate and creative, yet we are also proud to be an extremely international company, with Lufthansa Cargo as a major shareholder. The creative capacity in the company is maintained by "orchestrating" rather than "managing" company culture.'

The management team have tried to capture this in the company's core values – what they say are: 'that little bit of freakyness that defines time:matters!':

1. 'We are passionate: about our people and customers; committed to service, excellence, and courage; always trying to make the "impossible" happen.'
2. 'We want and accept responsibility: especially when things go wrong; we put competence above ego, and we're there when our customers or colleagues need us.'
3. 'We talk straight and do right: by expecting honesty; so, we put the fish [facts] on the table; and we never sacrifice integrity, respect and tolerance.'
4. 'We enjoy what we do: playing hard & working smart; in that undefinable mix of playfulness & professionalism; fuelled by a vision, lots of ambition and constant learning.'

In addition to creating a creative climate, time:matters hires people who have a 'make it happen' attitude, personal drive and the ability to solve complex A to B problems. According to Asbrand:

Innovation is central to us at time:matters because, without innovating regularly, what we offer will be copied by the competition. We cannot as such create a demand for increased shipments – there we are dependent on our customers' own businesses. But if we can create new service products that are unique, then our customers will want to use us for all their time-critical shipments.

Miller concludes:

Every day, I ask myself how time:matters can motivate its staff in a way which generates even more innovation. Our people want to be given responsibility, want the resources they need to be assigned; and want the freedom to act. Sometimes innovation requires the freedom that only a spin-off can offer. That's how time:matters started and now that's how Liefery will grow. It is important for managers to know when structure can get in the way of growth!

Reflective Questions

1. How does time:matters motivate, reward and recognize its staff, to innovate?
2. In what circumstances does innovation require a spin-off organization?

INNOVATION – PERFORMANCE AND CAPABILITY

INTRODUCTION

In previous chapters we have presented numerous tools for managing specific aspects of innovation, such as generating innovative ideas, or selecting the innovation portfolio. As we have stressed throughout, achieving effective innovation management will entail multiple interventions. And these actions must be coordinated, since each of the elements of the Pentathlon Framework is mutually dependent. So this chapter starts with the questions: What is the *innovation performance* of our organization? Is the organization innovative enough? Then it considers: Does the organization have the capability to innovate? And, if not: How can this *innovation capability* be developed? These are crucial questions that managers need to ask the moment their organizations decide that innovation is going to play a central role in, for example, generating growth.

Innovation should not just be considered in terms of outputs, such as new products or services. Far more, innovation should be viewed as an organizational capability – the ability to constantly develop products, services and business models, in ways that generate sustainable competitive advantage and growth. The need for innovation arises from a mismatch between the future we predict and the one we aspire to. Or, in the words of John Kao, an expert on corporate change: 'It's the capabilities by which we get the future we want as opposed to getting the future that we receive by default.'[1] Building innovation capability is challenging and it can necessitate deep-seated changes in how an organization functions. To successfully achieve such changes, change management principles are pertinent and this chapter explains how they can be applied to the context of innovation.

Every organization needs to utilize innovation in a different way and to a different extent, depending on the challenges it faces and the strategy it has chosen. Managers need to know what their organization is capable of. Innovation capability should be seen as preparedness and not just past performance. An army assesses its readiness not by the number of battles it has recently fought but by reviewing (and exercising) its capabilities – personnel, weapon systems, communications, transport and so on – to tackle the next battle (which will not be like the last).

This chapter covers the main aspects of this challenge, including:

- How to choose suitable measures to assess innovation performance.
- How to 'audit' an organization's innovation capability and identify priorities for improvement.
- Managing the changes that are necessary to build innovation capability.
- A main case study on Corning Inc., the US technology company.

ASSESSING INNOVATION PERFORMANCE AND CAPABILITY

To provide clarity, we will provide working definitions of the main terms connected with measuring innovation:

- *Innovation performance* is the output of new products, services, processes and business models and the financial impact of these.

- *Innovation investment* is the resources of an organization that are directly and indirectly linked to the development of new products, services, process innovation and business models. Typically, this will be financial investment, the time and effort of key employees, and the money spent on developing new markets. Companies need input measures as well as output ones.[2]
- *Innovation output* is typically measured by the revenues generated from innovative products, services and business models, and the savings generated by process innovation. If the financial figures are hard to obtain, then the numbers of innovations may be used as a proxy measure.
- *Innovation capability* is the sum of the underlying processes that enable innovation, from organizational culture and strategy, to ideas, their selection and their implementation.

The argument for using measures of innovation performance is simple, and some might say deceptively so, as the limitations of measures are often overlooked. To improve something, the first step is to measure current performance and compare it with some desirable standard, to see where it falls short. Then, changes are made and the performance is measured again, to check that improvements have been achieved and identify where further interventions are necessary. This is the way improvements are made to production processes, or sales methods, for example. However, improving innovation performance is not as straightforward. This is because the effect of improvements to innovation processes often cannot be fully assessed until some time afterwards. For example, changes to an NPD process may take several years to take effect (especially in the pharmaceutical sector, where drug development can take a decade). Similarly, moving to open innovation to source new technologies may take even longer. Such delays mean that feedback loops for managing innovation may be too slow to be of real use.

Economists' Measures

Economists mainly view businesses from outside and use data in the public domain to study innovation. Typically, they look at expenditure on R&D, patent counts, and the number of new products launched, as summarized in Table 9.1. These measures have both advantages and disadvantages.

Chapter 2 gave examples of typical R&D investment levels in different industries and these can be used as a benchmark. There is some benefit in making comparisons with direct competitors, whose circumstances may be comparable. For example, if your main competitors are making higher R&D expenditures, this raises questions. But it is not necessarily appropriate to match their figures. For example, your company may need to invest more than competitors to reach its growth goals. Or your company may be focusing on process innovations that are not accounted for under R&D spending. And the trend towards open innovation means that many companies are acquiring new products through partnerships, and R&D spending is a less complete measure of innovative activity than it used to be.

Table 9.1 includes two output measures and the first is patent counts. Strictly, patents are a means to an end and a patent only generates value when it is implemented in a product, or when it generates licence fees. In any case, patent

CHAPTER **9**

TABLE 9.1: Typical Measures of Innovation used in Economic Studies

Measure	Type of measure	Advantages of the measure	Limitations of the measure	Implications for managers
R&D expenditure as a percentage of sales revenues	An input measure	• Data on investment levels are normally published in company annual reports	• This is an 'input' measure, rather than a measure of R&D output	• R&D expenditure (and intensity) of comparable competitors is a useful benchmark
Number of patents, per employee, or over time	An output measure	• Data are readily available and can easily be analysed by industrial sector, country, etc. • Useful (but not complete) measure of performance in research labs	• Patents are a measure of invention not innovation • Some companies may chose not to apply for patents, as it is a time-consuming process and it does not always offer good protection to small organizations • Different patents are not of equal value: some can be valuable, others worthless	• It is useful to monitor the number and contents of patents filed by competitors • Patent counts are also used as an indication of a knowledge base in mergers and acquisitions
Percentage of sales from new products	An output measure	• Is a measure of the output of R&D (but not strictly of innovation, unless product success is considered) • With some desk research, competitors' performance can be easily monitored	• The meaning of 'new product' is equivocal (e.g. different degrees of product innovation were discussed in Chapter 1) and this can lead to measurement problems • Figures on the numbers of new products developed by companies are not easily available	• Companies need to carefully define what 'counts' as a new product • Few companies use this measure to check the performance of their competitors
Efficiency: output to input	A ratio measure	• Easy to calculate • It should show the productivity of an 'innovation system'	• Due to the lag between investment and output, ratio measures have limited usefulness for innovation performance assessment	• Assessing innovation capability is wider than just looking at inputs and outputs

counts are a poor measure because only a few patents are really valuable. The second output measure is percentage of sales from new products – a popular measure, as found by a recent survey.[3] Clearly, it is hard to estimate this figure for competitors.

Economists are keen on ratio measures. For example, the ratio of outputs to inputs is widely used to measure the *productivity* of both nations and manufacturers. Using ratio measurements for innovation has a limitation – the time lag between the investment and the resulting output mentioned earlier. It should be noted that economists do not capture any element of the actual innovation capability of firms.

Broader Measures of Performance

Companies need a richer palette of indicators than economists. To generate a broader understanding of innovation measures, it is useful to apply the *input-output model* to innovation, as shown in Figure 9.1.[4] *Inputs* include the time and resources assigned, such as people and funding. The *outputs* must ultimately be the financial value generated by innovations, although, as observed, economists often use surrogates such as patents. The *process* connects inputs and outputs and, for innovation, this consists of key processes such as generating, choosing and implementing innovations. It has been found that the amount invested in R&D (an input) is poorly correlated with sales and growth (an output measure),[5] because not all the money invested in R&D leads to successful innovations.

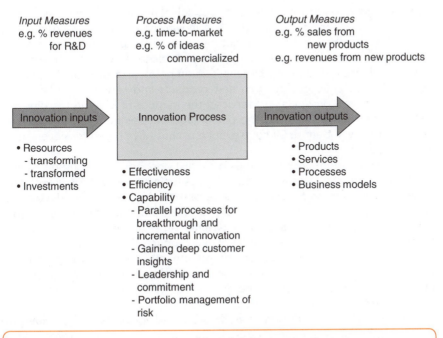

FIGURE 9.1: An Input-output Perspective of the Innovation Process

> **MINI CASE 9.1:** *Black & Decker – Measuring Innovation Performance*[6]

Black & Decker is famous for its power tools but it reserves a distinct brand – DeWalt – for its line of professional tools, such as drills and mitre saws. The company is well aware of the challenges of the professional market, in which the decision makers are looking for innovative, reliable and efficient tools and are not loyal to a single brand. John Schiech, president of DeWalt, chose a first-to-market strategy and has developed the core capabilities of his organization to support this strategy. For instance, he explains that deep customer insights are obtained by 'engineers and marketing product managers spending hours and hours on building sites talking to the guys who are trying to make their living with these tools'. Observing professionals working with power tools allows DeWalt to identify the problems and issues they face and develop products to solve these. Schiech says: 'It's only when you come with a breakthrough product that you can really change the game in terms of market share.' To be successful at breakthrough innovation, the company not only focuses on customer insights but also on rapid prototyping, in the 40–50 projects that are running at any one time. The first-to-market strategy has been very successful and performance is tracked using what DeWalt call *product vitality* – the percentage of sales from products launched in the previous three years. The level of this performance measure is typically around 30 per cent and some years it has even exceeded 50 per cent.

Selecting Measures

Measures are popular with managers but selecting the right ones is a challenge.[7] Our own case study research has shown that managers recognize this too,[8] although others have found that measures tend to be selected in an ad hoc fashion, rather than in a systematic way.[9] A recent survey of 1,075 companies by McKinsey[10] found the five most common measures to be (in order of priority): the revenue growth from new products and services; customer satisfaction with new products and services; the number of ideas in the pipeline; R&D as a percentage of sales; and percentage of sales from new products or services in a given period. Of course, none of these five measures covers innovation capability.

Choosing performance measures is context dependent – they should relate to an organization's business and the priorities for improvement. However, some general guidelines can be given. A range of measures should be selected that cover inputs, outputs and the process. Ratio measures are often useful, as they are easier to compare than absolute measures. An example of this would be taking the innovation rate as the number of new products ('new' is normally defined as less than three years old) compared to the number in the existing portfolio, rather than just the number of new products developed. Overall, the number of measures used must be appropriate because, as noted earlier, having too many measures wastes management time.

Prompted by the input-output model discussed above, Table 9.3 below provides a comprehensive set of measures for innovation, from which an organization can select the most appropriate ones. The measures listed go beyond finan-cial ones, as recommended in the well-known *balanced scorecard* approach of Kaplan and Norton (see Theory Box 9.1). A recent survey of 453 companies iden-tified the measures that are most widely used and so these have been included in Table 9.3.[11] Service organizations require specific measures,[12] which may also be relevant to manufacturing organizations that also offer services. Example measures for services are included in Table 9.3. Note that commonly used meas-ures such as patents and the percentage of revenues invested in R&D are less useful in service companies as benchmarking data are less likely to be available or to be reliable.[13]

In summary, organizations need to select measures that:

- Track the input resources being invested to different types of innovation (such as the golden ratio) and monitor whether these are sufficient to match the innovation strategy chosen.
- Identify if the level of innovation output is strong enough compared to the strongest competitors and leading companies in other fields.
- Help determine whether the innovation capability of the organization – the sum of the underlying processes that enable innovation – is increasing. This requires not only measures but also an assessment of the actions being taken to build capability.

THEORY BOX 9.1: *The Balanced Scorecard and Selecting Measures*

The well-known work of Robert Kaplan and David Norton of Harvard on the *balanced scorecard* has stressed the need for businesses to have a range of measures in addition to the classical financial ones. Such measures can help communicate management's vision and translate it into operational and individ-ual goals. The balanced scorecard approach recommends that every business needs to select measures that cover four categories:[14]

1. financial aspects
2. the customer perspective
3. the efficiency of internal business processes
4. an innovation and learning perspective.

Taking a broader, not just financial, perspective was also discussed in Chapter 6, where we rec-ommended that portfolio management should be based on a mixture of financial and non-financial approaches. Kaplan and Norton stress the importance of innovation, saying: 'We came to realize that innovation was a *critical* internal process.'[15] So their work supports the need to look for ways to assess innovation capability.

Research on business performance has shown that organizations use too many measures and thus fail to have the right focus, or measure things that are unimportant. Table 9.2 gives a set of questions to help guide the selection of a small group of activity measures that can be easily understood, and are reliable, appropriate and can be linked effectively to strategy.

Continued...

CHAPTER **9**

TABLE 9.2: Points to Consider in Choosing Performance Measures

	Aspect	Questions to ask about the potential measure
1.	Strategy	Is it directly related to the intended innovation strategy?
2.	Simplicity	Is it simple to understand and communicate?
3.	Action ability	Can and will it be acted upon?
4.	Appropriateness	Does it provide timely and appropriate feedback?
5.	Validity	Does it reliably measure what it is meant to?
6.	Reliability	Is it consistent, irrelevant of when or by whom the measurement was made?
7.	Clarity	Is interpretation of the measurement unambiguous?
8.	Behaviour	Will the introduction of the measure have any adverse behavioural affects?
9.	Cost-effectiveness	Is it worth the cost of collecting and analysing the data?

Source: based on Neely et al., 1997[16]

TABLE 9.3: Examples of Input, Process and Output Measures

Input Measures	Process Measures	Output Measures
Financial • Percentage of revenues invested in product R&D • Percentage of revenues invested in process R&D • Percentage of R&D budget invested in breakthrough and radical projects (the golden ratio) • Percentage of revenues invested in technology acquisition • Percentage of projects delayed or cancelled due to lack of funding	**Financial** • Average project costs • Project costs versus budget • Total cost of innovation efforts **Process efficiency** • Number of innovation projects • Number of projects at each stage • Average break-even time • Average time to market • Number of patents received/ number commercialized • Percentage mix of product/ process/service/business process innovation projects	**Financial** • Percentage of sales revenues from new products/ enhancements • Percentage of sales revenues from new services • Percentage cost savings/ revenues from process innovation • Return on innovation investment • Earnings from patent licensing • Profit from new products **Market parameters** • Market share trends • New product sales

TABLE 9.3: Continued

Input Measures	Process Measures	Output Measures
Customer or technology focus • Percentage mix of projects by their strategic drivers, e.g. meeting customer needs, reacting to competitors, technology versus customer driven, based on internal ideas etc. **Resources** • Number of people working on innovation work • Percentage of total employees involved in innovation projects • Number of ideas per source, e.g. ideas from employees, ideas from customers • Number of ideas generated per year for development into new products, services & processes • Number of ideas considered per year for new products, services & processes • Efficiency of links to external organizations	• Percentage usage of appropriate tools and techniques, e.g. advanced market research projects, computer-aided design, computer-integrated manufacturing etc. • Percentage of projects that entered development and were ultimately considered commercial successes • Percentage of projects killed too late, i.e., after significant expenditure • Percentage of employees actively contributing to innovation • Percentage of projects delayed or cancelled because of lack of resources **Learning** • Percentage of projects where post-project reviews are conducted • Number of improvements to innovation processes **Specific service measures** • Customer contact: time and degree of intimacy • Information exchanged with the customer • Customer throughput time • Staff satisfaction • Efficiency of innovations in products and service augmentations **Innovation capability** • Measures for capability are hard to define, so it is best assessed through an innovation audit (see text)	**Customer perspective** • Innovation rate – number of new products compared to total number in the product portfolio • Number of new products compared to competitors • Number of new services compared to competitors • Number of enhancements to service augmentations • Number of process innovations – number of innovations per year compared to the total number of major processes used in operations • Percentage mix of first-to-market, fast follower, and me-too products • Market share growth due to new products/enhancements • Market share growth due to new services **Intellectual property** • Number of new patents generated • Measure of importance of patents

Source: based on Goffin, 2001[17]

CHAPTER **9**

Assessing Capability – Innovation Audits

It is easier to identify measures for inputs and outputs than it is to identify measures of *innovation capability*, particularly as the latter is an emerging concept. Recent research has identified some key components of innovation capability to be: an organization's network of contacts, that is, open innovation, and its ability to generate deep customer insights;[18] plus having separate entities and processes for developing breakthrough innovations.[19] A company's full innovation capability is complex and so: 'Measuring performance is helpful, but it's only part of the story. To learn from our past successes and failures, we need to understand how they came about.'[20] Because of this, innovation capability is best assessed using an *innovation audit*. Innovation audits are different from financial audits, which are based on quantitative measures of financial performance, that is, output measures of past performance. Questions in innovation audits are mainly based on employees' and managers' perceptions. Although the answers are subjective, the range of answers from people throughout an organization (and even outside it) can help to identify an organization's strengths and weaknesses.

The innovation audit emerged in the 1980s. It was initially focused on creativity and took a multifunctional perspective, with audit questions to be answered by production, marketing, R&D, personnel and so on.[21] Later, audit tools have looked at all aspects of innovation management and their use has increased. The EU has given substantial financial support for companies to have innovation audits conducted by consultants – over 760 organizations in 18 countries have benefited from this.[22] The British Standards Institute developed an audit that looks at organizations, and product and service issues.[23]

Conducting Innovation Audits

The aims of an audit are to:

1. Identify an organization's innovation capability – the strengths and weaknesses of its innovation processes – by gaining the views of a representative sample of managers and employees.
2. Collect ideas on how to make improvements.

Innovation audits collect a mix of quantitative and qualitative data through survey techniques. They are best conducted by outsiders (who are neutral) interviewing a representative sample of employees, managers and, possibly, customers (all of whom can remain anonymous). Interpreting the results of an audit requires experience, which is one reason for using an experienced outsider to conduct the audit. Other reasons for using an outsider are that they can get employees' to comment candidly, and they can bring an informal element of benchmarking, by being able to compare the results with those they have seen in other organizations. That said, if outside resources are not available, innovation audits can be conducted by someone within the organization who is perceived as being trustworthy and reliable – and someone who others are willing of share their views of innovation with.

Since employees' views are collected using perceptional scales, the results are subjective, and the results for one organization cannot be directly compared with another. The cultural web (discussed in Chapter 8) can be used in conjunction with an innovation audit to collect information on how the culture of an organization impacts its innovation. The results of an audit may challenge the views of management and even disappoint them but the results should be seen as a call to action (see Mini Case 9.2 on Evotec).

▶ MINI CASE 9.2: *Evotec AG – Learning from an Innovation Audit*[24]

Evotec is a leading provider of biological, chemical and screening services, which help pharmaceutical companies accelerate the discovery and development process, manage risk, and reduce the time and cost of bringing new drugs to the market. The company has over 600 employees, many of whom are PhD scientists, based in Hamburg and in the UK arm, which was formerly Oxford Asymmetry International (OAI). Evotec has an impressive set of clients, which reads like a 'who's who' of the chemical and pharmaceutical industries and includes BASF, GlaxoSmithKline, Pfizer and Roche.

OAI used a team of consultants to conduct an innovation audit. Interviews were held with a sample of staff, covering all functions and levels and using a comprehensive set of audit questions. The results were revealing:

- staff rated OAI relatively low on creativity
- innovation was not perceived as sufficiently customer-led
- knowledge was not optimally applied in the company
- there was not enough communication between the two divisions (discovery and development)
- clearer rewards and recognition were needed.

Some of the management team were disappointed with the results and expressed the opinion that it did not reflect the OAI they knew and that the market view that OAI was already very innovative. Nevertheless, he audit seemed to show that management and employees viewed the potential for more innovation differently so the management team quickly set about making some significant changes.

The changes included major efforts to become more creative. For example, a knowledge management system was implemented to capture and share much of the expertise of individual scientists. This made the solution of clients' problems more efficient and helped identify innovations that would most impact the customer. OAI managers also worked on formal and informal communication. The bringing together of the two divisions in a new building made a big impact, as did a range of new reward and recognition schemes that spurred innovation.

Dr Mario Polywka, COO at Evotec, sees the innovation audit as an important catalyst:

> We probably would have made a lot of the changes such as implementing a knowledge management system anyway. However, the innovation audit helped galvanize our actions. We have seen a lot of returns on the investments we have made in our people, knowledge management, and communications. What is more, our customers have also seen many tangible benefits in the range and speed of services we offer to support drug discovery and development. For me, the biggest steps we have made are, first, that our employees now realize that being a service company involves significant technical creativity, but that also the way we do business, commercially and financially, is innovative in itself.

CHAPTER **9**

INNOVATION STRATEGY

- Does top management meet specifically to define innovation policy and to support innovation investment decisions?
- Do you have a clear/specific definition of innovation that is shared throughout the business?
- Is the main innovation strategy clear (for example, first-to-market or fast follower)?
- Do you actively monitor the operating environment to identify key trends and market drivers (for example demographics, legislation, changing needs, new technology, etc.)?
- Does the innovation strategy integrate all five areas of innovation management (ideas, prioritisation, implementation, people and strategy)?
- *What should top management do to make the innovation strategy clearer and more effective?*

IDEAS

- Is the general climate within all of our departments and functions supportive of the process of generating ideas?
- Do we take the opportunity to learn from and share experiences with other organizations ('open innovation')?
- Do we use structured problem solving approaches (such as brainstorming, TRIZ, scenario development, etc.)?
- Do we actively research, identify and capture customers' stated and latent (hidden) needs?
- Within our industry are we perceived to be a creative organization?
- *What should be done to improve the pipeline of ideas generation in our organization?*

PRIORITIZATION

- Do we have a specific system (as opposed to ad hoc arrangements) for screening and evaluating ideas?
- Does our portfolio prioritization process clearly link the choice of projects to our innovation strategy?
- Do we use both financial and scoring methods effectively and efficiently to evaluate our innovation projects?
- Do we have a clear and shared understanding of innovation risk – which allows us to objectively analyze projects?
- Is our current portfolio balanced (i.e. projects align with innovation strategy, they maximize value, and make the most efficient use of resources)?
- *What should be done to ensure the right projects are prioritised by our organization?*

IMPLEMENTATION (NPD, etc.)

- Do we have a systematic new product or new service development process? Are the steps integrated and do activities take place in parallel with each other?
- Do we ensure that customer and end user input is used throughout the process?
- Do we ensure that sufficient capacity is available in R&D, manufacturing, suppliers and support functions to allow fast and effective product development?
- Do we have a long-term (business) champion for each new product, new service, process and business model?
- Is our record of new products and services satisfactory when compared with our main competitors?
- *What should be done to improve the way our organization develops new products, new services, processes and business models?*

OUTPUT MEASURES

- Do new products and new services generate a significant amount of our total revenues?
- Have we introduced one or more new business models to the market in the last three years?
- Do we make our products and services more competitive through our process innovations?
- Are we are achieving significant growth through innovation?
- *What should be done to increase innovation output in our organization?*

PEOPLE AND ORGANIZATION

- Has management actively created and sustained a culture of innovation?
- Does our mission statement mention 'creativity', 'innovation' or both as being part of the corporate ethos?
- Is our employees' innovative and entrepreneurial behaviour encouraged, recognized and/or rewarded?
- Do we set aside budget and actively encourage training for staff in innovation-related activities?
- Do we have a budget set aside for 'blue sky' innovation projects and/or do we have a dedicated team working on innovation?
- *What should be done to improve the 'culture of innovation' in our organization?*

FIGURE 9.2: 'Fast Innovation Audit' Questions. See also www.som.cranfield.ac.uk/apps/innovationaudit/

Source: updated from: Goffin and Pfeiffer, 1999

The scope of the audit needs to be decided in advance, in terms of the number of people to be surveyed and the number of questions to be asked. Normally, a simple, fast audit will generate an initial idea of strengths and weaknesses and Figure 9.2 shows such a version, in which the audit questions have been grouped using the Pentathlon Framework. This determines in which of the five areas a company is stronger or weaker and whether output levels are sufficient. An 'app' of this audit is available at www.som.cranfield.ac.uk/apps/innovationaudit.

The fast audit can also be conducted as a workshop with managers, where their initial ideas for improvements and their views on the cultural web can also be collected. However, considering only the views of the management team is not sufficient (and can give a biased view). A representative sample from the whole organization is more revealing, as individual employees will give creative ideas for improving innovation. Direct interviews are more effective than distributing audit questionnaires, as vital information about the organization's workings can emerge in the discussion.

It should be stressed that Figure 9.2 represents a generic audit and some of the questions may not be appropriate for specific contexts, such as some service companies, or not-for profit organizations. A simple set of questions that can be integrated for service companies is given in Table 9.5. On our book's website (www.palgravehighered.com/gm), we give a comprehensive list of questions from a

TABLE 9.5: Innovation Audit Questions Recommended for the Service Sector

Number	Question
1.	Is innovation stated as part of your corporate objectives and business plan?
2.	Do you have at least two experiments or pilots of new service concepts being conducted at any one time?
3.	Do you regularly review your portfolio of service offerings to make sure that they are balanced in terms of novelty/innovation and risk?
4.	Is your objective to be the market leader by exceeding the value added of your main competitor?
5.	Does your financial reporting system reflect innovation as an investment rather than as a cost?
6.	Are you attracted by new technologies and considering how to apply them to your business?
7.	Do you provide support to staff who try out new ideas even if the ideas fail?
8.	Do you have a procedure for having staff 'mystery shop' the competition and report back?
9.	Do you provide training for staff in innovation-related skills?
10.	Do you expect to get at least 5% of export revenues from innovative services?

Source: Riddle, D., 'Managing Change in Your Organization'. International Trade Forum, 2 (2000), 26–8. Copyright © 2000 International Trade Centre. All rights reserved worldwide. http://www.intracen.org/publications. Reproduced with permission[25].

CHAPTER **9**

detailed review of the literature, from which relevant questions can be selected in designing a customized, or 'in-depth' audit.

An innovation audit identifies two things. First, it identifies the areas of the Pentathlon Framework in which an organization is strong and those in which it is weak. A typical result might be that the implementation processes are very efficient but that the front end fails to generate really innovative ideas. When related back to the Pentathlon Framework, most organizations perceive they are good in two or three areas and need to improve in the others. Second, an audit collects interviewees' ideas on how the innovation capability of the organization can be improved. The summarized results of the audit should be fed back to the organization and management. Once the weaknesses and ideas for improvement are known, then steps can be taken to make the changes needed. Typically, the more innovation ambition a company has (as discussed in Chapter 1), the more that change will be needed. This is because many organizations focus on incremental products and services. Companies that aim to change their golden ratio (the percentage of their investment in breakthrough and radical products) will require far-reaching changes in their innovation processes.

INNOVATION CAPABILITY – MAKING THE CHANGE

To increase innovation capability, significant changes may be needed in the way an organization approaches innovation, in its culture, and in its structure. Managers should be aware that in implementing these changes, resistance may be encountered. So they need to have patience and stamina because 'even starting to build an organization in which innovation plays a central role is often far more frustrating that most executives ever imagine it to be'.[26] Changes to organizational culture require management effort; much more than the superficial attempts usually made to manage culture.[27] Issues at the interfaces between departments may need particular attention (see Mini Case 8.10 on Fiat Iveco). Individual employees can be reluctant to accept change and so an organization can have an in-built inertia. The way in which an organization can best be changed depends on identifying those in favour of change and those against. Change management techniques help moderate resistance, as we will discuss.[28]

The Change Equation

Researchers, such as Michael Tushman at Harvard Business School, have found that three different factors are necessary to achieve organizational change: dissatisfaction, a vision, and a process for change. Each factor is necessary for change to succeed but none of them is sufficient on its own. Often, in management situations, one of the three factors is missing and so change is resisted. A memorable 'shorthand' is to express the relationship between these factors mathematically. The three factors are linked in the *change equation*, which should be read as 'the product of *D*, *V* and *P* needs to exceed *C*':

$$DVP > C$$

where *D* = dissatisfaction, *V* = vision, *P* = process and *C* = perceived cost of change.[29]

Note that the three factors, D, V and P, are multiplied together, and so if any are absent then the product will be 'zero'. All three are required to overcome resistance to change.

Perceived Cost of Change (C)

In applying the change equation, it makes sense to first identify what people perceive as the cost of change (C). People who resist change generally do not do so just to be awkward but because they perceive – rightly or wrongly – that the change, or the process of making it, will be 'costly' for them: that is, difficult, time-consuming, unpleasant, expensive, or any combination of these. The cost of change can be psychological, such as the fear of not being able to cope with new responsibilities, or that old skills will no longer be valued, or that their authority is being reduced.

In an organization, whole departments may perceive the cost of change to be high. For example, the techniques for identifying customers' hidden needs (discussed in depth in Chapter 5) are often seen as a threat by one department. And that department is marketing. Why? Because some marketing professionals perceive scouting groups and new techniques as a threat to their authority. So introducing hidden needs approaches needs to be treated as an exercise in change management.

Once the perceived cost of change from the perspective of all stakeholders has been identified, the costs of change can be addressed. Perhaps the costs can be reduced, or at least they can be discussed and then stakeholders may see them in a different light (see Mini Case 9.3 on how Ericsson encourages its employees to challenge the status quo). Attention should then switch to the other side of the change equation.

> **MINI CASE 9.3:** *Ericsson – Encouraging New Thinking*[30]

Ericsson, a Swedish company with a 140-year history and active in 180 countries today, is a world leader in communications equipment, software and services. It has 116,000 employees and, as over 25,000 of them work in R&D, it is not surprising that the company has an enviable stock of intellectual property – over 37,000 patents. In 2015 the company's sales were SEK 246.9 billion (€26.4 billion). Its products and services provide networks for more than 2.5 billion subscribers and a staggering 40 per cent of the

Continued...

world's mobile communications pass through networks delivered by Ericsson. However, as a large and successful company, the question is: How can a nimble, innovative and entrepreneurial spirit be kindled with 116,000 employees? One of the senior managers tasked with finding the answers to this question is Erik Chang.

Chang is head of strategy and operational development in Ericsson R&D Northeast Asia. His role is about creating and maintaining an innovation capability. He says: 'Being innovative is all about bringing R&D ever closer to the customer and being innovative in product and solutions for unmet customer need.' To do this, Ericsson is making extensive use of design thinking approaches and of R&D working in teams with marketing and sales to meet customers regularly. Chang says: 'We are also training and encouraging our engineers to challenge the status quo – we must provoke them to think in different ways.' As an innovation coach, he is widely involved in stimulating such thinking, and in designing NPD processes that will speed time to market.

An example of 'new thinking' is that when two engineers recognized that their development work was being slowed down by hardware simulations, they decided it must be possible to design a completely new way of conducting simulations that could be 10 times faster. Their questioning of 'accepted' timescales and practices led to a way to conduct the simulations overnight.

Inspired by the US west coast, Ericsson has also created its 'Innova' website, as a platform for collecting ideas and stimulating discussions. The original thought was to bring good ideas from Silicon Valley to Ericsson but now the site is generating ideas from around the world. Clearly, having a website to collect ideas is, on its own, no big deal. But the way Ericsson nurtures ideas has some clever variations. The Innova team has designed the 'governance' of Innova based on several elements. First, any promising project can receive venture capital-style funding. Venture capital funding means that the idea will never be granted full funding in one tranche; rather, it will only receive injections of cash at each phase. Second, and interestingly, the first funding is a prepaid $500 Visa credit card and one week's time – in which the idea's proposers must experiment and demonstrate the viability of their idea. Facing such a challenge brings out the best in people and if the initial week generates promising findings, then more funding and support is given. Here, the 'Innova squad' of internal innovation consultants can help the idea proposers, linking them, if necessary, to collaborative partners and universities. And innovations all follow a defined but flexible process. Chang summarizes: 'The new thinking we have introduced in Ericsson makes us aware that the way we do it today should not be the way we do it tomorrow.'

Identifying Dissatisfaction (D)

In overcoming the inertia to change that is inherent in every individual and organization, dissatisfaction with the status quo plays a key role. The reluctance to change must be overcome by galvanizing opinion on the need for innovation. This might be obvious to managers; so obvious in fact that they cannot understand why it is not seen as a priority by everyone in the organization. Change management experts often say that a *burning platform* issue is required. (The term comes from the Piper Alpha oil rig disaster in the North Sea. As the platform burned, workers were forced to jump from the inferno into a sea of burning oil. Fortunately, some of the workers who made this split second decision survived.) A burning issue in change management terms is an issue that readily motivates the majority to action, even if this involves difficult decisions.

In communicating the need to become more innovative, it is useful to consider:

- *Financial and market arguments:* Falling profits or stagnating growth can be pointers.
- *Customers' views on innovation:* These can identify end-users' frustrations and the need for all types of innovation (see Mini Case 9.4 on how Deutsche Bahn employees were encouraged to travel as 'normal' customers and identify customer 'pain points').
- *Employees' views:* People in organizations that are not particularly innovative normally recognize this and become dissatisfied (consider also the results of BuildCo's cultural web discussed in Chapter 8).

Where problems resulting from a lack of innovation affect different functions, 'shared dissatisfaction' will help overcome inertia.

> **MINI CASE 9.4:** *Deutsche Bahn – Pain and Personas* [31]

The German railway company Deutsche Bahn (DB) operates the long-distance railway system in Germany and to neighbouring countries in Europe. It has an annual turnover of €4 billion delivering 130 million 'passenger journeys' per year with its 45,000 staff.

Dr Michael Peterson, head of product management in the passenger transport long distance division, has been working to develop service innovations for the 10 million individual passengers DB serves each year. To do this, Peterson wanted to get to know DB's customers by interacting with them directly and he wanted his team to do the same. However, there was an assumption among DB staff that they already 'knew' their customers. This view clouded what was a lack of knowledge about the true customer experience. All Deutsch Bahn employees are issued with a card that allows them free travel and easy access to all the company's services. Due to this privilege, staff did not experience the same service as customers and wrongly believed they knew the customer experience. To refocus his team, Peterson requested his staff to 'put your DB staff travel-card into the drawer, buy your tickets yourselves, and experience our customer service'. As he says: 'There was some initial resistance but, after a couple of days, the team began to talk about the true customer experience. It enabled us to let go of our previous mindset and it had a dramatic effect on my team's ideas on innovation.'

Peterson and his team moved next to create 'personas' for their main groups of long-distance travellers. These are cartoons representing typical travellers and their needs:

> We didn't just focus on the 2 per cent of commuters who make up 30 per cent of our revenues, but on everyone and their reason for travelling. We then identified six personas, such as of course commuters but in addition businesspeople, young travellers, families and older people visiting family. These accounted for 95 per cent of long-distance travellers.

Next, DB identified the basic needs of each persona group, asking: What does a typical customer journey look like? What does our product look like to them? As a result of this work, it was recognized that the traveller's perception was of the 'end-to-end journey' but each part of this journey might be delivered by different divisions within DB. And detailed analysis identified a total of up to 350 'pain

Continued...

CHAPTER **9**

points' that could be associated with the customer experience of long-distance travel with Deutsche Bahn. Petersen says:

> To achieve a basic level of quality we needed to remove these pain points. We determined that 60 per cent of them were common across all persona groups. And then we set about eliminating them, one by one. For example, one pain point we got rid of was missing seat reservations for daily commuters. We recognized that this is important to them, also in terms of appreciation. This means that customers now can enjoy reserved seats on regional trains, to be rolled-out further, also to long-distance trains in the near future.

The focus on personas and pain points is expected to contribute significantly to big improvements in customer satisfaction but the customer orientation of Peterson's team has led to further innovations such as the inter-city express portal. This now allows for real-time information about the current train ride, information on changes in the schedule and automatically opens a train-bound ticket for other trains in case of incidents in the system. In addition, customers can learn about points of interests along the track, get to know their destination better and enjoy the latest news.

Peterson also believes that his team's customer orientation leads to more and faster innovation:

> The most energizing thing is this customer-centricity. DB is a complex organization, so different stakeholders previously fought over responsibility and initiatives. Now we have communicated the traveller personas to everyone internally, all DB staff can understand and help 'make life better for customers'. Suddenly, we have all the divisions around the table. And we provide them with extensive customer data, as our team is constantly engaged in direct interactions with customers, rather than working through market research agencies. My own team is now much closer to the traveller and this makes all the difference.

Case contributed by Julian Glyn-Owen.

Creating the Vision (V)

Every innovation management programme needs a vision, which should be not only inspiring but also realistic: 'When a vision is clear, consistently articulated, and widely shared, decisions throughout the organization can be made in a more consistent, directed way.' However, research shows that the way management communicates often only gives employees a vague idea of the vision.[32] For an organization with the right capabilities, the vision of being the industry first-mover can be appropriate (see Mini Case 9.5 on Dairymaster).

Overall, the innovation vision should address some or all of the following issues:

- How customers will directly benefit from the improved products, services and processes that will result from greater innovation performance.
- How quickly innovations will be developed: Is the organization first to market, or a follower? Should it be faster to market?
- The ways in which innovation will make significant improvements to an organization's competitive position.

MINI CASE 9.5: *Dairymaster – Milking Innovation* [33]

Dairymaster is a multi-award-winning Irish company that has become a world leader in the development and manufacture of dairy technology. Since it was founded in 1968 in Causeway, Co Kerry, it has grown exponentially. It now has operations in the UK and the US, and it exports products such as milking equipment, automatic feeders, milk cooling tanks and animal health and fertility monitoring systems to customers in 40 countries.

Dr Edmond Harty, CEO, says: 'Dairymaster has differentiated itself by constantly innovating. One of the secrets of our success is that we apply technology and innovation to make better products that offer farmers significant performance advantages.' An example of Dairymaster's innovation is its SwiftCool technology offering high-efficiency milk cooling combined with intelligent control and remote monitoring. For instance, if a relief milker is on duty, the farmer can access up-to-date information on the status of the milk tank using their mobile phone. If the relief milker has forgotten to start the cooling, the farmer can initiate the process remotely.

Another example of the way Dairymaster differentiates is its Swiftflo Commander system. This is the next generation of milking parlour control, integrating milking, feeding and animal health, as well as providing farmers with more information when and where it's needed – at the cow milking point. The system allows farmers to act immediately on information such as high somatic cell count (SCC) – a key bioindicator of milk quality. It also prompts the farmer to do a California Milk Test when high SCC values are detected. As a consequence, the diagnosis and treatment of cows is much faster. Other innovative features include speech technology (to update farmers effortlessly on information at a point when they can react to it), and an in-house designed touch-screen technology, which allows the system to be used even while wearing gloves.

A characteristic of all Dairymaster's products is that they solve real issues that dairy farmers regularly face. Dr Harty notes:

> In order for a cow to produce milk, it must have a calf. The cow's oestrus cycle is limited – approximately 21 days in length – and that period needs to be accurately identified. A single missed oestrus cycle can cost a farmer about €250 per cow. Clearly, eliminating such problems can make an enormous difference in a farm's profitability.

For example, the MooMonitor+ is a health and fertility monitoring device. Worn around a cow's neck, it monitors the cow's activity and behaviour, allowing it to determine whether or not the cow is in heat, or is sick. Sometimes described as the 'dairy satnav', it continually transmits information on individual cows and entire herds to smartphones and tablets via an app. MooMonitor+ helps optimize the animal breeding process, thus resulting in more calves and healthier cows performing at their peak levels.

Dairymaster's CEO won the Irish Ernst & Young Entrepreneur of the Year Award in 2012. The company subsequently won the world's top three awards for agricultural innovation, including the Eurotier Gold Medal for its Swiftflo Goat Rotary. Capable of milking up to 1,300 goats per hour, Swiftflo is designed to deliver optimum operator and animal comfort. The robotic presentation of the milking cluster directly under the goat's teats allows farmers achieve an attachment rate of less than 2.5 seconds per animal.

Increased demand for Dairymaster's products is largely due to its development teams' problem-solving techniques and methodologies, which have been honed over almost five decades of intensive R&D activity in all aspects of dairy farming and dairy herd management. Farmers value the high-performance capabilities of Dairymaster equipment and the technologically advanced solutions that make dairy farming more profitable by reducing long-term costs and labour inputs. Farmers also appreciate that better

Continued...

CHAPTER **9**

products can improve animal welfare. For example, Dairymaster's systems milk cows and goats in a more natural way – and faster – thus ensuring better udder health.

Another key factor in the company's continuing success is its personal approach. As Dr Harty observes:

> Accessibility to our customers ensures that communication doesn't end with the sale of a particular product. Our after-care service, ongoing interactions with customers – coupled with customer support and constant monitoring of product performance in the marketplace – give the company an up-to-the-minute understanding of all aspects of the industry as it evolves.

This in-depth industry knowledge has allowed parallel development of products to satisfy the different needs of dairy farmers in dozens of countries around the world. In many cases, these products ensure that farmers produce more food – and capture more value – from fewer resources.

Dr Harty says: 'In today's competitive economy, listening to the customer is critical. Our customers include farmers with herd sizes ranging from 40 to 10,000 cows. These customers' needs are constantly evolving. That's why we will never stop listening, and we will never stop innovating.'

Case contributed by Claire McBride.

Developing the Change Process (P)

Once people understand the need for an innovation and have a vision of what it will mean, they also need to believe that it can, and will, be achieved. Managers need to articulate a clear link between the current and the future state of their organization in order for employees to understand how the change can be achieved.[34]

The starting point of the change process is crucial. An innovation capability improvement programme is best linked to a particular project, the success of which can act as a signal that can fire up the whole organization. A project that is large and very high risk should not be selected; the project chosen should present a reasonable challenge. Change management experts talk of the importance of looking for the 'low-hanging fruit', which are projects where success quickly brings considerable returns. Mini Case 9.6 on the Sellafield nuclear reprocessing plant explains how a process innovation, in this case the introduction of project performance reviews, was analysed using the change equation. This was a valuable way to identify how post-project reviews could be made acceptable to employees at the company.

MINI CASE 9.6: *Sellafield – Easing the Way for Change*

Organizations that run nuclear installations tend, for obvious reasons, to be very conservative. Managers at the reprocessing plant at Sellafield in Cumbria, UK were tasked with working out how to overcome the expected resistance to the introduction of formal post-project reviews (PPRs) into the organization. They recognized that the crucial group to be persuaded were their colleagues in the project management community so they treated them as the key stakeholders.

Continued...

Perceived Cost (C)

The main costs were seen as:

- the difficulty of getting all the players together for a meeting
- the possibility of wasting time on what could be a short-term management fad
- the fact that some of the lessons would be painful to learn.

The first two costs were addressed by scheduling the reviews as part of the formal, documented project management process and holding them off-site in an informal atmosphere. Only project members would be present and they would decide what lessons there were to identify. A website would be set up to communicate results. However, nothing could be done to avoid the fact that the reviews are bound to be uncomfortable and possibly even acrimonious at times. So resistance would remain, as C could not be reduced to zero.

Vision (V)

The vision was not only of easier management of projects in future but also, crucially, that this innovation could be used as a way of raising the status of the project management function as a whole. To do this, a project management 'club' (a group of project management professionals at Sellafield) was proposed, which would meet regularly to discuss and identify best practices in project management in the Sellafield context. This group would report every six months to the technical director (later the executive management team).

Dissatisfaction (D)

Dissatisfaction with the status quo came from pressure from peers in the project management community recognizing that PPRs were 'the professional thing to do'. But, more subtly, the improved status that would come from contributing to the knowledge about project management at Sellafield, and having regular meetings with the technical director made not doing PPRs unattractive.

Process (P)

To make the process believable, the team looked for examples from other sites that could be used to demonstrate that PPRs really can be effective in practice, not just in theory. And before fully rolling out the process, a couple of pilots were planned to demonstrate how it could be done at Sellafield.

Leading Change Management

Just as a new product development project is dependent on a product champion, so change management is dependent on an effective *change agent*. In selecting the path forward, the change agent needs to be particularly careful to avoid trying to simply adopt best practice.[35] It is far better to consider the context of the organization in which change is deemed necessary and adapt ideas rather than simply adopting them. The way in which an organization can best be changed depends on identifying those in favour of change and those against. Plans should be made for both of these groups; how to make best use of allies and turn adversaries into allies. The change agent has a wide range of choices on how to go about change and needs to answer a number

CHAPTER 9

of questions. Do we need radical and fast change? Should it be organized to cascade down from senior management? Should external consultants be used to promote the changes? The answers to these questions flow into the plan for change. Performance measures should form an integral part of the change process, as they allow challenging but realistic goals to be set and progress monitored.

Leadership by the change agent is fundamentally important in pulling all the strands of innovation together, as 'an organization's capacity to innovate is affected far more by those who set the environment in which innovation is to occur and manage innovative activities than those who undertake the creative work'.[36] This means that top management will need to reserve sufficient time to drive and communicate the role and goals of innovation. An increasingly common approach is to create a specific role: innovation manager.

▶ MINI CASE 9.7: *Ferrovial and Amey – High-vis Innovation*[37]

The Spanish company Ferrovial is one of the world's leading infrastructure management and investment companies. It employs approximately 65,000 employees and operates in over 25 countries, generating €8.2 billion in revenues in 2015. Ferrovial Services includes the UK company Amey plc, which has 22,000 employees and revenues of £2.4 billion, earned from managing and running significant parts of the UK's infrastructure, such as roads, railways and airports.

Amey was founded as a quarrying company in 1921 but it has grown to offer a wide range of services. These include facility management and energy efficiency, infrastructure maintenance, environmental services including waste treatment and disposal, asset lifecycle management, maintenance of transport infrastructure, and maintenance of utility infrastructure (gas, electricity and water). Many of the front-office employees from Amey wear high-visibility safety jackets in their daily work in, for example, motorway maintenance. So, although many people in the UK do not know the company name, most people will unknowingly glimpse an Amey employee almost every day.

The management board at Amey asked four questions to help them develop their innovation strategy:

1. Do we have a consistent collective understanding of what we mean by innovation and why we need to innovate?
2. Are we clear about our innovation priorities and our appetite for risk/time horizon for innovation?
3. Do we have the most effective operating model in place and clear accountabilities for innovation?
4. Are there some quick, practical things we could do differently to improve our approach?

Working with the senior management team, David Epps, the strategy director, developed tools and methods. These clarified the nature of innovation at Amey – it was defined as the implementation of anything that added value for customers – and developed processes for managing the portfolio of innovation ideas, implementing the chosen ones, and creating the right culture. For implementation, a simple process was designed that used ideas from the Stage-Gate® philosophy but which were simplified for services. As can be seen from Figure 9.3, the first stage of this process was listening to customers to understand their unmet and future needs.

Continued...

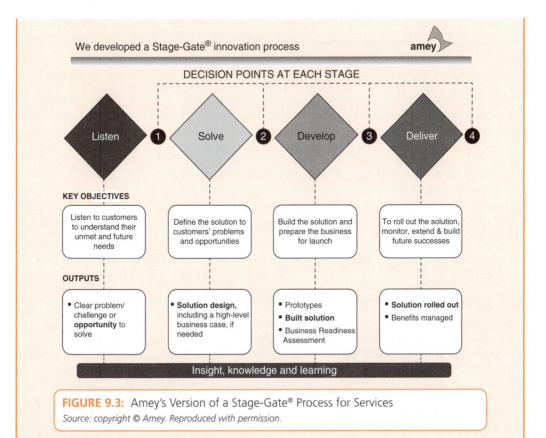

We developed a Stage-Gate® innovation process   amey

DECISION POINTS AT EACH STAGE

Listen — 1 — Solve — 2 — Develop — 3 — Deliver — 4

KEY OBJECTIVES

| Listen to customers to understand their unmet and future needs | Define the solution to customers' problems and opportunities | Build the solution and prepare the business for launch | To roll out the solution, monitor, extend & build future successes |

OUTPUTS

| • Clear problem/ challenge or **opportunity** to solve | • **Solution design,** including a high-level business case, if needed | • Prototypes
• **Built solution**
• Business Readiness Assessment | • **Solution rolled out**
• Benefits managed |

Insight, knowledge and learning

FIGURE 9.3: Amey's Version of a Stage-Gate® Process for Services
Source: copyright © Amey. Reproduced with permission.

In a company with so many frontline employees, Epps knew it was essential to get the full involvement of the employees from the 'sharp end' of the business. Therefore, he put a lot of time and effort into making an inclusive website, which explained innovation and championed employees' ideas, by giving many case studies of successful ideas. He know that the scheme was having effect when the number of ideas submitted to be considered by a management 'Dragons' Den' increased significantly. Epps says: 'Innovation must pervade all parts of Amey and become part of our culture. And when I saw that the vast majority of the employees receiving the company's annual innovation awards were wearing high-vis jackets, I knew we were getting there.'

The Role of an Innovation Manager

One of the first companies to create an innovation manager was AXA Ireland in 2000 (see Mini Case 3.8) and the new manager faced the challenge of defining the role as there was no precedent. Fifteen years later, innovation management as a subject is much better defined and many companies have started to create positions for innovation managers. And the first certified courses for innovation managers are starting to appear. The role varies from company to company but a key component is enabling change and overcoming resistance (see Mini Case 9.8 on someone who has experience of overcoming resistance to innovation in different sectors and organizations).

CHAPTER 9

> **MINI CASE 9.8:** *Magnus Schoeman – A Man for All Sectors*[38] *with video interview*

What does the role of 'innovation manager' entail? One person who is more than able to answer this question is Dr Magnus Schoeman. He has managed innovation in management roles in manufacturing, in a healthcare scientific setting, in the public sector, in the commercial service sector, and now as client executive with Atos.

First stops: having trained as a microbiologist and conducted post-doctoral research, Schoeman joined Rio Tinto Borax as a specialist on wood preservative products. In this position, he gained experience of new product development and, studying for an Exec-MBA in parallel with his job, gave him the opportunity to focus on innovation management methods and learn how to make Stage-Gate® Processes faster.

Next stop was a significant personal change; he moved to the UK's Department of Health, where he was responsible for working with scientists to commercialize new technologies emerging from research institutes. Schoeman says:

> This was a formative experience for me; scientists in the public sector had the luxury of not needing to be focused on commercial outcomes but the barriers to innovation were just as great as in the private sector. A major blocker was the mindset of researchers who felt that patenting inventions would stifle knowledge transfer.

Eventually, Schoeman did manage to take a number of new technologies to market – by working with the more cooperative scientists and addressing institutional issues such as reward schemes for inventors.

Next stop was the public sector, where he worked at the UK Passport Service to transform the processes and technologies connected with issuing documents. He says: 'In the public sector you have to learn to do more with less, as resources are always limited. However, that can be a good discipline – when people are challenged it is amazing the solutions they come up with.'

After the public sector, next stop was the UK Post Office, where he was responsible for innovation in the range of services offered at post offices and also the way in which they are delivered. He says of that experience: 'That taught me the importance in understanding customers' perceptions of services. Because they are intangible, understanding services is challenging.'

Schoeman is now with Atos, an international company that employs 100,000 'business technologists' worldwide. He works in a centrally important role in the organization, the 'client executive'. The role is focused on taking the end-customer perspective and driving the required digital transformation: that is, process innovation and business change. Typically, he helps organizations such as government departments understand how IT can deliver performance improvements. This involves working with the organizations to help staff members adopt 'helpful' behaviours towards new technologies. But is also involves constantly challenging the status quo. He says: 'For example, at Atos we investigate how technology can create new concepts and our "zero email" is an initiative to see how we can help reclaim time that organizations lose to low-value activities.'

Having experience of managing innovation in a full range of sectors, Schoeman has advice for innovation managers:

> There are some differences between the sectors that need to be considered but, fundamentally, innovation managers need to create the right culture and processes for driving innovation. No process equals 'no innovation'. But too rigid a process will stifle innovation. So, innovation managers need to strike the right balance between creating formal processes and achieving innovation by less formal ways, such as developing a supportive culture. You need to align processes and systems with the 'softer factors of recognition and reward'. There is no set way to achieve

Continued...

this, so that is where an innovation manager needs to develop their intuition, to sense how their actions are perceived. Innovation processes can make it possible but it is still the people, the teams and the enthusiasm that make things happen.

Going back to his first stop as a microbiologist, Schoeman likes to use a metaphor from immunology, saying: 'An innovation manager has to deal with organizational "antibodies". In any organization there are people, processes and a history that may cause resistance to innovation. Good innovation managers have to find creative and fast ways of dealing with these!'

Now visit www.palgravehighered.com/gm to watch Magnus Schoeman discussing his recommendations for innovation managers.

Companies like Ingersoll Rand, Hilton Worldwide, Arla Foods, Kimberly-Clark and MasterCard have all advertised for innovation managers in 2016. For example, Kimberly-Clark's post reports to a 'director innovation capabilities' and the role includes driving product and helping build innovation capability (see Figure 9.4). So being an innovation manager is an exciting, challenging role that few can aspire to.

MANAGER INNOVATION CAPABILITIES

Job Description Number#1600024

Reports to: Director Innovation Capabilities

Role Accountabilities

- Accountable to provide the business with the project management support and tools needed to accomplish the business goals
- Accountable for the daily activities and the results of the innovation project management process and tools team to drive continuous improvements and tight integration with IMF and Portfolio Management
- Drives the identification and implementation of a global Innovation Project Management support structure
- Ensures that projects are effectively and efficiently moved through the process including tracking mechanism to understand base line performance and improvement opportunities
- Accountable for improved project planning and execution in K-C
- Drive the use of customer feedback to continuously improve project management process and tools as appropriate
- Support Cross Functional Project Leaders and Program Leaders to develop sustainable project management capabilities
- Work closely together with the Global Network Leader to drive the use of our processes and tools around the globe

---

FIGURE 9.4: Recruitment Advert for Manager Innovation Capabilities at Kimberly-Clark[39]
Source: copyright © Kimberly-Clark. Reproduced with permission.

- Accountable for project leaders making use of project critical success drivers to ensure projects are being planned and managed to maximize in-market success
- Provide comprehensive technical expertise with deliverable based, critical path project planning and Microsoft Project Server
- Works closely with IT and Supply Chain/CI COEs to drive corporate project management skills through training and standard tools

Main Purpose of Role
- Provide the business with the project management support and tools needed to accomplish their goals
- Provide oversight of a team project management experts and implement a project management support structure around the globe
- Lead the global project management process and tool owners' team
- Interface with the various innovation teams and leaders to understand their needs
- The role will both serve the project teams and drive adherence to the project management standards

Key Leadership Behaviors and Skills
- Proven track record of leading teams
- Successfully lead innovation projects through multi-functional project teams.
- Strong interpersonal skills to build relationships with business leaders and project leaders
- Essential Knowledge/Experience
- Experience in leading high performance teams
- Proven ability in Innovation, multi-functional Project Management and general business management
- Proven ability in influencing without authority that can be applied to project teams and their functional leaders to drive flawless execution

Job Requirements
- Bachelor's Degree required
- At least 10 or more years with innovation, project management, or relevant work experience
- Experience leading others
- Proficient with Microsoft Project preferred
- Experience in Change Management preferred
- Demonstrated ability to build strong relationships
- CPG experience preferred

Kimberly-Clark and its well-known global brands are an indispensable part of life for people in more than 175 countries. Every day, 1.3 billion people – nearly a quarter of the world's population – trust K-C brands and the solutions they provide to enhance their health, hygiene, and well-being. With brands such as Kleenex, Scott, Huggies, Pull-Ups, Kotex, and Depend, Kimberly-Clark holds No.1 or No. 2 share positions in more than 80 countries. With more than 140 years of history of innovation, we believe in recruiting the best people and empowering them do their best work. If fresh thinking and a passion to win inspire you, come Unleash Your Power at Kimberly-Clark.

Kimberly-Clark is an equal opportunity employer and all qualified applicants will receive consideration for employment without regard to race, color, religion, sex, national origin, disability status, protected veteran status, sexual orientation, gender identity or any other characteristic protected by law.

The statements above are intended to describe the general nature and level of work performed by employees assigned to this classification. Statements are not intended to be construed as an exhaustive list of all duties, responsibilities and skills required for this position.

FIGURE 9.4: Continued

POSTSCRIPT

Overall, this book has presented a concise framework – the Pentathlon Framework – to make the complex topic of innovation management easier to analyse and manage. Innovation management is developing rapidly and the current hot topics are open innovation and business model innovation. These topics are important but they will not solve all the issues an organization faces. The Pentathlon Framework reminds us that the goal is not only to improve *innovation performance* but also to build *innovation capability*.

In preparing this book, we have had extensive contact with innovation managers in different sectors. All of them find their role difficult and challenging, because innovation performance and capability cannot be built overnight. Such managers have the mentality of a mountaineer, who yearns to ascend an unclimbed peak, or to climb a mountain by an untouched face. By definition, an innovation manager must thrive in working with the new, the unfamiliar, with ambiguity, and with the uncertain. If you want to become an innovation manager, industry has a real need for people like you.

Summary

This chapter proposed a systematic way to measure innovation performance and develop innovation capability, while stressing that organizations will need to find their own particular way of achieving better performance. A full set of measures for innovation performance were collected, based on the input-output model but the advantages and the limitations of using these measures were identified. To go further than traditional performance measurement, the innovation audit approach was described, which can be an appropriate way to gauge innovation capability. An innovation audit identifies the areas of the Pentathlon Framework in which an organization is strong and those in which it is weak and it also generates ideas for improvement. Once all these are known, the change equation is an important tool for identifying where resistance may be encountered and how this can be overcome in a positive way. This chapter's main case study describes Corning's moves to build its innovation capability.

Management Recommendations

- Select and use performance measures to understand and help communicate the innovation performance of your organization.
- Use an innovation audit to determine the strengths and weaknesses of your organization in innovation management. Determine the priorities.
- Develop an action plan to improve performance at both the project and organizational levels. Reserve enough top management time to take an active part in leading the implementation.
- Use change management techniques to gain acceptance for your plan.

- Be aware that there is no 'silver bullet' for building innovation capability and it is management's responsibility to explore the best ways of achieving it in their own organizations.

Questions for Students

1. An old management axiom states: 'You get what you measure'. With this in mind, what are the possible problems with these measures of innovation: number of patents; number of ideas; proportion of staff involved in innovation?
2. Can a company be too innovative? What would be the symptoms of too much innovation?
3. The full financial value of a new product or service offering cannot be assessed for many years. Suggest some measures of success that could be collected in the shorter term.
4. You have been appointed as innovation manager in a medium-sized company. What will be your five key tasks in the first few weeks?

Recommended Reading

1. Balogun, J., Hope Hailey, V. with Johnson, G. and Scholes, K., *Exploring Strategic Change* (London: FT/Prentice Hall, 2nd edn, 2003). Not specifically aimed at innovation management issues but useful coverage of change management tools and techniques.
2. PwC Consultants, *Breakthrough Innovation and Growth*, PwC Report, www.pwc.com/gx/en/innovationsurvey. Interesting document based on a consulting company's experience.

▶ MAIN CASE STUDY

CORNING INC – INNOVATION TO THE RESCUE[40]

Corning has a long and distinguished history in innovation. The company made the first light bulbs for Edison in the 1880s and did revolutionary work on manufacturing techniques for light bulbs in the 1920s. Later successes included synthetic glass-ceramics used in many applications from missile nose cones to tableware, cellular ceramics for catalytic convertors, and specialist glass for applications in TV tubes, LCD displays and smartphones.

The company prospered greatly in the 1980s and stepped up its investment in R&D from 4 per cent of sales in 1995 to 10 per cent by 2001. COO Peter Volanakis said in the late 1990s: 'We are not spending enough on growth. When our next big product

happens we need to invest more of that largesse in other areas.' Corning invested heavily in the technology and production of fibre-optic cables and was well placed to profit from the boom in telecoms in the 1990s (it was also working on the opportunities in the photonics market, with the intention of becoming a supplier of complete fibre systems). But this success was a double-edged sword, and when the bottom suddenly dropped out of the telecoms market in 2001, the company almost dropped out of existence. Sales fell from $6.9bn in 2000 to $3.1bn in 2002. Corning posted a $5.5bn loss and the stock price fell from $113 to $1. Yet the company was back in profit and growing strongly again by 2005.

Reorganization and Recovery

The basis of the recovery was a renewed and disciplined concentration on R&D. The first, bold step was to centralize R&D, closing a number of satellite labs inside and outside the US and consolidating at the central facility in New York. According to Joseph Miller, CTO of Corning at the time, this halved the R&D costs from $620m to $320m but also 'made it easier to identify and involve people from multiple disciplines for each project. This cross-functional, multidisciplinary approach allowed for the generation of more ideas and the integration of more technologies in developing new or improved solutions.' As another manager put it: 'All of a sudden we saw barriers breaking down between divisions as we scrambled to save the best and the brightest.' A Strategic Growth Organization (SGO) was created, reporting to the CTO and staffed by equal numbers of technical and commercial experts. Its role was to guide the programme and nurture new business areas. A Growth and Strategy Council (GSC) had oversight of the new body and interfaced with the rest of the company.

With the new structure came a new emphasis on the innovation process itself. A new five-stage process was launched and a team of facilitators was trained to spread it and other good innovation practices throughout the company. The process emphasized the expectation of long-term investment and cross-functional working and required the regular involvement of senior managers in the technical innovation process. The five stages were:

1. Build knowledge
2. Determine feasibility
3. Test practicality
4. Prove profitability
5. Manage the lifecycle.

To help with the selection of new projects, managers researched past successes and failures and formulated their own 'Recipe for Success'. Major new business projects would be expected to demonstrate that:

- The product was a key enabling component of a larger system
- The requirements were demanding
- The company had a deep understanding of the customer's needs

- The solution involved a unique material and a unique process
- The solution was protected by strong intellectual property and/or a unique capital investment.

Patience Rewarded

As Corning worked to pull out of the crisis at the turn of the century, it was able to profit again from its long history of innovation and from the company's culture of taking the long view. As CEO Wendel Weeks said in 2009: 'Usually the first idea is not the right one; it is the second or third. So that means you have to sustain your people through failure. You don't punish failure.' Two examples that underpinned Corning's recovery illustrate this.

In the 1960s, Corning had invented the fusion overflow process for making high-quality glass and developed it, aiming for the car windscreen market. It met little success so it was shelved, but not forgotten. Then, in the late 1990s, the process found an application in the market for desktop computer monitor screens. Corning saw the potential, although the volumes were not great, entered the market and continued to develop its capability, even during the crisis period, thanks to the active backing and guidance of the SGO and GSC. The breakthrough came around 2004 with the explosive growth of LCD TVs that required pure, high-quality glass, and in high volume. Corning was ready to respond and by 2010 Corning's Display Technologies business had built a 45 per cent market share.

Further back still, in 1952, Don Stookey, a Corning employee, had accidentally invented the first synthetic glass-ceramic. It was harder than steel and lighter than aluminium and found applications as diverse as the missile nose cones to 'Pyroceram' serving dishes. Pyroceram was opaque but the R&D teams set about applying the knowledge to develop a transparent material with the same properties. The result was a remarkably strong and durable new glass marketed in the 1960s as 'Chemcor'. Although this was a technical success, it too failed to find an adequate market and never went into volume production. That is, not until 2005, when Motorola launched the 'RAZR V3' flip phone, which had a glass screen instead of plastic. This stimulated Corning to set up a team to see if Chemcor could be made thinner while retaining its remarkable strength and damage resistance. The team imagined a small but profitable market. Work was underway when Steve Jobs approached the company looking for a glass screen for the Apple iPhone. The new material, 'Gorilla Glass', was developed rapidly and, as the smartphone market took off, it soon became one of the fastest-growing products in the company's history. It is now used in billions of handheld devices worldwide. The second, 20 per cent thinner version of 'Gorilla Glass' was launched in 2012. A third version, with three times the damage resistance, was launched in 2013. And an antimicrobial version was launched in 2014. Corning is continuing to innovate and has more than rescued itself. Few companies have achieved such a dramatic turnaround.

Reflective Questions

1. As part of its consolidation, Corning concentrated its R&D on one site. This reduced costs and improved central control, but what might the longer term disadvantages be?
2. In general, what types of businesses benefit from an international distribution of R&D and which do not?
3. What do you think of Corning's 'Recipe for Success'? Could it be too restrictive in the longer term?
4. What aspects of company culture helped Corning's recovery?

REFERENCES
AND NOTES

1 UNDERSTANDING INNOVATION AND INNOVATION MANAGEMENT

1. Drucker, P.F., 'The Discipline of Innovation', *Harvard Business Review*, 76(6) (1998), 149–57.
2. Birkinshaw, J., Bouquet, C. and Barsoux, J.-L., 'The 5 Myths of Innovation', *MIT Sloan Management Review*, 52(2) (2011), 43–50.
3. Baxter, D., Schoeman, M., Goffin, K. and Micheli, P., *Public Sector Innovation: The Role of Commercial Partnerships* (Steria Consulting/Cranfield School of Management, 2010).
4. Case based on:
   – www.cambridgeconsultants.com/news/pr/release/112/en, accessed April 2015
   – An interview with Andrew Dobson in November 2008
   – www.tataglobalbeverages.com/media-centre/news/news-detail/, accessed April 2015.
5. Schumpeter, J.A., *The Theory of Economic Development* (Boston, MA: Harvard University Press, 1934).
6. Porter, M.E., *The Competitive Advantage of Nations* (Basingstoke: Macmillan, 1990).
7. Rogers, E.M. *Diffusion of Innovations* (New York: Free Press, 1995), p. 11.
8. OECD, *The OECD Innovation Strategy: Getting a Head Start on Tomorrow* (Paris: OECD, 2010).
9. Priessl, B., 'Service Innovation: What Makes it Different? Empirical Evidence from Germany', in J.S. Metcalf and I. Miles (eds) *Innovation Systems in the Service Economy: Measurement and Case Study Analysis* (Norwell, MA: Kluwer Academic, 2000).
10. Djellal, F. and Gallouj, F., 'Innovation Surveys for Service Industries: A Review', in B. Thuriaux, E. Arnold and C. Couchot (eds) *Innovation and Enterprise Creation: Statistics and Indicators* (European Communities, 2001), p. 74.
11. http://uk.businessinsider.com/drivenow-launches-in-london-2014-12?r=US, accessed April 2015.
12. Wagner, K., Taylor, A., Zablit, H. and Foo, E., *The Most Innovative Companies 2014: Breaking through is Hard to Do*, Boston Consulting Group Report (October 2014).
13. See www.akzonobel.com/news_center/news/news_and_press_releases/2015/tool-predicts-impact-fouling-control-coating.aspx, accessed February 2016.
14. Pisano, G.P. and Wheelwright, S.C., 'The New Logic of High-Tech R&D', *Harvard Business Review*, 73(5) (1995), 93–105.
15. Making innovation hard to copy in Formula 1 Racing has been studied by Professor Marek Jenkins of Cranfield School of Management. He says, "In Formula 1 motor racing the teams are always striving to keep ahead of their competitors. Typically everyone improves by around 1/10 of a second every race that means you need to improve at a faster rate to pull ahead. If you can find creative ideas that the competition cannot easily detect – e.g. Renault's tuned mass damper which was located inside the nose of the car, or that they cannot quickly copy e.g. McLaren's F duct that required the other teams to complete further crash tests on their chassis, then you have some chance of staying ahead – at least for a few months." See also, Jenkins, M., Pasternak, K. and West, R. *Performance at the Limit: Business Lessons from Formula 1® Motor Racing* Cambridge University Press, 3rd Edition 2016.
16. Anonymous, 'Deutlich kleinere Dose, aber gleiche Erbiebigkeit', *Unilever Magazin DACH* (Germany, Austria and Switzerland) (Jahresheft 2014), pp. 16–17.
17. Op. cit., OECD, 2010.
18. Based on unpublished research by Goffin.
19. Case based on:
   – Sekhar, A., 'At Your Service: Your Wish is Their Command at Les Concierges', *Asian Business*, 37(5) (2001), 48–9
   – www.lesconcierges.co.in/, accessed April 2015
   – A telephone interview with Dipali Sikand conducted by Keith Goffin on 29 July 2015.
20. Booz-Allen and Hamilton, *New Products Management for the 1980s* (New York: Booz-Allen and Hamilton Inc., 1982).

Chapter 1 References and Notes

21. Deszca, G., Munro, H. and Noori, H., 'Developing Breakthrough Products: Challenges and Options for Market Assessment', *Journal of Operations Management*, 17(6) (1999), 613–30.
22. Ibid., p. 613.
23. Nagji, B. and Tuff, G., 'Managing Your Innovation Portfolio', *Harvard Business Review*, 91(5) (2012), 67–74.
24. Chan Kim, W. and Mauborgne, R., 'Value Innovation: The Strategic Logic of High Growth', *Harvard Business Review*, 75(1) (1997), 103–12.
25. Op. cit., Wagner et al., 2014.
26. Op. cit., Nagji and Tuff, 2012.
27. Op. cit., Wagner et al., 2014, p. 12.
28. Proportions a and b match the golden ratio when their ratio is equal to the ratio of their sum to the larger of the two values, that is: $\frac{a}{b} = \frac{a+b}{a} = 1.61803$). Such proportions are found to underlie the beauty of nature and many works of art.
29. For a good overview of quality management see: Slack, N., Chambers, S. and Johnston, R., *Operations Management* (Harlow: Pearson Education, 5th edn, 2007).
30. Op. cit., Wagner et al., 2014, p. 10.
31. Markham, S.K. and Lee, H., 'Product Development and Management Association's 2012 Comparative Performance Assessment Study', *Journal of Product Innovation Management*, 30(3) (2013), 408–29.
32. Ibid.
33. The idea to compare the phases of an innovation to a funnel goes back to at least to: Majaro, S., *The Creative Gap* (London: Longman, 1988).
34. Wheelwright, S.C. and Clark, K., *Revolutionizing Product Development: Quantum Leaps in Speed, Efficiency, and Quality* (New York: Free Press, 1992).
35. Mansfield, E., *Economics: Principles, Problems, Decisions* (New York: Norton, 5th edn, 1986).
36. Goffin, K. and Micheli, P., 'Maximizing the Value of Industrial Design in New Product Development', *Research Technology Management*, 53(5) (2010), 29–37.
37. Goffin, K., 'Enhancing Innovation Performance', *Management Quarterly*, 13 (2001), 18–26.
38. Griffin, A. and Hauser, J.R., 'Integrating R&D and Marketing: A Review and Analysis of the Literature', *Journal of Product Innovation Management*, 13(3) (1996), 191–215.
39. Quote from: Morita, A., 'The UK Innovation Lecture', Department of Trade and Industry (6 February 1992), Video Number INDY J1800NJ, 5/92.
40. Sakkab, N.Y., 'Connect and Develop Complements Research and Develop at P&G', *Research-Technology Management*, 45(2) (2002), 38–45.
41. In writing this section, the following innovation reports were reviewed:
    – Thuriaux, B., Eager, R. and Johansson, A., *Getting a Better Return on Your Innovation Investment*, Arthur D. Little Report (2013)
    – Op. cit., Wagner et al., 2014
    – IBM, *Leading through Connections: Insights from the Global Chief Executive Officer Study* (IBM: Portsmouth, 2012)
    – PwC Consultants, *Breakthrough Innovation and Growth*, (2013), www.pwc.com/gx/en/innovationsurvey/, accessed March 2016
    – Capozza, M.M., Kellen, A. and Somers, R., *Making Innovation Structures Work: McKinsey Global Survey Results* (2012), www.mckinsey.com/insights/innovation/making_innovation_structures_work_mckinsey_global_survey_results
42. Op. cit., PwC Consultants, 2013.
43. Ibid., p. 14.
44. Op. cit., IBM, 2012, p. 7.
45. Op. cit., PwC Consultants, 2013.
46. Case based on:
    – Ramaswamy, K. and Modi, M., 'Singapore International Airlines: Strategy with a Smile' (Thunderbird: the American Graduate School of International Management, 2001), Case Study 07-01-0012.

Chapter 1 References and Notes

    – Heracleous, L. and Wirtz, J., 'Singapore Airlines' Balancing Act', *Harvard Business Review*, 88(7/8) (2010), 145–9.

47. Op. cit., PwC Consultants, 2013, p. 26.

48. Figure 1.5 is based on searches conducted in the ABI Database of academic publications. The eight terms were used to identify the number of articles.

49. Cooper, R.G., 'Third-Generation New Product Processes', *Journal of Product Innovation Management*, 11(1) (1994), 3–14. The Stage-Gate® Process is now a registered trademark of Stage-Gate Inc.

50. Boag, D.A. and Rinholm, B.L., 'New Product Management Practices of Small High Technology Firms', *Journal of Product Innovation Management*, 6(2) (1989), 109–22.

51. Op. cit., Griffin and Hauser, 1993.

52. Kandybin, A., 'Which Innovation Efforts Will Pay?', *MIT Sloan Management Review*, 51(1) (2009), 53–60.

53. Griffin, A., 'Evaluating QFD's Use in US Firms as a Process for Developing Products', *Journal of Product Innovation Management*, 9(2) (1992), 171–87.

54. Anonymous, 'A Dark Art No More', in 'Something New Under the Sun: A Special Report on Innovation', *The Economist*, 13 October, 2007, pp. 6–8.

55. Op. cit., Kandybin, 2009, p. 54.

56. Rogers, E.M., *Diffusion of Innovations* (New York: Free Press, 1995).

57. Flurr, N. and Dyer, J.H., 'Leading Your Team into the Unknown', *Harvard Business Review*, 93(12) (2014), 80–8, quote at p. 82.

58. Bower, J.L. and Christensen, C.M., 'Disruptive Technologies: Catching the Wave', *Harvard Business Review*, 3(1) (1995), 43–53.

59. www.prnewswire.com/news-releases/bestseller-business-model-generation-sells-1-million-copies-worldwide-283074051.html, accessed March 2016.

60. Case based on:
    – An interview with David Gluckman conducted by Chris van der Hoven in March 2016
    – http://lumkani.com/, accessed March 2016.

61. Chesbrough, H., 'The Logic of Open Innovation: Managing Intellectual Property', *California Management Review*, 45(3) (2003), 33–58.

62. Birkinshaw, J., Bouquet, C. and Barsoux, J.-L., 'The 5 Myths of Innovation', *MIT Sloan Management Review*, 52(2) (2011), 43–50.

63. Internet 'hits' based on Google searches conducted in May 2015. The data on academic papers came from the analysis used for Figure 1.5.

64. Carson, P.P., Lanier, P.A., Carson, K.D. and Guidy, B.N., 'Clearing a Path through the Management Fashion Jungle: Some Preliminary Trailblazing', *Academy of Management Journal*, 46(6) (2000), 1143–58.

65. Birkinshaw, J., 'Beware the Next Big Thing', *Harvard Business Review*, 92(5) (2014), 50–7.

66. Op. cit., Anonymous, 2007.

67. Balachandra, R. and Friar, J.H., 'Factors for Success in R&D Projects and New Product Innovation: A Contextual Framework', *IEEE Trans. on Engineering Management*, 44(3) (1997), 276–87.

68. Van der Duin, P.A., Ortt, R. and Aarts, W.T.M., 'Contextual Innovation Management Using a Stage-Gate Platform: The Case of Philips Shaving and Beauty', *Journal of Product Innovation Management*, 31(3) (2013), 489–500.

69. Goffin, K. and Pfeiffer, R., *Innovation Management in UK and German Manufacturing Companies*, (London: Anglo-German Foundation Report Series, 1999).

70. Op. cit., Birkinshaw et al., 2011.

71. Op. cit., Deszca et al., 1999.

72. Moss Kanter, R., 'Innovation: The Classic Traps', *Harvard Business Review*, 84(11) (2006), 73–83.

73. Op. cit., Nagji and Tuff, 2012.

74. Anthony, S.D., Duncan, D.S. and Siren, P.M.A., 'Build an Innovation Engine in 90 Days', *Harvard Business Review*, 93(12) (2014), 61–8.

75. Op. cit., Wagner et al., 2014, p. 21.

Chapter 1 References and Notes

76. Op. cit., Flurr and Dyer, 2014.
77. Op. cit., PwC Consultants, 2013, p. 34.
78. Jelinek, M. and Schoonhoven, C.B., *The Innovation Marathon* (Oxford: Basil Blackwell, 1990).
79. Case based on:
    – Hunter, J., Chan Kim, W. and Mauborgne, R., 'NTT DoCoMo I-mode: Value Innovation at DoCoMo', INSEAD-EAC Case Study, Number 303-04301 (Fontainebleau, France, 2003)
    – www.nttdocomo.co.jp/english/corporate/, accessed July 2015
    – Several company reports as cited separately
    – An interview in 2005 with Daniel Scuka, co-founder of Wireless Watch Japan, www.wireless watch.jp
    – An interview in 2008 with the Fujitsu technical director
    – An interview in 2010 with John Lagerling, then-manager of the DOCOMO i-mode Global Strategy Department in Tokyo
    – Two interviews in summer 2015 with Lars Cosh-Ishii, Mobikyo, www.wirelesswatch.jp.
80. NTT DoCoMo, 'The Use of Cell Phones/PHS Phones in Everyday Urban Life', *NTT DoCoMo Report* (November 2000).
81. NTT DoCoMo, 'Current Trends in Mobile Phone Usage Among Adolescents', *NTT DoCoMo Report* (March 2001).
82. NTT DoCoMo, 'Children's Use of Mobile Phones: An International Comparison 2013.
83. https://twitter.com/Wireless_Watch/status/594351082123362304.
84. Adapted from www.nttdocomo.com/corebiz/imode/why/strategy.html, used with permission.
85. https://www.nttdocomo.co.jp/english/corporate/ir/management/message/

2 INNOVATION IN CONTEXT

1. Edmund Burke, *Reflections on the Revolution in France*, in, for example, *Oxford World's Classics* (Oxford: Oxford University Press 2009).
2. Schumpeter, J.A., *The Theory of Economic Development* (Boston, MA: Harvard University Press, 1934).
3. Solow, R., 'Technical Change and the Aggregate Production Function', *The Review of Economics and Statistics*, 39(3) (1957), 312–20.
4. Rodrigo, G.C., *Technology, Economic Growth and Crises in East Asia* (Northampton MA: Edward Elgar, 2001).
5. Steil, B., Victor, D. and Nelson, R., *Technological Innovation and Economic Performance* (Princeton: Princeton University Press, 2002).
6. Aghion, P. and Howitt, D., *The Economics of Growth* (Cambridge, MA: MIT Press, 2009).
7. Bhidé, A., *The Venturesome Economy* (Princeton: Princeton University Press, 2008).
8. Arena, R. and Dangel-Hagnauer, C. (eds) *The Contribution of Joseph Schumpeter to Economics* (London: Routledge, 2002).
9. Burda, M. and Wyplosz, C., *Macroeconomics: A European Text* (Oxford: Oxford University Press, 2001).
10. Kondratiev's book *The Major Economic Cycles* (1925) is out of print. For a description of his work, see Vincent Barnett's article in *Encyclopaedia of Russian History*, at www.encyclopaedia. com, accessed March 2016.
11. McGuigan, J.R., Moyer, R.C. and Harris, F.H., *Managerial Economics: Applications, Strategy and Tactics* (Cincinnati, OH: South Western/Thompson Learning, 2002).
12. Koratayev, A. and Tsirel, S., 'A Spectral Analysis of World GDP Dynamics', *Structure and Dynamics*, 4(1) (2010), 3–57.
13. Op cit., Burda and Wyplosz, 2001.
14. Hanson, J.A., 'Innovation, Firm Size and Age', *Small Business Economics*, 4(1) (1992), 37–44.
15. See, for example, Bound, J., Cummins, C., Griliches, Z. et al. 'Who Does R&D and Who Patents?', in Z. Griliches (ed.) *R&D, Patents and Productivity* (Chicago: University of Chicago Press,

Chapter 2 References and Notes

1984), pp. 21–54; and Klette, T.J. and Griliches, Z., 'Empirical Patterns of Firm Growth and R&D Investment: A Quality Ladder Model Interpretation', Institute for Fiscal Studies London, Working Paper no. 25 (1999).

16. Wakasugi, R. and Koyata, F., 'R&D, Firm Size and Innovation Outputs: Are Japanese Firms Efficient in Product Development?', *Journal of Product Innovation Management*, 14(3) (1997), 383–92.

17. Geroski, P.A., *Market Structure, Corporate Performance and Innovative Activity* (Oxford: Clarendon Press, 1994).

18. Audretsch, D. and Vivarelli, M., 'Firm Size and R&D Spillovers', *Small Business Economics*, 8 (1996), 249–58

19. Brynjolfsson, E. and Kahin, B. (eds) *Understanding the Digital Economy: Data, Tools and Research* (Cambridge, MA: MIT Press, 2000).

20. Ibid.

21. Case based on research on innovation in the biotech industry conducted by Jan Rosier of University College Dublin. NB, the company and the drug have had to be been disguised due to the ongoing market situation.

22. Figures are from the EU Industrial R&D Investment Scoreboard: iri.jrc.ec.europa.eu/research/scoreboard.html, accessed March 2016.

23. The fifth driver was added to the original model of: Sheth, J.N. and Ram, R., *Bringing Innovation to Market: How to Break Corporate and Customer Barriers* (New York: Wiley, 1987).

24. Case based on: Taylor, E., 'Super Market', *The Wall Street Journal Europe*, 5–7 December (2003), p. R4; www.future-store.org, accessed March 2015.

25. Wei, C. and Wenwei, S., 'Age of Disillusion Haunts Senior Citizens', *China Daily*, 28 September (2012), p. 6.

26. Jordan, M. and Karp, J., 'Whirlpool Launches Affordable Washer in Brazil and China', *The Wall Street Journal Europe*, 9 December (2003), p. A8.

27. Winter, A. and Govindarajan, V., 'Engineering Reverse Innovations', *Harvard Business Review*, 93(7/8) (2015), 80–9.

28. Wouters, M., Roorda, B. and Gal, R., 'Managing Uncertainty during R&D Projects: A Case Study', *Research-Technology Management*, 54(2) (2011), 37–46.

29. Nicolas, T., 'Innovation Lessons from the 1930s', www.mckinseyquarterly.com, accessed February 2009.

30. Abernathy, W.J. and Utterback, J., 'Patterns of Industrial Innovation', *Technology Review*, 80(7) (1978), 40–7.

31. Based on Abernathy and Utterback.

32. Rogers, E.M., *The Diffusion of Innovations* (New York: Free Press, 5th edn, 2003).

33. Gould, S.J., 'The Panda's Thumb of Technology', in M.L. Tushman and P. Anderson (eds) *Managing Strategic Innovation and Change* (New York: Oxford University Press, 1997), Ch. 5 (reprinted from *Natural History*, Jan 1987).

34. Christensen, C.M., Suarez, F.F. and Utterback, J.M., 'Strategies for Survival in Fast-changing Industries', *Management Science*, 44(12) part 2 (1998), S207–20.

35. Moore, G.A., *Crossing the Chasm* (New York: Harper Business, 2014).

36. Ibid.

37. Ryan, B. and Gross, N.C., 'The Diffusion of Hybrid Seed Corn in two Iowa Communities' *Rural Sociology*, 8 (1943), 15–24.

38. Op. cit. Rogers, 2003

39. Op. cit. Rogers, 2003, Ch. 6.

40. Based on Rogers, 2003, Ch. 1, op. cit.

41. Chesbrough, H., *Open Imperative: The New Imperative for Creating and Profiting from Technology* (Boston: Harvard University Press, 2003).

42. Quoted by Chesbrough, 2003, op. cit.

43. Quoted in Chesbrough, H.W. and Teece, D.J., 'When is Virtual Virtuous?', *Harvard Business Review*, 74(1) (1996), 65–73.

Chapter 2 References and Notes

44. After Chesbrough, 2003, op. cit. and Docherty, M., 'Primer on "Open Innovation": Principles and Practice', *PDMA Visions*, 30(2) (2006), 13–17.

45. A detailed account of the venture is given in Takahashi, D., *Opening the XBox: Inside Microsoft's Plan to Unleash an Entertainment Revolution* (Roseville, CA: Prima Publishing, 2002).

46. Ibid., p 151.

47. A recent digest may be found in: Chesbrough, H., Vanhaverbeke, W. and West, J. (eds) *New Frontiers in Open Innovation* (Oxford: Oxford University Press, 2014).

48. West, J. and Rogers, M., 'Leveraging External Sources of Innovation: A Review of Research on Open Innovation', *Journal of Product Innovation Management*, 31(4) (2014), 814–31.

49. Mortara, L. and Minshall, T., 'Patterns of OI in MNCs', in Chesbrough et al., 2014, Ch. 12, op. cit.

50. Gassmann, O. and Enkel, E., 'Towards a Theory of Open Innovation: Three Core Process Archetypes', *Proceedings of the R&D Management Conference (RADMA),* Lisbon (2004).

51. Op. cit., West and Rogers, 2014.

52. Chesbrough, H., *Open Business Models: How to Thrive in the New Innovation Landscape* (Boston: Harvard Business School Press, 2006).

53. Piller, F. and West, J., 'Firms, Users and Innovation', in Chesbrough et al., 2014, op. cit.

54. Vanhaverbeke, W. and Chesbrough, H., 'A Classification of Open Innovation and Open Business Models', in Chesbrough et al., 2014, op. cit.

55. Op. cit., Enkel et al., 2011.

56. Chatterji, D., 'Accessing External Sources of Technology', *Research-Technology Management*, 39(2) (1996), 48–58.

57. Roijakkers, N., Zynga, A. and Bishop, C., 'Getting Help from Innomediaries: What can Innovators do to Increase Value in External Knowledge Searches?', in Chesbrough et al., 2014, op. cit.

58. Nambisan, S. and Sawhney, M., 'A Buyer's Guide to the Innovation Bazaar', *Harvard Business Review*, 85(6) (2007), 109.

59. Ford, S., Garnsey, E. and Probert, D., 'Evolving Corporate Entrepreneurship Strategy: Technology Incubation at Philips', *R&D Management*, 40(1) (2010), 81–90.

60. Ford, S. and Probert, D., 'Trial by Market: The BT Brightstar Incubation Experiment', *International Journal of Entrepreneurial Venturing*, 2(2) (2010),185–200.

61. Chesbrough, H. and Winter, C., 'Managing Inside-out Open Innovation', in Chesbrough et al., 2014, op. cit.

62. Burgelman, R.A. and Valikangas, L., 'Managing Internal Corporate Venturing', *MIT Sloan Management Review,* 46(4) (2005), 20–34.

63. Based on discussions with Corina Kuiper, with additional information from Mol, C.J. and van den Hurk, P. 'Innovation is about survival', *Philips Research Password*, 27 (2006), 12–15, quoted in Ford et al., 2010, op. cit.

64. Teece, D.J., 'Business Models and Business Strategy', *Long Range Planning*, 43 (2010), 174–94.

65. See, for example, the special issues on business model innovation in *Harvard Business Review* (Jan-Feb 2011), *Long Range Planning* (2010, 2013) and *R&D Management* (June 2014).

66. Case based on:
    – Extensive work at Coillte by Ian Kierans (ian@advancedorganisation.com) including numerous interviews with Ciaran Black
    – www.coillte.ie/, accessed March 2016
    – www.compassclub.ie/, accessed March 2016.

67. Op. cit., Teece, 2010.

68. Johnson, M.W., Christensen, C.M. and Kagermann, H., 'Reinventing Your Business Model', *Harvard Business Review*, 86(12) (2008), 57–68.

69. Ibid.

70. Michel, S., 'Capture More Value', *Harvard Business Review*, 90(10) (2014), 80–5.

71. Op. cit. Teece, 2010; Baden-Fuller, C. and Haefliger, S., 'Business Models and Technological Innovation', *Long Range Planning,* 46(6) (2013), 419–26; Osterwalder, A., Pigneur, Y. Bernada, G. and

Chapter 2 References and Notes

Smith, A., *Value Proposition Design: How to Create Products and Services Customers Want* (Hoboken, NJ: John Wiley, 2015).

72. www.vestergaard.com/our-products/lifestraw-carbon-for-water, accessed February 2016.

73. Girotra, K. and Netessine, S., 'Four Paths to Business Model Innovation', *Harvard Business Review*, 92(7) (2014), 97–103.

74. Adapted from Casadesus-Masanell, R. and Ricart, J.E., 'How to Design a Winning Business Model', *Harvard Business Review*, 89(1/2) (2011), 101–7.

75. Case study based on Prahalad (see below); Menon, R., 'Aravind Eye: Infinite Vision', *India Today*, 17 March (2009); and www.aravind.org, accessed February 2016.

76. Prahalad, C.K., *The Fortune at the Bottom of the Pyramid* (Upper Saddle River, NJ: Pearson Education, 2005).

77. Ibid.

3 SERVICE INNOVATION

1. Raja, J.Z., Bourne, D., Goffin, K. et al., 'Achieving Customer Satisfaction through Integrated Products and Services: An Exploratory Study', *Journal of Product Innovation Management*, 30(6) (2013), 1128–44.

2. Hughes, A., Moore, K. and Kataria, N., *Innovation in Public Sector Organizations: A Pilot Study for Measuring Innovation Across the Public Sector* (London: NESTA, 2011), PSI/68.

3. Bitner, M.J., Ostrom, A.L. and Morgan, F.N., 'Service Blueprinting: A Practical Technique for Service Innovation', *California Management Review*, 50(3) (2008), 66–94, quote p. 93.

4. Biemans, W.G., Griffin, A. and Moenaert, R.K., 'New Service Development: How the Field Developed, Its Current Status and Recommendations for Moving the Field Forward', *Journal of Product Innovation Management* (2016), doi:10.1111/jpim.12283.

5. See, for example:
   – Forfas, *Services Innovation in Ireland: Options for Innovation Policy*, report commissioned by Forfas from CM International (2006)
   – NESTA (UK) *Service Innovation in Services*, NESTA report NI/15, July (2008)
   – Bradshaw, T. and Turner, A., *Excellence in Service Innovation*, CBI/QinetiQ Report on Innovation in UK Service Sector Businesses (London: CBI, 2008).

6. Sheram, K. and Soubbotina, T.P., *Beyond Economic Growth: Meeting the Challenges of Global Development* (New York: World Bank Publications, 2000).

7. Based on the *CIA World Factbook*, accessed under www.cia.gov/library/publications/the-world-factbook/geos/eg.html (2015). The statistics are mainly for 2014 (refer to website for the latest estimates).

8. United Nations, *Manual on Statistics of International Trade in Services* (New York: United Nations Publications, 2002), p. 7.

9. United Nations, *Manual on Statistics of International Trade in Services 2010* (New York: United Nations Publications, 2010), http://unstats.un.org/unsd/publication/Seriesm/seriesM_86Rev1e.pdf, p. 4, accessed December 2015.

10. World Trade Organization, www.wto.org.

11. Extracted from: Bureau of Labor Statistics, Employment by major industry sector, www.bls.gov/emp/ep_table_201.htm, accessed December 2015.

12. Extracted from: *The 2014 EU Industrial R&D Investment Scoreboard*, http://iri.jrc.ec.europa.eu/scoreboard14.html, accessed December 2015.

13. See, for example: http://blogs.wsj.com/moneybeat/2013/10/14/heavy-rd-spending-makes-unprofitable-twitter-a-high-risk-rapid-ratings/, accessed December 2015.

14. Forfas, *Services Innovation in Ireland: Options for Innovation Policy*, report commissioned by Forfas from CM International, Dublin (2006).

15. Storey, C. and Easingwood, C.J., 'The Augmented Service Offering: A Conceptualization and Study of its Impact on New Service Success', *Journal of Product Innovation Management*, 15(4) (1998), 335–51.

Chapter 3 References and Notes

16. Wagner, K., Taylor, A., Zablit, H. and Foo, E., *The Most Innovative Companies 2014: Breaking Through is Hard to Do*, Boston Consulting Group Report, October (2014), www.bcgperspectives.com/content/articles/innovation_growth_digital_economy_innovation_in_2014/.

17. Johne, A. and Storey, C., 'New Service Development: A Review of the Literature and Annotated Bibliography', City University Business School, Management Working Paper B97/2, April (1997).

18. Bitner, M.J., 'Servicescapes: The Impact of Physical Surroundings on Customers and Employees', *Journal of Marketing*, 56(2) (1992), 57–71.

19. Bennett, D.J. and Bennett, J.D., 'Making the Scene', in G. Stone and H. Farberman (eds) *Social Psychology through Symbolic Interactionism* (New York: Wiley, 2nd edn, 1981), pp. 190–6.

20. Case based on: Lunsford, J.L. and Michaels, D., 'Aircraft Designers are Masters of Illusion', *Wall Street Journal Europe*, 25 November (2002), p. A5; and McCartney, S., 'Easing Cabin Pressure', *Wall Street Journal Europe*, 29 June (2005), p. A5.

21. Lunsford, J.L., 'Boeing "Dreamliner" Sets Ambitious Course', *Wall Street Journal Europe*, 18 November (2003), p. A10.

22. Thomke, S., 'R&D Comes to Services', *Harvard Business Review*, 81(4) (2003), 71–9.

23. Ostrom, A., Bitner, M.J., Brown, S. et al., 'Moving Forward and Making a Difference: Research Priorities for the Science of Service', *Journal of Service Research*, 13(1) (2010), 4–36.

24. Rich, M., 'Hospital Design is Tied to Health', *Wall Street Journal Europe*, 28 November (2002), p. A8.

25. Chesbrough, H., 'Bringing Open Innovation to Services', *MIT Sloan Management Review*, 52(2) (2011), 85–90, quote p. 87.

26. Verma, R., 'An Empirical Analysis of Management Challenges in Service Factories, Service Shops, Mass Services and Professional Services', *International Journal of Service Industry Management*, 11(1) (2000), 8–25.

27. Case based:
    – Discussions with DialAFlight staff in 2006
    – www.lotusgroup.co.uk/dialaflight.aspx, accessed December 2015.

28. Case based on:
    – Baxter, D., Schoeman, M. and Goffin, K., *Innovation in Justice: New Delivery Models and Better Outcomes* (Steria Consulting/Cranfield School of Management, 2011)
    – www.starr-probation.org/uploaded_files/Dagmar%20Doubravova.pdf, accessed January 2016.

29. Christensen, C.M. and Tedlow, R., 'Patterns of Disruption in Retailing', *Harvard Business Review*, 78(1) (2000), 42–5.

30. Case based on:
    – Prystay, C., 'Long-Distance Learning', *Wall Street Journal Europe*, 5 July (2005), p. A6
    – www.careerlauncher.com/aboutus/#, accessed December 2015
    – www.satyaspeaks.com/?videos=runway-to-success, accessed December 2015
    – www.satyaspeaks.com/?videos=3-start-up-secrets-for-new-entrepreneur, accessed December 2015.

31. Case based on:
    – www.maskargo.com/about-us/overview, accessed December 2015
    – Khan, A., 'Perceived Service Quality in the Air Freight Industry', PhD thesis, Cranfield School of Management (1993).

32. Magnusson, P.R., Matthing, J. and Kristensson, P., 'Involvement in Service Innovation: Experiments with Innovating End Users', *Journal of Service Research*, 6(2) (2003), 111–24.

33. Op. cit., Bitner et al., 2008

34. Froehle, C.M., Roth, A.V., Chase, R.B. and Voss, C.A., 'Antecedents of New Service Development Effectiveness: An Exploratory Examination of Strategic Operations Choices', *Journal of Service Research*, 3(1) (2000), 3–17.

35. Tyrrell, P., *Fertile Ground: Cultivating a Talent for Innovation* (London: Economist Intelligence Unit, 2009).

36. Metters, R., King-Metters, K. and Pullman, M., *Successful Service Operations Management* (Cincinnati, OH: Thompson/South-Western, 2003).

37. Menor, L.J., Tatikonda, M.V. and Sampson, S.E., 'New Service Development: Areas for Exploitation and Exploration' *Journal of Operations Management*, 20(2) (2002), 135–57.

Chapter 3 References and Notes

38. Op. cit., Biemans et al., 2016.
39. Thomke, S. and Manzi, J., 'The Discipline of Business Experimentation', *Harvard Business Review*, 93(12) (2014), 70–9.
40. Downes, L. and Nunes, P.F., 'Big-Bang Disruption', *Harvard Business Review*, 91(3) (2013), 44–56.
41. Ramdas, K., Teisberg, E. and Tucker, A., '4 Ways to Reinvent Service Delivery', *Harvard Business Review*, 90(12) (2012), 98–106, quote p. 100.
42. Tether, B. and Miles, I., 'Surveying Innovation in Services: Measurement and Policy Interpretation Issues', in B. Thuriaux, E. Arnold and C. Couchot (eds) *Innovation and Enterprise Creation: Statistics and Indicators* (Luxembourg: European Communities, 2001), pp. 77–87.
43. Sørensen, F., Sundbo, J. and Mattsson, J., 'Organisational Conditions for Service Encounter-based Innovation', *Research Policy*, 42(8) (2013), 1446–56.
44. Lillis, B., Szwejczewski, M. and Goffin, K., 'The Development of Innovation Capability in Services: Research Propositions and Management Implications', *Operations Management Research*, 8(1/2) (2015), 48–68.
45. Hipp, C., Tether, B.S. and Miles, I., 'The Incidence and Effects of Innovation in Services: Evidence from Germany', *International Journal of Innovation Management*, 4(4) (2000), 417–53.
46. Johne, A. and Storey, C., 'New Service Development: A Review of the Literature and Annotated Bibliography', City University Business School, Management Working Paper B97/2, April (1997).
47. Case based on:
    – Smart, P., Goffin, K., Jaina, J. et al., 'Creating a Culture of Innovation at AXA Ireland', Cranfield School of Management (2006)
    – Company information gathered in regular interviews from 2000 to 2015
    – An interview with the HR manager, March 2014.
    – http://www.axa.co.uk/about/our-company/
    – https://www.axa.com/en/about-us/key-figures
48. Op. cit., Raja et al., 2013.
49. Szwejczewski, M., Goffin, K. and Anagnostopoulos, Z., 'Customer Support and New Product Development', *International Journal of Production Research*, 53(17) (2015), 1–20.
50. Goffin, K. and New, C., 'Customer Support and New Product Development: An Exploratory Study', *International Journal of Operations & Production Management*, 21(3) (2001), 275–301.
51. Op. cit., Raja et al., 2013.
52. Anagnostopoulos, Z., Goffin, K. and Szwejczewski, M., 'Design for Supportability: Leading edge practices', *AFSM International – The Professional Journal*, 26(3) (2001), 50–4.
53. Case based on:
    – www.jura.com/, accessed January 2016
    – A visit to Jura in 2009
    – Ownership of a Z5.
54. Hawksworth, J. and Jones, N., *Sectoral and Regional Impact of the Fiscal Squeeze* (London: PwC, 2010).
55. Schoeman, M., Baxter, D., Goffin, K. and Micheli, P., 'Commercialization Partnerships as an Enabler of UK Public Sector Innovation: The Perfect Match?', *Public Money & Management*, 32(6) (2012), 425–32.
56. Bason, C., *Leading Public Sector Innovation: Co-creating for a Better Society* (Bristol: Policy Press, 2010).
57. Fuglsang, L. 'Capturing the Benefits of Open Innovation in Public Innovation: A Case Study', *International Journal Services Technology and Management*, 9(3/4) (2008), 234–48.
58. Op. cit., Hughes et al., 2011.
59. Case based on:
    – Baxter, D., Schoeman, M., Goffin, K. and Micheli, P., *Public Sector Innovation: The Role of Commercial Partnerships* (Steria Consulting/Cranfield School of Management, 2010)
    – www.metoffice.gov.uk/news/in-depth/overview#origins, accessed December 2015.
60. Chalmers, D.M. and Balan-Vnuk, E., 'Innovating Not-for-profit Social Ventures: Exploring the Microfoundations of Internal and External Absorptive Capacity Routines', *International Small Business Journal*, 37(7) (2012), 785–810, quote p. 805.

Chapter 3 References and Notes

61. Lee, R.P., Ginn, G.O. and Naylor, G., 'The Impact of Network and Environmental Factors on Service Innovativeness', *Journal of Services Marketing*, 23(6) (2009), 397–406.
62. Meyer, H., 'A New Care Paradigm Slashes Hospital Use and Nursing Home Stays for the Elderly and the Physically and Mentally Disabled', *Health Affairs*, 30(3) (2011), 412–15.
63. www.emmaus.org.uk/what_we_do/our_impact, accessed March 2016.
64. www.sciencedaily.com/releases/2015/09/150929112121.htm, accessed March 2016.
65. Caincross, G., Brennan, C. and Tucker, J., 'Innovation in the Not for Profit Sector: A Regional Australian Case Study', *Journal of Economic and Social Policy*, 16(2) (2014), Art. 11.
66. See www.bosch-stiftung.de/content/language2/html/389.asp, accessed January 2016.
67. Omidyar, P. 'EBay's Founder on Innovating the Business Model of Social Change', *Harvard Business Review*, 89(9) (2011), 41–4.
68. Case based on:
    – Interviews with Jeff Gould in February and March 2016, conducted by Keith Goffin
    – http://rnli.org/Pages/default.aspx, accessed February 2016
    – http://rnli.org/howtosupportus/Pages/How-to-support-us.aspx, accessed February 2016. Readers interested in supporting this charity should visit this page.
69. Case based on:
    – www.som.cranfield.ac.uk/som/p18956/Knowledge-Interchange/Management-Themes/Innovation-and-Operations-Management/Innovation-and-Operations-Management-News/Case-Study-CitizenM-hotel, accessed March 2016
    – www.citizenm.com/, accessed March 2016
    – Several stays at the CitizenM Schiphol, Amsterdam.

4 DEVELOPING AN INNOVATION STRATEGY

1. Anthony, S., Duncan, D. and Siren, P., 'Build an Innovation Engine in 90 Days', *Harvard Business Review*, December (2014), 60–8.
2. Case based on:
   – Aramex 2014 annual report and www.aramex.com
   – Friedman, T., *The World is Flat* (New York: Farrar, Straus and Giroux, 2006)
   – Ghandour, F., The CEO of Aramex on Turning a Failed Sale into a Huge Opportunity, *Harvard Business Review*, March (2011), 11–16
   – Interview with Mohammad Alkhas, Aramex CEO for the GCC, 25 October 2015
   – CEO View: Fadi Ghandour of Aramex, INSEAD Knowledge, 26 August 2008
   – Fadi Ghandour: Culture is the ultimate differentiator. YouTube video, 13 August 2015, www.youtube.com/watch?v=eU5AD_1Fv3A, accessed March 2016
   – Aramex founder Fadi Ghandour on company strategy, YouTube video, 6 March 2013, www.youtube.com/watch?v=8RucAxBBdY4, accessed March 2016.
3. Courtney, H. Kirkland, J. and Viguerie, P., 'Strategy under Uncertainty', *McKinsey Quarterly,* June (2000), 1–6.
4. Thanks to Dr Richard Schoenberg for sharing his slides on strategic management; and to Dr Tazeeb Rajwani for suggestions on this theory box (both of the strategy department at Cranfield School of Management).
5. Raduan, C.R., Jegak, U., Haslinda, A. and Alimin, I.I., 'Management, Strategic Management Theories and the Linkage with Organizational Competitive Advantage from the Resource-based View', *European Journal of Social Sciences,* 11(3) (2009), 402–17, quote p. 406.
6. Ibid.
7. Warnier, V., Weppe, X. and Lecocq, X., 'Extending Resource-Based Theory: Considering Strategic, Ordinary and Junk Resources', *Management Decision*, 51(7) (2013), 1359–81.
8. Coulter, M., *Strategic Management* (Upper Saddle River, NJ: Pearson, 3rd edn, 2005), quote p. 109.
9. Van der Heijden, K., *Scenarios: The Art of Strategic Conversation* (Chichester: John Wiley, 1996).

Chapter 4 References and Notes

10. Schwarz, P., *The Art of the Long View* (New York: Doubleday, 1991).
11. Ringland, G., *Scenario Planning: Managing for the Future* (Chichester: John Wiley, 1998).
12. According to Schwartz and Ogilvy in Ch. 4 of: L. Fahey and R. Randall (eds) *Learning from the Future: Competitive foresight scenarios* (Chichester: John Wiley, 1998).
13. Op. cit., Schwartz and Ogilvy, 1998.
14. Phaal, R., Farrukh, C.J.P. and Probert, D.R., 'Strategic Roadmapping: A Workshop-based Approach for Identifying and Exploring Innovation Issues and Opportunities', *Engineering Management Journal*, 19(1) (2007), 16–24.
15. Willyard, C.H. and McClees, C.W., 'Motorola's Technology Roadmap Process', *Research Management,* 30(5) (1987), 13–19.
16. Groeneveld, P., 'Roadmapping Integrates Business and Technology', *Research-Technology Management*, 40(5) (1997), 48–55.
17. Barker, D. and Smith, D.J.H., 'Technology Foresight Using Roadmaps', *Long Range Planning*, 28(2) (1995), 21–8.
18. See, for example www.public.itrs.net, accessed November 2015.
19. www.foresightvehicle.org.uk, accessed November 2015.
20. Phaal, R., Farrukh, C., Mitchell, R. and Probert, D., 'Starting-up Roadmapping Fast', *Research-Technology Management*, 46(2) (2002), 52–8.
21. Albright, R.E. and Kappel, T.A., 'Roadmapping in the Corporation', *Research-Technology Management*, 42(2) (2003), 31–40.
22. Osterwalder, A. and Pigneur, Y., *Business Model Generation* (Chichester: John Wiley, 2010).
23. Kano, N., Saraku, N., Takahashi, F. and Tsuji, S., 'Attractive Quality and Must-be Quality', in J. Hromi (ed.) *The Best on Quality*, vol. 7 (Milwaukee: ASQC, 1996), pp. 165–86.
24. Kano, N., Nobuhiko, S., Takahashi, F. and Tsuji S. 'Attractive Quality and Must-be Quality' (1984), Hinshitsu – Journal of the Japanese Society for Quality Control, Vol. 14, No. 2, p. 39–48.
25. Kano, N., Nobuhiko, S., Takahashi, F. and Tsuji S. 'Attractive Quality and Must-be Quality' (1984), Hinshitsu – Journal of the Japanese Society for Quality Control, Vol. 14, No. 2, p. 39-48. Cited in Matzler, K. and Hinterhuber, H., 'How to Make Product Development Projects More Successful by Integrating Kano's Model of Customer Satisfaction into Quality Function Deployment', *Technovation*, 18(1) (1998), 25–38.
26. Foster, R., *Innovation: The Attacker's Advantage* (New York: Summit Books, 1986).
27. Roussel, P.A., Saad, K.N. and Erickson, T.J., *Third Generation R&D: Managing the Link to Corporate Strategy* (Boston, MA: Harvard Business School Press, 1991).
28. Op. cit., Foster, 1986, p. 27.
29. Op. cit., Foster, 1986, pp. 118, 183.
30. Utterback, J.M., *Mastering the Dynamics of Innovation* (Boston, MA: Harvard Business School Press, 1996).
31. Sood, A., James, G., Tellis, G. and Zhu, J., 'Predicting the Path of Technological Innovation: SAW versus Moore, Bass, Gompertz, and Kryder', *Marketing Science*, 31(6) (2012), 964–79.
32. Case based on:
    – The company's annual reports
    – Discussions with Isabelle Mari, directeur études stratégiques et marketing public, JCDecaux, conducted by Rick Mitchell in March 2016
    – www.jcdecaux.com/en/, accessed April 2016.
33. Kim, W. Chan and Mauborgne, R., *Blue Ocean Strategy* (Boston, MA: Harvard Business School Press, 2005).
34. Information from the company's website and others.
35. Schoenberg, R., 'An Integrated Approach to Strategy Innovation', *European Business Journal*, 15(3) (2003), 95–102.
36. Op. cit., Kim and Mauborgne, 2005.
37. Christensen, C.M., *The Innovator's Dilemma* (Boston, MA: Harvard Business School Press, 1997).
38. Bower, J.L. and Christensen, C.M., 'Disruptive Technologies: Catching the Wave', *Harvard Business Review*, 73(1) (1995), 43–53.

Chapter 4 References and Notes

39. For example, see Lapore, J., 'The Disruption Machine', *The New Yorker*, 23 June 2014.

40. Based on Kim, W. Chan and Mauborgne, R., 'Value Innovation: The Strategic Logic of High Growth', *Harvard Business Review*, Jan.–Feb. (1997), 103–12.

41. Gilbert, C., 'The Disruption Opportunity', *Sloan Management Review*, 44(4) (2003), 27–32.

42. Wessel, M. and Christensen, C.M., 'Surviving Disruption', *Harvard Business Review*, 90(12) (2012), 56–64.

43. Harris, R.C., Insinga, R.C., Morone, J. and Werle, M.J., 'The Virtual R&D Laboratory', *Research-Technology Management*, 39(2) (1996), 32–6.

44. Chesborough, H.W. and Teece, D.J., 'When is Virtual Virtuous?', *Harvard Business Review*, Jan.–Feb. (1996), 65–73.

45. Case based on telephone interviews with Wim Ouboter and Seth Bishop. For further details of the Micro products, see www.micro-mobility.com.

46. Case based on company documentation at www.cobrainter.com and interviews and personal correspondence with Cobra managers in May 2004, January 2009 and January 2016.

47. Teece, D.J., 'Profiting from Technological Innovation: Implications for Integration, Collaboration, Licensing and Public Policy', *Research Policy*, 15(6) (1986), 285–305.

48. Gladwell, M., *The Tipping Point* (London: Little, Brown, 2000).

49. Nayak, P.R. and Ketteringham J.M., *Breakthroughs!* (New York: Rawson Associates, 1986).

50. Cusumano, M.A., Myolandis, Y. and Rosenblum, R. (eds) 'Strategic Manoeuvring and Mass-Market Dynamics: The Triumph of VHS over Beta', in M.L. Tushman and P. Anderson (eds) *Managing Strategic Innovation and Change: A Collection of Readings* (New York: Oxford University Press, 1997), pp. 3–23.

51. Op. cit., Utterback, 1996.

52. Henderson, R.M. and Clark, K.B., 'Architectural Innovation: The Reconfiguration of Existing Product Technologies and the Failure of Established Firms', *Administrative Science Quarterly*, 35(1) (1990), 9–30.

53. Cooper, A.C. and Smith, C.G., 'How Established Firms Respond to Threatening Technologies', *Academy of Management Executive*, 6(2) (1992), 55–70.

54. Loutfy, R. and Belkhir, L., 'Managing Innovation at Xerox', *Research-Technology Management*, 44(4) (2001), 15–24.

55. Op. cit., Gilbert, 2003.

56. Op. cit., Utterback, 1996.

57. Case based on discussion with Group MD Nigel Bond, Lee Metters and those mentioned in the case.

5 GENERATING INNOVATIVE IDEAS

1. Floren, H. and Frishammer, J., 'From Preliminary Ideas to Corroborated Product Definitions: Managing the Front End of New Product Development', *California Management Review*, 54(4) (2012), 20–43, quote p. 24.

2. Markham, S.K. and Lee, H., 'Product Development and Management Association's 2012 Comparative Performance Assessment Study', *Journal of Product Innovation Management*, 30(3) (2013), 408–29.

3. An example of a paper that only considers product ideation is Floren and Frishammer, 2012, op. cit.

4. Meenakshisundaram, R., Purkayastha, D. and Fernando, R., *Innovation at Whirlpool: Creating a New Competency*, European Case Clearing House Case Study (2006).

5. Downes, L. and Nunes, P.F., 'Big-Bang Disruption', *Harvard Business Review*, 91(3) (2013), 44–56.

6. Weigel, T. and Goffin, K., 'Creating Innovation Capabilities: Mölnlycke Health Care's Journey', *Research-Technology Management*, 58(4) (2015), 28–35.

7. Brown, T., 'Design Thinking', *Harvard Business Review*, 86(6) (2008), 84–92.

8. Brown, B. and Anthoney, S.D., 'How P&G Tripled its Innovation Success Rate', *Harvard Business Review*, 89(6) (2011), 64–72.

Chapter 5 References and Notes

9. Ibid., p. 70.

10. Bonabeau, E., Bodick, N. and Armstrong, R.W., 'A More Rational Approach to New-Product Development', *Harvard Business Review*, 86(3) (2008), 96–102.

11. Miller, P. and Wedell-Wedellsborg, T., 'The Case for Stealth Innovation', *Harvard Business Review*, 91(3) (2013), 90–7.

12. *Schubladen* projects are unofficial (bottom drawer) projects, where a certain amount of time and funding are available in R&D to be invested as project teams think most appropriate.

13. Eling, K., Griffin, A. and Langerak, F., 'Using Intuition in Fuzzy Front-End Decision-Making: A Conceptual Framework', *Journal of Product Innovation Management*, 31(5) (2013), 956–72.

14. Ibid.

15. Op. cit., Floren and Frishammer, 2012, p. 24.

16. Bettencourt, L.A. and Bettencourt, S.L., 'Innovating on the Cheap', *Harvard Business Review*, 89(6) (2011), 88–94.

17. www.nobelprize.org/nobel_prizes/physics/laureates/1953/zernike-lecture.pdf, accessed March 2016.

18. Runco, M.A., *Creativity: Theories and Themes: Research, Development, and Practice* (Amsterdam: Elsevier, 2007).

19. https://en.wikipedia.org/wiki/Thinking_outside_the_box, accessed March 2016.

20. Amabile, T.M., 'How to Kill Creativity', *Harvard Business Review*, 76(5) (1998), 77–87.

21. Couger, J.D., *Creative Problem Solving and Opportunity Finding* (Danvers, MA: Boyd & Fraser, 1995).

22. Thomke, S. and Fujimoto, T., 'The Effect of "Front-Loading" Problem-Solving on Product Development Performance', *Journal of Product Innovation Management*, 17(2) (2000), 128–42.

23. Lovelock, J., 'Reflections of a Man of Singular Vision', *The Independent*, Section 2, 26 March (2014).

24. Hargadon, A. and Sutton, R.I., 'Building an Innovation Factory', *Harvard Business Review*, 78(3) (2000), 157–66.

25. Tyrrell, P., *Fertile Ground: Cultivating a Talent for Innovation* (London: Economist Intelligence Unit, 2009), p. 6.

26. Csikszentmihalyi, M., *Creativity: Flow and the Psychology of Discovery and Invention* (New York: HarperCollins, 1996).

27. Amabile, T.M., Hadley, C.N. and Kramer, S.J., 'Creativity under the Gun', *Harvard Business Review*, 80(8) (2002), 52–61.

28. Amabile, T.M., 'Minding the Muse', *Working Knowledge*, a Quarterly Report on Research at Harvard Business School, 4(1) (1999).

29. Nemeth, C.J., 'Managing Innovation: When Less is More', *California Management Review*, 40(1) (1997), 59–74.

30. Hayes, N., *Managing Teams: A Strategy for Success* (London: Thompson Learning, 2002).

31. This case study is correct as of 2005. Case based on:
    – An interview with Klaus Stemig
    – Articles in the press such as Martens, H., 'Sprung ins Dunkle'
    – *Der Spiegel*, (27) (2004), 97
    – Internal documentation from Allianz and Mondial.

32. Op. cit., Couger, 1995.

33. Op. cit., Tyrrell, 2009.

34. Op. cit., Runco, 2007.

35. Koestler, A., *The Act of Creation* (London: Hutchinson, 1964).

36. Goldenberg, J. and Mazursky, D., *Creativity in Product Innovation* (Cambridge: Cambridge University Press, 2002).

37. Goldenberg, J., Horowitz, R., Levav, A. and Mazursky, D., 'Finding Your Innovation Sweet Spot', *Harvard Business Review*, 81(3) (2003), 3–11.

38. Altshuller, G., *And Suddenly the Inventor Appeared* (Worchester, MA: Technical Innovation Center, 1996).

39. Op. cit., Runco, 2007.

Chapter 5 References and Notes

40. Ambrosini, V. and Bowman, C., 'Tacit Knowledge: Some Suggestions for Operationalization', *Journal of Management Studies*, 38(6) (2001), 811–29.
41. Case based on:
    – An interview with Olaf Dietrich conducted by Keith Goffin in January 2016
    – www.miele.de, accessed January 2016.
42. Nonaka, I., 'The Knowledge-Creating Company', *Harvard Business Review*, 85(7/8) (1991), 96–104.
43. Nonaka, I., Toyama, R. and Byosiere, P., 'A Theory of Organizational Knowledge Creation: Understanding the Dynamic Process of Creating Knowledge', in M. Dierkes, A. Berthoin Antal, J. Child and I. Nonaka (eds) *Handbook of Organizational Learning and Knowledge* (Oxford: Oxford University Press, 2001), 491–517.
44. Koners, U. and Goffin, K., 'Learning from Post-Project Reviews: A Cross-Case Analysis', *Journal of Product Innovation Management,* 24(3) (2007), 242–58.
45. Brailsford, T.W., 'Building a Knowledge Community at Hallmark Cards', *Research-Technology Management*, 44(5) (2001), 18–25.
46. Hae-Jung, H. and Doz, Y., 'L'Oreal Masters Multiculturalism', *Harvard Business Review*, 91(6) (2013), 114–19.
47. Op. cit., Hargadon and Sutton, 2000.
48. Saban, K., Lanasa, J., Lackman, C. and Peace, G., 'Organizational Learning: A Critical Component to New Product Development', *Journal of Product and Brand Management*, 9(2) (2000), 99–119.
49. Senge, P.M., *The Fifth Discipline: The Art and Practice of the Learning Organization* (London: Century Business Press, 1990).
50. Op. cit., Altshuller, 1996.
51. Zhang, J., Chai, K.-H. and Tan, K.-C., 'Applying TRIZ to Service Conceptual Design: An Exploratory Study', *Creativity and Innovation Management*, 14(1) (2005), 34–42.
52. Winter, A. and Govindarajan, V., 'Engineering Reverse Innovations', *Harvard Business Review*, 93(7/8) (2015), 80–9.
53. Govindarajan, V., 'A Reverse-Innovation Playbook', *Harvard Business Review*, 90(4) (2012), 120–4.
54. Washburn, N.T. and Hunsaker, B.T., 'Finding Great Ideas in Emerging Markets', *Harvard Business Review*, 89(9) (2011), 115–20.
55. Ronney, E., Olfe, P. and Mazur, G., 'Gemba Research in the Japanese Cellular Phone Market', Nokia Mobile Phones/QFD Institute, 11 May (2000), p. 4. Available at: www.mazur.net/works/nokia_gemba_research_in_japanese_cellular_market.pdf.
56. Rao, R., 'A Firm Footing', *Appropriate Technology*, 35(4) (2008), 61–3.
57. Balachandra, R., and Friar, J.H., 'Factors for Success in R&D Projects and New Product Innovation: A Contextual Framework', *IEEE Trans. on Engineering Management*, 44(3) (1997), 276–87.
58. Cooper, R.G. and Kleinschmidt, E.J., 'Major New Products: What Distinguishes the Winners in the Chemical Industry?', *Journal of Product Innovation Management*, 10(2) (1993), 90–111.
59. Op. cit., Markham and Lee, 2013.
60. Cooper, R.G., *Product Leadership: Creating and Launching Superior New Products* (Reading, MA: Perseus Books, 1998).
61. Athaide, G.A., Meyers, P.W. and Wilemon, D.L., 'Seller-Buyer Interactions during the Commercialization of Technological Process Innovations', *Journal of Product Innovation Management*, 13(5) (1996), 406–21.
62. Case based on:
    – www.bixolon.com/html/en/company/history.xhtml, accessed July 2015
    – Discussions with J.S. Oh in January 2015 and personal communications, July 2015
    – Discussions with J.S. Oh conducted by Kim Young-Jin in June 2016.
63. Oppenheim, A.N., *Questionnaire Design, Interviewing and Attitude Measurement* (London: Printer, 2nd edn, 1992).
64. Dillman, D.A., *Mail and Internet Surveys: The Tailored Design Method* (New York: John Wiley, 2nd edn, 2002).

Chapter 5 References and Notes

65. Green, P.E., Tull, D.S. and Albaum, G., *Research for Marketing Decisions* (London: Prentice Hall, 1988).

66. Sandberg, K.D., 'Focus on the Benefits', *Harvard Management Communication Newsletter*, 5(4) (2002), 3–4.

67. Deszca, G., Munro, H. and Noori, H., 'Developing Breakthrough Products: Challenges and Options for Market Assessment', *Journal of Operations Management*, 17(6) 1999, 613–30.

68. IBM, *Leading through Connections: Insights from the Global CEO Study* (2012), available from www-935.ibm.com/services/uk/en/c-suite/ceostudy2012/.

69. Op. cit., Markham and Lee, 2013.

70. Magnusson, P.R., Matthing, J. and Kristensson, P., 'Managing Service Involvement in Service Innovation: Experiments with Innovating End Users', *Journal of Service Research*, 6(2) (2003), 111–24.

71. Op cit., IBM, 2012, p. 7.

72. Kärkkainen, H., Piippo, P., Puumalainen, K. and Tuominen, M., 'Assessment of Hidden and Future Customer Needs in Finnish Business-to-Business Companies', *R&D Management*, 31(4) (2001), 391–407.

73. This case was based on:
    – http://buzzback.com/about/.
    – Discussions with Martin Oxley in September and October 2015.

74. Goffin, K. Lemke, F. and Koners, U., *Identifying Hidden Needs: Creating Breakthrough Products* (Basingstoke: Palgrave Macmillan, 2010).

75. Goffin, K., 'Understanding Customers' Views: A Practical Example of the Use of Repertory Grid Technique', *Management Research News*, 17(7/8) (1994), 17–28.

76. Leonard-Barton, D., *Wellsprings of Knowledge: Building and Sustaining the Sources of Innovation* (Boston: Harvard Business School Press, 1995), 194.

77. Comstock, B., 'Figure it Out', *Harvard Business Review*, 91(5) (2013), 42.

78. Case based on:
    – Prahalad, C.K., *The Fortune at the Bottom of the Pyramid: Eradicating Poverty through Profits* (Upper Saddle River, NJ: Pearson Education/Wharton School Publishing, 2005)
    – Bijapurkar, B. 'In Jugaad Land', *The Week*, 31 August (2008), 16–28
    – www.sewabank.com/introduction.html, accessed December 2015
    – http://economictimes.indiatimes.com/industry/banking/finance/banking/budget-2013-womens-bank-sewa-bank-plans-expansion-across-india/articleshow/18727649.cms, accessed December 2015.

79. Leonard-Barton, D. and Rayport, J.F., 'Spark Innovation through Empathic Design', *Harvard Business Review*, 75(6) (1997), 102–13.

80. Robson, C., *Real World Research* (Oxford: Blackwell, 1993).

81. Bettencourt, L.A. and Ulwick, A.W., 'The Customer-Centred Innovation Map', *Harvard Business Review*, 86(5) (2008), 109–14, quote p. 109.

82. Based on discussions with Chris Towns of Clarks and: Towns, C. and Humphries, D., 'Breaking New Ground in Customer Behavioural Research: Experience from Clarks/PDD', Product Development Management Association UK & Ireland Conference, London, November (2001).

83. Burns, A., Barrett, R., Evans, S. and Johansson, C., 'Delighting Customers through Empathic Design', 6th International Product Development Management Conference, 5–6 July (1999), pp. 157–71.

84. Rosier, B., 'From the Dreams of Children to the Future of Technology', *The Independent on Sunday*, 15 July (2001), p. 8.

85. See http://agelab.mit.edu/ and http://agelab.mit.edu/agnes-age-gain-now-empathy-system, accessed March 2016.

86. Herstatt, C., 'Search Fields for Radical Innovations involving Market Research', Technical University of Hamburg-Harburg, Germany, Working Paper No. 10 (2001).

87. Herstatt, C. and von Hippel, E., 'Developing New Product Concepts via the Lead User Method: A Case Study in a "Low-Tech" Field', *Journal of Product Innovation Management*, 9(3) (1992), 213–21.

Chapter 5 References and Notes

88. Von Hippel, E., Thomke, S. and Sonnack, M., 'Creating Breakthroughs at 3M', *Harvard Business Review*, 77(5) (1999), 47–57.
89. Von Hippel, E., Ogawa, S. and De Jong, J.P.J., 'The Age of the Consumer-Innovator', *MIT Sloan Management Review*, 53(1) (2011), 27–35.
90. Von Hippel, E., 'People Don't Need a Profit Motive to Innovate', *Harvard Business Review*, 89(11) (2011), 36–7.
91. Case based on:
    – Koerner, B.I., 'Geeks in Toyland', *Wired*, February (2006), 108–50
    – 'Development of a successful product series at Lego'. Keynote speech by Camilla Jeppesen, marketing manager, Lego, at the 22nd International Product Development Management Conference in Copenhagen (2015)
    – www.forbes.com/sites/parmyolson/2014/12/02/gadgets-we-love-lego-mindstorms-ev3/, accessed December 2015.
92. Alexy, O., Criscuolo, P. and Salter, A., 'Managing Unsolicited Ideas for R&D', *California Management Review*, 54(3) (2012), 116–39.
93. Malhotra, A. and Majchrzak, A., 'Managing Crowds in Innovation Challenges', *California Management Review*, 56(4) (2014), 103–23, quote p. 122.
94. Mount, M. and Martinez, M.G., 'Social Media: A Tool for Open Innovation', *California Management Review*, 56(4) (2014), 124–43.
95. Füller, J., 'Refining Virtual Co-Creation from a Consumer Perspective', *California Management Review*, 52(2) (2010), 98–122.
96. Jouret, G., 'Inside Cisco's Search for the Next Big Idea', *Harvard Business Review*, 87(9) (2009), 43–5.
97. Morgan, J. and Wang, R., 'Tournaments for Ideas', *California Management Review*, 52(2) (2010), 77–97.
98. Malhotra, A. and Majchrzak, A., 'Managing Crowds in Innovation Challenges', *California Management Review*, 56(4) (2014), 103–23.
99. Case based on:
    – www.ana.co.jp/asw/wws/uk/e, accessed September 2015
    – Discussions with Tsubasa Itani, September 2015.
100. Bartl, M., Ernst, H. and Fueller, J., 'Community Based Innovation: eine Methode zur Einbindung von Online Communities in den Innovationsprozess', in C. Herstatt and J.G. Sander (eds) *Produktentwicklung mit virtuellen Communities* (Wiesbaden: Gabler, 2004).
101. Herstatt, C. and Sander, J.G. (eds) *Produktentwicklung mit virtuellen Communities* (Product Development with Virtual Communities) (Wiesbaden: Gabler, 2004).
102. Damian, J., 'Pushing the Limits of Crowdsourcing', *Business Week*, 3 March (2009).
103. Bonabeau, E., 'Decisions 2.0: The Power of Collective Intelligence', *MIT Sloan Management Review*, 50(2) (2009), 45–52.
104. Thomke, S. and von Hippel, E., 'Customers as Innovators: A New Way to Create Value', *Harvard Business Review*, 80(2) (2002), 74–81.
105. Thomke, S. and Manzi, J., 'The Discipline of Business Experimentation', *Harvard Business Review*, 93(12) (2014), 70–9.
106. Attribute levels were based on internet searches in August 2016 for 'best gaming laptop'. Of course, in high-tech markets such as gaming laptops, these levels change very quickly. For example, the quality of colour reproduction is now becoming a key criterion, as games are offered in high definition quality.
107. Caroll, J.D., Green, P.E. and Charturvedi, A., *Mathematical Tools for Applied Multivariate Analysis* (Oxford: Academic Press, 1997).
108. Gustafsson, A., Herrman, A. and Huber, F., *Conjoint Measurement: Methods and Applications* (Berlin: Springer-Verlag, 2nd edn, 2001).
109. Burda, M. and Wyplosz, C., *Macroeconomics: A European Text* (Oxford: Oxford University Press, 2001), p. 446.
110. Rosen, W., *The Most Powerful Idea in the World* (London: Jonathan Cape, 2010).
111. Aeppel, T., 'Brothers of Invention', *The Wall Street Journal Europe*, 20 April (2004), p. A12.

Chapter 5 References and Notes

112. Kingston, W., *Enforcing Small Firms' Patent Rights* (Luxembourg: European Commission, 2000).
113. Ibid.
114. UK Trade Marks Act 1994.
115. Prystay, C., 'Crocodile Battle over Chinese Turf', *The Wall Street Journal Europe*, 2–4 April, (2004), p. A7.
116. Alexy, O., Criscuola, P. and Salter, A., 'Does IP Strategy Have to Cripple Open Innovation?', *MIT Sloan Management Review*, 51(1) (2009), 71–7.
117. Case modified with permission from: Weigel, T. and Goffin, K., 'Creating Innovation Capabilities: Mölnlycke Health Care's Journey', *Research-Technology Management*, 58(4) (2015), 28–35.

6 SELECTING THE INNOVATION PORTFOLIO

1. Cooper, R.G., Edgett, S.J. and Kleinschmidt, E.J., *Portfolio Management for New Products* (Cambridge, MA: Perseus Books, 2nd edn, 2001).
2. Based on Chapman Wood, R. and Hamel, G., 'The World Bank's Innovation Market', *Harvard Business Review*, 80(11) (2002), 104–12.
3. Nagji, B. and Tuff, G., 'Managing Your Innovation Portfolio', *Harvard Business Review*, 91(5) (2012), 67–74.
4. Ryan, G. and Ryan, P., 'Capital Budgeting Practices of the Fortune 1000: How Have Things Changed?', *Journal of Business and Management*, 8(4) (2002), 355–64.
5. Brigham, E.F. and Ehrhardt, M.C., *Financial Management: Theory and Practice* (Stamford, CT: Thomson Learning, 10th edn, 2002), p. 509.
6. Brealey, R.A. and Myers, S.C., *Principles of Corporate Finance* (New York: McGraw-Hill, 1996).
7. Perdue, R., 'Valuation of R&D Projects Using Options Pricing and Decision Analysis Models', *Interfaces*, 29(6) (1999), 57–74.
8. Dixit, A.K. and Pindyck, R.S., *Investment under Uncertainty* (Princeton: Princeton University Press, 1994), p. 109.
9. Op. cit., Ryan and Ryan, 2002.
10. Op. cit., Brigham and Ehrhardt, 2002.
11. Ibid.
12. Bernstein, P.L., *Against the Gods: The Remarkable Story of Risk* (New York: John Wiley, 1998).
13. Hacking, I., *The Emergence of Probability: A Philosophical Study of Early Ideas* (London: Cambridge University Press, 1975).
14. Op. cit., Bernstein, 1998.
15. Boer, F.P., 'Risk-Adjusted Valuation of R&D Projects', *Research-Technology Management*, 46(5) (2003), 50–8.
16. Mitchell, R., Hunt, F. and Probert, D., 'Valuing and Comparing Small Portfolios', *Research-Technology Management*, 53(2) (2010), 43–54.
17. Case adapted from Mitchell et al., op. cit.
18. For example, two papers by T.A. Luehrman: 'Investment Opportunities as Real Options: Getting Started on the Numbers', *Harvard Business Review*, 76(4) (1998), 51–67; 'Strategy as a Portfolio of Real Options', *Harvard Business Review*, 76(5) (1998), 89–99.
19. Two useful books on the subject are: Razgaitis, R., *Dealmaking using Real Options and Monte Carlo Analysis* (Hoboken, NJ: John Wiley, 2003) and Howell, S., Stark, A., Newton, D. et al., *Real Options: Evaluating Corporate Investment Options in a Dynamic World* (Harlow: Pearson Education, 2001). See also Boer, F.P., 'Valuation of Technology Using "Real Options"', *Research-Technology Management*, 43(4) (2000), 26–30; and Bowman, E.H. and Moskowitz, G.T., 'Real Options Analysis and Strategic Decision Making', *Innovation Science*, 12(6) (2001), 772–7.
20. Luenberger, D.G., *Investment Science* (New York: Oxford University Press, 1998).
21. Perlitz, M., Peske, T. and Schrank, R., 'Real Options Valuation: The New Frontier in R&D Project Evaluation?', *R&D Management*, 29(3) (1999), 255–69.

Chapter 6 References and Notes

22. Op. cit., Luenberger, 1998.
23. Cooper, R.G., Edgett, S.J. and Kleinschmidt, E.J., 'Portfolio Management in New Product Development: Lessons from the Leaders – 1', *Research-Technology Management*, 40(5) (1997), 18–29.
24. An accessible account of this field is Daniel Kahneman's bestselling book *Thinking, Fast and Slow* (London: Allen Lane, 2011).
25. Von Neumann, J. and Morgenstern, O., *Theory of Games and Economic Behavior* (Princeton University Press, 2nd edn, 1947).
26. Gilovich, T., Griffin, D. and Kahneman, D. (eds) *Heuristics and Biases: The Psychology of Intuitive Judgement* (London: Cambridge University Press, 2012).
27. Op. cit., Kahneman, 2011.
28. Janis, I.L., *Groupthink* (Boston: Houghton Mifflin, 2nd edn, 1982).
29. Mitchell, D.H. and Eckstien, D., 'Jury Dynamics and Decision-making', *International Journal of Academic Research*, 1(1) (2009), 163–9.
30. Saaty, T.L., 'Decision-making with the Analytic Hierarchy Process', *International Journal of Services*, 1(1) (2008), 83–98.
31. Ishikawa, A. and Nemery, P., *Multi-Criteria Decision Analysis* (Chichester: John Wiley, 2013).
32. Kaplan, R.S. and Norton, D.P., *The Balanced Scorecard: Translating Strategy into Action* (Boston, MA: Harvard Business School Press, 1996).
33. For example, Op. cit., Cooper et al., 2001.
34. Roussel, P.A., Saad, K.N. and Erickson, T.J., *Third Generation R&D: Managing the Link to Corporate Strategy* (Cambridge, MA: Arthur D. Little, 1991).
35. Op. cit., Cooper et al., 1997.
36. Mitchell, R., Phaal, R. and Athanassopoulou, N., 'Scoring Methods for Prioritizing and Selecting Innovation Projects', Proceedings of the Portland Conference on Management of Engineering and Technology (PICMET), Kanazawa, Japan (2014).
37. Ibid.
38. Hansson, S.O., 'Decision Theory: A Brief Introduction', http//people.kth.se/~soh/decisiontheory.pdf.
39. Op. cit., Mitchell et al., 2014.
40. Op. cit., Saaty, 2008.
41. Kandybin, A., 'Which Innovation Efforts Will Pay?', *Sloan Management Review*, 51(1) (2009), 53–60.
42. Graves, S.B., Ringuest, J.L. and Case, R.H., 'Formulating Optimal R&D Portfolios', *Research-Technology Management*, 43(3) (2000), 47–51.
43. Case compiled from discussions with Simon Bradley and Richard Blackburn, and the authors' personal experience
44. Op. cit., Nagji and Tuff, 2012.
45. Case study compiled from Sharpe, P. and Keelin, T., 'How SmithKline Beecham Makes Better Resource Allocation Decisions' *Harvard Business Review*, 76(2) (1998), 45–53.
46. Makridakis, S., Wheelwright, S.C. and Hyndman, R.J., *Forecasting: Methods and Applications* (New York: John Wiley, 1998).
47. Case adapted from Goffin, K., Lee-Mortimer, A. and New, C., *Managing Product Innovation for Competitive Advantage* (London: Haymarket Publications, 1999).
48. Case compiled from discussions with Christian Rasmussen and Hans Jørgen Klein of Grundfos.

7 IMPLEMENTING INNOVATIONS

1. Case based on:
   – Govindarajan, V. and Trimble, C., *The Other Side of Innovation: Solving the Execution Challenge* (Boston, MA: Harvard Business School Publishing, 2010), p. 123
   – Discussions with Roger Parker conducted by Rick Mitchell, January 2016.
2. Case based on:
   – Discussions with Simon Bransfield-Garth conducted by Rick Mitchell, November 2016
   – www.azuri-technologies.com, accessed April 2016.

Chapter 7 References and Notes

3. Royce, W.W., 'Managing the Development of Large Software Systems: Concepts and Techniques', *Proceedings of IEEE WESCON*, August 1970. Also available in *Proc. ICSE 9*, Computer Society Press, 1987.

4. Takeuchi, H. and Nonaka, I., 'The New New Product Development Game', *Harvard Business Review*, 2(1) (1986), 137–47.

5. Beck, K., Beedle, M., van Bennekum, A. et al. *Manifesto for Agile Software Development* (2001). Available from: http://agilemanifesto.org, accessed July 2015.

6. Boehm, B. W., 'A Spiral Model of Software Development and Enhancement', *Computer*, 21(5) (1988), 61–72.

7. Ibid.

8. Schwaber, K. and Sutherland, J., *The Scrum Guide: The Definitive Guide to Scrum: The Rules of the Game* (2011), available at www.scrum.org/Portals/0/Documents/Scrum%20Guides/Scrum_Guide. pdf#zoom=100.

9. www.agilemanifesto.org, accessed November 2015.

10. Cooper, R.G., 'Agile-Stage-Gate Hybrids', *Research-Technology Management*, 59(1) (2016), 21–9.

11. Renisdottir, T., 'Scrum in Mechanical Product Development: Case Study of a Mechanical Product Development Team using Scrum'. MSc, Chalmers University, available at http://publications.lib. chalmers.se/records/fulltext/191951/191951, accessed November 2015.

12. There are many good books on project management techniques. For example: Maylor, H., *Project Management* (Harlow: Pearson Education, 3rd edn, 2003); Baguley, P., *Managing Successful Projects: A Guide for Every Manager* (London: Pitman, 1995); Reiss, G., *Project Management Demystified* (London: Spon, 2nd edn, 1995).

13. Clausing D., *Total Quality Development* (New York: ASME Press, 1994).

14. Cohen, L., *Quality Function Deployment* (Reading, MA: Addison-Wesley, 1995).

15. Matzler, K. and Hinterhuber, H.H., 'How to Make Product Development Projects More Successful by Integrating Kano's Model of Customer Satisfaction into Quality Function Deployment', *Technovation*, 18(1) (1998), 25–38.

16. Op. cit., Clausing, 1994, p. 133.

17. Case based on:
    – Interviews with Radiometer staff conducted by Jawwad Raja and Thomas Frandsen
    – www.radiometer.com, accessed April 2016.

18. Nevens, T.M., Summe, G.L. and Uttal, B., 'Commercializing Technology: What the Best Companies Do', *Harvard Business Review*, 68(3) (1990), 154–62.

19. Datar, S., Jordan, C.C., Kekre, S. et al., 'Advantages of Time-based New Product Development in a Fast-Cycle Industry', *Journal of Marketing Research*, 34(1) (1997), 36–49.

20. Smith, P.G. and Reinertsen, D.G., *Developing Products in Half the Time* (New York: Van Nostrand Reinhold, 1991), Ch. 2.

21. Reinertsen, D.G., 'Whodunnit? The Search for New Product Killers', *Electronic Business*, July (1983), 62–6.

22. Ibid.

23. Case based on:
    – Material from Organon
    – Interviews with Erik Hoppenbrouwer in 2004 and 2015
    – https://us.fagron.com/en-us, accessed March 2016.

24. Binning, K., 'The Uncertainties of Planning Major Research and Development Projects', *Long Range Planning*, 1(4) (1969), 48–53.

25. Mahnic, V., 'A Case Study in Agile Estimating and Planning Using Scrum', *Elecron. ir Elektronica*, 5(5) (2014), 123–8.

26. Thomke, S., 'Enlightened Experimentation: The New Imperative for Innovation', *Harvard Business Review*, 79(2) (2001), 67–75.

27. Hartman, G.C. and Lakatos, A.I., 'Assessing Technology Risk: A Case Study', *Research-Technology Management*, 41(2) (1998), 32–8.

28. Bazerman, M.H., *Judgements in Managerial Decision-making* (New York: John Wiley, 1990).

29. Klein, G., 'Performing a Project Premortem', *Harvard Business Review*, 85(9) (2007), 18–19.

Chapter 7 References and Notes

30. Keizer, J.A., Halman, J.I.M. and Song, M., 'From Experience: Applying the Risk Diagnosing Methodology', *Journal of Product Innovation Management*, 19(3) (2002), 213–32.

31. Thomke, S., 'R&D Comes to Services', *Harvard Business Review*, 81(4) (2003), 71–9.

32. *Design Management Systems – Part 1: Guide to Managing Innovation* (London: British Standards Institution, 1999).

33. Cooper, R.G., 'Third-generation New Product Processes', *Journal of Product Innovation Management*, 11(1) (1994), 3–14.

34. O'Connor, P., 'From Experience: Implementing a Stage-Gate Process: A Multi Company Perspective', *Journal of Product Innovation Management*, 11(3) (1994),183–200.

35. Cooper, R.G., *Winning at New Products* (Cambridge, MA: Perseus, 3rd edn, 2001).

36. Stage-Gate® Process. Stage-Gate® is a registered trademark of Stage-Gate Inc.

37. Op. cit., Wheelwright and Clark, 1992.

38. Bowen, H.K., Clark, K.B., Hollaway, C.A. and Wheelwright, S.C., 'Development Projects: The Engine of Renewal', *Harvard Business Review*, 72(5) (1994), 110–19.

39. Koners, U. and Goffin, K., 'Learning from Post-project Reviews: A Cross-case Analysis', *Journal of Product Innovation Management*, 24(3) (2007), 242–58.

40. Schindler, M. and Gassmann, O., 'Projektabwicklung gewinnt durch wissenschaftsmanagement: Ergebnisse einer empirischen Studie die Konzernentwicklung der Schindler Aufzüge AG', *Wissenschaftsmanagement*, 1 (2000), 38–45.

41. Goffin, K. and Koners, U., 'Tacit and Explicit Learning in New Product Development', *Journal of Product Innovation Management*, 28(2) (2011), 300–18.

42. Case based on:
    – visits to Bosch Crailsheim from 2003 to 2009
    – An interview with Werner Mayer on 28 September 2009
    – Bosch website, www.boschpackaging.com/boschpackagingworld/eng/index.asp, accessed October 2009.

43. Gobeli, D.H. and Brown, D.J., 'Improving the Process of Product Innovation', *Research-Technology Management*, 32(2) (1993), 38–44.

44. Cooper, R.G., 'Overhauling the New Product Introduction Process', *Industrial Marketing Management*, 25(6) (1996), 465–82.

45. Op. cit., Govindarajan and Trimble, 2010.

46. Op. cit., Wheelwright and Clarke, 1992, p. 91.

47. Adler, P.S., Mandelbaum, A., Nguyen, V. and Schwerer, E., 'Getting the Most out of Your Product Development Process', *Harvard Business Review*, 74(1996), 4–15.

48. See, for example, 'A World of Work: A Survey of Outsourcing', *The Economist*, 13 November (2004).

49. Doz, Y. and Hamel, G., *Alliance Advantage: The Art of Creating Value through Partnerships* (Boston, MA: Harvard Business School Press, 1998).

50. Chatterji, D., 'Accessing External Sources of Technology', *Research-Technology Management*, 39(2) (1996), 48–58.

51. Alexy, O., Criscuola, P. and Salter, A., 'Does IP Strategy Have to Cripple Open Innovation?', *MIT Sloan Management Review*, 51(1) (2009), 71–7.

52. Adapted from Margulis, M.S. and Pekár, P. Jr, *The Next Wave of Alliance Formation: Forging Successful Partnerships with Emerging and Middle Market Companies* (Los Angeles, CA: Houlihan Lokey Howard & Zukin, 2003).

53. Harrigan, K., *Managing for Joint Venture Success* (Lexington, MA: Lexington Books, 1986).

54. Mortara, L., Slacik, I., Napp, J. and Minshall, T., 'Implementing Open Innovation: Cultural Issues', *International Journal of Entrepreneurship and Innovation Management*, 11(4) (2010), 369–97.

55. We are grateful to Dr T. Minshall of Cambridge University Engineering Dept. for permission to use these quotations.

56. Case based on a presentation by Katja van der Wal, London, 4 December 2008.

57. Bitner, M.J., Ostrom, A.L. and Morgan, F.N., 'Service Blueprinting: A Practical Technique for Service Innovation', *California Management Review*, 50(3) (2008), 66–94.

58. Berry, L.L., Shankar, V., Turner Parish, J. et al., 'Creating New Markets Through Service Innovation', *MIT Sloan Management Review*, 47(2) (2006), 56–63.

Chapter 7 References and Notes

59. Clark, G., Johnston, R. and Shulver, M., 'Exploiting the Service Concept for Service Design and Development', in J.A. Fitzsimmons and M.J. Fitzsimmons (eds) *New Service Development: Creating Memorable Experiences* (Thousand Oaks, CA: Sage, 2000).

60. Bitner, M.J., Ostrom, A.L. and Morgan, F.N., 'Service Blueprinting: A Practical Technique for Service Innovation', *California Management Review*, 50(3) (2008), 66–94.

61. Case based on: An interview with Synthiea Kaldi conducted by Keith Goffin in March 2004.

62. Based on Johnson, G. and Scholes, K., *Exploring Corporate Strategy* (Upper Saddle River, NJ: Prentice Hall, 2009).

63. Case based on: Discussions with Sachin Mulay and A.Vasudevan.

8 PEOPLE, CULTURE AND ORGANIZATION

1. PwC Consultants, *Breakthrough Innovation and Growth* (2013). Available at: www.pwc.com/gx/en/innovationsurvey, accessed January 2016.

2. Rao, J. and Weintraub, J., 'How Innovative is Your Company's Culture', *MIT Sloan Management Review*, 54(3) (2013), 29–37.

3. De Brentani, U. and Kleinschmidt, E., 'Corporate Culture and Commitment: Impact on Performance of International New Product Development Programs', *Journal of Product Innovation Management*, 21(5) (2004), 309–33.

4. Jamrog, J., Vickers, M. and Bear, D., 'Building and Sustaining a Culture that Supports Innovation', *Human Resource Planning*, 29(3) (2006), 9–19.

5. Bratton, J. and Gold, J., *Human Resource Management: Theory and Practice* (Basingstoke: Palgrave Macmillan, 3rd edn, 2003), p. 485.

6. Op. cit., Rao and Weintraub, 2013, p. 30.

7. Case based on:
   – Soupata, L., 'Managing Culture for Competitive Advantage at United Parcel Service', *Journal of Organizational Excellence*, 20(3) (2001), 19–26.
   – Soupata, L., 'Engaging Employees in Company Success: The UPS Approach to a Winning Team', *Human Resource Management*, 44(1) (2005), 95–8.
   – www.cbsnews.com/news/the-decisive-moment-how-going-public-changed-ups-forever/, accessed November 2015.

8. Leavy, B., 'A Leader's Guide to Creating an Innovation Culture', *Strategy & Leadership*, 33(4) (2005), 38–45.

9. Jelinek, M. and Schoonhoven, C.B., *The Innovation Marathon: Lessons from High Technology Firms* (Oxford: Basil Blackwell, 1990).

10. Ibid., p. 203.

11. O'Reilly, C. and Tushman, M.L., 'Using Culture for Strategic Advantage: Promoting Innovation Through Social Control', in M.L. Tushman and P. Anderson (eds) *Managing Strategic Innovation and Change: A Collection of Readings* (New York: Oxford University Press, 1997), pp. 200–16.

12. Zien, K.A. and Buckler, S.A., 'Dreams to Market: Crafting a Culture of Innovation', *Journal of Product Innovation Management*, 14(4) (1997), 274–87.

13. Based on ideas from Barsh, J., Capozzi, M.M. and Davidson, J., 'Leadership and Innovation', *The McKinsey Quarterly*, 20(1) (2008), 37–47; Jamrog et al., 2006, op. cit.; PwC, 2013, op. cit.; Wagner, K., Taylor, A., Zablit, H. and Foo, E., *The Most Innovative Companies 2014: Breaking Through is Hard to Do*, Boston Consulting Group Report, October (2014), www.bcgperspectives.com/content/articles/innovation_growth_digital_economy_innovation_in_2014/; and Rao and Weintraub, 2013, op. cit.

14. Beckhard, R. and Harris, R.T., *Organization Transitions: Managing Complex Change* (London: Addison Wesley, 1987),

15. Schein, E.H., 'Coming to a New Awareness of Organizational Culture', *Sloan Management Review*, 25(4) (1984), 3–16.

Chapter 8 References and Notes

16. Johnson, G. and Scholes, K., *Exploring Corporate Strategy* (Edinburgh: Pearson Education Limited, 5th edn, 1999).

17. Schein, E.H., 'Organizational Socialization and the Profession of Management', *Sloan Management Review*, 53(3) (1988), 53–65.

18. Ambrosini V., Johnson. G, Scholes K., *Exploring Techniques of Analysis and Evaluation in Strategic Management - 1st Edition* (Harlow: Prentice Hall Europe, 1998).

19. Ibid.

20. Heracleous, L., 'Spinning a Brand New Cultural Web', *People Management,* 1(22) (1995), 24–7.

21. Adapted with permission from: 'The Application of a Stage-Gate Process to Developing New Markets', Confidential MBA Thesis, Cranfield School of Management (2001).

22. Moss Kanter, R., 'Innovation: The Classic Traps', *Harvard Business Review*, 84(11) (2006), 73.

23. Bruch, H. and Menges, J.L., 'The Acceleration Trap', *Harvard Business Review*, 88(4) (2010), 80–6.

24. Case based on:
    – Houlder, V., 'Technology: Quiet Revolution', *Financial Times*, 26 March (1996), 143
    – www.ti.com/corp/docs/kilbyctr/nobel.shtml, accessed November 2015
    – Linganatham, T., 'Management of Technology and Innovation at Texas Instruments', presentation to MBA students at Universiti Teknologi Malaysia, Kuala Lumpur, November (1997)
    – www.skyrme.com/kmcases/ti.htm, accessed November 2015.

25. Boxall, P. and Purcell, J., *Strategy and Human Resource Management* (Basingstoke: Palgrave Macmillan, 2003).

26. Howard, R., 'The CEO as Organizational Architect', in M.L. Tushman and P. Anderson (eds) *Managing Strategic Innovation and Change: A Collection of Readings* (New York: Oxford University Press, 1997), pp. 631–41.

27. Sakkab, N.Y., 'Connect and Develop Complements Research and Develop at P&G', *Research-Technology Management*, 45(2) (2002), 38–45.

28. Johne, F.A. and Snelson, P.A., 'Success Factors in Product Innovation: A Selective Review of the Literature', *Journal of Product Innovation Management*, 5(2) (1988), 114–28.

29. Lim, B.C., 'Management of Technology and Innovation at Shin-Etsu', presentation to MBA students, Universiti Teknologi Malaysia, Kuala Lumpur, November (1997).

30. Hargadon, A. and Sutton, R.I., 'Building an Innovation Factory', *Harvard Business Review*, 78(3) (2000), 157–66.

31. Buckler, S.A. and Zien, K.A., 'The Spirituality of Innovation: Learning from Stories', *Journal of Product Innovation Management*, 13(5) (1996), 391–405.

32. Webber, A.M. and LaBarre, P., 'The Innovation Conversation', *Research-Technology Management*, 44(5) (2001), 9–11.

33. Szwejczewski, M., Wheatley, M., and Goffin, K., *Process Innovation in UK Manufacturing: Best Practice Makes Perfect* (London: Department of Trade and Industry, 2001), p. 36.

34. Ibid.

35. House, C.H. and Price, R.L., 'The Return Map: Tracking Product Teams', *Harvard Business Review*, 69(1) (1991), 92–101.

36. Oke, A. and Goffin, K., 'Leading Edge Knowledge Management at Oxford Asymmetry', unpublished teaching case study, Cranfield School of Management (2001).

37. This case is based on: discussions in October 2015 with VP Steen Lindby conducted by John Christiansen and Claus Varnes of Copenhagen Business School.

38. Drucker, P.F., *Innovation and Entrepreneurship* (Oxford: Butterworth-Heinemann, 1985).

39. Pavia, T.M., 'The Early Stages of New Product Development in Entrepreneurial High-Tech Firms', *Journal of Product Innovation Management*, 8(1) (1991), 18–31.

40. Bhide, A., 'How Entrepreneurs Craft Strategies that Work', *Harvard Business Review*, 72(2) (1994), 150–61.

41. Martin, M.J.C., *Managing Innovation and Entrepreneurship in Technology-Based Firms* (New York: John Wiley, 1994).

42. Op. cit., Drucker, 1985.

Chapter 8 References and Notes

43. Case based on:
    – Hawe, J., 'A New Style', *The Wall Street Journal Europe*, 26–28 September (2003), p. R2
    – www.qbhouse.com/singapore/index.html, accessed November 2015
    – McLannahan, B. 'For a snip these barbers cut both hair and time', FT.com, 16 February (2012), available at: www.ft.com/intl/cms/s/0/8cded488-57d9-11e1-ae89-00144feabdc0.html #axzz3nt6moTHP, accessed January 2016.
44. Amabile, T., 'Minding the Muse: The Impact of Downsizing on Corporate Creativity', *Working Knowledge: A Quarterly Report on Research at Harvard Business School*, 4(1) (1999).
45. Staw, B., Sandelands, L. and Dutton, J., 'Threat-rigidity Effects in Organizational Behaviour: A Multi-level Analysis', *Administrative Science Quarterly*, 26(4) (1981), 501–24.
46. Staber, U. and Sydow, J., 'Organizational Adaptive Capacity: A Structuration Perspective', *Journal of Management Inquiry*, 11(4) (2002), 408–25.
47. Op. cit., Balogun et al., 1999, p. 196.
48. Tyrrell, P., *Fertile Ground: Cultivating a Talent for Innovation* (London: Economist Intelligence Unit, 2009).
49. IBM, *Leading through Connections: Insights from the Global Chief Executive Officer Study* (Portsmouth: IBM, 2012).
50. www: opp.co.uk.
51. Op. cit., Bratton and Gold, 2003.
52. Cohn, J., Katzenbach, J. and Vlak, G., 'Finding and Grooming Breakthrough Innovators', *Harvard Business Review*, 86(6) (2008), 62–9.
53. Comstock, B., 'Figure It Out', *Harvard Business Review*, 91(5) (2013), 42.
54. Hae-Jung, H. and Doz, Y., 'L'Oreal Masters Multiculturalism', *Harvard Business Review*, 91(6) (2013), 114–19.
55. Katz, R., 'Managing Professional Careers: The Influence of Job Longevity and Group Age', in M.L. Tushman and P. Anderson (eds) *Managing Strategic Innovation and Change: A Collection of Readings* (New York: Oxford University Press, 1997), pp. 193–9.
56. For a good explanation of the theories, refer to: Mullins, L.M., *Management and Organisational Behaviour* (London: Pitman Publishing, 4th edn 1996).
57. Op. cit., Cohn et al., 2008.
58. Garvin, D.A., 'How Google Sold its Engineers on Management', *Harvard Business Review*, 91(12) (2013), 74–82.
59. Op. cit., Bratton and Gold, 2003, p. 13.
60. Op. cit., Bratton and Gold, 2003, p. 485.
61. Schoeman, M., Baxter, D., Goffin, K. and Micheli, P., 'Commercialization Partnerships as an Enabler of UK Public Sector Innovation: The Perfect Match?', *Public Money & Management*, 32(6) (2012), 425–32.
62. Torrington, D. and Hall, L., *Personnel Management: HRM in Action* (London: Prentice Hall, 1995).
63. Goffin, K. and Pfeiffer, R., *Innovation Management in UK and German Manufacturing Companies* (London: Anglo-German Foundation Report Series, December 1999).
64. Markham, S.K. and Lee, H., 'Product Development and Management Association's 2012 Comparative Performance Assessment Study', *Journal of Product Innovation Management*, 30(3) (2013), 408–29.
65. Birkinshaw, J., Bouquet, C. and Barsoux, J.-L., 'The 5 Myths of Innovation', *MIT Sloan Management Review*, 52(2) (2011), 43–50.
66. Weigel, T. and Goffin, K., 'Creating Innovation Capabilities: Mölnlycke Health Care's Journey', *Research-Technology Management*, 58(4) (2015), 28–35.
67. Op. cit., Boxall and Purcell, 2003.
68. Op. cit., Markham and Lee, 2013.
69. Ancona, D.G. and Caldwell, D.F., 'Making Teamwork Work: Boundary Management in Product Development Teams', in M.L Tushman. and P. Anderson (eds) *Managing Strategic Innovation and Change: A Collection of Readings* (New York: Oxford University Press, 1997), pp. 432–40.

Chapter 8 References and Notes

70. Pettigrew, A. and Fenton, E.M. (eds) *The Innovating Organization* (London: Sage, 2000), p. 251.
71. Case based on:
    – http://hope.haier.com, accessed March 2016
    – http://businesswireindia.com/news/news-details/haier-unveils-revolutionary-codo-worlds-first-pocket-washing-machine/44577, accessed March 2016
    – Discussions conducted by Lloyd He of China Institute for Innovation with David Teng, head of HOPE; Nick Huang, director of external partnership; and Zhengtao Wang, owner of the CODO washing machine micro-enterprise
    – www.wipo.int/wipo_magazine/en/2015/04/article_0006.html, accessed March 2016.
72. Goffin, K., Lee-Mortimer, A. and New, C., *Managing Product Innovation for Competitive Advantage* (London: Haymarket Business Publications, 1999).
73. Martin, M.J.C., *Managing Innovation and Entrepreneurship in Technology-Based Firms* (New York: John Wiley, 1994).
74. Wheelwright, S.C. and Clark, K., *Revolutionizing Product Development: Quantum Leaps in Speed, Efficiency, and Quality* (New York: Free Press, 1992).
75. Sosa, M.E. and Mihm, J., 'Organizational Design for New Product Development', in C.H. Loch and S. Kavadias (eds) *Handbook of New Product Development* (Oxford: Butterworth-Heinemann, 2008), pp. 165–97.
76. Anonymous, 'Face Value: The Mass Production of Ideas, and Other Possibilities', *The Economist*, 334(7906) (1995), p. 111.
77. Von Hippel, E., Thomke, S. and Sonnack, M., 'Creating Breakthroughs at 3M', *Harvard Business Review*, 77(5) (1999), 47–57.
78. Hershock, R.J., Cowman, C.D. and Peters, D., 'Action Teams That Work', *Journal of Product Innovation Management*, 11(2) (1992), 95–104.
79. Nicholson, G.C., 'Keeping Innovation Alive', *Research-Technology Management*, 41(3) (1998), 34–40.
80. Colarelli O'Connor, G., Corbett, A. and Pierantozzi, R., 'Create Three Distinct Career Paths for Innovators', *Harvard Business Review*, 87(12) (2012), 78–9, quote p. 78.
81. Gwynne, P., 'Skunk Works, 1990s-Style', *Research-Technology Management*, 40(4) (1997), 18–23.
82. Bernstein, E., 'The Transparency Trap', *Harvard Business Review*, 92(10) (2014), 58–66.
83. Govindaranjan, V. and Trimble, C., 'Stop the Innovation Wars', *Harvard Business Review*, 88(7/8) (2010), 76–83.
84. Op. cit., Gwynne, 1997.
85. Chesbrough, H.W. and Teece, D.J., 'When is Virtual Virtuous? Organizing for Innovation', *Harvard Business Review*, 74(1) (1996), 65–73.
86. Galvin, D. and Sucher, S., 'WingspanBank.com', *Harvard Business School Case Study*, No. 9-600-035, (2002).
87. Op. cit., Markham and Lee, 2013.
88. O'Reilly III, C.A. and Tushman, M.L., 'The Ambidextrous Organization', *Harvard Business Review*, 82(4) (2004), 74–81.
89. Dugan, R.E. and Gabriel, K.J., '"Special Forces" Innovation: How DARPA Attacks Problems', *Harvard Business Review*, 91(10) (2013), 74–84.
90. Henke, J.W., Krachenberg, A.R. and Lyons, T.F., 'Cross-Functional Teams: Good Concept, Poor Implementation', *Journal of Product Innovation Management*, 10(3) (1993), 216–29.
91. Wilson, K. and Doz, Y.L., '10 Rules for Managing Global Innovation', *Harvard Business Review*, 90(10) (2012), 84–90.
92. Thomson. L., *Personality Type* (Boston: Shambhala Publications, 1998).
93. Belbin, R.M., *Management Teams* (London: Heineman, 1981).
94. Hayes, N., *Managing Teams: A Strategy for Success* (London: Thompson Learning, 2002).
95. Sauermann, H. and Cohen, W.M., 'Motivated to Innovate', *MIT Sloan Management Review*, 50(3) (2009), 24.
96. Tzabbar, D., 'What Helps and Hinders Innovation?', *MIT Sloan Management Review*, 51(1) (2009), 17.
97. Tuckman, B., 'Developmental Sequence in Small Groups', *Psychological Bulletin*, 63(6) (1965), 384–99.

Chapter 8 References and Notes

98. Tuckman himself did not draw a diagram of how teams develop. However, based on his work, various 'teamwork wheels' have been drawn over the years based. The version we show originates from Cranfield School of Management.

99. Schein, E.H., 'Three Cultures of Management: The Key to Organizational Learning', *Sloan Management Review*, 71(4) (1996), 9–20.

100. Souder, W.E., 'Managing Relations between R&D and Marketing in New Product Development Projects', *Journal of Product Innovation Management*, 5(1) (1988), 6–19.

101. Nixon, B., 'Research and Development Performance Measurement: A Case Study', *Management Accounting Review*, 9(3) (1998), 329–55.

102. Goffin, K. and Micheli, P., 'Maximizing the Value of Industrial Design in New Product Development', *Research-Technology Management*, 53(5) (2010), 29–37.

103. Tsai, W., Verma, R. and Schmidt, G., 'New Service Development', in C.H. Loch and S. Kavadias (eds) *Handbook of New Product Development* (Oxford: Butterworth-Heinemann, 2008), pp. 495–530.

104. Case based on:
    – Discussions in March 2016 with general manager and vice president of the board of directors Anastassios Dimopoulos and section manager Spyros Sakellariou conducted by Evy Sakellariou of the American College of Greece
    – www.intracom-telecom.com/index.htm, accessed April 2016.

105. McDonough, E.F., 'Faster New Product Development: Investigating the Effects of Technology and Characteristics of the Project Leader and Team', *Journal of Product Innovation Management*, 10(3) (1993), 241–50.

106. Barczak, G. and Wilemon, D., 'Leadership Differences in New Product Development Teams', *Journal of Product Innovation Management*, 6(4) (1989), 259–67.

107. Colarelli O'Connor, G., Corbett, A. and Pierantozzi, R., 'Create Three Distinct Career Paths for Innovators', *Harvard Business Review*, 87(12) (2012), 78–9.

108. Op. cit., Markham and Lee, 2013.

109. Ibid, quote p. 78.

110. Case based on an interview with Massimo Fumarola, conducted by K. Goffin in May 2004.

111. www.huffingtonpost.com/ira-kalb/apple-watch-success-or-fa_b_8060310.html, accessed December 2015.

112. Cooper, R.G. and Kleinschmidt, E.J., 'Stage Gate Systems for New Product Success', *Marketing Management*, 1(4) (1992), 20–9.

113. Balachandra, R., Brockhoff, K.K. and Pearson, A.W., 'R&D Project Termination Decisions: Processes, Communication, and Personnel Changes', *Journal of Product Innovation Management*, 13(3) (1996), 245–56.

114. Meyers, P.W. and Wilemon, D., 'Learning in New Technology Development Teams', *Journal of Product Innovation Management*, 6(2) (1989), 79–88.

115. Prahalad, C.K., 'Best Practices Get You Only So Far', *Harvard Business Review*, 88(4) (2010), 32.

116. Dyer, J.H., Gregersen, H.B., and Christensen, C.M., 'The Innovator's DNA', *Harvard Business Review*, 87(12) (2009), 60–7.

117. Hill, L.A., Brandeau, G., Truelove, E. and Lineback, K. 'Collective Genius', *Harvard Business Review*, 92(6) (2014), 94–102.

118. Rigby, D.K., Gruver, K. and Allen, J. 'Innovation in Turbulent Times', *Harvard Business Review*, 87(6) (2009), 79–86.

119. Moss Kanter, R.. 'Innovation: The Classic Traps', *Harvard Business Review*, 84(11) (2006), 73.

120. Hill, L.A., Brandeau, G., Truelove, E. and Lineback, K. 'Collective Genius', *Harvard Business Review*, 92(6) (2014), 94–102.

121. Op. cit., Barsh, J., Capozzi, M.M. and Davidson, J., 'Leadership and Innovation', *The McKinsey Quarterly*, 20(1) (2008), 37–47.

122. Tushman, M.L., Smith, W.K. and Binns, A., 'The Ambidextrous CEO', *Harvard Business Review*, 89(6) (2011), 74–80.

Chapter 8 References and Notes

123. Flurr, N. and Dyer, J.H., 'Leading Your Team into the Unknown', *Harvard Business Review*, 93(12) (2014), 80–8.
124. Moss Kanter, R., 'Transforming Giants', *Harvard Business Review*, 86(1) (2008), 43–52.
125. Hamel, G., 'Moon Shots for Management', *Harvard Business Review*, 87(2) (2009), 91–8.
126. Blenko, M.W., Mankins, M.C. and Rogers, P., 'The Decision-Driven Organization', *Harvard Business Review*, 88(6) (2010), 54–62.
127. Angel, R., 'Putting an Innovation Culture into Practice', *Ivey Business Journal Online*, January/February (2006), available at http://iveybusinessjournal.com/publication/putting-an-innovation-culture-into-practice/.
128. Pfitzer, M., Bockstette, V. and Stamp, M., 'Innovating for Shared Value', *Harvard Business Review*, 91(9) (2013), 100–7.
129. Moss Kanter, R., 'Innovation: The Classic Traps', *Harvard Business Review*, 84(11) (2006), 73–83.
130. Op. cit., PwC Consultants, 2013, p. 21.
131. O'Reilly, C. and Tushman, M., 'Using Culture for Strategic Advantage: Promoting Innovation Through Social Control', in M.L. Tushman and P. Anderson (eds) *Managing Strategic Innovation and Change: A Collection of Readings* (New York: Oxford University Press, 1997), pp. 200–16.
132. Case based on:
    – www.time-matters.com/company/, accessed November 2015
    – An interview with F.-J. Miller conducted by K. Goffin in October 2015
    – www.lufthansagroup.com/en/press/news-releases/singleview/archive/2014/october/29/article/3332.html, accessed November 2015.

9 INNOVATION – PERFORMANCE AND CAPABILITY

1. www.bbc.co.uk/radio4/news/inbusiness/inbusiness_20081228.shtml, accessed April 2016.
2. Chan, V., Musso, C. and Shankar, V., 'Assessing Innovation Metrics', *McKinsey Quarterly*, 4 (2008), 1–11.
3. Wagner, K., Taylor, A., Zablit, H. and Foo, E., *The Most Innovative Companies 2014: Breaking Through is Hard to Do*, Boston Consulting Group Report, October (2014), www.bcgperspectives.com/content/articles/innovation_growth_digital_economy_innovation_in_2014/, accessed November 2016.
4. Slack, N., Chambers, S. and Johnston, B., *Operations Management* (London: Pitman, 4th edn, 2003).
5. Kandybin, A., 'Which Innovation Efforts Will Pay?', *MIT Sloan Management Review*, 51(1) (2009), 53–60.
6. Jaruzelski, B. and DeHoff, K., 'The Customer Connection: The Global Innovation 1000', *Strategy + Business*, 49 (2007), 69–83.
7. Holman, R., Kaas, H.-W. and Keeling, D., 'The Future of Product Development', *McKinsey Quarterly*, 3 (2003), 28–39.
8. Goffin, K. and Pfeiffer, R., *Innovation Management in UK and German Manufacturing Companies* (London: Anglo-German Foundation, 1999).
9. Adams, R., Bessant, J. and Phelps, R., 'Innovation Management Measurement: A Review', *International Journal of Management Reviews*, 8(1) (2006), 21–47.
10. Op. cit., Chan et al., 2008.
11. Markham, S.K. and Lee, H., 'Product Development and Management Association's 2012 Comparative Performance Assessment Study', *Journal of Product Innovation Management*, 30(3) (2013), 408–29.
12. Johnston, R. and Clark, G., *Service Operations Management* (London: Financial Times/Prentice Hall, 2001).

Chapter 9 References and Notes

13. Kleinknecht, A., 'Indicators of Manufacturing and Service Innovation: Their Strengths and Weaknesses', in J.S. Metcalf and I. Miles (eds) *Innovation Systems in the Service Economy* (Norwell, MA: Kluwer Academic, 2000), 169–86.

14. Kaplan, R.S. and Norton, D.P., *The Balanced Scorecard: Translating Strategy into Action* (Boston, MA: Harvard Business School Press, 1996).

15. Ibid., p. 97.

16. Neely, A., Richards, H., Mills, J. et al. 'Designing Performance Measures: A Structured Approach', *International Journal of Operations and Production Management*, 17(11) (1997), 1131–52.

17. Based on:
    – Goffin, K., 'Enhancing Innovation Performance', *Management Quarterly*, Part 13 (2001), 18–26
    – Updated to include: Markham and Lee, 2013, op. cit.

18. IBM, *Leading through Connections: Insights from the Global Chief Executive Officer Study* (Portsmouth: IBM, 2012).

19. PwC Consultants, *Breakthrough Innovation and Growth*, PwC Report, www.pwc.com/gx/en/innovationsurvey/, accessed February 2016.

20. Chiesa, V., Coughlan, P. and Voss, C.A., 'Development of a Technical Innovation Audit', *Journal of Product Innovation Management*, 13(2) (1996), 105–36.

21. Majaro, S., *The Creative Gap* (London: Longman, 1988).

22. Duhamel, M., *Promoting Innovation Management Techniques in Europe* (Luxembourg: European Commission, 1999).

23. *Design Management Systems – Part 1: Guide to Managing Innovation* (London: British Standards Institution, 1999).

24. Case based on:
    – An MBA project conducted in 2000
    – A visit to Evotec on 20 May 2009 with discussions with Dr Mario Polywka.

25. Riddle, D., 'Managing Change in Your Organization'. *International Trade Forum*, 2 (2000), 26–8.

26. Barsh, J., Capozzi, M.M. and Davidson, J., 'Leadership and Innovation', *McKinsey Quarterly*, 1 (2008), 37–47, quote p. 38.

27. Schein, E.H., 'Three Cultures of Management: The Key to Organizational Learning', *Sloan Management Review*, 71(3) (1996), 9–20.

28. O'Connor, P., 'From Experience: Implementing a Stage-Gate Process: A Multi-Company Perspective', *Journal of Product Innovation Management*, 11(3) (1994), 183–200.

29. Based on:
    – Beckhard, R. and Harris, R.T., *Organisation Transitions: Managing Complex Change* (London: Addison Wesley, 1987).
    – The change equation does not have an 'equals' (=) sign and so would more properly be known as the change principle; similar to the uncertainty principal in physics, which expresses an approximate mathematical relationship rather than an equation.

30. This case is based on:
    – An interview with Erik Chang in December 2015 conducted by Keith Goffin
    – http://thisisdesignthinking.net/2015/09/ericssons-innova-system-how-to-evoke-employees-entrepreneurial-spirit, accessed January 2016
    – www.ericsson.com/thecompany/company_facts, accessed January 2016.

31. Case based on: interviews conducted by Julian Glyn-Owen with Michael Petersen in January 2016.

32. Tushman, M.L. and O'Reilly III, C.A., *Winning through Innovation: A Practical Guide to Leading Organizational Change and Renewal* (Boston, MA: Harvard Business School Press, 2002), p. 49.

33. Case based on:
    – Interviews with Dr Edmond Harty conducted by Dr Claire McBride in March 2016
    – www.dairymaster.com, accessed April 2016.

34. Pettigrew, A. and Fenton, E.M. (eds) *The Innovating Organization* (London: Sage, 2000).

35. Balogun, J., Hope Hailey, V. with Johnson, G. and Scholes, K., *Exploring Strategic Change* (Prentice Hall: London, 1999).

36. Op. cit., British Standard, 1999.

Chapter 9 References and Notes

37. Case based on:
    – A presentation to MBA students by David Epps in 2015
    – An interview with David Epps in November 2015, conducted by Keith Goffin
    – Company website: www.amey.co.uk, accessed March 2016.
38. Case based on:
    – Interviews with Magnus Schoeman in 2009 and February 2016
    – http://uk.atosconsulting.com/en-uk/home/we-are.html, accessed March 2016.
39. www.careerbuilder.com/jobs-innovation-management?keywords=innovation+management&location, accessed February 2016.
40. Case based on:
    – Company annual reports
    – Miller, J.A., 'Out of a Near-death Experience into a Chaotic Global Economy: How Corning Rediscovered its Innovation Roots', *Research-Technology Management,* 54(6) (2011), 26–31
    – Henderson, R. and Reavis, C., 'Corning Incorporated: The Innovation and Growth Council', https://mitsloan.mit.edu/LearningEdge/CaseDocs, accessed March 2016
    – Interview for Bloomberg, reported in www.bloomberg.com/news/articles/2009-05-04/corning-lessons-from-the-bust-and-boombusinessweek-business-news-stock-market-and-financial-advice, accessed March 2016
    – *Wired* magazine, 9 December 2012, www.wired.com/2012/09/ff-corning-gorilla-glass/, accessed March 2016.

INDEX

Page numbers in **bold** indicate tables and in *italic* indicate figures.

Page numbers in **bold** indicate tables and in *italic* indicate figures.

Page numbers in **bold** indicate tables and in *italic* indicate figures.

Page numbers in **bold** indicate tables and in *italic* indicate figures.

Page numbers in **bold** indicate tables and in *italic* indicate figures.

Page numbers in **bold** indicate tables and in *italic* indicate figures.

Page numbers in **bold** indicate tables and in *italic* indicate figures.

Page numbers in **bold** indicate tables and in *italic* indicate figures.

Page numbers in **bold** indicate tables and in *italic* indicate figures.